DATE DUE

JUL █ 3 1995	
MAR 2 5 1996	
JAN 1 2 1997	
SEP 2 5 1998	

Fighting for the Confederacy

Purchased with a
grant from the
Knight Foundation

Brigadier General Edward Porter Alexander

Fighting for the
CONFEDERACY

The Personal Recollections of
General Edward Porter Alexander

Edited by
Gary W. Gallagher

THE UNIVERSITY OF
NORTH CAROLINA PRESS

Chapel Hill | London

Library of Congress Cataloging-in-Publication Data
Alexander, Edward Porter, 1835–1910.
Fighting for the Confederacy : the personal recollections of
General Edward Porter Alexander / edited by Gary W. Gallagher.
p.   cm.
Bibliography: p.
Includes index.
ISBN 0-8078-1848-8 (alk. paper)
1. United States—History—Civil War, 1861–1865—Campaigns.
2. Alexander, Edward Porter, 1835–1910. 3. United States—History—
Civil War, 1861–1865—Personal narratives, Confederate.
4. Confederate States of America—History, Military.
I. Gallagher, Gary W.   II. Title.
E470.A3725   1989
973.7′3013—dc19   88-37667
                                                          CIP

Manufactured in the United States of America

93 92 91 90   5 4 3 2

For my parents, William and Shirley Gray Gallagher,
whose influence on me has been far greater than they imagine—
and for my son, William Paul Gallagher,
who is a great joy in my life

Contents

Contents

Figures

Contents

Contents

ACKNOWLEDGMENTS

Four years have passed since Robert K. Krick first showed me excerpts from Porter Alexander's unpublished reminiscences and urged me to edit the whole work for publication. A cursory examination of portions of the manuscript revealed its importance, but I felt that Bob was the obvious person to do the editing. He pleaded other obligations, though I suspect the real problem was his reluctance, as a confirmed Jackson and Lee man, to spend several years working on a project associated with James Longstreet's First Corps. Whatever Bob's true motivation, I am thankful that he pressed me to undertake a task that proved to be an absolutely delightful experience. Bob also exhibited his usual generosity in supplying information about dozens of people identified in the notes.

In the course of editing *Fighting for the Confederacy,* I received help from many other generous people. Sue Alexander Butterfield and Alexander Porter Butterfield, granddaughter and great-great grandson of Porter Alexander, kindly granted permission for me to prepare an annotated edition of the manuscript. I especially remember a long telephone conversation during which Mrs. Butterfield recalled memories of visiting "Grandfather Porter" on Christmas holidays. On more than one occasion, Alexander P. Butterfield took time from a demanding naval career to answer my queries. Needless to say, without the cooperation of the Butterfields this book could not have been published.

Friends and colleagues responded to my many requests for assistance with uniform good humor. Barnes F. Lathrop and T. Michael Parrish spent many hours discussing editorial methods and problems. A. Wilson Greene and Warren W. Hassler, Jr., most unselfishly wielded their blue pencils on the introduction. Maury Klein, Alexander's biographer, was steadfastly encouraging and helpful. Thomas W. Broadfoot, Michael Owens, Stephen M. Rowe, and Ron R. Van Sickle employed their skills as bookmen to track down obscure materials. Those who helped to answer questions relating to notes included Keith Bohannon, Philip F. Callahan, Chris Calkins, Dennis E. Frye, Doug Harvey, Paul B. Harvey, Jr., John Hennessy, Dot Kelly, Jane M. Madsen, Michael P. Musick, Allan Purcell, Dorothy Rapp, Richard A. Sauers, Richard J. Sommers, and John E. Sunder.

Because the Alexander Papers are in the Southern Historical Collection at the University of North Carolina at Chapel Hill, I had the pleasure of working once again with Carolyn Wallace and Richard A. Shrader, who showed genuine interest in my project and went beyond the requirements of archival procedure to assist me. The Southern Historical Collection has been my researching home away from home for most of my scholarly life, and I cannot imagine a better place to pursue the past.

Matthew Hodgson and Iris Tillman Hill of the University of North Carolina Press were enthusiastic about this venture from the beginning. Undaunted by the size of the volume, they forgave several delays and agreed to include all of the illustrations and maps that appear in the original manuscript. In short, they were willing to publish *Fighting for the Confederacy* as it should be published—an admirable attitude in an era when university presses are subject to harsh budgetary realities.

My greatest debt is to my wife, Eileen Anne. She transcribed 1,200 pages of manuscript, helped proofread the entire typescript, and willingly sacrificed countless evenings and weekends over a period of three years. She knows Porter Alexander at least as well as I do, and by all rights her name should appear as coeditor. But she insists otherwise. I cherish our collaboration on this project. The hundreds of hours we spent together in Alexander's company (invariably with Nipper, our own loyal Buster, not far away) will remain among my most treasured memories.

Gary W. Gallagher
Pennsylvania State University
University Park, Pennsylvania
October 1988

INTRODUCTION

Brigadier General Edward Porter Alexander sat astride his horse on the south bank of the James River opposite downtown Richmond early on the morning of 3 April 1865. Decisive Federal assaults the previous two days had brought an end to the grueling siege of Petersburg and compelled R. E. Lee to abandon the Confederate capital. Chief of artillery in James Longstreet's First Corps of the Army of Northern Virginia, Alexander had just watched the last of his batteries cross the Mayo Bridge on its way out of the city. "It was after sunrise of a bright morning when from the Manchester high grounds we turned to take our last look at the old city for which we had fought so long & so hard," remembered Alexander. "It was a sad, a terrible & a solemn sight. I don't know that any moment in the whole war impressed me more deeply with all its stern realities than this. The whole river front seemed to be in flames, amid which occasional heavy explosions were heard, & the black smoke spreading & hanging over the city seemed to be full of dreadful portents. I rode on with a distinctly heavy heart & with a peculiar sort of feeling of orphanage."[1]

The evocative power of this passage from *Fighting for the Confederacy* might surprise readers who know Alexander principally through his *Military Memoirs of a Confederate: A Critical Narrative*. The latter quickly became a classic following its publication in 1907.[2] President Theodore Roosevelt acquired one of the first copies and hastened to write Alexander that "I have so thoro[ugh]ly enjoyed your 'Military Memoirs' that I must write to tell you so." Historian William A. Dunning, who read the volume at least twice in 1907, recommended it to his fellow scholar Frederic Bancroft as a "fascinating book." A reviewer in the *Army and Navy Journal* labeled it "one of the most valuable of all books on the war."[3] Later opinion echoed these early sentiments. Douglas Southall Freeman considered Alexander's effort "altogether the best critique of the operations of the Army of Northern Virginia." Another prominent historian of the Confederacy characterized it as "hard-hitting, authoritative . . . honest, fair, and sound." T. Harry Williams's opinion was that "probably no book by a participant in the war has done so much to shape the historical image of that conflict."[4]

As Williams and others noted, the title of *Military Memoirs of a Confederate* was a misnomer, for the book was really a general history of Lee's army rather than a record of Alexander's activities during the war. Alexander used available published sources and carried on a wide correspondence with former officers to make his treatment as accurate as possible. Almost completely unaffected by the mythmaking of the Lost Cause, Alexander had no special case to plead. His tone was detached, analytical, and very impartial; indeed, a common reaction among southerners was that Alexander had been too critical of Lee and Jackson. Maury Klein, author of the only scholarly biography of Alexander, accurately observed that no other Confederate writer "equaled the degree of objectivity attained by Alexander."[5] Occasionally Alexander himself took center stage in *Military Memoirs*—most notably on 3 July 1863 at Gettysburg—and in a few instances he paused to paint scenes that rival his dramatic account of those last moments at the Mayo Bridge. But on balance he kept himself out of the narrative and curbed his descriptive prose to create a straightforward scholarly work.

Over the years, historians and readers alike have expressed regret over Alexander's decision to tell so little of his own part in the war. Their frustration is understandable. Alexander's skill as an engineer, staff officer, and artillerist had placed him constantly at the side of R. E. Lee, P. G. T. Beauregard, Joseph E. Johnston, James Longstreet, and others of the southern high command. He participated in nearly all of the great battles in the East, and went west to Chattanooga and Knoxville with the First Corps in the summer and fall of 1863. Privy to so much, and endowed with far more than ordinary intelligence, he was potentially one of the best witnesses in the Army of Northern Virginia. Yet there were literally dozens of places throughout *Military Memoirs* where Alexander clearly stopped short of relating everything he must have known. "One could wish that he had written two books," mused T. Harry Williams, "a general history and a more personal narrative." In lamenting Alexander's omissions, Douglas Southall Freeman suggested that much "he could have said for the instruction of soldiers and to the enlightenment of students, he felt it improper to put in print." Whatever the reason for Alexander's reticence, his decision to tell so little of his own experiences seems one of the great lost opportunities in the literature on the war.[6]

Fighting for the Confederacy is Porter Alexander's true personal reminiscence.[7] Remarkable as it may seem in a field that has been studied so exhaustively, the 1,200-page manuscript lay virtually unknown for more than

eight decades—a good part of that time at the most famous of all reposito-
ries of southern primary materials.[8] Written several years before *Military
Memoirs,* it is a superlative work offering precisely the type of inside view
wished for by so many readers of *Military Memoirs*. It is utterly candid,
filled with memorable descriptions of people and events, and blessed with
ample portions of analysis, humor, and sheer drama. "If there is a better
unpublished source on Confederate affairs in the Virginia theater," a leading historian of Lee's army wrote of the manuscript, "I surely don't know of
it, and can't wait to see it."[9] What riches may yet surface cannot be predicted with any certainty, but in the last half-century only the reminiscences
of Henry Kyd Douglas and the journal of Jedediah Hotchkiss have
approached the quality of *Fighting for the Confederacy*.[10]

How such a treasure remained so obscure makes for an interesting tale.
Alexander spent considerable time studying and writing about the war
during the three decades after Appomattox. His first project was to have
been a history of the First Corps, undertaken at Longstreet's urging in 1866.
Approaching the task with his usual care, Alexander collected a large
amount of information. "What I want is not the general facts that everybody knows but the *details,*" he wrote a former member of Longstreet's
staff, "& they only exist in the memories of survivors & I have to elicit them
by correspondence & you *cannot imagine* how utterly hopeless a task this
seems."[11] Increasingly involved with business and frustrated by a poor
response from correspondents, Alexander abandoned his project on the
First Corps in the late 1860s. But he renewed his study of the conflict in the
1870s, and soon a stream of articles flowed from his active pen. Utilizing
material collected for his history of the First Corps, he published pieces in
the *Southern Historical Society Papers* on the Seven Days, Gettysburg,
Longstreet's division in 1861–62, Yorktown and Williamsburg, Fredericksburg, and the Confederate artillery. For the popular *Battles and Leaders of
the Civil War* from *Century Magazine,* he contributed essays on the artillery
at Gettysburg and Longstreet's Knoxville campaign.[12] Robert Underwood
Johnson, a principal editor of *Battles and Leaders,* fondly remembered
Alexander as one of "the two most lovable men I met in the long course of
our relations to the War Series." His "integrity and candor" were such that
Johnson felt he "might rely implicitly on anything . . . [he] said."[13]

By the mid-1880s Alexander's children had begun to press him to write a
memoir of his role in the war. Always he insisted that much as he would like
to accommodate their request, he simply could not budget the requisite time
for such a large project. Only rigorous discipline had enabled him to
complete his historical articles while pursuing a successful career as an executive with several railroads, banks, and other companies. Even after he
retired from railroading in 1892 to become a full-time planter, he somehow

remained too busy to undertake a full memoir. A turning point came in 1897 when President Grover Cleveland, who often hunted ducks with Alexander on the latter's estate in South Carolina, asked him to help arbitrate a boundary dispute between Nicaragua and Costa Rica. Being an arbitrator would entail long absences from home; but the remuneration was a thousand dollars a month in gold, and Alexander felt he could not pass up such a windfall for his family. After a difficult leave-taking from his wife, Bettie Mason Alexander, he sailed for Greytown, Nicaragua, in May 1897.[14]

Scarcely settled into his quarters in Greytown when a package arrived from his daughter Bessie Alexander Ficklen, Alexander opened the parcel to discover two blank ledger books and a letter urging him to begin work on his reminiscences. Early in June he asked Bettie to "tell Bess that I have begun to write in her blank books for my recollections of the war and try to do something every day when there is no special work on hand." Beginning with a long chapter on his youth, years at West Point, and life in the prewar army, Alexander found the task difficult. But when he got to the war, words came more easily, and the task became a labor of love yielding great satisfaction. "When I start writing on those times," he confided to his wife in late July 1897, "I hardly know where to stop." At first he envisioned a modest work that would fit in the four hundred leaves of Bessie's two ledger books, but his discussion of First Manassas rapidly filled page after page. Alexander optimistically predicted that his pace soon would increase, observing that "it is partly because Manassas being the first battle, when we were all new to it—there is much more temptation to detail than there will be after the narration has gotten used to battles." The first ledger book was en route to his daughter by the second week in August, its narrative complete through the aftermath of First Manassas.[15]

Alexander discussed his purpose and methodology in letters to his sister Louise Alexander Gilmer and Frederick M. Colston, a former subordinate in his battalion of artillery. "All my life my children have been begging me & I've been promising to write out my recollections . . . of the war," he began one letter to Colston, ". . . & down here I've found leisure enough to make a good start." Working from memory (Alexander's recall was extraordinary), with few supporting works except a one-volume abridgment of *Battles and Leaders,* he was "writing only for my children & intimate friends." Still, the perfectionist in Alexander bridled at the thought of inaccuracies: "I am as anxious to eliminate all mistakes as if it were for publication, & I know how easily mistakes can creep into *any* narrative, & particularly into one written as far from books of reference as I am here." He informed Louise that the recollections were not "to publish, but only for my children, so of course they are very personal." "But partly to tell them the real *story* of the war, & partly because I was often concerned in important affairs which they will be interested to understand," he went on, "I have written, along with my own little doings, a sort of critical narrative of the military game wh[ich] was being played, & I have not hesitated to criticise our moves as I would moves in chess—no matter what General made them." Alexander viewed his effort in Greytown as only a first draft. Once home in South Carolina, he would "go over it all at leisure, with all my military library at hand to put on finishing touches, & fill some few gaps." That might take as much as two years, after which he would have the whole thing typed for distribution to his children.[16]

The conviction that only those closest to him would see his narrative gave Alexander freedom to express unvarnished opinions about people and events. R. E. Lee, Stonewall Jackson, Jefferson Davis, and a host of lesser Confederates came in for substantial criticism. Where he thought the southern people as a whole had been wrong, as in their tendency to rely on divine intervention to sustain their cause, he bluntly said so. Nor did he excise profanities in quoting conversations. Descriptions such as those of Joseph E. Johnston in a white-hot fury on the Peninsula and Colonel Ellerbe B. C. Cash's violent outburst at First Manassas set *Fighting for the Confederacy* apart from the vast majority of northern and southern recollections. Alexander's honesty extended to portraying himself as a supremely self-confident, even arrogant young officer with scant patience for the failings of less gifted individuals. He completely avoided the ritual humility and saccharine praise of friend and foe alike characteristic of what might be called the John B. Gordon school of postwar writing.[17]

To his doubtless well-thumbed popular edition of *Battles and Leaders,* Alexander slowly added other reference materials. Some were his own, such as brief diaries that covered the last two years of the war, journals (also brief) for most of 1862, and an official diary for the First Corps covering 7 May–19 October 1864.[18] These stimulated his memory by providing essential details about his movements. Andrew A. Humphreys's book on the final year of the war in Virginia, William Swinton's history of the Army of the Potomac, Alfred Roman's biography of Beauregard, Edward A. Pollard's history of the Confederacy, and a few magazine articles also helped.[19] On specific questions, he sent queries to a number of former officers in the Army of Northern Virginia.[20] Where he was uncertain about something, Alexander either left a blank space or placed a question mark in the margin and continued with his narrative. Missing information and errors could be taken care of when he got home to his library in South Carolina.

For two years Alexander refought the war in his study in Greytown. Having filled the second ledger book and mailed it to Bessie early in 1898, he switched to foolscap and pencil. "I find I can get along so much faster than with ink in a small book," he reported to Bettie. In addition, this change would enable him to "revise & add notes" more easily. "I am *delighted* if you like my poor little 'recollections,'" he responded when Bessie praised the initial chapters, "but lots of them bring my eyes full of tears as I write." Many sweet memories clustered around the infrequent periods when he and Bettie had been together during the war. Among the happiest had come after the Confederate retreat from Pennsylvania in 1863, and when Alexander neared the end of his section on the battle of Gettysburg, he eagerly anticipated that reunion: "I'll only have to get back safe to Virginia & come & pay you that delightful little visit at Bowling Green." Three days of additional work on the battle intervened before he scribbled a postscript to this letter promising Bettie that "tomorrow I'll get to you at Mrs. Woolfolk's." Remembering friends also prompted emotional responses. "As I am living over all those old scenes, day by day & one by one," he said in reference to his brother-in-law Jeremy Gilmer, ". . . it comes over me more & more that of *all the friendships of my whole life* that with him was the most *intimate & sympathetic & perfect.*" An obituary for one of his artillerists called forth an anguished tribute to "my dear, splendid, old Captain Parker [who] is gone too! And nobody that ever went has gone to any higher or better place than he went to!"[21]

Clearly Alexander was engrossed in his subject, but the onset of war with Spain engendered doubts that he was avoiding more important service. "Do you know when I see Fitz Lee, Wheeler & the other boys going back into the Army as Maj. Genls.," he admitted to his daughter Bessie, "it makes me wonder if I ought not to have thrown up everything here & gone home months ago & gotten into it somehow." Aware that his association with Grover Cleveland would militate against his getting an appointment from Republican William McKinley, Alexander allowed James Longstreet to put in a good word for him. No invitation was forthcoming, however, and with fighting in progress just across the Caribbean in Cuba a subdued Alexander wrote his wife that he was "killing time studying Spanish & writing Recollections."[22]

That mood did not linger, however, as he tackled the great Confederate victory at Chancellorsville and moved on to Gettysburg and the Overland campaign of 1864. Surprised at how much he had to say about those operations, Alexander marveled in May 1899 that the manuscript "keeps just a growing & a growing." He sent the chapters on Gettysburg to Colston, who suggested that the treatment of Lee might be too harsh. "Every *criticism* I can *possibly* get is a great favor," Alexander answered. "As to what I write being considered an attack on Gen. Lee, I am afraid that there are but too many people who will insist upon regarding as an attack upon him anything wh[ich] admits or implies that he ever did make the slightest mistake in the world." John C. Haskell, Wade Hampton Gibbes, and John

Donnell Smith, all of whom served as artillerists under Alexander during the war, as well as other former comrades in the Army of Northern Virginia also reviewed parts of the narrative and supplied information.²³ Hoping to finish by the end of June 1899, Alexander lost time and patience when arbitration kept him from his recollections. In late July, with his deadline already a month past, he complained that he had not written a word for an entire week.²⁴

By late summer 1899 Alexander was devoting all of his energy to the recollections; even fishing, a passion throughout his life, could not entice him from his desk. He had decided that "*every body* better postpone *all* reading until I revise & get it all type written." Racing to complete a first draft before he left Nicaragua, he wrote Bettie on 31 August that once home "I'll buckle into [the] Recollex, wh[ich] I fear I cannot finish before I go. So much to write about the *last*." The "last," of course, was the Appomattox campaign, to which Alexander devoted nearly one hundred pages of his manuscript. In an arduous four weeks he traced the downward spiral of Confederate fortunes in Virginia—Five Forks, the fall of Richmond, Sayler's Creek, and the final painful scene at Appomattox. That September must have been hectic, yet during it Alexander fashioned some of his best prose. The task was finished by 1 October. Twenty-eight months had elapsed since he opened the first ledger book to begin *Fighting for the Confederacy*. Twelve hundred pages of narrative gave his children a precious legacy. He wrote Bettie that he had "been so busy heretofore writing at my Recollex that I w[oul]d never take time for any thing else." Now a reward was in order, and he meant to do some fishing.²⁵

Alexander left Nicaragua on 14 October 1899. He was worried about his beloved Miss Teen, as he called Bettie, because she recently had lost considerable weight, and he suspected she was "keeping things back" from him. Upon arrival in New York, he found his worst nightmare confirmed. Bettie Mason Alexander was dying. He rushed to Savannah, where Bettie was staying with one of their daughters. Guilt-ridden because of his absence in Nicaragua during her illness, Alexander kept watch at her bedside. His vigil ended with her death on 20 November. Alexander was staggered by the force of this blow, refusing entreaties from his children to move in with them and withdrawing to his plantation on South Island off the coast of Georgetown, South Carolina. There he mourned in isolation until April 1900, when news of the death of his daughter Lucy Roy Alexander Craig further rocked him. "My first loss seemed more peculiarly my *own* loss & so I seemed more able to bear it," he wrote. "But *this*—this falls with even more crushing weight & overwhelming desolation on others as well & it seems to me just unspeakable." Several months of profound grief followed, while Alexander groped for direction in his life.²⁶

Rallying by August 1900, Alexander settled on a plan for the future. His twin goals would be the improvement of his Sea Island properties and revision of his recollections. September 1900 found him still alone on South Island but "not lonesome—for I am so busy. I've actually *begun* in rewriting my Recollections & that puts an end to every idle moment—for I try to write a *little bit* every day."[27] At first he performed the fine tuning envisioned while he composed the chapters in Greytown. Using different colored inks and writing on the original manuscript, he corrected names, dates, and distances; he added a few sentences and altered others. Slowly his conception of the project evolved, however, and he decided that such tinkering would not be enough. Following his natural inclination to be both precise and definitive, he determined to convert his manuscript into a rigorous critique of the campaigns of Lee's army. "I want to tell the story *professionally,*" he informed a friend in the summer of 1901, "& to comment freely on every professional feature as one w[oul]d comment on moves of chess."[28] Convinced that he could not graft the needed changes onto his original manuscript, Alexander ceased to mark up chapters of the first draft and began fresh ones.

What had begun as a paternal favor became a scholar's quest. The Greytown recollections, which Alexander eventually presented to Bessie Ficklen, fulfilled the promise to tell his part in the war; the new work would be aimed at a larger audience. Alexander formed friendships with several eminent historians of the day—among them William A. Dunning, J. Franklin Jameson, and Frederic Bancroft—who applauded his shift in emphasis and spoke of publication.[29] Persuaded that most of his personal observations would be inappropriate in the new study, Alexander left them out in favor of more analysis and detail, thereby sacrificing much of the flavor and immediacy of the Greytown reminiscences. He also added material on Jackson's Valley campaign, Hood's Tennessee campaign, and other operations in which he had not participated. In all, Alexander discarded about one third of the Greytown draft and altered much of the rest. As published by Scribner's in 1907, *Military Memoirs* brilliantly achieved Alexander's purpose of examining with surgical precision the military side of the war in the Eastern Theater.

A comparison of *Fighting for the Confederacy* and *Military Memoirs* reveals striking contrasts. Most obvious is the greater proportion of personal material in the former and the more scholarly flavor of the latter. In quality of prose, six years of polishing resulted in a smoother, if somewhat duller, style for *Military Memoirs*. Because Alexander tempered many of his harshest judgments about personalities and deleted almost all of the profane quotations, *Military Memoirs* lacks the raw power of *Fighting for the Confederacy*. Chronological emphasis also differs significantly. *Fighting for the Confederacy* opens with a long chapter on Alexander's pre–Civil War life, virtually none of which is in *Military Memoirs,* and devotes far less space to the war before Gettysburg—about 33 percent as against 57 percent in *Military Memoirs.* Roughly 13 percent of each covers Gettysburg, but *Fighting for the Confederacy* allots 47 percent to the campaigns after Gettysburg compared with just 28 percent in *Military Memoirs.* The closing portions of the two books also differ markedly in effectiveness. The intensity of Alexander's treatment of the retreat from Richmond to Appomattox in *Fighting for the Confederacy* is one of the book's strengths, while the final chapters of *Military Memoirs* bear the marks of drastic cutting performed with scant regard for the integrity of the narrative.

Scholars interested in Alexander's writings were long confused by the intermingling in the Alexander Papers of the original manuscript of *Fighting for the Confederacy* and drafts of the chapters of *Military Memoirs.* When the papers first came to the Southern Historical Collection at Chapel Hill, the staff faced the difficult problem of how to make sense of various drafts "of a volume of Civil War recollections, published in 1907 as *Military Memoirs of a Confederate.*" The material consisted "of manuscripts written in blank books, of sheets of legal size paper fastened together in batches with paper fasteners, and of folders of typescript," all of which were repetitive and "confusing to organize and use." Most of it seemed to have been written "in the period 1900–1907, and some of it was extensively revised before publication." Unaware that Alexander had completed a full draft well before he did any revising, and bedeviled because the family had not treated the draft as a separate entity, the staff placed segments of the original Greytown manuscript and chapters from the later versions together in chronological files corresponding to the major campaigns of the war. This was a reasonable archival solution to a processing nightmare.[30]

One result was the disappearance of the two ledger books and hundreds of pages of foolscap of the Greytown manuscript into an intimidating mass assumed to be drafts of *Military Memoirs.* Canvassing the collection while editing a reprint of *Military Memoirs,* T. Harry Williams inferred that Alexander had begun writing after 1900 and intended to publish his work from the beginning. Alexander probably had shifted his emphasis from personal experience to analysis, Williams concluded, "to conserve space, to avoid controversy, and to give the book a broader appeal." Williams added that the manuscript, "if it could be pieced together as a continuous narrative, which would be difficult because of the repetitions, would be considerably longer than the book."[31] James I. Robertson, Jr., advanced another thesis to account for the absence of more personal description in *Military Memoirs.* Alexander had indeed written of his own activities, argued Robertson, but what appeared in *Military Memoirs* was almost entirely different. "Perhaps the Scribner's editors recoiled at the directness and/or bluntness of some of Alexander's original statements," he speculated, "or possibly the manuscript was too long and descriptive in the opinion of the publisher. In any event, someone other than Alexander wrote much of the finished narrative." Robertson thought it tragic that the original memoirs lay forgotten and pondered "how revealing and rewarding it would be if all that was omitted from *Military Memoirs of a Confederate* could be published in book form."[32]

Maury Klein first alerted students of the war to the existence of two quite different accounts. Commenting on Williams's wish that Alexander had written a personal narrative as well as *Military Memoirs,* Klein stated that "in effect he did just that, for the original Greytown recollections in their fading ledger books comprise a personal narrative." Klein later addressed Robertson's suggestion that *Military Memoirs* was ghostwritten by reiterating Alexander's authorship of both works. "The confusion vanishes when one examines Alexander's extensive papers in detail," wrote Klein, and he mentioned again that the "now faded ledgers comprise Alexander's personal memoir of the war."[33]

Klein performed a tremendous service in removing much of the confusion about Alexander's writings, but he failed to clarify the situation fully. Two major problems awaited anyone seeking the Greytown reminiscences in "faded ledgers" at the Southern Historical Collection. First, late drafts of chapters in *Military Memoirs* on Chickamauga and the Wilderness also were written in ledger books—gray ones with maroon leather corners. Second, and more serious, Bessie Alexander Ficklen's two light-brown ledgers held less than a quarter of the Greytown narrative.[34] The balance—everything from the latter stages of the campaign of Second Manassas forward—was on foolscap and other kinds of paper and was far harder to distinguish from drafts of chapters for *Military Memoirs.* The key to disentangling this material lies in Alexander's correspondence with family and friends while he was in Greytown. As he went along, he reported how many pages he had written on various parts of the war. For example, on 6 February 1899 he noted, "I've just finished Gettysburg *115 pages* & 2 maps, & I'll soon go on with East Tennessee campaign." Similarly, fourteen weeks later he wrote Bettie that ninety pages covering the period 1–20 May 1864 were wrapped and ready to be mailed home.[35] A search through the Alexander Papers for chapters corresponding in length to those mentioned in the letters reveals the entire manuscript for *Fighting for the Confederacy.* Without the clues provided by Alexander himself, identification would be virtually impossible.

Alexander's two books represent a unique achievement in the literature on the Civil War. Students have known for decades that only a handful of books by participants possess the enduring value of *Military Memoirs;* as an exercise in dispassionate analysis, it quite simply has no peer. *Fighting for the Confederacy* will redouble the debt owed to Porter Alexander. In its pages R. E. Lee stands revealed as a complex man displaying not only the gentleness, military brilliance, and nobility of legend, but also humor, frustration, anger, and pettiness. There is fresh information about many commanders on both sides—the existence of an ailment that rendered Gustavus Woodson Smith unable to ride a horse and evidence of Joseph Johnston's impressive physical strength, to name but two examples—together with severe criticism of Confederate civilian and military leadership. Information on the field artillery in the Army of Northern Virginia abounds. Well-crafted anecdotes illuminate the terror of civilians trapped in the capricious path of the conflict, the casual attitude toward death manifested by soldiers (including Alexander himself) numbed by prolonged exposure to killing, the grimness of daily life in the trenches at Petersburg, the animosity of Confederate soldiers toward blacks in the Federal army, and dozens of other facets of the war. Alexander's unabashed expressions of affection for comrades highlight the transcendent bond between soldiers of the same unit; his sense of humor and appreciation of irony add spice to an already vigorous narrative. Many of his purely descriptive passages, such as that last long look at Richmond on 3 April 1865, are haunting in their effectiveness.

Fighting for the Confederacy is a book to be savored, one of those wonderful volumes that is both instructive and pleasurable to read. All who traverse its pages will improve their understanding of the Civil War and the people who waged it. They will come to know Porter Alexander as well—and that is one of the great delights of this marvelous book.

EDITOR'S NOTE

The editorial goal of this project was to prepare an accurate, unabridged, and annotated text of the manuscript Alexander wrote while in Greytown, Nicaragua. The result, however, is not a literal transcription of the 1,200-page original. Writing in energetic spurts, Alexander began many sentences with "and" or "but," misspelled many proper names (he had no reference works in which to check many of them), paid little attention to paragraphs, pursued an erratic course with capitalization and punctuation, and left blanks where he lacked necessary information. A number of editorial decisions, none of which alters Alexander's account in any substantive way, were implemented in an effort to retain the flavor of the manuscript while at the same time helping the modern reader.

Alexander varied wildly in his use of capitals, and with several letters (especially c and s), it sometimes is impossible to distinguish between upper and lower case. Capitalization has been made uniform, following, for the most part, modern usage.

Punctuation in the manuscript also demanded attention. Alexander almost never used apostrophes (either in contractions or for possessives), neglected to put commas in series or other places where absolutely needed, often substituted dashes for periods at the end of sentences, and utilized a number of clumsy devices—for example, placing commas before parentheses and periods after the last word within parentheses. These problems have been corrected, as have constructions in which the original punctuation was distracting or obscured the meaning.

At some points in the manuscript Alexander wrote several pages without a break in paragraphs; at others he made a new paragraph with every sentence. Some of the former have been broken up and some of the latter combined to give the narrative better movement.

Alexander misspelled many proper names, often using two or three spellings for the same person or place. Had he composed the manuscript in his library rather than in Greytown, he certainly would have checked some of these spellings. All misspelled proper names have been corrected and variant spellings have been made consistent according to accepted usage. For example, Alexander used Nine Mile road, 9-Mile road, nine mile road, and 9-mile road in his account of the Seven Days; all have been changed to Nine Mile Road. With several place-names Alexander used common, though incorrect, nineteenth-century spellings—for example, Drury's Bluff for Drewry's Bluff, Spottsylvania for Spotsylvania, and Frazier's Farm and Frazer's Farm for Frayser's Farm. These have been retained. Apart from these problems with proper nouns, the manuscript is remarkably free of misspelled words. Most of the handful that do appear consist of one- or two-letter omissions; these missing letters have been supplied without the distracting addition of brackets, although brackets are used when it is necessary to supply an entire word or phrase to clarify Alexander's meaning. The only word that Alexander consistently got wrong was "bivouacked," which he spelled without the "k"; "bivouaced" has been retained as an idiosyncratic spelling. Late nineteenth-century conventions about words such as anybody, everything, breastworks, infantryman, and somewhere were fuzzy, and Alexander variously spelled them as one or two words. As a concession to the informal nature of the manuscript, they have not been made uniform. Similarly, alternating British, American, and French spellings for a number of words will be found throughout the text, as will a few archaic and colloquial variations.

The manuscript is filled with abbreviations for ranks, titles, and units, such as Gen, Col, Maj, Regt, Brig, Div, and the like; these remain in the text with periods added. Single letters used in place of a full name—J. for Johnston, L. for Lee—also have been retained. Alexander employed wh as an abbreviation for which, when, and what; wd for would; thru and thro for through; and altho for although. All of these words have been spelled out. Ampersands and &c. have been retained, but superscripts have been deleted.

The blanks Alexander left in his narrative where he was unsure of his information—usually about casualties or distances—are indicated in the text by a baseline rule: _____. Where possible, the missing information is supplied in a note. In the case of casualties, figures from Alexander's *Military Memoirs of a Confederate* are given, supplemented by more modern estimates if there is a serious discrepancy.

Alexander crossed out a number of passages in his narrative. It is impossible to state with certainty when he made these changes, but most probably came during the period after 1900 when he was turning the Greytown manuscript into a more scholarly work. In almost all cases the original language is retained and the deletion explained in a note. In a few instances where Alexander merely substituted a word or two with no change in meaning, the new language is retained and the original moved to a note.

Although Alexander was generally careful in citing numbers, a close reading of the statistics in some of his tables reveals small inaccuracies, such as totals that differ slightly from the actual sum of the individual numbers cited. No effort was made to double check all of Alexander's figures in order to correct minor discrepancies of this sort.

The illustrations in the manuscript of *Fighting for the Confederacy* are of two kinds: diagrams, sketches, and maps drawn in Alexander's own hand and illustrations clipped from other sources that Alexander pasted onto the pages of the manuscript. It is readily apparent from their physical appearance which illustrations are original and which are taken from other sources. Because the illustrations could not always have the same placement in published form that they had in the manuscript, indications of their exact placement in the manuscript have been inserted in the text in brackets. To aid in this, the illustrations have been numbered and given brief captions, an identification system of my devising rather than Alexander's. As is explained in the notes, five of the illustrations included here (Figures 12, 13, 14, 20, and 30) do not actually appear in the manuscript; they are maps that Alexander intended to supply but did not. The intended maps did appear in *Military Memoirs,* however, and the maps reproduced here are taken from that source.

As a participant's account, *Fighting for the Confederacy* stands very well on its own. It reflects Alexander's opinions and judgments. The endnotes are designed to present information necessary to a full understanding of Alexander's narrative, not to impose the type of pedantic scholarly apparatus that sometimes overpowers less impressive reminiscences. Where Alexander raises a question or alludes to controversy, the notes point readers to other material. Persons, books, poems, songs, and events are identified briefly within the context of Alexander's text. There are no summaries of the lives of generals, politicians, and writers who are covered in standard reference tools such as Ezra J. Warner's *Generals in Gray* and *Generals in Blue,* the *Dictionary of American Biography,* or Robert K. Krick's *Lee's Colonels.* Neither are there extended historiographical forays recapitulating what later writers have said about the topics Alexander covers.

Fighting for the Confederacy will meet the needs of the vast majority of those interested in Porter Alexander's personal reminiscences. It encompasses the entire original narrative, both text and illustrations. No observation, opinion, or scrap of analysis has been cut. Still, there are those who may need to see the manuscript *exactly* as written. The answer for them is a trip to the Southern Historical Collection.

Fighting for the Confederacy

Oh, life goes back through years, today,
And we are *Men* once more!
And yon old hill is Arlington,
And there the Alien Shore!
And over yonder on the heights
The hostile camp fires quiver;
And suddenly twixt us & them
Flows by *Potomac's* River.

O'er Stuart's head, in place of plume,
The long grain now doth wave.
Oft times we've seen the violets bloom
O'er Stonewall Jackson's grave.

Yet age remembers with a sigh
The days that are no more.

EARLY DAYS

I can recall vividly the occasion when I first heard the idea suggested that the Southern states would secede from the Union under certain circumstances. I think it must have been about 1848. I was a small boy, perfectly devoted to shooting & fishing, & I was the protege, in these amusements, of our excellent neighbor (in Washington, Geo.) Mr. Frank Colley, an old gentleman of 70, but not too old to start at daylight & ride 8 miles to Little River, & sit on the bank & fish all day for a single "sucker."

On one of these expeditions, Mr. Colley told me that secession was being talked of, & I remember well the spot in the road where we were, & the pang which the idea sent through me, & my thinking that I would rather lose my gun—my dearest possession on earth—than see it happen.

Two or three years later, at an election for delegates to a state convention, Toombs ran as a Union delegate against Gartrell as a secession candidate.[1]

My feelings were so much enlisted that I got into a quarrel with two of the "town" boys, Jim Hester & Ben Kappell, which came very near ruining my life.

I was told that these two had armed themselves with pistols & intended to whip me. I borrowed an old "pepper-box" revolver from our "overseer," John Eidson, loaded it heavily, & got 6 special "Walker's Anticorosive Caps" for the nipples, instead of the common "G. D.'s."[2]

It would be too long to detail the quarrel, but, indignant at being bullied by two older & larger boys, I at last came into collision with Jim Hester. He struck me over the head with a light "skinny-stick," breaking it. I drew my revolver &, aiming at his breast, pulled the trigger. It snapped failing to explode the cap. Hester drew a single barrel pistol, while I tried another barrel, which also snapped. This second failure made me think that the Walker caps were made of copper too thick for the hammer of my pistol, & that all six barrels would fail. At [the] same time—while he had drawn a pistol, Hester paused a moment, & made no motion to aim or fire at me.

This made me pause in the very act of pulling the trigger for a third trial; for I thought that if I continued to try to shoot, it would make him shoot, & that my pistol would continue to fail on account of my thick caps while his might not. I therefore stopped pulling on the trigger & waited to see what he would do. On this other boys ran in & took both of our pistols away. Some one said to the boy who took mine, "See if that pistol is loaded." He raised it over his head & pulled the trigger for the 3rd barrel (it was a self cocker). This time it went off loud & clear.

My father had very recently forbidden my staying at [the] play ground so as to be late at supper, & this little episode kept me until long after supper-time. My brother Charley knew that a difficulty was imminent & he hurried through supper & started out to the play ground, which was in an open lot west of the lawn in front of the house. As he left the house, he heard the report of my pistol (fired by the boy who took it from me) & ran out & met me just leaving the ground, the boys having separated Hester & myself, & started us both home.

Charley & I returned & met Father at the door. Hester's blow had made my nose bleed, & I had gotten my face bloody from it, & in reply to my father's rather angry questions, what was the matter, & why I was out so late, I told the whole occurrence. He was much shocked at it—so much so that I did not get the punishment I expected, & felt that I deserved. He & Mr. Hester, Jim's father (a most excellent man) forbade us both to visit the play ground for a long time, & meanwhile Jim & I made friends.[3]

But gratitude to a Providence which saved me so narrowly from a calamity which would have ruined my whole life, has led me ever since to avoid & eschew politics, as too prolific of quarrels for one who, like myself, is liable to become reckless of consequences when in a passion.

From my earliest recollection I was very anxious to go to West Point but my father would never listen to it until I was about 14 years old, when two of my sisters had either married, or were about to marry, graduates of the U.S. Mil. Acad., when he gave his consent. I can still recall the occasion. He was sitting in the front porch of the old family home at Washington, Geo., one summer evening about the year 1849, talking with Lawton & Gilmer.[4] I was in the "drawing-room" where some of my sisters were playing on the piano & singing & I had fallen asleep on the sofa, when some one, I forget who, came in from the porch calling me & I was waked & brought out on the porch. Then I was told that Father consented to my going to West Pt., provided I would promise to study hard enough to "graduate in the engineers." I was wide awake in a moment & ready to promise anything, & from that day all my thoughts & ambitions were of the army. Gilmer drilled me a little in the manual of arms occasionally that summer & in my studies special attention was given those which were taught at West Point.

My father soon went to see [the] Hon. Robt. Toombs, one of our near neighbors, & then the member of the House of Reps. for our district in Geo.—the 8th—to get his promise of the appointment in 1851 when I would be 16. But the place was already filled by W. R. Boggs[5] of Augusta, who would not graduate until 1853, so Mr. Toombs tried to get for me an apptmt. "at large" from the president. He *nearly* succeeded in 1852 but not quite—& I had to wait until Boggs graduated in 1853.

But this delay was doubtless the best thing for me in giving me better preparation & maturer mind, for I was only 18 in May '53 a few days before I entered as a cadet.

My father had been at great pains not only about my education but that of all of his children. When his four oldest daughters were growing up he brought out Miss Sarah Brackett from Mass. She came in March 1835 & stayed 8 years as a teacher for them, & it resulted in a large & prosperous "Seminary" under her control with a considerable corps of teachers all from the North, & scholars from all over the state. When the four boys came on next, he brought out several male teachers, of whom Mr. Russell M. Wright of Easthampton Mass., & Dr. A. M. Scudder (who moved to Athens & lived there all his life) were the most prominent. Scudder preceded Wright. I was under S. for only a year or two, & most of my education was under Mr. Wright, who lived & taught in Washington until the war when he had to return north, & still lives, I believe (1894), in Castleton, Vt.[6]

There is little to be said of my boyhood. I was passionately fond of shooting & fishing & my friendship with two old gentlemen, growing from this fondness, was a great source of amusement to my older sisters. They were Mr. Frank Colley, with whom I went fishing, & Mr. James Dyson, with whom I went hunting. My school intimates were Zeb & Dempsey Colley (sons of Mr. Frank C.; & Dempsey [was] killed in the war at Fredbg.), Ned Anthony, Henry Andrews & Garnett A., & Wylie & Jimmy DuBose (Wylie [was] killed in [the] Seven Days at Richmond [in] 1862).[7]

My father had two plantations—one in Liberty Co., Geo. ("Hopewell"), a rice & Sea Island Cotton place, near Riceboro; & the home place in Washington. There were about forty to 50 Negroes—little & big on each place.[8] They were all looked after by him & my mother as if they were children. Their clothes were all cut out & made up by the women under my mother's supervision, & she also taught all the young ones in Sunday afternoon "Sabbath-school." Provisions for the whole year were generally made on the plantations, & "hog killing" & curing was *the* event of the winter. If he had not raised enough hogs of his own, my father would buy from ten to thirty, from "droves" which were brought down from Kentucky & Tennessee by hundreds—driven slowly & kept fat on the way. As the most humane way of killing them, I was usually allowed to stay at home &

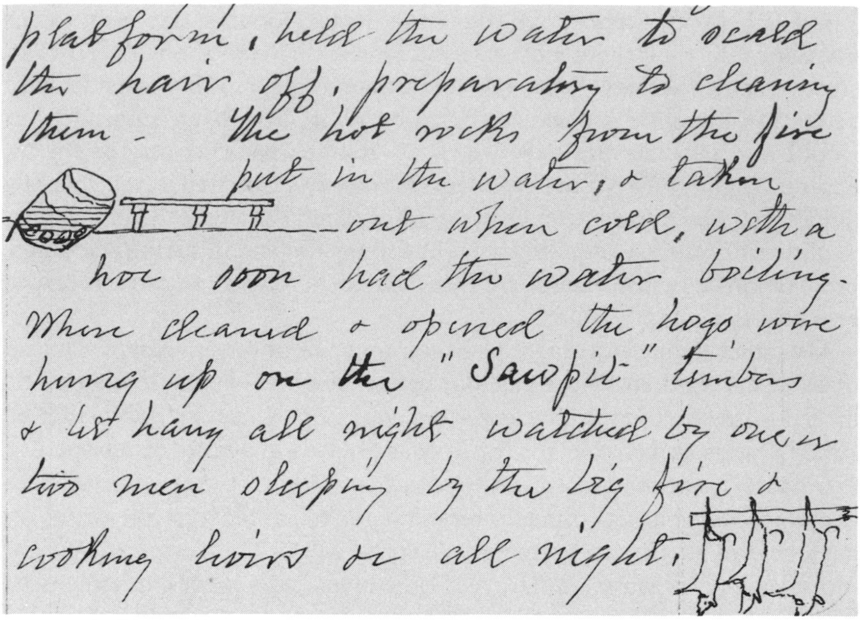
platform, held the water to scald
the hair off, preparatory to cleaning
them. The hot rocks from the fire
put in the water, & taken
out when cold, with a
hoe soon had the water boiling.
When cleaned & opened the hogs were
hung up on the "Sawpit" timbers
& let hang all night watched by one or
two men sleeping by the big fire &
cooking livers &c all night.

Figures 1 and 2. Hogshead and platform; Hogs on "sawpit" timbers

shoot them with a rifle.[9] A cold day was of course selected for the killing, a large fire of logs 6 to 8 feet long built up with about forty large stones in among the logs, & a big hogshead, in an inclining position at the end of a platform, held the water to scald the hair off, preparatory to cleaning them. [Figure 1 appears here in the manuscript.] The hot rocks from the fire put in the water, & taken out when cold, with a hoe soon had the water boiling. When cleaned & opened the hogs were hung up on the "sawpit" timbers & let hang all night watched by one or two men sleeping by the big fire & cooking livers &c. all night. [Figure 2 appears here in the manuscript.] About 30 or 40 hogs made a *"killing"* & there would be two or three every winter. All hands were at work making lard, sausages, spare ribs, hogs head cheese, jowls, "cracklings" &c. &c.

Of the servants on the Washington place I remember Adam, the lame shoemaker; Jack Ryans, the carpenter (& an excellent one), his wife Morots, the cook, & his children William, Stephen & Joel—all carpenters—James the driver, Tom, who succeeded his mother as cook—who died during the war—& Mary, who was sold at her own request to go with her husband—I don't remember where finally, but first to a Mr. Cozart; Charles, an old but very faithful man-about-lot & his family—his wife

Sukey, daughters Margaret, sold to go to Milledgeville with her husband, Eliza, Maria & Caroline, house girls, [and] son Jim; Old Bob & his wife Dilsey, super-annuated—who lived near the "big poplar"; Harry the gardener & his family—wife Rhina, sons July & Jacob, daughters Fanny [and] Hester. Then there was Emanuel the foreman at the plantation, wife Kitty, children Jane & Jerry. Then I remember but forget families & relationships [of] Lewis, deaf & a sort of blacksmith, Old Abram, Mercer, Little Johnnie, Mom Peggie, & several young ones growing up when I left home in 1853 for West Point. There was also a regular semptress Mary Ann & a regular washwoman Mary[10] & her daughter Sally.

Miss Sarah Brackett finally married Rev. Nehemiah Adams, a Presbyterian minister of Boston, Mass., & being in bad health came out & spent a winter with my father sometime in the fifties after the publication of *Uncle Tom's Cabin*. Dr. A. on his return north wrote a book (intended as a sort of reply I think to Uncle Tom) called "A South-side view of Slavery,"[11] which caused him some trouble with some of his friends at home.

Cadet Life

The winter of 1852 & 1853 I spent in Savh. taking lessons in French & drawing & staying with the Lawtons on South Broad St. In May '53 I started from Washn., Geo., for West Point, by rail via Augusta, Branchville, Wilmington, Weldon, Richmond, Aquia Creek, Washn. City, &c., taking 3½ days to the trip & stopping in N.Y. at [the] Astor House, then the fashionable hotel. I visited cousin John Hillhouse near Troy, N.Y., & entered at West Point with Bob Anderson from Savh. about June 12th.

At my examination for admission I measured 5'9½" barefoot & weighed about 150. My first room mates were Bob Anderson & Dick Meade from Petersburg, until we went into camp. In camp my tent mates were Tom Berry from Newnan, Geo., Dick Brewer from Annapolis, Md., & _____ Burnet from N.Y., who only remained a cadet until next January when he was found deficient. When we went into barracks in Sep. I was put in Co. D & roomed in Div. No. 7, Room 19 with Lawrence Kip from Albany, son of Bishop Kip of Cal. The Kips are related to our Hillhouse kin. Kip resigned at the approach of the June examination [in] 1854. In my 3rd class year I was a corporal in Co. B & roomed with C. H. Morgan of N.Y. a very good fellow.[12] My father & mother visited me during encampment in [the] summer of '54 & mother was ill for some weeks in a room on [the] 2nd floor of [the] east wing of Roe's Hotel, & my last sight of her dear face was there when she was able to be taken off. But she would not let me come the last morning to say good-bye. She died Feb. 28, 1855.

I came home on furlough in June '55 & stayed till Aug. 20th. During it I visited Cliff[13] in Athens at the Asbury Halls & went on a trip to Madison Springs & Toccoa & Tallulah Falls. In the party were Jack Church,[14] who had just graduated at West Pt., & his two sisters Mrs. Craig & Miss Annie Church, Jimmie Hull & Mrs. Rucker, whom he afterward married, & also Miss Cara Lucas, now Mrs. Hallonquist, a Miss Maria Heath from Richmond & several others whose names I cannot recall. I was much smitten with [the] charms of Miss Annie C. but it so happened that she did not reciprocate them & I never saw her again. She married a Whitner & died in Anderson, S.C., leaving a large family.

On my return to West Point I was made orderly sergt. of Co. D & roomed with Bob Anderson in [the] 2nd story, south west room, Division 7. Bob was sergt. major.

I remember my roll-call yet—all but the 4 corporals, thus: *Sergts.* Kimmell, Quattlebaum, Claflin; *Corporals* Sloan & 3 others whose names are forgotten; *Privates* Bacon, Bailey, Beck, Berry, Bevill, Brewer, Chamberlain, Coontz, Claflin, Cunningham, Enos, Ferguson, Gibbes, Gilmer, Holt, Hopkins, Ives, Johnson, Kennedy, Kerr, Laramie, Lee F., Lorain, Lyon, McFarland, Marmaduke, Mills, Mishler, Morgan, Napier, Parker, Ramseur, Randol, Ricketts, Rugg, Sanders W., Smith A., Stivers, Sweet, Tabor, Talbot, Taylor, Thomas, Vanderbilt, White R., Williams.[15]

As I write these names every one calls up a face & almost every one a story. Many of the stories, too, are tragedies—ending in death on the battlefield, one of which, that of Sanders W., will be told when I reach in my narrative the siege of Knoxville in Nov. 1863, when it happened that I with two regts. of infantry & a battery attacked a brigade of cavalry commanded by Sanders, & he was killed.

But one of these stories had even a darker end than one on the battlefield, & I will tell it here as it has no place in my narrative. It has never been published, & no story I have ever known has appealed more deeply to my sympathy. And I doubt if any one now living even recalls poor Kennedy's memory as often as I.

He was from Louisiana—I don't know what part—nor can I recall now his first name or initials, but he was a quiet modest fellow, with bluish gray eyes, neutral colored hair & a pleasant oval face & medium height & build. I don't know how hard he studied, but he was one of a large lot who were found deficient in Jan. 7, 1855, & were sent off.

When the war broke out Kennedy was in our western army somewhere & he was taken prisoner, but managed to escape from the Northern prison where he was confined & got across to Canada.

While there he joined in a wild, absurd, & utterly indefensible scheme to burn N.Y. City gotten up by some Confederate refugees there—on their own responsibilty & without any authority or countenance from Confederate authority. Kennedy & one or two others went to N.Y., & on a certain day Kennedy started a fire in Barnum's Museum on Broadway not far from the Astor House & the others started fires in one or two hotels. All of the fires were soon discovered & extinguished, but it was known that they were a Confederate effort to burn the city & large rewards were offered for those concerned in it. Kennedy had made his escape back to Canada & stayed at Niagara Falls. Some detective went there & managed to get into his confidence & roomed with him & at last persuaded Kennedy one day to walk across the suspension bridge with him. He had officers on the lookout with warrants & no sooner did poor Kennedy set foot on U.S. soil than he was arrested.

He was tried, sentenced & hung in old Fort Lafayette. The poor fellow tried to keep up his courage by jocularly asking old Col. Munroe in command of the Fort for a drink as he was led to the gallows & by singing a drinking song as the halter was placed about his neck.[16]

During my last year, June '56 to '57, I was captain of Co. D & occupied the tower room of Div. 8 with Tom Baylor[17] for [a] roommate, who was cadet quartermaster.

Utah Expedition

I graduated in '57, 3rd in my class & was made brevet 2nd lt. of engineers. After 3 mos. furlough I was ordered back to West Point as lt. of Co. A engineer troops & asst. instructor of practical military engineering.

In the fall of 1857 Gen. Albert Sidney Johnston started to Utah Territory with troops to install Gov. Cumming as governor; the Mormons, who had previously had Brigham Young for governor, having refused to recognise as govr. or receive anyone else.[18] Gen. Johnston got as far as Fort Bridger 100 miles east of Salt Lake & was compelled to go into winter quarters; the Mormons having fortified & obstructed the passes in the Wahsatch Mountains & having also captured & burned some of the provision trains sent out to supply him, by the contractors Russell, Majors, & Wadell.

It seemed as if there would be war with them, & it was proposed to send out strong reinforcements to Johnston as soon as they could be started in the spring. I applied to be sent with the co. of sappers & it was finally decided to send 64 picked men, out of the 100 in the co., Capt. Jas. C. Duane of the Engr. Corps in command & myself as lieut.[19] We accordingly left West Point about Apr. 1 for Fort Leavenworth, Mo., whence six columns of about 500 men each were to march for Utah as soon as grass in the plains would support the trains. On May 6 our column no. 1 marched from

Ft. L.—composed of our co. of engineer troops & about 8 co.'s of the 6th Regt. of Infantry commanded by Col. Andrews[20] of that regt. In the command were Capts. Armistead & Dick Garnett, both afterward Confederate generals & both killed in Pickett's Charge[21] at Gettysburg. Lt. Corley,[22] another officer, was Gen. Lee's quartermaster, when I was his chief of ordnance, & indeed afterward until the surrender at Appomattox.

The country was but thinly settled & we passed only one small beginning of a village after leaving Leavenworth. That was called Marysville & here one of my classmates, Magruder,[23] was murdered in column no. 3, which started about 4 weeks after us. He had been drinking & quarreled with some resident of the place about noon & about dark was shot dead from his horse while riding through the edge of the settlement, & I think the murderer escaped, & was never punished.

Our route was by Fort Kearny (300 m.), which we passed about May 26th, & thence up [the] south side of [the] Platte River to a place called afterwards Julesberg on the South Platte about 20 miles above the fork. Here the regular emigrant route across the plains, which we had so far followed, crossed the South Platte by a ford & then turned northwest & struck across to the North Platte at Ash Hollow & then followed [the] south side of that river to Ft. Laramie (700 [miles] from Lvwth.) & thence on to Sweetwater Creek, up which it ascended to [the] South Pass of the Rockies, whence it went southwest to Ft. Bridger.

We were ordered to take a more direct route which it was believed would be shorter. Lt. Bryan[24] of the Topographical Engineers had been over that part of it east of the Rocky Mts. & he was sent along with us as guide. Beyond the Divide only Frémont,[25] many years before, had ever gone.

So at Julesberg we kept on up the South Platte, some 20 miles, to the mouth of Lodge Pole Creek. We then forded the Platte & took our route up this creek—crossed the Black Hills at its headwaters & thence skirted the Medicine Bow Mountains, crossed the North Platte's headwaters & ascending Sage Creek we crossed the Rocky Mountain Divide at Bridger's Pass. Thence we struck for Bitter Creek & down its canyon to Green River, which we crossed, & thence via Rabbit Hollow we struck the emigrant trail coming from South Pass not far east of Ft. Bridger. Our route from Julesberg was practically the route now followed by the Union Pacific R.R., & in later years I have been able to recognise many localities where we marched & camped from the windows of the cars. I specially remember Pine Bluffs on Lodge Pole Creek, from which high elevation I got my first view of the Rocky Mountains [in] June 1858. They loomed high over the prairies with Pike's, Long's & one or two other snow peaks in sight & impressed my youthful imagination very deeply.

In 1885, when a govt. director on the Union Pacific, I was sent to investigate a massacre of Chinese miners by the American miners at some very extensive mines in Bitter Creek Canyon & recognised at once a spot at which we had camped by a sulpher spring & had gotten coal for our travelling blacksmith's forge from a near by bluff & where our first mail after leaving Leavenworth overtook us. Of course such a trip was full of delight & interest to me with my fondness for hunting & fishing & my romantic ideas of the Far West, the Indians, the trappers, &c., &c., & to this day I remember vividly a great deal about it & with great pleasure, but I can't go into detail here. I can only say here that at that time the plains were practically in their original wildness. Buffalo & all game were abundant. The Indians wore only breech-clouts & were armed with but bows & arrows, & were very frequently hostile & always suspicious & suspected. The Arrapahoes had been at war & defeated by Gen. Sumner[26] on Solomon's Fork in the fall of '57 & at first all fled from [the] approach of our column thinking we were after them. I was once sent on a scout with two soldiers, & not being able to get back at night I went to some 2 or 3 Indian lodges which I happened [to] pass near to spend the night & was the guest of a Sioux named "Spotted Tail," who afterward became the head chief of his tribe & was for many years the leading Indian on the plains.[27] We met on the trip Pawnees, Sioux, Cheyennes, Kioways, Arrapahoes, & Utes.[28] I hunted a great deal along the road, as Duane would march with the company all day on my agreeing to make all inspections of sentinels at night. I killed a great deal of game of nearly all kinds—buffalo, antelope, wolves, wild ducks, grouse, sage hens, &c., & I *hunted* a good deal for elk, mountain sheep, & grizzly bear but could never manage to get shots at any though we saw them, & some of each were killed by some of a half dozen tame Delaware Indians whom we had along as scouts & hunters.

I had a glorious chase after my first buffalo.[29] Our first sight of them was some 50 miles west of Ft. Kearny where one afternoon a bunch of about 15 bulls were seen about 2 miles to the front & left. Our 6 Delaware Indians saw them first & with two white wagon masters started for them & were more than half way to them when I started on a very fine grey horse I had. The buffalo soon took alarm & galloped off into the bluffs on the left which they climbed, & then getting on the level & hard table land, covered only with the short buffalo grass, they headed due south as fast as their legs could carry them pursued by all nine of us. But my horse was the only one equal to the occasion & though I had started a mile behind I gradually passed all the others & was soon at the very heels of the herd. My horse was very skittish & would never let me shoot from his back, & he was now so scared at the strange sight & strong smell of the big animals that it was with difficulty that by spurring & even beating him over the head with the Harpers Ferry Rifle I carried that I drove him in among them, for I determined to kill the one in the lead, for that would be the cow if there was a cow in the band & the cows make the best beef. But at last my grey let himself out, & going through the bunch so close that I could have touched them on either side he placed me alongside of the leader, both bull & horse at their best speed. I first dropped my reins & tried to aim from my shoulder to fire, but the motion prevented any aim & I remembered having been cautioned by old buffalo hunters to look out for buffalo turning suddenly when shot on their fore feet as a pivot & catching a horse on their horns, so I picked up, reins again in my left hand & resting [my] gun across my left arm. I sighted it as well as I could behind the buffalo's left shoulder & let fly. The bullet struck where I intended, passed nearly through & broke the shoulder on the opposite side, & the old bull—for there was no cow in the herd—fell with a real crash. I reined up my horse as soon as I could—he was so scared it was hard to stop him & he ran almost 400 yards beyond—& jumped off & picketed him by driving [a] picket pin (with lariat attached, which was always attached to [the] halter & hanging to [the] saddle bow) into the ground with my heel, & loaded my rifle running toward the buffalo, who had picked himself up & was making his way too toward me as well as he could. I ran up within 30 yards & shot him again, bringing him to the ground, just as the foremost Indian, their chief, a big fellow named Wolf, 6 ft. 2 in. [and] splendid looking, rode up & also fired but missed, his bullet knocking up the grass beyond. Few moments of my life have been prouder & happier than that and few compliments sweeter than the hearing Wolf tell the other pursuers, who had all given up the chase & gathered around, "He make good hunter; he not 'fraid.'" The Indians butchered the bull & packed the best parts on our horses & we returned to camp some 6 miles off.

I killed a great many buffalo afterward going & returning—about 2 dozen in all—all I cared to kill. Most of them I shot still hunting, in which way any number could be killed easily, as they were not shy unless they got the scent of horse or man. But on my return in the fall about 20 miles east of Fort Kearny I had another grand race, all alone, after the last buffalo that we saw. It took a whole afternoon & led me about ten miles, & when the old bull finally fell after chasing me nearly as much as I chased him he had four rifle balls & 6 revolver balls in different parts of his anatomy.

When we got near Bridger's Pass the 6th Infy. halted & encamped for two weeks or so to let our co. & an escort of 30 infantry go ahead to explore & cut a road in some difficult & obscure parts. We finally reached Fort Bridger about July 30th. Here we found that the Mormons had abandoned their proposed opposition to Gov. Cumming, that Gen. Johnston had moved in & occupied Salt Lake City peacefully & that the 6 columns of reinforcements on the march from Leavenworth were all being broken up & distributed elsewhere. Of our column, the 6th Infy. was ordered to continue its march & go to Oregon, while we of the sappers were to return to West Point. What was called "Steptoe's War"[30] had broken out in the spring, in Oregon, with the Coeur d'Alene & Yakima Indians, & the 36 men of our co., whom we had left at West Point, had been sent out by way of Panama to Oregon, where Gen. Wright[31] organised a campaign to avenge the Steptoe massacre.

So on Aug. 9th, orders to the above effect having arrived on the 8th, we suddenly found ourselves on the march eastward, back for West Point—instead of westward on to Salt Lake as we had planned. We made a rapid march without much incident—via [the] emigrant road & South Pass, as before stated. We passed Fort Laramie (402 miles) Sep. 2nd (20 marches), Fort Kearny (740 miles) Sep. 18th (35 marches) & arrived at Leavenworth (1019 miles) on Sunday, Oct. 3rd, in 47 marches. Looking over our itinerary I kept & have still preserved I see that our westbound route via Bridger's Pass was 49 miles shorter than our return route—between the common points Julesberg & Fort Bridger.

During the summer Duane & I, after a very small initial misunderstanding, had become very warm friends, & the friendship has never grown less. His son born during his absence was named for me & is now Dr. Alexander Duane of N.Y. City. While we were in Utah gold was discovered on Cherry Creek, near [the] present city of Denver, & on our return journey in the fall we met numbers of emigrants for that section of country going out & in a very few years Denver was settled & became a city with daily papers & an opera house.

West Point 1859 & 1860

We returned from Ft. Leavenworth to West Point via steamboat to St. Louis, & thence via Cincinnati & the Erie R.R. to N.Y. City & by boat to West Point, arriving about Oct. 13th. In addition to my company duties I was assigned as asst. instructor in engineering, & had classes in Prof. Mahan's[32] department until June '59. I was very intimate with Lieut. Kelton,[33] in charge of [the] Dept. of Fencing, Target Firing, &c., & when he went to Europe in June '59 I took his duties also until his return in the fall & during the encampment instructed all the different classes in one thing or another.

One Sunday in the early fall I accidentally met at the hotel Surgeon Albert J. Myer.[34] He, when a medical student, had written a thesis on [the] use of a telegraph alphabet as a means of communication for the deaf & dumb, suggesting too the use not of the Morse alphabet, which uses *four* separate or different signals & their combinations (dot, *dash, long dash* & interval), but the "Baine" or "chemical" alphabet which used but two signals—dot &

dash. Years after, when he had become a surgeon in the army & was stationed in Texas, he saw an account of a system of military signals devised by a Frenchman, who it was said could play on a violin & convey messages to his wife in another room.

That suggested to Myer the adaptation of the Baine alphabet for military signals & he brought the subject before the War Dept. The idea was approved by Genls. Totten, Huger & Lee,35 & Myer was ordered east & instructed to get up [an] apparatus & experiment, the belief being expressed that an apparatus which could be carried in a wagon could be devised which could be read four or five miles.

Myer was authorised, too, to select some officer to assist him in his experiments. Our acquaintance resulted in his selecting me. We spent the whole fall & until Christmas about N.Y. experimenting. Usually I would go down to Sandy Hook on Mondays & he would go to Ft. Hamilton. I would board in the light house with the keeper & Myer & I would signal to each other, 15 miles apart, all day & until near midnight every night—experimenting with different devises & methods—until Saturdays, when we would meet at [the] St. Nicholas Hotel in N.Y. & compare notes.

In January, having perfected the system, we took it to Washington City & submitted it to the War Dept. & to Congress with the result that Congress added to the army organisation a signal department, & Myer was appointed chief signal officer with the rank of major sometime about Mar. 1860.

During this time also I served for some weeks on a board for the trial of a number of breechloading small-arms which various inventors were offering the War Department. But by the end of March all this was over & I was ordered back to West Point. I got leave of absence however for two months & was married on April 3rd, 1860, at "Cleveland," near Comorn P.O. in King George Co., Va., the residence of W. Roy Mason, my wife's uncle.36 We spent the two months in Georgia & returned to West Point June 1st. We had a little delay in getting quarters but dear old Prof. Kendrick37—whom everybody loved—lent us a part of his quarters & on July 20th we moved in & gave a little house-warming. But before our guests arrived there came orders for me to proceed immediately to Oregon & relieve Lt. Robert,38 who was with the detachment of 36 of our men sent out there while we were in Utah. So we sold out our newly bought furniture & on Aug. 9th sailed from New York in the steamer *Northern Light* for Aspinwall. We reached there the afternoon of [the] 17th, had a wretched night at the miserable overcrowded hotel (I slept in a chair in [the] office of an adjoining warehouse, & there was a death from yellow fever in the warehouse during the night). Next day we went by rail to Panama & took the *John L. Stephens* for San Francisco, & by the kindness of a Mr. Campbell, a fellow passenger from N.Y. who was an official of the Line, we were given the "Bridal

Chambers" on the *Stephens*—a nice large stateroom & very nicely furnished & in the best part of the ship. It proved a great blessing, for Miss Teen took a low form of fever—called the Chagres fever—on the Isthmus & was very sick a week on the trip.

Among our fellow passengers I recall Dr. & Mrs. Bryerly from Balt. going to California to live. He had been a volunteer surgeon among the Russians during [the] Crimean War, & we liked him & his wife both so much that it has always been a grief that we have never been able to hear anything definite of them since. A Mr. Emory, who went only as far as Acapulco, going there as U.S. consul, was also very nice.

We were both also great friends with a big good natured young man named Drury Malone going out to try his fortune in the mines. And in 1892, being in California on the "Dalles Board"³⁹ & at the Palace Hotel [in] San Francisco, we saw Drury Malone's arrival & we hunted him up & had a very pleasant interview. He married a daughter of a man who had a sort of public garden & who became a millionaire, & Drury had become a very prominent individual financially & also politically. He invited us most cordially to visit him at a fine ranch he owns, but we could not make it suit to go. There was also a Mr. Gordon, with his wife & young lady daughter, who was a very wealthy sugar refiner & who told us of a park he was going to give the city of San Francisco.

We also took with us Maria Turner of King George Co., Va., who had been one of our bridesmaids,⁴⁰ but whose relations lived in S.F. And we took besides our combined house girl & cook Anne, whom we brought from West Point, but who preferred to stay in S.F. when we returned the following May. Maria Turner, I believe, also stayed out there & married.

On Aug. 26th we touched at Acapulco for coal & went ashore to eat a breakfast of squabs & fried plantains at a hotel kept by a French woman who waited on us dressed in man's clothes. We reached San Francisco about sundown on Aug. 30th, where we were met & most affectionately welcomed by my sister Louisa & her husband Capt. J. F. Gilmer of the Engineer Corps, who had been stationed in San Francisco for two years or more, & who took us to their house.

Gen. Albert Sidney Johnston was in command of the dept., & Gen. Halleck,⁴¹ who had been Gilmer's classmate & most intimate friend at West Point, & who having resigned from the army was now a prominent lawyer in S.F., was a near neighbor & very intimate friend of the Gilmers.

We remained in San Francisco until Sep. 8th when we sailed on the steamer *Cortes,* Capt. Hudson, for Fort Steilacoom, Washington Territory—situated near Puget Sound, about six miles from the site of the present city of Tacoma, that being the post of the detachment of sappers with whom I was to serve.

Our steamer however first went into the Columbia River & touched at Astoria & laid for a day or so at Portland, during which time I drove across to the ferry & visited Fort Vancouver. It was on the afternoon of Sep. 17th that we finally saw the little village called "Steilacoom City" over the beautiful quiet waters of Puget Sound, with grand old Mt. Rainier in the back ground, lifting its everlasting snows nearly three miles above the level from which we viewed them.

This little voyage from San Francisco was the severest trial which ever came to Miss Teen. Reduced by the Chagres or Panama fever, she was desperately sea sick the whole way & never ate a mouthful from San Fran. till the morning of the 17th, when on the smooth waters of the sound she took some raw tomatoes with mayonnaise dressing & commenced to revive. But she only weighed 95 lbs. when she landed.

Fort Steilacoom

The sappers with whom I came to serve were under command of 1st Lieut. Thos. Lincoln Casey,[42] of the engineers; & I had known him slightly at West Point before I went to Utah. His wife, Emma, was a daughter of dear old Professor Robert Weir,[43] prof. of drawing at West Point.

Perhaps this is as good a place as any to say that among all the many friendships which Miss Teen & I have made, in our varied journeyings, our friendship with the Caseys was one of the very dearest & it has proved the very longest of all in its duration. It continues today with poor Mrs. Casey, Tom having died last year, after being retired as brig. gen. & chf. of engrs., though still charged with, & having nearly completed one of the great works of his life, the Congressional Library in Washn. City.

Tom & Emma met us on the dock at Steilacoom City, & drove us up in the port ambulance to the fort, where we became the guests of his father, Lt. Col. Silas Casey[44] of the 9th Infy., who was in command of the post. I am tempted to linger a little over our six months' stay at Fort Steilacoom. As I look back at it, now it seems to have been the last of my youth. Never to, or during that time, did I begin to realize what care & responsibility may mean. I had a position for life, & an assured support in the profession I loved; & I had only to get the most pleasure that I could out of my surroundings.

I kept up some professional reading & study, & I worked a bit at two proposed patents, I had in mind, for projectiles, to give greatly increased ranges. (One was for a projectile with a hole through its long axis [Figure 3 appears here in the manuscript]; & one was for a flat projectile to *sail* like an aeroplane.[45] Some Germans are just perfecting this hole through the

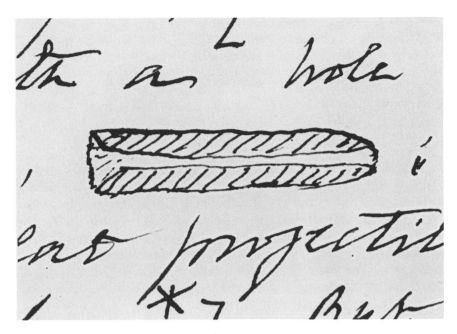

Figure 3. Projectile with hole through long axis

centre invention now, & getting very wonderful results. The aeroplane idea I am sure will also be utilized, probably to throw dynamite.) But my company duties were very light, & I had plenty of time for shooting, fishing, playing chess, & for social pleasures.

Our garrison consisted, beside the sappers, of two companies of the 9th Infantry. The other officers (besides the Caseys mentioned) were Capt. Thomas English; Lieut. David B. McKibbin—both married; Lieut. Arthur Schaaf; quartermaster Maj. "Nosey" Myers; Chaplain Rev. Mr. Kendig (married); Paymaster Maj. A. B. Ragan, with Mrs. Ragan & two adopted children (Frank & Wyly B.) & her brother, John Ector; the surgeon Dr. Brown & family, soon succeeded however by young Dr. Vansant and he later by Dr. Heger. In Col. Casey's household, beside Mrs. Casey, were also his two sweet daughters—Abbie, who while we were there married Capt. Hunt of the 4th Infantry; & beautiful Bessie, with her lovely eyes, who afterwards became Mrs. Robert N. Scott.[46]

Besides these families there was the family of the sutler, a Mr. Bachellor or Bachelder, who were visited by the ladies; & there were also Capt. Fauntleroy,[47] in command of the armed steamer *Massachusetts,* with his wife. The *M.* did not belong to the *navy,* but was kept by the army to protect the settlers & Puget Sound Indians from a very warlike Alaska tribe, the Stikines,[48] who sometimes made incursions in immense war canoes carrying 60 warriors each. Capt. F. was a Virginian—son of a former army officer, celebrated as a great rifle shot, & he had with him a Midshipman Barron, son of Commodore Barron, who I think fought a duel with Commodore Decatur.[49]

We stayed with Col. Casey as his guests for about two weeks. His quarters were a double cottage, 1½ stories, facing the centre of [the] parade ground; 4 rooms & 2 shed rooms on [the] lower floor, & 4 rooms in the ½ story above. On each side of it were 3 other cottages with 2 full rooms & 2 shed rooms below, & 2 rooms in the ½ story above. After looking around we found our only chance for quarters was to divide the cottage, next on the right to Col. Casey's, with Lt. Schaaf, who, being unmarried only needed half of the down stairs. He took the rooms on one's left, entering. The right front room, on entering, was our parlor & dining room. The rear or shed room was [the] kitchen. Upstairs (the upstairs rooms had no fire places) our bedroom was over our parlor (which was the side next to Col. Casey's), & Anne, our cook & housegirl, whom we had brought from West Point, had the room over Schaaf's parlor for her bedroom. It took us some little time to find all the furniture, bedding, &c., we needed to go to housekeeping; but we finally got fixed, sending 30 miles to Olympia, the capital, for some things, getting some in Steilacoom, & some at Nisqually, a fort or station of the Hudson Bay Company on the prairie about 6 miles to the south.

Mt. Rainier, in the southeast—across the parade ground—towered high above the Cascade Range which bounds the horizon there, apparently some 40 or 50 miles away. The country is one of interspersed prairie, & forests of fir, with many little lakes scattered about—a dozen or more within an hour's walk. Since the war the fort has been given to the territory for an insane asylum, & Miss Teen & I revisited it in 1892. Col. Casey's quarters, & our house on its right, & Tom Casey's on its left, were the only buildings left of all the officers' quarters existing in our day. But some of the old soldiers' barracks still stood, & the old trees about the vicinity; & we walked out to the little lake near by, where we used to walk in the old days of our honeymoon, & cut our initials on a tree with the dates '61 and '92.

One of our favorite walks, too, was to a little mill pond, about a mile north, on a stream flowing into the Sound—in a deep ravine. Here Miss Teen would sit on the bank & read, while I, out on a log, could always catch a fine string of brook trout in a little while.

Indeed we nearly lived on game & fish. I bought a nice pony which Col. Casey kept in his stable, for the privilege of joint use by his daughters, & once a week I would ride down to the mouth of the Puyallup River, where the city of Tacoma is now situated, &, leaving Charley, the pony, at the house of a Swede named Delinn, who had a little shingle mill on a little brook emptying into the Sound, I would walk up a mile or two to the Indian village on the Puyallup River & get an Indian to take me in his "Kynim" to paddle around the flats & creeks at the mouth of the river for a "cultus mimeloose Kulla-Kulla," or "for amusement kill ducks." I could usually get fifteen or twenty by the time he would land me at Delinn's, & if I cared to get any pheasants I could always get them in an adjacent crab apple thicket with Mrs. Delinn's little dog.

About 5 miles S.E. from the fort was a large lake, about one mile wide by four long, which was a great resort for wild geese to roost in. At least twice every week I would get up long before day & saddle Charley, & by dawn would be on the far side of the lake, to get a shot at the geese as they flew for their feeding grounds, & I usually brought in one or two, & one afternoon I walked out & back, & brought in 7. Occasionally, too, I would go deer hunting on the islands in the sound with Capt. Fauntleroy, but only once did we get a deer. Then I killed it, running in the woods, 100 yards off, by a wonderful chance shot, with the old small bore rifle of Capt. F.'s father— the bullet hitting it in the neck, & cutting the jugular vein.

Once, I was sent by Col. Casey on a three days' trip over to some settlements on White River, where it was reported that there were hostile demonstrations by the Indians, but the alarm proved unfounded.

Once every five or six days, I was on duty as officer of the day. Our guard had charge of a few very hard cases, deserters, &c., serving long terms. One day one of these fellows mutinied, & getting an iron bar cleared the upstairs room in which they were confined, & threatened to kill any one who came up. The sergeant of the guard ran over to my house for me, & I went over & advanced on the fellow with my sword when he retreated into his cell, where he gave up & submitted to hand-cuffs.

But *the* excitement of the winter was caused by the going crazy of my intimate associate John Ector, who lived with the Ragans in the cottage adjoining us on the right. As the Ragans were from Georgia & the old major a charming & hospitable gentleman, we became very intimate, & Ector & I used to be together a great deal & especially to play chess a great deal. Some time early in February 1861 his conduct began to be a little peculiar at times. He got excited upon religious subjects & began to show that exaggerated self appreciation which is so often a sign of incipient insanity. At last it became necessary to have him watched constantly, & one night they sent for me about 4 A.M. to come over, for he had a violent fit & had driven two soldiers who were nursing him & Maj. Ragan out of the house with a poker, breaking bones of one man's hand. I went over, hurriedly, in dressing gown & slippers, & got him in his room & disarmed him, but had to stay with him till breakfast time, at 8:30 A.M., when he insisted on going over to my house, to get my guns & pistol, to kill all the people on the post whom he thought were plotting against him. I got him out in the porch, & there a half dozen soldiers brought up behind a fence made a dash on him, & after a hard fight tied him. After that he had to be kept in an out house, in a straight jacket, & his feet fastened to a staple in the floor.

When we all came home in April & May (as has yet to be told), Ector was brought along—always with his arms in a straight jacket & his feet tied together [and] fastened to the floor of [a] cabin on the steamers, or [a] room in hotels, & transferred by main force when necessary, & generally making his vicinity known by howling & yelling, crying fire, or murder, or both, & vituperating every person he saw with a most extensive vocabulary of billingsgate & profanity.

Poor Major Ragan! Mrs. Ragan, Ector's half sister, was not very far from being crazy herself, even before Ector became so, & his affliction made her very excited & unreasonable & hard to do anything with. Then the major had a brother of his own with him (I forgot his name, a little old man), whom I had forgotten until now, & who could not help getting maudlin drunk whenever he could get a chance, & chances had to be allowed him or he would have D.T. And Mrs. R. had also a miserable pet poodle dog, named Annette, which she cared for as much as for her adopted boys, Frank & Wyly B. And the poor major had to make that trip from Fort Steilacoom to Georgia, with that menagerie, Mrs. Ragan, Ector, [the] major's brother, Frank, Wyly B., and Annette. Duly I will tell what happened to Annette on the journey, when I come to that. After getting to N.Y. he took Ector to an asylum in Phila., where he was cured within a year & came down to Georgia. And in 1874 he visited us in Opelika, [Ala.], & scared Miss Teen awfully, for she had no confidence in his recovery; & when I—manoeuvering to bring a long, long, tedious & trying visit to a termination—said I must go down to my office for awhile, Miss Teen nearly fainted at [the] idea of being left alone with him; & she believes to this day that I put her in great danger in making the suggestion. But fortunately it worked & Ector went off with me & did not come back.

For social amusements we had a very occasional "hop" at some sort of a semi public room or hall, I can't now recall exactly what, & once some wretched travelling minstrels gave a show to which Miss Teen & I took Bessie Casey, & I remember "Joseph Bowers" sang to the grinding of a coffee mill used in imitation of a hand organ. Once or twice we had attempts at sleigh rides with dry goods boxes on makeshift runners when we had a few inches of snow, but it usually melted in a day & we had to come back through the mud. Once the little pond we used to walk to froze over so hard that Col. Casey thought he might cut some ice, & he walked out there with Miss Teen, Bessie Casey, & an orderly. The orderly thought the ice was strong enough & walked far out where the water was very deep, when he broke through & would have drowned had not Miss Teen taken an oar & walked out near enough to give it to him while Bessie Casey ran back to the barracks—nearly a half mile—& brought help. The oar enabled the soldier to hold up until ropes were brought & he was hauled out.

Sometimes we had riding or walking excursions or picnics with some of the ladies & sometimes pistol practice for them, & Miss Teen generally beat them all. And as the spring approached she & I used to take long walks just to pick the beautiful yellow violets of which the woods were full. Bless the memories of old Fort Steilacoom! Though possibly they are seeming peculiarly dear today as I write them (Jun. 9th, '97) way down in Greytown, Nicaragua, where lonesomeness has its own abode, & homesickness its everlasting habitation.

Return to Georgia

But during our delightful six months in Washington Territory the fat was all getting in the fire in the East. Lincoln was elected president in Nov. '60. On December 17th, 1860, South Carolina seceded, & other Southern states rapidly followed—Georgia [on] Jan. 19, 1861; Alabama _____; Mississippi _____; Louisiana _____.[50]

Of course as soon as the news of the secession of Georgia reached us at Fort Steilacoom, some three or four weeks after the event, I knew that I would finally have to resign from the U.S. Army. But I did not believe war inevitable & I felt sure I could get a place not inferior in a Southern army, & I really never realised the gravity of the situation. As soon as the *right to secede* was denied by the North I strongly approved of its assertion & maintenance by force if necessary. And being young & ambitious in my profession I was anxious to take my part in everything going on. As it soon became clear that our detachment would be ordered to return to the East (for the Indian disturbances which brought them west were all over, & the East was now the theatre of activity), I waited for the orders to come & to get back to the East before resigning. About April 1st they came & on Apr. 9th Tom Casey with his wife & little boy, Miss Teen & I & Annie, Maj. Ragan & his menagerie before described, & our 36 sappers all embarked on the old *Massachusetts* about 3 P.M. She was to carry us up to Port Townsend & wait for the steamer *Cortes,* which would call there for us & bring us to San Francisco. Maj. Ragan was not ordered in but decided to resign & come. We had all been good friends in the garrison & they gave us [a] most regretful & affectionate good bye. Of all we left, I met again old

Col. Casey over in Brooklyn in 1869 & McKibbin over in N.Y. in 1884, except of course Bessie Casey whom we both see whenever we go to Washington City.

And with the farewells waved us from the wharf was one, inferior to none in affection, most dolefully howled by Ponto, a pointer McKibbin had given me. As is natural for one fond of hunting, I have many very devoted dog friends to welcome me in the spirit world, from old Rush the squirrel & possum dog—friend of my earliest youth—to poor Buster who died last year on South Island, but no dog's soul was ever given me more unreservedly than Ponto's.

We sailed in the afternoon of April 9th, 1861. Four years from that date and hour saw Gen. Lee come riding back from Appomattox C.H. to his camp, having just surrendered the Army of Northern Virginia to Gen. Grant.

Next morning, I think it was, we anchored off Port Townsend where the *Cortes* was to call for us, & we laid there several days. (I have exact dates in some little old note book in South Is.[51] but can only recall the most important ones.) While lying there one of our men was killed falling down the hold of the vessel accidentally. We buried him on shore, where there was a military post of one or two companies under command of Captain Hunt, Abbie Casey's husband.

At last the *Cortes* appeared & drew alongside & all baggage & passengers were transferred as fast as possible, after which the *Cortes* started for sea, & the *Massachusetts* to return to Steilacoom. An hour or so after the steamers had parted & were completely out of sight, Mrs. Ragan missed her poodle Annette & immediately there was a grand commotion & the ship was searched over; but in vain. Annette had been left on the *Massachusetts*! And Capt. Hudson of the *Cortes* refused absolutely to turn around & pursue the *M.* & recover her. Mrs. R. could never hope to see Annette again & her grief was sad to see. Poor Maj. R. tried hard to sympathise with her, but he had often described his experiences with Annette, when he brought her out from the states, kept shut up in their cabin & having fits the whole way, & he still had menagerie enough left to prevent his missing Annette very badly. I regret that I've never been able to learn Annette's fate, but I think it likely that the *Massachusetts* reached Fort Steilacoom without her.

The *Cortes* went into the Columbia River & up to Portland where it spent a day. I remember buying there "The Woman in White,"[52] just then out, to read on the voyage home.

Coming out of the river on our way down, we laid an afternoon at a landing on the north bank, & I went out to a mill pond a mile or so off to fish & saw there the greatest show of brook trout I ever saw in my life. They bit a little slowly at first but in a half hour it seemed as if all the fish in the pond were concentrated about the log on which I was fishing, & as soon as my hook with a bit of beef on it would touch the water a dozen would strike at it together. I caught 10 or 12 small to medium size, & then big fellows came & broke the three hooks I had with me one after the other—as fast as I could put them on—& then I had to give it up & leave them.

On the 20th of April we steamed in through the "Golden Gate" to San Francisco harbor, & as we entered we passed the steamer for Panama due to leave on that day going out (there were always 3 steamers a month—10th, 20th, & 30th). We had hoped to be in time to get on this steamer, but now knew we would have to be 10 days in San Francisco.

But as we touched the wharf a special messenger came aboard with special orders for me, sent by the "Pony Express" (which at that day filled the gap between the lines east & west of the Rocky Mts.), and which upset all of my calculations. I was relieved from duty with the detachment of sappers & was ordered to report to Lieut. Jas. B. McPherson[53] for duty upon Alcatraz Island in San Francisco harbor—in the construction of fortifications. When we landed & went up to Gilmer's another copy of the order awaited me there, & Gen. Albert Sidney Johnston had still a third for me. So it was evidently intended that I should not return east with the co.

I was very sorry for this, because it precipitated my resignation & compelled me to pay my own expenses on the journey, but I did not feel any doubt about what I had to do under the circumstances. Georgia had seceded. All the seceded states had united & organized a Confederacy, & the Confederacy was raising an army. The only place for me was in that army.

So in the course of a day or two I had a talk with McPherson, telling him that I felt bound to resign & go home, & asking that he would receive & forward my resignation & give me leave of absence that I might sail on [the] same steamer taking it & not be required to wait in California to receive its acceptance, which would detain me about two months.

McPherson's reply was remarkable for its foresight & appreciation of the real situation & its plain common sense, & the real kindness & affection which prompted it appealed to me very deeply. Mac. had served under Gilmer in Savh. soon after he graduated—in '53—& he was very fond of Gilmer & Sister Lou.[54] It seems to me that I can very nearly give his talk to me in his own words, my impression of it all is so vivid. He said:

> Aleck if you must go I will do all I can to facilitate your going. But don't go. These orders, sent by pony express to stop you here, are meant to say to you that if you wish to keep out of the war which is coming you can do so. You will not be required to go into the field against your own people, but will be kept out on this coast on fortification duty. Gen.

Totten likes you & wants to keep you in the corps & that is what this order means.

Now this is not going to be any 90 days or six months affair as some of the politicians are predicting. Both sides are in deadly earnest, & it is long & desperate & fought out to the bitter end.

If you go as an educated soldier you are sure to be put in the front rank[55] & where the fighting will be hardest. God only knows what may happen to you individually, but for your *cause* there can be but one possible result. It must be lost.

The population of the seceding states is only eight million while the North has twenty million. Of your 8 million over 3 million are slaves & may prove a dangerous element. You have no army, no navy, no treasury, no organisation & practically none of the manufacturers—the machine shops, coal & iron mines & such things—which are necessary for the support of armies & carrying on war on a large scale.

You are but scattered agricultural communities & will be isolated from the world by blockades.

It is not possible for your cause to succeed in the end & the individual risks you must run meanwhile are very great.

On the other hand, if you stay out here you will soon be left the ranking & perhaps the only engineer officer on the Pacific Coast; for every one of us older officers are sure to be very soon called in for active service. You will get promotion, for the chances of battle are sure to make many vacancies in our ranks.

You will have charge of all the government reservations. That on Lime Point has about ten thousand acres all growing up in wild oats. Buy a flock of sheep & hire a Mexican to herd them & in four years you will be a rich man.

The City of San Francisco too is filling in water lots, & the Engineer Corps is consulted & you will be able to make good investments. In short, remaining here you have every opportunity for professional reputation, for promotion & for wealth. Going home you have every personal risk to run & in a cause foredoomed to failure.

Nothing could exceed the kindness & real affection with which McPherson urged these views on me. He was one of the most attractive & universally popular men whom I ever met. There was a gentleness & refinement about him which was almost feminine.[56] He was one of those whom a man might love almost like a woman. Physically too he was a rarely fine specimen. The equestrian statue of him in Washington City is a wonderful success & conveys an excellent idea of him in face, figure & carriage. I never miss an opportunity to pass by it.

Of all the people I knew & talked with over the coming war his judgment & foresight was the clearest. It even seems as if there was a premonition of his own fate in his urging the promotion which the casualties of battle would surely bring. Poor fellow, he was killed before Atlanta July ____, 1864.[57] He had been Grant's right hand man at Vicksburg & Sherman's in his Georgia campaign. And he had been noted among Confederates everywhere for his kind & considerate treatment of the non combatants with whom he came in contact. No finer specimen of soldier or gentleman ever lived—or died.

His earnest talk impressed me deeply & made me realize that a crisis in my life was at hand. But I felt utterly helpless to avert it or even to debate the question what I should do. I could not doubt or controvert one of McPherson's statements or arguments; I could only answer this: "Mac, My people are going to war, & war for their *liberty*. If I don't come & bear my part they will believe me a coward—and I will feel that I am occupying the position of one. I must go & stand my chances."

Mac appreciated the situation & said, "I suppose in your situation I should feel as you do." And he gave me the leave of absence I wanted & was as kind & affectionate to me as a brother to the last moment when he bade me goodbye on the steamer.

Perhaps this is as good a place as any to say a little say about the war & its results &c.

I told McPherson we were going to fight for our "liberty." That was the view the whole South took of it. It was not for slavery but the *sovereignty of the states,* which is practically the right to resume self government or to secede.

I think it is even now admitted by all candid & unprejudiced Northern writers that when the states formed the Union by the adoption of the Constitution they reserved their sovereignty in that instrument itself. And it is beyond dispute that some of the states in their acts adopting the Constitution even more expressly stated that they reserved sovereignty—Massachusetts I think is one of these. But in such a partnership any right expressly reserved by one is equally the right of all, even if the constitutional reservation were of doubtful interpretation.

We had the right therefore to secede whenever we saw fit, & it was truly for our liberty that we fought. Slavery brought up the discussion of the right in Congress & in the press, but the South would never have united as it did in secession & in war had it not been generally denied at the North & particularly by the Republican party.

Well that was the issue of the war; & as we were defeated that right was surrendered & a limit was put upon state sovereignty. And the South is now entirely satisfied with that result. And the reason of it is very simple. State sovereignty was doubtless a wise political institution for the condition of this vast country in the last century. But the railroad, the steamboat & the telegraph began to transform things early in this century & have gradually made what may almost be called a new planet of it. Facility of communication & trade & commerce have entirely altered all the conditions of life.

As in ancient geological eras whenever the climate of a country changed, the fauna & flora of that country changed to conform to the altered conditions. Similarly our political institutions have had to change to conform to altered geographical, social, & commercial relations. Briefly we had the right to fight, but our fight was against what might be called a Darwinian development—or an adaptation to changed & changing conditions—so we need not greatly regret defeat.

I think it too a very fortunate result of the war that our Southern armies, though defeated in the end, scored so many brilliant victories in its course & gave the world so many fine examples of soldiers whom all nations & ages will honor for courage, loyalty, honor & the highest Christian principle. For at the beginning there was on each side a great deal of depreciation of the personal qualities of the other.

It would have been most unfortunate for the South, as the losing party in the game, not to have at least fully vindicated her courage & manly qualities, & the high type of the men her civilization produced. But, thank God! she did *that,* & left as a heritage to her sons of future generations, & not only to them but to the whole country, a record of which any nation may be proud. For each side may take equal pride in Lee who surrendered & in Grant who rose to the occasion by giving such honorable & generous terms, as I will tell in due course.

Have I ever regretted resigning when McPherson begged me not to? No, never. I have sometimes perhaps regretted the quiet, easy & prosperous life without a care for the future which my old position in the Engineer Corps would have brought me (I would now be the chief & able to retire in two years with a large salary for life), but I would not give up my recollections & experiences of life & action for anything that could possibly be given me.

But would I do it again now?[58] That is a harder question. When I was young I was willing to take risks & I would take them not only for myself but for those dependent upon me as well. I did not then as fully realize, as I now do, how inexorable are the *consequences* of mistakes—that sins may be repented of, &, we hope, forgiven, but mistakes laugh at repentance & go on piling up the consequences.

So that if I had now to take for my wife & children the tremendous chances of overwhelming disaster which I took in 1861, there would at least be much more deliberation about my choice than there was then. There is a popular story of an old Confederate whose philosophy commends itself to my maturer years & the experiences with which they have been fraught. It is said that the old soldier in question during a halt in a forced march sat on a stump & mentally passed in review his ragged clothes, his empty haversack, his worn out shoes & his sore & sockless feet, & then audibly remarked, "D—n me if ever I love another *country*!"

Fortunately for me, & even more fortunately for those dependent upon me, a kind Providence watched over me & brought me safely through the risks of battle, & not only that but the no less fearful risks of all the financial storms & stresses of the subsequent years so that at least we have never yet wanted for the necessities of life.

But of the other Southern officers who resigned from the U.S. Army as I did to take service with our native states, scarcely one I think in a hundred has been so fortunate & the fates of a great number have been sad tragedies.

So I wrote my resignation of my beautiful position in the Engineer Corps, & my sweet Miss Teen cried when I did it; although she knew it had to be done, & she had never said a word to discourage it. And McPherson gave me a written leave of absence to go east & await the acceptance of my resignation at home. And I may say here that my resignation was duly accepted to take effect May 1st, the date stated in it, & the notification of it was sent me by mail & duly received—the very last mail from Washn. City that I knew of. At that time too the resignations of many Southern officers were being rejected & the officers being discharged, for "resigning in the face of the enemy" or other disreputable reasons. So I considered the acceptance of mine as strong evidence of good will & regrets from the headquarters of the corps.

My steamer the "Golden Age" was to sail on May 1st. As I now had to pay my own way home & my wife's, McPherson & Maj. Bob Allen, the dept. quartermaster, persuaded the steamship co. to give us half rates home, which saved me several hundred dollars. Our cook Annie also decided to remain in San Francisco, where wages were about $30 a month, rather than return east, at our expense, to wages of $7.00 a month. Tom Casey's family & the sappers of course were coming on & Maj. Ragan & his menagerie. Lieut. Corley of the 6th Infy., with whom I crossed the plains in 1858 as before told, also turned up & came along, having resigned up in Oregon.

And a day or two after my arrival in the city I also met Lt. Wm. P. Sanders of the 2nd Dragoons, with whom I had been intimate at West Point & whose subsequent fate I have already referred to. Sanders's regiment was in Utah, but he had been sent in pursuit of deserters & had made a remarkably long & swift march & caught them & was taking a brief rest before starting back with them. He had two married sisters living in S.F., Mrs. Tevis & Mrs. Haggin, & a third, Mrs. Hunter & her husband, from somewhere in Kentucky, were to be our fellow passengers home on the *Golden Age.*

Tevis & Haggin[59] are still living I believe & for many years have been among the very richest men of California. Haggin is prest. of the Anaconda Copper, & the Ontario Silver, & I believe also the Homestakes gold mines.

I was with Sanders a great deal while in the city taking meals & playing billiards in his brothers-in-law's fine residences, & of course we talked a great deal about the political situation. Sanders was intensely Southern in all his views of it, more so I think than any other Southern officer in the army with whom I met during the whole period of the initiation of hostilities. His family were from Kentucky & Mississippi, & he frequently claimed connection or relationship with Jefferson Davis. I begged him to take passage on the steamer with his sister & myself, but he felt bound to return to his post in Utah first & deliver up his deserters & wind up all his personal affairs there, but he thought he could go overland & not be very far behind me in offering his services at Montgomery, then the capital of the newly created Confederacy.

He was on the steamer to see us off when we sailed & we said good bye with mutual promises & anticipations of an early meeting in the South. I have already told briefly of the result & more detail will appear in my account of the siege of Knoxville in Nov. 1863. But, for reasons which I have never heard, Sanders changed his mind completely & remained in the Federal army & came east & took an active part in the war.

He distinguished himself & was promoted & before Knoxville commanded a brigade of cavalry, which skirmished with our advance for several days & finally made a strong stand behind rail breast works about a mile in front of Burnside's[60] main line at Knoxville—near one of the two Armstrong houses. I attacked this line with a couple of batteries & two regts. of So. Ca. infantry lent me by Gen. Longstreet[61] for the purpose, & poor Sanders was shot through the stomach while vainly endeavoring to rally his men & hold his breastworks. He lived I was told afterward only 24 hours. Fort Sanders, which we afterward vainly attacked, was named for him. As the country was open and we were quite close I have no doubt that he & I actually saw each other during the fight, though too far off for personal recognition.

During the ten days we were waiting in San Francisco the great news came by pony express of the bombardment & capture of Ft. Sumter [on] April ____.[62] It is impossible to describe the tremendous excitement which this news caused. Until that event few seemed to believe that war was inevitable, or even very probable, and even among Northerners there were very many who thought that the South had justice & right & no little provocation on their side. But the news of the fight changed all that & in a twinkling Northerners now, to a man, Democrats & Republicans alike, were all for the war, & all united in saying, "The South struck the first blow!" In actual fact & truth nothing is more false & unjust, & while few historians as yet have admitted it, all will do so when prejudice has died out.

The whole attitude & position of the South was simply that it asked "to be let alone." It sent delegations to Washington proposing to adjust all financial obligations to the United States for all federal property within its limits & sought in every possible way a peaceful & honorable separation.

The first hostile act upon either side was *the act of Maj. Robert Anderson*[63] who, without orders or authority, & for actual reasons that God only knows, about Christmas 1860 spiked the guns of Fort Moultrie, where he was stationed, & moved secretly by night into Fort Sumter.

Fort Sumter was of no earthly or conceivable use to any state of the Union except South Carolina, or indeed to any other power on earth except to one having the design to conquer S.C. by arms. Anderson attempted to justify himself by saying he occupied Ft. S. because he feared S.C. might either take it herself or might attack him in Fort Moultrie. That is merely equivalent to saying that he struck the first blow for fear the other fellow would strike it. Such a fear may often be a sufficient reason, but it is adding insult to injury not to frankly admit the fact that the first blow has been struck by the first hostile act of aggression.

But the defensive case of the South does not even rest here. She made no hostile retort to Anderson's act, & she even permitted him to buy supplies for his garrison in Charleston market, though she immediately began to erect batteries both for offense & defense should the occasion require & she renewed her efforts in Washn. City to secure peaceful separation. Indeed Anderson was at first reprimanded by the prest. & sec. of war & was about to be ordered back to Ft. Moultrie when both president & cabinet were intimidated by the popular approval of Anderson's act by the North. But if any one act can be said to have made war inevitable it was Anderson's.

But the South never struck back before a second act was committed. I write this far away from all books of reference from which I might give exact dates & details but what took place in outline is as follows: South Carolina refrained from hostilities & permitted Anderson to supply himself with provisions in Charleston on the personal pledge of Secretary Seward[64] that the status should not be changed without fair notice being given. But meanwhile a fleet of transports & war vessels was prepared in New York to reinforce the garrison of Fort Sumter and after it had set sail for that purpose Seward notified So. Ca.'s representative of the fact, & as I recollect with an apologetic explanation (which practically admitted that it was a violation of his pledge) that he had been unable to prevent it.

But the fact remained that the sailing of this expedition was the 2nd act of hostile aggression. Yet nearly all present historians with a full knowledge of these facts unite in saying the South struck the first blow. But as already stated the onus of beginning it was on the South in the popular mind & all parties at the North were now a unit in support of war. And a similar effect on a smaller scale took place at the South. Virginia & some other states had not yet seceded & would not have seceded at all in all probability, had not the North committed itself to the policy of coercion.[65]

In army circles too were very many officers, some from states already seceded & some from states still in doubt & even a few from the North who had Southern wives or friends or political views, who were hesitating as to what they should do. My interview with McPherson had occured very soon after my arrival & at least two or three days before the news of Ft. Sumter came.[66] But now the die was cast for every body. Gen. Sumner suddenly arrived from N.Y., unannounced but with orders in his pocket to supersede Gen. Albert Sidney Johnston, whom the govt. evidently feared might try to turn California over to secessionists.

But the kindly feelings & confidence in each other's honor & integrity between the army officers themselves was not in the least lessened. On the contrary, the approaching prospects of war & separation only deepened mutual affection & regret. I have already mentioned Gilmer's intimacy with the Hallecks. When he sent in his resignation soon after I left he was compelled to wait the arrival of his successor from Washn. City in order to turn over to him & get receipts for the large amounts of public property for which he was responsible. Then, having rented his house (which he owned), he removed to Gen. Halleck's house while making his final preparations, but just before his date for sailing he was taken with an attack of inflammatory rheumatism which kept him in bed for six weeks. He was in S.F. therefore when the battle of Bull Run was fought, & he did not reach the South till sometime in August or Sept. after an adventurous time in getting through the lines via N.Y. City, Cincinnati, & Kentucky.

Our voyage on the *Golden Age,* leaving San F. on _____, & reaching Panama [on] _____,[67] was smooth & uneventful after the passengers got used to the alarms of fire & murder from Ector's stateroom before referred to. When he was being transferred from the cars to the steamer on the Aspinwall side he was led in his strait jacket & held by two men past a native who was carrying some over wraps, &c., & as he went by, howling & singing, he made a dive & caught my overcoat in his mouth & tore a great piece of it.

On the Atlantic side we took the steamer _____. There was a great deal of apprehension among the officers of the vessel & at least all the Northern passengers lest a Confederate cruiser or privateer might be lying in wait to capture our steamer, as it was well known that these steamers brought to the

East the whole gold product of California. The officers, in fact, made a little canvass of the passengers to know if a force could be organised to resist a capture, but the result did not encourage them. But no privateer showed herself, though everybody was always on the look out & every sail was an object of great interest.

I can only recall the name of two of our fellow passengers beside those of the army already mentioned. They were a Mr. & Mrs. Kettle of San Francisco. She was a daughter of somebody we knew—Bishop Kip I believe, I forget now whom—& was very nice & ladylike. He had been at one time a commercial traveller in the South for a Northern house & had, by his own account, once had, in Georgia, a narrow escape from a riding on a rail or some other hospitable entertainment which he resented & hoped Georgia would get well whipped for in the coming war. We had one consumptive passenger who came on at Aspinwall & died lying out on deck two days after & was buried at sea.

And up in the Gulf Stream we had one tremendous storm & quite a narrow escape from a wreck. We had abandoned our course & were heading the tremendous seas so as to ride them. The steamer (all steamers in fact nearly at that date) was a side-wheeler, & her big walking beam played up & down through the hurricane deck. A fireman oiling it was caught by the beam & crushed to death in the aperture in the deck through which it played. The engine had to be stopped to get the body out, & when the engine stopped the vessel fell off so rapidly that she was barely able when started again to avoid being caught broadside in the trough of the sea, which would have swamped her.

When the engine stopped we were in our berths, Miss Teen & I, & I, at least, was sick unto desperation. We heard some commotion & a woman came running by crying, "Oh Fire. Fire, the ship is on fire." Miss T. asked me to get up & go & see. I answered that I was too sick & did not care whether it was on fire or not. But she said if I did not she would go herself, for she was not ready to be burned. On that I got up & went to see. The alarm was caused by some one's misunderstanding the cry that a fireman was killed. So after the storm was over we had a second sea funeral.

We reached New York early on the morning of the 24th of May—which I think was Friday, & we went to the St. Nicholas Hotel. And that recalls another one of our passengers, a Mrs. Rion. She had occupied some domestic position in San Francisco, housekeeper perhaps, in the family of some of our acquaintances. I cannot recall which. She had been a first class or first cabin passenger, & she went to the hotel with us. She was very tall & thin, dressed in plain black, was quite old & entirely unused to travelling & taking care of herself. At the hotel she was apparently neglected by the servants & she came to Miss Teen to ask how she could procure some necessary attention, which Miss Teen took great pleasure in seeing to. We had been told by those who knew about her that she was the mother of a son who was the colonel of one of the new South Carolina regts. just raised since the secession of the state. This afterwards proved to be Col. Jas. H. Rion[68] of Winnsboro, who in 1871 helped to make me superintendent of the Char[lotte], Col[umbia] & Aug[usta] R.R., thereby stopping my going to Egypt as chf. engineer for the Khedive.[69]

I was very intimate with Col. Rion for a number of years during my R.R. life. He was one of the most distinguished lawyers of the state & was counsel for the C.C.&A. R.R. for many years & until his death, & he was even more intimate with my bro.-in-law, Col. A. C. Haskell,[70] who was president of that R.R. at the time. Col. Rion had been a protegee of John C. Calhoun's, who had educated him. I never heard where Calhoun brought him from but he had no known relatives in Carolina.

But on Col. Rion's deathbed he informed his family that his father was the Dauphin of France, whose fate has always remained a mystery since the execution of his father Louis XVI. He stated that his father became a lieut. in the British army & was stationed in Canada, where he married Col. Rion's mother. He stated that when Jno. C. Calhoun was secretary of war secret information of this marriage & of Col. Rion's legitimate birth was lodged with the U.S. govt. & also with the Austrian govt., & that Calhoun's care & education of him was due to his knowledge of his identity. He explained many little things in his life, which had seemed strange, as influenced by that; the only one which I can recall being that he had always declined any civil office (which had been often tendered him) because, although he might hold military office, civil office was incompatible with his rank.

There was a lot of curious & interesting detail connected with the matter which I forget, but Col. Haskell told me a good deal. But the whole matter has been kept a close secret by his family & doubtless they would object to any publicity being given to the matter.

After getting our trunks up to the hotel Miss Teen & I went out to do some shopping, as we had had no chance to do any for a long time & could not expect another one for a much longer. Canal St. was then the favorite place for ladies & we went there together. But while we were in the very first store we visited a man came running in with the exciting news of fresh hostilities on foot. After the fall of Fort Sumter Lincoln called out 75,000 troops "to put down the rebellion," & Virginia & all the other Southern states which were hanging back passed ordinances of secession & each side went to raising troops, but no further hostile acts had been committed. But on [the] night of [the] 23rd a strong Federal force was crossed over the Potomac to occupy Alexandria. In this force was Ellsworth's regiment, E.

being a young man who had acquired great notoriety, popularity & military reputation for having raised a volunteer military co. in Chicago & taught them great proficiency in a fancy Zouave drill & within a year had taken them to some of the principal Northern cities for exhibition & competitive drills. When the 75,000 troops were called for Ellsworth was made a col. & raised a Zouave regiment.[71]

Now in marching through the streets of Alexandria, Ellsworth saw a Confederate flag flying over a hotel kept by a man named Jackson,[72] & taking two men with him he entered the hotel & went up to the roof & took down the flag. As he came down stairs with it he was met by Jackson with a gun & shot dead. Jackson himself was also immediately shot dead by one of Ellsworth's companions.

This was the news now being spread of all over N.Y. City amid wild excitement. It was plain that any Confederate ran great risk of being mobbed if it was known that he was on his way south. I was also, I thought, liable to some special interference by orders from the War Dept., as I had heard of some cases of arrest of Southern officers seeking to go south, & threats against such "traitors," as they were called, were common in the papers. Moreover I was one of the very few, if not the only Southern officer who knew Myer's system of signals. Hence I concluded to lose no time in getting safely across the lines—& the only sure route was by going to Kentucky. That state had not seceded & had declared that it would stand neutral between the North & South, hence R.R. & mail service into it from both sections was uninterrupted.

So Miss Teen & I hurried up our shopping, got an early dinner, bought a little basket of fruit & took the Erie R.R. at 6 P.M. for Cincinnati. We both remember enjoying supper Sat. evening at Cleveland, where we got fine fresh lake trout, & by that time had sufficiently recovered from our sea voyage to have immense appetites. We reached Cincinnati about sunrise on Sunday, [May] 26. We had tickets to Louisville via the Ohio & Mississippi to Seymour, Indiana, but there was no train, being Sunday, until about 3 P.M. So we went to the Burnett House & spent the day.

We went to the station a little early in the evening, as I felt a little uneasy about my baggage marked U.S. Army having lain in [the] station all day checked through to L. When I took Miss Teen in the passenger car some man volunteered to select good seats & to turn one for us. I thought he was a train hand & I left him at this, while I went forward to see if my baggage was OK, & to my great satisfaction it proved to be so. When I returned my polite friend had taken a seat opposite Miss Teen & was giving her an account of the capture of Fort Sumter, which he claimed to have been present at. I was much interested as I had heard no details, & the polite man seeing my interest supplied them abundantly & threw in occasional comments indicating decided Confederate sentiments on his part. His voice was a little loud, & presently as the car began to fill neighboring passengers began to turn & listen to him. On this I spoke to him & asked him to lower his voice as we were attracting attention, which I was anxious not to do as I was on my way south.

He at once became very confidential & after asking where I was going, to which I answered Louisville, he began to tell me more & more of where he had recently been & what he had seen. "He had been in Montgomery at Mr. Davis's inauguration as president—& had afterward dined with Mr. Davis." Then I began to smell a mouse. "I was very fortunate in having met him, for he knew the private sentiments of all the public men in the West & should I get in any trouble he could be of great service to me." Then my mouse became a very large rat.

Finally he said he would tell me in confidence that he "was a cousin— German—of Lord John Russell[73] & that he was in this country on a very important political mission." Then the cat was out of the bag! My polite friend was either a spy who had seen my baggage & was after locating me, or he was a pickpocket or sneak thief of some sort who was on the lookout for a chance to rob us in some way, knowing we would be in too much hurry to stop to catch or punish him.

I don't know when I have ever spent a more anxious hour than I did then sitting & listening to this fellow's lies & wondering what his game was going to be & when he would begin to play it. I had some visiting cards in my pocket with U.S. Army on them. I went to the water cooler & quietly threw them out of the window. At every station I watched him closely to see if he was communicating with any detective or officer. I could not convey my suspicions to Miss Teen, for he was on the seat facing us & talking all the while. But I was keenly alert, & suddenly he asked a question which gave me an idea how we could escape him. He said, "At what hour will we reach St. Louis?"

I caught on in a second that he had misunderstood me when I told him I was going to Louisville & had thought I had said St. Louis—a very natural mistake as the O.&M. R.R. extends between Cin. & St. L. & we were on the regular through train. But at the supper house, Seymour, Indiana, we were to get off & spend the night & take a train from Indianapolis for Jeffersonville next morning. And here at the supper house we would give our polite & interesting friend the slip if he had not played his little game before we got there.

So not to undeceive him I answered promptly that we would arrive between seven & eight. But here Miss Teen in her innocence of all my fears & my scheme spoke up & said, "Not St. Louis, Louisville you mean." Fortunately he did not understand in the noise of the train, & the window being open, & said, "What did you say Madame?" But I told her quickly, "Wake war-war," which is the Chinook Indian for "don't say anything," & I spoke to him & said my wife had not understood what we were talking of & immediately asked some question about the St. Louis hotels. So he didn't catch on to his mistake & at Seymour he came out to supper with us, but I let some other passenger get a seat between us at [the] table & we ate very slowly so that at last he finished & said he would go on into the car & I nodded & said all right, & that is the last we ever saw or heard of him.

Arriving in Louisville devoutly thankful for escaping all our perils whether real or imaginary, we went to the Galt House, & then I hunted up Gen. Simon Buckner,[74] whom I had known in N.Y. & at West Point. For I had been a sort of protegee as a young officer of Lieut. John C. Kelton & Capt. G. W. Smith,[75] & Buckner was a special friend of these. I met at B.'s house Helm, a relative of Mrs. Lincoln's or Lincoln's (I forget which) & who was afterward a Confed. genl. & killed at Chickamauga,[76] but there was no other incident of interest.

We left Louisville that night about 11 & took dinner on [the] 28th in Nashville & breakfast on [the] 29th in Chattanooga. Here at the hotel I met Mr. Walker,[77] the Confederate sec. of war, on his way to Richmond, which had been made the capital of the Confederacy soon after Virginia came into it, & Mr. Davis & all his cabinet were moving there.

Secretary Walker informed me that a commission as captain of engineers awaited me & ordered me to report in Richmond as soon as possible. I promised to come as soon as I could take my wife to Washington & leave her there, for I had an idea that I would only be in Richmond a few days when I got there, & there was no telling where I would be sent for service, but doubtless somewhere in the field.

I can't recall certainly but I think we probably got to Atlanta that afternoon & spent the night with George Hull[78] & Cliff, George being then superintendent of the Atlanta & West Point R.R.

One thing I recall of this trip very distinctly was the comparative impressions made upon me by the camps & the preparations for war in the North & in the South. It was not calculated to make me doubt the truth of McPherson's prediction that the South could not finally maintain itself. My route of travel was through the most prosperous & thickly settled parts of N.Y. & Ohio. Every station was a town, many of very considerable size, & everywhere there were camps & soldiers in regiments & brigades. And they were all fine healthy looking men, with flesh on their bones & color in their cheeks, thoroughly well uniformed, equipped & armed.

Coming down through Tennessee & North Georgia the villages were few & small, & the troops I saw nowhere more than one or two companies together. These were generally poorly & promiscuously uniformed &

equipped & they were even still more poorly armed. The approved arm of that date for troops was the rifled musket, calibre .58. Of these I don't think I saw one. The old smooth bore calibre .69 was the best I saw anywhere. Then no one could fail to note a marked difference in the general aspect of the men. Our men were less healthy looking, they were sallower in complection & longer & lankier in build, & there seemed too to be less discipline & drill among them.

And, in fact, I think in every one of these characteristics, arms, equipment, health & ability to resist camp diseases & especially in discipline & drill, we remained inferior to the Federals up to the close of the war, except that in the matter of *small arms* we finally got even with them in 1863 by capturing enough rifle muskets to replace all our smooth bores. We also captured plenty of their cannon but we were *never* able to make as good artillery ammunition to use in them as they had in great abundance.

But I lived to see that our men had a spirit which more than made up for all their deficiencies, either of drill or equipment. In fact it was a never ceasing wonder to me to the very close of the war to see how they *did* fight— all the harder, it seemed, as they grew longer & lankier & more ragged & hungry looking.

I reached Washington, Geo., if I recollect right on Thursday, May 30th, about noon. We had of course a warm welcome, & of course the only subject of thought or speech was the war. I can't recall who composed the household certainly, & I only remember, beside my father, my brother J. H. & the two younger girls, Marion & Alice.79 And even J. H. was in camp— being a private in a co. of infantry being raised to form a part of the 9th Geo. Regt.

As I felt bound to get to Richmond as soon as possible I only spent the night at Washington, & the next morning I took my first war parting from my dear Miss Teen & started off, Friday, May 31, '61.

FIRST MANASSAS
OR BULL RUN

I arrived in Richmond Saturday night, June 1, & stopped at the Exchange Hotel. I reported for duty on Monday, & my commission as capt. of engineers was given me dating from [the] date of my resignation from [the] U.S. Army. I was ordered to await orders in Richmond & meanwhile to have a number of signal flags, &c. constructed so as to be ready to put a signal corps into the field on short notice. Mr. Davis remembered me from my having helped Myer exhibit the system to the military committee of the Senate in the winter of 1860–61, as before mentioned.

It did not take me long to get a manufactory of all sorts of signal apparatus under way & I reported as ready for orders in a very few days, being anxious to get into the field somewhere. We had armies in process of formation at Norfolk, Yorktown, Fredericksburg, Manassas, Winchester, & somewhere in West Va. besides the western & southern armies. I did not care specially *where* I was sent & made no special application, leaving it to the War Dept. to say where I could be of most use. I knew of Gen. Bob Garnett's applying to have me sent with him to West Va. & have ever since considered it a piece of very good luck that he was refused. For he was killed & his whole command routed at Rich Mountain, his first fight, in a very few weeks.[1] Meanwhile my orders were put off almost from day to day.

Richmond however was very far from dull, for troops from all over the South were arriving every day & resigned Southern officers out of the old army were coming in from every territory, & camps of instruction were formed near the city where raw troops were drilled, loose companies organised into regts. & regiments into brigades, field & staff officers were appointed & assigned, arms & equipments were issued, & as fast as any body was organised & equipped it was sent forward to one of the above named points.

My brother Felix[2] was at that time private secretary of Mr. Toombs, who was sec. of state—J.H.A.'s regiment, the 9th Geo., came through & went up to Winchester to Gen. Jos. E. Johnston.[3] My orders were still delayed from day to day & at last, about the end of June, I decided to telegraph for Miss Teen to come on & join me, as I thought I might be there another month & there was no reason why she should not be with me. She started promptly—under the escort of Dudly Dubose; but, alas! she was met at the station not by myself but by Lewis Webb with the news that I had been sent up to Manassas that very morning. That was our first sample of one of the minor "horrors of war." I had at last been very suddenly assigned to the staff of Gen. Beauregard,[4] as engineer & signal officer, & ordered to report by the first train. So poor Miss Teen was taken to the Webb's house, corner 9th & Leigh Sts., & she stayed there until long after the battle of Manassas.

I can't fix the exact date of my going to Manassas but it was about July 1st. Gen. Beauregard & his staff occupied a good sized two story house among some trees about 100 yards N.W. from the R.R. station at Manassas. I had never met any of them before but his aid Capt. S. W. Ferguson,[5] who had graduated in my class at West Point, having been turned back into it out of the previous class for fighting a cadet officer, Shoup,[6] who had reported him for something. But I was very cordially received & was given a room, & a bed, & a seat at the general mess table, & became at home at once. In fact I think Gen. B. had more courtesy of manner than any of the other generals with whom I ever served. He was of medium size or a very trifle short, but compactly built, quick & alert, of fine carriage & aspect, & of unusual strength & activity. His age must have been about 45 for he graduated in 1838. His hair was black, but a few months afterward when some sorts of chemicals & such things became scarce it began to come out quite gray.

Of the other staff officers I can now only recall Col. Thos. Jordan, adjt. gen., Cols. Porcher Miles & Chesnut of S.C. as volunteer aids & Capt. A. R. Chisolm of Chasn. as regular aid, and Dr. R. L. Brodie as surgeon & W. L. Cabell as qr.mr.[7] I will not attempt to tell how many troops he had nor their dispositions nor the names of the general officers, for it would make my narrative too long & cumbersome. I am not writing a history of the war, but only trying to preserve the principal pictures & impressions of it which linger in my memory, & to give only enough narrative of general events to give connection or to string my recollections upon.

Of course my first duty was to organise & instruct a signal corps & my second to study the topography of our probable field of action, & be prepared to utilize my men when they were able to work. First I went to Gen. Longstreet, who commanded a Va. brigade, near hqrs., & Gen. D. R. Jones[8] I think it was commanding a Miss. brigade, & got them to detail some ten or twelve intelligent young privates who would be suitable for promotion afterward. I can recall today the faces of most of them but the names of only two or three: Skipwith Wilmer from Miss., I think, was one & Leidy & Stuart were two others.[9] I formed these in a class for instruction & practise, & put in all my spare time in riding about & studying the country & was soon able to fix up several trial stations at which I put the men in camp in twos & threes & had them practising by day & night. Meanwhile I had bought myself two horses, Dixie, a rather large dark bay, & Meg Merrilies, a smaller bright bay,[10] & these horses I kept all during the war & had them taken from Appomattox to Washington, Geo., after the war.

I left Meg there when I went to Columbia in 1866, & she lived out her life there. Dixie got a scratch at Fredericksburg & quite severe wounds at Gettysburg & at Spottsylvania. In the fall of 1865 I rode her down to Savannah, & started on her from Sav. to ride to Macon along line counties through which [the] Central R.R. runs to record a mortgage of that road. While on this trip & near Warrenton I swapped Dixie, paying some boot, for a younger & stronger horse with a man who was running a large cotton plantation in the vicinity, as she was not standing the trip well & I feared she might fail me. Her new owner promised me to take good care of her & I suppose her bones are somewhere in that neighborhood.

Of course our little army knew that the Federals were organising an army to crush us & that they would very soon take the field. When they did, it was proposed that some advanced brigades & cavalry, which were about Centreville & Fairfax, should fall back before them, & the whole army should be concentrated on the south side of Bull Run, which should become our line of battle—our right flank resting at the railroad crossing at Union Mills Ford & our left at Stone Bridge, where the turnpike from Wash. City to Warrenton crosses some 3 miles after passing Centreville. This made our line of battle about 6 miles long. Bull Run was a good sized creek with wooded banks generally, but often the strip of wood along it was narrow & pastures, old fields, & cultivated grounds came sometimes up in a few yards, say a dozen, & sometimes receded 100 yards or more. The creek would average perhaps 30 feet in width & with alternate deep & shallow places. Infantry could find places to cross in almost any locality & there were several farm fords & roads along the line. The principal of these was called Mitchell's Ford, at which a country road from Manassas Junction to Centreville crossed. It was about 2½ miles from the right flank at Union Mills, & in between,[11] say in a half mile of, were two farm fords. The right hand or most eastern I will call Jones's (not remembering if it had any other name & D. R. Jones's brigade having been stationed at it) & it was about a mile from Union Mills Ford. The next was Blackburn's & it was within a half mile of Mitchell's Ford on the right or eastern side of it—our whole line runnning east & west & facing north towards Washington.

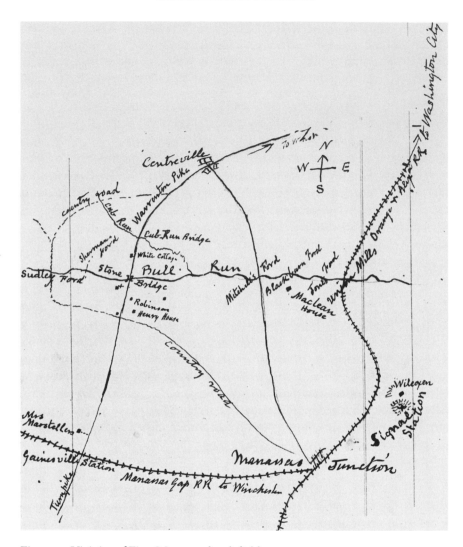

Figure 4. Vicinity of First Manassas battlefield

As I write this far away from all books of reference & maps I give everything from memory & may be inaccurate, but I will draw a little sketch which will at least give the general features so that the main points of the battle may be apprehended. [Figure 4 appears here in the manuscript.]

This is not true to any scale, but it was 6 miles in an air line from my signal station on Wilcoxen's Hill to Stone Bridge. I mark down on the map Mrs. (or Dr.) Marsteller's house, not that it has anything to do with the

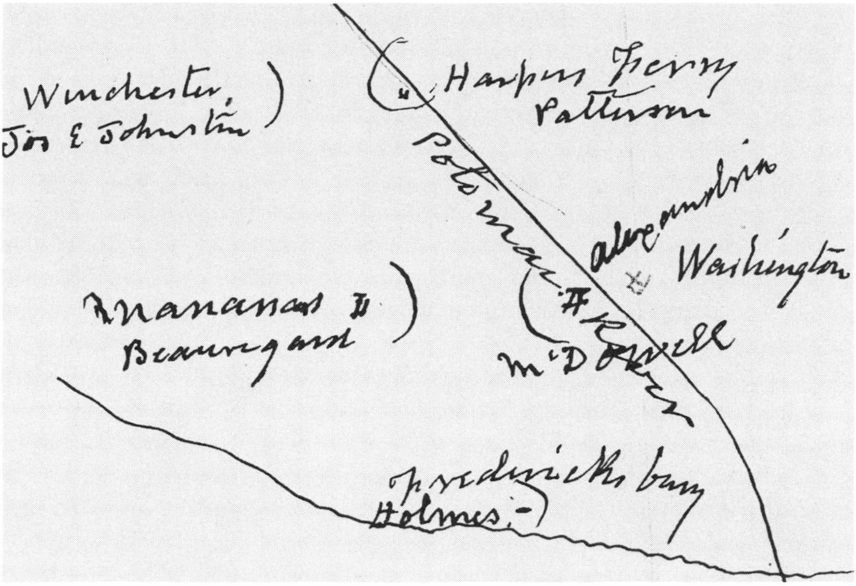

Figure 5. Strategic situation prior to First Manassas

battle but because it was there I unrolled the famous "bundles" in Jan. 1862 & first made the acquaintance of my delicious eldest child & daughter. To that house too Gen. Field was taken desperately wounded in Aug. 1862 in the battle of 2nd Manassas, he & his wife having also boarded there during the preceding winter.[12] Note also on the map the McLean house in rear of Blackburn's Ford, about which there will soon be something to say.[13]

As both sides were new to war & as war has its science, like chess, it may be interesting as I go on to keep one eye on the technical points of the game & to show briefly where they were successively lost & won. Now the very first great rule in the war is to try to mass all your force against fractions of the enemy's. Our General Forrest, noted for his successful cavalry fights in the West, is said to have expressed the idea in saying that he tried "to get there first with the most men." I doubt whether he ever really said it but he certainly often practised it.[14]

Now there was a beautiful chance on the chess board for either party to play this game on the other, for each party *had two armies in the field,* & might hope to be skillful enough to jump on one of his adversary's armies with both of his. [Figure 5 appears here in the manuscript.] We had Jos. Johnston at Winchester with about _____. At Harpers Ferry opposed to him was Patterson with _____. At Manassas Beauregard had _____, &

opposed to him was McDowell with about _____. We also had a small force, about _____, with Holmes at Fredericksburg.[15] As the Federals had [the] largest forces & best drilled & equipped they had the advantage of the move or the initiative. As Patterson had [a] roundabout & longer march to reach McDowell than Johnston had to reach Beauregard we had an advantage in position—what is technically called "interior lines" against their exterior.

Neither of us played the game as well as it might have been done. The Federals, indeed, did not seem to make any effort either to bring Patterson down to reinforce McDowell or to make him press Johnston closely & keep him from going to Beauregard.

We did indeed get Jos. Johnston down & about half of his men, & with their help at the last moment saved the battle by a very close shave, but it was not as easy as might be supposed to have the movement ordered. Beauregard himself could not order J. to come to his aid but had to persuade Prest. Davis to do it. Davis in Richd. felt reluctance to order Johnston, who was very sensitive about his prerogatives as a commander, & neither Davis or Johnston could keep in full touch of [the] situation & conditions at Manassas from day to day. But Beauregard wrote & telegraphed & sent staff officers with messages, & finally Davis left it to Gen. Johnston to use his discretion, & Johnston decided to come, on the night of the 18th I think it was, after we had had already a sharp skirmish at Blackburn's Ford, as will be told more fully soon. And McDowell most unwisely wasted the whole of the 19th & 20th in reconnaissances, not to mention the 18th, & thus gave time for a good part of Johnston's force to arrive.

So the "grand-strategy" of the campaign, as these preliminary movements may be called, was not specially brilliant on either side, but we had very much the best of it, such as it was. And the fault on both sides lay I think in each not having *one commander in chief over both its armies,* with authority & power to handle both as one without waiting to explain to, or convince, any body. Both of us learned better than that before the war was over.

As to our "line of battle" along Bull Run, it was never put to the test of an attack in front, but judged by experience acquired later it was not a *particularly* good one, & we did little or nothing to strengthen it. Later in the war we would have[16] straightened & shortened it, & had more & better roads behind it parallel to its direction, & we would have had rifle pits at important points & a few epandements for guns.

A day or so before the Federals actually started we knew they were about to come. Their general preparations could not be concealed & we had many friends in & near Washn. & Alexandria to send us word. More than one lady made more or less newspaper reputation by coming in from the country between our two lines to tell Gen. Beauregard what she knew about the enemy's movements, but I don't think any information received in that way cut any figure.

But before going on with my narrative I want to digress & tell about a curious little idiosyncracy which was developing itself, in both armies, & among both officers & men, under the test & stress of battle for the first time. I had already noticed it in reading the newspaper accounts of the little collisions which were beginning to occur in various directions, & had likened it in my mind to the way in which a person lays hold of an iron which he knows is hot, but does not at all know *how hot*—whether only uncomfortably warm, or hot enough to make the flesh sizzle. He does not grab it promptly with a full strong grip but picks it up & drops it for a time or two, till he gets the measure of the heat & sees whether he can stand it.

Well it was in very much that way that officers & men took hold of fighting at first. The men were strongly disposed after firing a volley to fall back a little to load, & officers getting a fair amount of success in a fight were slow to risk that in hope of greater.[17]

I give a few illustrations from memory not having references at hand. One of [the] first collisions was a charge through the streets of Fairfax C.H. before day one morning by a squadron of Federal cavalry under a Lt. Tompkins.[18] A Confed. co. of infy. quartered there were completely surprised & might all have been scattered or captured, their commander, a Capt. Marr,[19] being killed as he came out of a hotel where he had slept. But the Federals did not stay to see the effect of their random firing as they charged through & hardly drew rein until safe back in their lines.

The steamer *Pawnee* came down & shelled some little earth batteries we had at Aquia Creek with some old fashioned smooth bore guns in them, but were satisfied to draw off without either doing or receiving one bit of damage.

One day in June, Gen. Beauregard had sent Col. Maxcy Gregg of So. Ca. with his regt. of infy. & Kemper's[20] battery out to scout in the neutral grounds between the two armies. On [the] same day a Federal Gen. Schenck[21] had put a regiment or a good part of one in some passenger cars, & with an engine behind pushing them he also goes reconnoitering in the same territory—up the track of the R.R. which in time of peace was operated to London. It happened that Col. Gregg was crossing that track somewhere up in this neutral ground, when he heard the exhaust of an approaching engine. He quickly had Kemper's 2 guns unlimbered & trained, & pretty soon around a bend some 400 yards[22] off came Schenck's "railroad reconnaissance," as it came to be called. Kemper opened fire & aimed well, putting some 6 lb. shot right through the coaches full of soldiers & killing 8 & wounding 4. The engine stopped, cut loose from the cars, reversed & ran back to or towards Alexandria. Gen. Schenck & all hands scrambled out & scattered in the same direction, while Gen. Gregg, satisfied with his victory, resumed his march, not even stopping to visit & burn the abandoned cars.

Early in July, on _____, Gen. Butler at Fortress Monroe sent a small force, about 4,000, to feel of our forces about Yorktown under Gen. Magruder. They met here with about 1,400 men at Big Bethel & had the first engagement of the war. The Yankees attacked & were repulsed with [a] loss of about _____.[23] Among them were Capt. Greble of [the] 3rd Arty.[24] (with whom we had been very intimate at West Point, his wife being a daughter of Prof. French[25] the chaplain) & a Col. Theodore Winthrop of Boston, who was conspicuously brave & must have been a real fine fellow. I've read, since the war, a charming book he had written detailing adventures up in Washington Territory & Oregon among the Indians—& also other adventures down in Central America.[26] Hill[27] only lost one man, a private who volunteered to go out & burn a house between the lines. His name was Wyatt[28]—a fine young fellow & the first Confederate soldier, I believe, to die in battle.

Well when the Federals started back to Fortress Monroe their retreat soon became a rout in its haste & demoralisation. But meanwhile Magruder was himself falling back to Yorktown. A few cavalry which he had left to observe the enemy, seeing them retreating, followed, but Greble's lieutenant unlimbered a gun or two & made believe he was going to fire & they turned back. But he did not fire, for the battery had expended every round of ammunition in the fight & had not one left.

Perhaps I ought to say here that both Genls. Gregg & Hill were really more than ordinarily brave men. Both were conspicuously & notoriously brave & persistent & both had seen some service in Mexico about 14 years before. Gen. Gregg was killed at Fredg. Dec. 13, '62.

And perhaps it is as well, while on the subject, to mention here an incident of similar sort which occurred in the battle I am about to tell of, which will not otherwise come into my narrative. A Federal general, Hunter[29] I think, testified before a congressional committee on the conduct of the war that when they turned our flank, as I will tell in due course, he, riding ahead of the column, discovered a Confederate regt. in line of battle at [the] edge of a wood. He brought up a regt. of Brooklyn Zouaves, & each regt. fired a volley at the other simultaneously. And each regiment on firing retreated to load, leaving him the only person on the field but one single Confederate soldier shot down by the Federal fire.

And now we will return to our narrative which will disclose, on both sides, further & far more important illustrations of what I will call, for short, this "fire & fall back" tendency of new soldiers, however brave. In fact the making of *"veterans"* is simply getting over the feeling of that impulse. It only comes—like most of mankind's fears—from ignorance & imagination. As in my first illustration—the picking up of a hot iron—it is the uncertainty how severe the suffering may suddenly become which inspires it. When familiarity with parallel conditions has inspired confidence veterans almost learn to despise the dangers & to love the excitement of braving them.

Writing without access to books I can't give exact dates of McDowell's starting from Alexandria, & of [the] falling back of our advanced forces; but on July 18, Thursday, we were all in line of battle behind Bull Run, with a few pickets some half mile beyond in observation, & McDowell's advance division under Maj. Gen. Tyler[30] was about Centreville, & other divisions close up. The first man to be killed I believe was a sort of attache about some headquarters who lost his way in trying to find or follow up his officers & rode up to our picket on the road [from] Mitchell's Ford to Centreville. Seeing his mistake he turned & spurred his horse to escape & was shot down. He lived for a half hour or so, told who he was & gave his watch to one of the picket—which was perhaps superfluous, for it did not take long for the men on either side to find out that the pockets of the killed were often worth emptying.

Gen. Tyler, commanding the Federal advance (the father of Ned), was a graduate of West Point of 1819, & had resigned after distinguished service & had been equally distinguished in civil life for intellect, energy, & character. He seems to me to have been very little infected with the "fire & fall back" idea & to have had great faith in a bold policy, for it was reported at the time that he proposed to take Manassas Junction that evening & that his division should be the first one there.[31]

At any rate, about noon we discovered that his troops were approaching Bull Run in the vicinity of Blackburn's Ford. Gen. Beauregard had expected a battle along the line of Bull Run & had announced in orders that his headquarters would be fixed at McLean's house, some half mile in rear of this ford. And now I will stop the narrative a bit to tell of what I think is one of the most remarkable coincidences of the war.

McLean had married the widow of my wife's uncle Seddon Mason. This is near enough relationship in Va. to warrant recognition & family intimacy—especially if there are two pretty daughters as there were in M.'s family. So in my frequent excursions, studying the topography & roads, & locating signal stations (one of which indeed & an important one was quite near the house), I frequently called on the family, & took some meals with them & knew them all very well. The house, with all the usual farm outbuildings, kitchen, corn-crib, stables, servants' houses, &c., with quite [a] lot of shade trees, occupied a large knoll in the midst of corn fields (then in tassel) & pasture lands stretching on all sides for several hundred yards & down to the creek with its border of high timber.

Here—accordingly—about noon on the 18th were assembled in the shade of the trees about the premises Gen. Beauregard & all his staff. The surgeons too had located a hospital in the barn & stables in one corner of the grove, & couriers were coming & going, & all was ready for & in constant expectancy of the opening of a desperate battle—the first that most of us had ever seen.

I had gotten a good point of view & brought a chair from the house to make a good rest for my large spy glass, & I was closely studying the rolling hills across the creek when I saw a group of Federal officers ride out on an open hill some 1,500 yards off & hold quite a consultation. Evidently our position was most conspicuous with signs of life of all that they could see, & they decided to wake us up & bring out some demonstration of our position. So pretty soon I saw a battery appear on the hill with the officers & unlimber facing in our direction. I think I learned afterward that it was either under Benjamin (whom I fought often afterward—until [the] close of [the] war, in fact; I had known him at West Point & he was a good fellow & a first class artillerist) or B. [was] with it as lt.[32] My glass showed me everything as clearly as if I were quite close to them & I watched with great interest while they loaded one gun, aimed directly at us & then fired the first hostile shot I ever heard. It howled about 40 feet directly over our heads & struck in the corn-field beyond us. Then I watched them load again & aim & fire & the second shot fell short about 100 yards, striking in a peach orchard. Then they loaded three or four guns, taking quite a time & aiming very carefully, & then the[y] fired all three simultaneously—& in about five seconds all three arrived shrieking in chorus. One ploughed into the ground close by the house, one smashed into a corn & cob grinding machine standing in the yard, & a third came directly through the kitchen, a large log cabin close by the house in which our head quarter servants were just dishing up a dinner they had cooked for us. Fortunately not a soul was touched. But there was a general stampede of all the horses hitched about the yard, & an ambulance or two standing around & of a good many miscellaneous people—among them our darkeys, who tumbled out of the kitchen & rolled over each other getting out of the way. Our dinner was ruined by the mud daubing between the logs jarred out as the shell passed through both walls falling into the sliced up meat & dished up vegetables, & we went without dinner that day.

Well those were the very first cannon shot fired between the two great Virginia armies—the Federal "Army of the Potomac" & the Confederate "Army of Northern Virginia"[33] & they were aimed at McLean's house.

I don't recall seeing his family that morning & I guess he had taken them off. But I saw him frequently all that fall & winter & until we moved southward in March, & I have an idea that he acted as commissary for a while & had the title of major, but he dropped out of my sight early in 1862. And he had been both out of sight & out of mind for over two years when on April 11th, 1865, at Appomattox C.H., two days after the surrender of Gen. Lee to Grant, I rode into the village to confer with Gen. Gibbon[34] about turning over our surrendered artillery, when whom should I meet in the yard where Gibbon had his hd.qrs. but Maj. McLean. He was a short, stout little fellow & with a face easily remembered. I said, "Hello! McLean, why what are you doing here?" He replied, "Alexander, what the hell are *you fellows* doing *here*? I stood it on Bull Run till, backwards & forwards, between you, my whole plantation was ruined & I sold out & came way off here over 200 miles to this out of the way place where I hoped I never would see another soldier of either side, & now just look at this place"—& he pointed around to his yard full of tents & his fields stretching off low from [being] trampled & fences burned in the numerous camp fires, for the last guns were fired on his lands & in his house Gen. Lee surrendered to Gen. Grant. So the very first & the very last hd.qrs. & the very first & last collisions of these two great armies in a four years' war had taken place in the house & on the premises of the same individual—who fleeing from the turmoil & danger had moved meanwhile over 200 miles.

And now we can go back to McLean's house at Bull Run at which we left them shooting. They did not shoot much more there—but scattered their fire all around without doing any harm or drawing any response from our batteries, which were divided around with the different brigades. Then about 2 P.M. there suddenly broke out a roar of musketry along Bull Run near Blackburn's Ford. Tyler had sent a brigade to feel in the woods there, & they had come up very close to the creek when they saw & were seen by Longstreet's Va. brigade & both brigades opened fire, or rather the Federals fired one volley & fell back & our fellows fired several, the first at them & the others at the place where they had been seen. Then Longstreet sent a small force across the creek to follow them, which they did for some distance, picking up some hats & small things dropped & I think getting a prisoner or two, & exchanging some more shots with the retreating force. Then somewhere about three or four o'clock the Washington Artillery battn. of New Orleans, from a field between Mitchell's & Blackburn's Fords, some 10 or 12 guns, opened at the Federal battery which was still practising around at anything it could see, & the Federals got more guns & answered back & for an hour or more a sharp & very noisy duel raged between them. But I think there was little damage done on either side, for neither could see much more than the other fellow's smoke & so could not correct their aim or see where their shot went. Our side had some rifle guns shooting a shell, called the Burton & Archer, made in Richmond, but though the Washington Arty. made a very favorable report of their performance in this fight it turned out afterwards that they were really utterly useless, every one tumbling (or whirling over like a stick) & consequently having neither range or accuracy.[35]

And when this duel gradually died out the fight was over. During the afternoon Gen. Beauregard with his staff had ridden some along the lines, & when it was over we came back to McLean's. I remember the whole crowd of us being wrought up by the most terrible shrieking & groaning of some fellow at the hospital near the stable. I remember thinking that if being wounded hurt like all that, war was a sight more awful even than I had imagined. At last Gen. Beauregard told an aid to go to the hospital & ask the surgeons if they could do nothing to relieve the agony of that wounded man. The aid came back & reported that the man was not wounded but had cholera morbus—which much restored my courage.

The killed & wounded on each side as well as I can make out from reports were Confederate _____, Federal _____.[36] The effect of the fight was decidedly I think to encourage our side & to brace them up. There had really been nothing at all of what a veteran would call fighting, but our men had seen the enemy come up to our lines & recoil from them, & retreat from our fire. And from newspaper reports the enemy's retreat had been hurried & demoralized & I think had a decidedly depressing effect in their ranks.

It seems that Gen. Tyler was censured for what he did & I think he was soon after retired from active service.[37] But my own opinion is that McDowell lost his best chance of all in not attacking boldly & persistently at the earliest possible moment that he could. He had much the largest force & every hour that he delayed gave us a chance to get Johnston's army down. He ought to have counted on our doing this if possible & taken no chances. We were indeed trying it, as before stated, but it was far from working swiftly & easily & nothing short of the *three whole days'* delay saved our bacon.

Of the next two days, the 19 & 20th, I can recall very little. We were in almost hourly expectation of being attacked, & meanwhile we knew that Johnston was coming & every hour's delay brought him nearer. And sometime on the 20th, I think about noon, his troops began to arrive by train & he & his staff arrived.

I think Gen. Jos. E. Johnston was more the soldier in looks, carriage & manner than any of our other generals & in fact more than any man I ever met except Gen. Bob Garnett, who was killed at Rich Mountain. He had been my superintendent my first two years at West Point & possibly more youthful impressions had something to do with it, but his whole aspect was to me military discipline idealized & personified. And indeed his death illustrated it as perfectly as it could be done. His men behind some breast-works seemed a little restless under a heavy fire being poured at them to which Gen. Garnett did not wish them to reply. He remarked to one of his staff, "The men need a little example," & he got out in front of the breast-work & walked calmly & slowly back & forth in the rain of bullets till one struck him down killing him almost instantly. But that has nothing to do with Bull Run & I only put it in for poor old Gen. Bob, whom I used to hate when I was a cadet (though I never had the slightest reason for I believe he liked me), but who left no family & whose name is now never mentioned, but who had he lived I am sure would have won a reputation no whit behind Stonewall Jackson's.

And now I'll return to Gen. Johnston. His pictures, which are common, give an excellent idea of his strong & intellectual face. He was of medium stature but of most extraordinary strength, vigor & quickness. His aid Jimmy Washington & I once shared his room in Williamsburg in May '62 the night before the battle, & while undressing we got talking of sabre exercises. Gen. J. partially undressed & with arms & chest nearly bare took a sabre & gave us some illustrations, & though I have seen many much more powerful cavalrymen like Gen. Hampton,[38] Aleck Haskell, Col. Von Borcke,[39] &c., yet I've never seen a sabre whistle & sing like that one.

The general was very good to me from the first, and I was on his staff afterward & he tried to get me for his chief of arty. at Dalton in the spring of 1864, as I will tell more in detail when I come to that, & we were good, good friends to the day of his death. God rest his soul.

And that brings me to Sunday morning, July 21st. We had early breakfast & about sunrise both generals & all the staff started out on the Mitchell's Ford Road, but Beauregard ordered me to go to my high central station on Wilcoxen's Hill & to remain there in observation, keeping some couriers with me & reporting to him from time to time all I could learn of [the] enemy's movements.

He & Gen. Johnston had decided this morning to themselves cross Bull Run & attack McDowell. Ewell[40] was to begin the movement on our right, crossing & sweeping to the left. Then James Longstreet &c. in succession were to take up the movement as it came to them. But it turned out after-wards that the order sent Ewell to begin this movement never reached him, & before this fact was discovered McDowell has gotten *his* attack at work so vigorously on our left flank that our proposed attack was given up & everything concentrated to resist McDowell.

For this is what McD. did. When he left Washn. City his plan had been to turn our right. When he got on the ground he had found the ground less favorable for that plan than he had anticipated, so he stopped to reconnoitre

& that gave us our three days' delay. Now he had decided to leave a force along our front to observe us & to turn our left by way of Sudley Ford two miles above Stone Bridge. I have dotted on the map [see Figure 4] the country road by which his column marched. At sunrise it was probably approaching Sudley Ford where Evans,[41] who commanded our left at Stone Bridge, had a small cavalry picket. Meanwhile a heavy force moved up close to Stone Bridge & opened an artillery fire to occupy our attention while the flanking column came around our rear. So in the play for position on the field McDowell had the better of our generals & the battle was to be fought according to his plan.

The Federals had brought one very heavy gun, for field service, a 30 lb. Parrot rifle they called "Long Tom." Long Tom was on the pike opposite Stone Bridge & opened the day with a shot at my little signal station (marked with a red cross on the map [see Figure 4]) near the Stone Bridge, & the shot went through the tent but hurt nobody. Every where else things were quiet. I exchanged messages with all the stations when I got on Wilcoxen's Hill & then fixed my glass on the Stone Bridge station looking for the earliest developments there.

And while looking at them, as well as I remember about 8:30 A.M.,[42] suddenly a little flash of light in the same field of view but far beyond them caught my eye. I was looking to the west & the sun was low in the east, & this flash was the reflection of the sun from a brass cannon in McDowell's flanking column approaching Sudley Ford. It was about 8 miles from me in an air line & was but a faint gleam, indescribably quick, but I had a fine glass & well trained eyes, & I knew at once what it was. And careful observation also detected the glitter of bayonets all along a road crossing the valley, & I felt sure that I was "on to" McDowell's plan & saw what was the best part of his army.

But I had heard stories about reconnoitering officers seeing a little & reporting a great deal so I determined to be very exact in my reports. First I signalled to Evans as of most immediate consequence, "Look out for your left. You are flanked," & then wrote a note for Gen. Beauregard by courier as he was not near a station. I wrote this: "I see a column crossing Bull Run about 2 miles above Stone Bridge. Head of it is in woods on this side; tail of it in woods on other side. About a quarter of a mile length of column visible in the opening. Artillery forms part of it."[43] This message I hurried off by courier.

I afterward learned from Evans that my message was handed him at the same moment that his cavalry picket, which had been at Sudley, came to report itself driven in by a cavalry advance guard which had preceded McDowell's column. On getting it Evans had left a part of his force to observe Stone Bridge & with more than half of it he had moved off towards the left to meet the enemy. It was doubtless a portion of these who exchanged volleys with the Zouaves as described by Gen. Hunter & previously told.[44]

Both Beauregard & Johnston in their official reports mention the receipt of my note, & not long afterward too musketry firing began to be heard. Gen. Johnston's report mentions that on these developments the 7th & 8th Geo. Regts. under Bee & Bartow, the Hampton Legion & Stonewall Jackson's brigade, from various points in [the] rear—all belonging to Johnston's army & lately arrived—were ordered to hurry to the left.[45]

Briefly what took place out there was as follows. Evans's troops at least delayed the Federals & made them lose a lot of time deploying, & meanwhile the 7th & 8th Georgia arrived & put up a very hard fight. Indeed strange to say the casualties endured by these regiments before they retreated stand high on the list for regimental losses for the whole war, & I will interline these here when I can get the figures.[46] The fact is that while they were fighting heavily in front with the forces which had crossed at Sudley, Gen. Sherman[47] with a brigade which had found a ford between Sudley & Stone Bridge came in on their flank, & they still resisted obstinately for a while—not knowing any better. The Georgians' fight was quite a distance—$1/2$ mile or so—west of [the] Warrenton Pike. As they fell back & the Federals advanced the Hampton Legion had crossed the pike a couple of hundred yards or so, & they made an excellent stand & delayed the Federals considerably & then fell back still fighting & in good order though under sharp artillery fire.

But, while their fight was going on, the third body of troops hurried in that direction after the receipt of my report, Jackson's brigade, came up & took position on an elevated ridge stretching from [the] Robinson house [to] just in rear of [the] Henry house. Jackson recognized it as a good position & brought up some artillery, & the Hampton Legion & the Georgians & other remnants of the fight across the pike fell back on this line. Some of them stayed there too & fought well, but there were great numbers who thought they had done enough & kept on to the rear in spite of all efforts to rally them. Bee & Bartow were both killed in this vicinity, but before his death Bee had given Jackson his immortal soubriquet "Stonewall," rallying his men by saying, "See Jackson standing yonder like a stone wall." And in this connection I may as well tell here that late that evening, riding with Gen. Jos. E. Johnston, he used the same term in describing the fight made by "Col. Preston's regiment," which I think was in Jackson's brigade & was [the] 28th Va.[48] He was expressing his unqualified admiration & surprise at the way our raw troops had behaved, &, indeed, considering all the circumstances there can be no doubt that there was some fighting in our ranks there that day that was really superb & worthy of any troops that ever lived.

But my story must now leave this fight for a while & go back to the right flank, where I was watching its gradual development from my high hill & getting messages from my Stone Bridge station until the Federal advance, after driving back the Hampton Legion & the Georgians, compelled everything to quit the west side of the pike. And meanwhile Jos. Johnston & Beauregard with all their staffs had halted not far in rear of Mitchell's Ford, & the two generals themselves had gone alone on top [of] a moderate hill a few hundred feet to [the] left of [the] road where they could overlook a good deal of ground. And the Yankee batteries opposite kept up a scattering shelling of all our side of the creek.

Meanwhile, along about 10 o'clock[49] I suppose, when the dew was dried & the sun began to get warm, something else began to attract my attention. I could overlook the country to the west—our left—clear to the Blue Ridge thirty odd miles away, & now I began to notice clouds of dust begin to form low down at various scattered points in that direction. I could not be at all sure of the distances but I thought they were between 15 & 20 miles. I of course sent prompt messages to the generals by my couriers,[50] & by signals to all points, & I reported too what I could see of the fight, which was making more & more noise on the left. I could not see the movements of the troops at all, but by the clouds of smoke rising at different points I could tell what an extensive front the Federals were developing & that it was being advanced as well as widened. And as the sun got higher the dust clouds in the west also grew denser & taller, until they became veritable pillars in the air hundreds of feet high & covering many degrees of the horizon & evidently slowly approaching.

Indeed I have often thought it strange since—the development of that dust. It turned out to be made by the trains of Gen. Johnston's army—baggage, ammunition, quartermaster, commissary, hospital, &c. all being pushed rapidly down from the Valley to get under cover of our lines, & the condition of the air must have suited remarkably for the rising & hovering of the dust, for never afterward in all the war did I ever happen to see anything approaching these clouds, though many more trains were often moving.

My couriers returning kept reporting Genls. Johnston & Beauregard as still near Mitchell's Ford, & I could not understand why they did not go to the left where I was convinced the battle would be lost or won. At last I determined to go myself, thinking that perhaps my reports, being but moderate statements of only exactly what was visible, had not impressed them sufficiently. I found them out on a bare hill alone—their staff officers in sight near the main road. I was able then to make them see the columns of dust themselves from where they were—they had risen so high. Apparently Gen. Johnston was disposed to go there but Beauregard seemed to hesitate. But they decided to send one of Johnston's staff, Col. Whiting[51] of the engineers, with a lot of couriers to send back reports from time to time how matters were looking. Meanwhile too the roar of firing continued to increase & some half hour or so after Whiting had gone, on the sudden breaking out of a roar of musketry heavier than anything which had gone before it—equal I should say to ten thousand men engaged—Gen. Johnston said sharply, "I am going there," & jumping on his horse which was being held near by he set off at a gallop without another word to any one. Gen. Beauregard only stopped long enough to tell me to return to my high hill & keep him posted, by my couriers, of all movements right, left, or centre, & then he followed Johnston & all their staff officers & couriers, some 30 or 40 in all, apparently followed after them—the whole lot going a "calihooting." I wanted to go with them awfully, but I could appreciate the importance of intelligent observation of the fields so I went back to my place. But I will let my narrative go with Beauregard & Johnston for awhile.

They did not reach the field of battle on the left one moment too soon. Our lines had been driven back to the Henry & Robinson house hill where Jackson, almost the only brigadier left, was doing his best & keeping up a good fire, but the enemy was shelling him heavily from opposite hills, & from down in the hollow between large masses of infantry kept up heavy musketry—by file & in volleys. Both Johnston & Beauregard had to ride among our men & show them [an] example to steady them & keep them to the work. Johnston, if I remember right, particularly went in with the 4th Ala., a most excellent regiment. Beauregard had his horse killed under him & so I think did Ferguson & Chisolm of his staff. Once getting the lines steady, B. stayed with the line & J. went to a central point close in rear [of] the Lewis house to meet & direct other bodies of our troops which were being brought up as hastily as possible from other near points. Thus the battle was fought until some 2 o'clock, or later, in the afternoon when there arrived on the field from Manassas, where it had just gotten off the cars, a part of Kirby Smith's[52] command. They were directed by Gen. Johnston in such a way that they took the enemy's line on the flank & fired at rather close quarters into a Federal battery which had pushed right up to the Henry house, & they practically destroyed the battery—Griffin's, from West Point.[53] Many of the horses we had ridden as cadets were there & were killed or captured as well as the enlisted men who used to groom them. Almost as suddenly as I can tell it the whole Federal force fighting us there started to retreat, & the retreat very soon became a rout. One Federal account, which I saw, laid the whole business on a fat lieutenant who began to run & was followed at first by one or two, & those by others till everybody had to join in.

All this while, or very near it, I on my high hill had kept a sharp look out along the whole line. I can't recall the dust clouds as making any figure after my return from [my] interview with the generals. Possibly breezes arose to disperse them or possibly the smoke clouds of battle interested me so that I forgot them. I was able to form a fair idea of the enemy's progress by these clouds rising above the fields & low woods, & I could see that for some hours they had made practically little progress, though the fighting had with some lulls & swells gradually grown hotter. Suddenly along about two o'clock, as well as I can recall, farther out to our left than any fighting had yet shown, a battery of artillery went into rapid action, & I could see the shells from its guns bursting fast in the air along where the firing had been hottest. I knew the crisis of the battle must have come & that in one way or another it must soon be decided. I jumped on my horse & started for the field in a moment for I felt bound to be in it at the close whichever it was. As I galloped something like five or six miles I saw plenty of stragglers & fugitives along the road. President Davis arrived from Richmond & rode out, arriving[54] a few minutes after me. When he saw so many stragglers he thought we were whipped & he said to the officers with him, "Battles are not won where men leave their ranks in such numbers as this." Crossing a small creek near the Lewis house I came on a number of regimental hospitals. It had been a beautiful grassy meadow & shade trees on [the] edges. There were now perhaps a hundred dead & six or eight hundred wounded lying around in sight as I went by.

I soon found Gen. Beauregard—at the moment, all alone, watching a regt. of cavalry going to cross Bull Run where the fugitives by this time had all gone. He told me some things about the fight & sent me on one or two minor errands & then said: "Go across Bull Run to Gen. Kemper[55] who is conducting pursuit & tell him to follow the enemy up, but *not* to attack." There at once occurred to my mind the story in the papers of how our cavalry following Butler's retreat from Big Bethel to Fort Monroe had been bluffed with empty guns. But I hesitated about venturing any suggestion to my general, having heard several army stories wherein young lieutenants had made such ventures, & received sarcastic replies. But I took courage in the general's habitual courtesy to at least ask a question which would hint at a modification. I said, "Shall I tell him not to attack under *any* circumstances—no matter what the condition of the enemy in his front?" He replied, "I will send him Kemper's battery.[56] Tell him to await its arrival & not to attack unless he has decided advantage." I was very well pleased with this modification & went my way, crossing the Stone Bridge & going up the pike towards Centreville. At no great distance—[a] half mile perhaps—I overtook [the] rear of Kershaw's[57] column which was composed of [the] 2nd & 8th So. Ca. Regts.

As I got near the head of the rear regiment I saw a very fine looking sergeant major come out of woods on the left with a small man in citizen's dress & take him before the colonel at the head of the regiment. This turned out to be Col. Cash,[58] who in later years became very notorious not only in So. Ca. but all over the country. Between 1880 & '85 I think he killed in [a] duel Col. Shannon,[59] a very estimable & popular gentleman, under circumstances which created great feeling & for many years afterward, until his death almost, he was involved in broils & difficulties whose details I have forgotten but which were widely copied in the papers & made his name a notorious one.

At that time the colonel was a tall, stalwart fellow, apparently 35 or 40, red headed, red faced, light grey eyed, strong-featured &, as I approached him that afternoon, his face was as angry looking as a storm-cloud, & he had drawn his revolver & was trying to shoot the little citizen who was dodging behind the big sergeant major as Cash turned his horse about & tried to get at him, poking at him with the pistol & swearing with a fluency which would have been creditable to a wagonmaster. "You infernal s. of a b.! You came to see the fun did you? God damn your dirty soul I'll show you," & he spurred his horse to get around the sergeant major.

"What's the matter, Colonel," said I. "What are you trying to shoot that man for?" "He's a member of Congress, God damn him," said the colonel. "Came out here to see the fun! Came to see us whipped & killed! God damn him! If it was not for such as he there would be no war. They've made it & then come to gloat over it! God damn him. I'll show him," & again he tried to get at the poor little fellow who was evidently scared almost into a fit. "But Colonel," I said, "you must not shoot a prisoner. Never shoot an unarmed man."

I spoke authoritatively, for Beauregard had published an order that all officers of his staff spoke with his authority, & Cash recognized it & made no kick. "Turn him over to the provost guard," he said to the sergeant major; "and then go & hunt the woods for Senator Foster.[60] He is hiding here somewhere. Go & find him, & God damn you, if you bring him in alive I'll cut your ears off."

To finish up with the prisoner, on my way back from delivery of my message I overtook the provost guard with some 20 prisoners, among them the member of Congress. I made him walk by my horse while I questioned him. He was a Mr. Ely[61] from western New York, & had come out with quite a little party of congressmen & others in carriages to see the fun. The turn of the tide was so sudden that the party was scattered. All got away however but Mr. Ely. He recognised me as the one who had saved him from Cash & asked me, "What sort of a man is Col. Cash, Sir?" "Well," I said, "you keep out of his way, or he would as soon cut your ears off as not." Which was a fact, & the little fellow lived in terror of Cash as I heard afterward until he was safely sent down to Richmond, where he was soon exchanged or released.

When I got to the head of the column it had just reached the "White Cottage" & was being deployed into line. The enemy was trying to make a stand about Cub Run Bridge & a few bullets came whistling about & a gun was fired a few times at us. I gave my message, took a good look at the enemy & all around & started back. Within a hundred yards Kemper passed me going up at a fast trot. He went into action & almost his first shot killed a horse at the entrance of Cub Run Bridge. This partially blocked the road & made a panic among the Federals. Drivers of artillery, ambulances, wagons, &c. abandoned their vehicles, cut out their horses & took to flight. It was said that one of my class mates at West Point (Craig, whose father was chief of ordnance—he did not graduate, however) was killed on that Cub Run Bridge. The enemy abandoned at that place their big gun, Long Tom, & about a dozen other guns & a number of caissons, battery wagons, ambulances, &c.[62]

But we did not know of this until the next morning. Kemper had not been firing long & Kershaw's troops had not advanced when orders came from Gen. Beauregard recalling all of our troops back to the south side of Bull Run. The orders were sent by my classmate Captain, afterwards General, S. W. Ferguson, Gen. Beauregard's aid. I met him just *on* the Stone Bridge as I returned from Kershaw. Elzey's brigade was crossing to the north side & right in among [them] I met F. looking very blue—so I said, "Hello, Sam, what's the matter?" He said, "I'm going to bring everything back, to our side of the river. Some fool has sent some rumor about Yankees south of Bull Run way down about Union Mills and everything is ordered to come back."

It turned out afterward that somebody near Manassas had seen some of our own troops marching somewhere down there & had sent a report out to the battlefield to the generals. But though that was always afterward mentioned as one of the reasons why we did not pursue the enemy I cannot believe that it was really the reason. I attribute it very much more to that newness to battle to which I have already referred. The original message to Kershaw, which I carried, was sent long before the arrival of the false alarm from our right.

In fact the battle was treated as over as soon as the Federals retreated across Bull Run. It should have then been considered as just beginning—our part of it. It was, up to that time, the *enemy's fight.* They began it & were aggressive & we defended. Now was the time for our aggression, & there was plenty of time to do a lot before dark & a good moon to help after dark. One of our two generals should have crossed Bull Run at Stone Bridge with every man he could raise in that vicinity, & the other gone to Mitchell's Ford & crossed with all the forces in that vicinity & pushed for

Centreville. Then they would have promptly discovered how utterly demoralized the enemy was. As it was they never realized it fully at least for a day.[63] And we had plenty of fresh men who had not been engaged at all.

Of our whole force on the field, _____ of Johnston's, _____ of Beauregard's—only about _____ had been engaged & many of those were still fresh enough for us.[64] At Mitchell's Ford, Longstreet's & Bonham's[65] brigades did cross, Longstreet in advance. Bonham ranked L. & made him halt & let B.'s brigade take the lead. They then advanced until they came in sight of the Federal line—a few[66] officers & couriers riding ahead & the enemy firing a cannon shot or two. Gen. Bonham stopped the advance & Gen. Whiting of Gen. Johnston's staff, after conference with him, agreed that everything should return south of Bull Run.[67] None of Kershaw's men reached Cub Run & they did not know of the guns & things abandoned there. A regiment of cavalry also crossed Bull Run below Stone Bridge & charged & routed some Yankees retreating across a field, but they too I think were recalled with the rest.

When I returned to Gen. Beauregard I found him with Gen. Johnston & Prest. Davis, & they rode about for a while looking at the field & positions. I recall a few sights. The body of poor old Mrs. Henry,[68] very old & bed ridden, lay in her bed struck by one cannon ball & about three musket balls. The house was riddled from every direction. Her son & a servant who lived with her had had to run off & leave her early in the day, as she could not be moved & they would have been killed had they remained. Near by were abandoned 12 guns [of] Griffin's & Ricketts's[69] batteries with nearly every horse killed.

Not very far off to the right I saw in a pile three of [the] Hampton Legion killed by a solid shot. One of them had his arms raised & extended exactly as if he were aiming his musket. The shot had passed through his body from side to side just below his arm pits. Evidently he was aiming when struck, for had his arms been down they would have been cut off. It would seem as if the shot not only killed but stiffened at least the muscles of the arms in the positions in which they were.

Across the pike I noticed a well marked row of the enemy's dead showing where a regiment had fought. I noticed on their accoutrements that they were the 2nd Vermont. As I rode by one of the "Louisiana Tigers" of Wheat's battalion[70] was going from man to man stooping over each one. He had doubtless caught on to the fact that dead men's pockets sometimes had money, watches, & other valuables in them, but he had the decency to pretend that he was searching their cap boxes for caps as I came near him. I knew he was lying but I said nothing.

I was assigned to Gen. Johnston as a guide to direct him back to Manassas Junction, but gradually Prest. Davis & Gen. Beauregard joined in &

quite a crowd came back together by moonlight. The ride seemed long &
tiresome. It must have been half past nine when we got back to Manassas. I
cannot recall any supper though doubtless we must have had it.

Along about 11 P.M. or half past there came up to hd.qrs. an old West
Point friend, now a captain I believe & attached to Johnston's army, named
Robt. C. Hill from N. Ca. He was tall & slender, black hair & eyes & quite
a good looking fellow, but there was always a sort of suppressed excitement
in his manner & conversation which had gained him the soubriquet in the
Corps of Cadets of "Crazy Hill."[71] Hill told me that he had followed the
enemy's retreat & had been in the town of Centreville, & that the Yankees
had gone & had left the streets blocked & jammed with abandoned artillery. I took him upstairs where the president & the two generals were
discussing what to do on the morrow & put him in the room to tell his own
story. Not very long after he had finished & come out I was called up &
asked if that was "Crazy Hill" by Mr. Davis, to which I had to answer, "yes."
Mr. Davis had been sec. of war & knew a great deal about different cadets
& their reputations & he had heard of "Crazy Hill." He had at first been
greatly moved by Hill's story & started to write out orders for a general
advance in the morning, but a recollection of Hill & his nickname stopped
him, & learning that he was the man called "crazy" gave no more credence
to his story.

The actual facts of the matter I believe are that Hill *had* made his way as
far as Cub Run Bridge & had seen there the abandoned artillery, &c. But
he had probably not been to Centreville because no guns were abandoned
in the streets of Centreville. But Centreville was probably really evacuated
& abandoned by the enemy not later than between 12 & 1 o'clock.[72]

In fact the enemy's whole army practically broke up & disorganised
during that & poured back over the road to Washington a mass of fugitives.
Even a squadron of cavalry with a gun, following along the road & firing an
occasional shot, would have made it a panic. There is no legitimate excuse
for our not following. It is rarely that any army has such a chance as our
army had then and it ought to have played it for all it was worth.

In the panic our advance would have made it is likely that Washington
City would have been evacuated. I don't think we could have *taken* it had
they collected what they could & made a defence, but the panic would have
swept everything. We had them routed & on the jump, & just to make
history interesting & instructive we ought to have improved this rare occasion to the utmost.

It is customary to say that "Providence did not intend that we should
win," but I do not subscribe in the least to that doctrine.[73] Providence did
not care a row of pins about it. If it did it was a very unintelligent Provi-

dence not to bring the business to a close—the close it wanted—in less than four years of most terrible & bloody war.

And while on that subject I will say here that I think it was a serious incubus upon us that during the whole war our president & many of our generals really & actually believed that there *was* this mysterious Providence always hovering over the field & ready to interfere on one side or the other, & that prayers & piety might win its favor from day to day.[74] One of our good old preachers once voiced it in a prayer. I think it was Gen. Lawton who heard it & told me. He prayed, "Oh Lord! Come down we pray thee & *take a proper view of the situation,* & give us the victory over our enemies." But it was a weakness to imagine that victory could ever come in even the slightest degree from anything except our own exertions.

I may have to refer to this subject once more in telling of the "Seven Days" fighting beginning on June 26th, 1862, in which our great & glorious Gen. Jackson for once seemed to put all of his reliance on Providence & very decidedly slackened his own exertions, with the result that Gen. Lee's victory was shorn of the capture of McClellan's entire army.

When I waked up on the morning of July 22nd it was pouring down rain & it continued to pour all day—heavily. Our cavalry under Gen. Stuart[75] were early on the road & soon began to send back reports of the enemy's flight. The blockade of guns at Cub Run was found, & teams were procured & they were all brought up to Manassas, where I remember inspecting them with great pleasure.

The only other incident of the day which I recall was the arrival of the 9th Geo. Regt., in which was the Irving Guards, from Washington, Geo., in which my brother J. H. was a private. They came by train, arriving during the night of [the] 21st or early on [the] 22nd. They belonged to the same brigade with [the] 7th & 8th Georgia which were so badly cut to pieces, but it was their luck to be left behind.

We are now done with 1st Manassas, or Bull Run, where we won a great victory, but failed to play the game of war as it should be played from the moment that the battle was ours. There was some luck in our winning it, for the enemy was not badly punished when he ran; but we deserved to win for we had stood for many hours before a largely superior force & our raw men had behaved like veterans & had put up an exceedingly handsome fight. And if we got no other very material spoils from the fight we at least brought off a great morale, one to which we afterward added in almost every fight & never lost until Appomattox closed the book.[76]

3

FALL & WINTER
AFTER BULL RUN

It was on the morning after the battle of Bull Run that Gen. Beauregard sent for me & told me that I was to be promoted to the position of chief of ordnance of his army. His former chief Col. Samuel Jones[1] was to be brig. gen. & take the Georgia brigade. Gen. Jos. E. Johnston's chief of ordnance Col. Thomas[2] had been killed in the battle, & in a day or two he announced me as chief of ordnance of his corps also. And in fact the two armies were soon merged into one & my position now placed me on the staff of Gen. Johnston, who was commander in chief. Gen. Beauregard however remained attached & I continued to mess with himself & staff until after Christmas, when he transferred to the western army of Albert Sidney Johnston.

My duties as chief of ordnance were to keep the whole army always supplied with arms and ammunition—infantry, artillery & cavalry. It does not sound like very much to do, but there was an infinity of detail about it & I had to organise a complete system. First, I had to issue blanks to every organisation in the army for each one to report what arms it had, & what it needed. From these I could tell what kinds of ammunition each command would need & in what proportions. Then I had to organise a store house for general supplies of this kind at the R.R. station, & to see that each organisation of the army also had a train of wagons sufficient to carry a supply for at least one battle. Then I had to have weekly returns to my office from every regiment & battery & wagon train to have my eye, as it were, on the business everywhere & see what changes were taking place & that everything was as it should be.

We had great trouble from the great variety of arms with which our troops were equipped both in small arms & artillery. Every regiment & every battery would have some apparently of all possible calibres & would want every possible variety of ammunition. They objected always to swapping, & the matter only got better materially in the fall of 1862 when we captured enough rifled muskets from the enemy & enough good guns to supply all our deficiencies. [We] first got [a] full supply after Chancellorsville.[3]

At the beginning we had not over 10 per cent, if so many, of rifled muskets. The balance were old smooth bore muskets & some even had flint-locks. I soon had to organise a travelling repair shop, & I was lucky in finding a most excellent man to put in charge of it, old Major Duffey,[4] a jeweller of Alexandria. He was most earnest, honest & devoted, & an excellent mechanic. He started with two or three wagons of tools & arms needing repair & eventually had a train of over 60 wagons, mostly of reserve ammunition, & he was an institution of the army until the end of the war, going on with my successor as he began with me. Everybody knew old Maj. Geo. Duffey (G. C. I think were his initials),[5] with his good natured round face & his sympathetic Virginia voice, & I want my children to know him too. He & I will often be together—across the river. He has been over a long time already.

In charge of the big depot I had at Manassas was Capt. C. C. McPhail of Va. (whose beautiful sister was Mrs. T. M. R. Talcott on Gen. Lee's staff as an engineer). McPhail was an excellent officer & a great assistance to me.[6]

I remained in charge of the signals also but could not give it a great deal of personal attention. I instructed my brother J. H. in the system & soon afterward lieutenantcies were given to most of the men I had trained, & they were distributed about in our army & sent to other armies to introduce the system everywhere. A general signal officer for the Confederacy was wanted & I was offered the position with the rank of colonel, but I declined being unwilling to leave the field. It was accordingly given to a Col. Norris, who had been signal officer at Norfolk & was an excellent man.[7] I cannot now write any consecutive account of the matters that occupied me but will merely string together the few things which I can recall of the ensuing fall & winter regardless of their actual order.

First I remember that on two occasions I got from 3 to 5 days' leave of absence & went down to Richmond where my dear Miss Teen was staying with the Webbs at 9th & Leigh Sts. Once I went on some ordnance business. I have forgotten exactly what, but I took with me a N.Y. captain who had been captured to turn over to the authorities. We got in 2 hours after dark & I paroled him that night & lent him $10 to go to a hotel. He came up all right in the morning, & made beautiful promises about the $10.00 as soon as he could hear from N.Y., but that ten never came back. The second time I came was to see if I could get equipment to make a rocket battery of the Irving Guards. It was promised to me & some war rockets & tubes for shooting them were sent to me, but on trial I found they were too uncertain a missile & I gave up the idea & rustled around until I gradually got guns for them, & they became a fine battery of artillery commanded by Capt.

Lane, a young undergraduate from West Point, son of Lane who ran as V.P. on [the] Breckinridge ticket.[8] He still lives I believe in Oregon. It was a matter of very peculiar pleasure to me to get those boys from Washington—many of them old schoolmates & friends—into the artillery, which was much pleasanter service, free from all guard and picket duty.

I felt some doubt about the quality of the artillery ammunition & made an early opportunity to try some at target practise, & I found it in really dreadful shape. Our smooth bore shells & shrapnel would very frequently explode prematurely, & our rifle shot & shells would all tumble or fail to go point first, so they had no range at all & were worse than worthless. I devised methods to partly at least cure the bad shells already distributed to the batteries by leather washers & white lead under fuses, & I got the department in Richmond to work on new patterns all around. We gradually made great improvements, but the enemy were always far ahead of us in artillery ammunition of all kinds both in quality & quantity.

One of the camp excitements during the fall was the publication of Randall's poem "Maryland my Maryland"[9] & its being set to music & sung by the two very pretty Misses Cary, Hetty & Jennie, who were refugees, I believe, from Baltimore & were visiting friends in the vicinity.[10] It created immense enthusiasm & Gen. Beauregard had the poem printed on our headqrs. press (which printed all orders) & distributed to all who wanted.

Another little private excitement about headqrs. related to the getting up of a battle flag. During the battle of Bull Run, Gen. B. was unable to distinguish, at about 1,000 or 1,200 yds., whether one of our Confederate flags (1st issue) was ours or Federal. [Figure 6 appears here in the manuscript.] So he decided to adopt a battle flag & a lot of designs were suggested & discussed, & finally what after became our army battle flag was selected—the Maltese Cross in blue on a red field. Stars white in the blue. [Figure 7 appears here in the manuscript.] While this was considered a great secret & was never publicly mentioned, a pretended "prophecy" about the war was published in the Washington *Evening Star*—said to have been found in some old Catholic monastery in Maryland somewhere—as follows:

> Ere thirteen united
> Are thrice what they were
> Shall the Eagle be blighted
> By the fortunes of war.
>
> When sixty is ended
> And one takes its place
> Then shall brothers offended
> Deal mutual disgrace.

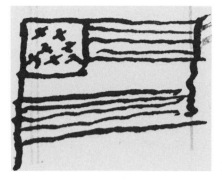

Figure 6. First issue Confederate flag

Figure 7. Army of Northern Virginia battle flag

> But whenever the Cross
> Takes its place mid the Stars
> They shall gain by their loss
> And thus end all their wars.

This reference to the cross was a strange coincidence, the cross being afterward put by Congress in our Confederate flag as a union. [Figure 8 appears here in the manuscript.] And there is a picture with a couplet which was published after the war & widely circulated which might well be considered the suggestion of a literal fulfillment of the prophecy. [Figure 9 appears here in the manuscript.] The banner is shown ascending in a night sky with stars around it & underneath is written:

> The warrior's banner takes its flight.
> To greet the warrior's soul

Let us at least hope that we *have* gained by our loss & have ended all our wars.

Twice, I think, during the fall & winter I was sent up to Leesburg to

Figure 8. Confederate flag with cross as union

Figure 9. Confederate flag surrounded by stars

select ground & lay off a few little forts to strengthen the position there. Quite a little battle was fought there, I think in Oct.

Some troops—about a brigade—under Baker, a prominent California political general, were sent across the river by Gen. Stone who commanded on [the] opposite side. They were attacked by a part of Evans's brigade, which was stationed about Leesburg, & were driven into the river where some were drowned & many killed, among them Baker. From all accounts our men did the best fighting & showed that they preserved the morale gained at Bull Run & added to it. Evans himself was not in the fight, which was made by the regimental officers of the _____, which were the only regiments engaged, & by a Col. Jenifer who had resigned from the old army—the inventor of the Jenifer saddle.[11]

It was after this fight when I was sent to lay out some works for the place. Gen. D. H. Hill was then in command there, & I remained with him several days. One of our works was on a hill which the enemy could reach with artillery from their side of the river, & they would often come out & practise at the working party but could never I believe quite hit them. Gen. Hill was very much amused one evening at two little boys living at a house in the line of fire but a little short. As he passed he saw them out on top of the barn watching the distant battery. When the rising cloud of smoke told that a gun had been fired the boys would shout with delight, "Now she's a coming." And then as the rushing shell screamed more or less close overhead & plunged into the hillside or burst in the air with a whizzing of fragments, they fairly danced on the flat-roofed shed saying, "Here she is. Here she is." Gen. Hill stopped as he rode by & said, "Boys ain't you afraid some of those shells will hit you?" But the little fellows answered with entire confidence, "Oh no, Sir. They aren't shooting at us."[12]

That was at my first visit. My second was made late in the winter when my wife was at Dr. Marsteller's near Gainesville, & I rode from there. I can only recall of that trip how bitterly cold it was & a very high wind blowing rails off fence tops as I rode along. And though it is out of chronological order I had as well tell here that about the first week in January I secured board for Miss Teen at Dr. Marsteller's, a very nice large house say a mile north of Gainesville, where Manassas Gap R.R. crosses [the] Warrenton Pike. Several other officers' wives were also located there, among them Mrs. C. W. Field & a Mrs. Swan of Baltimore, a very lovely woman of whom we became very fond during the winter. She had no children of her own & she was very devoted to our "little Bess." The latter I saw for the first time, after carrying her in my arms from the station to the house—a bright moonlight night with snow on the ground—when I unrolled a wonderful bundle of shawls & blankets, which her mother had reluctantly committed to my care when I met her in the car on arrival of the train at Gainesville. How well I remember waiting for that train—a long time—talking part of the time to a very pleasant & nice looking fellow whom I never saw, before or since—a Dr. Eliason, brother of Dr. Augustine Mason's wife & son of an old engineer officer of the old army.[13]

Well Miss Teen stayed at Dr. Marsteller's until about the end of Feb. or [the] first week in March when we all broke up, as will be duly told, to fall back toward Richmond. I used to ride from Centreville every Sat. afternoon along the Warrenton Pike & spend Sunday with her (see map [Figure 4])[14]—returning Monday morning.

Our army headquarters had been advanced from Manassas to Fairfax Court House soon after the battle of Bull Run & they remained there until about Nov. 1, when we moved back to Centreville where we spent the winter, & we built a few breast works there along a range of hills just north of the town. I saw a narrow escape from a sad accident there. The Washington Arty. got permission to do some target shooting from one of these works, & after sending out their officers to see that all was clear fired a number of shot, shell & spherical case over a large wood in a valley below at a tree in a clearing beyond the wood. After the shooting I rode with the officers to look about the target, when at the far edge of the wood just in our line of fire we saw a house. It seemed deserted, which we thought was fortunate as the officers sent out to examine had failed to see it & reported all clear. But when we rode up there were clothes hanging on a line, & we saw that a cannon shot had gone through the upper story & the side of the house was also peppered with case shot bullets. We dismounted, & opening the door & calling, out came a poor woman, evidently in very delicate condition of health, & three children, all scared nearly to death. A fourth child had run off somewhere in the woods, but it was soon found all right. The mother, when the shells began to fly over, had gotten the 3 children & taken refuge under the bed upstairs, & while they were under the bed a solid shot passed through tearing the mattress open. But most fortunately no one was hurt, but I believe the poor woman had a severe illness & premature delivery of an infant brought on by the terror & shock.[15] [Figure 10 appears here in the manuscript.]

For sometime during the fall of 1861 I continued to have general charge of the Signal Corps, in addition to my more important & exciting work as chief of ordnance. We had some long lines of signals running up to the Blue Ridge Mountains, but I can remember very little detail about that part of the business. But some chances offered in our immediate front which I became much interested in, & which gradually brought me into a good deal of secret service business. While our headquarters were at Fairfax C.H. our pickets held two hills from which a number of houses in Washn. City were in full view. These places were Munson's Hill & Mason's Hill. On the latter place was a nice residence with a commodious observation tower upon it, & I formed a plan to send an instructed signal observer to rent a room in some house in Washn. looking out towards this tower, & to establish a regular line of signals between his room & this tower; which it was easy to do.

A gentleman[16] living on the Battery in Charleston, but whose name I cannot recall, lent me a fine astronomical glass about 6 feet long & [with a] four inch aperature mounted on a tripod with which I could easily count the panes of glass in the windows in Washington City, and I mounted the glass in the observation tower on Mason's Hill.

The man to go into Washington & rent the room, & to send us the messages furnished him by our other friends in the city, was a splendid fellow, whom I grew very fond of, E. Pliny Bryan—a Marylander who volunteered his services to me & was at work for me for many months going in & out of the enemies' lines constantly. It would be too tedious to detail how we were to find & recognise the window of the room he rented, & how he from it—with a glass—was to locate our tower; but there was no difficulty in the matter, & the details were all carefully studied out, & his

Figure 10. Lt. Gen. James Longstreet late in life

signals were to be sent by a tin coffee pot, held just inside the window so that no one outside could see.

The accompanying letter, which I most accidentally stumbled upon in Greytown, Nic., a few days before writing this, tells how our plan was frustrated:

Headquarters First Corps, Army of the Potomac, Fairfax Courthouse, October 11, 1861.—His Excellency President Davis, Richmond, Va.—Mr. President: In compliance with your request, I have the honor to submit the following statement of the services being gratuitously rendered by Mr. E. Pliny Bryan, one of the earliest secessionists of the Maryland Legislature. He served originally as a volunteer private in the First Virginia regiment for a long period, including the battles in July and until he heard of the system of signals, when he offered his services unreservedly to me. With Gen. Beauregard's approval, I instructed him fully and sent him across the Potomac to live in Washington city, and communicate with us by signals from a window visible from Mason's Hill. This bold plan was only frustrated by our evacuation of that position while he was making his way through Maryland to Washington. He has returned safely, and is now only awaiting the perfecting of our plans before going back to Maryland to live, concealed on the shore at some suitable point, and communicate with us (both by boat and signals) information to be furnished by our friends in Washington. He is bold and intelligent, and well worthy of any recognition or reward you may deem suitable. I respectfully request something that may at least entitle him to our protection if arrested. In the same connection I beg leave to mention also a lady previously known to Mr. B., whom I design employing in Washington city in connection with him, with his full consent. She is most admirably adapted mentally, socially, and physically to her task, and has motives to serve us which will carry her to any necessary lengths. She claims to be married to an officer in our army, by whom she has two children whose legitimacy she wishes to establish, the father denying it and being about to marry another woman. His family is an influential one, and she desires to serve us to gain influence and an official recognition to meet their attacks upon her claims. Her present name is Mrs. Morris.

Begging your approval of my appointment of her in a way to jeopardize nothing, and a favorable remembrance of her services, should they prove of value, I am, very respectfully, your obedient servant, E. P. Alexander, Captain of Engineers.[17]

Gen. Johnston thought Mason's Hill too advanced & isolated to be safely held, & a new picket line was formed throwing it out on the very day that Bryan reached Washn. City. But, as we could not do that, we did the next best thing, by having a line across the Potomac down about the mouth of Bull Run. Bryan lived over on the Maryland side, with sympathizing friends who brought regular Northern papers & letters from friends in Washington. These friends were, at first, Mrs. Greenhow[18] & a wealthy man whose name I forget but who was very liberal in spending money to help us when needed. He was a strong Methodist & in our letters we always referred to him as the M.E. Institution.

The one thing we had done for us by our friends in Washn. City was to keep & send us regularly arrivals & departures of all Federal troops, &

clippings from newspapers which mentioned troops brigaded or associated together. From information of this sort I was able quite soon to construct a roster of the Federal army, showing every division of it with the brigades in each division & the regts. in each brigade. This of course enabled us to estimate the force of the enemy very accurately.

And why they could not, & did not, by similar processes correctly estimate our forces I have never understood; but it appears in all of McClellan's[19] official reports that he always enormously exaggerated our strength.

I will recur to this subject again further on in my narrative. Now I must finish with the secret service business. In my letter to the prest., given above, I have referred to "Mrs Morris." She was quite a handsome woman of about 30 years of age, with two children, who was sent through the Federal lines up near Leesburg by the enemy, & brought down to hqars. at Fairfax by our cavalry. She claimed to be the wife of a Capt. Mason from Leesburg, a relative of Tom Rhett's wife, Rhett being Gen. Johnston's adjutant, but Mason denied the relationship.[20] Beauregard's adjutant, Thos. Jordan, interviewed her on her arrival, & was at first suspicious of her being a Federal spy. He was finally satisfied however that she was not, & then he conceived the idea of sending her back as our spy, & he asked me to devise means of getting messages with more regularity than he had been able to do up to that time.

In reply to my letter to the prest. I was authorized to pay Mrs. Morris for services, & Bryan was made a captain in the Signal Corps—& the whole business was gotten to running. Mrs. Morris was sent back via Fortress Monroe & she went to Washn. City & boarded at Willard's Hotel, I believe, & we sent her money & she sent us letters—the best she knew how; & Bryan lived on the Md. shore, & an old Dr. Wyman,[21] or some such name, brought him the letters & papers from Wash., & two men whose names I forget (though I remember the faces—one small, dark & narrow, & one oval & fair & good-natured) acted on the south side of the river reading Bryan's signals & bringing the mail when it was crossed, which it was easy to do at night.

And this business was kept up successfully all the winter, but some time in the spring, I can't recall exactly, the enemy got wind of it far enough to arrest Mrs. Morris, & Mrs. Greenhow & a Mrs. Baxley,[22] who was also playing the spy in Washington, I believe, though I forget if I ever knew who sent her. But all three were shut up in the Old Capitol Prison together; & not only they but Dr. Wyman & the good natured-face man & Bryan himself, were all captured & were all locked up in the same edifice. But fortunately there was no evidence against any one of them &, about July, I think it was, they turned them all loose or exchanged them, & they all got safely back to Richmond. I was encamped near the city at the time & when these three ladies arrived the Confederate officials were very much at a loss what to do with them. I was sent for & appointed to interview them all, & find out what they wanted. One thing that each one wanted was that it should be understood that she had been pefectly discreet in every respect, but that the other two had flickered more or less. Evidently their common calamity had not drawn them together. But I believe each one had been as loyal & devoted as possible, & each one was satisfied now with very reasonable compensation—I forget the amounts but they were not very large & they were in Confederate money, which however was good enough then.

Mrs. Morris then went west somewhere. I don't know what became of Mrs. Baxley, and poor Mrs. Greenhow ran the blockade at Wilmington & was drowned. I never knew the details or the exact time. Pliny Bryan was sent down to Florida to worry the enemy's transportation on the St. Johns River, & was very successful, blowing up two boats, I believe, with torpedoes made of demijohns of powder. Then Beauregard had him up at Charleston harbor for some rush work on the enemy's ironclads, but the poor fellow sickened of yellow fever & died. He was a good man, & not afraid to take any risk which offered any chance of accomplishing results for our side. He & I will find each other across the river I am sure.

In connection with this secret service business, I set a trap to catch the enemy's spies, or messengers into our lines, of which I had great hopes, but all were frustrated by the loyalty & vigilance of our own people living between our lines & the enemy's. At a point on the Potomac called Evansport we were building, for a month, a masked battery which when completed would, & did, practically close the Potomac to the enemy's navigation. It was constructed in the midst of a dense thicket of cedars which competely hid it from the river, but could be cut down in a night & a full view given as soon as we were ready. The enemy got an idea we were trying something of the sort near a place called Limestone Point, & shelled about there a good deal, while we also made some false demonstrations there. About a week before we expected to be ready to unmask our Evansport battery I wrote an anonymous letter, or rather one under the fictitious name of Lazarus, to Gen. McClellan conveying the idea that I was a clerk, or courier, or employee of some sort about some important hdqrs. where I overheard many important conversations, & that I was willing to betray them to him if I could be promptly & well paid & given some means of getting letters to him.

And, as proof of what I could do, I told him all about the Evansport battery & about the false demonstrations made at Limestone. I gave many details & particulars & all exactly true. Then I went on to say that I had a brother in a cavalry brigade who would work with me, & that I would give him this, my first letter, & let him take advantage of his first opportunity in picketing or scouting to leave this letter where a Federal picket or scout would find it. And then I would expect Gen. McClellan to let me hear of its safe receipt by a letter to "John Lazarus Fairfax C.H. Va." put into a Confederate mail box anywhere in the Confederacy. And this letter must tell how I was to get paid, & how to send future dispatches, for I would only risk the dropping letters once.

This letter I carried in my pocket so that it would bear signs of having been handled & carried to correspond with its story, & then, when we were about ready to let the enemy find out about our Potomac batteries, I got Gen. Stuart, commanding our cavalry pickets, to make a scout & drive in the enemy's pickets & ride around a bit in their territory & then come back, meanwhile confiding the letter to a trusty private with instructions to place it so that the enemy would get it. This soldier thought the best chance was to confide it to an old Negro woman who had a cabin on the road. But a few days afterward there came up to hdqrs. a special messenger from a Major Munford[23] of cavalry on the picket line enclosing my letter (which I forgot to say was addressed on [the] outside to "Gen. McClellan—in care of any of his pickets who find this") & sending some very excited advice to watch the post office & hang who ever first inquired for a letter for Mr. Lazarus. It seemed that some good Southerner had seen the soldier stop behind & interview the old Negro woman, & had scared her into telling & giving up the letter. Then he had watched his chance to run the blockade & get it over to our pickets, thinking, of course, that he was frustrating a dangerous traitor.

But my opportunity to use some really valuable information as a bait was gone with the opening of the Evansport battery. I did try it however a second time, a few days or weeks later, but I cannot now recall the information which I used as a bait, nor exactly how the letter fell into the enemy hands again. I only know that both letters came back to my own hands without ever reaching the enemy, & I believe they still exist among my old papers. After the 2nd failure I never tried it again.

There were during the fall months some wonderful cock & bull stories in the Northern papers about traitors to the Federal cause in Washington. One was told with much detail that, on a certain night, a very important attack upon us had been planned, & the troops were beginning the move, when a display of rockets along the whole Confederate front showed that we were informed & upon the alert. I am quite sure there were no traitors in Washn. to speak of, but our little gang told of above, and I think I can also explain the rocket business. I had my signal stations scattered about on the high places, & of course under orders to report promptly all unusual occurrences. One night, I remember, about bedtime receiving a report that one or two or possibly more rockets had been seen over the Federal lines. I took the report to Gen. Beauregard & he asked me if I had rockets. I said yes, every station was provided, on which he told me to have every station send up one, & during the night to have one or two more little demonstrations of them. It took very few minutes to send the orders everywhere, & we soon had rockets apparently answering each other for a long distance right & left, & couriers were sent to shoot others, later, at other points. The next papers from the North brought the story above referred to. It was said McClellan complained to Lincoln that only he and Gen. Scott[24] knew of his plans, & yet they were allowed to become known to some one who must have betrayed them to us.

During this fall, Sep. to Dec., McClellan accumulated an immense army, some _____. We also did our best & probably had in northern Va. about _____,[25] but it was well for us that the Federals did not attack, for our new regiments suffered awfully from sickness, measles especially.

Hdqrs. during winter was at Centreville, & I remained with Beauregard's mess & staff until Gen. B. was ordered out west, sometime I guess about the time we broke up, early in March.

Gen. Johnston decided that he was a little too far to the front, &, as soon as the roads began to get passable, he prepared to withdraw back behind the Rapidan. So the wives were sent off (mine went to Richmond) & all baggage was reduced to the lowest, & early in March we moved slowly back to the south side of the Rapidan River. I was directed to blow up the old Stone Bridge—an arch of about 20 feet—when all had crossed, & Maj. Duffey & I mined the abutments & loaded them, & then the major remained & fired the mines at the proper time. I have always wanted to revisit that spot, which was quite a pretty one in those days, but I never had the chance, though I went across Sudley Ford, only two or three miles off, in Sept. '62. I will probably never see it again, but if any of my kids, or kid's-kids, ever travel that Warrenton Pike across Bull Run they may imagine Maj. Duffey & myself, on a raft underneath the bridge mining holes in the abutments, & loading them with 500 lbs. of gunpowder & fixing fuses on hanging planks to blow up both sides simultaneously.

On the march for the Rapidan I joined Gen. Johnston's mess & staff. I recall among them Thos. Rhett,[26] adjt. genl., & A. P. Mason (Penny), asst.; Jimmy Washington, aid de camp; old Col. Archie Cole, I can't be sure exactly what he was—some sort of a quartermaster I think, probably chief, & with Corley (who was afterward chief) for an asst. But Corley did not march or mess with us; nor did Bob Cole, who was chief commissary. But I think Dr. Choppin & Brodie,[27] the medical men did. On this march I first recall meeting some of the Haskell boys, Aleck, John, & Joe,[28] visiting Rhett at hdqrs. This must make them now almost my very oldest living friends & intimates, for of earlier days there are few if any left. Stevens[29] of the old Engr. Corps, Gen. Johnston's chf. engr., was also with us part of that time at least.

In this connection I forgot to say that my brother W. F.[30] had been with the army from sometime in the fall as maj. & qr.mr. of Toombs's brigade.

And I have vague recollections that when Gen. Toombs first joined the army he was not entirely a subordinate & respectful brigadier & there was at one time danger of some unpleasant trouble. But Beauregard & Johnston handled the matter with great good judgment, & all went well, in fact, until the next fall under Gen. Lee when Gen. Toombs was put in arrest for awhile, on the 2nd Manassas campaign, but not for long. After the battle of Sharpsburg, at which he was wounded in the hand by a pistol shot during the night retreat from Sharpsburg, he gave up his brigade & retired from service—after that, I believe, being in the Senate.

During the fall also my brother J. H. had been made a signal officer & sent off to Wilmington & other points south & west.[31]

When we got behind the Rapidan we were quiet for some weeks. Gen J. made his headquarters at the house of a Mr. Sidney Jones, about a mile east of the Orange R.R. bridge over [the] Rapidan, on [the] south side, a few hundred yards back from [the] river. I have very pleasant recollections of the hospitality & kindness of all the Jones family, & of the excellence of the table they provided for us. Jowl & spinach & I have been more than mere acquaintances, we have been friends, ever since we met at Mr. Jones's table. It pleasantly recalls Mr. Jones, to this day, whenever I see it.

When we abandoned Manassas & fell back, McClellan sent out an army corps or two to follow & see what we were doing, but they did not follow very far. In fact McClellan had made up his mind to attack Richmond from an entirely different quarter. He decided to make Fortress Monroe his base & to advance on the Peninsula between the York & James Rivers, his fleet supporting him advancing up the York to West Point, which he would then make his base of supplies within 30 miles of Richmond.

There was at first strong opposition to his plan in Washn. City by the prest. & the sec. of war, who objected to McClellan's army being taken from between our army & Washn. City. They feared that we would rush in & capture it, although it was girdled with line upon line of strong forts, armed with heavy arty. & with permanent garrisons. But at last he satisfied them by leaving about 40,000 men & he moved by water to Fortress Monroe with about 100,000. It was not at all bad strategy. In fact considering that we held Norfolk & had the iron-clad *Merrimac* there it was doubtless the very best strategy on the map, & the proof of the pudding showed it.

Practically without firing a shot, in two months he just manouvred us out of Norfolk, & of Yorktown; opened both the James & the York Rivers to his fleet of iron-clads; compelled us ourselves to blow up the *Merrimac;* brought our army down from the Rapidan; & established his own pickets within 6 miles of Richmond, & with only our army without fortifications, except a few very trifling ones, between him & Richmond. I say he did this without firing a shot, because there was no general battle, &, in the two minor ones which took place, we had not the worst of it, & neither of them were of any influence on the result. The simple presence of his tremendous force compelled our movements for fear worse things would happen to us.

But all his good strategy went for nought because he exaggerated our forces over 100 per cent, & was afraid to wade in & fight, as will appear as I go on. And I will give a page to a bit of a map by which any kid who reads may appreciate the points (see map [Figure 11]).

Now when Gen. Johnston on the Rapidan—enjoying good Mr. Jones's jowl & spinach—found that McClellan, instead of following him, had gone to Fortress Monroe with 100,000 men he felt beholden to get down that way himself, & with as many men as he could carry, & in the shortest possible space of time. So the whole army was just in motion by land & by rail; & the general & staff went by rail to Richmond, &, after all too few days there (where my wife & baby were, boarding with Mrs. Brock on Franklin St. about 3rd), we went on by boat down the James to a landing whence we could reach Yorktown. It was on this occasion that I "lost my horse" in Richmond for three days, by not being able to pick him out in a livery stable from others of [the] same color, which has seemed to some people an excellent joke.

At Yorktown, Gen. Magruder—known in the army as "Prince John"—was in command of some 8,000 or 10,000 men when McClellan started out for Yorktown with a large force. The Peninsula there is narrow—four or five miles maybe—& Magruder had stretched a line clear across, more than half the way behind a creek flowing to the James. And along the upper part of this creek were some dams, making overflows as obstructions. When McClellan's forces approached, Magruder actually bluffed them from making any serious attack upon him, by marching his men around & showing them successively at different places, making them appear much more numerous than they really were. And instead of attacking McClellan sat down & began a siege.

He should have attacked, without doubt strongly at several points, & he would certainly have carried one. And his fleet I think could have silenced our batteries on the river banks, had any serious effort been made. But I can hardly ever remember their making any demonstration even during the whole time of the siege.

One Federal regiment was sent against one of our dams & overflows, just about the time that our troops began to reinforce Magruder, & it behaved very well, actually crossing on the dam, & through the water, before our people were fully ready for them, & it actually got into our breastworks, but it was then severely punished & driven back with heavy loss.[32]

I can't recall a great deal about our stay in the Yorktown lines. Our hd.qrs. I remember vaguely as a large square house,[33] in a considerable clearing, in a wood, about [the] centre of the Peninsula, a short distance in rear of the line.

The sharpshooting between the two armies was exceedingly vicious wherever pickets or lines could see each other. It was the first time they were ever located near enough to each other for this & both sides went at it with vim, and the artillery too often took part. It made our lines in some places awfully uncomfortable. There was lots of rain, & the country was flat, & our dams & overflows cut off even what drainage there was.

Our infantry lines were mere ditches with dirt thrown out in front, & these ditches in many places nearly filled with water in which the troops had to sit & stand day & night. And in many places they could not even stand but had to keep crouched below the pile of dirt in front, for to stand up was to be exposed to the enemy sharp shooters. I remember some officer telling me of some friend of his, who waking in the morning from the uncomfortable dozing during the night stood up to yawn & stretch himself & was immediately shot through the heart by a sharpshooter. The Federals had an entire regiment armed with rifles with telescopic sights which were wonderfully accurate. We had no arms equal to those at all, but we had many good shots with the ordinary guns & from the accounts in Northern papers we made it nearly as hot for them as they did for us. One of their lieuts. of topographical engineers named Wagner from Pa., who was a class or so behind me at West Point, was killed by a very remarkable cannon shot by one of our batteries.[34] He set up a plane table to make a sketch upon, where the battery could see him though well over a half mile off. They fired at him & destroyed the table & killed him at the first shot.

In this flat wooded country there was no chance for signals & I think that I practically had nothing more to do with signals after this time. But I did send a spy into McClellan's line who went in, stayed a week with some of our loyal citizens living in there whom he knew & came out bringing a very full, accurate, & valuable report of the force the enemy had & how they were disposed & what they were doing. I am sorry I can't recall the brave fellow's name. He was a rather small, silent, good looking boy. We sent him in by a boat at night dropping down in the river to a point that this fellow knew when he landed, & then a week later it came back close to the same point at an agreed hour & he waded or swam out to it. I occasionally went about, through the lines to see everything, but most of my time was taken up in getting all the ammunition supply business for regiments & batteries well organised & working smoothly & efficiently.

Among my subordinate officers at different jobs about this time I recall a very striking character, T. Kinloch Fauntleroy from somewhere in West Virginia.³⁵ He combined in himself the reddest head, the most freckled face, the worst crossed eyes & the most terrible stammering I ever heard, with the most perfect sang-froid & self possession, & absolute freedom from self consciousness, that I ever met. It was told of him that once at a ball in a strange city he was introduced to a young lady who also stammered & asked her to dance the next dance. She stammered in reply that she was engaged, on which he supposed she was making fun of him & retorted, "d-d-dam fool—I couldn't help it."

He first entered the army as a private in a cav. regt. & was once detailed as courier at hdqrs., when we were at Fairfax, & Prest. Davis was there on a visit. Fauntleroy, lying on grass in the yard, with another courier, said he wished Mr. D. would make him a lieut. The other courier laughed & said, "Why don't you go & ask him?"—Mr. D. at the time sitting in the porch with one of the genls. F. immediately walked up in the porch & saluting Mr. D. asked him "please to make him a lieut." After a few questions Mr. D. told him that when he returned to Richd. he would send him a commission, when F. stammered, "N-n-n-now &c., Mr. President, can I *rely* upon you?"

Well he got his commission, but after being attached to a battery of arty. for six months, he was not popular & they got rid of him some how, & he was sent to Gen Johnston's headquarters for assignment, & I took him & put him in charge of a little outfit I had at Gordonsville altering old flintlock muskets to percussion. He once sent me a long telegram to Yorktown about his business & the telegraph operator getting his name & his business confused, put his signature to it as "T. Flintlock Fauntleroy." Gen. Johnston's staff got hold of it & Fauntleroy was ever afterwards known throughout the army solely as "Flint-lock Fauntleroy," flint-locks being notorious among small-arms for their hanging-fire qualities.

Sometime during the winter or spring, I had received two promotions & both had been dated back to carry rank & pay from [the] date of my becoming chief of ordnance. The first made me a "major" & the second "lieut. col. of artillery on ordnance duty," there being no ord. corps. And sometime also during these months I had acquired two appendages which stayed with me during the whole war. I had bought a second horse, "Meg Merrilies," a very pretty bay mare with a roan spot on one hip, & I had hired for an ostler & servant a 15 year old darkey named Charley—a medium tall & slender, ginger-cake colored, & well behaved & good dispositioned boy. In all the 3½ years I had him with me I had to give him a little licking but twice—once for robbing a pear tree in the garden of the Keach house, in which we were staying on the outskirts of Richmond below Rocketts, & once in Pa. just before Gettysburg, for stealing apple-brandy & getting tight on it.

Gen. Johnston appreciated that we could not afford to become entangled in siege operations with McClellan before Yorktown, for the river flank was too weak. He was willing to risk being assaulted by main force, but, as soon as it appeared that McC. would not venture that, he began to prepare to evacuate our lines and to retreat up the Peninsula & take position in front of Richmond.

As one of the preliminaries to this, I was temporarily taken from my ordnance work, and sent with Stevens, the chief engineer of the army, back to the vicinity of Richmond to select a line of battle for the army on the east side of the Chickahominy. We were three or four days in all on the business, & got to know very well all that country & many of its then peaceful & apparently prosperous citizens, where for three years the bloodiest battles ever fought on the continent were to be waged & every inhabitant & almost every living thing down to the very birds & rabbits were to be driven away. We stayed one night with Dr. Gaines & his family, & were probably the first officers he ever entertained at his house, which was a fine & large one, with orchards & gardens around. A mill he owned gave the name [to] the "Battle of Gaines's Mill"; and "Second Cold Harbor" as it was called, in 1864, also covered some of his grounds.[36]

I also recall a dinner at the quiet little one story country hotel, with a few cottages near, & lots of shade trees, called Cold Harbor; & how amused our party was at an old fashioned country bed, in one corner of the parlor, so high that it could only have been successfully assaulted with a step ladder.

We found a favorable location for a line of battle, with an especially strong left flank behind Beaver Dam Creek, near Mechanicsville, about which I will have more to tell when I come to the Seven Days fighting before Richmond in June. For Gen. Johnston finally decided to make his stand entirely on the south side of the Chickahominy, & our selected line was not used by ourselves, & the enemy took the beautiful Beaver Dam position for his own right. And some bloody blunders led to its being assaulted by two large, new, green Geo. & N.C. regiments, who were killed till they laid "like flies in a bowl of sugar" as a Federal writer described it at the time.

On the night of May 3rd, Gen. Johnston retreated from Yorktown, the Federals being just about ready to open, in a day or two, a tremendous artillery fire upon our works, from a long line of powerful batteries which they had erected. [Figure 11 appears here in the manuscript.] Our hd.qrs. took the road about sundown, as I recollect, & marched all night and until

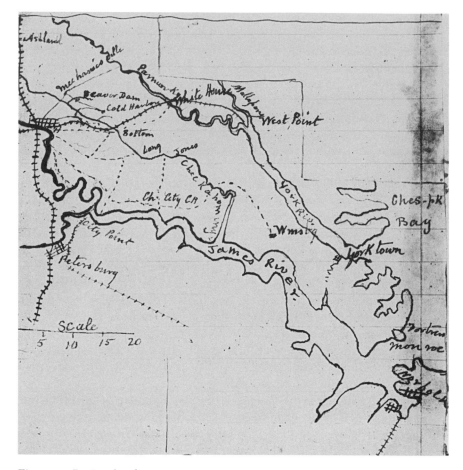

Figure 11. Peninsula of Virginia

afternoon of [the] next day before reaching Williamsburg; about _____ miles.37 It could hardly be called marching; it was wading in mud & slush from one to three feet deep. I have not a few remembrances of Virginia mud roads in winter time, cut into bottomless sloughs by the tremendous traffic of army trains & artillery, but none seem to me to approach the condition of the roads from Yorktown to Williamsburg on that occasion. It was a dark night, & there was no picking one's way, & the whole width of the road was filled with either wagons, ambulances, artillery, or infantry plunging & laboring through the mud, with frequent long halts when some gun, or wagon, stalled in some deep spot, & men from the ranks marching near had to swarm in & help the jaded horses pull them out, while everything behind,[38] if the road was at all narrow, had to come to a stop & wait. And so it went on all night—march or wade two minutes and halt ten or longer.

I recall a single incident of the night, and to tell it I must tell first a little about the Semmes family. I don't know where they orginally came from, but they were generally Catholics & they had several branches in different parts of the South, and, wherever I have known or heard of them, their men have been men of extraordinary force of character. Capt. Raphael Semmes,[39] of our privateer *Alabama,* was one of them of whom the South may well be proud. Highly educated, refined, brave, & magnanimous he was the very highest type of a naval officer. He sunk the U. S. warship *Hatteras* at night in the Gulf of Mexico & saved every soul aboard of her. He challenged the *Kearsarge*—much his superior in force & equipment—to a duel & would have sunk her, but for his very defective ammunition from being so long at sea, & away from supplies, in spite of her being chain clad over her vitals;[40] for he lodged a heavy percussion shell in her sternport—which failed to explode. His record is one of which the South may be proud in all her generations. He was the Stonewall Jackson of the sea. One of the best accounts of him is in a book, which is one of the two best books published about the war—Bulloch's "Secret Service of the [C].S."; the other one being "Johnson's" History of the Defence of Charleston Harbor & Fort Sumter (I may not have both titles exact but very near).[41]

I knew in Georgia three branches of the Semmes family. 1st, Alexander Semmes of Washington, Geo. He had a brother who, when a student at the Va. Univy. at Charlottesville, had unfortunately killed a professor who tried to arrest some of the boys skylarking one night. His name was Joe Semmes. The professor's name was Dr. Davis.[42] He was allowed bail, which his family forfeited & ran him off & kept him hidden in Texas & Georgia. He became a dreadful cripple from rheumatism, & he finally committed suicide along about 1847 in Washington, Geo., in his brother's house. 2nd, Tom Semmes was my father's next neighbor on the north, some 800 yards away, & his two sons, Alfonzo & Roger, were my very first playmates, & I went to school at a little house in their garden to a Mr. Ware for awhile, & then the whole family moved away to somewhere near Canton, Miss. But I mention them merely to speak of Mr. Tom Semmes's voice, which was the most remarkable I have ever heard for its carrying power. It was on a key of its own & cut through all other noises without any interference. If he, in his yard, raised his voice in giving instructions to his servants it could frequently be heard in our yard. He had two country plantations a mile apart or more & the foreman on each was named John. One day at some intermediate point he saw cows in a cornfield & calling for John both Johns came. The 3rd Semmes was Gen. Paul J. Semmes of Columbus, Georgia, who commanded a brigade in McLaws's division & was killed the second day at Gettysburg.[43] I have a vague idea that he served in Mexico but am not sure. At any rate he was well known in Georgia as a man both of military tastes & accomplishments before the war, & though of no military education he was one of the first generals created. And it is due him to say that there never was a braver or a better.

This is a long preliminary to a very short & simple anecdote of Gen. Semmes, but I knew him so well that I want you to know him too, any how, & it will help give you an idea of the night. Gen. S. had a voice not unlike Mr. Tom's, &, though not so remarkable as that, anyone who once heard it would always know it. About the middle of that night we were passing a sort of flat open place with scattered low bushes and on the right what seemed to be a low bank with a ditch on each side a few yards off the road— on which a few figures seemed to be groping & bogging along. I had had poor luck in trying to find better riding, off along the sides, & was just working the middle of the road, when I heard Gen. Semmes's voice clear & sharp from the bank through the darkness, "Get out of the road, Sir," & some man in reply said—"But I can't. Here's a big ditch on both sides. I can't get off of here." "By God! you can and you will," said Semmes and immediately there was a tremendous splash & floundering in the water & that was all.

Along about 2 P.M. on [May 4th][44] we passed a good sized, bastioned front earth work called Fort Magruder, one of a row of some four or five making a line across the Peninsula there some mile or two east of Williamsburg, & then we went on into the town to the hotel about the middle of a very long straight street which seemed to be about the whole town. After a bit of a meal, breakfast & dinner in one, I was sent back to carry some message to some one out on the road near that fort, & while I was there a force of the enemy with a battery emerged from a wood only 600 or 800 yards away & opened fire on everything in sight on the open ground & on the fort—which had no one in it.

I had passed a Georgia brigade, halted, a few hundred yards back, & I galloped back to them to get them to hurry back to the fort before the enemy knew it to be unoccupied. I met them starting to march back & I begged the leading col. to take the double quick, but he declined saying the men were too jaded & the ground too bad. I really think now that he was near about right, but I went on to the second regt. in the line which was under Lt. Col. John Weems,[45] whom I used to know in Washington, Geo. On my telling him of [the] situation he gave [the] command "Double Quick" & his poor tired fellows responded in spite of mud & water & went splashing along, passing the leading regiment, when we saw some of our cavalry forces enter the fort & open fire. So the infantry came down to the walk again. The enemy were quickly driven back & all was quiet for the night, which we spent at the hotel. Jimmy Washington, Gen. Johnston, & I occupied [the] same room & I remember Gen. J. giving us a very pretty exhibition of sabre exercise when we were retiring, apropos of some conversation about it.

Next morning, May 5, it was apparent from slow progress of our trains that we must make some delay at Wmsburg. to let them get ahead & Gen. Longstreet was directed to halt his corps & keep back any advance of the enemy. A good deal of fighting resulted, lasting more or less all day, & generally we had it all in our favor, & no trouble at all in keeping the enemy back, & I think we captured a Federal battery[46] but condition of [the] roads prevented bringing it off. But on one occasion in the evening our men were a little "too brash" & got a back set over which the enemy crowed a great deal & which gave Gen. Hancock[47] a great reputation. Rather late in the afternoon Hancock found his way to some of Magruder's old defensive works on our extreme left which were unoccupied, & he moved forward into them with a brigade or two. Gen. D. H. Hill was out on that flank, & had had no fighting & was spoiling for some, & decided to charge him.

That was not war. We were on [the] defensive, merely fighting to delay the enemy for the day, to let our trains get ahead. It was our role to make the enemy take the offensive, which is generally the hot & bloody end of the battle. For it is better to lie down & shoot at them coming a half mile than to have them lie down & shoot so at you. Now the day was practically already gained, & we had no business to do any unnecessary fighting, & Hancock's occupying those old works did us no harm whatever. But Gen. Hill charged him in them & I believe with only two [brigades] suffered much.[48] But they made a handsome charge, as the casualties show, & had they been in sufficient force they evidently had spirit enough to have driven the enemy off. This fighting about finished up the day, for the enemy did not try to follow up his success.

During the day Gen. Johnston spent two or three hours with Gen. Longstreet on the field & all of us accompanied him. I remember seeing a man with a severe scalp wound coming back from the firing line & Gen. Johnston spoke to him saying, "My man, I hope you are not badly hurt." The man, wiping the blood from his eyes (the wound was just at top of his forehead), answered, "No, General, damn 'em. They all shoot too high."

That night Gen. J. stopped for a while at the old College "William & Mary," I believe it is, Gen. Ewell's brother being its president,[49] & about ten or eleven we started on another night march. All night we struggled out of one mud hole into another, passing a place called "Burnt Ordinary" about sunrise. I felt a curiosity to know what that name could mean. It turned out that country stores are called ordinarys in that part of the world—which seems simple & natural enough after one once finds it out. I can't recall any halt until about noon, when we were at Barhamsville, not very far below White House, on the York, or perhaps abreast of it. But a force of the enemy had been landed there by steamers & Hood's Texas Brigade had met them feeling out towards our road & had driven them back to [the] shelter of their gun boats.⁵⁰

Gen. J. had evidently rather expected to have a hard fight here for I recall a very large force concentrated & ready. But about 4 P.M. our scouts brought in reports of the enemy showing that there would be no fight, on which Gen. J. mounted & started for New Kent Court House some ____ miles off.⁵¹ I will remember that ride as long as I live. The general seemed for some cause to be in a terrible temper—the only occasion I ever saw him exhibit it. He was splendidly mounted & without saying a word to his staff he set out, at the first, at full speed or as near it as could possibly be made through the mud & around all the wagons, guns, ambulances, &c. which encumbered the road. Evidently he was trying his best to leave every one of his staff & couriers out of sight.

But I promptly made up my mind that he should not leave me unless he deliberately told me that he wished to be alone, & I suppose all the rest thought the same way, so the whole lot of us started after him, some 15 or 18 in all. My old Dixie was never anything extra as a horse but she was good & honest, & what in threading by the wagons & guns, & looking ahead & picking which side of [the] road to take, I gradually got through & ahead of every body else, & closed up about 20 yards behind the general. Close behind me came Penny Mason, & perhaps one courier. At one place we got into a long sort of lane—[a] road with fence on each side—& just ahead of us went an ambulance. As Gen. J. neared it, at a full gallop, he took the left side of the road to pass it. But the ambulance driver could hear the approaching splashing without being able to see, as the ambulance curtains were all down, & wishing to give more room for the rapid riders to pass, he also at the same moment swerved out to the left, heading the general off & pocketing him in a fence corners where he had to rein up his horse so suddenly that he almost went over its head. There he stood penned, unable to get out forward or back, for the driver had also stopped the ambulance, & I drew up just behind looking on. I don't think I ever saw any one fly into such a fury in my life. I had never before heard the general use an oath, but now with his face as red as blood, "God damn you!" he shouted, "what do you mean? Give me a pistol & let me kill this infernal blanketty blank," at the same time reaching over the fence corner to me. I had my revolver in my belt, but I pretended not to, & held back & looked around, while the poor ambulance driver, scared almost into a jabbering idiot, whipped at his team, & presently got the ambulance along & let the general out of his corner. Then he started on as before & soon after dark we got to the little

hotel in a little country village where we spent the night. The staff &
couriers were arriving for an hour afterward.

This was May 6, '62.[52] In a few days afterward I next recall our headquarters located at the house of a very queer character, a Dr. Harrison, with
a small farm, and a large, low, shady house near the Nine Mile Road &
some where about five miles from Richmond. I remember finding in the
house one day a pile of copies of a pamphlet published by the Dr., defending
his character against imaginary or possible aspersions, & giving his views
upon many social & moral subjects, in what were like schoolboy composi-
tions on them. I can't recall any particular subject but my recollection is
that, for instance, "The Love of Fame" might have been one. They were
about of that wildly exciting character. But the funniest thing was a collection of letters from his neighbors & acquaintances. He had addressed a
number of them a lot of questions as to what they thought of him, morally,
socially, & intellectually, & their replies were religiously published. Evidently they were all more or less dumbfounded at being, as it were, brought
to book in black & white as to their private opinions about him, & some
evidently considered it a prelude to a personal difficulty being forced upon
them, & were more or less ready to meet it. Evidently the poor old gentleman was a chronic case of that incipient degree of insanity, in which the
man's own personality is magnified into something of extreme importance.
But we were very hospitably quartered & treated, & he never catechised
any of us as to what we thought of him, & if I recollect aright his place was
headquarters till after Seven Pines, when Gen. Johnston was wounded &
Gen. Lee succeeded to command of the army.

Along about the middle of May I was taken sick with the measles. I forget
whether my wife, & our little Bess, were already in Richmond, or whether
they were at Farmville, Va., & came down for the purpose, but she nursed
me through the attack at a house on [the] S.E. corner of Grace & 2nd
Streets, where, I remember, they had neither tea or coffee & gave the
boarders only sassafras tea. And this brings me to the Battle of Seven Pines,
on May 31st & June 1st.

On May 30th I was getting over my measles & was sitting up when news
reached me that the two armies were now so close together that a great
battle might occur any day. This decided me to return to hd. qrs. at once &
finish my convalescence there, so I sent for my horse & rode out in the
afternoon. Soon after my arrival a terrific thunderstorm came up & continued till late at night, & feeling very weak & tired I went to bed very early.
Next morning only did I learn that Gen. Johnston had ordered an attack
upon a considerable force of the enemy who had crossed to our side of the
Chickahominy. I give a little map to explain the situation,[53] for this fight
affords a most striking illustration of how people may misunderstand each

other in important affairs; & of the supreme importance, in such matters, not only of having everything thoroughly understood, but of the commanding general supervising by his staff the actual execution of all orders in order to guard against accidents & misunderstandings.

I will leave this fight for a moment to illustrate my meaning. I have told before how at Bull Run Gen. Beauregard intended to attack McDowell's left flank early on the morning of the battle. Our extreme right flank under Ewell was to cross Bull Run & begin the attack & successive commanders to the left were to take it up. The written order to begin was sent Ewell by a courier, but was lost in some way I've never heard explained. At any rate Ewell never moved, & our two generals, not four miles off, waited for hours & never knew of the miscarriage till it was too late to correct it. If a staff officer had been sent to see Ewell put in motion there could have been no mistake.

Another illustration occurred in the battle of Shiloh. When Gen. Albert Sidney Johnston planned & ordered this battle it was intended to fight it a day sooner than it was fought—on _____ instead of _____.[54] And when in a conference of the generals & corps commanders the plan of march & attack upon the enemy was formulated, it was supposed to be understood that Gen. Polk[55] would put his corps, which was to lead in the march, in motion immediately, without waiting to receive the formal written orders which were to be prepared for each corps commander. But it developed afterward that Gen. Polk did not so understand it, & did not proceed to do it. And that important fact was not discovered until the day was too far spent for it to be rectified. When the battle came to be fought Grant's army was saved from destruction by the arrival at the last moment of Buell's[56] army. Had the battle been a day earlier Buell could not possibly have arrived in time to save it.

To return now to Seven Pines. Three roads led east from our lines into the territory occupied by the enemy on our side—the south—of the Chickahominy: the "Nine Mile," the Williamsburg & the Charles City, in order from our left to our right. The first two intersect at Seven Pines, & about & in front of the intersection the enemy had established himself, & partially fortified a position with abattis & breast works. G. W. Smith's division was on our front on Nine Mile Road, D. H. Hill's on Williamsburg. Longstreet was in reserve some two or three or four miles in rear of Smith; & Huger's division was in reserve just out of Richmond in rear of Hill. On [the] Charles City Road, which branched out of [the] Williamsburg Road about half way between Hill & Huger, there were only pickets of either army. Huger's division was ordered to march down this road till abreast of Seven Pines, then sweep to the left through the woods & take the Seven Pines position in flank & envelop its rear. As soon as Huger's attack developed

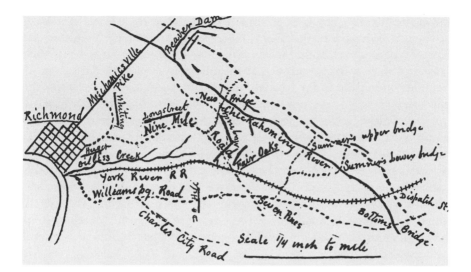

Figure 12. Battlefield at Seven Pines

D. H. Hill was to attack Seven Pines also, in front. Meanwhile, on Nine Mile Road Longstreet's division was to march down & pass through G. W. Smith's line & was then to mass & form ready to join in the assault on Seven Pines as soon as D. H. Hill's guns were heard.

It was an excellent & well devised scheme, & apparently as simple as any plan could be. Properly carried out it is hard to see how it could have failed to overwhelm all the enemy south of the Chickahominy, by a concentrated attack of superior numbers. But note how a single misconception brought chaos over the whole & made of the fight two isolated attacks of single divisions upon equal or superior numbers & in one instance quite well fortified. One of these attacks—the one on the fortified position—was successful, the other a failure.

Gen. Longstreet entirely misconceived his orders, & instead of marching straight down the Nine Mile Road & massing in front of G. W. Smith, *he crosses over to the Williamsburg Road, to get behind D. H. Hill.* Of course he would not have done it had he not conceived himself ordered to do it.[57] And, in crossing over, his troops met & blocked the road of Huger's troops en route for the Charles City Road, where they were to open the ball. It is said that when they met Huger asked Longstreet which of them was the older & ranking maj. genl., & entitled to take precedence; & that Longstreet said that he knew himself to be the senior, on which H. surrendered the road to him.[58] It afterward turned out that Huger was the senior. Now the terrible rain during the night had made a river of every brook, & a quagmire of every road, & all marches were greatly delayed in consequence. So it happened that D. H. Hill, listening for Huger's guns on the enemy's flank, & listening in vain from 8 A.M. to about 1 P.M., then decided to go it alone, & through all the mud & water attacked the enemy's fortified line in his front. Meanwhile, hdqrs., keeping no eye upon the execution of orders, did not know at all how everything was being mixed up. One little incident will illustrate how complete was the misconception. Sometime during the morning Gen. G. W. Smith, surprised at the non arrival of Longstreet's division, sent a messenger to Gen. Johnston asking where Longstreet was & why he did not arrive. Gen. J. ordered his aid, Lieut. Washington, to go & find Longstreet & to put him in communication with Smith, & he told Washington that he would find L. somewhere down the Nine Mile Road. So W. rode down that road & actually passed through Smith's line & his pickets & went on until he rode into the Federal pickets & was taken prisoner.

That was the first intimation received by the Federals that something was on foot. It appears in their reports that when they found that they had captured Gen. J.'s aid they at once guessed that we were preparing an attack & that they set to work to prepare for it.

No hint of all this misconception & the difference it made in the battle, appears in the official reports of the action. Smith made some reference to it in his original report, but at Gen. Johnston's request withdrew the report & struck that part out. But within the last few years he has published a book upon the battle giving the whole matter even down to photographs of Gen. Johnston's request that he would suppress all mention of it in his report.[59] The enemy's capture of Washington, too, is the strongest possible confirmation of the whole story.

The responsibility for the blunder seems to me to rest solely upon Gen. Johnston. He evidently failed to make Longstreet understand fully & exactly what he was to do, & he failed to keep an eye upon the doing. The result was that Huger never got down the Charles City Road at all, but that D. H. Hill went in alone in a front attack on a strong position, under great difficulties of muddy roads & fields hampering his assault, while crowded up behind him were two whole divisions [for] which there was no room to deploy or to use effectively in any way.

Nevertheless Hill was successful in carrying the enemies' position & in capturing some of his batteries & some prisoners. He especially used up the division commanded by my old friend Gen. Silas Casey, under whom I had served at Fort Steilacoom from Sep. 1860 to March 1861. The genl's. headquarters were captured & his ambulance with his name on it was a familiar sight to my wife & myself all that summer in Richmond. His chief of artillery Bailey[60] was killed, a superb soldier & one of the most attractive men I ever met. He was in the class ahead of me at West Point, but he was very nice to me and I had grown intimate with him & very fond of him. Had he lived he would have made a mark I am sure. He was killed among his guns fighting them to the last when our men charged in. I inquired about it from our men who were in the charge.

But, attacking directly in front as we did, we got comparatively few prisoners, & the enemy fell back towards [the] Chickahominy, & took new positions, Hill being himself too much cut up to press their retreat very seriously. Meanwhile, Gen. Sumner, commanding a Federal corps on [the] north side of the Chickahominy, hearing the battle, without waiting for orders, crossed his corps over to the south side over the Grapevine causeway & bridge, a military road the enemy had just constructed. The river was rising rapidly from the tremendous rain & Sumner just did succeed in getting over before parts of it were carried away & all communication between the two sides was cut off for 12 hours.[61]

So the end of Hill's battle, say three o'clock in afternoon, left the enemy backed up towards the river, but reinforced by Sumner's whole corps, just arriving.[62]

And now we will go back to G. W. Smith on the Nine Mile Road. Gen. Johnston had joined him there sometime during the day. I don't know exactly when, but I don't think Gen. J. went over to the Williamsburg Road at all that day. On my arrival the evening before I had heard nothing of the expected battle, & had retired early. Next morning Tom Rhett—adjt. genl., posted me, & my first care was to get the ammunition supply trains all right. By that time Gen. J. & all the rest of the staff had left, except Rhett, & he & I rode down together & found Gen. J. & G. W. Smith & all the staffs near where New Bridge Road branches to [the] left from Nine Mile.

From some peculiar condition of the air & direction of the wind the noise of Hill's fight had not been heard, or had not impressed the generals, & it was only when a messenger finally came from Hill, about 3 P.M., I guess, that the situation was known. Then part of Smith's troops were put in motion down the Nine Mile Road, & Gen. J. & the staff rode near the head of the column. In less than a half mile we passed the enemy's line of abandoned breastworks, & behind it his deserted camps, showing that we had lost a favorable moment for attack when they were about to retreat, because of [the] loss of positions captured by Hill.

Passing these, we got out in a large open country, & were well out in it, when suddenly fire was opened on us by a battery some 1,000 yards off in our left & rear. At first I could not believe that it was the enemy. I thought that a part of our troops advancing on our left, near the Chickahominy, coming out of the woods there, had seen us so far out as to mistake us for retreating Federals, & I proposed to Rhett that I should be allowed to gallop across to them & stop them. But he presently convinced me that it must be the enemy, by showing Whiting's brigade[63] forming to charge the battery.

It was, indeed, a part of the original force of the enemy on the south side which had fallen back towards the river on Hill's taking Seven Pines, & it was now reinforced by Sumner's whole corps, being near the Grapevine Bridge Road.

So we all stood & watched Whiting's charge, which was met by a musketry fire so heavy that a very large force of the enemy was indicated, & Whiting was driven back with severe loss. I can't recall any more details of the attack, but several other partial assaults were made before darkness fell, & a general long range fire at each other was kept up by both sides all the while. Gen. Johnston & the staff stood out in the field watching until a little before sundown when the general received a musket ball in his shoulder & in a moment or two afterward a fragment of shell broke some of his ribs & brought[64] him to the ground. A litter was brought up, & he was put on it & started back to hd.qrs. Darkness soon stopped the firing, after which I followed & overtook the litter bearers. The general seemed to suffer great pain & was angry with the litter bearers, occasionally, for shaking him up. But really it was no easy job in the darkness & deep mud holes to get along at all, & our progress was so slow that my recollection makes it near eleven o'clock when we finally reached hd.qrs.

His wound left G. W. Smith in command of the army. I had always been a great friend of Gen. G. W. & believed him a great soldier. In the Mexican War he had been a lieut. in what was afterwards my old Co. A, engineers, & had had an unusual amount of hard & close fighting, & he came out of that war with several brevets, & a reputation for personal gallantry second to none in the army. But, some how, in our war, the fates were against him. He started with high rank but had never had a chance in battle until this fight. I have shown how things were mixed up by Longstreet's going to the wrong place—practically losing the whole day, for Smith at least. The next morning he did not renew the assault. Even if he wished to do so some hours of daylight would have been necessary to properly dispose his troops. Smith was a martyr to physical ailments which greatly reduced his energy, &, especially made riding almost impossible.[65] I don't know whether he intended to attack or not, but about noon Gen. Lee came out from Richmond to replace Gen. Johnston in the command. I had ridden down & reported to Gen. Smith, but now had to report to Gen. Lee. That ended my service on Gen. Johnston's staff.

But in March 1864, when he took command of our western army at Dalton, he applied for me as his chief of artillery, as I will tell more in detail when I come to that time. And as long as he lived I never had a warmer or kinder friend than Gen. Johnston, nor he a more affectionate admirer than I. He was a great soldier. I used to think at the time that his one fault was impatience of detail. But to study his fine campaign in front of Sherman in 1864 would seem to imply that he was specially excellent in detail. At any rate the enemy considered his marches & retreats as superlatively well planned & conducted.

After Gen. Lee took command he decided not to renew the attack, but the enemy themselves made some advances as we were preparing to withdraw, & there were some sharp local fights but nothing of consequence.

There now began a gradual break up of Gen. Johnston's staff & organisation of Gen. Lee's. Lee brought some men, perhaps Walter Taylor, Marshall, Long & Venable,[66] his aids, &c., with him, but I can't recall exactly; & Johnston's heads of departments, of course, stayed on. For at first it was supposed that Johnston would return to command as soon as his wounds healed. And, soon after Seven Pines, I recall Gen. Johnston removed into Richmond, & I myself with some of his old staff, located at a house called the Keach house, on the north side of the River Turnpike Road, on the hill, beyond the creek, beyond Rocketts.

Gen. Lee's hd.qrs. were in a camp somewhere, not a great ways off, but my recollection is not clear. Our troops were extended on a line from the Chickahominy, near New Bridge, away out to the Charles City Road, & began fortifying a line of battle, & the enemy, some three quarters of a mile in front, also fortified themselves. And thus it was until Gen. Lee attacked them, beginning June 26th.

The only intermediate incident which I can recall was a very remarkable conversation which I had, with Capt. Jos. C. Ives,[67] who was on Prest. Davis's personal staff. But first let me tell a little about Ives.

He was a tall, slender, handsome man about 32 years of age, had graduated at West Point in '52, in topographical engineers, & had married one of the Semmes connection in Washington City. He himself was born in N.Y., appointed from Conn. When the war broke out he was surveying & exploring in southern New Mexico. My sister, Mrs. Gilmer, was then in California, & heard that when the U.S., about June or July 1861, required all officers to take the oath of allegiance over again, Ives was one who took it. Afterward when she found that Ives had resigned & entered the Southern army, she conceived a violent prejudice against him; & she accused him of being a Federal spy. In 1862, summer or fall, Genl. Gilmer, after being wounded at Shiloh, became chief engineer & lived in Richmond—my sister with him. She was very intimate with Mrs. Davis, & strongly impressed Mrs. D. with her distrust of Ives.

And Ives made the matter worse by being concerned in some social scandals, which more than prejudiced the ladies against him. In fact, Mrs. Davis not being able to convince the president herself that Ives was a spy & traitor, Mrs. Gilmer sought an interview with him & tried it. But it was a signal failure & she only recd. a rebuke from Mr. D.

And indeed the accusation was utterly unfounded. Ives was far above any such suspicion as a soldier, whatever his moral character in other respects. And nothing could afford more absolute proof that he was no spy than the astounding & continuous ignorance of the enemy of our strength. They overestimated it about threefold. They never had any spy worth a cent. After the war Ives went abroad, became very dissipated, & is said to have killed himself drinking in a very few years. But whatever were Ives's faults he was undoubtedly a man of rare intellectual ability & of trained military acumen. In the field I believe he would have made a name as a general. [He] died in N.Y. [in] 1868. So much for Ives. Now for my talk with him.

When Gen. Lee took command there was really very little known of him generally. He had made great reputation in Mexico as a staff officer & an engineer, but in our war he had had, as yet, but one command, & that had been unfortunate. He had been sent to West Va., where Floyd & Wise,[68] two of our political generals, were at loggerheads, but the Federals had manouvred & fought all three of them out of the country. Then he had been sent to fortify the South Atlantic coast, & yet the enemy had easily taken Port Royal. And now that he was put in command of the army, some of the newspapers—particularly the Richmond *Examiner*—pitched into him with extraordinary virulence, evidently trying to break him down with the troops & to force the president to remove him.

This paper was edited by John M. Daniel,[69] celebrated long before & afterward for his personalities; & they finally cost him his life. Some year or two, or more, after the war he published an account of a Mrs. Grant's leaving her home in Richmond (on account of a quarrel with her mother) & going to a relative in Baltimore, with insinuations against the young lady's character. Next morning her brother waylaid Daniel—who was known to be armed & prepared for him—& shot him dead on the sidewalk in front of his office from an upstairs window on the opposite side of the street. A Richmond jury afterward acquitted him.

Daniel's attacks upon Gen. Lee were as bitter as he could make them, & were repeated almost daily. I can recall but little of them now, that little being that henceforth our army would never be allowed to fight. It would only be allowed to dig, that being the West Point idea of war, & West Point now being in command; that guns & ammunition would now only be in the way, spades & shovels being the only implements Gen. Lee knew anything about, &c., &c. I can't recall any reply ever being made in any paper to these assaults and Gen. Lee himself never seemed even remotely conscious of them.

But one afternoon I accidentally met Ives riding out from Richmond to look around the camps & lines, & being on very good terms with him I joined him & we rode a pretty fair circuit of the whole business. Coming back home Ives asked me if I thought that the persistent attacks in the papers had had any effect in the army—if the confidence in Gen. Lee of the men & officers generally had been weakened by them. I replied that I had, myself, seen no evidence of it, but that, being myself one of his staff officers, it would not likely be exhibited to me even if it existed. "But," I said, "Ives tell me what you think about the matter yourself. Has Gen. Lee the audacity which is going to be required in the command of this army to meet the odds which will be brought against it? Look at the situation today. McClellan, immediately in our front, has already a largely superior force with reinforcements behind at Fort Monroe. McDowell is at Fredericksburg with near 40,000 men & there is nothing to keep him, as soon as he is ready, from coming right on down on our flank. Here we are putting up some little lines in our front, but we are leaving the enemy to take his own time, & to perfect all his plans, & accumulate all his forces, & to choose his own battle. We are as it were saying 'Whenever you are ready, Mr. Enemy, we propose to give you the hardest kind of a fight, but you can take your time about getting ready.'"

"Now with our inferior forces & resources such a course as that must finally end in defeat. Our only hope is to bounce him & whip him somewhere before he is ready for us, and that needs audacity in our commander. Has Gen. Lee that audacity?"

Ives heard me through fully, & then stopped his horse in the road, to make his reply more impressive, & turning to me he said, "Alexander, if there is one man in either army, Federal or Confederate, who is, head & shoulders, far above every other one in either army in audacity that man is Gen. Lee, and you will very soon have lived to see it. Lee is audacity personified. His name is audacity, and you need not be afraid of not seeing all of it that you will want to see."

I frequently recalled Ives's words afterward—to the very close of the war—for if ever a prophecy was literally fulfilled this was. And while I am on it this is as good [a] place as any to stop & talk about it a little bit, even though it will have to recur, more than once, in the narrative of different battles.

I think that military critics will rank Gen. Lee as decidedly the most audacious commander who has lived since Napoleon, & I am not at all sure that even Napoleon in his whole career will be held to have overmatched some of the deeds of audacity to which Gen. Lee committed himself in the 2 years & 10 months during which he commanded the Army of Northern Va.

On two occasions, I am quite sure, he will be adjudged to have overdone it. He gave battle unnecessarily at Sharpsburg Sep. 17th, 1862. The odds against him were so immense that the utmost he could have hoped to do was what he did do—to repel all assaults & finally to withdraw safely across the Potomac. And he probably only succeeded in this because McClellan kept about 20,000 men, all of Fitz John Porter's corps,[70] *entirely out of the fight* so that they did not pull a trigger. And Lee's position was such, with a great river at his back, without a bridge & with but one difficult ford, that defeat would have meant the utter destruction of his army. So he fought where he could have avoided it, & where he had nothing to make & everything to lose—which a general should not do.

Then perhaps in taking the aggressive at all at Gettysburg in 1863 & certainly in the place & dispositions for the assault on the 3rd day, I think, it will undoubtedly be held that he unnecessarily took the most desperate chances & the bloodiest road.

There was still another occasion when I recalled ruefully Ives's prophecy that I would see all the audacity I wanted to see, & felt that it was already overfulfilled: but when, to my intense delight, the enemy crossed the river in retreat during the night, & thus saved us from what would have been probably the bloodiest defeat of the war. It was on the 6th of May 1863 at the end of Chancellorsville, & I will tell of it in detail when we come to that battle. Here I will only say that Hooker's[71] entire army, some 90,000 infantry, were in the Wilderness, backed against the Rapidan, & had had nearly three days to fortify a short front, from the river above to the river below. And, in that dense forest of small wood, a timber slashing in front of a line of breastworks could in a few hours make a position absolutely impregnable to assault. But on the afternoon of the 5th Gen. Lee gave orders for a grand assault the next morning by his whole force of about 40,000 infantry, & I was all night getting my artillery in position for it. And how I did thank God when in the morning the enemy were gone!

And again, even at the last, on March 25, 1865, when we were reduced to about 40,000 men holding about 30 miles of line stretching from the Chickahominy on the left, to near Five Forks below Petersburg, against 120,000 men massed all along our front, within rifle shot, in strongly fortified lines & forts behind each other, two, three, & four deep, he took the aggressive, & sallied out & captured some of the strongest parts of their line on Hare's Hill, in a desperate effort to cut the enemy in two & destroy his two halves separately. The effort failed, but it was worth all it cost merely as an illustration of the sublime audacity of our commander, & the enduring confidence in each other between him & his men, & their glorious fighting qualities to the very last. For this was within 15 days of our final surrender at Appomattox.

I have often wondered how Ives got his insight into, & his appreciation of Gen. Lee's qualities, in this regard, & I once asked Mrs. Davis, whose strong disapproval of Ives has not been at all mollified by his death or by time. She promptly refused Ives the slightest credit for it, and declared that he was merely repeating Mr. Davis's estimate of Gen. Lee. There had doubtless been many military conferences between the two, but it seems to me a remarkably strong & clear estimate of character to have been formed from anything short of actual performances, of which Gen. Lee had before given little or none.

SEVEN DAYS

This brings us to the Seven Days fighting about Richmond. I will give a little map[1] & will outline briefly the principal events & can then in a very small space outline my personal experiences during their occurrence.

Early in June, Gen. Stonewall Jackson, whose reputation up to this time had simply been that of a desperate & stubborn fighter (having only fought so far in the battle of Bull Run), suddenly broke loose up in the Valley of Virginia & not only astonished the weak minds of the enemy almost into paralysis, but dazzled the eyes of military men all over the world by an aggressive campaign which I believe to be unsurpassed in all military history for brilliancy & daring. It seems indeed to me to be only approached by Napoleon's best Italian campaigns. I write away from all books of reference & cannot therefore go into any details, but in general terms what he did was about as follows.

There were two Federal armies out after him in the Valley, one coming up the Valley from the north & one over the mountains from the south west, both superior to him in numbers. Meanwhile, too, McDowell with about 40,000 was at Fredericksburg about 100 miles to his east. But McD. was out not for Jackson, but for Richmond & to co-operate with McClellan against Lee. And he was just about to move too when Jackson began his performances by bouncing upon the army in front of him in the Valley— under Banks[2] I believe—& giving it a complete defeat at Strasburg on _____[3] & chasing it down the Valley nearly or quite to the Potomac River. This alarmed the Federals for Washington & McDowell was stopped from his proposed advance to Richmond & was ordered to send a strong body of troops to get behind Jackson & unite with the force advancing from the southwest under Frémont.[4] But Jackson hurried back from the Potomac so rapidly as to get between these converging enemies & to defeat each of them separately & to drive each of them back. These battles took place on Jun. 8 & 9th.[5]

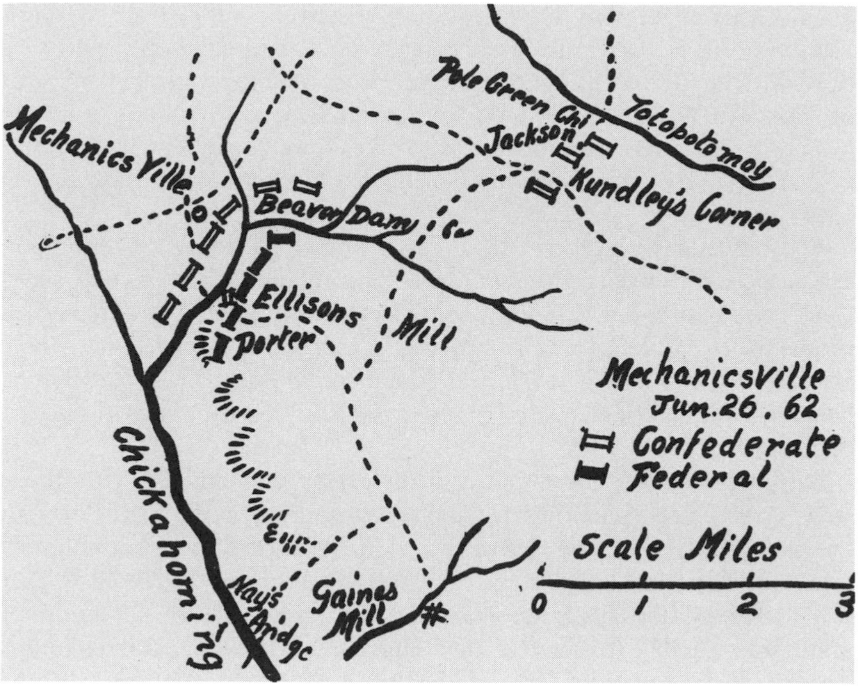

Figure 13. Battlefield at Mechanicsville

Gen. Lee now conceived the plan of bringing Jackson down from the Valley swiftly & secretly & having him surprise & fall upon the Federal right flank. This was posted at Ellison's Mill on Beaver Dam Creek in the same beautiful position—absolutely impregnable to a front attack—which we engineers had selected for our own left-flank had we taken line of battle north of the Chickahominy. Thence the Federal line ran down the Chick. to below the Nine Mile or New Bridge Road, crossing where it crossed & ran over past Seven Pines.

Gen. Lee issued a regular battle order setting forth his whole plan in detail & I cannot explain it better than by simply copying the official copy of it which I received as chief of ordnance. This order & the map will make all clear.[6]

Meanwhile also elaborate efforts were made to deceive the enemy by making him think that our game was to reinforce Jackson strongly up in the Valley, & have him make a vigorous attack on Washington itself. For this purpose Whiting's division (2 brigades, his own & Hood's) was withdrawn from our lines, & sent by rail up to Jackson. Also Lawton's big brigade, arriving from Savannah, was also railroaded up to Jackson. But all was so planned that by railroad & by marching, they would all be back, & all of Jackson's original men with them, concentrated at Ashland on the evening of Wednesday, Jun. 25th. There the battle order took them in hand at 3 A.M. on June 26th, & started them to march around the enemy's flank at Beaver Dam & to cross the creek above it & to take the enemy in rear, while A. P.7 & D. H. Hill crossing by Meadow Bridge & Mechanicsville roads threatened its front.

And now I shall have to tell, as my narrative proceeds, of how upon several occasions in the progress of the fighting during the next six days, Gen. Lee's best hopes & plans were upset & miscarried, & how he was prevented from completely destroying & capturing McClellan's whole army & all its stores & artillery by the incredible slackness, & delay & hanging back, which characterized Gen. Jackson's performance of his part of the work.

But little has been said about it in the press. As compared with Longstreet's alleged shortcomings at Gettysburg nothing at all. Gen. Fitzhugh Lee, in his life of Gen. Lee, devotes pages to the latter, & does not remotely refer to the former.8 But to suppress it robs Gen. Lee of the credit of what seems to me perhaps his greatest achievement. As it was, within a month of taking command he scattered all the tremendous forces concentrated for his destruction & practically deposed McClellan, the "Young Napoleon" of the Federals. But think of the moral effect on the country, & the world had he captured this entire army of 100,000 men with all its stores & arms & artillery. And this he would indoubtedly have done had the Gen. Jackson of those six days been the same Gen. Jackson who had marched & fought in the Valley but a few weeks before, or the same who upon every other battlefield afterward—Cedar Mountain, Second Manassas, Harpers Ferry, Sharpsburg, & Fredericksburg, to his lamented death at Chancellorsville in May '63—made a reputation unequalled in military annals. And just to think—it was practically all done within less than 12 months.

We of Gen. Lee's staff knew at the time that he was deeply, bitterly disappointed, but he made no official report of it & glossed all over as much as possible in his own reports.9 Indeed, I never thoroughly understood the matter until long after, when all the official reports were published, & I read Gen. Jackson's own statements of times & things, & those of the officers under him & compared them with what I knew of the whole situation.

The question naturally arises, what was the matter with him? Although the public has heard little of the matter, it has by no means entirely escaped comment and I will give presently some of the things which have been said10 by Gen. D. H. Hill, his brother in law, & others of his friends.

For myself I think that the one defect in Gen. Jackson's character as a soldier was his religious belief. He believed, with absolute faith, in a personal God, watching all human events with a jealous eye to His own glory—ready to reward those people who made it their chief care, & to punish those who forgot about it. And he specially believed that a particular day had been set aside every week for the praise of this God, & that a personal account was strictly kept with every man as to how he kept this day & that those who disregarded it need expect no favors, but that those who sacrificed all other considerations, however recklessly, to honoring Him by its observance, would be rewarded conspicuously. And I see in Gen. Jackson's whole conduct during the Seven Days a sort of faith that he had God on his side & could trust to Him for victory without overexerting himself & his men.

The only quotation I have at hand concerning Gen. Jackson's conduct during the fighting is from Gen. D. H. Hill, who was Gen. Jackson's brother-in-law & was in his command at the time. In an account of the movements [on] June 30th & July 1st ending with the Battle of Malvern Hill, published in the Century War Book, Gen. H. says—speaking of the affair at White Oak Swamp [on] June 30th (which will be more fully explained later):[11]

> Our cavalry returned by the lower ford & pronounced it perfectly practicable for infantry. But Jackson did not advance. Why was this? It was the critical day for both commanders, but especially for McClellan. With consummate skill he had crossed his vast train of 5,000 wagons & his immense parks of artillery safely over White Oak Swamp, but he was more exposed now than at any time in his flank march. Three columns of attack were converging upon him, and a strong corps was pressing upon his rear. Escape seemed impossible for him, but he did escape. . . . Gen. Lee through no fault in his plans was to see his splendid prize slip through his hands. Longstreet & A. P. Hill struck the enemy at Frazier's Farm (or Glendale) at 3 P.M., and, both being always ready for a fight, immediately attacked. Magruder, who followed them down the Darbytown Road was ordered to the assistance of Gen. Holmes on the New Market Road, who was not then engaged, & their two divisions took no part in the action. Huger, on the Charles City Road, came upon Franklin's left flank but made no attack. . . . So there were five divisions within sound of the firing, & within supporting distance, but not one of them moved. . . . Maj. Dabney in his life of Jackson[12] thus comments on the inaction of that officer: "On this occasion it would appear, if the vast interests dependent upon Gen. Jackson's co-operation with the proposed attack upon the centre were considered, that he came short of the efficiency in action for which he was everywhere else noted." After showing how the crossing of White Oak might have been effected, Dabney adds: "The list of casualties

would have been larger than that presented on the 30th, of one cannoneer wounded, but how much shorter would have been the bloody list filled up the next day at Malvern Hill. This temporary eclipse of Jackson's genius was probably to be explained by physical causes. The labor of the previous days, the sleeplessness, the wear of gigantic cares with the drenching of the comfortless night, had sunk the elasticity of his will, & the quickness of his invention for the nonce below their wonted tension."

And Gen. Hill adds his own solution of the mystery as follows: "I think that an important factor in this inaction was Jackson's pity for his own corps, worn out by long & exhausting marches, & reduced in numbers by its numerous sanguinary battles. He thought that the garrison of Richmond ought now to bear the brunt of the fighting."[13]

This seems to be [to] me a most remarkable excuse to be tendered by a friend. It was indeed whispered about in the army afterward that Gen. Jackson had said that he did not intend that his corps should do all the fighting, but it was regarded as a slander. I don't think Major Dabney's excuse that his inaction was due to physical exhaustion will at all bear analysis. For three successive nights & two entire days, since the battle of Gaines's Mill, he had been in camp near that battlefield. He had especially done nothing all day Sunday—although every hour then was precious. My own solution of the matter is that he thought that God could & would easily make up for any little shortcomings of his own & give us the victory anyhow.

But in this connection I will quote only one sentence more from Gen. D. H. Hill: "Had all our troops been at Frazer's Farm there would have been no Malvern Hill." And perhaps it is as well to put here also, what Gen. Franklin said about it—who was opposite Jackson on the 30th at White Oak Swamp. It is also from the Century War Book.[14]

And now I can go back to my narrative & outline of the principal events which is to be completed before taking up the story of my small individual experiences.

Gen. Jackson started down to Richmond for a personal conference with Gen. Lee on the approaching event, by rail on Saturday, June 21. The train was due to arrive in Richmond about daylight Sunday morning & the conference might easily have been held on Sunday. But Gen. J. was unwilling to travel on Sunday, at least when such momentous events were in hand. So before midnight he left the train at Louisa C.H., spent the rest of the night with a friend, attended church, two or three times the next day, Sunday, & then, after 12 o'clock Sunday night, mounted his horse & rode the balance of the way to Richmond, about 60 miles—I have not at hand the details of the hour of his arrival, the time of the conference & the time of his return to his command, but all were from 24 to 48 hours later than they need have been, & Gen. Jackson had more over the personal fatigue [of] a very trying horseback ride of ____ miles.[15] But I believe neither Prest. Davis or Gen. Lee disapproved, & I have no doubt that Gen. Jackson thought that such a conspicuous respect for the Sabbath at such a time would do more to give us a victory than all that his whole army could accomplish without special Divine aid. Wednesday night found himself & his whole command concentrated at Ashland.

He was ordered to march for the enemy's flank at 3 A.M. on Thursday but the official reports which mention the hour of starting all concur that it was after sunrise.[16] The distance he had to go to the enemy's flank was about ____ miles,[17] & early that morning the whole of Gen. Lee's army on the south of the Chickahominy was alert & listening for Jackson's guns & ready to take their respective parts as laid down in the order of battle already given. I remember seeing Mr. Davis & his staff on the hills overlooking the Chickahominy, near the Mechanicsville Road, where Gen. Lee had made his temporary head qrs., & my recollection is that he came as early, at 10 or eleven o'clock, & was on or about the ground all day. For hour after hour passed & nothing was heard of Jackson. At last about 3 P.M., when it was plain that the day was almost[18] gone, our extreme left flank, A. P. Hill's division, crossed the Chick. at Meadow Bridge & started the ball without him, hoping he would still turn up by the time the fight became hot. Hill, on crossing, moved down stream & soon cleared off the small Federal forces about Mechanicsville & opened that road, when D. H. Hill brought over a part of his division & joined him.

They found themselves confronted by the Federal right flank under Fitz John Porter, behind Beaver Dam Creek, near Ellison's Mill. It was the very position told of selected by the engineers[19] & myself for our own flank, had we fought on that side of the river, & they had fortified it with infantry breast works, & pits for guns, & by cutting down all timber in range to give unobstructed fire. The valley of the creek was rendered impassable by the fallen trees & brush, & by the creek on one side of it, & the mill race on the slope of the eastern bank, just in front of the enemy's line. Briefly there was no cover in front within musket range, say 400 yards, & the enemy's line could not be reached by an assaulting force, & his men were quite well sheltered from fire. But there were our people in front of it, & the day was drawing to a close & our major generals were all brash to do something. And the full strength of the position, particularly the inaccessible feature of it, was not apparent to the eye until one had entirely crossed the plain[20] swept by their fire & gotten actually up to the valley of the creek. A. P. Hill's men, advancing confidently were at first allowed by the enemy to approach quite closely, when a sudden & tremendous fire of infantry &

artillery at short range drove them back with some loss. We then brought up artillery, & a very severe duel ensued between, perhaps, fifty guns about equally divided between the two sides & there was also some heavy musketry, but at rather long range. A. P. Hill seems now to have recognised the strength of the position—at least he did not again force his infantry close upon it.

But somehow it happened that two regts. of Ripley's brigade of D. H. Hill's division were ordered to charge it.[21] It was a tragic illustration of the absurdities which often happen upon battlefields. Fitz John Porter had about 25,000 men sheltered & inaccessible & about 1,500 are launched into his fire & told to charge him home. The regiments sent were big green regiments never before under fire but full of the spirit & prestige given to our whole army by our former successes.

Had those green regiments been given anything to do which was within the bounds of possibility it seems reasonable to believe that they would have done it, & in doing it acquired a self confidence which would have made them ever afterward as near invincible as soldiers can get to be. For their charge was indeed a glorious one. Across the level meadows which stretched from Mechanicsville to the edge of the rather deep & narrow Beaver Dam valley, where even every occasional scattered shade tree had been previously cut down by the enemy to give a free field of fire, they swept without a break through all the fire the enemy could throw. And when they finally reached the rather steep descent into the valley, with its swamp & felled timber & creek & race—all within 200 yards of Fitz John Porter's intrenched 20,000—they knew too little of war to turn back but plunged on down & into the entanglement.

There is no wonder that, as the Federal officer wrote, their dead laid "like flies in a bowl of sugar." The following details from the official reports will assist in forming a correct idea of the affair.[22]

Where was General Jackson with his 20,000 men? The official reports show that he went quietly into camp before sundown at Pole Green Church with the noise of the musketry & artillery at Beaver Dam only 3 miles away ringing in his ears. He had marched only 14 miles over good roads & had no opposition except that a single squadron of Federal cavalry had opposed his crossing of Totopotomoy Creek for a little while & then made their escape without loss. A further advance that afternoon of 3½ miles would have completely cut off the retreat of Fitz John Porter's whole corps. Not until [the] next morning did Fitz John retire[23] safely bag & baggage to the position behind Powhite Creek not far from Gaines's Mill 3 miles below. Comfortably the next morning Gen. Jackson made the 3½ mile march, which closed the trap Gen. Lee had designed for the capture of Porter, & then turning to his right advanced towards where Porter had been the night before. Presently seeing some skirmishers approaching he fired on them with artillery. They were the advance of A. P. Hill's men who had discovered the enemy's retreat & were following. Jackson's fire took the arm off of Capt. Heise[24] of Columbia, S.C., a gentleman I knew well in after years.

Gen. Lee now had 3 divisions, A. P. Hill, D. H. Hill, & Longstreet, across the Chick. & united with Jackson, having his own & Ewell's divisions & the two brigades of Hood & Whiting united under the latter, say 5½ or 6 divisions—& about 50,000 men.

The enemy had excellent engineers & had found a new position nearly as strong as Beaver Dam. I will quote from Gen. Fitz John Porter in the Century War Book:

> The position selected was east of Powhite Creek, about 6 miles from Beaver Dam Creek. The line of battle was semicircular, the extremities being in the Valley of the Chickahominy while the intermediate portion occupied the high grounds along the bank of the creek, & curved around past McGehee's to Elder Swamp. Part of the front was covered by the ravine of the creek. The east bank was lined with trees & underbrush which afforded concealment & protection to our troops, & artillery. . . . Our new line of battle was well selected & strong though long & requiring either more troops to man it than I had, or too great a thinning of my line by the use of the reserves. The east bank of the creek, from the valley of the Chick. to its swampy sources, was elevated sloping & timbered. The bed of the stream was nearly dry, & its west bank gave excellent protection to the first line of infantry, posted under it, to receive the enemy descending the cleared field sloping to it. The swampy grounds along the sources of the creek were open to our view in front for hundreds of yards, & were swept by the fire of infantry & artillery. The roads from Gaines's Mill, & Old Cold Harbor, along which the enemy were compelled to advance, were swept by artillery posted on commanding ground.[25]

In this strong position Porter had about 30,000 men & 75 guns. Slocum reinforced Porter at 4 P.M. with 10,000 & French & Meagher after sundown with 4,000.[26]

Lee's forces crowded the available roads & their advance was slow, but about noon, A. P. Hill got into action with a small advanced force of the enemy at Gaines's Mill, & drove it back upon the main body—& before two o'clock we were up against the enemy's line, A. P. Hill on our right, with Longstreet behind him, Jackson on our left, & all the rest in reserve and in between.

Strong as was Porter's position we had men good enough & enough of them to have beaten him on the very first charge, had one grand simul-

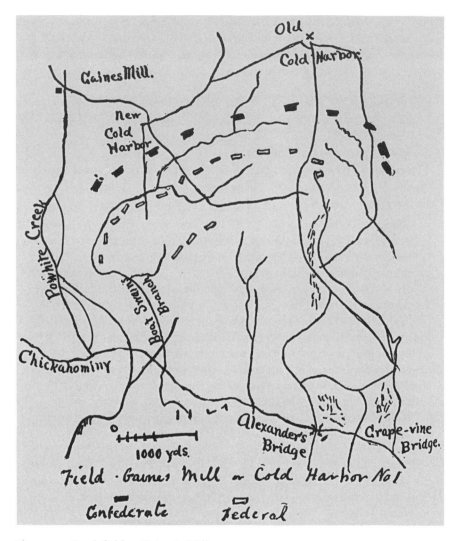

Figure 14. Battlefield at Gaines's Mill

taneous effort been made. But somehow, God only knows how, every body else seemed to stand still & let A. P. Hill's division, from 2 o'clock until near or quite four, wreck itself in splendid, but vain & bloody, isolated assaults.

But I will again let our adversary, Fitz John Porter tell about it.[27] (He was my old instructor in cavalry drill & tactics at West Point & was one of the best soldiers in all the Federal army.) He first says (in [the] same article already quoted) about Jackson's strange inactivity opposite his right flank,

"The advance column of these troops came a little earlier than those under Longstreet & A. P. Hill, *but were more cautious, and for some hours not so aggressive"* (the italics are mine). Not only was a great deal of useless blood shed caused by the loss of those hours, but the precious daylight was lost, necessary to gather the fruits of victory when finally won. And this is his description of A. P. Hill's fight:

> Soon after 2 P.M., A. P. Hill's force, between us & New Cold Harbor again began to show an aggressive disposition, independent of its own troops on its flanks, by advancing from under cover of the woods, in lines well formed & extending, as the contest progressed from in front of Martin's battery to Morell's left.[28] Dashing across the intervening plains, floundering in the swamps, & struggling against the tangled brushwood, brigade after brigade seemed almost to melt away before the concentrated fire of our artillery & infantry; yet others pressed on, followed by supports as dashing & as brave as their predecessors, despite their heavy losses, & the disheartening effect of having to clamber over many of their disabled & dead, & to meet their surviving comrades rushing back in great disorder from the deadly contest. For nearly two hours the battle raged, extending more or less along the whole line to our extreme right. The fierce firing of artillery & infantry, the crash of the shot, the bursting of shells & the whizzing of bullets, heard above the war of artillery & the volleys of musketry, all combined was something fearful.
>
> Regiments quickly replenished their exhausted ammunition by borrowing from more bountifully supplied & generous companions. Some withdrew, temporarily, for ammunition, & fresh regiments took their places, ready to repulse, sometimes to pursue, their desperate enemy for the purpose of retaking ground from which we had been pressed, & which it was necessary to occupy in order to hold our position.

It was only after A. P. Hill's division was worn out to a frazzle, and when Fitz John Porter had received a reinforcement of a fresh division under Slocum, that the rest of the Confederate divisions began to be put in, & even then attacks were disjointed & partial until near about sundown, when at last Gen. Lee had gradually gotten every thing in, & when a charge by Hood's Texas Brigade finally carried one of the strongest parts of the enemy's line. This break was promptly followed by others at many places, & the bloody victory was ours. But the lateness of the hour, & two fresh brigades sent to him across the Chick., enabled Porter to make an excellent retreat & with wonderfully little loss.

Had Jackson attacked when he first arrived, or during A. P. Hill's attack, we would have had an easy victory—comparatively, & would have captured most of Porter's command. Gen. D. H. Hill wrote in the Century article before quoted, "Porter's weak point at Gaines's Mill was his right flank. A thorough examination of the ground would have disclosed that, & had Jackson's command gone in on the left of the road running by the McGehee house, Porter's whole position would have been turned & the line of retreat cut off."[29]

Had our army been as well organised at this time as it became afterward, & as seasoned to battle, the morning after the battle—Sat., June 28th— would doubtless have brought us active movements for new dispositions. For though the enemy had successfully withdrawn his defeated men & guns to the south side of [the] Chick., we had his whole army cut off from their base of supplies, at the White House on the Pamunkey River, & it was plain that they would have to move, & that immediately. It was a question whether they would go to the James River near City Point, where their fleet & supplies could meet them; or whether they would seek to recross the Chick. lower down & go back to the York.

Ewell's division & Stuart's cavalry were sent down the Chick. on the north side to reconnoitre & see what they were doing. They were abandoning & burning what they could not move & it was clear that they had adopted the first mentioned alternative. The other divisions all laid in camp or bivouac all of the 28th, recovering from the wear & tear of the battle, caring for wounded, & burying dead of both sides.

And here is as good a place as any to note the defects in our organisation above referred to, & which were subsequently changed, not all at once, but, little by little, by the next Dec. Our infantry was now all organised into divisions generally of four to six brigades each (though Whiting had only two), but these divisions were not organised into corps. Jackson, indeed, coming from the Valley, had practically a corps, & it was spoken of as a corps, but one of its divisions was called Jackson's, the other two being Ewell's & Whiting's. All the other divisions received orders direct from Gen. Lee. They were Longstreet's, D. H. Hill's, A. P. Hill's, Magruder's, Huger's, Holmes's, McLaws's.[30]

This gave too many independent commands to be efficiently handled by the commanding officer. Later we gradually organised them at first into two corps, of about 4 divisions each, & still later into 3 corps of 3 divisions each. Longstreet's was always the 1st Corps, Jackson's the 2nd, & A. P. Hill's was the 3rd—& the last formed.

Our artillery, too, was even in worse need of reorganisation. A battery was attached, or supposed to be, to every brigade of infantry. Beside these, a few batteries were held in reserve under old Gen. Pendleton.[31] Naturally our guns & ammunition were far inferior to the enemy's, & this scattering of the commands made it impossible ever to mass our guns in effective numbers. For artillery fire loses effect if scattered.

Later, we organised our artillery into battalions, of 4 to 6 batteries each,

& we put about 5 battalions to each corps of 3 divisions. One battalion would usually march with each division of infantry, to be near it in case of need, & the other two battns. were in reserve, under a chief of arty. for the corps, who had command of all.

And it is a remarkable fact, stated in Birkhimer's *History of the Artillery of the U.S. Army,*[32] that the Army of Northern Virginia was the first ever to so organise its artillery, & this organisation has since been adopted by most of the modern armies of Europe. The enemy were a bit ahead of us in organising their infantry. They had larger armies & felt the need more. But they were behind us in organising their artillery. They soon however came into something not very different, but called artillery brigades, instead of battalions, &, having more of it to handle than we had, they added what, I am sure, is an improvement, in having a general army reserve, to be drawn on for all special demands & to furnish promptly fresh batteries in case of loss, & in which crippled batteries can be refitted.

All this is said in partial explanation [of] how McClellan got away from us. We had men enough, & good enough, to have gotten him & all he had, if we had only been organised up to the standards which we finally reached. But as yet we were green & had to learn by experience.

And so Saturday night & Sunday morning the 29th found all the troops who had fought at Gaines's Mill on the 27th still on the same field. But now Gen. Lee knew pretty well McClellan's plans, & he started to go for him. The shortest & most direct road in pursuit of the enemy was assigned to Jackson; & his command was increased by giving him D. H. Hill's division. This made him 4 divisions—Hill, Ewell, Whiting, & his own under command of _____. Their effective force was about _____.[33]

With Longstreet's & A. P. Hill's divisions, which had suffered most severely in the battle, Gen. Lee himself recrossed the Chickahominy, & passed in rear of Magruder's & Huger's divisions[34] standing on the south side between McClellan & Richmond, away around to our extreme right flank about 14 miles, where they encamped that night on the New Market Road in about 3 miles of Frazer's Farm. During Saturday night & all day Sunday great fires could be seen burning at numerous points in the enemy's lines & it was clear that he was destroying immense stores of provisions, forage, &c; & some heavy explosions where the R.R. crossed the Chickahominy told also of a great destruction of ammunition. It was plain that we had the enemy on the jump, & that a great opportunity was before us.

But General Jackson with his great force did not move, & the only reason that he did not is that it was Sunday. It is usually stated that he was delayed by necessary repairs to the Grapevine Bridge which was his shortest line of advance, but I have the authority of Gen. Hampton for saying that the necessary repairs were very slight & were executed Sunday morning by a lieutenant & not over twenty men. D. H. Hill in [the] Century War Book says, "New Bridge was repaired on Saturday [the] 28th—our troops were then ready to move in either direction." He also says that Jackson's whole force also crossed Sunday afternoon but that is a mistake. Only one brigade crossed.[35] And it is certain that during the afternoon a brigade was sent across & encamped on the southern bank. Even had there been no road there at all he could have crossed at New Bridge or Nine Mile Road with very little increase of distance.

Meanwhile Magruder's & Huger's divisions directly opposite the main Federal position were to press the enemy directly in their rear. McClellan of course had a strong rear guard along his fortified front, & until it moved out, these divisions could do little. But on Sunday morning, Heintzelman's corps,[36] oppposite to Magruder, fell back to Savage Station, & Magruder followed & attacked him there. Had Jackson been across the Chick. & joined him there was a great opportunity, but Magruder alone was too weak & he was repulsed.

Nothing else was done on Sunday. But Gen. Lee was concentrating everything for one grand attack the next day, with his whole force, upon the enemy at Charles City cross roads. Jackson with four veteran divisions was to follow direct down the Nine Mile Road & attack the enemy's right flank, which rested on that road where it crossed White Oak Swamp, a small branch running through swampy wood land. Huger's division opposite the centre of the enemy's line on [the] Charles City Road was to attack direct & also McLaws. Magruder's division was withdrawn from [the] vicinity of Savage Station & sent around to reinforce Longstreet & A. P. Hill on the New Market Road opposite the enemy's left. And Holmes's division, under the excellent but super annuated & deaf old general of that name, was sent down the river road towards Malvern Hill, a magnificent amphitheatrical position commanding all the principal roads, & over which the enemy would have to pass.

I will tell the sad story of lost opportunity beginning with Holmes on our right. At 10:30 A.M. on Monday [the] 30th he drew near Malvern Hill with near about 6,000 men, & 6 batteries of artillery. The commanding hill itself was occupied by about 1,500 Federal cavalry. Our own cavalry had been on the hill the day before. We may get a glimpse in this fact of the chances lost by inactivity on the 28th.

Holmes might easily have taken & occupied this hill, but his troops were all green, & they were a good deal demoralised by some shelling of the woods by Federal gunboats in the James & he remained quiet. About 4 P.M. he began to see troops passing over Malvern Hill & he opened fire on them with six rifle guns.

He was now promptly answered by 30 Federal guns which immediately[37] silenced him, & so demoralized him that he sent for reinforcements & himself fell back towards Richmond, abandoning 2 guns & 6 caissons. But his whole loss was but 2 killed & 49 wounded. The force which engaged him was but 1,500 infantry & 30 guns. Holmes's appeal for reinforcements put Magruder's division out of the fight. On its march to Longstreet it was diverted to go to Holmes, &, through a confusion of names in some local roads, it lost miles of marching & counter marching & was all day miles off from where it could do any good, & was almost broken down with fatigue by night.

Next we come to Longstreet's & A. P. Hill's divisions. Longst. early found the enemy's line of pickets & by 11 A.M. got his division ready for the attack, with A. P. Hill close at hand for support. But he was ordered to await the opening of the battle by Huger & Jackson to his left. At half past two he heard guns in Huger's front, and he put some batteries to firing at the enemy, to signal his readiness.

Gen. Lee had come in person to Gen. Longstreet's position, & President Davis from Richmond was also there, all in momentary expectation of a decisive battle. The enemy was superabundantly supplied with excellent artillery, & their return fire became so hot, that an infantry brigade, Jenkins's,[38] was ordered to try & silence one of the batteries, by sharp-shooters, which had actually burst shells right in the party of the generals & their staff. This, little by little, brought on a fight which lasted until night & involved both Longstreet & A. P. Hill for all they were worth. It was desperate & bloody, but successful in the end. It involved, I believe, more actual bayonet, & butt of gun, melee fighting than any other occasion I know of in the whole war. McCall's Pa. Reserves were in it (the bayonet business) on the Federal side & Wilcox's Alabama & Field's Virginia brigades on the Confederate.[39] But in the end we captured Gen. McCall & 3,000 prisoners & 18 guns & darkness alone stopped us. And we were but two divisions & those the worst cut up of any, at Gaines's Mill, only 3 days before. And five other divisions, close up to the enemy, stretching off to our left heard it all, & listened, & went into bivouac for the night without pulling a trigger.

Huger found the enemy in his front strongly posted. He opened some artillery, which was promptly answered by superior force, & his infantry was not put in.

And now we come to Jackson. He had only about 5 miles to go & before 10 o'clock his advance had found the enemy's rear at White Oak Swamp, guarding the crossing with a battery. He had, as before stated, D. H. Hill's division, 5 brigades, Whiting's div., 2 brigs., Ewell's div., 3 brigades, & his own old div., 3 brigades, [and] Lawton's 1 brigade.[40]

All this infantry was halted & about 2 hours consumed in bringing up about seven batteries comprising some 31 guns.⁴¹ The salient features of the situation will be best understood from a little sketch which I make from memory of the locality, which I frequently visited afterward. [Figure 15 appears here in the manuscript.] Jackson's road ran straight down a rather steep hill, crossed the swamp & made a long & gentle ascent on other side. His left side of the road was all dense forest until some distance across the branch. On his right, on his side [of] the creek, was a considerable clearing with a good ridge running at right angles to the road, & parallel to the creek, giving [an] excellent place for artillery; & here (A) Jackson placed his guns, at first under cover until all was ready. Then about noon they suddenly developed & opened on the Federal battery at B. They soon overwhelmed that battery, & disabled a gun, which the rest of the battery withdrew & abandoned. Munford's cavalry regt. went across to get this gun but was fired on by other artillery in position behind the forest which bordered the creek, above the road, on the enemy's side. See C on the sketch. Our cavalry retreated through the swamp below the crossing, and it is at this point in his narrative of these events that Gen. D. H. Hill makes the comments upon Gen. Jackson's subsequent inactivity which I have already quoted.

For, when these new Federal batteries opened, the Confederate batteries were ordered to open fire in their direction *guided by the sound,* for the forest in their front completely hid them from view. And, for all the rest of that day, that absurd farce of war was played, our guns firing at the enemy's sound & their guns firing at ours. The enemy had the good luck to wound one of our cannoneers. Whether we hit anybody or not I cannot find out. And all four divisions of infantry laid there all day in the roads & slept there all night & never fired a musket.

Among these troops was Hampton's brigade & Gen. H. has on several⁴² occasions told me the following circumstances. He himself with one or two of his staff⁴³ went exploring, across White Oak, below the road & on our left, & he soon found himself upon the flank & rear of the infantry rear guard posted on that side of the road & very close to them. He drew off unobserved & went to Gen. Jackson & told him that it was easy to lead infantry to surprise & rout them, & asked permission to take his own brigade there & attack. Gen. J. asked if he could make a bridge across the branch. H. said no bridge was necessary, but one would be very easy to build. Gen. J. said, "Go & build one." Hampton soon finished it & came back to report it. Gen. J. was seated on a log, his head down, & cap over his eyes. When H. reported Gen. J. raised his head, looking under his cap brim, & said, "H m-m?" (that unspellable interrogative). Gen. H. repeated about his having built the bridge, [and] Gen. J. said, "Um-h-m-m" (the unspellable assertive) & resumed his first position. Gen. Hampton waited for

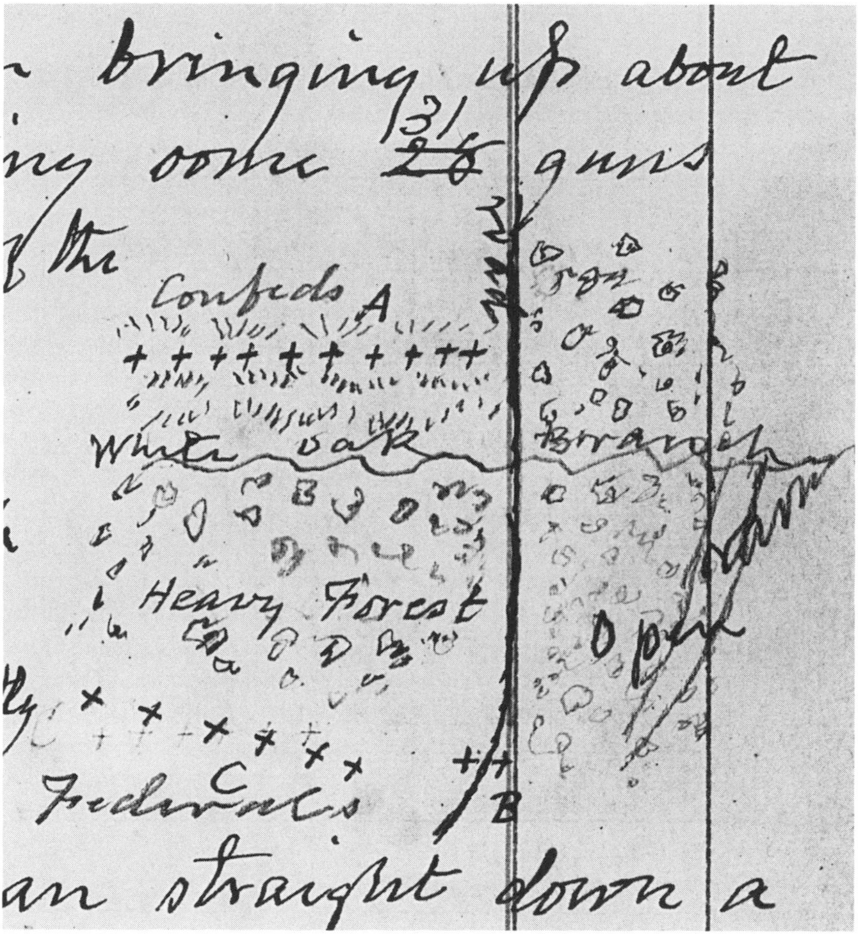

Figure 15. Terrain at White Oak Swamp

further remarks, until the situation seemed awkward, & then went back to his brigade.

I have already quoted what our opponent Gen. Franklin said about our inactivity—& there is nothing more to add. But when one thinks of the great chances in General Lee's grasp that one summer afternoon, it is enough to make one cry to go over the story how they were all lost. And to think too that our *Stonewall Jackson* lost them. He had been great & grand & glorious before & he was so, too, many a time again, until he gave his life in battle within less than eleven months afterward.

But never, before or after, did the fates put such a prize within our reach.

In spite of all the odds against us, it is my individual belief that on two occasions in the four years we were within reach of military successes so great that we might have hoped to end the war with our independence, had we gathered the rich victories which seemed easily possible.[44] *Possibly* there were *three* such occasions. If so the first was at Bull Run [in] July '61, when a vigorous pursuit *might* have caused the abandonment of Washington. But of that I am less impressed than of either of the other two chances. This chance of June 30th '62 impresses me as the best of all.

The Confederacy at this moment[45] was about in its prime & had more men available than ever before or after. And think of the moral shock to the North of the destruction & capture of McClellan's entire army, & the immense material gain to us in guns, muskets, stores, &c. The 3rd or last chance was Jun. 13, 1864—to be told of hereafter. I would probably never have known of this last chance we seem to have had but for certain statements in Swinton's history of the Army of the Potomac.[46] But all about that I will tell in order when I come to it.

In this connection it may be noted that I do *not* count Gettysburg as a place where the end of the war might have been the result of a victory, although many writers do,[47] in whose judgment I generally have more confidence than I have in my own. But it has seemed to me always that the fact that our nearest railroad point to replenish supplies & ammunition was at Staunton, Va., about 150 miles by wagon road, was bound to put a short period to our stay in Pa. whatever our success in battle might be, so I don't myself exactly figure on Gettysburg as one of the places where, as we might say, the "war was lost."

But there is one thing about the accounts of Gettysburg which any one who has read some recent ones will note, & about which in this connection I would like to say a word. Great blame is attached by some writers to Longstreet[48] about Gettysburg. Gen. Fitzhugh Lee is a typical instance, in his life of Gen. R. E. Lee. But little or nothing is ever said in print of this failure of Gen. Jackson's just detailed. Fitz Lee's book has not one single word about it. Yet, even apart from general considerations of the truth of history it ought to be told in *justice to Gen. Lee.*

Yet it is hardly correct either to say that the failure to reap the greatest results was in no way Gen. Lee's fault. No commander of any army does his whole duty who simply gives orders, however well considered. He should *supervise their execution,* in person or by staff officers, constantly, day & night, so that if the machine balks at any point he may be most promptly informed & may most promptly start it to work. For instance on Jun. 30 I think he should have been in person with Huger, & have had reliable members of his staff with Jackson on his left, & Longstreet & others on his right, receiving reports every half hour or oftener, & giving fresh orders as needed.

But it is time to get back to my narrative. Next day we began to pay in blood for the lost opportunities & tried in vain to get them back. During the night the enemy moved on to Malvern Hill, & there, in that most magnificent position of all he had found yet, he had concentrated his whole army, infantry & artillery, including especially his siege & reserve train of 100 guns.

I will not attempt any description of the ground further than to say that it gave room for the development of over 300 guns, with good protection for themselves & their infantry supports & with but narrow & obstructed approaches on our side. Fitz John Porter says in the Century War Book: "This new position, with its elements of great strength, was better adapted for a defensive battle than any with which we had been favored. . . . The ground in front was sloping, & over it our infantry & artillery, themselves protected by the crest & ridges, had clear sweep for their fire. In all directions the land over which an attacking force must advance was almost entirely cleared of forest & was generally cultivated."[49]

I don't think any military engineer can read this description of this ground without asking in surprise, & almost in indignation, how on God's earth it happened that our army was put to assault such a position. The whole country was but a gently rolling one with no great natural obstacles anywhere, fairly well cultivated & with farm roads going in every direction. Why was not half our army simply turned to the left & marched by the nearest roads out of the enemy's view & fire to strike his road of retreat, & his long, slow & cumbersome trains, a few miles below, while the rest in front could threaten & hold his battle array but without attacking it.

I have myself, on the ground afterward, discussed the feasibility of this in company with Gen. Wade Hampton, & Gen. J. F. Gilmer, chf. engineer, & we examined & found short, easy, & covered roads in every way favorable.

But Gen. Lee, though himself distinguished as an engineer, & for engineer work, in Mexico, had but few engineer officers close to him, & seemed to have such supreme confidence that his infantry could go anywhere, that he took comparatively little pains to study out the easier roads.[50]

In the Mexican War fought with smooth bore, short range muskets, in fact, the character of the ground cut comparatively little figure. But with the rifled muskets & cannon of this war the affair was very different as was proven both at Malvern Hill, & at Gettysburg; as will appear when we come to that fight.

There were with our army several residents of that neighborhood who had some appreciation of the military strength of the Malvern Hill position. A Rev. Mr. Allen, with Gen. D. H. Hill, on the day before, had described to him "its commanding height, the difficulties of approach to it, its amphitheatrical form & ample area, which would enable McClellan to arrange his 350 field guns, tier above tier, & sweep the plain in every direction." And Gen. Hill describes his telling Gen. Lee about it as follows: "Jackson moved over the swamp early on July 1st, Whiting's division leading. Our march was much delayed by the crossing of troops & trains. At Willis's Church I met Gen. Lee. He bore grandly his terrible disappointment of the day before & made no allusion to it. I gave him Mr. Allen's description of Malvern Hill & presumed to say, 'If Gen. McClellan is there in force we had better let him alone.' Longstreet laughed & said, 'Don't get scared now that we have got him whipped.' It was this belief in the demoralisation of the Federal army which made our leader risk the attack."[51]

I have not the data at hand for it, nor is it necessary to go into the details of the battle. A good many efforts were made to bring a heavy artillery fire to bear upon the enemy, but all were failures in the end, partly for lack of organised battalions of guns, & partly because the enormous development of the enemy already in position, & with the range of our few possible points of approach, & with heavier metal & better ammunition, could practically crush our isolated batteries as fast as we could get them on the field. Only since writing this have I seen Gen. Pendleton's report. We *had,* under *him,* organised battalions—several—including perhaps 20 batteries. He reports that he could neither find Gen. Lee nor any place on the field where he could get in with his guns. His report will convict him of having practically hidden himself out all day where nobody saw him, & no orders could find him.[52]

But, in spite of our disadvantages, it was marvellous how gallantly & desperately our men fought, both our infantry & artillery, the brigade batteries. Communication along our line was very difficult, through the woods & swamps, & under incessant shelling, not only of the enemy's guns on the field, but of his gun boats on the James, with their great rifles. This made simultaneous action very difficult, & many assaults in the afternoon were greatly scattered, but, for all that, there is abundant evidence that we gave the enemy some very anxious moments, & compelled them to bring into action about all of their force. At times & places our infantry were actually in among their guns & almost had temporary possession. At one time, Gen. Fitz John Porter himself, who was practically in command of the field on his side, had such apprehensions of falling into our hands as a prisoner, that he records that he took from his pocket & tore up his "diary & despatch book of the campaign," as he rode, bringing up reinforcements to his line.[53] I rode in person over the field, the next morning, & was amazed to see by our dead how far our lines had penetrated at some points. I recall a handsome young Louisianian as decidedly in advance of all others & far inside the line of their guns. And, to illustrate the severity of the fire at some points, I recall meeting a Maj. Johnson, quartermaster (an old resident of Alexandria, Va.),[54] with one half of one of the steel breast plates, which were found frequently on the enemy's dead at this time, which had been struck by 6 musket balls, one canister shot & one rectangular fragment of shell. The musket balls had only made shallow dents in it. The canister shot had made a dent so deep that the metal was cracked & torn, but the shot did not get through. But the fragment of shell had cut a clean hole about 2 inches by one.

But perhaps the best brief account of the fighting is Gen. Fitz John Porter's:[55]

> The spasmodic, though sometimes formidable attacks of our antagonists, at different points along our whole front, up to about 4 o'clock were, presumably, demonstrations or feelers to ascertain our strength preparatory to their engaging in more serious work. An ominous silence, similar to that which had preceded the attack in force at Gaines's Mill, now intervened, until, at about 5:30 o'clock, the enemy opened upon both Morell & Couch[56] with artillery from nearly the whole of his front, & soon afterward pressed forward his columns of infantry, first on one, & then on the other, or on both. As if moved by a reckless disregard of life equal to that displayed at Gaines's Mill, with a determination to capture our army or destroy it by driving us into the river, regiment after regiment, & brigade after brigade rushed at our batteries. But the artillery of both Morell & Couch mowed them down with shrapnel, grape, & canister; while our infantry, withholding their fire until the enemy were within short range, scattered the remnants of their columns, sometimes following them up & capturing prisoners & colors. As column after column advanced, only to meet the same disastrous repulse, the sight became one of the most interesting imaginable.
>
> The havoc made by the rapidly bursting shells, from guns arranged so as to sweep any position, far & near, and in any direction, was fearful to behold. Pressed to the extreme as they were the courage of our men was fully tried.

Oh, the rivers of good blood that flowed that evening all in vain, & all, as I verily believe, because Gen. Jackson had remembered the Sabbath day to keep it holy, & then trusted to the Lord for victory. For the magnificent fighting of our men, which "pressed to the extreme" the whole Federal army concentrated upon such an advantageous field would, surely, the day before, have destroyed its far strung out divisions, in flat & wooded country giving but little chance to use artillery. And our losses[57] in this connec-

tion would not have been one half, & we would have become possessed of
every gun McClellan had. For we would have driven his men into the river,
as Fitz John Porter expressed it.

It is a somewhat remarkable fact that Gen. McClellan himself was not
upon a single one of his battle fields, & there was some comment upon it in
some of the Northern papers. He was on Malvern Hill in the early morning
but passed on to the river & was aboard one of the gunboats in conference
with the naval officers at the time of the battle.

Our losses on this field were about 6,000 men.[58] Fitz John Porter implies
that our whole army was engaged, & in one assault, which they attempted
to make simultaneous; though his own narrative indicates that it was rather
a rapid succession of separate brigade charges than one united advance.
Really the whole of the serious fighting was done by 14 brigades.

First, D. H. Hill on our left went in with his 5 brigades, G. B. Anderson's,
Rodes's, Ripley's, Garland's, & Colquitt's.[59] These five fought practically
alone for an hour & a half, & were beaten; when, about sunset, 9 brigades
of Huger's & McLaws's divisions beginning just on Hill's right made their
attempt. Hill writes of it: "I never saw anything more grandly heroic than
the advance of the 9 brigades under Magruder's orders. Unfortunately they
did not move together & were beaten in detail. As each brigade emerged
from the woods from 50 to 100 guns opened upon it tearing great gaps in its
ranks, but the heroes reeled on & were shot down by the reserves at the
guns which a few squads reached. . . . It was not war—it was murder."[60]
These brigades were Mahone's Va., Wright's Geo., Barksdale's Miss., Ransom's N.C., Cobb's Geo., Semmes's La. & Geo., Kershaw's S.C., Armistead's Va., & G. T. Anderson's Geo.[61] These 14 brigades were practically
fought to a frazzle. The rest of the army was practically not engaged.[62]

Next morning the enemy were gone & the melancholly field was ours, to
collect our wounded & to bury our gallant dead. But the divisions which
had not been engaged followed after McClellan & found him at Harrison's
Landing with his fleet to protect his flanks, & in a strong position. Gen.
Lee decided it to be too strong for assault, & after a few days looking
about, as I recall it, the army gradually got back to its camps within our
original lines about Richd.

It was said that, at first, the enemy had failed to occupy at Harrison's
Landing an important commanding hill from which artillery could have
swept their whole encampment. But that, before our pursuing infantry
came up, Gen. Stuart of the cavalry not only occupied it, but began to shell
them with a single battery, on which they sent a strong force of infantry &
drove him off & held it in force. I think it was Gen. Hampton who told me
of this, & who thought that had Gen. Stuart waited for our infantry to

come up before bringing on the fight, something might have been done, but I am not sure.[63]

And now, having sketched out the battles & the general movements & results, I may descend to narrate the very small personal part I bore in them. And not having preserved a single personal note, or record, I have only the memory to fall back upon of the few special occasions which in some way made special impressions.

My general business, & the most important in a time of so much fighting, was the seeing to it that no gun or musket should ever run out of ammunition. Besides the regular supplies in reserve carried by every brigade, which I was always posted about, I had some extra trains arranged to be near each fight, & I may sum up nearly the whole business in saying that everything worked smoothly & well, & there was never a breath of complaint anywhere of our men's ever being short of ammunition—either for small arms or artillery. I had a very excellent & active assistant in good old Maj. Duffey, & this fact enabled me to find time for a little special work which Gen. Lee committed to me.

Some weeks before this campaign began, Doctor Edward Cheves of Savannah conceived the idea of making a balloon for military observation.[64] Dr. C. was an uncle of my friends the Haskell young men, John, Aleck, Joe, &c. He was wealthy & he was a very remarkable & skillful mechanic & chemist & engineer. He bought up all the silk to be found in Sav. & Charleston, experimented with various substances for varnish to make the silk approximately gas tight (finally using old rubber car springs dissolved in oil) & at last completed a very excellent balloon & brought it on to Richmond about Jun. 24th. The enemy had had balloons in daily use during the whole campaign, from the beginning of the siege of Yorktown. In fact they began to use them, during the fall of 1861, before Washington City, & they continued their use up to about May 1863, after which I cannot recall seeing them. This would imply that they did not finally consider them of much value. If so I think their conclusion a decided mistake.

I am sure that on certain occasions *skilled observers* in balloons could give information of priceless value. Balloons ought frequently to permit the discovery of marching columns, such as I made at Bull Run, as told in my account of that fight, & which was made from a high hill 8 miles off—a sort of poor & accidental substitute for a balloon. And the very knowledge by the enemy of one's use of balloons is demoralizing, & leads them, in all their movements, to roundabout roads & night marches which are often very hampering. But the observers in the balloon should be *trained staff officers,* not the ignorant class of ordinary balloonists, which I think were generally in charge of the Federal balloons.

Well, on the receipt of this balloon, Gen. Lee ordered me to take charge of it, & to go up in it, to observe, specially, any transfers or crossings of the Chickahominy—from one side to the other—during the approaching battles on the north side, & also any indications of any disposition of the enemy to assume the aggressive on the south side. And I was ordered to provide signals to be displayed to indicate whatever I might see.

We could not get pure hydrogen gas to fill the balloon, & had to use ordinary illuminating gas, from the Richmond Gas Works; & we could only use such starting points as we could reach from the Gas Works without going through woods or very narrow roads. With illuminating gas the balloon would only lift my weight with about 1,000 feet of line to hold it by. The balloon would leak gas so fast also that it would not keep up at the full height more than three or four hours, when it would gradually begin to lose, & after 6 or 7 hours it had to be emptied & refilled, which took some hours. For signals I got up four big, black-cambric balls, stretched over telegraph wire hoops, & I devised a little signal code of one or more of these balls, hung out below the balloon, & copies[65] were given to all the principal officers all along our lines.

But I was not at all enamored of my prospective employment. When a boy I had had no fear of high places at all, but while at West Point as a cadet I had had a serious fall over a cliff on [the] left bank of "Indian Falls" opposite West Point one winter Saturday afternoon when I "ran it" across the Hudson, on the ice, with first-class-man Deshler of Ala.—afterward killed at Chickamauga[66]—& ever after that fall high places gave me an almost irresistible impulse to jump. And now, when I thought of going up 1,000 feet I had a feeling that nothing could keep me from jumping. And finally, as I was about to step into the basket, as a sort of dismal joke to keep my courage up, I said to the man whom Dr. Cheves had sent to take care of the balloon & to superintend the filling, &c.—"I'd advise you not to stand immediately beneath this basket, for the chances are that, at about 500 feet, I'll jump out; & if I fell on you it would not help me any to speak of, & yet might be a little rough on you." "Oh," answered the man, "you're afraid of that feeling people have on steeples & precipices, but you needn't be. You never have that in a balloon." " Why?" said I. "Well," he answered, "the reason is this. When on a steeple or a precipice one feels that the centre of gravity is below him & that if once started from the perpendicular the tendency is to go further & the whole business to pitch over, or it is unstable equilibrium. But here one has the instinctive feeling that the centre of gravity is up above, in that big swelling globe; & if one started to swing out the tendency is to come back, & that makes stable equilibrium."

Now, whatever the merits of this reasoning, it is certainly a fact that one's feelings in such a situation are entirely *instinctive,* & that in a balloon the whole instinct & feeling is one of the most perfect & absolute security. The balloon had not risen 50 feet before I felt as safe & as much at home as if I had lived in one for years. I had thought before hand that I could only hope not to jump by avoiding looking directly downward. Now it was most fascinating to do it & watch how small the people seemed to grow. If balloons were plenty I could imagine one's acquiring the "balloon habit," & going up every day just to gaze down.

Well my first afternoon in the balloon was during the terrible battle of Gaines's Mill. I ascended from a point about 2 miles out on the Williamsburg Road &, while I could seldom see the troops, the smoke of the firings gave a very fair idea of the action, & I saw & signalled the crossing of Slocum's division to reinforce Porter during the action. The troops of the enemy on our side of the river made no move. During the next several days I made several ascensions both by day & by night, when the locations of camp fires would betray troops who could not be seen by day, the object being to locate the routes over which the enemy was retreating.

When the enemy got away from his original lines, & we could not follow with the balloon by land, I had it filled & towed down the James River by a little armed tug, the "Teaser." On the night of July 3rd we made such a trip, & I ascended from her deck, an hour or more before day, from the James River away down near Malvern Hill. After sunrise when the balloon began to get very weak we emptied & folded her, & the captain, Davidson,[67] offered to run down a little further & land me where I could get out & probably make my way to Gen. Lee to report, & he started to do so, when, unfortunately, the *Teaser* ran hard aground on a mud bank out near the middle of the river. The tide was falling, & it would be some three hours before it would release us. I saw a few straggling Federal soldiers in the swampy woods along the bank, & I landed with a boat & took two or three prisoners, & was about to re-embark for the *Teaser* with them, when a sentry we had put out fired his musket, & around the bend, a few hundred yards below, came a large Federal gunboat, the *Maratanza*. The *Teaser* had but one gun, a rifled 32. She took one shot at *Maratanza*, but I don't think she hit her. Then Davidson kindled a fire on the *Teaser*, & lashed down his safety valve so as to try & explode her boiler, & he & his men jumped overboard & swam & waded to shore, while the *Maratanza* showered grape & canister after them & after us in the woods indiscriminately. Prisoners & all we took to the shelter of the woods & trees, & all escaped damage, but the *M.* sent a boat which boarded the *Teaser*, extinguished the fire, loosed the valve, got a tow line out, & then the *M.* pulled her out of the mud & carried her off, balloon & all. So, I left the sailors & the prisoners to make their own way to Richmond while I struck out for the army, which I soon found, & Gen. Lee also, & made my final balloon report.[68]

In between whilst I had been around every day, also, with my ordnance trains & on the 30th had seen the splendid fight of Longstreet & A. P. Hill at Frazier's Farm, & the next evening, in the rear of our lines of battle at Malvern Hill, had a taste of how the enemy's big guns could shell the woods. I can appreciate the story told by Gen. Lawton of an ambulance driver who swore at a big shell which crashed near him: "You d—n s–n of a b—h. You haint got no eyes, & would as soon hit a ambulance driver as anybody else."

As I watched the fight of Jenkins's South Carolina brigade at Frazier's Farm a fine, tall, handsome, young fellow dropped out of ranks & came back toward me. As he seemed weak I went to meet him & found he had been shot through the lungs, the bullet passing clear through. He had been the color bearer. I had a small flask of some of my father's "Old Hurricane" brandy of 1811, & I gave him a drink, & helped him on toward where an ambulance could be had. He asked me, rather apologetically, if I thought he had any chance of recovery. I told him about poor Bob Wheat who was killed at Gaines's Mill only three days before, but who had been shot through the lungs at Bull Run in July '61, & though he was exceedingly stout & thick, so that the hole was fully two feet long through him, had yet gotten well very easily & soon. He was evidently cheered & said, "Of course, I'm willing to die for my country, if I must; but I'd a heap rather get well & see my mother & my folks again." Poor fellow, I hope he did, but I never knew. It was a close call, anyhow. I did know his name & regiment, but they soon escaped my memory in all the many kindred things occurring for so long.

Only about a week before the battles began my wife, with our little girl, Bess, & Mary, her excellent nurse, had come down to Richmond from Farmville, where she had been for some weeks. I got board for her with a Mrs. Taylor, a sort of half crazy woman, on Church Hill, near the bluff over the James. So she was in the city during all the battles & could hear the musketry & artillery every day & saw the long strings of ambulances with their loads of wounded. My own camp & headquarters were at the Keach house, on the hills beyond Rocketts & the creek (north side of the river pike), not over a half mile away, so I was able to see her or to communicate almost every day.

And, not long after the fight, we had an officer's mess organised at the Keach house for several of us with our wives. I think that Thos. Rhett & A. P. Mason (Penny) of Gen. Jos. E. Johnston's staff were among them, and I know that good old Col. Archie Cole, quartermaster, & his beautiful wife & her little pet Mexican dog "Pickalingo," were a part. And then I brought over my little crowd from Mrs. Taylor's. And I remember here one day calling, at a near by house, on my old classmate & most special friend Dick

Meade—now in [the] Confederate engineers. He was lying down, sick with fever contracted in the Seven Days in the woods & marshes, & in a day or so he was removed to Petersburg—to his family—& he died there a few days after. I will attach a letter Gen. Lee wrote his mother. He was one of the best & the most intimate friends I ever had, being my very first room-mate on the day of my entry at West Point.[69]

During the battle of Cold Harbor (or Gaines's Mill) on [June] 27 my friend John C. Haskell lost his right arm at the shoulder. He was an aid of Gen. D. R. Jones and had carried a message across the Chickahominy to Gen. Lee & had then volunteered to join in the charge about to be made by Hood's brigade. His horse was killed near the Federal breastwork where Hood's men carried it & he going on then on foot recd. his wound. Gen. Hood tells in his book that wishing to send a message [and] all of his staff being already employed, he called out for a volunteer when Lt. Jno. C. Haskell came up & offered his services, but as a cannon shot had just carried away the young man's right arm at the shoulder he advised him to seek a hospital.[70]

Another event of that charge which I could not stop my narrative to tell but it is worth record was the death of poor Bob Wheat—already referred to. Bob was the son of a clergyman of Alexa. & Memphis,[71] I believe, & when a small boy ran away to Mexico with the Voltigeur Regiment.[72] He became well known there to lots of old army officers & was very popular. After that war he was in some fillibuster war in Central America, Walker's,[73] I believe, & distinguished everywhere for bravery. I had frequently heard of him before I ever saw him at West Point in 1859, where he came to submit a new patent of a gun. It was an immensely long gun, with chambers in the trunnions to carry two extra loads of powder intended to go off after the ball passed them, under the impulse of the load in the breech, & thus give her a tremendous velocity. It is all very pretty in theory but the gun would not work.

Next Bob turned up at Manassas in June 1861 in command of the "La. Tigers," a battalion of wharf rats &c. which he had recruited in New Orleans. This command, & one other, the "Black Horse Cavalry" Co., greatly impressed the Northern newspaper correspondents by their names in the first year of the war, & the advertising that they got in the papers as terrible fighters was absolutely ludicrous. For while the Black Horse was an excellent company from Fauquier Co., Va., I believe, the Tigers were noted for disregard of discipline & after Wheat's death were soon broken up. The first military execution I ever witnessed was the shooting of two of them for forcing a guard & releasing a friend of theirs who had been arrested. This was near Centreville in the fall of 1861.[74] At Bull Run, as before mentioned, Wheat had been shot through & through the lungs but had recovered wonderfully. He was rather short,[75] very thick-set, dark complexion, splendid eyes, & a handsome face & most cordial & attractive manner. Longstreet's adjutant, my excellent friend afterward, Gen. Moxley Sorrel[76] told me that just before the charge was made in the afternoon of June 27th he called Wheat aside & said, "Bob, there's just two drinks left here in my flask. Divide them with me." Wheat replied, "Moxley, something tells old Bob that this is the last drink he'll ever take in this world & he'll take it with you." Very soon after the charge was ordered & in it Wheat fell, only living long enough to exclaim, "Bury me on the field, boys!" His was one of the most attractive personalities I ever met.[77]

Very few of the reports distinguish between the casualties of the different battles, of which there were four, beside a sharp affair of Magruder's at Savage Station on Sunday the 29th,[78] about which I have never known the particulars except that it was an isolated attack on a strong rear guard by $2\frac{1}{2}$ brigades[79] & it was repulsed, as might have been expected. No *small* force of ours could have hoped for any real success, & all such inadequate attacks were mistakes.

Of the other four actions, three were assaults by main force right where the enemy wanted us to make them. The first, Ellison's Mill, was an entire failure & very bloody—but fortunately was in a small scale. The second, Cold Harbor or Gaines's Mill, was also a bloody failure at first—being made piecemeal. Finally made in force it was a success. The third, Malvern Hill, was an utter & bloody failure. Ellison's Mill & Malvern Hill could both have been turned, & Gen. D. H. Hill asserts that the enemy's right at Cold Harbor could have [been] better assaulted than the centre or left where our attack was made.

As the war went on we learned to try more turning operations, & fewer direct rushes right where the enemy had fixed up to receive us. And it is instructive to look back to the earlier actions & note wherever there was an opportunity to have done better than we did,[80] generally a turning game instead of a forcing game would have been better play. We will see beautiful examples of the turning game at Chancellorsville & at [the] Wilderness & a rather sad example of the forcing game at Gettysburg.

5

SECOND MANASSAS CAMPAIGN

We had nearly a whole month of quiet after the Seven Days. McClellan fortified himself strongly in his camp at Harrison's Landing, &, not only that, but he crossed over & occupied some hills on the south side of the James also; being practically forced to do so by an attempt by Gen. Pendleton, Gen. Lee's chief of arty., to shell his camps at night with some long range guns from the south side. I cannot recall a single incident of interest as occurring during that month. I find in the War Records that on one occasion I got the following order from Gen. Lee, but I cannot remember what resulted:[1]

Hd. Qrs., Army Northn. Va. July 5, 1862
9 P.M.

Lt. Col. E. P. Alexander
            Chief of Ordnance
Colonel:
            Gen. Lee directs me to say that Genl. Pendleton is absent & he does not know who is in charge of the Reserve Artillery; he therefore desires that you will go at once & ascertain the condition of the Reserve Artillery & have it put in condition to move to Malvern Hill early tomorrow morning.
    The artillery will be held in readiness to move, everything ready for active service, but you will not move the artillery without further orders from these headquarters. You will also see that your ordnance train is ready to move at the same time, if necessary.
    If the artillery is ordered down the general desires that you go with it.
Yours, &c. A. P. Mason
Asst. Adjt. Genl.

    I was occupied in re-accumulating supplies of ammunition, & in improving our armament of small arms, & of artillery, by our captures in the recent battles, as well as by all the arms we could make or get in through the blockade.² The great point desired was to equip all our infantry with the rifle musket, calibre 58/100 inch instead of the old fashioned smooth bore round ball musket, calibre 69/100ths, which nine out of ten of our men had to start out with. The former has a range of 1,000 yards, the latter of only about 200. The enemy were armed entirely with the former, & we were at a great disadvantage until we did the same. My recollection is that Gettysburg was our first battle in which we were at last entirely rid of smooth bore muskets. The captured Federal guns, & artillery ammunition too, were much superior to most of ours, & we had a great swapping around both in infantry & artillery, after the battles, for many weeks. I overhauled too all the ammunition supply service of the whole army, & I enlarged the reserve train under Maj. Duffey, & generally got everything ready for an active & extensive campaign. And all the time my wife & baby were with me at the Keach house & I had a rarely happy time of it. But about Aug. 1st Gen. Lee began to get a move on him, for his situation was getting to be a very critical one.

The three separate armies which the Federals had had—one at Fredericksburg under McDowell, about 18,000; one in the Valley under Banks, 11,000; & one coming from West Va., about 13,000, under Frémont—had all been united into one, and Gen. John Pope had been brought from the West to command it.³ And now I am going to stop my narrative & tell a little about Gen. Pope, which will put subsequent events in a clearer light as we come to them; & I am also going to make a digression to point out some facts about the position into which we had practically driven Gen. McClellan, which have never been commented on in print that I have seen, but which are, I think, of decided military interest.

First, about Gen. John Pope. He had been a captain of topographical engineers in the old army, & I had happened to hear two things about him. When a very young officer he had been stationed in Savannah, & there was extant there a story that his conduct to some young lady had led to his having his face slapped & being tabooed in the society of the place. Then in 1858 on the Utah expedition, where I met a great many officers of the line, I heard no end of fun made of two topographical engineer officers, Pope & Abert,⁴ for their ridiculous official reports. One, I forget which, had furnished the celebrated Capt. Derby (John Phoenix),⁵ with a subject for a celebrated picture. He had written in his report, "The birds carolled forth their songs of love from the neighboring mullen stalks & I could not resist the temptation of firing off my mule." Derby had circulated a picture of the officer touching off the mule with a port-fire like a piece of artillery. That, however, may have been on Capt. Abert.

Pope though figured in an army song, a parody on Moore's "Hope told a flattering tale."⁶ He was stationed for some years on the "Llano Estacado" or Staked Plains of Texas trying vainly to get water by boring artesian wells.[7] The song had it:

> Pope told a flattering tale
> Which proved to be bravado,
> About the streams which spout like ale
> On the Llano Estacado.

Briefly it may be said that Pope's general reputation in army circles, as I happened to know them, was that of a blatherskite, & shortly before he was promoted to the command of this new army (Jun. 27th) over the heads of many prominent & distinguished major generals in the East—like McDowell, Franklin, Porter, Sumner, &c.—he had telegraphed some very sensational & absurd yarns about what he had accomplished with some cavalry out about Corinth, Miss. The old army officers now among the Confederates used to smile to think how Pope had managed to impose himself upon Mr. Lincoln, & how bitterly many of the old officers, who knew Pope & who were overslaughed, would necessarily feel about it.

Well Pope had arrived early in July & began to concentrate & organise his army; & also to make known his qualities. Indeed his promises & his subsequent performances almost read like a plot from a comic opera. I will give in full his first general order to his army:

> Headquarters in the Saddle, 1862
> Gen. Orders No. 1[8]

This order was reprinted in all the Southern papers, &, with it, a sort of defiant reply of the South, that a general who did not know his headquarters from his hindquarters had better be kept out of Gen. Lee's way. How speedily the prophecy was verified & how Pope's "hindquarters" proved to be his vulnerable point will appear in my narrative.

And now I want to say something about the position into which we had driven McClellan's army, on the James River; so near City Point at the mouth of the Appomattox River that it may practically be considered as the place itself. In all the military criticisms on the different Virginia campaigns which I have ever seen, I have never seen pointed out, or commented on, the tremendous advantages offered the attacking army by that location. Grant finally got into it in June 1864, and, although he did not play its advantages for one half what they were worth & so prolonged the struggle for some months, yet the Confederacy was practically gone when he had once fortified himself in that position.

Let me state briefly[9] what constitutes advantages in a military position & then point out how eminently this position possessed them. In the text books on the subject the whole art of war is condensed into a few axioms,

& it is perhaps of interest to note that the best compendium of this art, which I have ever seen, was written & published by Gen. Halleck, several years before the war; having been prepared as a course of lectures before some club or society in Boston,[10] I forget now exactly what. Halleck, by the way, was the classmate & most intimate friend of my bro.-in-law Gen. Gilmer, & I think I have mentioned my meeting him at Gilmer's house in San Francisco in 1860 & '61.

He had been in command of the western Federal armies, & now, on July 11, 1862, he had been summoned to Washington City & practically placed in supreme command; a position which he held till superseded by Grant in the spring of 1864.

The first of all the maxims for the conduct of a campaign is to oppose fractions of the enemy's army with the whole unit of your own. In other words compel the enemy to divide while you unite, & strike him divided. Or as our Gen. Forrest put it in plain Confederate vernacular, "Git thar furst with the most men."

Now if one could hold a small circle & compel his enemy to occupy a larger one[11] he would possess the greatest possible facility for playing this game. He could for instance threaten the enemy's right until he forced him to draw his reserves to that vicinity, when he could precipitate himself upon the weakened left flank & crush it long before help could come away around from the right.

The second great axiom in the art is if possible to act against your enemy's communications, without exposing one's own. The simple fact that no army can subsist for long without daily supplies of food & ammunition from the rear, indicates at once the vital importance of keeping its communications to the rear free from interruption.

Now look at this little rough sketch & see how perfectly a Federal army holding the junction of the James & Appomattox Rivers holds these two immense advantages over a Confederate army charged with the defense of Richmond & the portion of Virginia north of it. [Figure 16 appears here in the manuscript.] The railroad line shown was practically the only one available for the supply of Richmond from the south in 1862. There was, indeed, another route open to Chattanooga by way of Lynchburg, but it was a mountain route, with heavy grades, & through a section where there were many disloyal people in the mountains who frequently burned bridges; & Richmond could not have been held without the railroad to Weldon. The Confederate govt. appreciated this, & in 1863 themselves built a line from Danville to Greensboro, N.C.; which gave Rich. a second route to the south, & which supplied it in 1864 when the Weldon Road could no longer be used. But even then Richmond was immediately evacuated when Petersburg could no longer be held.

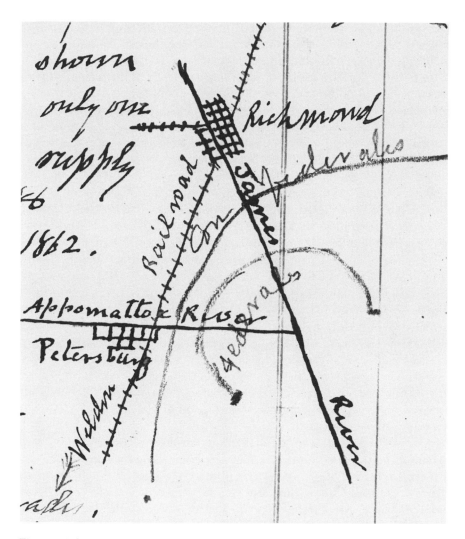

Figure 16. Strategic situation on the Richmond-Petersburg front, 1862

Then it must be stated also that the James River was large & deep enough for monitors, which gave the enemy quiet & assured possession, & which could proceed to Richmond itself, could they once, by a land force, drive us from our batteries at Chaffin's & Drury's Bluffs where our line crossed the James. Of course the enemy had plenty of bridges & ferries for free communication, & the wooded country enabled him to make strong interior defensive lines, with abattis for protection if attacked.

Perfectly safe therefore himself against our taking the offensive, he had the centre of a circle, which forced us to occupy a long circumference broken by two rivers, & he threatened our only line of communications while his own were absolutely secure from attack.

In fact it has always seemed to me that any expert in the science of war, given a map of Virginia & asked to select the best line of attack upon Richmond, should promptly put his finger on this position covering the junction of those two rivers & say, "Occupy this position & Richmond is yours." And it would seem that of all men then in either army, Gen. Halleck, the author of a most excellent book on this art, would be the man of all others in the United States to appreciate it.[12]

But the evidence seems clear that it was Halleck himself who considered McClellan in a faulty position, & who took his army away from there, by water, & carried them back up the Potomac. McClellan himself protested & begged to be allowed to remain, & to be reinforced. And in his recollections, written after the war, he claims to have always appreciated the great advantages of that line to which, too, he ascribes Grant's final success, but says that, against all his protests, his army was carried back to reinforce Pope, who was in no danger until his own withdrawal from the James released Gen. Lee's army from Richmond.[13]

And on the whole I candidly believe that the bringing to Washington of Halleck & Pope really prolonged the war for perhaps two years. Our only hope would have been in the fact that McClellan himself was a too hesitating & cautious fighter, as will appear further on. But briefly I consider it one of our very narrow escapes, by pure good luck, when McClellan was removed from the James.

And now I will take up the condensed narrative of principal events in what we call the first Maryland campaign, comprising the battles at Cedar Mountain, Second Manassas, & Sharpsburg, or Antietam. I will not try to go into detail, for I am writing where I have no records accessible, or almost none,[14] & my own personal part in it was very uneventful & very few scenes linger in my memory. My duties as chief of ordnance required me to see that every infantry man, artillery man, & cavalry man in the army was always supplied with ammunition, according to his calibre & his expenditures & losses. In such an active campaign, covering so much ground, & so far away from railroads, & even across the Potomac & in the enemy country, & with such heavy fighting, this was a work of some magnitude. And I feel no little pride in saying that it was all smoothly & efficiently done, & even to the end of that last dreadful day at Sharpsburg, there was never a lack of powder or lead at any point on the line. My principal assistant was good old Major Duffey, to whom, too, I had given a lieut. as assistant (I forget his name), and I had overhauled & increased his train to something over 100 wagons if I remember aright.

Heretofore, in all our marches & movements, I had messed, slept, & travelled with Gen. Johnston's whole staff. Since Gen. Lee had been in command headquarters had remained near Richmond. In the coming campaign I foresaw that I could manage my business much more efficiently if I had my own wagon, tent, & cook, so as to be footloose to go & come when & where I chose. So early in July I began to fix myself up with a team & driver, tent, camp-equipage, travelling desk, &c., &c. When I could, I encamped near Gen. Lee, & when needed I could be with any division in the army. My cook & factotum was Charley, hired the winter before at Centreville as groom from his master (whose name I have long forgotten) living near Aldie, Va. My driver was a most faithful old fellow named Abram, small & pure black from King William County, Va. His owner, too, I have long forgotten. With just these two I made all of that campaign, & at its close, when I gave up my position as chief of ordnance, & went to command a battalion of artillery, I took them with me to the battalion headquarters. In fact when in 1864 I left the battalion, being further promoted as chief of arty. of Longstreet's corps, & again to have my own camp & mess with my staff, Charley & Abram were the nucleus of the new organisation.

And while on the subject perhaps I had as well say that they stayed with me to the end of the war, when Abram was captured a few days before the surrender, & I never saw or heard of him again. But Charley was on hand & wanted to follow me even to South America. So his further history will come later. But Abram's memory remains green in the expression "Drive on Abram," still to be heard when survivors of the dear old battalion meet & recall the camps & marches of our old campaigns. For Abram's wagon usually led the march.

Our campaign opened early in August. Pope was concentrating east of the Rappahannock the three armies of Frémont, 13,000, Banks, 11,000, & McDowell, 18,000 inf. & 5,000 cavalry. The best return I can find of their numbers would make his whole available force about 47,000.[15]

To Pope came orders from Halleck to make some demonstrations toward our railroad at Gordonsville so as to attract a part of Gen. Lee's troops from Richmond, in order that McClellan might safely weaken his army by beginning to ship it to the Potomac. Nothing could have suited Gen. Lee better. No sooner did Pope send some of his troops across the Rappahannock, than Lee sent Jackson with his own division, Ewell's & A. P. Hill's to look after him. In fact there is a doubt in my mind whether Lee did not himself start Jackson up to Gordonsville before he ever heard of Pope's demonstrations; intending on his part to *force* Halleck to withdraw McClellan in order to defend Washington, & meanwhile, too, intending to take advantage of his interior position & try & crush Pope before McClellan could reach him.

Certainly that whole game was formulated in his mind at the very commencement of the campaign & it was executed with a dash & brilliancy equalled by few campaigns in the world, & with as much success as could possibly have been hoped for, considering the odds & all the circumstances, for Pope had the easiest game to play. Lee lost some time by heavy rains & a freshet in the rivers & Pope did get reinforcements of 3 corps from McClellan (3rd, 4th & 5th I believe) & one, the 9th, from No. Ca.,[16] but yet Lee cleaned him up, & ran him off the last battle field while two whole corps, Sumner's & Franklin's, were just 1 & 2 days away. It was a beautifully played game on Lee's part anyway.[17]

And now I'll try & outline briefly the different steps. Jackson crossed the Rapidan with his three divisions & on Aug. 9th had a very sharp battle with Banks's corps on the slope of Cedar Mountain. He drove Banks off the field; but he himself suffered sharply, & he recrossed the Rapidan. Among our casualties was Gen. Winder killed—a very promising officer. One of my special friends, Col. Snowden Andrews, of the arty.,[18] received here one of the most desperate wounds from which any one ever recovered. A shell exploded by him & a fragment cut open his side so that his liver protruded. But he still lives to tell how he saw it & pushed it back, & got well in spite of all predictions.

On Aug. 13th Gen. Lee himself left Richmond by rail to join Jackson & took with him Longstreet & his division, and Stuart with the cavalry also followed. That still left R. H. Anderson's, D. H. Hill's, McLaws's & Walker's[19] divns. to observe McClellan's diminishing forces, but they were to follow Longstreet as soon as it was apparent that McClellan was gone. I cannot fix the date, exactly, on which I started, but soon after Gen. Lee got to Gordonsville he wired me to come & bring my train with me. So I put Maj. Duffey in motion that very afternoon, & [the] next day with my light personal wagon I followed. I can remember very little detail about that march. It was a long, stern chase I had, pursuing our men, who were doing wonderful marching around & beyond the enemy, & I only caught up with them after the battle of 2nd Manassas when I was able to replenish all their ammunition & fix them up as well as when they started, & then by sending back empty wagons to Gordonsville, the nearest rail point, I soon got my own train full again.

Gen. Lee of course was very anxious to attack Pope before he could receive all the reinforcements coming to him, & Gen. Longstreet states that he "gave orders that his army should cross the Rapidan on the 18th & make battle. . . . But for some reason not fully explained our movements were delayed, & we did not cross the Rapidan until the 20th. In the meantime a dispatch to Stuart was captured by Pope which gave information of our presence & contemplated advance. This, with information Pope already

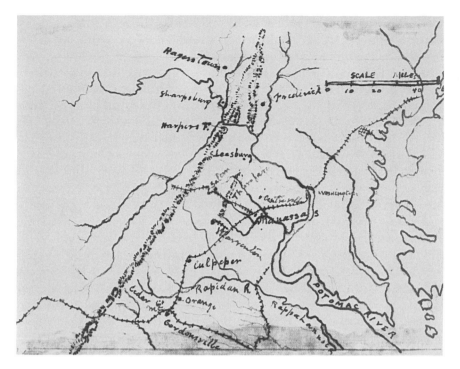

Figure 17. Virginia and Maryland

had, caused him to withdraw to a very strong position, behind the Rappahannock River, & there instead of at Culpeper C.H., where the attack
was first meant to be made, Gen. Lee found him."²⁰ [Figure 17 appears here
in the manuscript.]

So far Pope had handled his army very well indeed. It was his policy
indeed to avoid a fight except with great advantages of ground, & these the
position on the Rappahannock gave him. Gen. Lee came up to the river on
Aug. 21st & felt the position strongly in some severe artillery duels across
it. But in spite of his pugnacity he thought better of attacking (which would
have been pie for Pope like Malvern Hill was for McClellan) & decided to
turn him by a long march, striking his communications far in the rear with
one half of his army while the other half, protected by the river against an
assault, waited for the results. It was a bold & beautiful play. For back at
Manassas Junction 24 miles behind Pope's line of battle were enormous
stores & depots of Pope's army. But while the game was in progress the two
halves of Lee's army would be necessarily far apart & unable to help each
other, & only hard fighting & good marching could save them. From Aug.

21st to 24th Lee was reconnoitering & feeling Pope & was held back too by a freshet in the river, but on the 25th Jackson was able to cross at a point, Hinson's Mill, four miles above Pope's right flank. None of his officers were informed where he was going. His men carried 3 days' cooked rations & a few frying pans. A few ambulances & a few wagon loads of ammunition only were taken along. And Munford's 2nd Va. Cavalry picketed all roads leading to the enemy & screened the march. I should have mentioned, by the way, before that Stuart with part of his cavalry had before this gotten in rear of Pope's line, & had given him a little lesson as to the necessity of looking out for his rear, by capturing his own headquarters wagon, with his baggage & valuable correspondence showing the reinforcements which were coming to him; & this had doubtless stimulated Gen. Lee in his earnestness to get at him.

Jackson had with him his own division under Taliaferro,[21] Ewell's, & A. P. Hill's, say 21,000 infy. men & 2,500 cavalry (14 brig. [of] infty., 2 brig. [of] cav., 18 light batteries).[22] His first day's march was from Jeffersonton via Hinson's Mill & Orlean to Salem—over 26 miles. To give an idea of how much of a march this is I will say that Duane & I coming home from Utah in the fall of 1858 tried to make a good march of it, & having empty wagons let the men put their muskets in the wagons so that they marched light, & had perfect roads, & there being only 64 men, they marched without the annoyance of alternate stoppings & hurryings always attendant on long columns. Under these most favorable possible conditions we averaged 22 miles per day, & the one longest march we ever made was 27 miles. So that 26 miles, including the fording of the Rappahannock, & carrying arms, knapsacks, 60 rounds ammunition, & three days' rations over a very uneven country for a column of 25,000 men with ordnance & artillery & ambulances is a very remarkable march. But in this connection it must be said that such heavy marches will always lose some men from the ranks—not quite able to keep up. And another thing I cannot resist thinking & saying—Ah, if only Gen. Jackson had marched like that from Ashland on June 26.

But perhaps his own conscience had had it out with him about the whole Seven Days business for there was never again in him any trace of his Seven Days behavior.

At dawn on the 26th he started again from Salem, & now he turned sharp to his right flank & marched for Manassas Junction, Pope's great depot of supplies. Parallel to his march most the day before, & between him & Pope, were the Bull Run Mountains, a low outlying development of the Blue Ridge chain. These he crossed at Thoro'fare Gap & soon after he was overtaken by Gen. Stuart with 2 brigades of cavalry (Fitz Lee's & Robertson's[23]) who had crossed the Rappahannock that morning & made a forced march to join him. Together they pushed on & during the night[24] reached Manassas, a distance of 25 miles[25] from Salem, & captured a small force there of 8 guns & 300 men.

During this afternoon of the 26th Pope was waked up to the fact that something was going on in his rear, & he began to abandon the line of the Rappahannock & to come back with his whole army by different roads to see what it meant. And when he found it was only Jackson with 3 divisions he was pleased & made sure that Jackson would be destroyed.[26]

So on the morning of the 27th Pope has gone from the Rappahannock to meet Jackson, & Longstreet with the rest of the army, some thirty-thousand men, he says, started to follow Jackson. Gen. Lee gave him his choice to follow on the straight Warrenton Pike after Pope or to follow Jackson's right angled route & he chose the latter, as less apt to be delayed by an enemy's rear guard in strong positions. His marches were not quite up to Jackson's & he reached Thoro'fare Gap late in afternoon of the 3rd[27] day, the 28th, Jackson having passed it in the morning of his second day. We will leave Longstreet there while we bring Jackson up to the same hour.

He devoted the 27th to plundering & burning the Manassas Depot. Ewell's div. was thrown out towards Bristoe Station to look out for Pope's approach, & in the afternoon it was attacked by Hooker & fell back slowly, fighting until dark when it rejoined Jackson.

Early in the morning of the 27th I forgot to say a New Jersey brigade under a Gen. Taylor[28] had arrived near Manassas by train from Washn. City to drive off what the Washn. authorities supposed to be a cavalry raid. Taylor formed & attacked before he found out any better, & he was killed & many of his men captured & also his train, which was burnt, as also the Bull Run R.R. bridge.

Jackson now knew that by morning of the 28th Pope would be concentrating everything on him. So during the night he marched out toward Bull Run & even sent A. P. Hill's divn. across it & as far as Centreville, but it came around & recrossed Bull Run at Stone Bridge & before the afternoon Jackson had, as we may say, ambushed his army south of Bull Run & west of the Warrenton Turnpike nearly parallel to that pike & not more than a mile[29] off in a large wood. Hill's going around by Centreville was probably only intended to mystify the enemy.[30]

It is worth while to pause here for a moment & take note[31] of Jackson's strategy in thus halting his army & taking position to give battle to the whole of Pope's army, in this open country, when he might have gone on a considerable distance towards Thoro'fare Gap, through which Longstreet was coming to meet him. The main object of his flank movement had been to break up Pope's position, behind the Rapidan, which was too strong to be attacked. He had accomplished this & incidentally destroyed vast quantities of stores & now had Pope's entire army racing back to find him & to reopen their communications. Naturally then he might wish to avoid being brought to battle until Longstreet could be near enough to help him, and Longstreet on this day, the 28th, was still far beyond Thoro'fare Gap. He only approached it at sundown on that day, as stated [above], & found a division of the enemy there, under Ricketts, opposing his passage. So Jackson with his three divisions had to contemplate standing off Pope's whole army, of about five corps or fifteen divisions,[32] for all of 24 hours, with all the chances that Pope might detain Longstreet longer, or even crush him separately.

But there was a strong reason why he should fight as soon as it was possible to do so. Two additional whole corps of McClellan's veterans from the James, Franklin's & Sumner's, were on the way, but had not yet arrived, to reinforce Pope. If any choice was left to Pope, he might not make the battle until these had arrived. It was worth taking even desperate chances, & the occasion found the man equal to it. Jackson was no longer the Jackson of the Seven Days, but the Jackson of the Valley. Perhaps the experiences of that campaign had awakened him to at least a sub-conscious appreciation that the Lord helps best those who do not trust in Him for even a row of pins, however devoutly they may talk about it, but who appreciate the whole responsibility & hustle for themselves accordingly. However that may be, the Jackson of the Seven Days was never seen on Earth again. In less than nine months he was to lay down his life, shot by mistake by the fire of his own men, but meanwhile here at 2nd Manassas, & at Harpers Ferry, at Sharpsburg, at Fredericksburg, & at Chancellorsville he was to wipe out from men's memories the fact that he had ever been, even temporarily, anything but the Jackson of the Valley.

So now we see him, at midday of the 28th, in line of battle parallel to the Warrenton Pike & in gun shot of it on the west, ready to try conclusions with whatever might seek to pass on that road. He had not very long to wait. In the latter half of the afternoon King's[33] division of McDowell's corps came along hunting for him. Being attacked, they met it half way, & the ground giving their artillery a good chance, they put up an unusually hot fight which lasted until dark & in which our Gen. Ewell lost his leg— leaving Lawton in command of his division. During the night King abandoned his ground & fell back toward Manassas. Late in the evening Jackson's men had been cheered by hearing Longstreet's guns at Thoro'fare Gap, about 20 miles off,[34] & they knew that help was coming. During that night, Longstreet had sent three brigades through another gap, Hopewell, three miles north, & another brigade or two to occupy the heights on each side of the Thoro'fare road, & when the morning dawned Ricketts's division had retreated without a fight & gone towards Bristoe. So Longstreet pushed on with his troops & Gen. Lee went on with him & by noon they had practically connected with Jackson.

Meanwhile Jackson had been doing some of the most desperate fighting ever done. When Pope learned by his attack on King that Jackson had stayed to fight him he thought that he saw victory in his hands. Jackson was almost sandwiched in between Reno's[35] & Heintzelman's corps on the east & McDowell's & Sigel's corps & Reynolds's[36] division on the west, & Porter's corps was close by in front. Pope attacked at dawn with two corps, Sigel's & Heintzelman's. About noon Reno's corps joined in until about 1:30 P.M. From then until about 4:30 there were intermittent calms & squalls. About 5:30 Reno & Heintzelman renewed their attack on his left & McDowell & Reynolds on his right, Sigel having had all the fight taken out of him during the morning.

It will be noted that Porter's corps was not engaged on the Federal side nor Longstreet's on the Confederate. This happened by our cavalry's reporting the advance of a heavy body of Federal infantry soon after Longstreet's arrival on the ground, & he, expecting to be attacked awaited it. Porter either knew or guessed that a much larger force than his own was before him, & he also preferred the defensive & wanted to be attacked. For this he was court-martialed & cashiered. In 1878 however he got a rehearing, & a board of officers on the testimony of Longstreet & other Confederate officers justified & commended his conduct & he was put on the list of retired officers. No one knowing Fitz John Porter personally would believe that he could deliberately fail in his duty as a soldier. But no one who knew how Pope was regarded by many of the best officers of the old army can doubt that they found some consolation in the fact that it was Pope who was whipped. Gen. Lee had desired to disregard Porter's proximity & to have Longstreet go to support Jackson's battle soon after his arrival, & doubtless that would have been safer play. Later in the evening, however, near sundown, Longstreet did make an assault with a small force, gained some ground & captured a gun, but later abandoned both & fell back to his original position.

This attack cut no figure as help to Jackson's fight, & it is due both to Jackson & his men to say that these three divisions successfully held off four corps & one division (say ten divisions) from dawn till dark of a long summer day. There was said to have been bayonet fighting at some points, & at one place where there was a rocky hill & an old railroad cut & embankment Starke's[37] Louisiana brigade, its ammunition temporarily running low, defended itself partly by throwing stones at the enemy's lines.

Next morning, Aug. 30th, Gen. Pope thought that Lee's army had begun a retreat to the south. Some of his men who had been captured & paroled from within the Confederate lines brought reports to that effect & his reconnoitering officers confirmed it. It was ten o'clock before he found out any better, his whole army, meanwhile, recuperating from the severe fighting of the 29th. And, on his part, Gen. Lee believed for a time that Pope had either begun to retreat or was preparing to do so. He thought Pope's position & force too strong to be immediately assaulted but he was preparing to pursue vigorously at the earliest moment. About noon Pope, realizing that there was still the bulk of Lee's force before him, formed a powerful assaulting force practically comprising the whole of his army of five corps & one extra division & moved upon Jackson's position. The heavy lines & columns made a magnificent sight as they advanced across the open fields, but their direction was such that from some hills in Longstreet's front they were exposed to an oblique, & almost an enfilading fire.

Longstreet saw this, & immediately brought forward all his available artillery, & opened fire on them. Since the experience of the Seven Days, Gen. Lee had begun to throw his isolated batteries together into battalions of artillery. Usually four batteries (three of 4 guns each & one of 6, making 18 guns in all) constituted a battalion, which was commanded by two field officers. But one of Longstreet's battns. was an unusually large one, comprising 5 batteries—22 guns—under Col. Stephen D. Lee and Maj. Del Kemper.[38] Col. Lee was an excellent officer, as may be guessed from his becoming lieut. general within the next two years. And the battalion itself we will hear much more of also, as I succeeded Lee in the command of it on his promotion early in November. Lee's battalion was conspicuous for its brilliant service upon this occasion. It had a beautiful position in easy range & the weight of its fire was very effective in breaking up the enemy's lines & columns. They endeavored to reform again & again, but were again & again broken & confused by the constantly increasing Confederate fire. While in this condition Longstreet's whole force of infantry was at last launched against them, & even Jackson's tired veterans also took the offensive. The enemy was still in superior force & fought well, but they were gradually driven back everywhere & before darkness ended the fighting they had lost from a half to three quarters of a mile of ground.

During the night Pope retreated across Bull Run. The next day he was joined by Sumner's & Franklin's corps near Centreville, but as Lee moved after him in pursuit he fell back toward Washington City. At Ox Hill on Sep. 1st a part of Jackson's forces encountered a strong rear guard & received a temporary check, but Pope made no halt outside of the strong chain of fortifications guarding Washington on the south. The following are the best returns I can find of the forces engaged & the casualties of this campaign.[39]

It is now but a short task to bring up the narrative of my personal movements & close the chapter of this campaign. I have already told briefly that I followed Gen. Lee from Richmond to Gordonsville with my big train of ammunition wagons, & moving there found the army gone, & that I followed after them but only overtook them after they had fought the battle & driven Pope within the fortifications of Washington City. I cannot now fix my place on the road at any single date. I recall passing through Orange C.H., fording the Rapidan, going through Culpeper C.H., & taking the road via Waterloo to Warrenton & passing that place. At Culpeper I heard of the fighting going on at Manassas & that I could take the straight road to Warrenton, & next day or day after I could hear the guns & from the top of one high hill saw the distant smoke of some small affair which occurred in the pursuit of Pope. I approached the battlefield by the Warrenton Pike, & a few miles before reaching it I came to the gate leading in to Dr. Marsteller's house, at which my wife had boarded in January & February. My horse Dixie had made many a trip to that gate & within it, coming from the other direction, during those months & she no sooner saw the gate than she recognised it, & at once proposed going in. I consented, anxious to know something of the fortunes of the family. On reaching the house, several hundred yards through woods & fields, I found it a hospital full of Confederate wounded. The family had all left & no one I saw could tell me where they were. Among the wounded I found General Charley Field, whose wife was my wife's first cousin, & she also had wintered at the Marsteller's house & had I believe the same room in which the general now laid with a desperate wound in the hip & scarcely expected to recover. He did survive but he carried the bullet for twenty years, & it was then cut out nearly behind the knee on the opposite side of its entrance, having gradually worked down as bullets often have a way of doing. His wife was staying at Farmville at the time of the battle & had a remarkable dream about the occurrence. I will tell her story of it to the best of my recollection, having very frequently conversed with her about it.

She dreamed of seeing her husband, with his brigade, out in an open field, fired on by the enemy & Gen. Field fell. He was carried to a house, &, the building being already full of wounded, was laid under a tree in the yard. Soon the surgeons examined the wound, &, believing it mortal, did little or nothing more than to examine, passing on to other sufferers where prompt attention might save life. He laid under the tree all night. A surgeon's operating table stood near & amputations were going on upon it all night, the sights & sounds distressing Mrs. Field in her dream very much. In the morning she saw the surgeons re-examine the wound & heard them say that if he lived ten days he would recover.

Next morning on waking she was much excited, & having some clothes out with a sempstress[40] being made she sent for them & began to pack her trunk. During the day news came of the battle & Gen. F. was reported in papers as killed. Other lady boarders at the hotel, hearing it first, sent for a Methodist minister to break the news to Mrs. F. As soon as she realized that he had come to tell her bad news she told him that she knew all about it, & insisted on being put on the next train for the front. At the end of the R.R. she was promptly forwarded in an ambulance, & she reached Gen. F.'s bedside several days before the ten days had elapsed of which she had dreamed of hearing the surgeons speak.

She and Gen. Field always asserted that on comparison they found a wonderfully accurate agreement of all the details of her dream with the actual occurrences. Gen. F. also mentioned in talking to her how he was himself distressed during the night by the proximity of the operating table. But she would not tell him about the ten day opinion until after that day had passed, though he had asked her specially, "Nimmie is that all you dreamed?" She would evade a direct reply, but after the tenth day she told him what she had dreamed saying that she would not tell him until the danger was over. He answered, "Yes, the surgeons did say that very thing, & I overheard them, & I was trying to find out if you had dreamed that also when I questioned you, but I did not want to tell you until the time was over." Before I get through with my story I shall have more to tell of Mrs. Field's wonderful warning dreams.[41]

After leaving the hospital I passed through the battlefield & rode over the whole extent of it looking at the ground. The wounded had all been removed & our own dead buried, & some of the enemy's, but there were still a good many lying about & the entire vicinity was deserted.

I received word somewhere & some how, now forgotten, not to follow the army towards Washington but to cross Bull Run at Sudley Ford, leaving the turnpike & turning up toward Leesburg, & somewhere in that direction I began in a day or two to meet our army, which having chased Pope within the fortified lines about Washington had now started up the Potomac to cross into Maryland, as is to be told more fully in the next chapter.

I will only close my recollections of this march with the last details I can recall. Among the first troops I met was Gen. McLaws's division, & somehow I was commissioned to deliver him some order from either Gen. Longstreet or Gen. Lee, but I cannot recall what it was. I only remember that he did not relish it for some reason &, although he obeyed it, he exhibited his distaste of it, which I thought at the time to be in bad taste. I think it must have required some extra marching for his men for I afterward got to know him more intimately, & to appreciate that few of our generals equalled him in his care for their comfort & the pains he took in many matters of little detail. It gave him the reputation of being slow, but he made up for it in having his division always in the best possible condition.

I remember also fording the Potomac at a ford I think called Edwards. I recall a little island near the Virginia shore, & all that day I rode in company with Gen. Semmes—him of the penetrating voice & the short temper. And we became, I think, rather special friends from that day until his death at Gettysburg, only then ten months in the future.

SHARPSBURG CAMPAIGN

The consternation in Washington City over the defeat of Pope's army was almost if not fully as great as that which prevailed when McDowell's defeated troops raced back from Bull Run. Gen. McClellan had arrived in person from the James River but a few days before, with the last of his troops. But as fast as they arrived all of his troops were placed under Pope's command & rushed to the front. Not to put too fine a point upon it, Lincoln & Halleck had believed in Pope, & had been prepared to shelve McClellan entirely as soon as it could be decently done. There is some reason to believe that political jealousy cut some figure in their feelings toward him, but his shortcomings as a general were enough to justify them in a desire to change, even though they had not been as fully exemplified at that time as they were soon after at Sharpsburg.

But McClellan was still very popular in the army, and now, in their distress, Lincoln & Halleck turned to him to save them. McClellan has written of it as follows:[1]

> Next morning (Sep. 2nd) while at breakfast at an early hour, I received a call from the President, accompanied by Gen. Halleck. The Prest. informed me that Col. Kelton[2] had returned & represented the condition of affairs as much worse than I had stated to Halleck on the previous day; that there were 30,000 stragglers on the roads; that the army was entirely defeated, & falling back to Washington in confusion. He then said that he regarded Washington as lost & asked me if I would, under the circumstances, consent to accept command of all the forces. Without one moment's hesitation, & without making any conditions whatever, I at once said that I would accept the command, & would stake my life that I would save the city. Both the President & Halleck again asserted that it was impossible to save the city, & I repeated my firm conviction that I could & would save it. They then left, the President verbally placing me in entire command of the city, & of the troops falling back upon it from the front.

The city really was not then & never was in the slightest danger; certainly not after the autumn of 1861, for now it was entirely surrounded with a line of fortifications impregnable by assault if defended even by the debris of a defeated army. With Pope's debris were Sumner's & Franklin's corps which had not been engaged. McClellan rode out that same afternoon, & at the outer fortifications met Pope & took command & gave Pope permission to go into the city. Poor Pope, that evening, was indeed an object of pity. He had gone up like a rocket & had put on airs & boasted what he would do. Now he came down like a stick, & his rival took his command from him on the road. He was afterward sent out to Minnesota to fight the Sioux Indians, who were committing massacres out there, & I think he bore no further part in the war. But there is one thing which may be said in Pope's favor. He was not afraid to fight his men, & when he did fight them he did his best apparently to get in all he had at the same time. And that was what McClellan never learned to do.

When Pope got into his fortified lines Gen. Lee turned his troops toward Leesburg. His army had acquired that magnificent morale which made them equal to twice their numbers, & which they never lost even to the surrender at Appomattox. And his confidence in them, & theirs in him, were so equal that no man can yet say which was greatest. And no old soldier need ask a prouder record than is implied in that fact. By going into Maryland Gen. Lee could at least subsist his army for awhile upon the enemy, & he doubtless hoped, too, for a chance to force the Federal army to come out & fight him under favorable conditions. And so, on Sept. 7th[3] Gen. Lee was at Frederick City, Maryland, with his whole army, & we laid there & took a much needed rest for man & beast for four days. And even that was scarcely enough, for stragglers were lining the roads, &, what with these & the killed & wounded at Second Manassas, divisions had sunk to little more than brigades, & brigades nearly to regiments.

I have two or three recollections of Frederick. For one I recall a delightful visit to a book store, & buying that charming book "Father Tom & the Pope," & a *Harper's Magazine* for May 1862 with a very amusing article upon caricatures.[4] And I remember some neighboring farmer with a delightful little hand machine for making fresh cider while you wait, giving me just all I could drink. And either coming to it or leaving it I ran across a little country pottery, the first I had ever seen. And I almost envied the potter the fun he seemed to have with his wheel, turning so many pretty things so beautifully. I bought three little dishes for my mess chest & when he figured it all up, carefully, at only 14 cents for the three I could hardly suppress my emotion. However, I handed him a nice new Confederate one dollar bill. He gave me for change one half of a one dollar Maryland bank bill, cut in two with scissors, to make it into change—25 cts. in silver, & he was trying to hunt up 11 cents more for me in pennies when I recovered sufficiently to tell him to keep the balance.

But it was from no distrust of the value of the Confederate money which I had given him, that I felt ashamed to take any more change. It was only that his prices were so low. I thought the Confederate money far better than greenbacks. I saw my first green-backs while on this very march from Richmond to the Potomac. I still had something to do with the secret service & a few hundred dollars of green backs was committed to me by the order of Gen. Lee for use as occasion required, & I disbursed it all by giving it to trusty scouts whom Gen. Stuart selected & handled. But I can recall the very slight respect I felt for the green paper, while our Confederate bills seemed to me as real money as gold or silver.

Frederick City always recalls to my mind Whittier's very pretty little poem "Barbara Frietchie."[5] But it has been abundantly proven that no such incident, nor anything even remotely resembling it, ever occurred. Gen. Jackson arrived at his camp near Hagerstown in an ambulance having been severely bruised by a new horse rearing & falling backward with him. He first entered the town the next day, Sunday, to attend church. A few days later, passing through Middletown, two pretty Union girls waved small Union flags at him, & his only remark was, "We evidently have no friends here." In fact there was an entire difference in the way in which the two armies used to regard such demonstrations of hostility by non combatants. I cannot recall a single instance where any of our men or officers ever regarded them as any thing but amusing. I recall a Chambersburg Barbara Frietchie who came out to the gate of her yard as my battalion of artillery passed through going to Gettysburg in 1863. She had a small flag which she waved vigorously almost in the faces of the cannoneers passing on the side walk. The wag of Parker's[6] battery paused in front of her for a moment & then jumped toward her & said, "Boo." Possibly some one said "Boo" to the original Frederick City Barbara but the story could have had no better foundation than that.

On the 9th of Sep., Gen. Lee issued a confidential order for a movement upon Harpers Ferry. There was a garrison of about 11,000 infantry & 2,000 cavalry at this place & Gen. Lee wished to capture them. He had talked of it with Longstreet but L. advised against it, saying that the men were worn with marching & scant rations, & that there was danger in dividing the army with the enemy near and in his own country. But Gen. Lee apparently thought that the bird in hand at Harpers Ferry was worth bagging any how, & Jackson, liking the idea, was given command of the expedition. I must say that I think the movement was, as planned, an excellent one. Easy to execute—involving no risk, so far as one could foresee, & the game was worth the candle. But two little things happened which rather made a mess of it. One was that, in execution, one feature of the programme was changed & in quite an important particular. Longstreet's division, instead of being halted at Boonsboro along with D. Hill's, was ordered on to Hagerstown. Here it was too far away when wanted, & could not be gotten back in time, as will appear later. The other little event was that a copy of Gen. Lee's order for the whole movement fell into the hands of Gen. McClellan. Usually the latter was so slow & cautious that there was reason to anticipate abundant time to capture Harpers Ferry & forget about it, before he would know what we were doing & where we all were. But here on Sep. 13th he received an official copy of Gen. Lee's order giving him the fullest details. It was a shabby trick for fate to play us.

I think that this is how it happened. D. H. Hill's division had recently been considered a part of Jackson's corps & orders were sent it from Jackson's headquarters. It was *now* to go with Longstreet—detached from Jackson. And somehow two copies of Gen. Lee's order, dated Sep. 9th, were made out somewhere, & one reached Hill & was duly preserved, & the other was found in one of our old camps & was taken to Gen. McClellan on the 13th. Meanwhile on Sep. 10th we all broke up at Frederick & marched on our respective roads. I went with Gen. Lee's headquarters & Longstreet's & D. H. Hill's divisions on the Boonsboro Road. The rest of the army was split into three commands to surround Harpers Ferry on all sides—& all these were to be under Jackson's control. Walker's small division of two brigades was to occupy Loudon Heights, in [the] S.E. angle of [the] Shenandoah & Potomac. He crossed at Point of Rocks on the night of [the] 10th & took the height unopposed by noon on [the] 13th.[7] McLaws's division was to occupy Maryland Heights, north of the Potomac, & Jackson, crossing above, was to get possession of Bolivar Heights in the S.W. angle of the rivers.

It happened on the march that I met my brother-in-law Gen. Lawton, &, our roads lying together for a good many miles, we rode together for several hours in very pleasant fraternal conversation. He was now in command of Ewell's division, in Jackson's corps, since Ewell had lost his leg at Second Manassas. And he told me that he was the only division commander in Jackson's corps not at that moment in arrest. It seems that Gen. Jackson, at times, was something of a martinet—& this was one of his times. All, I believe, were arrested because Gen. J. had seen some of their men straggling on the march; & Lawton was in hourly fear lest Jackson might perhaps catch one of his men somewhere in the rear up an apple tree & send an aid ahead & tell Lawton to consider himself in arrest. But he got through safely & was one of the few of Jackson's generals with whom there was never the least unpleasantness.

And our army was indeed straggling badly. Provisions were scarce, but green-corn & apples were abundant. That diet, however, weakened the men, caused sickness & had much to do with the straggling. But Gen. J. very soon released his unfortunate generals, and nothing came of it, though I can recall that A. P. Hill's arrest caused a great deal of talk. Possibly Gen. Lee may have smoothed matters down or possibly Gen. Jackson saw the point of Gen. Early's reply; who, when he received a note with Gen. Jackson's compliments, & desiring to know why he saw so many stragglers in rear of Early's division that day, answered with his own compliments that it was probably because Gen. Jackson rode in rear of the division.

We camped that night, I think, near Boonsboro & the next day Gen. Lee & his staff not only went on to Hagerstown themselves but he took Longstreet's division with him, which as will be seen later turned out unfortunately. The only thing about the march which I recall was stumbling on a flock of beautiful fat young quail on a rocky, briery hillside, & getting an old musket & a few loads of bird shot I had picked up somewhere & killing a nice little mess of them. I brought Maj. Duffey's train with me & we all encamped on [the] south side of the town. We were there two days. The only incident I can recall was meeting Dr. McGill & his pretty daughter, strong Southern sympathisers. The dr. had once been arrested & it was said that the young lady had assaulted the arresting officer with a riding whip.

But meanwhile McClellan had discovered that four of our seven divisions had recrossed the Potomac & a fifth was down at Maryland Heights, & the other two were isolated at the gap in the Blue Ridge near Boonsboro, &, having 7 corps in his army, he sent about two to make trouble for McLaws & the other five hunted up Longstreet & D. H. Hill. It was even easier for him than he thought. Longstreet was at Hagerstown, fully 13 miles from Hill, & Hill's division was less than 6,000 effective men. Had Longstreet's men rested there with Hill & made some slight fortifications of the mountain pass they might have held their ground. So, early on the 14th, we were all hurrying back to Boonsboro as fast as we could while the smoke of D. H. Hill's guns from the mountain pass told us of the trouble he was having.[8]

I was riding with Gen. Lee when we came within a mile or two of the fight & some one discovered a small party of people on what seemed to be a sort of old tower on the mountain top about a mile north of the pass. There were some indications that it might be a signal party of the enemy sending messages of our approach, &, itching to have some personal part in a fight, I suggested to Gen. Lee that I might take a few men & go recapture it. He approved & had eight men sent with me from some brigade, I forget whose. I got in cover of some woods & then struck up the mountain side &, after a hard, hot climb, at last got up & around the tower (which seemed to have been built originally for a windmill) before the party on it knew of my approach.[9] But they were plainly all natives of the vicinity attracted by the firing & up there to see the battle. I was quite disgusted at the peaceful character of my capture & left them after seeing that the position gave no valuable view of the enemy's ground, & I pushed on to the front & right, towards the firing. At length I reached a point among some large rocks & scattered trees where the ground fell rapidly in front, & out in the green meadows about a mile away there was deploying a whole Federal army corps, the 1st[10] as I afterward learned. Rodes's Ala. brigade was a short distance in front of me down the slope & stretched a couple of hundred yards or so to the left. From some point about 300 yards I judged to my right, but hidden by trees was a battery, which I afterward found to be Lane's[11]—the Washington, Geo., boys, which was practising carefully with some three or four rifle guns at the Federal lines evidently preparing to assault us. They made some beautiful shots & several times forced portions of the lines to leave the fields & hide in the woods with shells bursting right over & among them as they ran. But there was not enough artillery to stop so large a body of men, & it soon appeared that their line overlapped ours so far that their advance would envelope our flank & turn it.

Meanwhile they sent out in front a long line of skirmishers from the Pa. Bucktails,[12] for with my glasses I could see the tail each man wore on his hat. These fellows came ahead sometimes running, sometimes crouching behind bushes, or fences, & Rodes's skirmishers in front began to pop at them, & they returned it & their bullets began to whistle & hit all about, though they were over 600 yards off. I was always an excellent rifle shot & I entered into the game with delight. I put all my eight men behind a big rock to loading & handing me their guns & began to fire at the rate of about 8 shots a minute. I don't think I hit many, for distances varied rapidly, & all had to be guessed, but I did distinctly see one fellow drop at my shot. And I drew a good deal of fire to my rock & have still preserved an old calibre .69 elongated ball which struck the rock in a few inches of my head. After awhile the skirmishers got into the woods where our line was & then I could only shoot at long range, 800 yards or over, at lines of battle which began to advance, & before long they too were in the woods & then Rodes's line of battle turned loose & it began to be a real hot fight. And after awhile I saw away up at my level & only about 400 yards away a heavy line of battle which had passed clear around Rodes's left flank & were now swinging around to take him in reverse. I reopened my little fire at them but only for a few minutes, for Rodes's men were soon falling back & changing front to meet them, & I saw that the enemy's force was so superior that the utmost we would be able to do would be to delay them until night, which was now fast coming on. So I now dismissed my little escort & made my way, to the right, to the main road where I found Gen. Lee. It was clear that we could not continue the battle at that point the next day. D. H. Hill had fought desperately but Longstreet arrived too late to prevent the enemy getting several vantage points. One of Hill's best brigadier genls. was killed, Garland.[13] He was engaged to be married to Sallie Grattan.

Gen. Lee ordered me to take my ordnance train by [the] nearest country roads to ford the Potomac at Williamsport & to come down on the Virginia side to Shepherdstown, where I would hear of him & the army on [the] Maryland side of the river near Sharpsburg. It was now after dark but near full moon. I hunted up my own wagon & Maj. Duffey & his train & lost no time in starting, & we marched all night, forded the river at dawn & then went on until near noon before we made camp not many miles from Shepherdstown. I shall always remember that night march for my first experience in really suffering from sleepiness. I would doze on my horse until I would suddenly almost fall from the saddle, & the only relief would be to get down & walk & almost go to sleep while walking. Only twice afterward in all the war can I recall a more wretched night—at Chancellorsville & on the retreat to Appomattox.

And it happened too, that night, that without knowing it I & the whole train ran a very narrow escape of being captured by a brigade of cavalry under Col. Davis,[14] who were themselves making a nocturnal escape from surrender at Harpers Ferry. They crossed our track & captured 45 wagons of ammunition of Longstreet's ordnance train.[15] And now I must tell what was going on at Harpers Ferry.

On the morning of the 14th the three commands sent to surround it were all in position, & each of them having signal men with them Gen. Jackson took command wig-wagging his orders. He seemed to think that there was no danger of McClellan interfering, for his first orders to Walker & McLaws were not to fire unless forced to, for he would summon the enemy to surrender & if refused would allow 24 hours for removal of non-combatants. But I think that the real reason of this proposed delay was because it was Sunday, & Gen. J. was always reluctant to begin a fight on that day.

Fortunately, as it turned out, for even 12 hours' delay would have lost us the battle of Sharpsburg, Gen. Walker was less pious, & he determined to get himself forced to fire. So he paraded some troops about ostentatiously until the misguided enemy fell into his trap & fired at them, & then his artillery opened & that gradually involved Jackson & McLaws also, & from 5 P.M. all cannonaded away merrily until about dark. Both Walker & McLaws had had trouble to get their guns to the mountain tops. McLaws only succeeded by putting 200 men to drag up each gun. And both, from their high peaks, proved to be too far for efficient work. But, learning by this afternoon's practice, both got advanced & better positions lower down during the night, & were ready for business at day-light. All this occurred while we were fighting at Boonsboro. And McLaws's rear too was found &

much trouble made for it by some of McClellan's men, so that he was in a very close place. And after night fell Davis found an unguarded road on [the] north side of [the] Potomac & he took his cavalry brigade & escaped, as I have already told.

So now we come to the morning of the 15th. We had really been driven from Boonsboro the night before, for this was about the one battle of all the Army of Northern Va. ever fought where we abandoned the field as soon as night would permit us. And Harpers Ferry had not yet fallen. But most fortunately our artillery had, during the night, all been gotten into good advanced positions, Jackson's as well as the others, & when they opened at daylight their fire was fairly effective. Still from all my experience of artillery fire scattered over a considerable territory, as it was here, I should not have anticipated so speedy a surrender. I should have thought it would take a day, or possibly more, to force a surrender. But, at 8 o'clock A.M., the Federal flag was lowered & a white flag raised by the comdg. officer, Gen. Dixon S. Miles.[16] Unfortunately it was not seen for some minutes by some of the batteries of Ewell's division,[17] & Gen. Miles received a fatal wound from a fragment of shell after the white flag was raised. He was an old army officer & had fought in Mexico & Indian wars. The enemy surrendered about 12,000 men, about 73 guns[18] & large stores of ammunition. The day was consumed in arranging the formalities of surrendering & paroling the men & turning over the property, & when night came Gen. Jackson started for Shepherdstown & all the troops were to follow him next morning, except A. P. Hill's division who were to stay until they had finished the surrender business & sent the paroled prisoners off. McLaws of course had come across from Maryland Heights, the surrender having relieved him from a very dangerous position.

So that now our whole army was back on the Va. side of the Potomac except Longstreet's & Hill's divisions. These could have been easily retired across the river, & we would, indeed, have left Maryland without a great battle, but we would nevertheless have come off with good prestige & a very fair lot of prisoners & guns, & lucky on the whole to do this, considering the accident of the "lost order." And that seems to have been, perhaps at first,[19] Gen. Lee's intention. For Jackson was first ordered to halt on the Va. side, but early on [the] 16th the orders were changed & he & every body else was ordered to come across the river to deliver battle. For the onus was on McClellan to attack. And this, I think, will be pronounced by military critics to be the greatest military blunder that Gen. Lee ever made. I have referred to it briefly once before, but I will give the reasons now more fully.

In the first place Lee's inferiority of force was too great to hope to do more than to fight a sort of drawn battle. Hard & incessant marching, & camp diseases aggravated by irregular diet, had greatly reduced his ranks,

& I don't think he mustered much if any over 40,000 men. McClellan had over 87,000,[20] with more & better guns & ammunition, &, besides that, fresh troops were coming to Washington & being organised & sent him almost every day. A drawn battle, such as we did actually fight, was the best *possible* outcome one could hope for. Even that we only accomplished by the Good Lord's putting it into McClellan's heart to keep Fitz John Porter's corps entirely out of the battle, & Franklin's nearly all out. I doubt whether many hearts but McClellan's would have accepted the suggestions, even from a Divine source. For Common Sense was just shouting, "Your adversary is backed against a river, with no bridge & only one ford, & that the worst one on the whole river. If you whip him now, you destroy him utterly, root & branch & bag & baggage. Not twice in a life time does such a chance come to any general. Lee for once has made a mistake, & given you a chance to ruin him if you can break his lines, & such game is worth great risks. Every man must fight & keep on fighting for all he is worth."

For no military genius, but only the commonest kind of every day common sense, was necessary to appreciate that. It has seemed to me strange that no writer on the subject, that I have ever seen, has noticed the characteristics of the ford by which Jackson, Walker, & McLaws all crossed to reach Sharpsburg & by which alone the whole army retreated on the night of the 18th.

The river, along here, is paralled by the C&O Canal on the Maryland shore, the tow path being on the bank between the two. At Shepherdstown there had been a fine bridge, on stone piers, but it had been burned long before. This little sketch, from memory, shows [the] situation. [Figure 18 appears here in the manuscript.] The ford was about one mile[21] below the town, at Boteler's Mill; the road to reach it ran along the face of high bluffs much of the distance, & in many places was so narrow that a horseman, I know by experience, could not easily pass a wagon. The ford itself was deep & rocky.[22] On the Maryland side rolling hills gave room for no end of guns which could command the roads on both [the] Va. & Md. sides, as well as the ford itself. A few wagons wrecked would block the road completely at many points. But it requires no argument to see that no army could retreat over such a road as that under fire. And every feature of the whole business was well known to the Federals. In addition to all this it must be borne in mind also that our whole army was not yet united. A. P. Hill's division was still at Harpers Ferry. And, as a matter of fact, it will be seen that it did not reach the field until about the last minute possible to arrive & save the battle. When all these facts are considered I think no one will deny that Ives had not been very far wrong when he said that audacity's name was Lee.

So now on the morning of the 16th we have everybody crossing back into Md. to join Longstreet & D. H. Hill, who had taken position behind

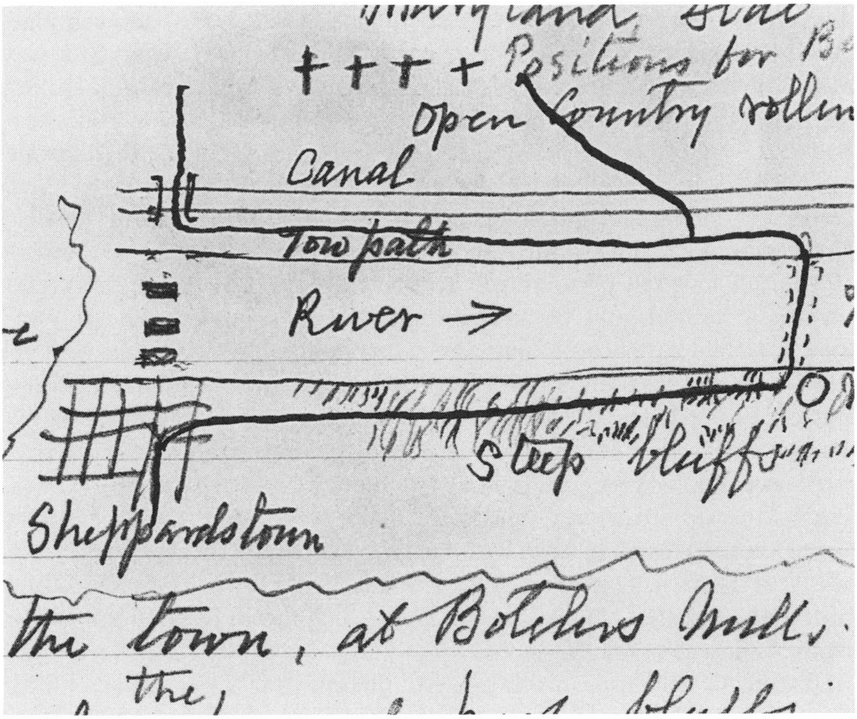

Figure 18. Potomac River near Shepherdstown

Antietam Creek, McClellan's forces beginning to show on the far side, & some scattering artillery practise at each other going on. And one thing worth noting was that our men had time to have done some quite effective little fortifying their positions, at some points, but I don't think a lick of it was done anywhere. But they began to learn very soon after, & in a year from that time they did not need to be told, but would build themselves very fair little lines with bayonets & tin cups, & using fence rails for a basis, whenever they saw even a remote possibility of a fight.

And now let me bring up the ordnance reserve train & the story may proceed. I left it in camp the night of [the] 15th, between Williamsport & Shepherdstown. I remember reaching S. along about ten o'clock perhaps, & I inquired for & soon met in the street my wife's "Uncle Gerrard," whom I had never met before, but who lived somewhere in the vicinity. I had time for only a short interview with him but it was very cordial & pleasant, the doctor (Gerrard Mason) being a most attractive specimen of an attractive class of men, the educated & refined country physician. He had been John Brown's attendant physician when the poor wretch, badly wounded, was tried, convicted, & executed.[23] After meeting Dr. Mason I left Maj. Duffey with the train parked near the town & set him to issuing ammunition to ordnance wagons of brigades & batteries who needed it, & then I rode across the river, by the route sketched, & found Gen. Lee with Jackson, Longstreet, Lawton, & others in a little wood near Sharpsburg on [the] left of the pike. Gen. Lee, immediately on seeing me, called me to him & ordered me to go in person direct to Harpers Ferry, & take measures to have the captured guns & ammunition sent back immediately to Winchester, except so much & such calibres of ammunition as might be suitable for immediate use in the coming battle.[24] I was disappointed at being sent off where I would not see this coming battle, which I had not the smallest doubt would be a great victory, & I hankered to have some personal part. But looking back at it now, & with a better appreciation than I then had of the situation, I must say I ought to consider myself lucky in having escaped the chances of that day. I had enough fighting afterward to satisfy all the regrets I felt at the time in losing its experiences, & had I been knocked over there I would have still been losing the lot of good things I've had in the last 36 years.

So I left the field immediately[25]—with no time to talk to any one or look at the position. I hurried back to Maj. Duffey's train, took from him all his empty wagons & emptied a few more, whose contents I knew would soon need to be issued, & started for Harpers Ferry that same afternoon. The distance is about 13 miles.[26] I can't recall where I camped that night but I was in Harpers Ferry soon after sunrise next morning, passing A. P. Hill's division starting for Sharpsburg near by on the road. My first care was to inspect all the ammunition surrendered, & select loads of most useful kinds to load my wagons & start them back to Maj. Duffey. It was scattered in several places, & quite a lot of it, too, was out along the lines in which the Federal troops had fronted Jackson on Bolivar Heights. Hill had left a quartermaster & Thomas's brigade[27] in charge, & he too had a fair supply of wagons, so I had no trouble in then loading every thing not likely to be needed at Sharpsburg into a wagon train for Winchester. I can only recall about the amount of ammunition surrendered that it was quite a large lot, but a part of it was ammunition for some 24 mountain howitzers, which helped make up the total of 73 pieces surrendered in all.[28]

Sometime towards four o'clock in the afternoon going along the line of the Federal positions, looking up scattered ammunition & small arms, I got on a high hill giving a very extensive view up the river, & I could see in the distance the clouds of battle smoke rising from the field at Sharpsburg, & even the small balloon like swelling puffs that showed where shells burst in the air. I cannot recall whether the sound was very audible or not. The direction of the wind would determine that. Neither can I recall feeling any apprehension whatever of defeat. Under Lee his soldiers thought that some victories might be better than others, indeed, but all fights would be victorious.

I think I encamped at Harpers Ferry or not far off that night & started back early next morning. I certainly returned by a different road & one nearer the Potomac than the one I went by. The country was more wooded & broken & I shall never forget a purchase of some ducks I made on the road. I came upon a very pretty farm house, on a hill, surrounded with shade trees, & big apple trees loaded with big apples, with a nice spring near by, &, near the spring, a big flock of the cleanest, prettiest, fattest looking ducks I ever saw. Even chickens are generally very scarce in the vicinity of armies, & as to ducks these are the only ones I can recall seeing between Bull Run & Appomattox. I immediately went up to the house to negotiate. There were no men about but a very nice, neat, bright-eyed matron of 35 or 40 came out to see me, & very cheerfully agreed that I should have six green headed drakes, just full grown, out of the flock. My wagon had come up & Charley & Abram soon captured the ducks. Then I asked her what I should pay for them. Fifteen cents apiece, she said, was the regular price, $6 \times 15 = 90$. I produced a dollar bill. Her face fell, & she said she had not a cent of change. Never mind the change, I said, but if she would let me I would pick a half dozen apples.[29] At that time I considered Confederate money better than greenbacks, indeed fully equal to gold. But as it began to depreciate later & gradually went down to fifty & sixty for one I have often felt worried about that duck trade, & wondered whether she still had that dollar, or whether she looked on me as a cheat. And if I had only known where to find her I would have sent her a gold dollar long long ago. About noon I got back to Shepherdstown, & there learned that we had repulsed all attacks on the 17th & that the enemy had not renewed their assault, but that Gen. Lee was preparing to retreat across the Potomac that night & that no one without special business was now permitted to go across.

So now, I will go back with my narrative, & will put in a little map of the field to make it clear & try & tell briefly the outline of the battle of Sharpsburg. [Figure 19 appears here in the manuscript.]

As has already been told, Longstreet's & D. H. Hill's divisions retreated from the South Mountain or Boonsboro battlefield on the night of the 14th, Sunday. About noon on [the] 15th they halted after crossing Antietam Creek & took position between the creek & the village of Sharpsburg, which are nearly a mile apart. The enemy followed them up quite promptly & appeared on the other side of the creek before dark. News of the sur-

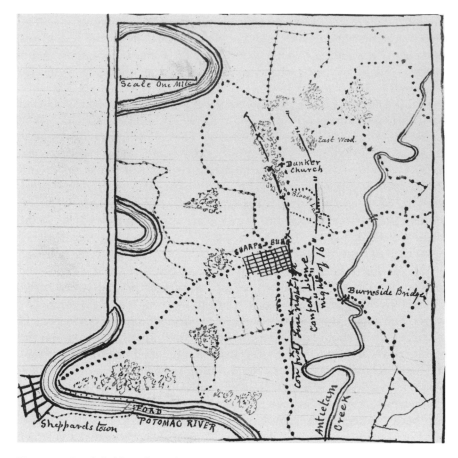

Figure 19. Battlefield at Sharpsburg

render at Harpers Ferry reached Gen. Lee that night. That was the time for him to have taken those two divisions & recrossed into Va. & saved the blood shed for no possible good on the 17th. Next morning 2 of Jackson's 3 divisions, J. R. Jones's & Ewell's under Lawton, were at Shepherdstown & after a short halt were brought across, & later Walker's division (of only two brigades) also came over. By noon an immense Federal force was apparent on the other side of Antietam Creek. Lee's right rested on this creek at Burnside's[30] Bridge a mile to the right & front of Sharpsburg, & gradually leaving the creek further & further in its front, it bent back toward a big loop of the Potomac. The line was about three miles long in all & the country generally open & cultivated, giving the Federals a fine chance for their excellent long range artillery from the heights on their side of the creek. And now McClellan's chance had come. He must have known that Lee's whole army was not yet on the field, & he should have begun his attack at the earliest moment & pushed it with all possible vigor & all his force. He did cross a considerable force opposite to our left flank but there was no collision until nearly sundown when Hooker's corps had a sharp fight until dark with Hood's division. During the night two of Jackson's brigades reinforced Hood.

Next morning, the 17th, McClellan's chance was still as good as ever. A. P. Hill's division was still at Harpers Ferry 12 miles away. McLaws's division had been marching all night & had halted near the river for breakfast. McLaws was forever afterwards called slow, because he did not come into the battle until about ten o'clock. I don't know the details necessary to pass judgment about his slowness, but when he did come his men were in good condition & did beautiful & successful fighting. Four of McClellan's corps were massed on his right on the south side of Antietam Creek—the 1st under Hooker; the 12th under Mansfield;[31] the 2nd under Sumner & the 6th under Franklin. These last two corps were the two which reached Pope too late for Second Manassas. Opposite our centre was Fitz John Porter's corps, the 5th. It was directly on the creek at the crossing of the pike, with a heavy skirmish line across and with a lot of Pleasonton's[32] cavalry & horse artillery, all within a mile of the village of Sharpsburg which was behind our line. Burnside's corps, the 9th, was opposite our right flank, which rested on what was called the Burnside Bridge.

Had McClellan attacked along our whole line at dawn we had not the force to have withstood him long. He let us get through the day only by making partial attacks & giving us the chance to concentrate nearly all we had to meet each one in succession.

First on the left at dawn Hooker's & Mansfield['s] corps came on together. At first they forced Hood back, but reinforced by the rest of Jackson's command they were repulsed with severe fighting in which Gen. Mansfield was killed. Then Sumner's corps came in to help, & Gen. Lee was compelled to withdraw Walker's division which had been originally posted on our extreme right. They were hurried to the left, & our lines twice driven back were again advanced & restored. Then Franklin's corps was put in, & again the enemy forced us back, but just as things were looking very blue McLaws arrived. He was put right at them & again the enemy were driven back. After a while they made still a fourth assault, but they had been badly cut up & could no longer muster a force to drive us, from the four corps which had been engaged. And some congenital defect made McClellan keep Fitz John Porter's fine, large corps entirely out of action, though it stood there looking on about 20,000 strong within a mile of our centre.

After this fourth failure the fight on our left was allowed to cease except scattered sharpshooting & artillery fire, & Burnside was ordered to attack our right. There was very little left there but Toombs's small brigade guarding the bridge, & he successfully resisted for some time all efforts to drive him off, or to carry the bridge by a charge. But at length, two brigades being sent to cross at a ford a half mile below, Toombs was flanked out, & then Burnside's whole corps, about 14,000 men, crossing & deploying, Sharpsburg & our whole line of retreat seemed to be at their mercy. Only about 3,000 men including Toombs were available for the defence, & the Federals started a bold advance. But they had waited just exactly a few minutes too long. Hill had been marching from Harpers Ferry under whip & spur, hearing the guns & knowing how he would be wanted. It was said at the time that he used a rapier like sword, which he wore, to prick forward laggards until its point was bloody, but, whether that be true or not, he had made a very rapid march, losing a good many stragglers perhaps, but arriving in the nick of time with just the requisite force. When one thinks how glad Lee and Jackson must have been to see him in this desperate crisis it is easy to understand how his name should be one of the last on the lips of either upon his death bed. A. P. Hill's division included five brigades, but only three had arrived when he hurried them to D. R. Jones's assistance. They not only repelled Burnside but they followed him & drove him back to the creek. Toombs with only about 500 men had delayed him long enough to save the battle. It was now near sundown & that ended the hard fighting of the day.

I have given but the merest outline of it, but as a suggestion of many of its desperate details I will quote briefly from Gen. Longstreet in the *Century Magazine:*[33]

> With new troops & renewed efforts McClellan continued his attacks from time to time. The line swayed forward & back like a rope exposed to rushing currents. A force too heavy to be withstood would strike & drive in a weak point till we could collect a few fragments & in turn force back the advance till our lost ground was recovered. A heroic effort was made by D. H. Hill, who collected some fragments & led a charge to drive back & recover our lost ground at the centre. He soon found that his little band was too much exposed on his left flank & was obliged to abandon the attempt. Thus the battle ebbed & flowed with terrific slaughter on each side.
>
> The Federals fought with wonderful bravery & the Confederates clung to their ground with heroic courage as hour after hour they were mown down like grass. The fresh troops of McClellan literally tore into shreds the already ragged army of Lee but the Confederates never gave back.
>
> I remember at one time they were surging up against us with fearful numbers. I was occupying the left, over by Hood, whose ammunition

gave out. He retired to get a fresh supply. Soon after the Federals moved up against us in great masses. We were under the crest of a hill occupying a position that ought to have been held by from four to six brigades. The only troops there were Cooke's[34] 27th regiment of N.C. infantry & they were without a cartridge. As I rode along the line with my staff I saw two pieces of the Washington Artillery, but there were not enough men to man them. The gunners had been either killed or wounded. This was a fearful situation for the Confederate centre. I put my staff officers to the guns while I held their horses. It was easy to see that if the Federals broke through our lines there the Confederate army would be cut in two, & probably destroyed, for we were already badly whipped, & were only holding our ground by sheer force of desperation. Cooke sent me word that his ammunition was out. I replied that he must hold his colors up as long as he had a man left. He responded that he would show his colors as long as there was a man alive to hold them up. We loaded our little guns with canister & sent a rattle of hail into the Federals as they came up over the crest of the hill.

That little battery shot harder & faster, with a sort of human energy, as if it realized that it was to hold the thousands of Federals at bay or the battle was lost. So warm was the reception we gave them that they dodged back behind the crest of the hill. As the Federals would come up they would see the colors of the N.C. regiment waving placidly & then would receive a shower of canister. We made it lively while it lasted. . . . After a little a shot came across the Federal front plowing the ground in a parallel line. Another & another, each nearer & nearer their line. This enfilade fire, so distressing to soldiers, was from a battery on D. H. Hill's line & it soon beat back the attacking column.

When at last night put a welcome end to the bloody day the Confederate army was worn & fought to a perfect frazzle. There had been no reserves all day. But on the Federal side Porter's corps had hardly pulled a trigger & Burnside's was comparatively fresh. In view of this, it seems strange that Gen. Lee did not take advantage of the night & recross the river into Virginia. For he knew too that McClellan had reinforcements coming to him & liable to arrive at any hour. But with sublime audacity the only question he debated with his generals, when they met at his headquarters after dark, was whether or not he should himself attack McClellan in the morning. Fortunately for somebody he decided to stand on the defensive. But surely military historians will say that McClellan again threw away a chance which no other Federal commander ever had, before or since. For he decided to wait for the considerable reinforcements now within a day's march. And when Lee appreciated his game he saw that there was nothing left to do but to return to Va. So all preparations were duly made & during the night of the 18th the whole army recrossed without accident, loss, or trouble. But I have always been proud of the fact that Gen. Lee did dare to stand & defy McClellan on the 18th. It not only showed his audacity as a commander, & his supreme confidence in his army; but it showed that in spite of distance from railroads, & of the excessive amount of fighting in the previous three weeks, his chief of ordnance still had plenty of ammunition at hand.

When McClellan found Lee gone he sent a force in pursuit which came near the river & opened with artillery upon everything in sight on our side. Now among the things in sight was my ordnance train under Maj. Duffey, & their first intimation of danger was the bursting of Federal shell among them. But they got up a very lively movement in very short order, & got away without any serious harm, though several of the vehicles got holes through unessential parts. To meet this fire old Gen. Pendleton, Gen. Lee's chief of artillery, deployed some reserve batteries he had had somewhere on the south side of the river & this artillery opened upon the enemy.[35] But meanwhile the enemy sent two brigades of infantry across the river to capture these batteries, & they—having a very small[36] infantry support—had to limber up & save themselves by flight, & Gen. P. with them, losing 4 guns. News of the affair reaching Gen. Lee he ordered A. P. Hill's division to turn back & meet the enemy. Hill did it most effectually, driving them into the river & shooting them down as they forded & swam so that their loss was quite severe.

The reported strength & losses of the two armies in this campaign are as follows:[37]

Our loss in general officers included _____ killed & Lawton, _____ wounded.[38] Lawton was shot through the leg, the bullet passing between the two small bones below the knee. He suffered a great deal from the wound for a long time, one or both bones being injured. He was made qr. mr. general early in 1863 & thence forward had his headquarters in Richmond, where my other brother-in-law, Gen. Gilmer, had already been chief of engineers for some time. Both brought on their wives & kept house. And my brothers W. F. and J. H. were also located there—W. F. as chief clerk to Lawton, & J. H. in Gilmer's office. W. F. had remained qr. mr. of Toombs's brigade as long as Gen. Toombs was in command of it. But after his wound at Sharpsburg, which was a pistol bullet through the hand received during the retreat across the river in the night of the 18th, he went into the Senate & never returned to the field. Of the officers killed I was a very great friend of one G. B. Anderson of No. Ca. He was a six footer of fine figure with specially good legs which gave him a very graceful seat on horseback, & his face was as attractive as his figure, with brown hair, blue gray eyes & general good nature in every feature. I had gotten to know & to like him at Ft. Leavenworth in 1858.

Chapter

7

THE FALL OF 1862

The first camp which I can remember after we got back from Sharpsburg was near Stephenson's Depot, some 5 miles north of Winchester. Most of the time, it was in a meadow, a few hundred yards from the station to the northeast. We were in the immediate vicinity for about a month, though, toward the last, Gen. Lee moved out of the meadow, to a small wooded hill very near by to the southeast. But for quite a while his camp was within 100 yards of mine in the meadow, & I kept mine there until the army moved. The time was devoted to much needed rest & recruiting & drilling, & there were also I think some reviews. It was at this camp I think that Gen. Wolseley[1] of the British army paid us a visit. He ever afterward was a great admirer of Gen. Lee, & ranked him among the greatest generals who ever lived. And he appreciated that Lee was as noble in character as he was great. A dim picture arises in my mind of some review or parade which Wolseley attended, & of seeing there, on horseback, attended by some of Gen. Stuart's staff Miss Belle Boyd,[2] who acquired & cultivated the newspaper reputation of being a Confederate spy. I believe that once, when she was residing somewhere outside our lines, she rode into them & told of seeing some Federal troops pass her house; but that was about the amount of it all, & the information was most likely of little value.[3] Of course no woman could make an efficient spy, & the scouts whom we selected & sent on such errands were the best men, carefully chosen for special qualifications.

It was really wonderful how our numbers increased during this month. Brigades which had been reduced until they looked like only small regiments began again to look like brigades. Not only did the tens of thousands of stragglers left along the roadsides in our marches come back, but a good many fresh men from home came on, & were incorporated in the old regiments, & we began to feel that again we had an army. For our successful defense at Sharpsburg & our last day's defiance of the enemy had given us renewed confidence that we could not be whipped. Meanwhile

McClellan sat quietly on the north side, likewise employed in getting rein-forcements & supplies & getting his army in the best possible shape. He must be given credit for knowing how to do that, even if he never learned how to fight it. President Lincoln was constantly urging him, & on Oct. 6th even ordered him to "Cross the Potomac, and either give battle to the enemy or drive him south." But he always had good excuses for delaying a little longer, & we were able to stay where we were until the latter part of October.

Personally I was as pleasantly & as independently situated as if I had been a corps commander. In my own department I had complete control, & I marched & camped as I chose. And my fondness for shooting could not resist the temptation offered by the great numbers of quail which swarmed every where. I first began to shoot occasional birds with my revolver, & at last I had gotten an old rifle musket calibre .58, &, for shot, I would make Charley mash up bullets flat & then cut them into strips & squares, & with these I killed quantities of quail, & I nearly lived on them. While encamped in the meadow near Stephenson's I killed 120 in a single field of broom corn, close by, of about 2 acres extent. I remember Charley's coming to my tent one Sunday morning & saying, "Mars Ned, I was a chopping up some bullets for you just now, & the ginerl (Lee) come by, & he say, 'Charley, your Mars Ned can't never kill no birds with dem shot that you chop up on Sunday.' So I dun stop chop em today, but I'll chop em soon tomorrow morning for you."

Another bit of Gen. Lee's dry humor comes to me with my memory of his camp after it was moved on the wooded hill. I was visiting it one night & got into conversation with Col. Talcott on some mathematical problem, & we went to his tent to work it on paper. Col. Marshall was there, who cared little for mathematics; & after a while he produced a demijohn & pro-posed a drink. We told him to go ahead, & we would join him presently. He took a glass in his left hand & the demijohn by the handle in his right, raising it up so as to rest it behind his right shoulder. Then, raising his elbow, the neck of the demijohn came down over his shoulder, & the whiskey poured into the glass. Altogether, I don't think there can be any possible attitude of a man with a demijohn & a glass so utterly reckless & dissipated—so suggestive that the man proposes to drink all there [is] in the demijohn, by goblets full at a time, as that adopted by Marshall to pour out his drink. And as he poured a pretty stiff one, & looked the very quintes-sence of toughness, Gen. Lee opened the tent fronts & looked in—I can't at all recall now for what purpose. But I remember well how worried Marshall was over the incident, & how Talcott & I teased him, telling him how he had looked, & what Gen. Lee would likely do about it. And next day Talcott told me the sequel. At breakfast in the morning Marshall complained of a head ache, & Gen. Lee remarked that, "Too much application to mathematical problems at night, with the unknown quantities x & y represented by a demijohn & tumbler, was very apt to have for a result a head ache next morning."

Still another incident of this camp has been told me by Col. A. C. Haskell, who at that time was adjutant of Gregg's So. Ca. brigade.

I have before mentioned Lawton's telling me, on the march from Frederick City, that Jackson had all his maj. gens. in arrest except himself, & that he would probably be arrested too if Gen. Jackson should come along in rear & find any of his men straggling. Among those arrested then, or perhaps a few days before, was Gen. A. P. Hill, who was greatly loved & admired in his division, & particularly so by Gen. Maxcy Gregg, & there was a very strong feeling upon Gregg's part that Jackson was tyrannical & unjust. Now on this same march some of Jackson's staff placed in arrest two most excellent cols. of Gregg's brigade, Col. Hamilton of the 1st So. Ca. & Col. Dixon Barnes of the 12th.[4] Both were brave and excellent officers & the 12th Regiment was particularly distinguished for conduct both on the march & in battle. The circumstances of Hamilton's arrest I do not remember but those of Barnes's were as follows. The staff officer, riding past this regiment in the road saw men picking apples from a tree in a field by the road. "What regt. is this?" he asked, & was answered, "12th So. Ca." He called for Col. Barnes & ordered him under arrest. The fellows getting the apples did not belong to Barnes's regt. At Harpers Ferry, as the brigade was formed to charge the enemy's intrenchments, Col. Barnes came & begged to be released from arrest & allowed to lead his regt. Gregg did not feel that he could permit it, but A. P. Hill coming up took the responsibility & put him back at head of his regiment. The enemy surrendered just before the charge was to have been made. But when A. P. Hill arrived on the field of Sharpsburg about 4 P.M. on the 17th (having marched from Harpers Ferry since 9 A.M.), & charged & broke Burnside's fresh 15,000 men with Gregg's, Branch's, & Archer's brigades,[5] numbering under 3,000, it was the 12th S.C. under Col. Barnes who led the charge & the gallant col. laid down his life.

Gen. Gregg smarted under all this so much that he preferred charges against Gen. Jackson—based on these facts but in exactly what form I do not know. They were forwarded by regular course through Gen. Jackson to Gen. Lee. My story is growing longer than I anticipated but at last we get to the camp in the meadow. Gen. Gregg had heard nothing from his charges for some weeks, & while we were there he sent his adjt., Lieut. Haskell, to ask if any action had been taken on them. Haskell had just received a new overcoat from home & he got himself up as nicely as possible & rode up to the camp with his overcoat on. He says that Gen. Lee was standing outside his tent near a fire, it being quite a cool day in early Nov., & several of his staff were about, that I was one of them, & that I and one other fellow had on our overcoats. But he says that when he approached & shook hands with Gen. Lee the genl. said in what seemed to him a very sarcastic tone, "Good morning, Lt. Haskell, I am always glad to see my young men so well protected against the cold weather." Now I have always believed that the general only meant to be a little facetious & not at all sarcastic, but when Haskell returned to his camp he took off his overcoat & gave it to a soldier, & he never wore an overcoat again during the whole four years of the war, though for nearly two years he was in the cavalry & particularly exposed.

And now to finish about Gregg's charges. As soon as Haskell told Gen. Lee that he was sent by Gregg on that matter Gen. Lee grew very grave & took him into his tent. There he told him to tell Gen. Gregg that he, Gen. Lee, desired the matter to go no further, that our cause could not afford to have our good men in ill will toward each other. On that message Gen. Gregg dropped the matter & his charges were sent back to him through Gen. Jackson. And barely a month after, on Dec. 13, when Gen. Gregg received his mortal wound Gen. Jackson came to his dying bed & a last private interview took place between them which was surely a reconciliation. And Jackson himself had then less than five months to live.

But at last McClellan had gotten all the men he wanted, & could not think of any more supplies they wanted, & so he had to begin to get a move on him. Gen. Lee was waiting for him at Stephenson's Depot but he concluded not to go that way, but to cross the Potomac at or below Harpers Ferry & thus threaten Lee's communications. So about Oct. 27th the news came that McC. was across the Potomac east of the Blue Ridge, near Loudon. On this Gen. Lee himself, & with Longstreet's corps, moved to Culpeper C.H., but leaving Jackson still in the Valley. I, of course, came with Gen. Lee['s] headquarters, & camped near them on [the] S.E. edge of Culpeper after we got there, though on the march I went with Maj. Duffey's train by roads further from the front than those used by the troops. It was several days' march & glorious weather, & I recall it as a regular picnic. I little dreamed that it was my last march as chief of ordnance, & that I was about to exchange my charming position on the staff for one in the fighting line. The fact was that I was myself perhaps a little too good a Presbyterian, & disposed to let happen what would, as if all events were ordered by a Divine intelligence. So during the whole war I never sought either a promotion or a duty, but simply obeyed all orders. And I valued Gen. Lee's approval & good opinion far more than general reputation or even high rank in our volunteer army. For my highest ambition was directed toward position in our regular Engineer Corps, after we had conquered our independence. Perhaps my passive accceptance of whatever orders came was illogical, but it had its advantages, & I have certainly no cause to quarrel with its results. I had the whole four years of the war entirely free from any anxiety, or care where I was to be sent, or how employed, & I had, all the while, delightfully independent positions, congenial duties, & pleasantest possible associations.

On the night of Nov. 7th we had a severe snow storm, & next morning the snow was eight inches deep every where. My camp was on the edge of a pine thicket, the limbs of which were loaded nearly to breaking, & I had stayed in at some office work, when, about ten o clock, I was called on by Captains Moody, Jordan, & Woolfolk[6] of S. D. Lee's big artillery battalion. They came as a committee representing all the officers of the battn. & told me that Col. Lee had just been promoted brig. gen. of infantry & was ordered to Vicksburg, & that he had recommended Gen. R. E. Lee to appoint me to succeed S. D. Lee[7] in command of the battn., & he had recommended the officers of the battn. to try & secure me. So this committee had been appointed, first, to see me, & then to see Gen. Lee. As I was both complimented & pleased with the idea, & as I was prepared on principle to accept all orders, I thanked the committee very warmly & told them that Gen. Lee could do whatever he thought best for the good of the service. Soon after they left Steve Lee came to see me. He was a cadet lieutenant of my company when I was a plebe, was a splendid, handsome six footer, was always universally popular every where,[8] was a natural-born soldier, & was one of the few young men who afterward deservedly rose by hard fighting to the rank of lieut. gen.; & he & I had long been friends. He, too, came to urge me to accept the position, & I remember the line of his argument. He said, "The Battalion is about the biggest & the best in the army, & the officers are all fine fellows. The chances are that before long you will get some opportunity like I had at Second Manassas, &, with but little loss, render conspicuous service & get promotion. That fight is what has promoted me, & yet I hardly lost over a dozen men." "But," he added, "old fellow, pray that you may never have to fight another Sharpsburg! Sharpsburg was just Artillery-Hell!"

Of course I made him the same reply that I had made to the committee— & he also left to go & see Gen. Lee. In an hour afterward Gen. Lee sent for me, & to him too I said that I only wished to serve where he thought I could be of most use. "But," he said, "whom can I put in your place as chief of ordnance?" I answered that there was an officer in Richmond, in the arsenal there, whom I had never seen, but with whom I had been in almost daily correspondence, for months, upon the details of the army supply, & I had formed that opinion of him from his letters that I would most confidently recommend him as gilt-edged & highly qualified in every respect. There never was anything done more easily & quickly. Gen. Lee telegraphed

Richmond & Col. Briscoe G. Baldwin,[9] my nominee,[10] was sent immediately up to him. And the personal impression he made was if possible even more favorable than that his letters had made upon me. A broad shouldered handsome six footer, with brown hair & eyes & a presence & bearing which inspired liking & confidence, Gen. Lee never changed him, & he was chief of ordnance to the close at Appomattox. And the friendship which he & I had declared in our correspondence, before we ever met, was a pleasure all through the war. His fate afterward, alas, was one of the tragedies which closed over many of those who in the war were excellent & devoted soldiers, & whose lives had we been successful had every promise of prosperity. I have never known the details but only heard that insanity & suicide finally ended poor Baldwin's life, as they did also the life of Col. Corley, who was Gen. Lee's quartermaster during the whole time he commanded the army.

So the very next day I struck my tent & moved over through the town to the camp of the battalion, now to be known as "Alexander's," about a mile out on the N.W. side, in the edge of a large oak wood. And within a day or two I had installed Baldwin & turned over to him dear old Maj. Duffey & his train. But some of these times all of our ghosts will get together yet, some moonlight night, & march & camp & pick up arms & issue ammunition around those old Virginia roads & battle fields, just to revive once more the sentiments of those old days, which even our ghosts will love to do.

And now let me give some idea of my dear, my beautiful battalion. It was composed of six batteries. The Madison Light Artillery of Port Gibson, Miss., Capt. Geo. V. Moody, 6 guns; the Bedford Arty. of Bedford Co., Virginia, Capt. _____ Jordan, 4 guns; the Brooks Light Arty. of Charleston, So. Ca., Capt. A. Burnet Rhett, 4 guns; the _____ of Caroline Co., Va., Capt. Pichegru Woolfolk, 4 guns; the _____ of _____ Co., Va., Capt. _____ Eubank, 4 guns; & the _____ of Richmond, Va., Capt. W. W. Parker, 4 guns—total 26 guns.[11]

I was already acquainted fairly well with most of the captains in the battalion, from having frequently issued ammunition to them & gotten reports of armament, &c., so I did not go among them entirely as a stranger. Captain Moody, the senior, had commanded a heavy battery in works about Manassas Junction in July 1861. He was a magnificent specimen of physical manhood, over six feet in height & weighing about 200 lbs., straight & muscular, a large, strong face, blue eyes & no colored hair. He always dressed well & I think rather prided himself in a carriage & general appearance not unlike Gen. Lee's. He was a good soldier & disciplinarian, & needed to be, as his company was rather a tough one, having many ex-stevedores & boat hands from the Mississippi River. He & I were always most excellent friends, but he was not an easy man to get along with generally, & was often in more or less hot water with his brother captains.

One case perhaps I had as well tell of here, as I will not wish to stop at Gettysburg, when I get there, with any side shows. Various little things between Moody & Capt. Woolfolk had kindled feeling & a few days before Gettysburg some question, of precedence in the march, I believe it was, led to a challenge from Moody to Woolfolk, which was sent on July 1st while we laid in camp at Fairfield. Woolfolk accepted, to fight with muskets at ten paces at sunrise next morning. Of course I only knew of this afterward. Well that night orders came to march at midnight for the battlefield at Gettysburg & the duel was postponed until after the battle. In the battle Woolfolk was wounded & laid up for some months. Before he recovered Moody also received a slight wound & had a severe fit of illness, so that he had to be left near Knoxville & was taken prisoner. He was sent to Chicago & kept in prison nearly the whole of 1864. In the fall of that year Woolfolk was captured visiting his mother near Milford, Va., & he was kept a prisoner until after the war, when he settled in Richmond. Moody was with Prest. Davis shortly before his capture in Georgia at the break up. He then returned to his old home, Port Gibson, Miss., & resumed his profession, the practice of law. Within about two years, I think, as he sat writing at his desk one night, he was shot dead from the street by an assassin, who was supposed to be a man whom he had recently shown up in court to be a great scoundrel. And, within a year or two of this occurrence, poor Woolfolk was one of those killed in the noted "falling of the Capital" in Richmond in which, also, my brother-in-law Lewis Webb perished.[12] So the two men, Moody & Woolfolk, never met again after the time fixed for the duel.

Captain Moody was a native, I believe, of Vermont. He had a brother who was said to have been a prominent preacher at Chicago when Moody was a prisoner there.[13] And it was said that they quarreled because Capt. M. resented his brother's appealing to him to take the oath of allegiance to the U.S. & the brother resented his refusal. Woolfolk was also a very handsome & fine looking man—as tall as Moody, but of lighter figure, black hair & eyes, jolly, careless, hospitable, sociable, & always fond of a laugh. And he paid me the great compliment of naming after me a son born to him during the war Edward Alexander Woolfolk. And still another of my captains did the same thing—only it was a daughter & the name had to be kept in the middle, Nellie Alexander Parker.

No compliments which I have ever received in my life seem to me more worthy of pride than these proofs of my having won the esteem & some share of affection from as true & gallant men as these.

Of Captain Parker words fail me to express my high conception, both as a man & as a soldier. One could not be with him an hour & not recognise him as a man the law of whose life & conversation was Christianity. And it was not so much a Christianity of doctrine & belief, but one of doing & being. The whole of his doctrine & belief, that I could ever discover, was that if he died he would go at once to heaven, & that was only manifested by an absolute insensibility to danger in battle. It was not that he did not fear danger but there just was not any to fear. And one of his brave lieutenants, Saville, who was not a professing Christian told me of the captain's once actually reproving him after a battle for showing a coolness in action which the captain thought he had no right to feel. He said, "Saville, I don't see sir how you *dare* to expose your life as you do, knowing that you have not made your peace with your maker."[14] I have had him get up & come to me at night, when there might be some distant unusual firing, and ask permission to take some guns & go out to see if he could find some fighting, not that he loved fighting but only that he might be of some use, or "do some good," as he expressed it.

He was a physician by profession, & his battery was largely composed of boys from families among his patients. In fact there were so many of them that it got to be called the "Boy battery." He returned to his profession after the war & at this writing is still alive, & doing no end of good still, though not exactly as he used to propose doing it with his guns. But no physician ever lived, I believe, whose [*sic*] has done more charity practice than Doctor, Captain, & later Major Parker. And if I am ever closely questioned at Peter's Gate I shall promptly offer, as my best credentials, the fact that Captain Parker named a daughter after me.

Two of my other captains were only with the battalion a little while, Burnet Rhett and _____ Eubank. Eubank I think was elected to Congress, & was there the rest of the war. He was [a] rather stout, solid, farmer looking man, very popular at home & probably the oldest of all the officers. He was succeeded by his first Lieut. O. B. Taylor,[15] who was of only medium build, & plain & unassuming manner, but a most excellent & reliable gentleman. He really threw his life away, on the retreat from Richmond, but a few days before the surrender. The battalion was surprised on the march by a charge of Custer's[16] whole brigade of cavalry. Only Taylor in the lead was able to unlimber his four guns & fire a round or two of canister, when the enemy swarmed in among them. Taylor, called on to surrender, answered, "I'll be damned if I do," & was shot dead, firing, I believe, with his own revolver at the same time.

Rhett left us to go to So. Ca. as a field officer in some regiment there, & I know no details of his later history. He died, in Charleston, a few years after the war, & his handsome widow & children own the "Rhett's pond" place, near Flat Rock. When Rhett left there was some trouble about getting a captain in his place. He had two lieuts.—Gilbert, first, & Fickling,[17] second, & there never were two better, braver, more unassuming men, but neither of them wanted the captaincy. Gilbert acted for some months, but finally got Fickling to take it over his head, & they went safely through the war in that way, & no company ever had better officers. Fickling was about 6 feet 4 in. in height. After the war he was a machinist & locomotive engineer on the C.C.&A. R.R. in Columbia, S.C. So far as I know he is still living.

Gilbert has for many years been the oldest & most reliable conductor on the So. Ca. R.R., with his home in Charleston & highly esteemed by all who know him. That's all of the original captains except Jordan. Medium build, brunette style, pleasant face & manners, gives my recollection of his tout ensemble. He was promoted major before very long & was succeeded by his first lieut., Jno. Donnell Smith[18] of Baltimore. Smith was tall, & wore glasses. His was the most intellectual & cultivated mind in the battalion, & he was also one of the most conscientious & careful men in everything regarding his duty, & he was also a man of most refined tastes. He was not only one of those for whom I felt great admiration & liking, but one of those for whom I learned a real affection which will last as long as my very bones. His family is one of the oldest & best in Baltimore, & there was nothing but his own sympathies with our cause to lead him to share the hardships & dangers of the war. He has never married—a great pity—& he has devoted his life since the war to the study of botany, in which, particularly, I am told, in the ferns, he is the highest authority, & has the finest collection extant.

But I am giving, I fear, more space than I have to spare to these sketches of my captains & I must try & abridge, though the temptation is great to linger over individual memories of many men toward whom I feel, not only the ties of comradeship, but a sort of everlasting gratefulness because they fought under my command & fought so well.

There was also with the battalion a major, two doctors & an adjutant,[19] & in the course of time I got a quartermaster & a commissary. The major was _____ Lewis of the Confed. Marine Corps.[20] He had been, I think, in the U.S. Marines, & he was a very nice good-looking fellow, but he was soon transferred somewhere else & then I got my glorious Frank Huger. My adjutant's name was Smith.[21] I'll have to tell as I go what became of him, but I just want to say here that the only *real* adjutant I ever had was Joe Haskell, whom I did not get until the next July. But Joe Haskell & Frank Huger were the most loveable comrades that the Lord could make in the pattern of man. My doctors were Gray & Monteiro,[22] both excellent & capable.

Monteiro told a story which is worthy of record, & I will repeat it. It is recalled whenever I read of the pension list. He says that he was one of several men, sitting together in a hotel in Washn. City, & discussing the approaching war, about the time, in 1861, when it became apparent that war could not be avoided. Some one spoke of the immense expense which would attend it, & of the great destruction of property which would result. A man sitting in the party, but whom Monteiro did not know, spoke up sententiously & said, "Yes, but that won't be the worst feature of the war." "No," said some one else, "think of the blood which will be shed & of the lives which must be sacrificed!" "That won't be the worst feature, either," said the sententious man. "No," said another, "families will be divided. Brothers will be fighting brothers & fathers against sons." "That won't be the worst feature either," said the man. "Well what will be the worst feature then, my friend?" said one of the party. "Why," said the man, "the worst feature will be the damned lot of *heroes* the war will make. It will take this poor country forty years to get rid of them." That man was surely a descendant of the prophets, but even he foresaw only dimly. For he thought that forty years would end the calamity, where as they have nearly past & the numbers on the pension lists still increase yearly, & now reach near a million of heroes & heroes' widows. And the widows are going to outlast the heroes for at least a half century.

Another story of Monteiro's illustrates how the soldiers used to appreciate that it's an ill wind which may not blow good to some one. About midnight of the night after the battle of Gaines's Mill, Monteiro, having attended to all his wounded laid down in a fence corner on the battle-field to sleep until day-break. He noted the dead body of a Federal lying close by, but soon dozed off. The ground was hard & uncomfortable, & after an hour he waked & was a little disturbed to notice that his dead companion had turned over, & was now facing him when he had originally had his back toward him. It seemed a little uncanny, but Monteiro soon dropped asleep again, for perhaps an hour. Then he waked & now his dead friend had again rolled over & turned his back to him. This was too much, & Monteiro had about decided to change his fence corner when he noted the approach of a battle-field prowler who came up to the dead man, & felt in his pockets on the upper side, & then rolled him over to get at those on the under side. Monteiro said [to] him, "My friend, please lay that Yankee on his back, & turn all his pockets wrong side out, or else neither he or I will get any rest here tonight."

Beside those already mentioned one other of the lieutenants often acted & was finally promoted captain, Lt. George Poindexter[23] of Moody's battery. He was from Virginia & had been a cadet of the V.M.I., was a big fine looking fellow & an excellent officer. He survived the war & has been & still is a successful insurance agent at different places in the South, & all of my children will doubtless recall him easily. This will have to do to give an idea of my new comrades & surroundings. The younger lieutenants, the non commissioned officers & the privates were altogether as fine a set of brave, loyal & uncomplaining soldiers, as ever went on a battlefield. There was not a black sheep in the whole lot of them. Some of Moody's boys could not resist liquor, if it made itself conspicuous, but even then they were good-natured & took their little punishments like men, &, whenever it came to fighting, the whole lot did it to the queen's taste. Of all my earthly experiences the dearest in its memories and its ties, outside of those of family, are the memories & ties of the old battalion.

And perhaps I may as well tell here of one thing of which I am so proud that I want to tell it somewhere. The battalion, some months after my promotion to brigadier general, made an application to be given a permanent battalion organisation & to bear the name "Alexander's Battalion" as a permanent designation. There was thought to be some legal objection to permanent organisation, & it was not done; but I valued the application very highly as indicating that my affection for the battalion was reciprocated & I have always perserved the paper. One effect of the change was to bring me the promotion of a grade. As chief of ordnance I had the rank of lieut. col. I was now made colonel of artillery to rank as such from Nov. 8th.

8

THE BATTLE OF
FREDERICKSBURG

Within a few days after I had given up my position on Gen. Lee's staff & taken command of my battn. of artillery, news reached us that Gen. McClellan had been deposed from command of the Army of the Potomac & succeeded by Gen. Burnside. No one was surprised then, & still less should anyone be surprised now when McClellan's inability to fight an army stands out so clearly in the light of his whole career, & particularly in his Sharpsburg campaign. Burnside did not want the position, but took it with the advice of his friends, to keep it from being offered to Hooker; of whom the old army influence by no means approved. Burnside was a man almost universally popular, though few thought him, & he did not apparently think himself, any great general. In my mind his name is associated with "Benny Havens's" near West Point, for he was old Benny's greatest admiration of all cadets ever at the Academy. He had graduated long before me, & had left the army but old Benny was always talking, even in my day, of "Ambrose Burnside."

The Federal army gave McClellan immense demonstrations of affection in telling him good-bye, & he devoted a day to receiving them. The men liked him because he had them well cared for, & they believed he would never expose them in action unnecessarily, which was most certainly true. But there was no kick against Burnside. Burnside was understood to have changed McClellan's plan of campaign for one of his own device—McC. had started to operate on a line towards Gordonsville. Burnside changed direction to Fredericksburg. It was certainly a great improvement, giving him a water base & a nearer one, & chances for new water bases, if successful, as he advanced on to Richmond. But he lost his campaign, & his excellent chances, from the miserable slowness & hesitation with which he executed his first step. He had six army corps of infantry, over 100,000 men. Lee was with Longstreet at Culpeper with about 30,000 men, & Jackson was up in the Valley with about the same number. Our pickets held the line of the Rappahannock, & there was a regiment of cavalry, perhaps, and a field battery at Fredericksburg.

On Nov. 17th the leading corps of Burnside's army arrived at Falmouth on [the] north side of the Rappahannock opposite Fred. but made no serious effort to cross. The news came to Gen. Lee about the _____[1] & on the 20th Longstreet's columns began to arrive on our side of the river. Burnside could easily with his immense force have crossed & at least occupied the town & a fortified camp on our side of the river. His excuse was the absence of his pontoon trains but he could have torn down houses & made boats or forded plenty of men to have taken the town. And at that time our army was, indeed, dangerously divided; Jackson being still in the Valley. And he did not come down to join us until about Dec. 3rd. Of course my battalion came down with Longstreet's infantry from Culpeper, & I encamped it west of the Plank Road, a mile or so out of town, nearly opposite Mr. Guest's[2] house. I had been dined at that house, & also at Marye's, Stansbury's & Lacy's,[3] when last at Fredbg., with my wife a few weeks after our wedding.

Very soon after my arrival I was directed to assist Gen. Lee's engineer officers in locating & constructing some pits for artillery at various points along the range of hills overlooking the town & valley of the river. The idea was that the enemy was likely to shell the town at any time, & our pits were ordered to be located so as to fire upon their batteries, if they did. But, in selecting the positions, I persuaded the engineers always to advance the guns to the brows of the hills so as to be able to sweep the approaches to the hills if it became necessary. And this brought about a little incident with Gen. Lee which, in the end, I enjoyed immensely. One day when the pits were nearly finished I was with a party working upon one on Marye's Hill, when Captain Sam Johnston,[4] Gen. Lee's engineer in charge of the whole business, came up to tell me that Gen. Lee was inspecting the line man near by, & was blaming him for not having located the pits further back on the hill. He said, "You made me put them here. Now you come along & help me take the cussin." So I rode with him & when I came up Gen. Lee said, "Ah, Col. Alexander, just see what a mistake Captain Johnston has made here in the location of his gun pits, putting them forward at the brow of the hill!" I said, "Gen., I told him to put the pits there, where they could see all this canister & short range ground this side [of] the town. Back on the hill they can see nothing this side [of] the river." "But," he says, "you have lost some feet of command you might have had back there." I answered that that was a refinement which would cut no figure in comparison with the increased view, but he rather sat on me & had the last word, though I knew I was right & did not give it up.

Well, when the battle came on, Burnside's most powerful effort was made at that exact point, & the guns there never fired a shot at their distant view, but thousands of rounds into infantry swarming over the canister & short range ground, & contributed greatly to the enemy's bloody repulse. And a few evenings afterward, visiting Gen. Lee's camp, I took the opportunity, when the general was near enough to hear, to say loudly to Johnston, "Sam, it was a mighty good thing those guns about Marye's were located on the brows of the hills when the Yankees charged them!" I was half afraid the general might think me impertinent, though I could not resist the temptation to have one little dig at him. But he took it in silence & never let on that he was listening to us. I was however frequently put at location jobs afterward, &, thence to the close of the war, I never got but one more scolding (Oct. 7th, 1864) which I will tell of when I get to it.

Longstreet's corps at this time consisted of four regular divisions of infantry—Hood's, Pickett's,[5] McLaws's, & Anderson's, & beside these Walker's temporary division of his own & Ransom's brigades was attached to us. Each division had some artillery attached to it, & these division batteries had in the fall gradually been made into battalions, & these battalions marched with the divisions & fought under control of the generals commanding them. Gen. Lee had on his staff a so called chief of artillery, Gen. Pendleton, but at this period his duties consisted principally in commanding a collection of some nine or ten batteries in 3 battalions called the Reserve Artillery, belonging to no corps, but kept ready to reinforce either which should need extra help. Later this command was broken up, & Gen. Pendleton after that was more directly looked on as the official head of all the artillery of the whole army. We made returns to him & drew supplies through him. And, later, each infantry corps had its own chief of artillery who, more & more, took direct command of all the battalions of the corps in battle, as well as on the march & in camp. But, at this time, I am not sure that even the title of "chief of artillery" of a corps was used. At first it was little more than a title given to the ranking battalion commander. But in battle he occupied himself principally with his own battalion. In Longstreet's corps the senior artillery officer was Col. Walton, who commanded the Washington Artillery from New Orleans—three small companies manning only 9 guns.[6] His battalion & my 26 were called Longstreet's reserve artillery, & I made my returns & received orders through Col. Walton.

As I had had so much to do with selecting the line & positions I was practically allowed to choose for myself whether I would take any of the gun-pits on the line, in the approaching battle. But I decided not to take any. I never conceived for a moment that Burnside would make his main attack right where we were the strongest—at Marye's Hill, & I determined to keep most of my guns out in reserve, behind our left flank, expecting the brunt of the attack to fall there; but foot loose & ready to go any where. I thought he would try to turn our left flank on the river above Falmouth where his superior artillery, & a cloud of sharpshooters, on the north side could certainly destroy a part of our line near the river bank & enable his storming columns to make a lodgment. The ground is there yet to be looked at, and I submit that Burnside made a great mistake in not directing his attack there. I placed one light battery, Parker's, up that way, in the Stansbury yard & I placed Rhett, who had some heavy 20 pr. Parrott rifles, in pits on a high central hill near the Plank Road which overlooked our whole line & the plateau in rear of it, as a nucleus for a second line in case [we] were compelled to fall back or change front. The other four batteries I determined to hold in reserve in a little hollow west of the Plank Road whence I had roads in every direction.

Our pickets & the enemy's occupied opposite sides of the river in full view & short range but without firing on each other. It was the first time in the war, I believe, that this had ever happened. Before that they would keep up constant sharpshooting whenever they were within a half mile. But now both sides were willing to postpone killing each other until the grand struggle should be prepared. And, afterward, it became the general custom, to the close of the war, for pickets not to fire when there were no active operations on foot. So we built our batteries on our side & the enemy built a lot on his side, all without disturbance; and, beside our batteries, we very quietly constructed a good many rifle pits, on the edge of the town along the river, preparing to make it warm for them whenever they came to cross. As to the front of Marye's Hill, Gen. Longstreet says that I reported to him that a chicken could not find room to scratch where I could not rake the ground. I don't recall it, but very possibly I said something of the sort.[7] It was exaggeration, but the ground was so thoroughly covered that I never thought Burnside would choose that point for attack.

At this time the enemy got to using his balloons on us again. We had not seen them since the Peninsula campaign. Now he used two of them constantly, endeavoring to locate our roads & encampments.

Jackson had joined us from the Valley about the 3rd. On the afternoon of Dec. 10th I received notice that the enemy intended to move on us the next morning at day break. Stuart had had some scouts within his lines & they had brought the news. Orders had been issued to the whole army that two guns, fired near headquarters, would be a signal upon which all troops must move to their assigned stations. About 4 A.M. on the 11th, clear, cold, & still, the shots rang out, putting our 60,000 men in motion for their positions, & letting the enemy's 120,000 know that we were ready for them. Fredericksburg was the most dramatic of all our battles; the opposing hills & intermediate plain affording some wonderful & magnificent scenes.

And I expect few who heard those two cannon shot, that cold morning, and rose & ate & hastened to their posts by starlight ever forgot the occasion.

The town itself was held by Barksdale's brigade (four[8] Mississippi, & one Florida, regts.) of McLaws's division. McLaws was about the best general in the army for that sort of a job, being very painstaking in details, & having a good eye for ground. He had fixed up his sharpshooters all along the river to the Queen's taste. It was not expected that we could prevent the enemy from crossing but only designed to delay & annoy him as much as possible. Barksdale's men had reported, early in the night, the noise of boats & material being unloaded on the enemy's side, & long before daylight they could hear boats being put in the water & work commenced. But they were ordered to let the enemy get well committed to his work & to wait for good daylight before opening fire. Meanwhile, the guns which served as a signal to us, were also taken as a signal by most of the population of Fredericksburg to abandon the town. By every road there came numbers generally on foot, with carts loaded with bedding, &c. preparing to encamp in the woods back of our lines until the battle was over. The woods were full of them, mostly women & children. A few persons remained in the town, & though it was severely shelled, as will be told presently, no one I think was killed. But Gen. Couch, in the *Century,* speaks of the Federal soldiers looting the houses, & implies that no objection was offered by the officers.[9]

Soon after day there rose from the river the merry popping of Barksdale's rifles. He had waited patiently until the light was good & the enemy getting careless, & he then opened suddenly a deadly fire upon them which ran them all to cover immediately. They deployed a large force of sharpshooters to try & keep down his fire & opened with their artillery & made many fresh attempts to continue their bridge-building, but were invariably driven back with loss. Meanwhile the morning wore on, calm, clear, & cold, but a very heavy smoky mist, something like that of an Indian summer, hung in the river valley in the early hours, gradually disappearing as the sun got power. The troops were all at ease along the line of battle, & looked across at the Federal army grandly displayed on the open slopes & bare hills on the north side; & listened to the fight of the sharpshooters on the river bank, which rose & fell from time to time, & in which from daylight a few Federal guns were taking a hand.

At last, near noon, Burnside out of all patience with the delay, thought to crush out the sharpshooters with one tremendous blow. He already had about 170 guns in position extending from Falmouth, above, to nearly two miles below Fredericksburg. He ordered that every gun within range should be turned upon the town & should throw fifty shells into it as fast as they could do it. Then I think was presented the most impressive exhibition of military force, by all odds, which I ever witnessed. The whole Federal army had broken up their camps, packed their wagons & moved out on the hills, ready to cross the river as soon as the bridges were completed. Over 100,000 infantry were visible, standing apparently in great solid squares upon the hilltops, for a space of three miles, scattered all over the slopes were endless parks of ambulances, ordnance, commissary, quartermaster & regimental white-topped wagons, also parked in close squares & rectangles, & very impressive in the sense of order & system which they conveyed. And still more impressive to military eyes though less conspicuous & showy were the dark colored parks of batteries of artillery scattered here & there among them. Then, in front, was the three mile line of angry blazing guns firing through white clouds of smoke & almost shaking the earth with their roar. Over & in the town the white winkings of the bursting shells reminded one of a countless swarm of fire-flies. Several buildings were set on fire, & their black smoke rose in remarkably slender, straight, & tall columns for two hundred feet, perhaps, before they began to spread horizontally & unite in a great black canopy. And over the whole scene there hung, high in the air, above the rear of the Federal lines, two immense black, captive balloons, like two great spirits of the air attendant on the coming struggle.

To all this cannonade not one of our guns replied with a single shot! We were saving every single round[10] of ammunition we had for the infantry struggle which we knew would come.[11] I had come forward to Marye's Hill to watch events & I sat there quietly & took it all in. And I could not but laugh out heartily, at times, to catch in the roar of the Federal guns the faint drownded pop of a musket which told that Barksdale's men were still in their rifle pits & still defiant. The contrast in the noises the two parties were making was very ludicrous. In fact the sharpshooters scattered in their pits were very little hurt. The one casualty which was severe was caused by the falling of the chimney of Mr. Roy Mason, Jr.'s, house, which fell upon a Mississippi company held in reserve behind the house, and killed, I was told, seven, who were buried in the yard.[12] But when Burnside advanced his bridge-builders again, on the cessation of the cannonade they were driven back just as promptly as before.

Then the Federals, at last, resorted to what they should have done at first, before daylight in the morning. They ran two or three regiments down into the pontoon boats, & rowed across. They suffered some loss of course but, as the boats drew near our shore, they got under cover of the bank & out of fire. The rest was easy: to form under cover & then take the pits singly and in flank. But Barksdale was now ready to withdraw anyhow. Two or three miles below the town, where there was no cover on our shore, the Federals had already completed a bridge, & were crossing in force. So Barksdale was now ordered to withdraw back out of the town, which he did very succesfully, having however a few isolated men cut off & captured. And so the whole day passed with no more fighting, & at night everything slept on the line of battle. I recall that the night was very cold & indeed the cold spell lasted throughout the battle. I was told that there were one or two cases of pickets without fire being frozen to death (one in [the] 15th So. Ca.).[13]

The next day was rather uneventful. It was entirely occupied by Burnside in crossing over his army & ours lay quietly on its arms. We could not attack him, for our advance would have been swept by his artillery on the north side, besides which the ground he occupied near the river was also very strong & favorable for defense. Our rifle guns however would fire occasionally at bodies of infantry exposing themselves within range & the enemy's batteries would retaliate at them; & the opposing picket lines in the valley had bullets to spare for any body who would show himself within a thousand yards. Joe Haskell joined me & offered his services as an aid which I gladly availed myself of, & found him exceedingly useful as well as a delightful companion. Our friendship, commenced then, has only grown closer every day since.

Again we slept in position & then dawned Saturday the 13th, which we all knew would bring the struggle. In the early morning all the valley was shrouded in the strange sort of Indian summer mist before referred to. About 9 o'clock the heights on each side became visible & perhaps about ten the plain could be seen from the hills. Infantry pickets & sharpshooters all along the line began firing as soon as they could see, and the Federal heavy batteries from the hills north of the river began to feel for us also. We let them do most of the shooting, but occasionally Rhett's 20 pr. Parrots, or a Whitworth rifle of Lane's battery (the company from Washington, Geo.), from a high hill on our left—or some other rifle gun which got a chance, would try a shot at something offering an attractive target. But we devoted very little fire to their batteries.[14]

Some half mile to the rear and a little to the right of Marye's Hill was a very high & commanding hill called Telegraph Hill (afterwards Lee's Hill) overlooking the entire field down to Hamilton's Crossing—five miles away—where Jackson's right flank rested. Gen. Lee made his headquarters on this hill, & on it were some half a dozen, or more, guns in scattered pits. And among these guns were two 30 pr. Parrot rifles. It was the only time in the war that we ever had such heavy guns in the field. They were, however, the right things in the right place here, & filled a great want, until they, unfortunately, both exploded towards the middle of the day, one at the 37th round & one at the 42nd. At one of the explosions Genls. Lee & Longstreet & many staff officers were standing very near, & fragments flew all about them, but none was hurt. And, to finish with these guns, one of these

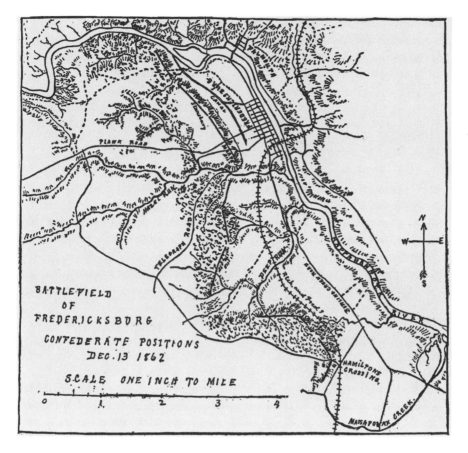

Figure 20. Battlefield at Fredericksburg

fragments furnished a good story on a green youngster serving on Pickett's staff. He had brought a message to Gen. Lee & he saw the base of one of these large guns, with all in front of the trunnions blown away. He told Gen. P. that "the Yankees had thrown the biggest shell at Gen. Lee that he ever saw. It was about 6 feet long & three feet in diameter with two knobs on one end as thick as his leg & it must weigh over two thousand pounds."

About ten o'clock, the firing in Jackson's front began to indicate serious battle. From Gen. Lee's hill the enemies' lines of battle, preceded by a heavy skirmish line & accompanied with many batteries, could be seen advancing across the plain upon Jackson's position on the wooded hills about Hamilton's Crossing. And there was one very petty little incident. "Sallie" Pelham,[15] as we called him at West Point, major commanding Stuart's horse artillery, was with our cavalry upon the enemy's left flank. When their long lines of infantry advanced & when Pelham found himself almost in their prolongation the temptation to enfilade them was irresistible. With only two guns he galloped forward to where an old gate stood on a small knoll & opened fire on them & soon began to produce a good deal of confusion & delay. They brought up battery after battery to crush him, until he sustained the fire of six 6 gun batteries, when he retired without much damage. Gen. Lee told of the action in a dispatch to Richmond that night[16] in which he spoke of "the gallant Pelham," by which name his memory is still dear to all survivors of the Army of Northern Virginia. Poor fellow, he was killed in the April following, charging with a cavalry squadron, up on the Rapidan, just before Chancellorsville.[17] He was a very young looking, handsome, & attractive fellow, slender, blue eyes, light hair, smooth, red & white complexion, & with such a modest & refined expression that his classmates & friends never spoke of him but as "Sallie" and there never was a Sallie whom a man could love more!

Having started on Jackson's fight I will finish it before I take up Long-street's, for the two were entirely distinct. As the Federals advanced, in three lines of battle after the little Pelham episode, Jackson's artillery along his whole line opened on them very effectively. They developed a very heavy artillery fire in reply, & their infantry pushed on in very handsome[18] style & making a fine show. But, when they came near enough to receive Jackson's infantry fire, their advance was checked. Several efforts were made to push them on but all failed except at one point upon the line of A. P. Hill's division. I have never known exactly how it came about, but his second brigade from the right, Gregg's, was not in the line between Archer's, the first, & Thomas's, the 3rd, but was back some 200 or 300 yards in the woods, which were quite swampy where the straight line would have been. The error was probably due to the fact that a considerable part of Jackson's force had only arrived that morning from Port Royal, 18 miles below Fredericksburg, where Burnside had been making some demonstrations. So the character of the field was not thoroughly known to all of his officers.

It happened that Meade's[19] division had the luck to strike that soft spot where it met no infantry fire, & of course it went in. Naturally Archer & Thomas soon began to crumble away on the left flank of Archer & the right of Thomas. Gregg, in the rear, did not seem to know the gap existed, for when the advancing Federals surprised his brigade he thought they were friends & was actually trying to stop his men from firing upon them when he received his mortal wound. Some of the men, & officers too, of Archer's right—finding their left falling back, at first actually fired upon the fugitives, believing that they were deserting their posts without cause. A severe fight now took place in the woods. Gibbon's division, & part of Birney's,[20] reinforced Meade. But Jackson had Early's division in reserve &

sent it to repair the breach. They struck like a cyclone & not only whirled the enemy—all of them—out of the woods, but pursued him far out into the plain across the railroad & toward his bridges. That was the end of the battle on the right. After that there was nothing but sharpshooting & some shelling. Gen. Jackson did propose a night attack upon the enemy, & Gen. Lee gave him permission to try it, but after more careful study he decided not to venture it. So now we can take up Longstreet's fight.

About 11 that morning, I had gotten a little uneasy lest all the fighting would go Jackson's way & none of it come ours, for we were practically doing nothing, while the noise Jackson was making now filled the heavens. So I rode over to Gen. Lee's hill to find out what was going on. It took but a few minutes to see that we had no occasion to be jealous of Jackson's luck. The town was evidently already crammed as full of troops as it could hold, &, beside these, dense black columns still pouring into it, or headed for it, were visible coming up the river from below & also moving down to the bridges from the north bank. Evidently more than half of Burnside's whole army was preparing to assault us, & the assault too was not going to be where I had imagined it would be—up along the river bank—but it was going to come right out from the town, & strike where we were strongest. If we couldn't whip it we couldn't whip anything, & had better give up the war at once & go back to our homes. From that moment I felt the elation of a certain & easy victory, & my only care then was to get into it somehow & help do the enemy all the harm I could.

And, very soon, I thought I saw a good chance. I got glimpses of a heavy column of infantry on the north side evidently in motion across a bridge and into the town. My knowledge of the town made me quite sure that they would march up a certain street. Intervening hills, trees, &c. would prevent my seeing even the tops of the houses on the sides of the street, but they would not prevent my cannon shot from a distance flying high over those obstacles & then coming down in the street & bouncing along it where they would meet that advancing column. In fact all three streets must have been full of men anyhow. The only question was whether we could afford to use ammunition in that way, where it could, indeed, worry the enemy & kill some of them, but yet where we could not certainly know what we were doing, & where there was no special issue to be determined.

While I was debating this in my mind I saw a long line of battle advance from the eastern side of the town toward Marye's Hill. A long cut of an unfinished railroad ran obliquely across the open ground they had to cross. They were evidently receiving some long range infantry fire, & also a few shells, & as they came up to this railroad cut, say ten feet deep, the whole brigade of them swarmed into it. They had hardly done so when one of the 30 pr. Parrott guns, right by me, roared out, & I saw the bloodiest shot I ever saw in all my life. The gun exactly enfiladed the cut & it sent its shell right into the heart of the blue mass of men where it exploded. I think it could not have failed to kill or wound as many as 20 men. The sight of that shot excited me so that I felt bound to have some share, so I determined to send forty shot, anyhow, down that street. So I did not wait to see any more, but started for my battalion to get Moody's Napoleons for the job. After a little reconnoitering I was able to locate them upon the prolongation of the street leading to the bridge & then we fired the forty shots at an elevation to take them nearly to the river. What harm they did, of course, we could not tell, but there were lots of people about where they fell & bounced. The enemy's batteries across the river opened on us & dropped some of their shell very close, but we had no one hurt.

Meanwhile Burnside had ordered his troops in Fredericksburg to carry Marye's Hill. Of his six corps of infantry, two were already in the town, & two more, just below, were brought up during the action which followed. Our line here was held by McLaws's division, with three brigades in line of battle at the foot of the hill: Cobb's[21] Georgians; Kershaw's South Carolinians; & Barksdale's Mississippians, in order from left to right[22] with Semmes's Georgians in reserve. Walker with his own & Ransom's brigade were also in reserve close by in the rear. The Washington Artillery, 9 guns, were in the pits above & also near the Plank Road was Maurin's battery—4 guns of Cabell's battalion.[23] A sunken road, for a part of the way, gave the infantry a beautiful line, &, where that was lacking, McLaws, with his usual painstaking care & study of detail, had utilized ditches & dug trenches & provided for supplies of water & of ammunition & care of the wounded. But there was one feature of the ground which was very favorable to the enemy. There was a little sort of flat ravine running parallel to our position, & about four hundred yards in front of it, in which there was perfect cover from our sight & direct fire, for twenty thousand men or more, & this covered ground could be reached without any serious difficulty.

So the military dimensions of the task were as follows—to charge out of cover, over 400 yards of open ground, broken by a few scattered houses & garden fences, under the direct fire of fourteen guns & three brigades of infantry (say 5,000 muskets)—mostly under cover of pits & walls or trenches. To be sure there were in reserve, behind, three more brigades of infantry & say 22 guns—four of them in pits, but the rest, & the infantry, would have had to fight out in the open. But these reserves were not found necessary to repel the attacks, although toward the last, one brigade of them, Cooke's North Carolina, was brought into action. Had the case been reversed I cannot believe but that the morale of the Army of Northern Virginia would at least have taken them over the guns at the first dash. The difficulties do not begin to compare with what our men went through at either Malvern Hill or Gettysburg, where we went over the guns at the first go, charging those times as far & against five times as many men & guns.[24] I don't wish to seem to brag about our men unduly, but I think that any professional military critic will say that that ravine ought to have enabled the Federals to, at least, have crossed bayonets with us. As it was, none of their lines of battle came within 75 yards,[25] though a few officers & individuals got up nearer—the nearest to about 30 yards.

The first assault was made by a column of 6 brigades who advanced from the ravine above mentioned, each one after the first letting the one in advance get 200 yards' start. Practically every brigade broke up & retreated at or about the 100 yards line: which was where our infantry fire began to get in its full strength. For our men would not fire at long range but would purposely let them get nearer. The fugitives crowded behind the scattered houses, fences and in little depressions here & there, whence they fired back at our guns & line of battle. There were enough of them to keep the air, as it were, swarming with bullets, but the pits & banks enabled us to hold on in spite of them. Meanwhile, too, their siege guns, from the north bank, concentrated & pounded at us, their very best & heaviest, but we just paid no attention to them & let them shoot. One of them however killed Gen. T. R. R. Cobb, with a fragment of shell, smashing his thigh. He was a great loss to us. A man more brave, noble, & lovely in character & disposition, never lived, & he was making his mark as a soldier as rapidly as he had made it in civil & political life before the war.

It is not necessary to go into detail as to the different Federal charges, & how they brought up reinforcements, & made a number of efforts, but none of them any stronger or more serious looking, to us, than the first. A popular impression has seemed to prevail that the Irish Brigade of Thomas Francis Meagher exceeded all others in its dash & gallantry. But while it may be true that his men went as far as the farthest, Gen. Meagher's official report of the battle shows that personally he was not in the charge, but that as it began he "being lame" started back to town to get his horse & he was soon joined in town by the remnants of his brigade whom he led back to the river bank.[26]

So the battle in front of Marye's Hill would occasionally rise to the intensity of a charge, & decrease to severe sharpshooting & more or less shelling, from about noon till late in the afternoon. About half past three a note came to me from Col. Walton saying that the Washington Artillery was nearly out of ammunition, & calling upon me to relieve it with an equal number of guns from my battalion. Had I not been new to my command, I would have proposed to send in ammunition, & men too, if necessary, but to object to the exposure necessary of both his teams & mine in his gun's being withdrawn & my guns going in. For all the pits were in open ground & some were a little troublesome to get to. But it was my first fight in command of troops, & I was only too glad of the chance to get into those pits, & I determined at once, not only to go, but, once there, to stay to the end of the fight, if it were a week. So I at once selected 9 guns—Woolfolk's 4, Donnell Smith 2, & 3 of Moody's—& started with them for Marye's.

As we came up to the Plank Road, I asked Joe Haskell to ride up to Rhett's battery, which was firing at the time right over the route we had to take, & order it to stop until we passed; as its shells sometimes exploded prematurely. As he spurred ahead we both saw a Parrott shell from the enemy coming which had struck about 100 yards off & ricocheted & was now whirling end over end like a stick. I was just in the line of it as we could both see. Haskell reined up his horse expecting to see me cut down. I merely realized that I had no time to dodge, & wondered where it would hit. It passed under the horse's belly somehow—without touching & struck about fifteen feet beyond her. When we got nearly to Marye's Hill, keeping in low places & under cover as much as possible, the leading driver in trying to avoid the bodies of two dead men in the road got into a narrow deep ditch with both his team & the guns, & made some delay in righting things. Meanwhile the Washington Artillery ran up their teams, limbered up & came out. It was only a few minutes however before we were on hand & went in at a gallop. The sharpshooters & the enemy's guns all went for us, but we were emulating greased lightning just then & we got off very lightly, some 6 men & 12 horses, I think it was, only who were struck. Then we dismounted ammunition chests, & sent running gear & horses back under cover.

Up on Gen. Lee's hill they did not know that Walton had asked me to relieve him, & Gen. Lee, happening to look & see his guns coming out, thought they were retreating. He caught Longstreet's arm & said, "Look there, what does that mean?" Longstreet turned to Maj. Fairfax[27] of his staff & said, "Go & order Walton to go back there and to stay there," but in a few minutes they saw my guns going in, & then they understood.

Meanwhile it happened that the enemy had just brought up a fresh division under command of Gen. Humphreys,[28] of my old corps—the engineers, a splendid old soldier; and they were preparing to make an extra effort. Just as they were getting good & ready for the charge, back in the flat ravine, before mentioned, word was sent back to them that our artillery on the hill had been withdrawn. This raised their hopes, & Humphreys, to diminish the temptation to stop & fire, which is the bane & danger in all charges, ordered that his whole division should go with empty muskets, & rely on the bayonet alone. And so it resulted that we were hardly in our pits & good & ready, when there arose a great hurrah back at the Federal ravine

& there swarmed out some three or four long lines of battle and started for us in fine style. That was just what we wanted. Our chests were crammed full of ammunition, & the sun was low; so we set in to improve each shining hour, & get rid of as much as possible of that ammunition before dark. It was for just this sort of chance that we had been saving it up since the beginning. So now we gave them our choicest varieties, canister and shrapnel, just as fast as we could put it in. It was plainly a disagreeable surprise to them, but they faced it very well & came along fairly until our infantry at the foot of the hill opened. There were now six ranks of infantry for a part of the way, & their fire was very heavy.

Then Humphreys broke all up.[29] General Couch, in describing this charge of Humphreys's division, in the Century War Book, writes as follows: "The musketry fire was very heavy & the artillery fire was simply terrible. I sent word, several times, to our artillery on the right of Falmouth that they were firing into us & tearing our own men to pieces. I thought they had made a mistake in the range. But I learned later that the fire came from the guns of the enemy on their extreme left." This last fire mentioned came from Parker's battery near the Stansbury house. His line got no further than the others had come & his men scattered about, & laid down & fired from behind houses, but the charge was over.

And then, between sundown & dark still one more division, Getty's,[30] was sent in on Humphreys's left. If they had not started with a cheer I don't think that I, at least, would have known they were coming; for I could not see them, but only—when they began to fire—the flashes of their muskets. I was in a pit near the right with one of Jordan's guns, & we had almost ceased to fire for lack of a good target, when this disturbance began, & I ordered them to fire canister at the gun flashes. The gunner, who was a Corporal Logwood,[31] from Bedford Co., Va., aimed & stepped back & ordered fire. But I was watching his aiming, & I thought he had not given quite enough elevation to his gun, so I stopped the man about to pull the lanyard & told Logwood to give the screw another turn or two down. He stepped to the breech to obey, but as he reached out his hand there was a thud, & the poor fellow fell with a bullet through & through the stomach. We had to remove him from under the wheels, & then I aimed the gun myself, & fired until after it got dark when, gradually, the whole field became quiet. Poor Logwood lived for two days, but his case was hopeless from the first.

That was an awful night upon the wounded; especially on the Federal wounded left between the lines, where their friends could give them no relief or assistance. Gen. Couch writes of it, "It was a night of dreadful suffering. Many died of wounds & exposure, and as fast as men died they stiffened in the wintry air, & on the front line were rolled forward for protection to the living. Frozen men were placed for dumb sentries."[32]

I cannot recall at all when or where or how I either ate or slept during the whole battle from our breaking camp on the 11th. We probably had a tentfly & a fire close behind the line somewhere. The next day was Sunday & we imagined of course that Burnside with his immense force would make another & even a more tremendous effort somewhere. So during the night we filled up again with ammunition, & we worked some on our pits, strengthening & repairing damages, & when morning came were all good & ready. That Indian summer haze again hid everything from view till the sun got high, but we could hear commands & movements of troops within it, &, as soon as it was possible to see, a swarm of sharpshooters along the enemy's front began to make it warm for us. Their artillery also, from the hills across the river, began a regular target practice at us, slow & deliberate, & as nicely aimed as they could do it. Some of our rifles not so situated that they could get at a storming column would occasionally retaliate at anything they thought they could hurt, but all our guns, along the infantry line, got under cover & laid low, waiting for an assault which we felt sure would come. Indeed, it turned out afterward that Gen. Burnside formed a column of seventeen regiments, which he proposed to lead himself in a charge upon our lines; but was induced to abandon any further attack by the views of his principal officers. I think he would have failed had he tried it, not on account of the strength of our position, which was nothing extra as I have before explained; but because we had already demoralized his whole army.

So we waited & waited, but the whole day passed without anything serious, anywhere along the line. But I remember the day as a very disagreeable one, for I had to move about a great deal, having guns at so many different places; & the sharpshooting & shelling everywhere made me quite unhappy. There was a particularly bad nest of sharpshooters in a brick tanyard, on the east side of the Plank Road, where it crossed the little canal. They cut regular loop-holes through the brick walls & from them they had a very annoying fire on certain parts of our line. And the loop hole in the corner on the Plank Road could see up the road some 300 yards to where our line crossed the road, & as we had built no breast-work, or obstruction, across it the fellow at the loophole had a fair shot at every man who crossed. To be sure a man could run across, but the sharpshooter kept his gun already sighted at the spot, & his finger on the trigger, & he only had to pull & the well aimed bullet was on its way. He had several shots at me during the day, & though he missed me every time, I acquired a special animosity to him.

That night a train from Richmond arrived with a large supply of ammunition. I visited Longstreet's headquarters, & having told how they had had us under hack all day in sharpshooting & shelling, because we were saving ammunition, Gen. Longstreet gave me permission to use a few score shell the next day to get even with them. Now it had happened too that some of the enemy's long range guns, up towards Falmouth, had accidentally dropped a few shells short, where they had either hurt or scared some of their own men. So these guns had all been ordered to stop firing entirely.

As before, Monday morning was again thick and hazy, but when the sun was about an hour high the nest of sharpshooters in the tanyard announced their ability to see by opening a very lively fusillade. I happened to be nearby, & I at once determined to try & rout them. But the building was so nestled in the hollow, & hidden by intervening low hills & trees, that only from one gun, one of Moody's 24 pr. howitzers, could even the peak of its roof be seen. But I knew that if I only skimmed the top of the low intervening hill the shell would curve downward & probably get low enough for the loop holes. The howitzer was on the south of the Plank Road & some 400 yards off. I got the line of the obnoxious corner loophole on the roof & sighted in that line, & then fixed an elevation which I thought would just carry the shell over the low hill, aiming myself, & taking several minutes to get all exact. Then I ordered fire. Standing behind we could see the shell almost brush the grass, as it curved over the hill, & then we heard her strike & explode. At once there came a cheer from our picket line in front of the hill, & presently there came running up an excited fellow to tell us. He called out as he came—"That got 'em! That got 'em! You can hear them just a hollering & a groaning in there."

I examined the place the next day, after the enemy had left. I had made a perfect shot. The shell struck within a foot of the corner loop hole, making a clean hole over a foot in diameter, & exploding as it went in. It knocked off most of the head of the sharp shooter, & the walls of the room on all sides were scarred by fragments of shell & brick. They left his body in the room, & doubtless others were wounded by fragments, from the account of the groaning, but were carried off. But not another shot was fired from the tanyard that day, & in a very little while orders were evidently extended over their whole line to cease sharpshooting. For we soon found that we could expose ourselves freely anywhere, & never a musket would be fired at us; even though our sharpshooters continued to revenge themselves for the day before by shooting at everything in sight.[33]

And I simply spent the whole day going about our line, getting on all the high places with my glass, & studying out where any of the enemy were sheltering themselves & then doing a little target practise at them from the nearest gun. During the morning two of Gen. Lee's staff, Baldwin, chief of ordnance, & Sam Johnston, the engineer who built the pits, as before told, came & spent nearly an hour with me. While together we discovered that quite a little body of the enemy were lying down in a shallow depression about 400 yards from another of Moody's 24 pr. howitzers, which were my favorite guns. Partly to make the enemy unhappy, & partly to show my companions how effective the gun was, I carefully aimed & fired four shrapnel (each of which contained 175 musket balls) so as to burst each one about 15 feet above the ground & about as many yards in front of the little hollow. While we would not see into it, the bullets & fragment would probe it easily. From the very first shot, we saw, at the far end, men helping three wounded to get out to the rear, but our infantry sharpshooters opened on them & ran them back. The next day, Baldwin & Johnston visited the spot together to study the effects, & told me that they found 13 dead which they were sure from the fresh wounds & blood were killed by those four shrapnel.

The following extracts from a *Century* article by Gen. J. W. Ames, will afford a conception of the battlefield on the Federal side:

> On Saturday, Dec. 13, our brigade had been held in reserve, but late in the day we were hurried to the battle, only to see a field full of flying men, & the sun low in the west, shining red through columns of smoke—six deserted field pieces on a slight rise of ground in front of us, and a cheering column of troops in regular march disappearing on our left. But the day was then over, & the battle lost; & our line hardly felt bullets enough to draw blood before darkness put an end to the uproar of hostile sounds, save desultory shell firing. For an hour or two afterward, shells from Marye's Heights traced bright lines across the black sky with their burning fuses. . . .
>
> We were roused before midnight, formed into line with whispered commands, . . . & marched away from the town. There were many dead horses at exposed points of our turning, & many more dead men. Here stood a low brick house with an open door in its gable end, from which shown a light & into which we peered when passing. Inside sat a woman, gaunt and hard featured, with crazy hair & a Meg Merrilies face, still sitting by a smoking candle though it was nearly two hours past midnight. But what woman could sleep, though never so masculine & tough of fibre, alone in a house between two hostile armies—two corpses lying across her doorsteps, & within—almost at her feet four more! . . . We now began to take note through the misty veil of the wreck of men & horses cumbering the ground about us. . . . Just here was the wreck of a fence which seemed to have been the high tide mark of our advance wave of battle. The fence was a barrier which, slight as it was, had turned back the already wavering & mutilated lines of assault. Almost an army lay about us, & scattered back over the plain toward the town. . . . About eighty yards in front the plowed field was bounded by a stone wall, & behind the wall were men in gray uniforms moving carelessly about. This

picture is one of my most distinct memories of the war—the men in gray behind this wall, talking, laughing, cooking, cleaning muskets, clicking locks—there they were! Lee's soldiers!—the Army of Northern Virginia. . . . The enemy riddled every moving thing in sight: horses tied to the wheel of a broken gun carriage behind us; pigs that incautiously came grunting across the road; even chickens were brought down with an accuracy of aim that told of a fatally short range & of a better practice than it would have been wise for our numbers to face. They applauded their own success with a hilarity we could hardly share in, as their chicken-shooting was across our backs leaving us no extra room for turning. But this was more wantonness of slaughter, not indulged in when the higher game in blue uniform was in sight. The men who had left our ranks for water, or from any cause, before we were pinned to the earth came back at great peril. Indeed I believe not one of them reached our line again unhurt. . . . I was called back to the dull wet earth, & the crouching line, by a request from Sergeant Read, who "guessed he could hit that cuss with a spy-glass" pointing as he spoke to the batteries which threatened our right flank. Then I saw that there was commotion at that part of the Confederate works, & an officer on the parapet with a glass was taking note of us. Had they discovered us at last, after letting us lie here till high noon, & were we not to receive the plunging fire we had looked for all the morning? Desirable in itself as it might be to have "that cuss with a spy glass" removed, it seemed wiser to repress Read's ambition. The shooting of an officer would dispel any doubts they might have of our presence & we needed the benefit of all their doubts. Happily they seemed to think us not worth their powder & iron.[34]

Possibly I was the "cuss with the spy glass," for I carried a very large one in a special holster on my saddle—not an opera or field glass, but a fine large & long spy glass, which I found of infinite value, many times as powerful as the best glass of the opera type ever made. No one else in the army had such a glass, & no one without experience & practice, such as I had had in signal service, could use such a glass well without a rest. But the writer was exactly correct in his reason for their escape from some shrapnel shot. That was on Sunday & we were saving ammunition for expected charges. The fellows who were on that ground [the] next day were not so fortunate. Yet even from the infantry sharpshooting he reports that his command had about 150 casualties among 1,000 men.

I kept up my amusement at the enemy's expense until sundown, & then rather reluctant to stop, I planned to give them a surprise during the night by suddenly sending a few dozen shells down the streets of the town about midnight. But I could not do that without Gen. Lee's & Longstreet's permission, which I could see they might not readily give, as it might cause a general alarm, so I gave it up. But I have ever since regretted it for during the night Burnside's whole army was recrossed over to the north side of the river. The streets of the town were necessarily swarming with troops, guns, ambulances, &c. all night, & a sharp fire on them would perhaps have made commotion enough to have disclosed the move to us & enabled us to attack it, & almost ruin them. And I lost the chance to save myself riding three or four miles after night! But who could have imagined that Burnside with his immense army would turn back so easily! Of Longstreet's corps only about four brigades had done any fighting, though four corps had been opposed to us. And, though Jackson had about three divisions engaged, it was for but a short time, as fights go.

Early next morning we noted the unusual quiet in the enemy's lines, & a force of skirmishers was ordered forward, about sunrise, to investigate. We found them all deserted & then we knew how it was. I went with the skirmishers through the town & down the river bank. On the opposite shore we saw a Federal picket & they seemed to us to look a little mortified. They were looking at our approach, when we saw them, from a place where they could have gotten cover by stooping. They stood up purposely, apparently to let us see them, but they did not shoot at us, & were evidently willing to go back to the no-picket-firing truce which prevailed before they crossed the river. We were glad enough to do it—so we did not fire either, & walked out boldly. Then they came forward in the open, & we scanned each other curiously for some minutes, & then we turned & went back toward our lines. We were near enough to have exchanged banter, but no word was said on either side.

One amusing incident happened to me as we entered the town. Quite a few citizens of the place, from one cause or another, had remained in the city during the whole period of the battle, taking refuge in cellars when either we or the Federals shelled it. As I went in with the skirmish line, I saw a citizen coming with a musket & bayonet, marching in front of him a Federal soldier. The prisoner was a rather small Dutchman, in bran[d], new uniform & with a most complete & extensive equipment of knapsack, haversack, canteen, overcoat, rubbercloth, tin cup, bags of ground coffee & sugar, & all sorts of little tricks I never saw before. And everything was that neat that it was plain the man was one of the old maid types, with a genius for making himself comfortable. And that was how he came to be a prisoner. His captor gave me the impression, but I don't know how, of being a clerk in a drug store. "Where did you get this man?" said I, as he came near. "He slipped into my cellar last night & went to sleep there. All the rest of the Yankees went across the river during the night, & he never knew it. I found him still asleep there this morning & I just took him prisoner & marched him out to give him to you all." "Very good," I said, & turning to the prisoner I asked him, "To what regiment do you belong?" "One hundred forty fort Pensilvany," said he, with a very Dutch accent. Immediately his captor levelled the bayonet on him, & actually yelled, "God damn you! Did not I tell you, if you said that again I'd bayonet you! You damned lying—" & he was apparently really about to give the fellow a taste of the steel when I stopped him. "Hold on! What's the matter? What are you threatening the man for?" "Why, didn't you hear what he said?" "He only answered my question. I asked his regiment & he was obliged to reply." "But didn't you hear what the son of a bitch said? That he said the *hundred & forty-fourth* Pa.? Don't you see that it's just a dam Yankee trick. That they've just left this fellow here on purpose to tell that lie, & try & demoralize our men by making them think there are 144 regiments in their army from Pa.?" "Pshaw," said I. "They've got over 200 from some states, but it isn't half enough yet to whip this army. So don't stick him but take him along to the line. Our boys would not care if he was in the 500th regiment." So I sent him on & hope the prisoner made the trip safely, but I never heard more of either of them.

As soon as the news of the enemy's retreat reached headquarters, orders were sent to break up the line of battle, & to return [to] our old camps, or to form new ones. I got my battalion, again, all together in our old camp, & spent most of the day, afterward, going over the field where the enemy had charged & studying the effect of all the little accidents of ground, houses, fences, &c. upon their columns. Evidently there was a great tendency among their men to stop & take shelter, & go to firing whenever they could get any cover. Even board fences, which would not at all stop a bullet, would have crowds trying to shelter behind them, as was shown by the number of bodies left there. In fact the dead lay thicker behind one such fence than anywhere in the open ground. Some of their wounded were still alive, & among them I noticed one with a wound which one would have supposed must be instantly fatal, as it was directly through the brain. But he was still alive after nearly three days, & said, "Captain, captain" when spoken to. Ambulances were sent at once for all who were alive but the dead were not buried for several days.

Fredericksburg was the easiest battle we ever fought. I have already referred to the small proportion of our force which was engaged. Our casualties were _____ killed, _____ wounded, _____ missing. Total _____. These occurred principally in _____ divisions, numbering about _____ men present for duty, a percentage of ____. Two Confederate generals were killed & ____ wounded.[35]

The Federal losses were 1,296 killed; 9,642 wounded; 2,276 missing. Total 13,214. Of this total about _____ were in the two corps which were opposite Jackson & _____ were in the four which fought Longstreet. One

Federal general only was killed.³⁶ The total is a light percentage to have turned back such a superior force. I have already referred too to the fact that none of their charges at Marye's Hill reached our line, & compared them to our charges at Malvern Hill & at Gettysburg, in which we at least got in among the guns. Still another of our unsuccessful charges, interesting in this connection, was at Franklin, Ten., _____ 1864. There _____ divisions, about _____ men, charged a strongly fortified position with abattis & obstructions in front which were practically impassable under fire. They advanced across _____ yards of open ground under fire of about _____ guns & about _____ infantry. They only gave up the assault after losing _____ killed, _____ wounded, & _____ missing. Total _____ or, ____%. But the most striking feature of the battle was the mortality among the Confederate generals, as showing how they were accustomed to lead their men & to fight with them rather than to be repulsed in a charge. Of ____ majr. generals, & ____ brigadiers engaged, there were killed ____ & wounded ____.³⁷

Among the killed at Fredericksburg were two of my special friends—Ed Lawton,³⁸ a brother of Gen. Lawton's & adjutant of his old brigade, & Dempsey Colley, one of the older boys about Washington, Geo., when I was a small boy. Lawton fell mortally wounded at the farthest point of our advance where Jackson's men pursued the enemy toward their bridges, after repulsing them as has been told. He consequently fell into the enemy's hands & died in one of their hospitals some days after the battle. The Federals treated him with every possible kindness & courtesy, and after his death sent his body down to the river to be delivered to us under an escort with arms reversed and a band playing the dead march & all possible military honors. No more noble & promising life than his ever fell a victim to war.

Poor Dempsey Colley, I have already referred to as one of the very closest & best of all the friends of my boyhood. He was peculiarly generous, unselfish, pure minded, & high minded. And he had a peculiar genius for quaint & striking expressions & comparisons, many of which I can still recall. For instance, "This is a better dog before breakfast than that dog is all day." "I had rather have this horse than a whole cowpen full of that horse." "Now you'll see me kill that hawk so dead he will smell bad in a minute." Poor Dempsey, he ought not to have been killed. He never cared for politics even remotely, & war ought to have let him alone. In my mind his memory recalls squirrel hunts in the old Georgia woods & midday dinners of fried chicken & biscuits by deep shady springs wherein big watermelons had been put to cool, and perhaps a little fire and some barbecued squirrel. And I love to think that ghosts are probably not forbidden in those old woods & though they may not eat watermelons, & such, any more I trust that they will have their own compensations, & with eternity on our hands I know Dempsey & I will put in some of it on Fishing Creek and Little River.

I can recall very little of our camp-life after the battle until sometime early in January when we were sent back, nearly to Hanover Junction, to establish ourselves in winter quarters, where the horses could be better fed during the enforced inactivity of the winter. I recall two pieces of poetry inspired by the situation & founded on fact which appeared in the papers about this time, & which I will stick in an appendix I will have to provide. Both, I believe, were by Jno. R. Thompson. First was "Richmond is a Hard Road to Travel." This was enormously popular in the army, generally summing up, as it did, all the Federal commanders who had come to grief in trying to get to that city, one after the other, McDowell, Banks, McClellan, Pope, & Burnside, & also the naval attempt with the monitors. And it reflected the self confident morale of our whole army which could not imagine itself beaten. But it told another lesson too which it did not occur to us to learn. It told of the persistence of our enemy. However badly beaten he never relaxed, & always came back again. To the long list given in the song there came to be added Hooker & Meade & still they persisted & sent Grant. And Grant, repulsed again & again, & again, until the losses of his one army in less than one year nearly equalled those of all his eight predecessors in three years, still stuck to his task until we were finally worn out. So that song embodies some instructive history. The other song, "Music in Camp," founded on an actual incident of the friendly picket lines along the Rappahannock at this time, is something akin to Bayard Taylor's "Crimean Incident," but is a finer piece of poetry. Indeed the war produced few to equal it.[39]

Among my minor recollections is one of Christmas day, when my little darkey Charley, now growing tall & long legged, came & asked permission to go to Gen. Lee's hdqrs. "to catch the general for Christmas gift." I gave him the permission & he came back & told me, "I cotch im & he gin me a dollar." And then on the last day of the year I got a furlough of about three days & ran down to Richmond to see my wife & baby. They were living in a house on South Broad Street on the top of Church Hill, where General & Mrs. Gilmer, Mrs. Phoebe Pember,[40] & _____ were living in a joint mess. Oh the happy times when the last battle is just over & the next one far out of sight & thought in the future!

WINTER AFTER
FREDERICKSBURG

Early in January I marched my battalion from Fredericksburg with orders to select winter quarters on the north side of the North Anna River a few miles north of Hanover Junction. I found an excellent camp in a large oak & hickory wood at Mt. Carmel Church some two miles from the river & a mile or so from the railroad at a station then called _____,¹ but now changed to Ruther Glen. An open field gave a park for the guns, a pine thicket gave shelter for the horses, & the woods enabled the men to make very comfortable little cabins & furnished abundant fuel. And, best of all, less than a half mile away was a very comfortable farm house occupied by a most excellent couple of old people living entirely alone, Squire & Mrs. Wortham. And I easily & promptly arranged with them to board myself & family. So before I had been there a week I had been joined by my wife & our little 14 months old daughter, now running about & beginning to talk. And then began nearly four months of what seems, as I look back upon it, to have been one of the happiest periods of all my life. Could I have foreseen that there were still over a quarter of a million battle casualties to be distributed in the two armies within two years, with the final loss of our cause, I might have been in very different spirits. But ignorance is bliss, & it's foolish to be otherwise in a case like this; & I shared the general feeling that after one or two more defeats the enemy would surely give it up.

For a nurse I had bought a colored girl of about 17 in Richmond during the fall, giving, I think, about a thousand dollars for her. She was named Amy _____ & came from North Carolina, but probably not of the most select circles, for she told my wife that her former mistress dipped snuff & swore terribly & poor Amy herself was woefully ignorant of many very ordinary ways of civilized life. But she was cheerful & good natured, & soon grew very fond of her charge, & she remained with us until after the war, when we no longer cared to have her, & she never, that I remember, even had a scolding.

———

Gen. Pendleton's reserve artillery was encamped a few miles away, & one of his officers, Lieut. George Hobson of Lynchburg, also got board for his wife with the Worthams. They also had a little girl, Jennie, about Bessie's age, & we found them very agreeable company & we became great friends. Poor Hobson was killed during the ensuing summer, & we have lost sight of the wife & child ever since.[2] We took advantage of the vicinity of Gen. Pendleton to get him to come over one afternoon & baptize our Little Bess.[3] She grew & developed rapidly & enjoyed the excellent country fare & the big yard to play in, & one of the pictures which remains very vivid in my recollection is of her running around in the yard & eating a cold boiled partridge, brought to her from camp by my boy, Charley. There were plenty of these birds about, & I shot a good many, & I fished some, as spring came on, in a small creek near the house; & whenever weather permitted Miss Teen & I would take long walks over the plantation.

The few incidents I have to record of these four months are the best proof of how peaceful & happy they were. The first incident was one called in both armies the Mud March. After Burnside got safe back across the river he still was not happy. He evidently felt that he had not accomplished what had been expected of him. And after thinking over the matter for about a month he determined to make another effort & this time by another route.

So on or about Jan. 15 he put his whole army in motion to move up the river; intending to cross at some of the upper fords & turn our left flank. But the winter rains, & freezes & thaws, had converted all Virginia roads into bottomless quagmires. For about two days his army floundered in them, in vain efforts to make a practicable advance, & then gave it up & floundered back to their camps. And that was the end of Burnside. On the 25th of January he was superseded in command of the army by Gen. Hooker. When Burnside made his start Gen. Lee was speedily informed of it, & made his preparations to meet it. One of them was to order my battalion to move up to a church, whose name I forget, some ten miles to the left & rear of Fredericksburg. The mud was fearful, but we made the trip & were there on time, & spent a day there. By that time what had happened to the enemy became known, & we were permitted to flounder back to camp ourselves. On the advance I remember that a lot of Moody's men got hold of whiskey somewhere on the road & turned up very drunk. I had about fifteen of them with each man's hands tied behind him strung on a prolonge rope passed under one arm of each, & kept them so for 24 hours, the ends of the rope tied to roots of two trees at night so that they could lie down.

There were a few peddlers, about that time, who made a regular business of peddling whiskey in the vicinity of the army camps. But I had the luck to catch one outfit of them, which I wound up so effectually that I was never troubled with them anymore. Two fellows, with a two horse wagon, two barrels of whiskey and a barrel of gingercakes, encamped one day in a wood not far from my camp & made their presence known to the men. A squad of Moody's men soon paid them a visit &, pretending to have left their money in camp, began to drink on credit promising that one man would presently go & bring the money. After working that game as far as it could be worked, they sent a man back, but with private instructions to come & report the whole thing to me. So I sent a guard & arrested the outfit. I confiscated the whiskey & turned it over to the surgeons, for hospital stores. I confiscated the wagon & mules, & turned them over to the quartermaster. I arrested the two men as evaders of the conscript law. I put them under the camp guard, & fed them on their confiscated ginger cakes for two days, until I got a chance to send them under guard to the conscript camp at Richmond. I delivered them safely there & never heard any more of them.

Sometime in February, I think, Hood's & McLaws's divisions of infantry, of our corps, passed us marching to Richmond. Gen. Longstreet had been ordered to make an expedition, down to Suffolk, with these divisions to keep the Federal force at Norfolk in close quarters & enable the Confederate commissaries & quartermasters to gather forage and provisions in the good agricultural districts in that vicinity. The expedition was a very successful one in that respect & was accomplished without much fighting.[4] There was however quite a lot of skirmishing & sharpshooting & the enemy's gunboats would often shell the positions held by our men. I recall an incident which was told through the army on their return. Jenkins's So. Ca. brigade was not only about the largest brigade in Hood's division but it was noted for its good uniforms & its excellent discipline & military bearing even in small matters. One day they were marching down a road by the side of which the Texas brigade was lying at rest. As they passed, a stray shell[5] from a gunboat came along and cut off the right feet of four men marching abreast, who, of course, all fell in a heap. Some of the Texans immediately cried out, "There! You see that's what you get for keeping step!" But they did not rejoin the army until after the battle of Chancellorsville, & that, I think, was bad play in the game of war. We did indeed win the battle, but that result was not something we could have fairly counted upon doing with one fourth of our army absent. And the narrative of that battle will show that accidents, at critical moments, permitted to us great advantages & probably largely affected the result. I suppose it was intended to bring these two divisions back in time for the battle but the time was miscalculated & they only returned about May ____.[6]

One incident of the winter which I recall was the receipt of notice that a cavalry raid was being made by the enemy, toward Richmond, & I was warned to look out, not only for my command, but also for the railroad bridge over the North Anna River—about two miles in our rear. So, to do both at the same time, I marched my command to the end of the bridge on our side, where I posted the whole battalion on fairly good open ground, where we could have, at least, held an enemy at bay for some hours. But the raid did not pass near us at all. The position near the end of that bridge gave a long view over open country to the eastward, down the valley of the river. I recall one occasion when I went there, with some of Parker's rifled guns, to try some new fuses sent from Richmond. As our glasses showed nothing in sight we began to fire some shrapnel shell over the open ground to the eastward, bursting them in the air a mile or so off. We had only fired a few rounds when I heard a yell of delight from one of Parker's little powder monkeys—"Ha—Routed em! Got them running!" Looking, I saw a considerable gang of Negro plow men, who had evidently been plowing in some depression where they were hidden from view, but not from fragments of shell. They had everyone left their plows, but mounted their mules & were making wonderful time off towards the high grounds on the right to the intense amusement of the boys. Fortunately it was a bloodless victory.

In the latter part of the winter, a court martial was ordered to sit at my camp, & I was made president of the court. We used the church, Mt. Carmel, for a place of sitting, & were in session for near a month; quite a lot of prisoners, from different commands, being brought before us. There were two capital cases, both from Woolfolk's battery. One of them was a young fellow, named Howard,[7] who had deserted & gone to his home where he was caught by a conscript guard. The other was a substitute, named Wilson,[8] who had only joined us the week before he deserted, showing himself to be a regular bounty-jumper. One of Woolfolk's men had gotten permission from the War Department to put in a substitute & to be discharged. He had agreed to pay the substitute a thousand dollars, but it was directed that I should hold back a large portion of the money & only pay it to Wilson in installments. When it came before me I didn't like either Wilson's name or his looks. So I gave him a fair warning. I said, "Wilson, if you are one of these bounty-jumpers you had better go & try somewhere else; for if you desert from this command I shall offer the whole seven hundred dollars of your bounty which I retain, as a reward for your capture; & if we catch you we will shoot you for a deserter, certain." Well, Wilson did not scare a bit. He deserted in less than a week. But I had told Woolfolk to let all his men know that if Wilson deserted there was his own $700 reward offered for his capture. So his comrades were quietly watching Wilson very closely. He had not been gone an hour when it was known, and in a few hours afterward he was recaptured. And then I considered him mine to shoot, after certain tedious formalities, & I set to work to keep him safe, putting him in irons.

When these cases came before the court both were clear cases of desertion & sentence of death was pronounced upon each. But the proceedings & findings were not allowed to be made known, until they were passed upon & approved by Gen. Lee. I knew that this would take a long time & that meanwhile, suddenly some day, we would be breaking up camp & going into active fighting. My men had no muskets to guard prisoners with, but only swords, & I was afraid, on an active campaign, the prisoners might escape. Howard, I felt very sorry for. I would have been willing to give him chances. Woolfolk always believed his story that he did not intend to desert for good & all, but only to go to see his folks a bit—and may be a sweetheart. But unluckily for him he was caught before he was ready to come back of his own accord. But Wilson had scamp written all over him, & was clearly a professional bounty-jumper, & I itched to see him made an example of. So I sent both of them down to Richmond to "Castle Thunder,"⁹ with a letter to the provost marshal, saying that they had been tried for the gravest crime, & were awaiting result, & I asked him to take *special care of them until I sent for them.*

I will anticipate & tell the result at once. About July ____ on the retreat from Gettysburg we arrived near Culpeper C.H., & on the march I happened to meet & ride with Col. H. E. Young¹⁰ of Charleston, Gen. Lee's judge advocate general. In conversation, Young told me that the proceedings of my court had at last been acted upon, & approved; & that an order was being issued for me to execute the two deserters¹¹ in a few days, which order would reach me the next day. That afternoon we went into camp rather early, in a broom-grass old field; & we were hardly in camp when Howard walked up to my tent, & reported himself for duty. My heart sank at the sight of him. Orders were already signed directing me to shoot him. He told me that he had simply been turned loose from Castle Thunder along with a good many others, & told to come & meet the battalion, coming back from Pennsylvania, & he came—on foot a good part of the way. He knew nothing of Wilson.

Now, I *believed* that if I went promptly to Gen. Lee, & begged him, he would commute Howard's sentence. I had thought a great deal about doing that anyhow, when the time came, & I had Wilson to make an example of. But now I felt sure that Wilson had gotten away, for Howard had had plenty of chances to escape & had come along to camp. I did not know how Gen. Lee would feel about there being *no* example of punishment for desertion. And I just could not, now, contemplate shooting Howard. If I asked Gen. Lee and he refused to pardon him there would be no help. It was very unmilitary, but I determined that Howard should escape that night. When he reported I had told him he could not return to duty, but must be kept under guard until his sentence was published, & he was now in the guard tent, though not ironed. Captain Woolfolk was the officer in charge of the guard. I had a conversation with him telling him how I wished that Howard would escape & the next morning, sure enough, *he was* gone. I have never heard, as I should like to do, what became of him. Next day the orders came to execute the two. I sent to Castle Thunder for Wilson & the keeper could not tell anything whatever about him. There was no record of his discharge or anything else about him, & I have never heard of him since either. So the means I took to make sure of him were what saved the scoundrel's worthless life.[12]

One other incident of this winter which I recall was a message sent me from Gen. Jackson through Gen. Pendleton that he had applied to have me made one of his brigadiers, to command the large brigade which had been Lawton's. General Pendleton brought me the message & advised me to write to Gen. Lawton & Gilmer in Richmond to see that the application was favorably acted upon, as influences there were often more potent than applications from the generals in the field. But I was on principle opposed to either seeking or shirking any assignment whatever—whether it carried promotion or not. So, though exceedingly delighted with the high compliment, I told Gen. Pendleton that I could not conscientiously move in the matter at all & the appointment was not made. And I was really better pleased to have it so, for I was more ambitious for reputation in the rather scientific branches of engineering and artillery, than for mere rank. And I felt more confidence in myself & believed that I could be more useful in these branches where we had so very few educated & trained officers. And surely all is well that ends well & I have never for a moment regretted that I stayed with the artillery. The officer too who was promoted, Col. Jno. B. Gordon,[13] most richly deserved promotion for his brilliant service in D. H. Hill's desperate fighting at Seven Pines, Malvern, & Sharpsburg. At Sharpsburg he had received 5 wounds & not to promote him would have been a *scandal*.

Chapter

IO

BATTLE OF CHANCELLORSVILLE

On Monday, April 27th,[1] 1863, I went up by rail to Milford Station, about half way to Fredericksburg, to visit some of Jackson's artillery who were in winter quarters near there, and to see some new fuses tried, which had been sent up from Richmond for experiment. I spent the night with my friends there, & next afternoon, instead of returning to camp, at Mount Carmel, I decided to run up to Fredericksburg & spend the night with my former comrades on Gen. Lee's staff. In that way it happened that I was there on the morning of Wed., April 29th, when we were aroused at daybreak with the news that Hooker was throwing a pontoon bridge across the river below Fredericksburg, where Burnside's lower bridge had been located in December. The character of the ground here permitted him to do this at any time, practically without opposition, & we could make no attack upon him until he ventured to move out from the river. But it was clear that the building of this bridge meant business, & that we were about to try the fortunes of another great battle.

The first thing to be done was to telegraph down to our winter quarters, and to order all the artillery—my own battalion of course included, to march immediately for the front. My second in command was now my glorious & beloved Frank Huger, who never shirked a care or danger or grumbled over a hardship in all his life, & with whom all my intercourse was always as that of the most affectionate brothers. Sometime during the spring Maj. Lewis had been transferred to some naval duty, & Huger was sent in his place. On getting the orders to march immediately for the front, Huger sent my boy Charley to Mr. Wortham's to get my two horses, & to tell my wife the news. But she was all unwilling to have me go off to battle without coming to take leave of her, so she refused to let the horses go. Huger, however, then sent over Adjutant Smith, who at last convinced her that keeping the horses would not bring me, so she was finally prevailed upon to let them go.

And now, that my narrative may be better understood, I must give an outline of Hooker's plan of campaign. When Burnside was relieved, his corps, the 9th, was taken from the Army of the Potomac & he went to the West with it. But its place was supplied by two other corps, the 11th & 12th. This gave Hooker 7 corps—1st, 2nd, 3rd, 5th, 6th, 11th, & 12th—averaging about 18,000 men each, & his cavalry brought up his whole force to 139,000. Gen. Lee's force was six divisions of infantry, averaging about 8,000 each, & 2 divisions of cavalry, about 3,000 each. For this campaign the most of Hooker's cavalry force was despatched on a raid toward Richmond, & to break up our communications, & the largest part of ours were sent in pursuit of them; & we were able to prevent their accomplishing any serious harm. Of his seven infantry corps, Hooker left three, the 1st, 3rd, & 6th under Gen. Sedgwick,[2] to make a crossing just below Fredericksburg, & to make demonstrations which would hold us on the defensive; while with the four other corps he made a circuit, crossing the river some 18 miles above us, & then moved down taking us in flank. As he moved down & drove in our left, uncovering successive fords of the Rappahannock, he would establish short communication between the two halves of his forces, & could then, suddenly, & without our knowledge, reinforce his turning column by the 1st & 2nd Corps, giving him 6 corps upon our left flank. On the whole I think this plan was decidedly the best strategy conceived in any of the campaigns ever set on foot against us. And the execution of it was, also, excellently managed, up to the morning of May 1st. At that time Hooker had reached Chancellorsville on our side of the river and only about twelve miles from Fredericksburg, & had with him five corps of infantry, while two were threatening our front at Fredericksburg.

And now I have to tell the marvelous story of how luck favored pluck & skill, & how we extricated ourselves by the boldest & most daring strategy of the whole war; combined with some of the most beautiful fighting which it witnessed; and how we sent Hooker's great army—the greatest this country had ever seen—back across the river foiled & demoralized if not defeated. For the first day & a half, while awaiting the arrival of my battalion, I played engineer & staff officer for Gen. Lee. On the morning of May 1st[3] I was supervising the preparation of a line of battle across the Plank Road at an important point about five miles from Fredericksburg whence the Plank Road forked & a road from our rear came in on the left. The previous day had been spent in getting together our somewhat scattered troops, and in awaiting the full development of the enemy's plans; for it was soon apparent that the crossing below Fredericksburg was not the most serious part of them. And now, on the [1st],[4] the presence of a heavy force on our left was being rapidly developed, & a division of our infantry was being placed to make a stout resistance at the fork of the road above mentioned.

About 8 A.M.,[5] as I sat on my horse directing a working party preparing a position for a battery, I was agreeably surprised to see my small darkey Charley ride up on one of my own horses by the road which here came in from the left. The battalion was approaching by that road, and he had ridden on ahead to hunt me up. And I was very glad to see him, to get news from my wife, & to be rid of the longer need to borrow horses from my friends. And Charley had thoughtfully hung a haversack of lunch over his shoulders too, which I unfortunately omitted to take from him on sight, being at first too much interested in hearing about Miss Teen and how she had tried to keep the horses, which had excited Charley very much. He had not half finished telling me when, from a pine & cedar thicket about only 200 yards in front, there came the crash of a volley of musketry, & all about us the bullets hummed like a swarm of bees. I did not get my lunch, & the rest of Charley's story, until late that evening, for with the exclamation, "Hoo! They are shootin!" Charley disappeared in the direction from which he came so fast that nothing but a bullet could have caught him. But our working parties, dropping their tools, & picking up their muskets, soon made the thicket so hot that the enemy cleared out at double quick, leaving too some dead & wounded.

And soon afterwards Frank Huger & the dear battalion arrived, and as I rode among them, guns & men & officers, my spirits rose with a delicious sense of the wicked power of which I was in control, & which I was soon going to turn loose upon our enemy. We supposed at that time that we would fight a defensive battle along that line.[6] And then in a moment all was changed. Up the road from Fredericksburg comes marching a dense & swarming column of our shabby gray ranks, and at the head of them rode both General Lee & Stonewall Jackson. Immediately we knew that all our care & preparation at that point was work thrown away. We were not going to wait for the enemy to come & attack us in those lines, we were going out on the warpath after him. And the conjunction of Lee & Jackson at the head of the column meant that it was to be a supreme effort, a union of audacity & desperation. I have had to tell in my account of the Seven Days how Jackson, there, was, for a while, not Jackson; being temporarily under the shadow of a superstition, but, as if to make up for it, he had ever since been almost two Jackson's, & now at the beginning of this, his last battle—for the sands of his active life had run down to about only 36 hours—when he rode up with Gen. Lee, about noon on May 1st, as a fighter and a leader he was all that it can ever be given to a man to be. How splendidly the pair of them looked to us, & how the happy confidence of the men in them shone in everyone's face, & rang in the cheers which everywhere greeted them.

And now let me tell a little more about the execution of Mr. Hooker's plan, which, as I have already said, was most excellently conceived, & had up to this point, also, been excellently well carried into effect. He was at Chancellorsville at noon on the same May 1st with 5 corps & that was all right.[7] But it was all wrong to stop at Chancellorsville—at least for the man who had to fight Lee & Jackson. But that is just what Hooker did. And what made him do it seems to me largely to have been the moral oppression of knowing who were his antagonists, & feeling himself outclassed. His cavalry had found a mare's nest the evening before. It had skirmished with our cavalry & reported that our cavalry was covering some movements of Jackson out southwest from Chancellorsville. It was absurd, for Jackson then was below Fredericksburg in front of Sedgwick. Had he been out to the S.W., Hooker would have had practically an open road to move down & join Sedgwick himself. But Jackson had the reputation of making mysterious moves, of diabolic ingenuity, & Hooker thought this was one of them, & he became demoralised & hesitated. It should be explained that Chancellorsville is situated a mile or two within an extensive forest called the Wilderness, stretching northward to the river & westward for many miles. The original forest was cleared off, to make charcoal for some iron furnaces, fifty odd years before, & the second growth, which covered it, was small but dense, & hard to penetrate. Chancellorsville was a single large, brick, two-story house, with pillars in front, & quite an extensive clearing around it. And there were a few, but only a few, other clearings scattered here & there through the Wilderness.

These forest conditions naturally had their effect upon the military features of the Chancellorsville position. There was no room for a large artillery force—of which force the Federals had an excess. But, on the other hand, defensive lines were quick & easy to make, & to hold, &, by cutting a little abattis in front of them, an entanglement would result which only rabbits could get through. But Hooker's move, clearly, should have been to get his men through the Wilderness country & out into the more open fields beyond, where his superior artillery could be deployed, & to push his advance as rapidly as possible towards Sedgwick. And, after some delay, he finally did, indeed, order four of his five corps to move forward towards the open country. But he was now just a trifle too late.

Gen. Lee had left, at Fredericksburg, one division, Early's, & one brigade, Barksdale's, his reserve artillery under Gen. Pendleton, & a few other batteries to hold the lines against Sedgwick, & now, with Jackson & the remaining four & three-quarter divisions had started to attack Hooker wherever he could find him. When the head of the column reached the fork of the road where my battalion was located, a short halt was made to arrange fighting dispositions in front, for the enemy's pickets were but a short distance ahead. The two roads which here separated[8] were known as the Pike on the right & the Plank Road on the left.[9] The Pike ran nearly straight to the Chancellorsville house, about 5 miles. The Plank Road, after diverging a mile or two to the left swept around & came back into the Pike through the woods nearly at right angles at the same place. One division, or so, of our force was sent straight forward along the Pike. The rest of the column, with both Lee & Jackson, proceeded along the Plank Road. A strong skirmish line was now thrown about four hundred yards in front, with the remainder of a brigade in support, & then came my battalion of artillery leading the column. But I was first ordered to detach a section of two guns to go back to Fredericksburg to occupy two of the pits upon Marye's Hill in which we had fought in December. The Washington Artillery had also been left there but lacked two guns of having enough. I sent First Lieut. J. Wilcox Brown[10] with a section from Parker's battery.

Within a mile of the forks of the road we met the enemy's pickets, & from there on, our skirmish line kept up a lively fire with the enemy who fell back slowly, making all the delay that they could. To lessen that delay I went ahead with Woolfolk's battery & followed the skirmishers closely, opening fire to help them at every opportunity. I recall one sad accident, of a premature explosion of one of the guns, as it was being loaded in an apple orchard on the right of the road, blowing off the hands of the poor fellow handling the rammer. In about *two* miles of Chancellorsville, we got into an extensive open country & at the far side of it we saw a great display of Hooker's force, & I brought up more guns, & more infantry was deployed, which we moved steadily forward towards them. But they soon began to disappear in the woods & we recognized that they were being withdrawn. That is just what had happened. Hooker had[11] become so demoralized at the idea of having a Jackson in his rear that he countermanded his order for an advance, & withdrew his troops back to Chancellorsville at the first sign of a resolute advance upon him by the Jackson who was in his front.

We had, really, but little fighting on our road, & long before sundown we occupied the edge of the forest; & with one gun, dragged by a "prolonge" rope, hitched to the limber, & a small squad of infantry skirmishers on each flank, I went down the road to the last turn, whence I could see the Chancellorsville house, & the black masses of troops about it, & was harmlessly fired on by a gun behind a breastwork across the road about 300 yards off. Meanwhile our column which followed the pike had had a rougher time. They had struck strong forces in good positions, & the roar of their battle, which we heard, indicated desperate fighting & the detailed accounts of it, which we soon afterward received, convinced me that the force which we had on that road would not have been adequate for the work, had not Hooker called back his men. It was in that fighting that I first recall hearing of Gen. Miles[12] as a Federal brigadier, & one particularly noted for his hard fighting by our own men.

I recall one incident of the afternoon, which might have made me a little trouble afterward, but for the death of Gen. Jackson. When I went down the road through the woods, with my gun & prolonge rope, we passed the knapsacks of a whole Federal regiment, laid in order and abandoned by the side of the road. When we came back after getting the glimpse of Chancellorsville, the sergeant, acting as chief of piece to the gun, stopped & got himself a nice rubber overcoat off one of the knapsacks. I made no objection, as we were retiring leisurely, & I knew that the business of the day was over. When we came out to the edge of the wood, I rode up to Gen. Jackson to report about the masses of men I had seen about the Chancellorsville house. He noticed this sergeant with his new rubber coat. "Where did that man get that coat?" "From a row of knapsacks left by a regiment down the road there," said I. "Put him immediately under close arrest for stopping to plunder on the battlefield," said he. Of course, I did so, but I felt equally guilty with the man; for though he had asked no permission, I had looked on without objection. And the next afternoon, when we expected to go very soon into a severe action, I let myself be persuaded by Capt. Woolfolk to take the responsibility of returning the sergeant to duty as he was an excellent gunner. All of this was very unmilitary, & I have often wondered to this day what would have happened to me had Jackson lived. If it is allowed in the next world I'll ask him yet.

We bivouaced that night in the open woods on the right of the Plank Road, near where the furnace road diverged to the left, our guns & horses being just out of the road.[13] One of the little incidents I have always remembered was Capt. Parker's giving me a tin cup full of scalding hot but genuine coffee. I never before knew how good coffee could be, & to this day, I never drink a cup of real good coffee, but the picture comes up of the good captain approaching in the fire light with the cup in his hand, & I hear his gentle voice, & he sits down by me under a tree & while I am cooling & drinking it he explains in his short quick sentences where the coffee came from, & exhibits one or more little buckskin bags full of ground coffee & sugar already mixed. And, alas! They were all taken from the bodies of the dead, left by the enemy in his retreat. What would General Jackson have said & done had he known about it? And will he make any fuss about it if we tell him of it on the other side when I ask him about the sergeant business?

Generals Lee & Jackson bivouaced together very near us, in grave consultation, & receiving reports of the much more severe fighting which our right flank had had. In fact, our situation that night was a very desperate one, &, before taking up the narrative of the next day, I must explain it, & show the audacious strategy, so promptly devised & adopted during that night. I do not know whose was the suggestion, nor at what hour of the night it was decided upon. But between midnight & daylight Lee & Jackson were up & alone together sitting over a little fire & in close conference, and the movement I have to describe was started as soon after daylight as the men could get their little breakfasts.

This was our situation. In our rear, about three miles below Fredericksburg, threatening our communications, & our lines all the way from the town to Hamilton's Crossing, was Sedgwick with the 6th Corps, an unusually large one, now mustering about 25,000 men. They were intrenched in a position where they could not be attacked, but whence they could attack any part of our long line in an hour's notice. They were held in check only by Early's division & Barksdale's brigade with Pendleton's reserve & a little other artillery, distributed thinly, & without reserves, along the six miles of line they had to hold. Early was below the town, & Barksdale opposite & above. Early had about 8,000 men, & Barksdale about 2,000. In front of us, at Chancellorsville, laid Hooker with 5 Corps, the 2nd, 3rd, 5th, 11th, and 12th—about 90,000 men. The 1st, with about 15,000 more, was coming up on the north side to join them; &, very fortunately for us, Hooker was *waiting for their arrival before taking an active offensive.* As far as we had been able to locate the line held by Hooker's force it was naturally strong, & was already partly fortified. But it stretched off to the west, parallel to the Plank Road, far beyond our observation. I have already told some of this before, & that Lee had started from Fredericksburg with about four & three quarter divisions to attack Hooker wherever he could find him. One brigade of these, Wilcox's of Anderson's division, he had left about 6 miles below, opposite Banks's Ford of the Rappahannock, in observation, & he now had, consequently, four & a half divisions in hand, say 36,000 men, with which to attack Hooker's 105,000 intrenched in the Wilderness, for the 1st Corps was within reach & arrived before the battle.

One of the axiomatic rules of warfare is to avoid dividing one's forces in the presence of one's enemy. For it gives him opportunities to oppose your fractions with his whole units, & to crush them in detail. We were already necessarily divided into three fractions—36,000, 2,000, & 10,000; but standing somewhat back to back, facing respectively west, north, & northeast.

But rules are for the play when antagonists are some what equally matched. Where the disparity is as great as that under which we labored, the only good of rules is to indicate the lines which must be transgressed to find any chance of safety. And in this case Gen. Lee promptly decided upon a still further division and separation of our army, in hopes of finding & perhaps surprising some weak part of their line. Our largest fraction, of 36,000, was to be subdivided. Gen. Lee himself would retain about 12,000 in our present position, in front of Hooker, & endeavor to keep him interested by demonstrations along his front, while Jackson, with all the remainder, by a roundabout road, should endeavor to pass unobserved entirely around his right flank & take it in the rear. It was supposed, & it turned out to be the fact, that Hooker's flank did not extend over three miles to his right. A road called the Furnace Road & some other cross roads would take us there by a march of about 14 miles.[14] So, early that morning, Stuart with his cavalry had started ahead to clear the route, & to picket between it & the enemy, so that the movement should not be observed. About sunrise Jackson's column started, & the general asked me to ride with himself and his staff at its head. His own chief of artillery, Col. Crutchfield,[15] a most excellent officer, was also along, with two or three of Jackson's own battalions; mine being the only organisation from Longstreet's corps.

It would seem that with only ten miles to go, & the roads being in average fair country cross-road condition, we should have reached our goal in five hours—say by 11 A.M. But no one who has ever marched with a long column can form any conception how every little inequality of ground, & every mud hole, especially if the road be narrow, causes a column to string out & lose distance. So that, though the head may advance steadily, the rear has to alternately halt & start, & halt & start, in the most heartbreaking way, wearing out the men & consuming precious daylight, often beyond the calculations even of experienced soldiers. I think that that was the case in this march, or more extraordinary efforts would have been made for an early start, & to save every possible minute along the road, than any I can now recall. Not that any time was deliberately lost—not a minute—or any unavoidably that I know of. But here was a fighting column of only three divisions of Jackson's best men, with Jackson at their head, without baggage, but only ambulances & ordnance wagons, & with daylight worth a million dollars a minute, as will appear when we study the fight—starting at sunrise, which was about 5:10 A.M., and it took just 12 hours or till 5:10 P.M., to make their ten mile march, to form, & to begin the battle. I have never seen any criticism upon or discussion of the time consumed by this march, or the effect upon the result of darkness falling at the very crisis of the action, but to me it seems that some of the most valuable lessons of the battle are to be learned from their study. And, in my own mind the extraordinary consumption of time was due largely, not to the *badness* of the road, but to its narrowness. And for such marches I am sure much time could be saved by formations of eight men abreast, or more, depending on width of road, & special care in marching to have them kept so, & to prevent checking the men behind.

I can recall few special incidents of the march. Cheering was forbidden, & all noises suppressed as far as possible. Gen. Jackson was grave & silent,

& there was not very much conversation in the party. Of course, every one knew that serious business was close ahead, but, judging others by myself, we felt entire confidence that it would come out all right, & as to personal risks we were somewhat used to them, & simply put them out of mind. At one place we passed Fitz Lee, with some of his cavalry, guarding a road which led into the enemy's lines, & we all halted while Fitz took Gen. Jackson forward to a point where, without being himself seen, he could overlook quite a portion of the enemy's position. When he came back from the view there was a perceptible increase of eagerness in his air, & he hurried the head of the column over to a cross road we had to follow from there.

At last, I should say, somewhere about two o'clock we struck into the Plank Road a mile or so west of the enemy's extreme right flank; and here we turned toward them, & after marching, perhaps a half mile, we halted in the midst of the densest part of the Wilderness forest.[16] And here it occurs to me to say, that Hooker may be said to have lost this campaign from having sent off his large cavalry force, under Stoneman,[17] to raid our communications. Had all his cavalry been with him we could not possibly have made this long march across his front & around his flank. And on the very next campaign—that of Gettysburg, we made a somewhat similar error, & had the bulk of our cavalry on a raid around the enemy, when a great many good critics think they would have been far more valuable acting in immediate connection with us. The leading division of our column was under Gen. Rodes, one of the finest looking & most excellent officers of the army. It was promptly formed, as it came up, in line of battle at right angles to the road, extending into the woods on each side, & with a strong skirmish line about 200 yards in front. The second division, under Colston,[18] as it came up was formed parallel to Rodes & about 200 yards in his rear; & the third, A. P. Hill's, similarly, 200 yards in rear of Colston. My own battalion was put as a reserve with Hill's division, while Crutchfield massed Jackson's artillery to advance down the road with the leading divisions.

As I recall it, all these dispositions took a long, long time, waiting for the rear of the column to come up. For one part of the column toward the extremity had had to have a little skirmish. Some of Sickles's 3rd Corps had somehow gotten a sight of some of our ordnance wagons & artillery on the Furnace Road, somewhere about noon. He sent word to Hooker that Lee was retreating in the direction of Gordonsville; & also sent two divisions forward to investigate. They had quite a skirmish with our rear guard but fortunately everything was then by. But they practically cut our communication with Gen. Lee. While we were waiting in the woods, for the column to form, three or four of the enemy's men who had been off, probably scouting for chickens, buttermilk, &c., & were now finding their way back, walked right into our lines, & to their great surprise found themselves prisoners. I saw one of them—a major brought out of the woods. He asked with lively curiosity whose were all the troops that he saw, & when he was told that they were Jackson's, said, "My God. The report in our army is that he had gone to Cumberland Gap."

It was about six o'clock[19] when the rear of our column was practically up, & Gen. Jackson at last gave the order to Rodes to move. Immediately a bugle sounded "Forward," & it was taken up & echoed through the woods by other bugles in every direction. These bugles do not seem to have been heard by the enemy—or if heard they were attributed to their own cavalry. For the first intimation they are said to have received of our advance was the appearance of deer, turkeys, rabbits, &c. running out of the woods ahead of our lines. We had over a mile & a half to go to reach the Federal line & it took about three quarters of an hour for the lines to get through the dense woods. A picket post fell back before us, & when we got near their flank a strong line of skirmishers was in the woods to meet us. It was quickly driven back however, & then we struck the edge of quite an extensive tract of fields & open grounds, with small patches of woods here & there, extending for two miles towards Chancellorsville. On the edge of this open ground the enemy's line ended & he had thrown up some hundreds of yards of breastworks perpendicular to the Plank Road & stretching to his rear, & some of his batteries were quickly brought into action to oppose us.

But, now that the cat was out of the bag, there was no longer any embargo on noises & the mingled roar of our musketry, & the famous Confederate yell, shook the woods. The Federal right flank was held by Howard's[20] 11th Corps. Howard was an excellent officer. His corps was composed almost entirely of Germans. A few stood their ground, & fought well for awhile; but within twenty minutes the whole corps was thrown into such a wild panic as was never seen in either army before or after; not even after Bull Run in '61. That is how daylight came to be worth, as I said before, a million dollars a minute; for it was now after 6 & the sun set at 6:50. Our lines of battle had been, practically, broken up by the advance through the thick woods, & they did not halt to reform but pressed forward, the men singly & in groups, firing, stopping to load, & then pressing forward again. They made havoc in the flying crowds, whenever they got in range of them, & Crutchfield got some chances with his foremost batteries to contribute to the demoralisation—but they were all gone with the rapidly advancing front before I could get up.

I recall one incident of the advance. I passed one of the wounded enemy lying by the roadside calling out loudly & rapidly "water! water! water!" As I passed opposite to him I noticed that he was shot through the forehead &

the brain was protruding. I asked, "What state are you from?" He changed his cry & began to shout "New York! New York! New York!" just as he had been shouting "water" & kept it up as long as I could hear.

The following extract from a Federal account, by Gen. Alfred Pleasonton, will give an idea of the panic:

> I hastened back to my command at Hazel Grove; when I reached it the 11th Corps, to our rear & our right, was in full flight, panic stricken beyond description. We faced about—having then the marsh behind us. It was an ugly marsh, about 50 yards wide; & in the stampede of the 11th Corps, beef cattle, ambulances, mules, artillery, wagons & horses became stuck in the mud, & others coming on crushed them down, so that when the fight was over the pile of debris in the marsh was many feet high.[21]

But now, in the full tide of victory, in the very crisis of this his most wonderful battle, all unseen by human eyes, the last sands of life of our great & beloved Stonewall Jackson were falling in the glass.

We had swept over nearly two miles, of more or less open ground, & now came into a considerable body of the Wilderness forest, extending on both sides of the generally straight Plank Road. On our left it was unbroken all the way to Chancellorsville, about a mile. On our right, for a half mile next to Chancellorsville was an extensive clearing, a narrow neck of which ran out obliquely toward us, crossed a branch & opened into another clearing called the Hazel Grove position, already mentioned in the extract quoted from Pleasonton. This included a beautiful position for artillery, an open grassy ridge, some 400 yards long, extending N.E. and S.W., & only about 200 yards from the forest through which our line was now approaching it, & was quite near. This position was within the lines of the 3rd Corps (Sickles), some of which was out of position, having gone out to the front, as before told to investigate our wagons on the Furnace Road. But Pleasonton was there with his cavalry & some artillery, &, finding other batteries of the 3rd Corps, he covered the ridge with guns, 22 in all, & double shotted them with canister & waited [for] our approach.

Most unfortunately just at this time General Jackson had thought it necessary to check his advance for a short while, in order to get the troops better in hand, & in line; and to put A. P. Hill's division into the lead with its fuller cartridge boxes. It was during the delay caused by this change that Pleasonton got together & posted his guns, & that the last million dollar minute of daylight died out. And there was a lull in the firing, & General Jackson, on the Plank Road, restless & impatient, with two or three of his staff & several couriers, rode ahead of his line of battle down the road towards the enemy. From all accounts he must have gone some two hundred yards or more when some musket shots were fired on the party by a picket of the enemy. They turned & galloped back. Meanwhile, the troops at the road had now been changed, & some of these, on the south side of the road, took the galloping horsemen approaching in the dark for enemy's cavalry, & began to fire upon them, & shot dead Capt. Boswell of the staff & a signal sergeant named Cunliffe.[22] The general obliqued across the road to get into the woods on the north side & was met by the volley of a company from that side. Three balls struck him. One lodged in his right hand, one went through the left wrist & the left hand, & one shattered the whole bone of the left upper arm. He dropped his reins, bushes swept off his cap & badly scratched his face. He reeled in his saddle & was caught by his signal officer, Capt. Wilbourn,[23] & lifted from his horse to the ground, some ten or twenty yards in front of his line of battle. Members of his staff, & Gen. A. P. Hill with his staff were promptly around him; his sleeve was ripped up & his wounds bound with handkerchiefs, to stop the flow of blood. A litter was brought & he was placed in it & the party started to move back behind the line of battle, the litter borne on the shoulders of four men, in the Plank Road.

Just at this moment there was a crash of musketry a little ways to the right,[24] followed instantly by tremendous broadsides & volleys of artillery, & extending from far on the left clear down to the Plank Road, which was enfiladed with a heavy fire of canister & shell. What had happened was this. A. P. Hill's division, having taken the front line on our right flank had promptly begun to move forward. And they had come out upon the Hazel Grove clearing & discovered Pleasonton's guns, & had fired a volley at them. Had it been daylight, at that close range a single volley would have left the guns, without men or horses, to be captured & turned on their former owners in a few minutes. But musketry fire requires daylight to make it effective, especially at artillery; while canister fire with guns at infantry does not. So the volley of our infantry was comparatively harmless, in the dim light, & in the next minute they received a terrific discharge of canister, & then all the guns, now shrouded in smoke were firing as rapidly as they could be loaded. Beside the guns which Pleasonton had in position at Hazel Grove, another lot of artillery was also in position in the cleared ground immediately south of the Plank Road, & these guns also opened when Pleasonton did, firing down that road, & into the woods on both sides. By this last fire one of Jackson's litter bearers was cut down in the Plank Road, but as he fell Major Watkins Leigh,[25] of A. P. Hill's staff, caught the litter & prevented the general from being thrown out. But the hail of shot was so severe that the litter bearers put down the litter & took shelter in the wood behind trees, while the general's aid, Captain James Power Smith,[26] laid down by him on the ground in the road, holding him down & sheltering him as much as possible, while canister shot struck fire all around in the flinty road, & shell crashed & exploded on all sides. Gen. A. P. Hill was wounded, by this fire, & Col. Crutchfield, Jackson's chief of artillery, lost his leg.

After several minutes, the weight of the fire being diverted in another direction, Capt. Smith assisted the general to rise, & supporting him, got him into the woods, on the south side of the road, where he sank exhausted. The litter was brought & four men again lifted him on their shoulders, & started to carry him to the rear, when one of them was again shot down. This time the litter turned, & the general received a very heavy fall, & groaned as if in great pain. Finally an ambulance was brought, and he was placed in it, & started back, to return by the route we had come, & to be taken to the railroad at Guinea Station. His wounds were not necessarily mortal but he had an attack of pneumonia & died at that station on Sunday May 10th.

The enemy's fire, the darkness, & the wounding of both Jackson & Hill, put an end to all further efforts to advance. Gen. Stuart was now the ranking officer present, & he was promptly notified & took command. I had followed Hill's division closely with my battalion, & had it massed in a field, on the south of the road, a few hundred yards in rear of the line, when a courier from Gen. Stuart came to call me to him. I found him on the Plank Road, at the point where Jackson had been shot. He told me of Crutchfield's being wounded, which left me the ranking artillery officer on the field & he ordered me to take command of all the artillery & to be ready to attack the enemy at day break every where along the line. As he had just taken command he could tell me nothing at all about the positions, or the roads, & I had to find out for myself about them, during the night. Fortunately it was a glorious, clear, calm, full-moon night. I took a courier, to hold my horse when I wanted to go out to the picket line or to explore thick places, & started immediately. I shall never forget that night. From about nine o'clock to three, I was hunting out our line of battle in the woods, from the extreme right to the extreme left, & trying to get views or ideas of the enemy's positions in front, & then following out all the roads within our limits by which our guns could be moved. At several places we could hear axes & picks in the enemy's lines at work, indicating that he was strengthening his position & cutting abattis in front of his line of battle.

Several times during the night there occurred false alarms on the enemy's line. There would be a musket shot or two, & then several, & then whole brigades would fire tremendous volleys in our direction, & I would get behind a tree & wait for them to quiet down. The woods covered us so, everywhere, that there was but poor chance for our guns to do much. Only at a single point could I get a view of the enemy's line. I have already described the Hazel Grove position—as I came to know it afterwards. At the time I did not even know of its existence. But I found that night what I called a *"vista"*—a straight clearing about 100 feet wide & 200 yards long through a dense body of second growth pine, which gave a view of a part of the enemy's line & batteries at Hazel Grove. Of course I selected this as a position for a good battery. Then, to give a hot fire down the Plank Road, I decided to put two four gun batteries across it, about 200 yards apart, the rear one to fire only solid shot over the front one's head as our shell were liable to explode prematurely sometimes. I wanted to make as much noise as possible, to encourage our boys & demoralize the enemy, even if there was no good chance for very effective aiming.

Beside these three positions I picked out two more. One was only a thin place in the woods, where an old farm road gave access & room to handle four guns. They could not see the enemy's line, but they could rake a wooded valley which I knew that it must cross. The other was nearly behind the "vista" position. It was an isolated little clearing, but little more than 100 feet in diameter, on the top of a little conical hill. The tops of the second growth pines, all around on the slopes were high enough to obstruct the direct view, but would not obstruct the fire, & I knew both distance & direction to reach the Hazel Grove ridge.

Beside these places there actually was no other where a battery could be unlimbered. It was fully three o'clock when I finished my explorations. The sun would rise about five, & daylight would begin about four, so I had just an hour to get the batteries & conduct them to their positions. Since midnight everything had been quiet, & our men, lying on the ground in line of battle with their guns in their hands, or by their sides, overcome with the fatigue & excitements of the previous day, looked like an army of dead men in the pale moonlight, & irresistibly suggested the thought of how many must indeed be left stretched in death in those dark woods before the rapidly coming day was many hours old. For our situation was apparently a desperate one. We were a body now of but little over 20,000 infantry, with Hooker's 100,000 between us & Gen. Lee. And Lee only had 12,000 in hand to help us. Nothing but a combination of desperate fighting & good luck could save us. But I was saved from any great uneasiness or distressing apprehensions as to the result by being, by that time, almost utterly drunk with sleep. I could hardly keep in my saddle & would doze & dream & fall forward in my saddle as I rode along back to the rear to get the batteries for the different positions. Most of these were massed in some open fields, the horses still in harness & the men lying scattered around the guns; & it took me a little while to wake up some who could tell me where to find Col. Lindsay Walker,[27] who would select the batteries for me. At last I found him, wrapped in a blanket & lying under a little haw bush. I waked him & told him what I wanted. He said it would not take five minutes to get the batteries in the road, as all were ready hitched, & only the men had to be roused; & he started off to do this. In ten seconds I was in his blankets & sounder asleep than I had ever been before, or ever before even realized that it was possible to be.

For there is a sort of higher power of sleep, with qualities as entirely different from the ordinary as light is from heat. I don't think that mere fatigue, or loss of ordinary sleep, produces this higher power of sleep, because I have never been able to obtain it except in connection with the excitement attendant on a battle & not more than three or four times even then. This was my first experience of it & the recollection of no pleasure of all my life is more vivid & enduring than that of this letting myself, as it were, sink under a dense fluid which penetrated alike eyes & ears & pores until it pervaded the very bones bringing with it, instantly, everywhere a trance of delicious rest & freedom even from dreams. It does not seem possible to dream, but yet the oblivion is half conscious. Could death ever come as that sleep did it would be delicious to die. Walker was not gone ten minutes but when he waked me I came back from a long ways. But I came easily & felt at once refreshed wonderfully, as if by a strong cordial. Within the hour I had every battery in position, with full instructions & guns ready, loaded & aimed & ready for the word. And there was no long delay in the word being given.

I have seen many actions ordered to commence at daylight but this is one of the very few which was punctual to the minute. I don't think there was any eating breakfast that morning. I cannot recall, either, any eating the night before, nor indeed for several days. I suppose that I & everybody else had a haversack with provisions, & we ate as we marched along.

The action was commenced by advancing our infantry until it developed the enemy's line. This was found close at hand everywhere, & was generally strengthened by trenches, breastworks of logs, & with trees felled in front. Tremendous musketry fire was at once opened by both parties, & all the guns I had located joined in for all they were worth, & the enemy showed up in more than equal force. I remember thinking at the time that the roar of the battle would be easily heard at Mr. Wortham's & would tell them all what was going on. And I was interested afterward to hear that our little 18 months old daughter was greatly excited over it, & made the longest sentence she had yet produced, "Hear my papa shoot Yankee. Boo!"

I went back & forth from battery to battery, & while on one of the little roads in the woods had the narrowest escape of my life from a shell taking my head clean off of my shoulders. A flying shell can only be seen if the eye is almost exactly in the line of its flight. I saw this plainly come out of the bushes within ten feet & it seemed to pass my ear within two inches.

I recall an incident which took place on the Plank Road. I was standing by Captain Parker, who had two of his guns there at work, when one of our infantryman came out of the wood, just at the guns, with two prisoners. They turned down the Plank Road to pass to the rear—our man in the middle, with his gun at "right-shoulder-shift," & a prisoner on each side. They had not walked ten steps when, with a rushing screech, a percussion shell cut our man's left leg cleanly off at the knee,[28] & then, striking on the road a few feet in front, it exploded with a bang & a great whizzing of fragments. The poor fellow fell backward, dropping his musket & partially catching on his hands behind, holding up the bloody stump & shouted angrily to the prisoners, "Pick me up! Why in hell don't you pick me up?" But the two prisoners, scared almost to death, jumped like lightning to get behind the nearest trees on the roadside. At the same instant there came running up one of Parker's littlest boys, a regular little powder monkey, bringing ammunition from the limber in the rear to the gun in front, and he also shrieked out in a jeering treble at the terrified prisoners, "What in hell are you running from your own shells for?" It all took place in an instant, showing a surprising appreciation of humor under some drawbacks. Doubtless the prisoners felt towards their shells as Lawton's ambulance driver did towards the gunboat shells at Malvern Hill which perhaps I have already told in my account of the Seven Days. "You dam son of a bitch," he said, after a shell which went whistling by. "You've got no eyes & would as quick hit a ambulance driver as anybody else."

For a long time our best efforts made very little impression upon the enemy's line, but, somewhere between one & two hours after starting in, our right flank succeeded in carrying the Hazel Grove ridge. Gen. Stuart, who was at the spot at the moment, sent me word to immediately crown the hill with 30 guns. They were close at hand, & all ready, & it was done very quickly; all of my own battalion not already in action being in the number. The position turned out to be one of great value. It gave us fire over a larger part of the Chancellorsville plain, & we could even see the Chancellorsville house from it, about 2,000 yards away. But the part of the enemy's line next [to] the Plank Road was held with obstinacy for some time. They had built about 25 pits for guns, in one long row, on the edge of the sort of plateau, looking over the stream which ran across the Plank Road. Against their fire & the strength of their breast works, we might have never gotten them out but for our beginning to crumble their line on its left. Finally Gen. Stuart & I went together over to the Plank Road, & decided to try taking some guns straight down the road & out into the open, their infantry having been forced back near the road. So we limbered up a section & started, ordering another to follow close behind.

Stuart was in fine spirits & was singing "Old Joe Hooker, would you come out the Wilderness." As we came out where the woods on the right ended, we found that we could see the Chancellorsville house, & we saw, off to our right, one of our brigades with a battleflag & Virginia state flag move out from the woods & advance towards the left end of the enemy's gunpits. The two guns with us were at once brought into action, & Gen. Stuart galloped back to send forward more, while I rode rapidly to the Hazel Grove position to bring forward all from there. By the time we could get over, the enemy had abandoned his 25 gunpits, & we deployed on the plateau, & opened on the fugitives, infantry, artillery, wagons—every-thing—swarming about the Chancellorsville house, & down the broad road leading thence to the river. That is the part of artillery service that may be denominated "pie"—to fire into swarming fugitives, who can't answer back. One has usually had to pay for this pie before he gets it, so he has no compunctions of conscience or chivalry, but feels like the women in Southey's poem, who "all agreed that revenge was sweet, and young prince Crocodiles delicate meat."[29] Some of our shells soon set fire to the big Chancellorsville house itself, & the conflagration made a striking scene with our shells still bursting all about it.

When the last of the fugitives had disappeared we ceased firing, & ordering the guns to follow as they could limber up, I galloped forward to the house. Several wounded Federal officers were lying near who had been quartered inside, & hastily removed when it caught fire. And I remember noting a beautiful Newfoundland dog which had been killed, also lying in the yard. And after a while Gen. Lee & his staff rode up & once more these two portions of the army were united.

And now I must make the situation clear by telling what the other parts of the army had been doing while we were on our turning movement. Gen. Lee, with Anderson & McLaws, had simply threatened & skirmished all along that portion of the enemy's front which faced towards Fredericks-burg; merely to hold him in position. And when our attack this morning finally forced Hooker to fall back, & take an interior line, they had pressed his withdrawal as heavily as possible, & their troops from the south & south east were now meeting ours coming from the west.

But while we were having it all our own way up here quite a different scene was about to be enacted down at Fredericksburg. I have already described the situation there—Early's division & Barksdale's brigade spread over six miles, trying to hold in Sedgwick's corps. Saturday evening Sedgwick got orders from Hooker to attack & fight his way up towards Chancellorsville, in order to take us in the rear. During the bright moon-light night he silently withdrew the greater part of his force from opposite Early's front & concentrated in Fredericksburg in front of Barksdale. Here he was joined by Gibbon's division of the 2nd Corps, which had been left at Falmouth when the rest of that corps went up to Hooker the day before—

thus giving him fully 30,000 men. Early Sunday morning he attacked Marye's Hill, but was repulsed with severe loss, although the length of line held by Barksdale had stretched out his brigade more than double the distance it should have had to hold. Two or three efforts were made with like result, & then the enemy sent up a flag of truce, ostensibly to make some proposition about removing their wounded, but really only to see what force was there. Their messengers were thoughtlessly allowed a chance to see how thin our lines were. Really only about two regiments of infantry were on the front attacked by a division. After this was known an overwhelming force, about 11 A.M., was rushed upon them, & the position was actually over run. But our men, infantry & artillery, fought to the last, the infantry using their bayonets & the guns firing until the enemy were in their pits, & severe loss was inflicted upon him. As before told, Brown's section of Parker's battery was a part of this artillery. They behaved magnificently, & were all captured with their guns except a straggler or two who managed to get away. The Washington Artillery of New Orleans also lost all their guns & so many men that their three companies could never afterwards man more than about 8 pieces.

But, though the position was lost, valuable time was gained; for by the time Sedgwick had thus opened his road out of Fredericksburg, Stuart had finished his task at Chancellorsville & cut his way to a union with Lee. And now it remains to explain the lucky accident by which we had gained this success in spite of the enormous odds against us in numbers, as well as in position. It is all very simple. The enemy simply did not avail himself of more than about one half of the force he had at hand. He had six corps— less Gibbon's division. He only fought about three corps.[30]

And the reason why he did not put in more men was that, by a lucky cannon shot, a half a brick from one of the pillars of the Chancellorsville porch was thrown with great violence, & struck Hooker in the stomach. It seems to have had the effect of a pugilist's blow on the "solar plexus" & to have "knocked him out" for some hours. There were unfriendly stories that Hooker was also partly intoxicated, but his friends denied it strenuously. But the fact was that several strong appeals were sent for reinforcements, & reinforcements in profusion were at hand, but no orders could be issued. For some hours there was practically no head to the army. Had he been killed outright, or desperately wounded, the next in rank would have acted. But, as it was, he filled the position of commander of the army, but was utterly unable to exercise a single function. Did ever a narrower chance influence great results? How many lives, & whose, were saved by that brickbat?[31]

As I remember I was for nearly two hours about the Chancellorsville house, & I recall the hearty greetings of Gen. Lee & his staff & our friends in Anderson's & McLaws's divisions. And here Col. J. Wilcox Brown,[32] commanding one of Jackson's battalions which had not been with us the day before, joined us, & as his commission as colonel was older than mine, I surrendered the position of acting chief of artillery, & rejoined my own battalion. Meanwhile our lines were being extended through the woods in order to locate the enemy in his new position. It was not far off & it was held in great strength—a short line about 3 miles long with both flanks on the river & covering a great horse shoe bend, in which was ample space for his army and a good ford called United States Ford, giving free access to the north bank.

But before all this was developed, & while we were expecting soon to follow the enemy & renew the attack, news was brought to Gen. Lee that Sedgwick had taken Marye's Hill, & was advancing in our rear. On receipt of this news, McLaws's division of infantry & my battalion were ordered to march immediately down the Plank Road to meet him. We had every reason to anticipate that the last end of that day was going to be even hotter for us than its beginning. For now surely was their chance, if the Federal army ever expected to whip us. We were out in the open country with no breastworks or trenches to help us, & we were right between their two great divisions & liable to attack from both directions. And they had three men to our one. At Fredericksburg, as before explained, had been only Barksdale's brigade & Early's division. When Sedgwick carried Marye's Hill he nearly destroyed Barksdale, & he interposed between Early & Gen. Lee. Early was practically cut off, & was thrown out in the woods to Sedgwick's left, where Sedgwick had in fact left him while he pushed on up toward Chancellorsville[33] leaving only a good rear guard to look after him. Between Sedgwick & our rear at Chancellorsville was nothing but the remnants of Barksdale and Wilcox's single brigade, which had been left near Banks's Ford, but which now threw itself across the Plank Road to dispute Sedgwick's advance.

I have always felt surprise that the enemy retained Sedgwick as a corps commander after that day, for he seems to me to have wasted great opportunities, & come about as near to doing nothing with 30,000 men as it was easily possible to do. He gave his men a rest after taking Marye's Hill, & when he did advance it was so cautiously done[34] that Wilcox's Alabama brigade alone delayed him until about five o'clock in getting to Salem Church—about four miles only from Fredericksburg. At this point Wilcox had had a hot fight, with two divisions of the enemy, & they had just gotten possession of the church when McLaws's division arrived. With a little help from McLaws, Wilcox was able to drive the enemy back & recover the position. After this, Sedgwick seemed to make no further effort to advance, but went into camp to wait for another day. We formed a line of battle across his road & went into bivouac on it. In the selection & formation of this line, which included my whole battalion, all the daylight was consumed. There was[35] too I think some little shooting but nothing of any special consequence.

Early next morning Gen. Lee had come down to join us, & had brought Anderson's division with him, & it was understood that we were going to attack Sedgwick & crush him. And it was reported that Early's division (which, as before told, being below Fredericksburg, had been cut off by Sedgwick's advance up the Plank Road) had now come around through the woods & connected with our right. Early in the morning we had orders to be ready to attack. We were already full of ammunition & needed no more preparation, & we lay quietly waiting, & at last, wondering why the ball did not begin. About ten o'clock Gen. Lee in person with his staff came up to where I was on the line, & for the first time (& the only time in my life, but once—in Oct. '64) I saw him in a temper. I could not comprehend at the time whom it was with, or what it was about; & I never have exactly found out yet. But the three ideas which his conversation with myself & others in my presence seemed to indicate as uppermost in his mind were as follows. 1st. That a great deal of valuable time had been already uselessly lost by somebody, some how, no particulars being given. 2nd. Nobody knew exactly how or where the enemy's line of battle ran & it was somebody's duty to know. 3rd. That it now devolved on him personally to use up a lot more time to find out all about the enemy before we could move a peg.

I remember thinking that the quickest & best way to find out about the enemy would be to move on them at once, but the old man seemed to be feeling so real wicked, I concluded to retain my ideas exclusively in my own possession. And so off he went to the right, & we just spent the whole day quietly & there was no fight at all in our front. About 6 P.M. an advance was made on the enemy away around in his rear, & his line was carried. We advanced also & had a little artillery practice. But night prevented any valuable results & even caused loss of one or more regiments of our men, getting astray in the darkness, & marching into the enemy's lines.

As well as I can guess the matter, it was as follows. Gen. Lee wanted to find the enemy's left flank. He knew that their right flank (which was in front of *us*) rested on the river; but where was their left? When he left the place where I had the unhappiness of seeing him, he went off to find that flank. And he spent the whole afternoon finding out that the enemy had entirely abandoned Fredericksburg & Marye's Hill & that their left flank was on the river too, as well as their right, their whole line being merely a horse shoe. I can't account for the loss of that day in any other way.

But all's well that ends well! I've sometimes thought that if we had given Sedgwick a big fight that morning the noise of the guns & musketry must have stirred Hooker for very shame to put his big force in motion at Chancellorsville. Nothing but another brick, either in his hat or his solar plexus, could have stopped him from doing it. And he had so much force that if it were all put in motion it stood an excellent chance to accomplish some results.

When our people finally did attack Sedgwick's, way around on their left, I did a little shelling of their lines just for fun, & not only that, but I got the range & direction of Banks's Ford, where they were evidently to recross the river during the night; & I marked it in a gunpit I had built on a high wooded point, and I sat up there all night long firing shell at that ford. The country is hilly & banks were far too high for me to see the water, but my shell would curve over the hills & their fragments would all find the ground somewhere. Of course random fire like that could do no very serious harm, but from some Federal accounts afterward I was encouraged to believe that I had caused a good deal of annoyance[36] & that compensated me for the loss of rest.

The next day, Tuesday, May 5th, I received orders to go & reconnoiter the place where the enemy's left flank rested on the river below U.S. Ford, & to move my battalion up to that vicinity. Gen. Lee intended to attack Hooker in his intrenchments the next day, & wanted me if possible to get a bit of enfilade fire upon his line. We had his pickets kept in as close as we could, and then I found locations for some half dozen guns, which would have an oblique fire on his line, but it had been too well located to give us a chance for effective enfilade. And when I saw how the enemy had been throwing up dirt & strengthening himself; & reflected how easy it was in that Wilderness thicket to make a line impregnable by abattis in front, it made me very unhappy to think of seeing our infantry sent to charge such a tremendous force in those intrenchments. But for myself there was nothing to do but to try & make it hot for the enemy's left flank next day, so, as soon as it was dark enough to hide me, I was on the ground where the pits were to be, with a hundred of my men; & we set to work to build them & get fixed in them before daylight. I did not sleep any all night long, but I went for a while into a rather nice, frame country house, close by, and advised its occupants to be ready to leave the vicinity at daylight, as shells from the enemy's left battery which went over our heads would be all around their house. Before daylight we had all the pits ready for occupation, & we moved in the guns, & the ammunition chests, & sent off the horses. As it became light enough to see we were putting on the last touches, when, suddenly, there was a volley fired at us by a battery, not on the line we had made ready to attack, but on the opposite side of the river, on our right flank, & not over six hundred yards off.

And that volley was followed by others until there were two or three batteries apparently making it warm for us. As I did not know exactly what it meant I would not reply at all at first, but just made everybody keep under cover in the pits, & I went off to our infantry line on the left to find out what was the matter.

Ah! what good news it was! The enemy had gone! During the night he had vacated his lines! He had crossed the river, & was on his way back to his encampments! The campaign was over! There was to be no bloody assault of those strong intrenchments! The guns which were firing at my pits were guns placed to protect the retreat of his wagon trains at a point where the road on the north side might have been shelled from our side. If I could only get my guns safe out of the pits we could go back to Fredericksburg. But that was more easily said than done, for now that the battle was over I did not want another one of my men to be killed or hurt, & I could not hope to bring up horses & limber up without some casualties. For an experiment I took some two or three of my other batteries to a point whence I could reach the enemy's position, but without being in sight, & for about ten minutes I gave him a hot fire as a retaliation for his fire on my pits. That had the effect of reducing his fire to only an occasional shot, & that we put up with very quietly. For he could not hurt us. He could only delay us—till dark at the farthest. I also found a place where I could see his wagon trains passing, over a mile away, on the other side, & I also found the Washington, Georgia, company of artillery, Lane's, who had a Whitworth rifle & to kill time I put it to practising on the wagons, & made them go at a gallop. And in the afternoon it began to rain. Then I left Capt. Woolfolk in charge of the guns in the pits, & I took the rest of the battalion over on the Plank Road & within three miles of Fredericksburg. And there we pitched a tent & went into camp, in a rain, now pouring hard & steady, but, oh God! with such thankful hearts! And Woolfolk joined us before dark having gotten out under cover of the rain, & neither man nor horse on our side was hurt, for all our getting caught in such a snap in those pits. And oh what a big supper we did cook & eat, though I was almost reeling sleepy before it was ready, & I was anticipating another high power sleep that night.

And as soon as we finished eating we began to spread blankets for bed, when in the pouring rain we heard a hail. Frank Huger put his head outside & answered. Some one said, "Can you tell me where is the camp of the Somethinth Virginia?" "No. We have just come in here ourselves from up river, & have seen no other camps at all." "Who are you?" "Alexander's battalion of artillery—who are you?" "I am Surgeon Blank of the Somethinth Virginia, & I have here in the ambulance with me Col. Blanker who has lost his leg." "Well," said Frank, "You can't get anywhere tonight. You just get right out & bring the colonel in here, & get some supper & spend the night with us."

So we set our boys to rustle up some more supper, & the colonel, whose leg had been amputated about the knee, was helped out of the ambulance & we fed them, & though there was barely room for the five of us to crowd inside the tent, we were all as jolly & cheerful as could be, & by all lying on edge we all five could sleep together on the floor. And then I had a whole solid night of that delicious high power sleep. My very bones remember it vividly today, & also the exhilaration of the awaking in the morning. I am very sorry that I cannot remember the names of the colonel & the doctor for they were such nice fellows and we grew very fond of each other & parted affectionately in the morning, but we never ran across each other again.

And now my head & heart were both full of but one thing. How I could get down to Mt. Carmel & see my wife & baby. As it was not likely that the enemy would be aggressive again very soon, I thought it possible that Gen. Lee might let us return for awhile to our winter quarters. But that was thought to be too far off, and I was ordered instead to go & encamp on the railroad at Milford Station; only about fifteen miles from Fredericksburg. That however turned out to be even more pleasant than Mount Carmel, for Captain Woolfolk's mother lived within a mile of the station, & she immediately invited us all to make our home with her. Within a very few days we were most comfortably installed there, where we found as dear, kind, & hospitable friends as we ever met in all our lives—before or since. And that is saying a very great deal.

There is very little more to say about the battle of Chancellorsville. The most striking feature to me of the military history of the battle is the perfect collapse of the moral courage of Hooker, as a commander in chief, as soon as he found himself in the actual presence of Lee & Jackson. Hooker had been noted for personal bravery, as I have heard from Gen. Jos. E. Johnston, from his entry in the regular army as a young man. He was on some accounts—I never knew exactly what—neither highly esteemed nor much liked in the old army circles which I knew, but he was given full credit for personal courage. And as a division & corps commander he had become noted among the others of the Army of the Potomac as a bold & hard fighter. And it was because Lincoln considered him the most so[37] in the army that he placed him in supreme command. And none of its commanders ever planned or executed better than he did up to his reaching Chancellorsville, & finding that Lee was on the war path after him. Then he became timid, believed absurdities & gave us the time to make the turning movement on him. That was his first blunder. His second, permitting us to defeat a part of his army while the next stood idly by, we will attribute solely to the brick in the solar plexus, & excuse him for it. But why did none of his staff take the responsibility? Or none of the other corps commanders? I can only attribute the general fear to take responsibility to the moral effect of Lee's prestige. And surely something like that is necessary to excuse Sedgwick's timidity—to which I referred as I went along.

But Hooker's third & last blunder was the greatest of all. He lost confidence even in being able to repulse Lee with his whole army united behind a short line which any engineer would pronounce *impregnable*. Besides a powerful artillery force, he had men enough to put them about 15 deep for every yard of line. And he ought to have known Lee's aggressive audacity enough to at least wait a day or two more & see if he could get him to attack.

Had it been Grant in command he would not have dreamed of giving up the fight. But Grant had been built up by successes in the West, & the Army of the Potomac had never had the luck necessary to properly educate a general. When we come to write of Gettysburg, Meade too, one of the bravest of men personally, will be found permeated with the same timidity we see here in Hooker.

Hooker's total casualties were:
Killed 1,575   Wounded 9,594   Missing 5,676   Total 16,845
Confederates
Killed 1,665   Wounded 9,081   Missing 2,018   Total 12,764[38]

And now it only remains to tell the experiences of poor little Miss Teen after she had to give up my horses & let me go to the battle without telling her good-bye. Really it was better so, although it was very bitter to her when she began to hear on Friday afternoon the distant booming of the guns & knew that the contest was beginning. Saturday there were only occasional shots until late in the evening & then until after dark they could hear heavy cannonading. But it was not until Sunday morning that they could distinguish the rolls & crashes of musketry & realise that the crisis must now be at hand.

Old Mr. Wortham made several trips to the railroad but could get no news, for our battle was far off even from Fredericksburg, & the operators had removed to Guinea Station. But on Monday morning there arrived one of Parker's men who made his escape when the enemy captured Brown's section on Marye's Hill. He thought every one but himself was killed of that section, & he had heard of Jackson's wound & some dreadful stories of slaughter & calamity for all the rest of the army, & he said that in another day the whole Yankee army would be along. Poor old Mr. Wortham was greatly wrought up & told Miss Teen that he would have to immediately hitch up his wagon & take herself & Mrs. Hobson & Mrs. Wortham toward Richmond. But before doing so he rode to the railroad station to get the latest news from the telegraph operator, & by that time correct information had been brought to Guinea's & wired along the line & the poor old gentleman did not have to emigrate. He was a good old man & did his best for the poor forlorn ladies in his charge, & his wife did too, & a little corner of my heart will be warm for them as long as it is warm for anybody. And about Thursday Miss Teen was made happy by a telegram from me, & about Saturday I came in person to take her up to Milford to Mrs. Woolfolk's, where she could have the horses once more under her eye. [Figure 21 appears here in the manuscript, between Chapters 10 and 11.]

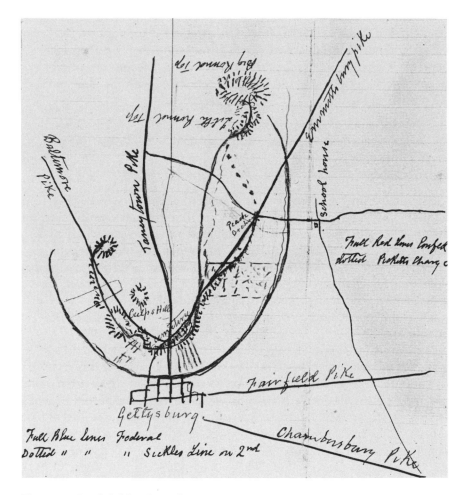

Figure 21. Battlefield at Gettysburg

II

THE GETTYSBURG
CAMPAIGN

We were now entering upon the third summer of the war. So far we had been able to hold the territory of the South practically intact. The enemy had lodgments upon our borders, but we still held the Mississippi River & all important railroads connecting Virginia with Georgia & the Gulf States. What we had lost to the enemy so far was only of outlying provinces which we could never have hoped to keep intact. But they were like wounds only skin deep & not affecting our power of resistance. Indeed, as the territory occupied by our principal armies became more compact, & the distances between these armies was diminished our power of resistance, according to all the rules & axioms of the great Game of War, was approaching its maximum.

And before taking up the history of the game, as we actually played it during this critical summer of 1863, I want to point out a variation which we might have played; & which Longstreet claims that he urged upon President Davis; & which, I think, must be pronounced by all military critics to have been much our safest play. Indeed, as will appear in due course of the narrative, we actually did make the play in September, after our return from Gettysburg, & with very fair success even then, although the circumstances were much less favorable than those prevailing in May.

No axiom of war is more obvious & of more frequent application than that pointing out the advantages possessed by the party occupying the *interior lines* or the center of the circle, against the adversary who operates around the circumference, or on the exterior lines. The principle is the same whether the question be one of a single battlefield, as is to be illustrated in the account of the field of Gettysburg; or of the whole territory occupied by opposing armies. The party having the interior lines can concentrate at any one point by shorter routes & consequently in less time than the party on the exterior. This offers opportunities to overwhelm portions of the exterior line, or isolated armies upon it, by sudden concentrations & attacks.

Our forces & resources were far inferior to those of the enemy upon the whole, but *the one single advantage* which we possessed was that of the interior lines. We could reasonably hope to transfer a large force from our Army of Northern Virginia to our Army of Tennessee, or vice-versa, much sooner than the enemy could discover & transfer an equivalent force to meet us. Such a manouvre, by the axioms of the game, was our best hold. And it was this manouvre which Gen. Longstreet states that he urged upon President Davis, as soon as he, Longstreet, then in Petersburg, with two divisions of his corps, knew that Gen. Lee with his reduced force had inflicted a demoralizing defeat upon Hooker's whole army at Chancellorsville. He states that he pointed out the fact that these divisions were not now needed with Lee, & were already well started on a trip to the West. And he goes into some detail as to other troops which could have joined him and as to the opportunity of taking the enemy by surprise & striking him terrible blows in the West.[1]

Unfortunately for the reception which this claim of Longstreet's has met among Confederate writers, his book, in several places, has given offence by alleged egotism & by seemingly harsh criticisms of Gen. Lee, & consequently much that he has had to say on this as well as on some other matters has been sneered or discredited in the Southern press. But looked at purely as a technical military question [of] which of the two plays in May 1863 was the most judicious for the Confederacy—to transfer as fast as possible heavy reinforcements to the West, or to invade Maryland & Pennsylvania—I must confess that the former seems to me so very much the best that I can excuse one who suggested it at the time for some warmth & earnestness in now pointing out its possibilities.[2] Any rising enthusiasm, however, which my old personal Confederate sympathies may engender, over the things which apparently might so easily have been—either on this occasion or many others—does not long survive the reflection that had things been otherwise, I might not have been here to enjoy the experience of them. As the battles all went, I had the good luck to survive them, & the result has been a long life filled with happiness to myself & family. But who can say what would have been the result, to me & mine, even of a series of Confederate victories on different lines & in other places? So let us all gratefully accept things as they have happened & take up the narration of them without any more delay.

I have told of my going into camp near Milford Station, after the battle of Chancellorsville, & staying with my wife at the house of Mrs. Woolfolk. This was on a little hill, overlooking the valley of the Mattapony, a short mile north of Milford Station, & about 500 yards or so east of the railroad. I always look out at the house, from the car windows, as I pass to this day to recall afresh the pleasant hours spent there, & the good friends we found. And in that house, on Sep. 20, '63, our twins were born.[3] Three of Mrs.

Woolfolk's sons were in one of my batteries. Capt. Pichegru Woolfolk was its captain, a fine, handsome, black-haired & eyed six footer, good natured & full of fun & joke but high-strung & fearless in face of any danger. James, somewhat small, with a queer old face, & a defect in his palate which gave him a remarkable sort of pirated voice and great quaintness to his dry humor, was first lieut.; & Ned, a younger & blonde six footer, was a sergeant. Still another brother, Clarence, was a lieut. of infantry in a regiment in Jackson's corps.4 Mrs. W. the mother was a widow, & with her were living her daughters-in-law Mrs. Pichegru & Mrs. Clarence. The whole family were as nice & hospitable as it was possible to be. They took us to board, at first, for a month, but begged my wife to stay along with them when we started on the Gettysburg campaign, & she remained there not only through that, but until December, when we had gone down to Georgia & up to Knoxville.

From this time until the close of the war I kept, not a diary, but a memorandum of dates of marches & principal events, so that I can henceforth be somewhat more minute & accurate in details than I could generally heretofore. It begins, "1863, June 3, Wednesday. Left Milford at 2 P.M. Marching via Spottsylvania C.H. & Summerville Ford of Rapidan." I recall the morning vividly. A beautiful bright June day, & about 11 A.M. a courier from Longstreet's headqrs. brought the order. Although it was only to march to Culpeper C.H. we knew that it meant another great battle with the enemy's army, which still confronted ours at Fredericksburg. I remember the hurried preparations, the parting with my wife & little daughter, & the looking back as long as even the tops of the locust trees & oaks about the house could be seen. And I can recall, too, the pride & confidence I felt in my splendid battalion, as it filed out of the fields into the road, with every chest & ammunition wagon filled, & every horse in fair order, & every detail fit for a campaign. It was just a month to the very hour almost that Pickett's charge at Gettysburg was repulsed. And late that afternoon or early next morning we passed over the ground where eleven months later, in May '64, we were to have a desperate struggle with Grant for twelve days at Spottsylvania C.H. I recall our camp that night near a house on the right of the road, but I cannot locate it.

My next entry in what I may call, for short, my diary is, "Jun. 6th, Sat. Arrived Culpeper C.H. 11 A.M.—60 miles. Went in person with Hood's division to Ellis's Ford."

This requires a little explanation. While Gen. Lee was headed for the country north of the Potomac, and as I recollect it, our destination was generally understood, at least by the officers, yet he was not averse to picking up a fight anywhere on the road that a chance offered. Our corps being at Culpeper was some 8 or 10 miles from the Rappahannock River and across that river was Hooker & all his army. They might nearly all still be about Fredericksburg, or they might have divined our plan & some of them might be on the march up to confront us. Ellis's Ford was on the Rappahannock in a direct line to Hooker's army & Hood's division was ordered to go & bivouac near it that night, and at dawn the next morning he was instructed to surprise the enemy's picket which held the ford and to cross the river. I cannot now recall what was intended to be done after getting the division across, but my recollection is that no other infantry was near at hand nor was any more artillery thought necessary than Henry's[5] battalion, of 18 guns, which always marched with Hood's division. So my own battalion was left at Culpeper C.H., and I was sent in person rather as an engineer to aid Gen. Hood in making his dispositions to force the crossing & to hold his position afterward if attacked. Longstreet had no engineer officer on his staff & I was frequently pressed into that service for odd jobs.

So I left my battalion to go on & camp about a mile northwest of the town, on the same ground where I had first joined them six months before, & I rode alone to overtake Gen. Hood, already marching toward Ellis's with his division. With his staff we rode ahead of the troops, escorted by a few of our own cavalry, & sometime during the afternoon we stealthily approached the river & spent nearly two hours in inspecting the ground & approaches & the large picket, & reserve near by, which the enemy had on the opposite bank. And a great part of the time a severe thunder shower poured on us, which helped to keep the enemy from discovering us.

Then, very wet & uncomfortable, we found a house, a mile or so away, where we went to bivouac until it was time to move for the attack at dawn. But about midnight we were waked with orders to abandon the enterprise, which I for one, was not sorry to do, because I did not have my own battalion with me. I remember on this trip talking a great deal with Hood about our chances in an invasion of the enemy's territory & the impression I gathered of Hood's view was that we were taking a lot of chances. The only one, however, which impressed me was the question of being able to keep up an ammunition supply in Pennsylvania by wagons from Staunton—our nearest rail point. But, like the rest of the army generally, nothing gave me much concern so long as I knew that Gen. Lee was in command. I am sure there can never have been an army with more supreme confidence in its commander than that army had in Gen. Lee. We looked forward to victory under him as confidently as to successive sunrises.

My next entry is "*Tuesday, Jun. 9th.* Drawn out for cavalry battle but not engaged." Gen. Stuart had concentrated about 8 miles from Culpeper at Brandy Station the largest cavalry force which we had ever gotten together, some 8,000 men.[6] And here early in the morning on Jun. 9th he was attacked by Pleasonton, with about as many cavalry, supported by two brigades of infantry, who forced crossings at dawn at several fords on the river and took some of Stuart's commands by surprise. The fact was that, although Ewell's corps had left Fredbg. ahead of ours, & was pushing on towards Winchester, & only A. P. Hill's corps was left at Fredbg., Hooker had not discovered the movement, even though on Jun. 6th he had made Sedgwick bridge the Rappahannock & make some demonstrations of attack. But he had also ordered Pleasonton to make a heavy demonstration on Culpeper & find out what was there. Pleasonton did it in fine style, & but for bad luck in the killing of Col. Davis,7 leading his advance, would probably have surprised & captured the most of Stuart's artillery. But as soon as Stuart's people could get together they were able to hold their own & after hard fighting all the morning, in the afternoon Pleasonton, as we put it, was forced to withdraw. He had however gained the information he was sent for, & Hooker immediately withdrew from Fredericksburg, & moved up to keep between us & Washington City. In the early part of Stuart's battle it had looked as if he might need help, & my battalion moved down toward the fight, & remained there most of the day, but we were never called upon to show ourselves.

I recall nothing else of our stay at Culpeper & my next entries are as follows. "Monday, June 16. Marched from Culpeper at 2 P.M." "Tuesday, June 17. To Flint Hill, via Sperryville & Gaines Cross-roads. Arrested postmaster in gap for selling liquor to command." The incident was as follows. On the march I met a man with a barrel of apple brandy mounted on a sort of sled. I suspected him of designing to open a little road side bar, to sell to the passing troops of all kinds, & charged him with that intention. He swore that he would never do such a thing, but was only taking the liquor to his own home. I gave him a warning & went on, but soon sent back an officer to watch him. In about an hour he overtook me with the culprit who had been caught in the act. His brandy had been confiscated to our medical stores. I told him that I would conscript him, & I tied his hands to the rear of a caisson & let him march there until we went into camp, about 12 miles off, that evening. Then I let him go. He pleaded govt. occupation as postmaster at some country office there, as a bar to conscription, but I only threatened that to give him a good scare.

The diary entries continue as follows. "Jun. 17th, Wed. Through Chester Gap of Blue Ridge, via Front Royal & across the Shenandoah at Morgan's Ford. 63 miles from Culpeper." I remember the camp & a delightful swim in the clear cool river after the hot & dusty march. And that recalls that since leaving Culpeper my battalion & the Washington Artillery had always marched together under the command of Col. Walton of the W.A., who ranked me & who was really the chief of artillery of the corps, being the ranking arty. officer. I was but the third in rank, Col. Cabell's[8] commission also being older than mine. Cabell was attached to McLaws's division, Dearing's[9] battalion to Pickett's & Henry's to Hood's. Each of these had 18 guns. Walton's Washington Artillery 9,[10] and my 26 composed the "reserve," so called, & usually went together. Now, when different commands march together it is a custom of service to let them alternate in having the lead on successive days; for the marching is easier, & the camp earlier, with choice of ground. But Walton, somehow, ignored that custom & always gave his own battalion the lead. At this camp some of my captains became indignant & wished me to protest but I refused. Moody prepared to go over & challenge one of Walton's captains, but I objected to any one's taking any notice whatever of the matter, to which all at last agreed, consoling themselves by saying that they would get in front when the fighting began. My relations with Walton were always very pleasant and friendly, & I really suppose his never giving us the lead was merely from inadvertence & of course I never complained. But we had an ample revenge at Gettysburg as will duly appear.

Another reminiscence of this camp is a painful one—an undignified punishment I gave a sergeant, one of the best in the command, & who was killed at his gun soon afterward at Gettysburg. To prevent straggling on the march I had occasional roll-calls on the road, and that day I had found this sergeant & some half dozen privates absent. The privates I put to marching around a ring, carrying fence rails, for an hour or so after getting into camp. I sent for the sergeant intending only to reprimand him, but the reprimand as I spoke it seemed so mild & disproportional to what the privates had to undergo that on [the] spur of the moment I told the sergeant to climb a tree & sit up there for a while. Some of the men guyed him—"I sees your legs a dangling down," & before very long I let him come down, but it is the one punishment I ever gave which I always after regretted—as tending to mortify.

"Jun. 18th. To Millwood, & encamped on road to Winchester. Arrested spy & also citizen for taking horse." At my camp, the night before, an intelligent, & apparently reputable & prominent resident of the vicinity, had called & told me a long story of a neighbor of his—a young man—who was a deserter, he said, from some Va. infantry regt., & who had been arrested as a spy by Ewell's men when they defeated Milroy & captured Winchester, a few days before, but who had escaped from Ewell's provost guard. He said the man was then at his home a few miles ahead on our road. So, in the morning, I sent a guard ahead & they arrested the man just about to mount a fine mare standing at his door & with saddle bags on the saddle. The house was one of the largest & finest country houses I saw in the Valley, but I cannot recall the man's name. As the charge against him was very grave—of being both a deserter & a spy—& as my guard were not equipped with any weapons but old sabres, I had irons put on the prisoner until I could transfer him to the corps provost guard, which was within a couple of days.[11] He was very angry & swore vengeance against me, but I never heard what became of him after we transferred him. His father called to see him once at our camp, & I offered him the use of my tent for a private interview, but the prisoner refused to accept any courtesy.

The case of the citizen arrested for taking a horse was rather peculiar. One of my private soldiers brought him to my tent & accused him of stealing his horse. But the charge was made in such broad Dutch brogue that I only partially understood the details. The man was evidently a man of some means & position, & what had happened was this. Dutchy was a driver, & had ridden one of his horses out to get some grass. At a suitable place he had dismounted & cut some, & given to the horse to eat, while he went off where it was long & cut & tied up a bundle. When he came with it his horse was gone. Going toward camp he met our mail carrier starting for Winchester, & told him to ride fast & to look out for the horse. A mile or two along the road, [the] mail carrier, looking down a country road, leading at right angles, saw a man with two horses, both saddled, but exchanging the saddles. He rode up & one was Dutchy's horse, so he arrested the man & brought him & both horses to camp, & then he started again for Winchester. The prisoner *claimed* to have found the horse, not eating grass, as Dutchy left him, but straying down the road. Dutchy swore his horse would never have left grass uneaten. The prisoner asked permission to write a note to the gentleman on whose place we were encamped, whom I had already met, & who was a county lawyer of prominence. He did so—the house was very near & soon there came back a reply that Mr. _____ (the prisoner), I can't recall the name, was a gentleman of the highest standing, & far beyond any suspicion of stealing a horse. On this I apologised for the mail carrier's arresting him & I let him go. I had not then seen the mail carrier, nor heard about the change of saddles.

That night, I not only heard that, but the lawyer who had sent me the note, so strongly endorsing the gentleman, came down & told me that he really did believe that the man *would* steal a horse, but knew that whatever he wrote to me would probably have to be shown to him, & he didn't want to have any difficulty with him, & consequently gave him a good character. Said the man had been a soldier, but had put in a substitute & gotten himself discharged; & that since his discharge he had been concerned in some financial matters which he, the lawyer, thought shady. Hearing this I was sorry I had let him go. But I had another chance as will soon appear.

"Jun. 19th, Friday. Went to Ashby's Gap & selected line of battle." This was another little job of engineering for Gen. Longstreet. Our corps was holding the gaps in the Blue Ridge, while Ewell's Corps was already across the Potomac & making a regular raid up the Valley, by Hagerstown & Chambersburg, toward Carlisle & Harrisburg; while A. P. Hill's corps coming up from Fredericksburg (which he could not leave until Hooker had been drawn up towards the Potomac) passed in our rear & crossed the Potomac & followed on after Ewell. We would protect his flank, & then follow after him when he was safe over. So McLaws's div. was holding Ashby's Gap, Hood's div. some of the others, & in front of them was Stuart with our cavalry keeping off the enemy's cavalry under Pleasonton. And P. had a large force, & was aggressive, & the fighting was growing harder & drawing nearer every day. And it was thought not impossible that infantry might come to help Pleasonton, & some hard & important fighting might suddenly and soon take place in the gap itself. So I was sent up in person to select a line of battle for McLaws's division, & positions for Cabell's batteries; & I spent a day up there with them, finding a beautiful & strong line, & no end of delicious wild strawberries growing all around it. As Col. Cabell ranked me, I felt somewhat awkward at making suggestions to him about positions, &c., but the old man was not only a superb soldier, but a delightful gentleman also, & on this occasion & on others somewhat similar I learned a great affection for him.

"Jun. 21, Sunday. Marched battalion to Shenandoah." On Saturday night the news from the cavalry in front of the gaps was so threatening that Longstreet sent me word to come with my battalion & cross the Shenandoah to the entrance of Ashby's Gap.

I started long before day, there being some moonlight, & was riding at the head of the battalion, some three miles on the way, when just at the peep of dawn I met in the road, travelling fast on a good horse, the gentleman who had gotten mixed up with Dutchy's horse on the 18th. He passed so rapidly that I had to call after him to stop him. I told him that on reflection I had decided to report the whole matter to Gen. Longstreet, & that the general was near Ashby's Gap where I was going, & I wanted him to go with me. He accommodated himself promptly & without complaint to the situation, & at once asked what sum in money I would think a sufficient deposit to secure his return. I said $500. He asked me to send a guard with him to a neighbor's house, not very far off. I did so, & in an hour he returned with the money, which he handed to the quartermaster as a sort of bail. And then he started for Longstreet's hdqrs. alone on his fast horse.

We marched to the place directed & stayed there all day but were not called on for any service. And late in the afternoon our man presented himself with one of Gen. Longstreet's staff officers, who brought me a personal message from the general, asking me to drop the matter, which, of course, I very willingly did. For the gentleman was a relative of the staff officer, & really all that he had done was to take up a stray horse. And I would not have stopped him in the morning had I had a moment for reflection. It was the quick impulse of a moment seeing him suddenly passing in the dim light. Then having done it, I stuck to it, but was glad of a graceful retreat. And the gentleman himself behaved very nicely & we parted friends—I have never heard of him since. I forget whether we spent that night near Ashby's Gap or not. But we were back at Millwood on Tuesday & on Wednesday we marched via Winchester, & encamped at Bunker Hill, 21 miles.

In passing through Winchester I called on my wife's pretty cousin, Mrs. John Stephenson, & had a warm welcome & a nice lunch & heard some amusing details about their experiences under the Federal occupation of the town. One story was told of a young lady, who was not allowed to buy hay, for the family milk cow, without a permit. She applied at headquarters for the permit, but it was refused unless she would take the oath of allegiance. She demurred to that, but Gen. Milroy[12] insisted, saying that "this wicked rebellion must be crushed," to which she answered, "If you expect to crush this rebellion by starving John Harman's[13] old cow you may try it & be damned to you."

The next day, Thursday, Jun. 25, we forded the Potomac at Williamsport, & encamped on the north bank after a march of 23 miles. A. P. Hill's corps had come up from Fredericksburg, & crossed & gone ahead of us, & now, our corps was following but with one of our divisions, Pickett's, still some distance in our rear.[14]

About this time Gen. Stuart, who as explained before was on the eastern slope of the Blue Ridge, in front of the passes held by Longstreet's infantry, & fighting off the enemy's cavalry, started off on an expedition which has been very much written about & which must be explained in describing the campaign.

When Hooker found that our infantry was crossing the Potomac, he crossed also, to keep between us & Washington City. Stuart, instead of crossing above Hooker & keeping between him & our infantry, struck east, crossed the Potomac, below where Hooker had crossed it, and got between Hooker & Washington City. Of course he could not maintain himself there, but he was able to burn & destroy wagon trains with supplies, & to create a good deal of confusion; & by rapid movements he eluded all their efforts to crush him, & rode north, clear around Hooker's army, & finally joined Gen. Lee on the afternoon of July 2nd at Gettysburg. When he started, he left behind him two brigades, Jones's & Robertson's, to act between Longstreet's & Hill's infantry & the enemy; Ewell already having two small brigades, Jenkins's & White's in advance.[15] But these two brigades did not prove sufficient to keep Gen. Lee as fully posted as he desired to be about the enemy's position and movements during Stuart's absence. His official report of the campaign make[s] reference to this & it has ever since furnished ground for criticism of the movement. Gen. Stuart's friends have shown, however, conclusively, that he had asked Gen. Lee's permission to make the movement & that Gen. Lee had allowed him discretion in the matter. And they have also claimed that Gen. Lee was at no serious disadvantage in the opening of the action at Gettysburg, & so no special harm can be shown to have resulted.[16]

Yet in my humble opinion, it was bad play to let our cavalry get out of touch & reach of our infantry. The first axiom of war is to mass one's strength. Then & then only can its fullest power be brought into play. As before stated, in the account of Chancellorsville, I think Hooker's defeat was due to the absence of his cavalry on just such a useless raid as this. We ought to have recognized Hooker's error & avoided repeating it. I cannot say exactly what would have happened, but our force in hand at [the] opening of the fight would have been greater—& that might easily have changed the whole result. We took unnecessary risk, which was bad war, & the only bad war, too, I think, in all our tactics. Every thing else in the advance was excellently planned & executed—& I can now proceed with my narrative.

Friday, June 26, we marched from Williamsport via Hagerstown to Greencastle, Pa., & encamped on [the] northeast edge of the village. The next day we went on & passing through Chambersburg encamped on a stream about a mile northwest. I recall two incidents of the passage through Chambersburg. The entire population of the place lined all points of observation, to see the troops pass. A few houses had U.S. flags displayed, of which our men took not the slightest notice—either here or anywhere else that we ever encountered them in the possession of non-combatants. This, it may be said in passing, was in strong contrast with the behavior of the Federal troops everywhere & always; during the war & since—almost to this very day. It is a feeling which I cannot myself understand, but it is like the feeling with which fervent believers in some religions regard the emblems of faith of other sects, & seek to insult & destroy them—as the old Spanish priests would an idol or Scotch covenanters would a cross. As we marched through Chambersburg, one of the houses, with a little garden in front, not only had a U.S. flag hanging from a window, but a good looking stout Dutch girl, in the porch, had a little one in her hand. She was waving this defiantly, &, as I happened to be passing, in an excess of zeal she came forward & stood in the front gate, & began to wave it almost in the faces of the men, marching on the side walk. One of the very first of these chanced to be a member of Parker's battery with quite a reputation as a wag. He stopped square in front of her, stared at her a moment, then gave a sort of jump at her & shouted "Boo." A roar of laughter & cheers went up along the line, under which the young lady retreated to the porch.

The other incident I did not witness, but it ran through the corps, & for months afterward furnished road-side slang almost as popular as "Here's your mule."[17] While the residents of one house were all looking on from the porch, at the street full of guns & the side walks of hurrying infantry, a large yellow dog in the backyard caught on to the fact that something unusual was transpiring, & came through a gate into the front yard to see about it. And when he did see, his rage knew no bounds. He charged up to the front fence & reared up on it, & he cavorted up & down, barking furiously, as dogs do when they are sure that the gate is shut & there are no holes. And a little girl on the front step shrieked out in evident terror, "Ma! Ma! Don't let Beave bite the army!"

For two days, Jun. 28th & 29th, we laid at Chambersburg. The only incident I recall is my giving my darkey, Charley, a small licking for getting drunk, on some apple jack he had managed to purloin from our hospital stores. That was the second & last time I ever had to punish him. The first was a year before at Keach's near Richmond for robbing the Keach's pear tree.

June 30th, Tuesday. We marched from Chambersburg, &, after much delay along the road by troops & trains of our infantry, we went into camp, before 2 P.M., at a little village called Greenwood, on the road to Gettysburg, & only 9 miles from Chambersburg. We had had some rains & the roads were very muddy. The infantry would seldom[18] be able to use them & generally marched in the fields along side where they would trample broad paths in the wheat, now nearly ripe. It was a clear hot day, and, about noon, seeing a house with a pump in the front porch, I rode up to see if we could get a drink. The Dutch owner was in the porch when I came up & was in a state of abject despair. The infantry ahead of us had not only made a path along the edge of his wheat field, but in trying to pump their canteens full of water at his well had pumped the well dry & [left] the porch very wet & very muddy. I could see deep trouble in his face as I came up & in the meekest manner possible asked if I could get a drink of water. He almost shouted, "No! Dere ain't no water! De well is done pump dry! And just look at dis porch vere dey been! And see dere vere dey trampled down dat wheat! Mine Gott! Mine Gott! I'se heard of de horrors of war before but I never see what dey was till now!" That sounds like a made up anecdote, but it is verbatim & literatim as I saw & heard it myself.

The Dutch in that section of country were very unsophisticated people, but generally apparently very industrious & very prosperous, & a sturdy & desirable population. Big barns, & fat cattle, & fruits & vegetables were every where. Owen, adjt. of the Washington Arty., tells a story of this march in his book which is so good that I repeat it. They stayed, one night, with a couple who fed them so generously that when they left in the morning a silver half dollar, which some one had, was voted to be given to the husband. He beamed with delight as he called his wife, "Katrina! Take dis money & put it wid dat oder one vot you got last Christmas. By Jiminy! Ain't dis war big luck for some peeples!"[19]

Gen. Lee was encamped close by us this afternoon & after we were in camp I remember a long visit at his headquarters to my old comrades of his staff & I recall the conversation as unusually careless & jolly. Certainly there was no premonition that the next morning was to open the great battle of the campaign. Greenwood was a little village right among big rolling hills in a gap through the Blue Ridge Mountains. At the eastern outlet of the gap was Cashtown, some five miles[20] from Greenwood; & about ten miles beyond that, by a good turnpike, was Gettysburg. Evidently we had been stopped at Greenwood, because we were not wanted any further east, for we could easily have made many miles more that afternoon. And there were signs of the close proximity of Hill's corps, & I think we also knew that Ewell's, which had been far to the north east, almost to the Susquehannah River, was also under orders to come in for concentration at or about Cashtown. And when all our corps were together what could successfully attack us? So, naturally, we were all in good spirits. We remained in camp all next day at the same place. I wrote a long letter to my wife, telling her that of course we would have to have a battle before very long, but, as yet, there was no prospect of it.

A new officer, recently elected to be a lieut. in Rhett's battery (now under command of Lieut. Gilbert, R. having been promoted & transferred), arrived from Charleston. I can't recall his name.[21] He has never served with artillery before, &, being new to the duties, asked me to let him look on for a few days, to learn the ropes, before going on regular duty. I consented & assured him that there would be plenty of time. And, the next afternoon, I could but laugh to recall it, as I saw him standing behind a little sapling, & looking at the Federal batteries at the Peach Orchard, only about 500 yards off, & knocking his battery to pieces around him as badly & as fast as I ever saw it done in my life. He stuck to it until it was over, but finally concluded that he did not fancy the artillery & returned to his old cavalry regiment in So. Ca.

There took place on this day, also, a quarrel between my two captains, Moody & Woolfolk, which I only learned of afterward, but will tell the whole incident here. It arose over some question of precedence in taking the road in the morning, & the one entitled to it not being promptly ready, but I never learned the details. But on this day, July 1, Moody sent a challenge to Woolfolk, which was accepted, the time fixed for next morning, & the weapons rifled muskets at ten paces. But the orders we received that night, to march to Gettysburg, caused the meeting to be postponed until after the battle.[22]

In the battle Woolfolk was wounded badly, & was sent home. Before he returned to duty, Moody, in Dec. '63, was left sick at Knoxville, & made a prisoner. Before he was exchanged, in the fall of '64, Woolfolk was captured on a visit to his home & was never exchanged. And, soon after the war, Moody was assassinated at his home in Port Gibson, Mississippi—shot down at his desk at night by a man he had abused in the courthouse that day—he was a lawyer. Not far from the same time, but a little later I believe, Capt. Woolfolk was killed in Richmond, in the Capitol building, along with a great many others, by the falling of the gallery in a courtroom, which carried down the floor of the room beneath. So the two men never met again after their quarrel.

And now let me explain how the battle was brought on at Gettysburg. First, there had been a change of Federal commanders. Gen. Lee in advancing up the Cumberland Valley had left behind him a Federal garrison of about 10,000 men at Harpers Ferry. Gen. Hooker wished to withdraw that garrison & send it with the 12th Corps (about 9,000) to operate in Gen. Lee's rear. It might not have been a bad move; but Gen. Halleck disapproved of it, & on this Hooker asked to be relieved. The command was given to Gen. Meade, who was doubtless one of the best men available. This change took place on June 28th.

When Meade took command the most of his army was some 15 or 20 miles south & east of Gettysburg. Some may have been 40.[23] He began moving slowly in that direction as Lee's troops were known to be further north & west. About June 29, Gen. Heth[24] of Hill's corps heard that there were plenty of shoes in the stores in Gettysburg, & he asked permission of A. P. Hill to go there & get some for his men, who were in great need of them. I think he first sent a brigade on this errand on June 30th, but the brigade found a strong cavalry force had just occupied the town, & did not attempt to drive them out. But, however this may be, on July 1st Heth's whole division started to Gettysburg to get shoes, & Pender's[25] division followed to help in case of trouble. The strength of the two divisions was about 12,000 men. But no very serious trouble was anticipated,[26] for Hill's 3rd division, Anderson's, was left behind, & also Longstreet's two divisions which were near by.

The Federal cavalry at Gettysburg was Buford's division,[27] about 3,000, & early that morning there also arrived the 1st & 12 Army Corps of infantry, some 23,000 men, under Gen. Reynolds.[28] And here the absence of Stuart, with the bulk of the cavalry, does seem to me to cut some figure. Had they been with us Gen. Lee would doubtless have been too well informed of the enemy's exact location to have permitted two divisions to blunder into an attack upon two corps & a division of cavalry. For, without going into details, the fact is that Heth & Pender were getting a genteel whipping, by the very superior force they had inadvertently pitched into,[29] with great spirit, when unexpected help came to them as will presently be told. But before it arrived Heth's two leading brigades had been almost ruined. The brigade of Davis lost all its field officers but two, & a great many men were captured.[30] Gen. Archer & a large part of his brigade were also captured. Heth was wounded & the effective force of his whole division for the rest of the battle was greatly impaired. The Federal General Reynolds was killed, & was succeeded by Howard. It is safe to say that Heth & Pender would have had to retire but for the arrival on the field, about 2 P.M., of Rodes's division of Ewell's corps coming from Heidlesburg on the N.E. Rodes's 6,000 men[31] made things more even, but the enemy still had a superiority, & Iverson's,[32] one of Rodes's brigades, was caught in a corner & lost three regiments captured out of five. But, about 3:30 P.M., Early's division of Ewell's corps also arrived, making the infantry forces about equal. Rodes had not been ordered to Gettysburg but to Cashtown.[33] Hearing the firing, however, he had come to it. Early's line of march brought him naturally near the field.

A general advance of the Confederate line, reinforced by Early, about 4 P.M. swept the entire Federal line from their advanced position, & drove them through the town. But they made a fairly good retreat, losing only some 5,000 prisoners & 2 guns.[34] Just beyond the town, & over looking it, stands Cemetery Hill. It forms part of a ridge, presenting the most beautiful position for an army which I have ever seen occupied. Good positions were abundant in that section, it being remarkably well cultivated & having numerous extensive ridges, with open rolling lands between. But the position here offered was unique. Briefly, it was in the shape of a fish hook. A straight shank, some two miles long,[35] reached to Big & Little Round Top mountains, forming a very strong left flank, with superb view & command over all the open ground in front, & unlimited positions for the Federal's strongest arm, their fine artillery. Opposite the town the hook gradually bends around, & then runs off the point some 2,000 yards long,[36] in a rocky ridge overlooking a creek, very steep in front in many places, & masked by woods from artillery fire of an assailant, but permitting its use at canister range by the Federals. This was, perhaps, the strongest part of their whole position. The whole length of this line was 4½ miles,[37] just right for their force, & stretching us too much for ours. Plenty of stone fences & wood permitted rapid arrangement of breast works every where.

On this line Howard had kept as a reserve, during the fighting in front, one brigade of the 11th Corps with a battery.[38] The fugitives from the defeated line were here rallied & reformed, by Gen. Hancock, who had been sent to the front by Gen. Meade, when he heard of the death of Genl. Reynolds. Our troops pursuing, stopped in or near the town, & did not attack them. This delay has been sometimes criticised. I think any attack we could have made that afternoon would have failed. Heth's & Pender's divisions had been much crippled, as already told, & even Rodes had lost nearly 3,000 men out of 8,000. Only Early's was even comparatively fresh & he had but two brigades disposable, the other two watching a road on which the Federal 12th Corps was near. Ewell's 3rd division (Johnson's),[39] did not arrive until sundown. By that time two other Federal corps were arriving, the 12th & the 3rd. Gen. Lee did order Gen. Ewell to carry the position if he thought it practicable to do so, but warned him not to bring on a general engagement. Gen. Ewell thought the position too strong for assault, & Lee and Col. Long agreed in this opinion.

And now, when any further attack that evening was abandoned, there occurred, in my judgment, the crisis of this battle, & this campaign, & of all that depended upon it. It arose in Gen. Lee's consideration of the question whether or not to resume offensive battle on the morrow. He says in his report that it had become "*in a measure* unavoidable." As the statement is qualified let us look at it purely as a military question, whether or not he could now have avoided further offensive battle. The reasons he gives are as follows:

> It had not been intended to deliver a general battle so far from our base, unless attacked, but, coming unexpectedly upon the whole Federal army to withdraw through the mountains, with our extensive trains, would have been difficult & dangerous. At the same time, we were unable to await attack as the country was unfavorable for collecting supplies, in the presence of the enemy, who could restrain our foraging parties by holding the mountain passes with local & other troops. A battle had therefore become, in a measure, unavoidable, & the success already gained gave hope of a favorable issue.[40]

Now when it is remembered that we stayed for three days longer on that very ground, two of them days of desperate battle, ending in the discouragement of a bloody repulse, & then successfully withdrew all our trains & most of the wounded through the mountains; and, finding the Potomac too high to ford, protected them all & foraged successfully for over a week in a very restricted territory along the river, until we could build a bridge, it does not seem improbable that we could have faced Meade safely on the 2nd at Gettysburg without assaulting him in his wonderfully strong position. We had the prestige of victory with us, having chased him off the field & through the town. We had a fine defensive position on Seminary Ridge ready at our hand to occupy. It was not such a really *wonderful* position as the enemy happened to fall into, but it was no bad one, & it could never have been successfully assaulted. As Gen. Jackson once said, "We did sometimes fail to drive them out of position, but they *always* failed to drive us." The onus of attack was upon Meade anyhow. We could even have fallen back to Cashtown & held the mountain passes with all the prestige of victory, & popular sentiment would have forced Meade to take the aggressive.

I cannot believe that military critics will find any real difficulties in our abstaining from further assault on the following day, or in pointing out more than one alternative far more prudent than an assault upon a position of such evident & peculiar strength. I never think over the situation that night without recalling Ives's estimate of Gen. Lee, that "his name was audacity." For I have a great idea of the immense advantages in battle which position may sometimes confer. And I surely think that Gen. Lee never paid his soldiers a higher compliment than in what he gave them to do on this occasion.

Sometime during the day, already, Longstreet's two divisions, Hood's & McLaws's, had been ordered forward. They bivouaced during the night about four miles off. It has been asserted by some that Longstreet was ordered to asault at sunrise but I do not find this assertion credible.[41] Had Gen. Lee desired this, the one way to accomplish it would have been to have himself provided guides & ordered Longstreet's troops put in position during the night. It takes a little time to hunt out & reconnoiter a position which has to be attacked & the enemy's position here was never thoroughly developed until morning.

There was one other occurrence of this night which I have never seen a comment upon, by any writer, & yet it seems to me to involve one of the vital points of the battle. Ewell's troops were all placed beyond, or N.E. of Gettysburg, bent around toward the point of the fish hook of the enemy's position. It was an awkward place, far from our line of retreat in case of disaster, & not convenient either for re-inforcing others or being reinforced. And as has already been explained this part of the enemy's position was in itself the strongest & it was practically almost unassailable. On the night of the 1st Gen. Lee ordered him withdrawn & brought around to our right of the town. Gen. Ewell had seen some ground he thought he could take & asked permission to stay & to take it. Gen. Lee consented, but it turned out early next morning that the position could not be taken. Yet the orders to come out from the awkward place he was in—where there was no reasonable probability of his accomplishing any good on the enemy's line in his front & where his artillery was of no service—were never renewed & he stayed there till the last. The ground is there still for any military engineer to pronounce whether or not Ewell's corps & all its artillery was not practically paralysed & useless by its position during the last two days of the battle.

Back at our camp at Greenwood we knew nothing of the fighting until late in the afternoon. Then rumors began to arrive, & at last about dark, came orders for us to start at 1 A.M. for the field—following Walton & the Washington Artillery. All the accounts we had of the fighting represented it as having been very hard & bloody on both sides, & though we had finally gotten the ground & the town, we heard enough to assure us that the little dispute was not entirely settled.

We had a little breakfast and corn coffee before starting, & then a lovely march over a fairly good pike by a bright moon, & some time after sunrise we turned off to the right from the pike, &, getting on a country road of near parallel direction, we all halted in a sort of very thin wood, with grass under the trees, as I have it put in my notes, at 9 A.M. But when one is up long before day[42] & marching he is very apt to think it much later than it really is. I don't remember consulting my watch, & the distance by the map is only about 15 miles[43] & I remember the sun as low in the sky. So I doubt whether it was really much after seven. We were a mile, or so, short of reaching Seminary Ridge. Our guns halted in column by the road side, & we made the drivers unhitch the horses & let them graze, but keeping the harness on, & we rested & nibbled a bit at the lunch we had handy. As soon as we halted Col. Walton rode on to the front to report our presence to Gen. Longstreet. In about a half hour he returned, &, riding up to me, told me that Gen. Longstreet wished me to report to him in person. I could but feel sorry for Walton, who evidently felt himself overslaughed & that I was going to be practically put in charge of the artillery on the field. And, as I rode off to the front, he stopped with his battalion & dismounted, & I saw him no more that day.[44]

I found Longstreet with Gen. Lee on Seminary Ridge, from which we had a view of the town & of [the] enemy's line above it & toward our right. My recollection is that a lot of our infantry was halted not far off, & some of their generals were around, & quite a lot of staff officers. In Gen. Lee's presence Longstreet pointed out the enemy's position & said that we would attack his left flank. He told me to take command of all the artillery on the field, for the attack, & suggested that I go at once, first, & get an idea of the ground, & then go & bring my own battalion up. But he told me to leave the Washington Arty. in bivouac where they were. And he specially cautioned me to keep all movements carefully out of view of a signal station whose flags we could see wig-wagging on Little Round Top. In ten minutes after I reported, I had my orders, & was off to examine all the roads leading to the right & front, & to get an understanding of the enemy's position &

how & where we could best get at it. I rode fast—having a courier or two with me, & I don't think it took me much over an hour to get a very fair idea of the ground & roads & to find Cabell's & Henry's battalions, & give them what instructions were needed. Then I rode back to bring up my own battalion. They were still grazing their harnessed horses, when I rode up & had the bugle blow "boots & saddles." And then my men had their revenge for marching in the rear, for we had to file our whole length along by the W.A. men & guns. And every man of ours was strutting & telling his neighbor, "I told you so. We've got in front at last." And the whole thing really only worried me, for the W.A. men were as good as any on earth & their officers too, and they were all good fellows, besides, with no nonsense or affectation, & they got into this position from no fault of their own but only from Walton's thoughtlessness—who had been their old colonel before the war.

I do not remember looking at my watch this whole day, & all my ideas of the hours are guesses, but it seems to me that before 11 A.M. I had gotten my battalion down in the valley of Willoughby Run, in a few hundred yards of the school-house, where I had to wait on the infantry & Cabell's & Henry's battalions before going further. I had come there by a short & quite direct road, which at one point passed over a high bare place where it was in full view of the Federal signal station. But I avoided that part of the road by turning out to the left,[45] & going through fields & hollows, & getting back to the road again a quarter mile or so beyond. Then I recall riding back for something, & finding the head of one of our divisions of infantry standing halted in sight of the signal station. It had been put on that road to march, but told, as I had been, to keep out of view. Finding that the road brought them into view they halted & sent back for orders or a guide. Finally, after a delay which must have been much over an hour, orders came, and, I believe, a guide to lead them by "Black Horse Tavern." I've never forgotten the name since. And that, I see by the map, was apparently four miles to get less than one.[46]

That is just one illustration of how time may be lost in handling troops, and of the need of an abundance of competent staff officers by the generals in command. Scarcely any of our generals had half of what they needed to keep a *constant & close supervision on the execution of important orders.* And that ought always to be done. An army is like a great machine, and in putting it into battle it is not enough for its commander to merely issue the necessary orders. He should have a staff ample to supervise the execution of each step, & to promptly report any difficulty or misunderstanding. There is no telling the value of the hours which were lost by that division that morning. Of course I told the officers at the head of the column of the route my artillery had followed—which was easily seen—but there was no one with authority to vary the orders they were under, & they momentarily expected the new ones for which they had sent & which were very explicit when they came after the long, long delay.

It has since appeared that if our corps had made its attack even two or three hours sooner than it did, our chances of success would have been immensely increased. The key to the whole position was Little Round Mountain, & the enemy's 5th Corps, which alone prevented our taking it, was barely arriving on the field when our assault was finally made; & was barely raced to the position in time to encounter our attack, by Gen. Warren[47] who, fortunately for them, visited the signal station opportunely & discovered our approach. I have already said that I don't think Gen. Lee could have ever ordered or expected an attack by our corps at sunrise, for the preliminary detail for any attack seems to have been left till morning. But, by ten, or eleven o'clock at latest, it was entirely practicable for us to have delivered our attack in good shape. And Confederate writers, with almost one accord, put the blame of whatever delay there was on Gen. Longstreet.

The long & the short of the matter seems to me as follows. Longstreet did not wish to take the offensive. His objection to it was not based at all upon the peculiar strength of the enemy's position for that was not yet recognized, but solely on general principles—perhaps the same referred to implied in Gen. Lee's report where he says that he "had not designed to give battle so far from his base unless attacked." But Gen. Lee overruled him & ordered him to prepare for the assault. Then Longstreet asked permission to delay it until one of the brigades of Hood's division—Law's[48]—which had been left on picket the day before at Guilford Ct. House could rejoin the division. He says that Gen. Lee consented to this delay.[49]

At last somewhere about 3:30 or 4 P.M. Hood's & McLaws's divns. were united in the valley of _____ Run[50] near the little school house, & Hood took the lead to move to the attack. And, after he had actually started his movement, some scouts, which he had sent out, came in & reported that if, instead of attacking the enemy's line running from the Peach Orchard to Round Top, he would march around the base of Round Top to the right, he would strike in on the enemy's rear among their parks & trains. Hood promptly sent the information to Longstreet & asked permission to make the movement. L. replied that Gen. Lee was already fretting over the delay which had occurred & he was unwilling to add to it by offering further suggestions. Henry's battalion moved out with Hood & took positions near the Emmitsburg Pike & became at once hotly engaged & with superior force.[51]

And here I must explain that the enemy's position this afternoon was not exactly in the fishhook line which I have described. At the "bend" of the hook, where the ridge was less well defined & partly flattened out, a lower & still less defined ridge angled off in front of the main ridge which makes the shank of the fishhook & climbs up into the Round Top mountains. Gen. Sickles's corps, by a misconception of orders, had taken position along this ridge, instead of on the main shank. Along this ridge ran the Emmitsburg Pike. Sickles formed along this pike until he reached a cross road, where there was a large peach orchard, & there he turned off to the left & rested his flank in some broken ground in front of the foot of Little Round Top. And neither Little or Big Round Top was occupied, except perhaps with pickets & the signal station. Meade did not like Sickles's position, & was just about to bring him back to the "shank" line (as I may call it) when our attack began. While on the subject I may say that in my judgment it was no harm to Meade to have our charge expend its first fury upon an advanced line in front; where the shank line in rear gave such fine opportunity for artillery to cover the retreat of troops from the front. And Sickles claims that his advanced position is what gave Meade the victory, and in my opinion he has reasonable ground for thinking so.[52]

Each of our divisions formed a double line of battle. Two brigades in the front line & two in the rear. McLaws was on our left, & the middle of his line was about opposite the Peach Orchard, where Sickles's line made a large obtuse angle back to his left. A wood enabled us here to come up within about 500 yards.[53]

Hood, on McLaws's right, first moved out to cross the Emmitsburg Pike and attack Sickles's left flank in the rough ground in front of Round Top. Henry's battalion moved out with him, & they were both heavily opened on by the enemy's artillery from the Peach Orchard & beyond. To help them out I immediately put in Cabell's whole 18 guns, as one battery, from the edge of the woods about 700 yards from the Peach Orchard, & then, selecting 18 of my own 26, I put them in action at the nearest point, Warfield's house, where McLaws's line was within 500 yards of the Peach Orchard.[54] This gave me 54 guns in action—all I had except 8 rifles, which I held for awhile as a reserve. I never remember hearing of any conference or discussions among our generals at this time as to the best formations & tactics in making our attacks, & our method on this occasion struck me as peculiar even then, & I don't think it was the best. [Figure 22 appears here in the manuscript.]

A diagram attached will illustrate the essential positions of the two armies. Now the weakest part of Sickles's line was the angle at the Peach Orchard. And it was the nearest, & time was of great importance, for it was late in the afternoon. I think the best & strongest assault would have been for both divisions, in a decidedly shorter line, to have simultaneously assaulted the Peach Orchard. But, as it was, Hood moved first and alone, &

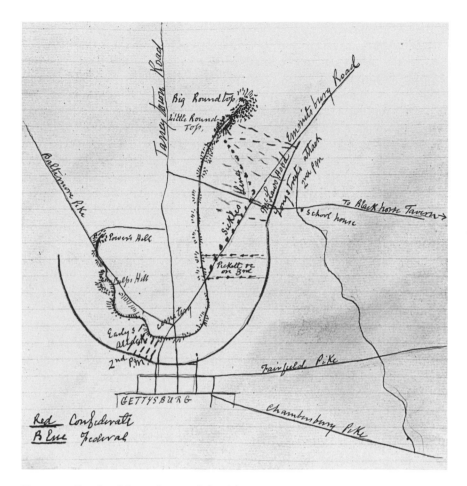

Figure 22. Battle of Gettysburg, 2 July 1863

had a long & desperate fight upon Sickles's left flank, before McLaws was launched upon the Peach Orchard. I had hoped, with my 54 guns & close range, to make it short, sharp, & decisive. At close ranges there was less inequality in our guns, & especially in our ammunition, & I thought that if ever I could overwhelm & crush them I would do it now. But they really surprised me, both with the number of guns they developed, & the way they stuck to them. I don't think there was ever in our war a hotter, harder, sharper artillery afternoon than this. I believe I have written about Gen. S. D. Lee's telling me—when I succeeded him in command of the battalion—that I might pray never to see another Sharpsburg, that "Sharpsburg was artillery hell." Well, at Sharpsburg the casualties of the 6 batteries in the battalion were for the whole campaign about 85 men [and] 60 horses; [at] Gettysburg, 144 men [and] 116 horses, two thirds in this afternoon.

Gilbert's (Rhett's) battery of 4 guns had two fairly struck by the enemy's shot & dismounted. Of less than 75 men[55] in action he had 40 killed & wounded, an unusual proportion of the wounds too being noted by [the] surgeon's report as severe. Gen. Hunt, Meade's chief of artillery, specially writes of the losses of Bigelow's Mass. battery which "sacrificed itself for the safety of the line."[56] It lost 37 out of 104—partly in a hand to hand fight with infantry. But Gilbert's were almost all by artillery fire. Within a half hour after beginning, Capt. Moody reported that he was short of force to handle his 24 pr. howitzers on the rocky ground, & asked permission to try & borrow some volunteers from Barksdale's Miss. brigade lying close in our rear. I went to Gen. Barksdale & we soon got 8 fine fellows. Five of the 8 that night were dead or severely wounded. And at last seeing that the enemy was in greater force than I had expected, I sent for my 8 reserve rifles, to put in the last ounce I could muster. While they were coming McLaws's infantry at last charged the Peach Orchard, & the enemy abandoned it & fell back.

When I saw their line broken & in retreat, I thought the battle was ours. Of course, I had known it was going to be all along, but now the hard part of it was over. All the rest would only be fun, pursuing the fugitives & making targets of them. I rode along my guns, urging the men to limber to the front as rapidly as possible, telling them we would "finish the whole war this afternoon." They were in great spirits, cheering & straining every nerve to get forward in the least possible time, &, our other two batteries coming up just then, all six batteries were going for the Peach Orchard at the same time. We spread out all through & about it, & all the batteries were soon in action again. And when I got to take in all the topography I was very much disappointed. It was not the enemy's main line we had broken. That loomed up near 1,000 yards[57] beyond us, a ridge giving good cover behind it & endless fine positions for batteries. And batteries in abundance were show-ing up & troops too seemed to be marching & fighting every where. There was plenty to shoot at. One could take his choice & here my guns stood & fired until it was too dark to see anything more, & both sides were glad to stop & rest. Once I rode back to try & get up some of Cabell's guns, but he had suffered so heavily in horses that I don't think any of his batteries moved forward before night.

I cannot attempt to give any details of the fight made by our infantry that afternoon further than to say that I think it not only contests with Pickett's charge the palm of being the most brilliant & desperate part of the whole battle of Gettysburg, but that it is not excelled in these qualities by any record of our war—nor, for that matter, of any other war. Made in the peculiar way that it was, all of Hood's men & part of McLaws's had to bring their front parallel to that of the enemy. This always produces a certain amount of confusion, & more especially in broken ground & where two lines follow each other. In reading the reports by the subordinate officers one cannot but be struck by the manner in which during this fighting the continuity of the lines was broken & regiments & brigades were separated & stretched out, & often found their flanks exposed. Hood was wounded—losing his arm early in the action, & Law took command of that division.[58] But generally every brigade fought on its own hook.

Law's brigade on the extreme right overlapped Sickles's line and ascended Little Round Top. As before stated they were just too late to find it unoccupied, Warren having succeeded in bringing up the 5th Corps. This, once in position, made it impregnable. Kershaw gives an instance of how little confusions often cause serious troubles as follows. In the right wing of his brigade, the right regiment—the 7th—had overlapped the one next on its left. To correct this he ordered the 7th to "move by the right flank." Meanwhile owing to the obliquity of the lines, his left wing was nearest to the enemy, & charging the enemy's batteries in rear of the Peach Orchard, but out of Kershaw's view from intervening obstacles. The enemy's cannoneers had deserted their guns, & their caissons were actually beginning to run away when there came up the line, through the noise of the battle, the command which Gen. Kershaw had given to the 7th Regt. only, the command "Move by the right flank." The left wing stopped its advance on the enemy's batteries, & moved by the right flank. Immediately the retreating enemy ran back to their guns, & as Gen. K. states it, "opened on these doomed regiments a raking fire of grape & canister at short distance, which proved most disastrous, &, for a time, destroyed their usefulness. Hundreds of the bravest & best men of Carolina fell victims of this fatal blunder."[59] Imagine the difference of Kershaw's men using the guns on the fugitive enemy! It is things like this which are to be expected when any complicated tactics have to be executed in battle.

I never myself thoroughly comprehended all that was done by those two divisions, that afternoon, until a few years ago, when as the guest of Mr. John Russell Young, I was one of a party of both Confederate & Federal generals who visited Gettysburg, & went all over the field under the escort of a professional guide, Capt. Young.[60] His exact knowledge of the ground & study of the history of the battle enabled him to give wonderfully minute & accurate statements of all that took place. Standing on Little Round Top, I first heard him tell the story, in full, of how many troops Meade drew from other parts of his line, & hurried to his left, to stop the progress of these two divisions. I had myself never seen or heard a full & consecutive statement of them before. And, as I heard of the successive corps, divisions, brigades, & batteries concentrated on these two lone divisions—for whom there was no possibility of help or reinforcement, for there was absolutely nothing in their rear but Walton's *nine* guns, & they over two miles away[61]—there came to my recollection a story I had heard at the time but had long forgotten. One of our infantrymen said that he had overheard the enemy's commands that afternoon & that they were "Universe, Forward! By Kingdom into line! Nations guide right!" And, although Capt. Young drew no direct comparison of the forces in his narrative, no listener could fail to be struck with the absence of any account of reinforcement to the Confederates, to offset the great list on the other side, & all could appreciate it when he finally told a variation of the story I had already recalled. His version of it was that when the Confederates saw how the reinforcements continued to pile on them, some of them exclaimed, "Great God! Have we got the Universe to whip?"

To express it as briefly as possible & as nearly as I can find the exact figures, our two divisions' 13,000 infantry with 62 guns took the aggressive against a strong position & captured it, fighting successfully for three hours against 40,000 infantry & 100 guns, & holding the ground gained. I think that a greater military feat than the partial success gained by Pickett's charge, where the infantry fighting was scarcely a half hour. But both events illustrate the superb capabilities of our army at Gettysburg. None of Longstreet's three divisions were any better than any other divisions of the other corps. But Longstreet's had the luck not to have wasted their fighting edges in any preliminary or minor affairs, & they were able to show what a division could do. If the whole fighting force of our army could have been concentrated & brought to bear together upon that of the enemy I cannot doubt that we would have broken it to pieces.

But now there came into play one of the well recognised forces in all military affairs—the difficulty in securing concentration of effort over long lines. To read military history is calculated to make one think that it should be stated not as a difficulty but an impossibility, & that certainly seemed to be the case at Gettysburg. Our line was like a big fishhook outside the enemy's small one. Communication between our flanks was very long—roundabout & slow while the enemy were practically all in one convenient sized bunch. Reinforcements from their extreme right marched across in ample time to repulse our attack on their extreme left. But Ewell's men could hardly have come to our help in a half a day—& only under view & fire.

Our only hope was to make our attacks simultaneous. But that is the thing which always looks beforehand very simple & easy, & always proves afterward to have been impossible, from one of a hundred possible causes. On this afternoon of the 2nd it would seem that after Longstreet's long delay in beginning his attack that Hill & Ewell would have been thoroughly prepared & that our whole force would press the enemy everywhere at once. Had this been done I think the chances are that we would have gained the battle. For the enemy during the afternoon actually abandoned his lines on his right wing for a long distance, taking Ruger's division[62] & possibly [other units] over to the left to oppose Hood & McLaws & leaving his breastworks unoccupied. Johnson's division of Ewell's corps penetrated there & finding the lines deserted went forward some distance as far as the Baltimore Pike—nearly reaching the camp of the enemy's reserve ammunition train. Then suspecting some trap they fell back but they occupied a portion of the lines all night, but were attacked & driven out at sunrise next morning.

Of Ewell's other divisions, Rodes & Early, Rodes does not seem to have been engaged at all. Early attacked near the town & made a desperate & gallant fight, at first carrying a part of the enemy's line & guns. But they brought up reserves & Early received no help on either right or left & he was driven back with heavy loss of brave men. A. P. Hill was also expected to cooperate in this simultaneous but scattered assault. Of his three divisions, one, Anderson's, was fresh. It made an attack not far to the left of McLaws & some of his brigades penetrated as far as the enemy's main line. But it was too weak in itself to accomplish anything against the forces which it met. The other two divisions, which had been so badly cut up the day before were not engaged.[63]

The fighting gradually ceased as night compelled it. And then how much there was to do! The first thing was to care for the wounded of both sides, for there were many of the enemy's within our lines beside all of our own. Most of our own dead, too, were promptly buried; but the enemy's dead were left where they lay. Then our poor horses needed to be taken off somewhere & watered & brought back & fed, the crippled ones killed, & harness taken from the dead, & fresh ones scuffled for with the quartermasters. Then limbers & caissons of all guns must rendezvous with ordnance wagons containing the particular kind & calibre of ammunition which its gun needs, & the boxes must be opened & cartridges, shell, fuses, primers, &c. be packed in the ammunition chests replacing all expenditures of the afternoon. The men must get something to eat—not only for tonight but tomorrow too. And then the scattered batteries & battalions must all be gotten together & in hand. And when it is sure that all are fit & ready to resume action at dawn, they must be put near their probable positions, & some chance given the men to get a little sleep.

Soon after the firing ceased, while I was going about in the Peach Orchard overlooking all this detail, I was agreeably surprised to hear my boy, Charley, asking after "Mars Ned," & he came up on my spare horse

Meg & with very affectionate greetings & a good haversack of rations. Dixie, the horse I had been riding, had received a severe gash in the hip from a fragment of shell, & I had had my right knee skinned by a bullet which passed behind one leg & in front of the other as I was walking between Gilbert's guns. It gashed both pants & drawers & let my knee stick out very disreputably, looking, not like a bullet hole, but like a big tear. Beside Hood disabled we had lost two most excellent generals, Barksdale, who had done so splendidly at Fredericksburg, & Gen. Semmes, whom I thought the most promising major general among all the excellent brigadiers in the whole army—with his wonderful voice which I've told of before.

During the evening I found my way to Gen. Longstreet's bivouac, a little ways in the rear, to ask the news from other quarters & orders for the morning. From elsewhere the news was indefinite, but I was told that we would renew the attack early in the morning. That Pickett's division would arrive and would assault the enemy's line. My impression is the exact point for it was not designated, but I was told it would be to our left of the Peach Orchard. And I was told too to select a place for the Washington Artillery which would come to me at dawn.

Fortunately it was a glorious moonlight night, greatly facilitating all the necessary moving about. By one o'clock I had everything in shape for the morning, & nothing more to do but to try & get a little sleep myself. What with deep dust & blood, & filth of all kinds, the trampled & wrecked Peach Orchard was a very unattractive place, but I secured two good straight fence rails, &, lying sidewise, partly on & partly between them, placed about four inches apart under one of the trees, & with my saddle for a pillow & with the dead men & horses of the enemy all around, I got two hours of good sound & needed sleep. For I had only had about the same amount the night before.

At three o'clock I was up & began putting the different battalions & batteries into position. In all the smoke & confusion of the afternoon before I had not been able to learn the exact location of all the enemy's line, &, in the very early dimness, I put over a dozen guns to the left of the Peach Orchard in a line which prolonged ran toward high ground I could see against the sky, where part of Anderson's divn. had been fighting the night before. I supposed this ground to be in front of the enemy's line. But, after getting the guns all unlimbered, I thought I had better make sure, &, going out that way, by the increasing light I saw the enemy's artillery all over it. It scared me awfully, for did they discover the chance I had given them to enfilade us, they would surely rake us awfully before we could get out. But fortunately they did not seem to be able to see us clearly, & by quick work I got the line broken up, & thrown back in such a way as not to present a good target, before a gun was fired. All the vicinity of the Peach Orchard, any how, was very unfavorable ground for us, generally sloping toward the enemy. This exposed all our movements to his view, & our horses, limbers, & caissons to his fire. If any who read this ever go over that ground, & then see the beautiful ridge positions from which the enemy could answer us, with more & bigger guns, & better ammunition, I know we will have their sympathies. I studied the ground carefully for every gun, to get the best cover that the gentle slopes, here & there, would permit, but it was generally poor at the best & what there was was often gotten only by scattering commands to some extent. And from the enemy's position we could absolutely hide nothing. I will quote presently from Gen. Hunt, Meade's chief of artillery, how it all looked from his point of view. This to any artillerist will tell its own story of our great exposure & disadvantage in position.

As soon as it became light enough to see, some of the enemy's guns began to pot at us, & I think one of the very first shots wounded some of the Washington Artillery, whom I was placing near the Peach Orchard. But it was our policy to save every possible round for the infantry fight, & I would never allow more than one or two shots in reply, if any; leaving the honor of the last to them, & trying to beguile them into a little artillery truce. It worked excellently, & though, occasionally, during the morning, when we exhibited a particularly tempting mark we would get a few shots we got along very nicely.

Not very long after sunrise Gen. Pendleton came up & paid me a visit and commended all of my arrangements. In his official report of the battle he says, "On Longstreet's line by Alexander's activity [I found] much already accomplished."[64]

I quote this because among the very unjust, &, indeed, absurd criticisms which poor Gen. Longstreet's detractors have brought against him, in connection with this battle, is one to the effect that Gen. Lee's orders were disobeyed & neglected the handling of our artillery in Pickett's charge. Now the orders which I received, both from Longstreet & Pendleton, were quite specific, & were carried out to the letter, as I will show, & even more effectively, I think, than could have been reasonably expected beforehand. Moreover they were identical with the usual practice, both of our army and the Federals, in attacking each other in position, from the beginning of the war to the end of it. And, as things turned out, the result of any other method would probably have been the loss of our artillery, &, possibly, a rout of the whole army. I will go a little into detail in this matter for there has been a great deal of most "egregious folly" written in some of the books & papers published on the subject.

My orders were as follows. First, to give the enemy the most effective cannonade possible. It was not meant simply to make a noise, but to try & cripple him—to tear him limbless, as it were, if possible. Note Gen. Longstreet's expression in a note to be quoted in full presently, "drive off the enemy or greatly demoralize him." When the artillery had accomplished that, the infantry column of attack was to charge. And then, further, I was to "advance such artillery as you can use in aiding the attack." Now, I could not hope to bombard effectively with anything less than the whole force of artillery at my disposal, for my range was to be generally over 1,200 yards, & I had not the ammunition to make it a long business. It must be done inside of an hour if ever. One word about our ammunition. The average gun carries in its limber & caisson about 125 rounds. This includes canister, only good at short ranges, & all varieties of shell, shrapnel, & solid shot. We went on this campaign with ordnance reserve wagons carrying, to the best of my recollection, a good deal less than 100 rounds per gun extra. I have tried in vain to find exact records, and many of these details, which were once the occupation of my life, have faded out of my mind. Perhaps we had in all an average of about 200 rounds per gun. Now a gun in action will easily fire from 30 carefully aimed shots in an hour, to 100 hurriedly aimed. During the previous afternoon, we had had 62 guns in action for from 1 to 4 hours, & had refilled our chests from the trains. Our reserve wagons, I knew, must be now very nearly empty of all but canister. And then, though no one cautioned me about it, my own good sense made me appreciate that it would be very imprudent not to keep to the last extremity enough ammunition to cover a retreat back to Virginia, for we were 150 miles from Staunton, the nearest point at which we could get a fresh supply. From these elements it is very easy to work out, even without exact figures, the conclusion that we had no artillery ammunition to waste.

And here I can't refrain from stating the military proposition that the Federals made a great mistake in accepting the little artillery truce[65] into which I worked them that morning. They had ammunition in abundance— literally to burn—& plenty more close at hand. They did not need to be told our situation. If they had cared to inquire they knew exactly how many reserve ammunition wagons we brought across the Potomac. They might have guessed too how we felt about it from our very anxiety to save it. And they ought to have forced us to begin using it as long as possible before we were ready. For 9 hours—from 4 A.M. to 1 P.M. we lay exposed to their guns, & getting ready at our leisure, & they let us do it. Evidently they had felt the strain of the last two days, but for all that they ought to have forced our hand.

In this connection I pause in my narrative a moment to refer to a story which occasionally crops up in print. It is that during the night of July 2nd Gen. Meade had determined to retreat. This is said to have been testified by his chief of staff, Gen. Butterfield, before the Committee on [the] Conduct of the War.[66] There is also evidence of the existence of a report in the

Federal army that a force under Beauregard was approaching to re-inforce Gen. Lee. And it is a fact that some weeks before Gen. Lee had written three letters to Prest. Davis, begging that Gen. Beauregard should be sent in person to Culpeper, with even any few old troops which might be scared up out of jails or hospitals just as a source to start rumors from, for he appreciated the absurd insanity of fear felt for the safety of Washington City. Now Mr. Davis does not seem to have realized the value of this suggestion, for it was surely worth, at least, having Beauregard give a few days to it. And Mr. Davis wrote at last a letter to Gen. Lee saying that it was impracticable to get any force under Beauregard. And in his office the immense blunder was made of sending that letter by a courier & not putting it in cipher. The courier was captured on July 2, in Greencastle, by Capt. Ulric Dahlgren,[67] who appreciated the importance of this letter, & hurried to Gettysburg with it, reaching there toward midnight & delivering the letter to Meade.

Of all that there is no doubt. And Dahlgren was soon after jumped three grades to the rank of a colonel, & he is said to have told his friends that his promotion was for capturing a letter & delivering it to Gen. Meade in time to prevent him from retreating from Gettysburg. However this may be it is instructive to note how careless it is to send valuable information around without putting it in cipher.

And now I may return to the visit paid me by Gen. Pendleton in the early morning, when he looked over & approved my dispositions. As I rode with him & talked over matters he told me that Col. R. L. Walker, A. P. Hill's chief of arty., had nine 12 pr. howitzers for which he had no special use as their range was too short. Gen. Pendleton asked me if I could make use of them. I jumped at the idea, & thanked him & said, "yes, I had the very place for them." And I rode on with him immediately, and had them turned over to me, under the command of a Maj. Richardson.[68] I did not tell Gen. Pendleton what I wanted with them & he probably supposed that I was going to stick them somewhere around in my firing line, like all the rest of my guns. But I had another purpose in view. I intended not to let them fire a shot in the preliminary cannonade, & to keep them under cover & out of view, so that with fresh men, & uninjured horses, & full chests of ammunition, these 9 light howitzers might follow Pickett's infantry in the charge, more promptly, & also, perhaps more *safely* than guns out of the firing line could do. I say more safely, because one function of a firing line of artillery, in a case like this, is to cover the retreat of the storming column in case it fails to make a lodgment upon the enemy's line. If the guns from the firing line advance prematurely, & are caught in a repulse, they may not only be lost, but turned on their former owners at most critical moments, & with fatal effect.

So I led Maj. Richardson & his 9 howitzers to the best protected little hollow I could find behind a piece of woods & left him there with orders simply to wait until I sent for him. As I intended to take personal charge of him, when the time came, no further orders were necessary. I had with me a courier, named Catlett,[69] whom I also cautioned to note exactly where Richardson was left.

The proposition of Gen. Longstreet's critics is that a considerable force of his artillery should have charged along with his infantry. But that general suggestion does not go into detail, & there are many important details to be considered. First it must be borne in mind that our Confederate artillery could only sparingly, & in great emergency, be allowed to fire over the heads of our infantry. We were always liable to premature explosions of shell & shrapnel, & our infantry knew it by sad experience, & I have known of their threatening to fire back at our guns if we opened over their heads. Of course, solid shot could be safely so used, but that is the least effective ammunition, & the infantry would not know the difference & would be demoralized & angry all the same.

Of course, also, the infantry would not fire over the heads of the artillery. Hence it results that each arm must have its own fighting front free, & they do not mix well in a fighting charge. Again it must be remembered that artillery on the march presents such an immense target to infantry, and to other artillery in position, that within their respective ranges it requires very few minutes to disable it. For every horse in a battery team is fast to the limber or caisson, & brings the rest of the team to a stop, when crippled, until he can be cut out. This halts them under fire every time they are hit, & makes easy more hits. Charges can be made for short distances, particularly where the ground admits of a gallop, or where there are occasional covered places for rest & breathing; but on this field every condition was adverse. Fences, ditches, & wheat fields with soft ground were frequent. There was not a sheltered foot of ground in the whole wide expanse we would have to traverse, for rest or cover from one of the enemy's long line of guns in position, extending from Cemetery Hill to Round Top. It scarcely needs to be pointed out that if any guns were advanced entirely out upon the flank of the assaulting column, they would be exposed, not only to the enemy's artillery, but also to the rifle musketry of his sharpshooters & infantry line of battle, which would bring it to a stand still in a few minutes & soon destroy every horse & man.

Briefly, the peculiarities of the topography, which are of most extreme importance upon every battle field, here left no reasonable method of making our attack at the point selected but the one adopted. Of my original force of guns I could spare none from the firing line. I had 75 which I placed to fire on the point of attack & its near vicinity. Then, a few extra, I forget the exact number, were held to protect our right flank, which was, indeed, attacked by cavalry during the action. When I got the 9 extra howitzers, I, at first, intended merely to follow behind Pickett's infantry, without attempting to fire a shot, until I got as close as I could go without getting within infantry range. There, I would have halted & unlimbered, to cover his retreat if he were repulsed; or to limber up & follow quickly if he made a lodgment. Meanwhile, too, all the batteries in the firing line had similar orders—to limber up & follow any success, as promptly as possible.

Later, I changed my plan a little about the Richardson howitzers, & I may as well anticipate the order of events & tell here what happened. I got afraid that Richardson might get in trouble bringing his guns through some open, but rocky woods he had to pass. So, just to be sure, I decided to bring him beforehand & get him where he would be hidden but all ready & to move him out in front of Pickett instead of behind him. Of course in that position I could not go very far. But I could get through a gap in our firing line, & at the best location I could find in advance, short of their infantry fire, I would unlimber & fire a few rounds before Pickett's men passed on forward in between my guns. The change proposed cut no essential figure, but it avoided a possible delay in the guns getting out. So I told Catlett to go & bring up the major & the guns. He was gone for some time & came back & said they were not where I had left him. I did not think Catlett could have gone to the right place, & I said, "He would not dare to leave there without orders. You go again & find him & don't you come back without him."[70] Again he was gone a long time, & at last, after our cannonade opened, he returned & said that Richardson was certainly gone, & that he had looked all around but could not find him. After the battle I found that Gen. Pendleton, himself, had sent & taken four or five of the guns, & disposed of them elsewhere without any notice to me. The remainder Maj. R. admitted having moved "a short distance" because he said he found himself in the range of shell from the enemy, thrown at some of A. P. Hill's guns, which had quite a considerable fight of their own to be told about presently. But, wherever he went, it was where Catlett, who was an excellent & reliable man, could not find him. I reported it all to Pendleton & Longstreet, & felt quite like preferring charges, but we were soon sent out West & that was the end of it. [Figure 23 appears here in the manucript.]

And now, while I am on the subject, I am going to make one criticism of my own upon how the artillery of the Second Corps was handled on this occasion, & also another upon the military engineering displayed in the selection of the point of our attack.

First—as to the artillery of Hill's corps, next on our left. Col. Walker, their chief, told me that he had 63 guns in action. He had them on Seminary Ridge, which was very favorable ground, affording good cover for his movements, & also for limbers & caissons. He advanced no guns, either

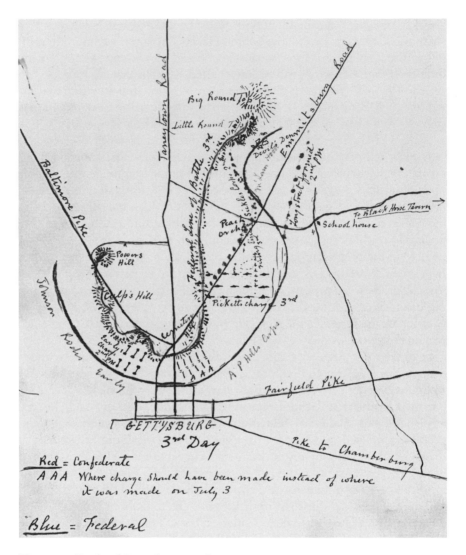

Figure 23. Battle of Gettysburg, 3 July 1863

before, during, or after the charge that I ever heard of, though the left half of the column was in Hill's front. And I feel quite sure that he had no reasonable opportunity to do so, or he would have done it. Between eleven & twelve o'clock there was a severe artillery duel, between Hill's guns & the enemy, which seemed to me to begin in a fight between the skirmishers over a barn. The artillery on each side was disposed to help its skirmishers, & the barn was set on fire. At last, at least 100 guns, on the two sides, got into a duel which lasted nearly a half hour & then finally died out. I would not let one of my guns fire a shot. For myself, I think it was a mistake to use that much ammunition prematurely if it could have been avoided. This duel made a great deal of noise while it lasted, & many writers have imagined it to have been a part of the cannonade to prepare the way for Pickett. But there was about an hour between them in which there was scarcely a shot anywhere, except among the sharpshooters between the lines.

The great criticism which I have to make on the artillery operations of the day is upon the inaction of the artillery of Ewell's corps. Our position on the exterior line, as I have before explained, placed us under many & serious disadvantages. But it gave us one single advantage. It enabled us to enfilade any of the enemy's positions, near the centre of their line, with our artillery fire. Now, a battery established where it can enfilade others need not trouble itself about aim. It has only to fire in the right direction & the shot finds something to hurt wherever it falls. No troops, infantry or artillery, can long submit to an enfilade fire. But, both the infantry & artillery lines which we were to attack could have been enfiladed from somewhere in our lines near Gettysburg. There is where the use of a chief of artillery for the army comes in. He visits & views the entire field & should recognize & know how to utilize his opportunities. The chief of each corps only sees his own ground. I never had an idea of the possibility of this being done at the time, for I had but the vaguest notion of where Ewell's corps was. And Ewell's chief doubtless had as vague ideas of my situation & necessities. But Gen. Lee's chief should have known, & given every possible energy to improve the rare & great chance to the very uttermost. Only one of Ewell's five fine battalions, & he had some of the very best in the army, & under officers second to none in either army, participated in our bombardment at all. It only fired a few dozen shots, for, apparently, it could not see what it was doing. But every shot was smashing up something, &, had it been increased & kept up, it is hard to say what might have resulted.

The Federal artillery officers, among whose guns these shots fell, published an account in the Phil. press which I will endeavor to secure & attach as an appendix.[71] It will tell the whole story, & enable one to appreciate what we lost by Ewell's five battalions not being utilized as they might have been. Let it be remembered, too, that enfilading guns need not be close, & need not be on hill tops, nor even be able to see where their shot are going. They may fire from a ravine, where they cannot themselves be seen, & they only need the direction & the approximate distance. Signals from other points can tell them when they are about right, & then, safe themselves, they can do the most effective artillery work in the world. That neglect was a serious loss. Every map of the field cries out about it.

Now, one more criticism, & I return to the much more agreeable narrative. But the technical problems of all battlefields are of deep interest to me, &, particularly so, are those of this great field. And, as a student of such technical questions, I think that all military engineers, who will study that field, will agree that the point selected for Pickett's attack was very badly chosen—almost as badly chosen as it was possible to be. I have no idea by whom it was done—whether by a general or staff officer, or a consultation of officers. There was a rumor, in our corps, that Ewell & Hill each reported against assault in his front, & so, by a process of exhaustion, it came to Longstreet's.

Briefly described, the point we attacked is upon the long *shank* of the fishhook of the enemy's position, & our advance was exposed to the fire of the whole length of that shank some two miles. Not only that, that shank is not perfectly straight, but it bends forward at the Round Top end, so that rifled guns there, in secure position, could & did enfilade the assaulting lines. Now add that the advance must be over 1,400 yards[72] of open ground, none of it sheltered from fire, & very little from view, & without a single position for artillery where a battery could get its horses & caissons under cover.

I think any military engineer would, instead, select for attack the *bend* of the fishhook just west of Gettysburg. There, at least, the assaulting lines cannot be enfiladed, and, on the other hand the places selected for assault may be enfiladed, & upon shorter ranges than any other parts of the Federal lines. Again there the assaulting column will only be exposed to the fire of the front less than half, even if over one fourth, of the firing front upon the shank. These considerations are alone enough to determine the question, even if the exposed approach should be 1,400 yards wide & destitute of cover. But I believe it is certainly much more favorable.[73] Upon that point, I have never had an opportunity to examine the ground, however, & I only give my impressions.

For awhile, Longstreet's critics tried to make it appear that he disobeyed an order to put McLaws's & Hood's divisions also in the storming column with Pickett. But it has been pointed out, in Gen. Lee's report, that although there had been at first a desire, on his part, to use some of these troops in Pickett's charge, it had been abandoned, & Heth's division under Pettigrew[74] (Heth being wounded) & some other of Hill's troops were substituted for them. For, indeed, it would have been simply impossible to hold the firing line, upon which our guns were placed, if either Hood or McLaws were taken away, to be placed in the column with Pickett. They could only have been withdrawn under observation, & fire from the enemy upon Round Top, & a cloud of skirmishers could have followed their withdrawal & soon driven back a large part of our firing line.

So now we can come back to our little line of guns, & take up the narrative of events. After Gen. Pendleton's visit I saw & conversed with both Gen. Lee & Longstreet, & most of their staff officers, & got more exact ideas of where Pickett was to direct his march. Dearing's battalion, which accompanied P., arrived & I placed it also on the line. Dearing himself, who was a fine, handsome fellow, had reached the field many miles ahead of his guns, the afternoon before, & had helped me look after things. As I got better ideas of the ground, I found a good many little changes desirable in our locations, & I made them all without any casualty that I can recall but one.

Capt. Carlton,[75] taking position on a pretty grassy slope, had a 20 pr. rifle shell knock one whole buttock off a lead horse in making a turn. I never saw so much blood fly, or so much grass painted red before, & the pretty drill Carlton was wishing to show off was very much spoiled. My battalion, of course, while I was acting as chief, was under my dear Frank Huger; & I had with me, acting as aid, young Fred Colston,[76] who was our ordnance officer—& who was very active & enthusiastic & a great help to me. Col. Walton had come upon the field but he stayed with his own battalion & took no supervision over any other guns.

Pickett's men were in the woods behind my line of guns, resting, I believe, & eating. I recall one incident of a ride this morning to our extreme right flank, to visit the guns assigned for its protection. I came upon two lieutenants, of a Miss. regt., apparently robbing the dead body of a Confederate officer, lying in the road. I stopped to reproach them & they said, "He is not dead, damn him, he is drunk. It is our surgeon & he is drunk too off whiskey issued for the wounded; and it's not the first time, either. We are just taking his instruments to take care of them." I said, "Toss him about! Roll him! Shake him! See if you can't arouse him." They did so but he would no more arouse than a dead man. Then I said, "Every officer owes it to discipline to report such a case. Give me all your names." When we returned to Virginia I preferred charges against the surgeon. He was left in Pa. in charge of our wounded, at houses near the battlefield, when we retreated to Virginia, & the case only came on for trial, by our military court, next spring in East Tenn. The poor fellow's friends had prevailed upon the two lieutenants to say that it was possible he might have only been under the influence of opium, & not drunk; & in spite of my testimony the court, I am exceedingly glad to say, divided, which operated as an acquit[t]al. Three judges composed the court, but only two were present. I am very grateful for the result because I had perhaps too much youthful indignation at a crime to which I never had any personal inclination, and I had made the charges too severe: "Misbehavior before the enemy," or something like that, which might even have allowed him to be shot.

It was understood that Gen. Longstreet would give the signal for the cannonade to open—two guns, to be fired by the Washn. Arty., near the Peach Orchard. And he had instructed me to take a position whence I could see best, & I was to determine the moment & give Pickett the order when to charge. One of Pickett's couriers was sent to remain with me & carry the order when I gave it.

I had, at first, taken no very special thought as to how long I would let the fire continue, before telling Pickett to go. Some 20 to 30 minutes I supposed would be about right. Not shorter than 20, for the longer the time the more punishment the enemy would have. But not longer than 30, because they had a long charge, & I must allow plenty of time for them to cover the distance within the hour. For I did not like to use up more ammunition than that would consume before having the crisis of the matter determined.

I had no expectation whatever of seeing anything special happen in the enemy during the cannonade, either to make me lengthen or shorten this period. In fact if I had thought very seriously on the subject & figured up that the enemy had as good & as many guns as we; & great advantage in position & ammunition over us I might not have felt as cheerful & sanguine as I did. But the fact is that like all the rest of the army I believed that it would all come out right, because Gen. Lee had planned it.

And now I received a sudden shock. A courier brought me a note from Gen. Longstreet which read as follows:77

> Colonel. If the artillery fire does not have the effect to drive off the enemy, or greatly demoralize him, so as to make our efforts pretty certain, I would prefer that you should not advise Gen. Pickett to make the charge. I shall rely a great deal on your good judgment to determine the matter & shall expect you to let Gen. Pickett know when the moment offers.

That presented the whole business to me in a new light. It was no longer Gen. Lee's inspiration that that was the way to whip the battle, but my cold judgment to be founded on what I was going to see. Gen. A. R. Wright of Geo. was with me when the message was brought.78 I showed it to him & after talking over the situation I wrote to Gen. Longstreet—about as follows (I kept no copy at the time, but wrote out afterward what I remembered very vividly; Gen. Longstreet's two letters I preserved):

> General. I will only be able to judge of the effect of our fire on the enemy by his return fire, for his infantry is but little exposed to view & the smoke will obscure the whole field. If, as I infer from your note, there is any alternative to this attack it should be carefully considered before opening our fire, for it will take all the artillery ammunition we have left to test this one thoroughly, & if the result is unfavorable we will have

none left for another effort. And even if this is entirely successful it can only be so at a very bloody cost.

After a while there came this reply:

> Colonel. The intention is to advance the infantry, if the artillery has the desired effect of driving the enemy's off, or having other effect such as to warrant us in making the attack. When the moment arrives advise Gen. Pickett, and of course advance such artillery as you can use in aiding the attack.

Gen. Wright read this & said, "He has put the responsibility back upon you." I said, "General, tell me exactly what *you* think of this attack." He said, "Well, Alexander, it is mostly a question of supports. It is not as hard to get there as it looks. I was there yesterday with my brigade. The real difficulty is to stay there after you get there—for the whole infernal Yankee army[79] is up there in a bunch."

Now, I had already decided in my own mind that I could see nothing during the cannonade upon which any safe opinion could be founded; & that the question, whether or not that attack was to be made, must be decided before the cannonade opened. I had tried to avoid the responsibility of the decision, but in vain. Gen. Lee had originally planned it, & half the day had been spent in preparation. I determined to cause no loss of time by any indecision on my part. As to the question of supports, that I supposed would be the one to which Gen. Lee himself would have given his own special attention—far more than to any particular features of the ground. And I had heard a sort of camp rumor, that morning, that Gen. Lee had said he intended to march every man he had upon that cemetery hill that day.

But before deciding absolutely, I rode back for a little interview with Pickett himself. I did not tell him my object, but just felt his pulse, as it were, about the assault. He was in excellent spirits & sanguine of success. Then I determined to let Gen. Longstreet know that I intended to put Pickett in. I wrote him just these words: "General. When our artillery fire is at its best I shall order Gen. Pickett to charge."

And then, feeling more responsibility, I began to revise my calculations about when to give Pickett the order to start. To be too soon, seemed safer than to be too late, so I fixed in my own mind on 20 minutes—with a possibility of even shortening it to 15, if things looked favorably at the time.

And now let me explain what troops were formed for the charge & how. Pickett had his three brigades in two lines, as Hood & McLaws had formed the evening before. In fact that always seemed to be the favorite Confederate method everywhere. The Federals, with more men, often had several lines.

Before Marye's Hill, at Fredbg., they had six. Pickett put two brigades in his front line, Garnett & Kemper—Garnett on his left. Some 200 yards in rear of the right centre Armistead's brigade formed the second line. This division was not quite one half of the whole storming column. Joining it on the left Heth's divn. under Pettigrew extended the front line, & behind their left centre came two brigades of Pender's under Trimble.[80] Then, a little in rear of Pickett's divn. was Wilcox's brigade (of _____ division)[81] which was ordered to support the charge promptly. It was not ordered however to move at the same time & as part of the column; but to come along very soon after & help anywhere it might be needed. Exactly who, if anybody, was to give Wilcox orders when to move forward I do not know.

Along in rear of where the left half of this column was formed, under cover of the woods, was Anderson's division of Hill's corps, forming part of his line of battle along Seminary Ridge.

The strength of these commands that morning from the best estimates I can find are about as follows—Pickett 5,000, Pettigrew 4,000, Trimble 2,000, Wilcox 2,400, Anderson 5,000. Anderson had no orders to advance, but, of course, in case of any emergency of success or failure, could be brought forward. And there were also 2 brigades of Pender's (about 2,500 men) holding Hill's line on towards Gettysburg.[82]

I have already told that Johnson's divn., of Ewell's corps, had taken possession of some of the enemy's trenches, on our extreme left, the evening before, while Geary's[83] & Ruger's divisions were being used elsewhere. Gen. Lee had intended to have Johnson make a simultaneous attack, when Pickett's attack was to be made. But the enemy took the aggressive early in the morning, & Geary, Ruger, & a brigade of the 6th Corps attacked Johnson & before eleven o'clock recovered their lines in full.

And now that all the preliminaries are explained & we are only waiting for the cannonade to begin, I will quote from Gen. Hunt, as promised, his description of what he could see of our preparations from his side of the line. As a free spectacular display, it was all very well, but we would greatly have preferred not to have exhibited so much. Gen. Hunt says:

> Between 10 & 11 A.M., everything looking favorable at Culp's Hill, I crossed over to Cemetery Ridge, to see what might be going on at other points. Here a magnificent display greeted my eyes. Our whole front for 2 miles was covered by batteries already in line or going into position. They stretched—apparently in one unbroken mass—from opposite the town to the Peach Orchard; which bounded the view to the left; the ridges of which were planted thick with cannon. Never before had such a sight been witnessed on this continent, & rarely if ever abroad. What did it mean? It might possibly be to hold that line, while its infantry was sent to aid Ewell, or to guard against a counter-stroke from us; but it most

probably meant an assault on our centre, to be preceded by a cannonade, in order to crush our batteries & shake our infantry; at least to cause us to exhaust our ammunition in reply, so that the assaulting troops might pass, in good condition, over the half mile of open ground which was beyond our effective musketry fire. With such an object, the cannonade would be long, & followed immediately by the assault, their whole army being held in readiness to follow up a success.

From the great extent of ground occupied by the enemy's batteries, it was evident that all the artillery on our west front, whether of the army corps or the reserve, must concur as a unit. . . . and beginning on the right I instructed the chiefs of artillery, & battery commanders, to withhold their fire for 15 or 20 minutes after the cannonade commenced, then to concentrate their fire, with all possible accuracy, on those batteries which were most destructive to us—but slowly—so that, when the enemy's ammunition was exhausted, we should have sufficient left to meet the assault. I had just given these orders to the last battery on Little Round Top, when the signal gun was fired, & the enemy opened with all his guns. From that point the scene was indescribably grand. All their batteries were soon covered with smoke, through which the flashes were incessant, while the air seemed filled with shells, whose sharp explosions, with the hurtling of their fragments, formed a running accompaniment to the deep roar of the guns. Thence I rode to the artillery reserve, to order fresh batteries & ammunition to be sent up to the ridge, as soon as the cannonade ceased, but both the reserve & the train had gone to a safer place. Messengers however had been left to receive & to convey orders, which I sent by them; then I returned to the ridge. Turning into the Taneytown Pike I saw evidence of the necessity under which the reserve had "decamped" in the remains of a dozen exploded caissons, which had been placed under cover of a hill, but which the shells had managed to search out. . . . In fact the fire was more dangerous behind the ridge than on its crest.[84]

It was just one o'clock, by my watch, when the double boom of the signal guns from the Washington Artillery broke the silence; & it was, indeed, a grand & exciting moment to hear our long line of guns break loose as if impatient of their long restraint, & roaring in very joy of battle. Every gunner had his target selected, & we must have made it pretty hot for the opposite line from the word go, for Gen. Hunt's orders not to reply for 15 or 20 minutes, I am very sorry to say, were immediately forgotten. I hope he court martialed every rascal of them for it afterward; for how much more all of us Confederates might have enjoyed that 15 minutes. But, instead of giving a beautiful exhibition of discipline his whole line from Cemetery Hill to Round Top seemed in five minutes to be emulating a volcano in eruption.

Lots of guns developed which I had not before been able to see, & instead of saving ammunition, they were surely trying themselves how much they could consume. I could not now go along my line & see how they were faring, but Woolfolk's rifles, near which I had taken my place to observe the enemy's line, had several casualties very soon.

In ten minutes after the opening I had recognized a force of artillery at work on the enemy's line which I thought it madness to send a storming column out in the face of, for so long a charge under a mid-day July sun. I saw at once that I must wait longer than my proposed 15 minutes, & hope meanwhile to silence some at least of their guns. And so I waited, 15, 20, 25 minutes—I would have liked to have waited longer. I would only too gladly have waited an hour longer—but I was afraid to risk getting out of ammunition. I could not be sure that Pickett's column might not waste ten minutes or more[85] in dressing ranks, alignments, guides, or some little tactical niceties, & every minute now seemed an hour. I could not take any more chances. But instead of simply giving the single order "charge," I thought it due to Longstreet and to Pickett to let the exact situation be understood. So I wrote as follows, & sent it to Pickett at exactly 1:25 P.M.: "If you are coming at all you must come at once, or I cannot give you proper support, but the enemy's fire has not slackened at all.[86] At least 18 guns are still firing from the cemetery itself." This was the point of direction of the storming column. The brigade of direction was Fry's,[87] the right brigade of Pettigrew's line. It was to march on the cemetery & the rest of the line was to dress upon it.

Perhaps I should say that my idea of exactly where, & how big, the cemetery was may easily have been mistaken. I should have repeated too that about ten minutes after the fire opened Catlett had come with the news that the 9 Richardson howitzers could not be found. These would have cut quite a figure in giving Pickett support, as they had full chests of ammunition. Now their absence contributed greatly to render delay imprudent and dangerous.

I had hardly dispatched this note, when I began to notice signs of some of the enemy's guns ceasing to fire. At first, I thought it only crippled guns; but soon, with my large glass, I discovered entire batteries limbering up & leaving their positions. Now it was a very ordinary thing with us to withdraw our guns from purely artillery duels, & save up every thing for their infantry. But the Federals had never done anything of that sort before, & I did not believe they were doing it now. Knowing what a large reserve force they always kept, I supposed that they were only relieving exhausted batteries with fresh ones, as I had relieved the Washington Arty. at Marye's Hill. But the fresh ones not promptly appearing, I said, "If they don't put fresh batteries there in five minutes this will be our fight." I spent the five minutes with my glass studying their lines every where. Some batteries still kept up their fire, but there was not a single fresh gun replacing any that had withdrawn. Of course, I knew that what were withdrawn were still there— just behind the hills—& that nothing but a desperate infantry fight could ever decide the day; but I felt encouraged to believe that they had felt very severe punishment, & that my fire had been generally well aimed & as effective as could be hoped. For surely here was a new departure in their conduct.

So I wrote another note to Pickett & sent it at 1:35—ten minutes after the first note. "For God's sake come quick. The 18 guns are gone. Come quick or I can't support you." I sent two written & one verbal message to that effect, for I was afraid of their losing time in little preliminaries, & I wanted to get them inspired to disregard everything but getting there.

And now, before going on with the narrative, I will quote, from some of the Federal accounts, what will give some idea of the effect of our fire in their lines, & will also explain the withdrawal of their guns, which I had just noted.[88] Gen. Hunt writes as follows:[89]

> I now rode along the ridge to inspect the batteries. The infantry were lying down, on its reverse slope, near the crest, in open ranks, awaiting events. As I passed along a bolt from a rifle gun struck the ground, just in front of a man of the front rank, penetrated the surface & passed under him, throwing him "over & over." He fell behind the rear rank, apparently dead, & a ridge of earth, where he had been lying, reminded me of the backwoods practise of "barking" squirrels. Our fire was deliberate, but, on inspecting the chests, I found that the ammunition was running low, & hastened to Gen. Meade to advise its immediate cessation, & preparation for the assault which would certainly follow.
>
> The head quarters building, immediately behind the ridge, had been abandoned, & many of the horses of the staff lay dead. Being told that the general had gone to the cemetery, I proceeded thither. He was not there, &, on telling Gen. Howard my object, he concurred in its propriety, & I rode back along the ridge ordering the fire to cease. This was followed by a cessation of that of the enemy, under the mistaken impression that he had silenced our guns, &, almost immediately, his infantry came out of the woods, & formed for the assault. On my way to the Taneytown Road, to meet the fresh batteries which I had ordered up, I met Maj. Bingham[90] of Hancock's staff, who informed me that Gen. Meade's aids were seeking me with orders to cease firing; so that I had only anticipated his wishes. The batteries were brought up, & Fitzhugh's, Weir's, Wheeler's, & Parson's were put in near the clump of trees. Brown's & Arnold's batteries had been so crippled that they were not withdrawn & Brown's was replaced by Cowan's.[91]

Meantime the enemy advanced, & McGilvery opened a destructive oblique fire, reinforced by that of Rittenhouse's six rifle guns,[92] from Round Top, which were served with remarkable accuracy, enfilading Pickett's lines. The Confederate approach was magnificent, & excited our admiration, but the story of that charge is so well known that I need not dwell upon it, further than as it concerns my own command. The steady fire from McGilvery & Rittenhouse, on their right, caused Pickett's men to "drift" in the opposite direction; so that the weight of the assault fell upon the positions occupied by Hazard's[93] batteries. I had counted on an artillery cross-fire that would stop it before it reached our lines, but, except a few shots here & there, Hazard's batteries were silent until the enemy came within canister range. They had, unfortunately, exhausted their long-range projectiles during the cannonade, under the orders of their corps commander, & it was too late to replace them.

Gen. Hunt's last sentence is a dig at Gen. Hancock, comdg. the 2nd Corps. Hunt, as chief of artillery of the army ordered Hazard, chief of arty. of [the] 2nd Corps to cease firing. Hancock ordered him to resume it. It is a mooted question of army organisation, today, whose orders should prevail, if a corps commander & the army chief of arty. should differ. As I am taking a shy at every technical question which comes up, I give my views on this too. I think a corps commander should be supreme in his corps, & the army chief must submit, or get the commander in chief to interpose & overrule the corps commander. The army chief ought to have, of course, a reserve of his own, & that should answer all his purposes. Hunt had such a reserve, & a large one. We had no such general reserve after we organised our 3rd Army Corps, Hill's; not that we did not want it, but we could not maintain it.

I rather think too that I concur with Gen. Hancock's idea that the Federal policy at Gettysburg should have been to keep their batteries firing at least as long as ours were. For they had superiority in number, & calibre of guns, &, of even greater importance, in quality and quantity of ammunition. Their policy should have been always to fight us to exhaustion if we would give them the chance. Exhaustion would have come to us first.

And now I must go back & tell what followed on my notes to Gen. Pickett. On getting the first one Pickett rode to Longstreet, who was near by, & showed it. Longstreet read it & made no comment. Pickett said, "General, shall I advance?" Longstreet still made no reply. His staff officers who were near by noted that he turned his face aside. He, himself, told me afterward that he knew the charge must be made, but he could not bring himself to give the order. Pickett paused a few seconds, saluted, & said, "I am going to move forward, Sir," and immediately rode to his division, & put it in motion. My "come quick" notes arrived after the event was determined, & the orders given; but they of course brought him some comfort & encouragement.

Some five or ten minutes after sending my last note Gen. Longstreet rode up all alone. I was expecting Pickett every moment, & was all impatience for him to come, for the fire of our own guns was also now much reduced, & I was not sure how much was due to exhaustion of ammunition, & how much might be only because the enemy had nearly ceased firing. I had given no orders to cease or slacken at all, whether the enemy did or not, & I wished the fire kept going to our utmost capacity until the crisis was past.

So when Gen. Longstreet came I told him how the enemy had withdrawn their guns, & we would certainly get a favorable start; but I expressed impatience at Pickett's delay, & I told him of the Richardson guns being taken off, & said I feared the support I could give might not be all I wished, & had counted upon. By the way this was the first that Gen. Longstreet knew of my having had these guns at all. I had been hoping to give him a little agreeable surprise with them when I ran them out into the field. Gen. L. spoke at once, & decidedly, "Go & halt Pickett right where he is, & replenish your ammunition." I said, "General, we can't do that. We nearly emptied the trains last night. Even if we had it, it would take an hour or two, & meanwhile the enemy would recover from the pressure he is now under. Our only chance is to follow it up now—to strike while the iron is hot." He answered, "I don't want to make this attack—I believe it will fail— I do not see how it can succeed—I would not make it even now, but that Gen. Lee has ordered & expects it." He made these statements, with slight pauses in between, while he was looking at the enemy's position through his field glasses. I had the feeling that he was upon the verge of stopping the charge, & that with even slight encouragement he would do it. But that very feeling kept me from saying a word, either of assent or dissent. I would not willingly take any responsibility in so grave a matter, & I had almost a morbid fear of personally causing any loss of time. So I stood by, & looked on, in silence almost embarrassing. After sending my last "hurry up" notes to Pickett at 1:35 P.M., I do not recall looking at my watch again that day. So I cannot be absolutely sure, but I think it was not earlier than 1:50, nor later than 2 P.M., when with great relief & delight, I saw Pickett's line approaching at a good fast gait.94

Ahead of his men rode good & lovable Gen. Dick Garnett. I had crossed the plains with him, & Gen. Armistead also, in 1858, & grown very fond of them both. Their favorite songs, "Willie Brewed a Peck of Malt" and "Wife, Children & Friends," have been among mine ever since. Now that Pickett was actually started, my work was to begin again, so I left Longstreet, as he returned Garnett's salute, & after riding a few yards with the latter, & wishing him good luck, I turned to ride down my line of guns. Garnett had not been well, and only got out of an ambulance, that morning, to lead his brigade for the last time.

As I came to each gun, I examined its remaining ammunition. If it had enough long range projectiles left to give some 15 shots, more or less, I ordered it to limber up, & move forward after the storming column—if necessary taking sound horses from other teams near by, for an unusual number of horses had been struck, owing to our lack of cover. If the gun had less shots than its neighbors it was ordered to wait until the infantry had gotten a good distance in front, then, aiming well over their heads, to fire at the enemy's batteries which were firing at our infantry [while] our infantry got close up to the enemy, then they should cease but stand ready to cover their retreat if necessary. It was an individual question with each gun & battery, where all could not go, to get the best which was left most immediately to the front. My general recollection is that I got a gun or two from nearly every battery I visited, perhaps an average of two guns out of five. I went to the end of [the] line in the Peach Orchard at Haskell's guns and turned back & joined those first started. I got together the most advanced & moved them out towards the Emmitsburg Pike toward Pickett's right flank. By the way, I could not see either flank of Pickett's line when it passed me, from the rolling ground & small bushes, fences, &c. His two brigades must have had a front of about 1,100 yards, Pettigrew's about 1,200.⁹⁵

Very soon after our infantry showed itself, we could see the Federal batteries begin to reappear & open fire upon them, & before the charge was finished they had seemingly half as many guns showing as they had had before the cannonade. The volume of their fire did not seem great & certainly it failed entirely to check or break up Pickett's advance. They moved rapidly & cleared a good deal of space even while the enemy were realizing the situation & getting back their guns. As to exactly how much damage they were able to accomplish it is difficult to arrive at exact conclusions.

The particular guns which are said to have hurt them most were the rifle guns from Round Top, which enfiladed the assaulting line when it got near the Emmitsburg Road, as Hunt describes. I had some rifles, near the Peach Orchard, to fire on these Round Top guns, but of course could never silence them, in their choice position. One of the pictures of the war, stamped in my memory, is one of Kemper's men, whose entire mouth & chin was carried away by one of these flanking shots. I came upon him, sitting up in a fence corner, as I was advancing the guns I had gotten together toward the right flank of the column. We had to halt while the cannoneers threw down gaps in the fence for the guns to go through, &, as I halted my horse, this poor fellow looked up at me, & I even noted powder smut from the ball showing on the white skin of the cheek.

As we rose with these guns out of a little depression, approaching the pike, we saw a movement of troops out in advance of the enemy's line to our right of Pickett's right flank. It was evidently intended to take the assaulting column in reverse, & I think the troops were probably Stannard's Vermont brigade.[96] I at once put my guns in battery & opened fire, having a good oblique range upon them. And now I got my first chance really to look at our advancing lines, which had, so far, done no firing, except by a skirmish line in front. The enemy's infantry had now opened upon it & it was opening in reply. Then there was soon nothing to see but volumes of musketry smoke, & the crashing roar which went up—it seemed to me the heaviest I had ever heard—told that the matter was now being brought to the final test. We could see lines of the enemy closing toward Pickett, & those we fired into as fast as we could load & everywhere that their smoke seemed thickest. And that our fire was well aimed & effective appears from the following quotation from Col. Edmund Rice's account in [the] Century War History which presents an interesting inside view of this collision:[97]

From the opposite ridge, three quarters of a mile away a line of skirmishers sprang lightly forward out of the woods, &, with intervals well kept, moved rapidly down into the open fields, closely followed by a line of battle—then by another & by yet a third (this third must have been Wilcox, & he probably soon halted).[98] Both sides watched this never to be forgotten scene—the grandeur of attack of so many thousand men. Gibbon's divn., which was to stand the brunt of the assault, looked with admiration on the different lines of the Confederates marching forward, with easy swinging step, & the men were heard to exclaim: "Here they come!" "Here they come!" "Here comes the infantry!" Soon little puffs of smoke issued from the skirmish line, as it came dashing forward, firing in reply to our own skirmishers in the plain below. . . .

Pickett's separate brigade lines lost their formation as they swept across the Emmitsburg Road, carrying with them their chain of skirmishers. They pushed on toward the crest, and merged into one crowding, rushing line, many ranks deep. As they crossed the road Webb's[99] infantry, on the right of the trees, commenced an irregular hesitating fire, gradually increasing to a rapid file firing, while the shrapnel & canister from the batteries tore gaps through those splendid Virginia battalions. . . . By an undulation of the surface of the ground to the left of the trees, the rapid advance of the dense line of Confederates was for a moment lost to view; an instant after they seemed to rise up out of the earth, & so near that the expressions on their faces was distinctly seen. Now our men knew that the time had come & could wait no longer. Aiming low they opened a deadly concentrated discharge upon the moving mass in their front. Staggered by the storm of lead, the charging line hesitated, answered with some wild firing, which soon increased to a crashing roll of musketry running down the whole length of their front, & then all that portion of Pickett's division, which came within the zone of this terrible close musketry fire, appeared to melt & drift away in the powder smoke of both sides. . . . A Confederate battery near the Peach Orchard commenced firing, probably at the sight of Harrow's[100] men leaving their line & closing to the right upon Pickett's column. A cannon shot tore a horrible passage through the dense crowd of men in blue, who were gathering outside the trees; instantly another shot followed & fairly cut a road through the mass. My thoughts were now to bring the men forward; it was but a few steps to the front, where they could at once extinguish that destructive musketry, & be out of the line of the deadly artillery fire. Voices were lost in the uproar, so I turned partly toward them, raised my sword to attract their attention, & motioned to advance. They surged forward, & just then as I was stepping backward, with my face to the men urging them on, I felt a sharp blow as a shot struck me, then another; I whirled around, my sword torn from my hand by a bullet or shell splinter. My visor saved my face, but the shock stunned me. As I went down, our men rushed forward past me, capturing battle flags & making prisoners. Pickett's divn. lost nearly six-sevenths of its officers & men. Gibbon's division, with its leader wounded & with a loss of half its strength still held the crest.

From my position I could not see what happened with the left half of the assaulting column. But I afterward learned that as it advanced its unsupported left flank was unable to withstand the severe fire concentrated upon it & it began to crumble off when half way or two-thirds across to the enemy's line. Those nearest the centre however kept on & Fry's brigade, which was next to Pickett & was the "brigade of direction," reached the enemy's breast works with Pickett & actually had them in possession. Armistead's brigade had here united with the two brigades in front, & gallant Gen. Armistead had leaped the enemy's line & led a charge upon a battery beyond it & was killed waving his hat on one of the enemy's guns. Garnett was killed near by & Fry & Kemper desperately wounded.

I kept up my fire until the cessation of both musketry & artillery around the point of Pickett's attack, & fugitives running back from there, showed me that the attack had failed. Then, suddenly, I began to realize more fully than I had before, what might happen if the enemy should take a notion to follow up our fugitives[101] from the field with a strong advance. Immediately I stopped firing, for, in that case, every round of ammunition would be worth its weight in gold, & sent orders to all my guns, everywhere, to hold their positions, but not to fire a shot, & to try and re-establish our little artillery truce. Some of the enemy's guns did not seem exactly to understand it at first, but gradually they took to the idea. Some ten minutes after the crisis was all over, here came along Wilcox's brigade. As they passed us I could not help feeling a great pity for the useless loss of life they were incurring, for there was nothing left for them to support. They did not go far however, before that became so apparent that they were taken back. For such an attack as Pickett had to make the supporting lines should follow quick & fast; or as Josh Billings[102] recommended for marriages, "Begin early & repeat often if necessary."

I had with me at the advanced guns, when we ceased firing, Lieut. Colston, & possibly a courier or two, & I remained there to observe what the enemy would do. Soon after Wilcox withdrew, Gen. Lee rode up, entirely unattended. He must have intentionally separated himself from his staff & couriers or some of them would surely have been with him or followed him in a few minutes. And I have no doubt whatever of the object of his visit. He expected Meade to follow the fugitives of Pickett's division, & he intended, himself, to have a hand in rallying them, & in the fight which would follow. He had the combative instinct in him as strongly developed as any man living. No soldier could have looked on at & listened to the fight we had just been making, without a mighty stirring of every fibre in his frame, & a yearning to have some share in it. And the general had come out determined, if there *was* any more, that he would be in the thick of it. I've sometimes felt sorry that there wasn't! I'd like so to have seen him in it!

He had been with me but a few minutes when there came riding out to join us—also alone, Col. _____ Fremantle[103] of Her Majesty's Coldstream Guards. Of him I had heard early that morning, as having joined our army—a visitor anxious to see a fight. He had entered the Confederacy in Texas, & had come on to Richmond, & thence hurried after us, hoping to see the coming battle. He and Gen. Lee remained there with Colston & myself for an hour or more. Fremantle asked many questions, & I talked to him a good [deal] about the action, but Gen. Lee did not introduce me to him. A vague suspicion at the time came into my mind that it *might* be on account of my disreputable pants with my naked knee showing; & I was, moreover, in my grey shirt sleeves without coat, or mark of rank except that I *may* have had stars on [my] shirt collar. And I was sorry afterward that he did not introduce me, when there came out, in *Blackwood's Magazine,* an account of what F. saw of the battle, with much detail of what Gen. Lee did & said while we were all there together.[104]

One incident seemed, particularly, to impress him. He says that an officer spurred his horse, for shying at the bursting of a shell, & that Gen. Lee reproved him for using harsh measures, & told him that gentler ones were more effective. The officer was Lieut. Colston. His horse did not shy at the bursting of a shell, but it was thus. We heard loud cheering in the enemy's lines to our right. Gen. Lee thought it might mean preparing for a charge. He told Colston to ride out in that direction & see if he could discover what they were doing. Colston's horse, accustomed to be on the march with mine, balked at having to go off alone. Gen. Lee never could bear to see a horse maltreated, &, when Colston began spurring, he said, "Oh don't do that. Use gentle measures. I had a foolish horse once, & gentle measures always had the best result."[105]

A great many of Pickett's fugitives passed by us, & Gen. Lee spoke to nearly all, telling them not to be discouraged, & saying, "Form your ranks again when you get back to cover. We want all good men to hold together now." He also used the expression "It was all my fault this time." Four men came bearing a litter on their shoulders, on which an officer lay covered with a blanket. Gen. Lee rode up & asked, "Whom have you there?" They answered, "Gen. Kemper." Gen. Kemper, hearing Gen. Lee's voice, pulled the blanket from over his face. Gen. Lee said, "Gen. Kemper, I hope you are not badly hurt." "Yes, General," said Kemper, "I think they have got me this time." "Oh, I trust not! I trust not," said Gen. Lee.

Not a staff officer or courier found him, though doubtless many were looking for him back along the lines. Colston after a little reconnaissance, off to the right, reported that the cheering was for some officer who had ridden along the Federal lines. After about an hour or so, it being pretty clear that the enemy were not going to advance, Gen. Lee & Col. Fremantle left, & I also went to look over the other batteries, & begin, little by little, to get things into shape. A few horses at a time could be watered, & a little ammunition brought up, & scattered guns & batteries united. Then some pickets were gotten out in front, for the enemy put out some, & we began to be annoyed by sharpshooters. I ventured to let the men give the sharpshooters a few shell occasionally, which always taught them respect; & the enemy's artillery seemed to consider that no violation of our truce. But again I think they were wrong from a military point of view. They were the nearest to their abundant depots, & they should have shot at us, mercilessly, whenever they could. I saved ammunition all the war. But that was because our supply was always scant. But it is generally the poorest economy in the world to save ammunition in battles.

One of my guns, of Capt. Parker's battery, had such a hot skirmish with the sharpshooters, during the afternoon, that they had to use water to cool their gun off, but they held their ground. At dusk I began to quietly & silently move the batteries from the battlefield, back about where our infantry formed on the afternoon of the 2nd. Our infantry too was now established on a line, here, where it would be out of observation of the enemy. And at last, somewhere about ten o'clock at night I came off with the last battery, & going down past the school house I found somewhere within a mile, but I can't be sure where, a big barn which was our hospital, at which Frank Huger now had the whole battalion united,[106] &, the fighting being now over, I came back to my command. Ah, what a delightful sleep that night on some wheat straw in that barn!

That night Gen. Lee decided that he must return to Virginia, & began at once to dispatch his trains & his wounded. But, to give them a good start he determined to keep the army 24 hours longer. So the next day I was started at a very early hour, with some engineer officers[107] and staff to select a line of battle for our corps upon which to fight if the enemy should attack.

As it was the Fourth of July there was an idea that Meade would be inspired to try & win a real victory. We found a good line & occupied it but Meade did not come, &, in the afternoon, the march was commenced along towards sundown. An order of march was issued, & it was to be practically without halting until we approached the Potomac.

About an hour by sun[108] I was directed to go to the turnpike leading from Gettysburg to Fairfield, & take that road immediately behind a certain division, Heth's I think. When we approached the road it had begun raining, & the road was full of passing troops & trains. We parked in a little meadow, &, managing to get an old door off some old ruin of a structure near by, we put it on the ground, on a little knoll, some thirty yards from the road, & four of us sat on it, Huger, Colston, the adjt., & myself. Every once in awhile one of us would go to the road & ask, "Is this Heth's division?" It wasn't & nobody knew, either, where Heth's div. was, or when it was coming. After it got to be night we were all so overcome with sleep that we tried to lie down together on the door, & to pull our rubber coats over us, but the hard steady rain soaked through them, & every half hour we took turns going down to the road all that livelong night. It was daylight when Heth's divn. at last came along, & sunrise when we got strung out on the road.

This was now Sunday, July 5th. The march was very slow & tedious. Travel a little ways, & stopped by the thing in front of you stopping—it may be for a few seconds, it may be a half hour. Nothing is more wearying. Our carriages were light of ammunition, but we had lost enormously in horses. We were authorized by Gen. Lee to send out & impress horses from citizens, & told to offer payment in Confederate money, or to leave a descriptive list of animals taken, signed by an officer, on which the bereaved citizen could found a claim for damages upon his government. Had I foreseen our eventual taxation to pay our share of all these war claims, I might have given my men less liberal orders about the valuations they were permitted to put in. My diary says our march this day was via Fairfield & Fountaindale to Monterey Springs. I recall little of the road but a single incident. In the afternoon, up in a mountain district, riding a little ahead, I came on a country store kept by a woman. I went in & asked her if she would sell for Confederate money, & she said yes. She had nothing on her shelves but a few little remnants, but I thought I might get a little thread & yarn & take [it] back to Virginia, to my wife, where such things could hardly be gotten at all. I had gotten about a pocketful of some such little stuff (about a dollar I think I paid her), when a company of our cavalry came up & dismounted & the store soon filled. I fear the old lady did not get even Confederate money for all the rest of her remnants.

About midnight I remember passing a large hotel, well lit up & up in the mountains. This was Monterey Springs. To stretch my limbs & try & shake off the sleepiness making me nod in the saddle I dismounted & walked in but it seems as much a dream as a recollection. We made no stop, that I recall, except to water horses, or as the column blocked all night, & went on also all the next day, Monday, the 6th, via Waterloo & Ringgold, & came to Hagerstown about 4 P.M. This by the roads travelled is about 45 miles made in about 36 hours.[109]

During the day I had an accession to my staff. Capt. Stephen Winthrop had held a captain's commission in Her Majesty's 23rd Regt. (but I am not[110] at all *sure* that I have the number correct) & had sold out & come over to America to see some fighting.[111] He brought excellent letters to Richmond, for with real British pluck he decided to help the little fellow rather than the big. He did not care a pin for any other issue of the war, than which were the best fighters, & our side had the best general reputation abroad. So the Richmond people gave him a commission in the Inspector-General's Department, & sent him up to Longstreet to be assigned to duty. He arrived about the beginning of the battle, & was assigned to duty with Col. Walton. But he did not fancy the assignment, for some reason, and, on the march from Gettysburg, he negotiated with Gen. Sorrel, Longstreet's adjutant, to be transferred to me. Sorrel asked me if I would consent— which I did very willingly, & he joined me about noon on the 6th. He was well built, stout & very muscular, good grey-blue eyes, a full, oval face, with a British mouth & nose, good natured, jolly, & brave. He was an excellent and admirable representation of his country, & proved in every way an agreeable accession to our mess; & he remained with me & on my staff until the winter before the surrender.[112] His strongest personal peculiarity was his fondness for killing things. It was not cruelty—that is he did not go out to kill things unnecessarily—but destructiveness! If anything had to be killed he loved to do it.

That very afternoon he got a chance to show the stuff he was made of. As we approached Hagerstown, we heard some fighting ahead, between our cavalry & a cavalry force of the enemy. I rode ahead to see if any artillery was needed, &, meeting Gen. Stuart, I accompanied him into & through the town, & out beyond, where the skirmishing we had had before developed into some severer fighting, as he came upon larger forces; which, however he drove off entirely.

It happened that Winthrop's horse had become lame, & he had gone back to one of the batteries for a fresh horse, at the moment when I rode ahead to the sound of the fighting. When W. with his fresh horse came back he rode on to find me, but, in going through the streets he missed me, but came upon a regiment of cavalry, drawn up to charge down a pike, upon a Federal battery. Winthrop rode up, introduced himself, & asked permission to ride with them in the charge, & carry their colors, which in compliment to his country they granted. He & the adjutant led the charge, & Winthrop's horse was killed by canister quite close to the guns, but the charge was repulsed. He got another horse, & went in a second charge—this time with only his sabre—& got into the melee, in which he ran one of the enemy through, coming out with his sabre bent & bloody all over.

While we were fighting at Hagerstown, with part of Kilpatrick's[113] division of cavalry, another part of the same & Buford's division of cavalry made a strong attack at Williamsport upon Gen. Imboden's[114] brigade of cavalry, with our trains & wounded, which I had escorted from Gettysburg via Chambersburg—starting before us as already told. Imboden had met there, also, fortunately, a wagon train with some fresh ammunition which had been hurried down from Winchester, almost at a gallop, & without an escort. Imboden made a most gallant fight, many even of the wounded from the wagons participating, & the trains were saved & the enemy repulsed.

About sundown we went into camp, at last, a mile or two from Hagerstown to the S.E. It had been intended, the next day, to ford the Potomac, but the river was swollen by the recent rains, & was too high. It would require several days to build a bridge at Falling Waters. We had left a ponton bridge, there, when we advanced, but the enemy had destroyed it. We at once set to work on a new one, making new ponton boats from timber in part, I believe, procured by taking down barns. But, meanwhile, a great opportunity would be presented to the enemy. Here we would be penned up, with a river at our backs, with ammunition greatly reduced, & fresh supplies cut off, & defeat now would be ruin. A chance was offered Meade, as great as McClellan had missed the year before at Sharpsburg. We expected him to be on us in forty-eight hours, & vigorous efforts were made to be ready for him.

Early the next morning, Tues., July 7, I was sent for to join Gen. Lee's engineer officers in a reconnaissance of the country, & the selection of a line of battle upon which the army could make the best possible fight. We spent three full & busy days on this work, the enemy not following us nearly as closely as we expected. There was no very well defined & naturally strong line, & we had to pick & choose, & string together in some places by make-shifts & some little work. And, on the last day, at one point, where we differed, Gen. Lee came out to see the ground, & decided in my favor, of which I was very proud. I enjoyed the work those three days, & also the fine ripe cherries & raspberries which grew everywhere. And I specially recall one day, when we got at some farm a lot of corn, Irish potatoes & other vegetables, & some fat chickens, & took them by my camp about noon, & late in the afternoon came back to one great big camp kettle, where everything was cooked up together. It was unanimously voted that no one had ever seen that dish equalled before. I don't believe anyone who ate of it, & there was enough for all, will forget it in a thousand years.

I recall another incident of that camp. When I came home, the first afternoon, I found waiting for me an old Dunkard farmer, from somewhere in the vicinity, whose horse had been impressed by my men. He said he was a poor man & needed a horse in his crops, & that my men had told him that I had some footsore horses—from lack of horse-shoes on the rocky roads—& that I would probably have to abandon them, & he came to ask if I would give him one of these. I told him yes, I had two hoof-sores, & I would give him both. He thanked me, but said one would do. Then I asked him how he would take his pay for his horse, in Confederate money—the best we had & we were doing our best to make it good—or would he take a receipt on which he could collect from the U.S. He said the one lame horse would be pay enough. I felt sorry for the old fellow, & pushed him to take either money or a receipt. He declined both, respectfully but firmly—though I offered to make the receipt give his horse a character he would be proud to exhibit. At last, being pushed, he said, "Well, Sir, I am a Dunkard. With us the rule is 'an eye for an eye, a tooth for a tooth, & a horse for a horse,' & the church would discipline me if I violated our rule." "Well then," I said, "take two hoof-sores. I make you a present of them.[115] The Lord who made horses knows that yours is worth more than these two together, or you tell the church I gave you one." At last I got him persuaded, & he went off with his two horses. But that night, after we were all in bed, hoofs were heard approaching, & I got up expecting a courier with orders. It was my old Dunkard with one of the hoof-sores. "Well Sir," he said, as he hitched him to a fence near by, "this afternoon you talked so as to make that two horses for one sound all right, but I've been thinking it over since, and I don't think I can make the church see it that way, & I would rather not try." So saying he dismounted & walked off rapidly, refusing any further discussion of the matter. What a people those Dunkards ought to be for places of trust, from R.R. conductors to bank presidents & trustees!

Up to now, the enemy had pursued us as a mule goes on the chase of a grizzly bear—as if catching up with us was the last thing he wanted to do. But, at last, on Friday morning the 10th, the whole of Meade's army drew near, & some Georgia troops, who were camped over near Funkstown, were, somehow, caught in a tight place & suffered quite severely on a small scale. The whole army was immediately ordered to take position upon the selected line of battle. One incident of this morning which has always remained with me very vividly, was an interview I had with Gen. Lee, in a little oak grove, near the line, where he had dismounted, & was all alone, when I came up to get some direction. His greeting was specially friendly & almost affectionate, & after the matter upon which I had come was finished he detained me, & asked many questions about our lines, & seemed to try to draw out my opinion, & to take satisfaction in the confidence I felt that we could hold them. Only on one other occasion in the whole war did I ever see him in anything like this mood. It was in the fall of 1864 when Butler placed our prisoners under fire in the Dutch Gap Canal, of which I will tell in due course.

As fast as we got the troops upon our line of battle, everything, infantry & artillery, went to work fortifying it & making it stronger. I was given general charge again of all the artillery of our corps & left my own battalion to Huger as at Gettysburg. And, as we got things into shape, oh! how we all did wish that the enemy would come out in the open & attack us, as we had done them at Gettysburg. But they had had their lesson, in that sort of game, at Fredbg. & did not care for another. I remember two points on our line distinctly. Downesville, a little village near the Potomac, of only a few houses, was the key point of our right flank, & there I put the greater part of my own battalion, thinking likely that Meade's principal effort would be directed there, whence our bridge could be threatened. And the boys seeing me anxious about it assured me that future history would proudly record that "Downesville never surrendered." The other point I recall is St. James College grounds, where we had some good artillery positions & could also utilize the college buildings in defence.

But Gen. Meade showed no disposition to attack us. If he had he would not have had any easy task, though with his superior resources & forces, & the rare chance of ruining us which success would have given he certainly should have tried it for all he was worth. Or—if from Gettysburg he had marched hard & fast for Harpers Ferry, he might there have crossed the river & opposed us from the south bank & compelled us to again attack him in position. When it is remembered that Vicksburg had surrendered to the enemy upon July 4th, it does seem as if the cumulative moral effect of such another immense victory, as the destruction of Lee's army would have been, would surely have ended the war, & have made of Meade its greatest hero, & a future president. But the man who either could not see it—or feared to play the game with the opportunities he had—did not deserve it. Fortunately it finally came to one who did deserve it & was worthy of it.

At last on July 13 President Lincoln sent positive orders to Gen. Meade that he should attack. So on Tuesday morning, July 14, Meade moved forward upon our works. But the mule had not yet caught up with the bear. Downesville had lost its chance of becoming a great name in history. On the night before the bridge had been completed, &, moreover, the river had fallen to a point where the ford at Williamsport allowed some crossing, and Gen. Lee had ordered the army withdrawn.

But, oh, it was another awful night. I was now back with my battalion, & we were marching all night in awful roads, in mud & dark, & hard rain, & though we had only three miles to go, we were still some distance from the bridge at sunrise. The rain was now over, & the sun rose clear, &, about that time, a sudden alarm of Federal cavalry made me put some guns in position on a hill on the road side. Here they had a few shots at the cavalry, who were driven off, but our Gen. Pettigrew was killed in the melee which ensued when they surprised the train in march.[116]

The whole night had been spent in groping & pulling through the mud, a few feet at a time, & then waiting for the vehicle in front of you to move again. And men would go to sleep on their horses, or leaning in fence corners, or standing in the mud. At last, not long after sunrise, we came to the ponton bridge. It had a very bad approach, steep & on a curve—a bad location & several wagons, caissons, &c. had gone into the river during the night, though big fires were kept up to light it. But we got over fairly well & 3 miles beyond at a place called Hainesville we were glad to camp—once more on Virginia soil.[117]

Wednesday, July 15, we moved on to Bunker Hill where we camped for five days.[118] While at this camp I succeeded at last in getting as my adjutant my dear Jos. Haskell, Smith, who had been with me so far, being transferred into ordnance service somewhere south. Haskell was with me to the last day of the war, not only admired but loved by everybody on the staff, & in the command. Nature has not got any more admirable or attractive type than that in which the whole family of the six Haskell brothers in the war was stamped. One, Charles, a captain in the _____ So. Ca. was killed at Gettysburg. The same mail which carried this news to the family, at Abbeville, S.C., also brought news of the death of another brother, Edward, and of Capt. Langdon Cheves, the brother of their mother, both killed in battle on Morris Island, Charleston.[119] The mother had driven into Abbeville, 12 miles from their home in the country, & received the mail, & opened it in the carriage driving back. Langdon, the oldest brother, at this time was a captain in McGowan's So. Ca. brigade in Wilcox's division.[120] Alex, who had been Gen. Gregg's adjt., was about now transferred to the

7th So. Ca. Cavalry, which he afterward commanded. John, who had lost his right arm at Gaines's Mill leading a charge over the enemy's breast works, was now majr. of Henry's battalion of artillery with Hood's division, & soon after succeeded to command the battalion as lt. col.

I remember one other incident of the stay at Bunker Hill. The gash in the hip, received at Gettysburg by my mare Dixie, had not healed up. A great excrescence of proud flesh had grown projecting several inches, & looking very badly. Capt. Parker volunteered to cut it out & dress it so that it would heal, & he performed the operation for me with entirely successful results. But it was necessarily exceedingly painful to the poor animal, & in her very desperate struggles, against the ropes & men we had holding her, she came very near killing my faithful old Negro driver Abram by knocking him in the head with her own skull. It dropped him senseless but fortunately the African forehead proved as solid as the equine.

Monday, July 20th, we marched from Bunker Hill to Millwood, 24 miles. I afterward made a complaint of the order of march—I think it was upon this occasion. Of all tiresome things to soldiers there are few more disagreeable than to be ordered to march, & gotten out to the road, & then to be held waiting indefinitely. And, besides tiring the animals, by keeping them in harness, it loses time when they might be grazing. On the day in question, whenever it was, orders came that Ewell's corps should march at 4 A.M., Hill's at 6 A.M., & Longstreet's at 8 A.M. So, at 8 A.M., I had hitched up & had my battalion moved out to the pike by which we all were to travel. But each corps with all its trains would occupy about 12 miles of road, & it took it nearly four hours to stretch out. Consequently, Hill could not march until about 8, nor our corps until near 12.[121] I mention it only to illustrate how important in a big army is the detail, which only a large & well trained staff can supply.

On the march, that day, I remember coming upon a sheep, fallen out of a commissary drove, & exhausted by the heat. I had it put in our headquarters wagon & Winthrop butchered it scientifically when we got to camp & we enjoyed some very fine mutton.

For some cause, I was behind when we reached Millwood, & the battalion had started to encamp in a very beautiful sort of grove or park, around a very fine residence, with great pillars about the front porch— altogether one of the most elegant country places I ever saw—a little N.E. of the village. As I came up, a polite note from the proprietor was brought asking if we could avoid injury to the shrubbery & beautifully kept grass, &c. I had already stopped the unharnessing, & ordered the whole business to move out, & go to a piece of woods close by, equally good for our purposes. So while they were moving off, I rode up to the house to apologise to the owner for our unauthorized invasion. He was quite a striking character. He saw me coming & opened the door for me himself. He was very short & thickset, with a fiery red head which was cropped to the closest possible prizefighter's length. I said I had merely come to apologise that my command should have ever intruded so unnecessarily, & to say that I had ordered them out as soon as I saw it, & even before his note had been received. The old gentleman then started to accept my apology, & to say that he was sure from the first that it was merely some mistake. But, when he started to speak, I found that I had struck the worst stutterer I had ever encountered in my life. But he carried it off with a manner which was equally rare. He did not hurry, & he looked me calmly & benignantly in the face & made me feel that he knew I was far too much of a gentleman to regard his unfortunate failing, &, therefore, for us it did not exist. And so we had quite a pleasant little interview & he offered me the courtesies of his house if I remained near,[122] which I did not. I am not sure of his name but I have an idea that it was Burwell.

On Tuesday the 21st we marched 13 miles & camped near the Shenandoah, which was now too high to be forded, & had a ponton bridge over it. We crossed this bridge the next morning at dawn & moved up into Chester Gap, which was threatened by a cavalry force of the enemy's. At a certain point in the gap we halted & remained there all day ready to help defend it, if any attack was made. I have an idea that there was some fighting a few miles off, but none in our vicinity. At night we resumed our march, & travelled all night, & until about 8 A.M., when we camped for the day. Next day, after a march of 15 miles, we encamped near Culpeper—to the west of it—on the farm of a very celebrated old character, in that section, Maj. Jack Pendleton.[123] On this march I remember, by the way, finding a wasp nest, & borrowing a fish hook & catching a nice little string of small fish, with the wasp grubs, from a creek we forded.

Maj. Pendleton's notoriety in his county was largely for violence of temper, & I had a specimen of it. An order came down from hd.qrs. not to put our horses out to graze, but to have grass cut for them. It was a very injudicious order, not only for the extra work put upon the men, but it was wasteful. Grass long enough to cut can be made into hay for the winter. Short grass cannot. And there are ten acres of short grass good for nothing but grazing to be found for one acre of grass suitable for cutting. The only grass long enough to cut, within a mile of my camp, was a beautiful large meadow running up to Maj. Pendleton's house. So I sent a detail up with some grass hooks, for a supply for our big lot of horses. In about ten minutes the men came, almost flying, back from Maj. P. with a double barrel shot gun, & a volley of oaths that would have done credit to a Gatling gun. He had sworn he would shoot the first man who cut the first blade of his grass.

I had a few muskets in some of our wagons, & I had a few of our guard armed with them, for moral effect, & for a show of superior force, &, as Joe Haskell was of very nice manners & pleasing address, I put him in charge of the party, & gave him instructions, & he went back. First he left his armed guard out of sight, but within call, & then went up to the gate, where the major met him. Haskell showed him the order from Gen. Lee, not to graze our animals, but to cut grass. Told him that, personally, I thought the order injudicious, but had to obey it. That I knew of no other grass convenient, but if he could show or tell me of any I would consider it. His only reply was that he would shoot the first man who cut a blade. Then Joe told him he regretted to have to display force, but had no choice. He had seen for himself that we had orders, & we were bound to execute them. And he gave a signal & up came our fellows with the muskets. Then the old man came down a peg. "Would I wait until he could ride & see Gen. Lee?" "No, but I would not cut any large supply, only one feed for my horses." That was accepted, & the old fellow went off. I don't know whether he used another Gatling volley of oaths or not, but he certainly brought back a note relieving me from obedience to that order. It was in talking about this that I afterward told the general about how the marching orders at Bunker Hill caused us to lose some hours of grazing. Of course he had to leave details to subordinates & in that way they sometimes got out of the best shape.

We camped at Pendleton's for a week, & then on Fri., July 31, we moved 7 miles over near Somerville Ford of the Rapidan. The next day, we crossed the Rapidan, &, on Sunday, Aug. 2nd, a short march of 8 miles took us to a nice camp, on the right of the road, some 2 miles or so north of Orange C.H. at which we remained for over five weeks. This march, then, practically terminated the Gettysburg campaign & I will close the chapter with some further detail of casualties & some miscellaneous remarks. The official losses of the two armies were as follows:

	Killed	Wounded	Missing	Total
Confederate Army	3,072	14,497	5,434	23,003
Federal [Army]	2,592	12,709	5,150	20,451
Both Armies	5,664	27,196	10,584	46,454

The casualties make Gettysburg the bloodiest battle of the whole war. The nearest approach is _____.[124] To give some idea of the work done by different sub divisions I put together the following table of casualties:[125]

General Review of the Battle

As I progressed with my narrative I have touched, more or less fully, upon nearly all the controverted points in the popular discussion of Gettysburg, which I have ever seen, & I trust that the spirit in which all I say is suggested will be appreciated. It is not at all that of personal criticism of any of the generals, or other officers discussed. General Lee's reputation, for instance, either as a soldier or as a man, does not seem to me involved, to any appreciable extent, in a technical discussion whether or not, for the summer of 1863, the safest Confederate play in the great game of war, was what we might call the Pennsylvania gambit, which he did play, or the Tennessee gambit which Longstreet claims to have suggested. Victory was possible under either, very easily, and we have the benefit of our backsights in the discussion, where he had only that of his foresights. But as the games of chess of the greatest masters who ever lived[126] would be but little interesting and but half understood, if the narrative of their moves is not accompanied by even a feeble effort to point out, at different situations, the technical questions arising, & discussing the solutions attempted, so, I have thought that both the interest & the comprehension of my long & detailed narrative will be greatly lost if it is not kept in touch with the military problems & features of the successive situations.

I will, therefore, now recapitulate, briefly, the principal technical questions which I have touched upon in the progress of my narrative, &, also, discuss somewhat one or two others of interest to which the narrative did not directly lead.

1. The question of all, at the inception of the campaign, was whether to play what I've already called the Pennsylvania, or, the Tennessee gambit. By the rules of the game, the Tennessee, with its interior lines was the safest game. But, perhaps, one consideration which may have influenced Gen. Lee was that Pa. was nearest the enemy's vitals. There was reason to believe that, if we could take Washington, the moral effect on the enemy would be much more potent than to capture Cincinnati. And the narrative of the battle I think has put it beyond all question that it was not the *choice of the gambit* which lost the game. We took into Pa. an amount of fight, so to express it, which would have defeated Meade's army, if it had been judiciously concentrated & applied, & not expended upon physical obstacles, and at non-vital times & places.

2. Hooker seems to me to have lost a great chance when he found, at Fredericksburg, only A. P. Hill between himself & Richmond; Longstreet at Culpeper, & Ewell in the Valley. By all means, he should have marched to Richmond, overwhelming Hill as he went; which would have been sure & easy with his immense force. A somewhat similar situation was presented to Sherman in 1864, when, at Atlanta, he found Hood threatening Nashville in his rear. He knew that Hood could do nothing serious, even if he took Nashville, so he let him alone, & marched for Savannah. But, as I have before written, the Federals were ridiculously & insanely afraid of our

capturing Washn. City; in spite of their superb triple circle of fortifications. Gen. Lee appreciated their weakness, and boldly played upon it—indeed I think he must sometimes have enjoyed very hearty laughs over his successful but marvellous audacity in practising on the enemy's fears.

3rd. The next point in the game was Stuart's cavalry move, around Hooker's army. I've already said that I am sure that was bad play, on general principles. We should have *always* had our *whole* army in *easy reach, & supporting distance* of each other. Such a raid could cut no real figure on the grand result, & was taking chances for no good.

4. When Heth's division was authorized to go to Gettysburg to get shoes, I think it should surely have had a similar caution to that given Gen. Ewell, on the afternoon of the first day's battle, when he was directed to occupy Cemetery Hill but cautioned *"not to bring on a general engagement."* The principle involved in such cautions, which are very often given, is not to waste the fighting spirit & power of the army on side issues. It is simply that of saving & concentrating every energy for the vital point at the critical time. This fighting spirit in the troops, after a period of rest, is something as real, though not as tangible, as ammunition, & should be economised in the same way. Even the best divisions, after one really severe & bloody action, cannot be expected to exhibit the highest development of spirit, particularly on the offensive, until after a little rest; during which new officers & fresh leaders among them acquire influence, & replace those who have been lost. Note the better spirit of Pickett's fresh division in his charge than that of the troops badly cut up two days before.

5. On the first day we had taken the aggressive. Although a casual reading of Gen. Lee's report suggests that the aggressive on [the] second day seemed forced upon him, yet the statement is very much qualified by the expression "in a measure," & also by the reference to the hopes inspired by our partial success. I think it must be frankly admitted that there was no real difficulty, whatever, in our taking the defensive the next day; & in our so manouvring afterward as to have finally forced Meade to attack us.

I think it a reasonable estimate to say that 60 per cent of our chances for a great victory were lost by our continuing the aggressive. And we may easily imagine the boon it was to Gen. Meade (who was neither a man of any high degree of decision, or of aggression; & who was now entirely new to his great responsibility, & evidently oppressed by it) to be relieved from the burden of making any difficult decision, such as he would have had to do if Lee had been satisfied with his victory of the first day; & then taken a strong position & stood on the defensive. Now the gods had flung to Meade more than impudence itself could have dared to pray for—a position unique among all the battlefields of the war, certainly adding fifty per cent to his already superior force, and an adversary stimulated by success to an utter disregard of all physical disadvantages & ready to face for nearly three quarters of a mile the very worst that all his artillery & infantry could do. For I am impressed by the fact that the strength of the enemy's position seems to have cut no figure in the consideration [of] the question of the aggressive; nor does it seem to have been systematically examined or inquired into—nor does the night seem to have been utilized in any preparation for the morning. Verily that night *it was pie for Meade*!

6. There seems no doubt that had Longstreet's attack on the 2nd been made materially sooner, we would have gained a decided victory. Nor is there any doubt that it could have been—or that Gen. Lee much desired it to be made very much earlier. But he yielded to Longstreet's request to wait for Law's brigade; and the delay caused by Longstreet's infantry being taken in sight of Round Top seems to have entirely escaped his attention, & that of all his staff. He was present on the field all the time, & was apparently consenting to the situation from hour to hour. Longstreet is bitterly blamed for asking for delay,[127] & subsequent events showed that it lost us a great opportunity. But it seems to me that while he might blame himself for it general criticism must be modified by the fact that Gen. Lee's granting the request justified it as apparently prudent, at the time.

7. I have sufficiently discussed, in my narrative, the very great mistake made, in my judgment, in the selection of the point of attack. Here again, as when the question of the aggressive or the defensive was up, on the night of the first day, there seems a lack of appreciation of the immense figure which the character of the ground may cut in the results of an aggressive fight. Not only was the selection about as bad as possible, but there does not seem to have been any special thought given to the matter. It seems to have been allowed almost to select itself as if it was a matter of no consequence.

8. Similarly, I have told in my narrative how each chief artillery officer, of each corps, was left to his own devices; & the one advantage of our exterior position, that of enfilading parts of the enemy's line, was not utilized. I will refer again to this subject under the next head.

Finally, we come to consider the constitution of the storming column. I have written, in my narrative, that Gen. Wright remarked to me when I showed him Longstreet's note, that the success of the attack "was solely a question of supports." In the account I wrote for the *Century Magazine,* I said, "Our men were good enough; the only trouble was that there were not enough of them."[128]

That Gen. Lee himself expected the attack to be at least better supported than it was is very certain. I quote from Gen. Imboden a very graphic account of an interview with him after midnight of the last day, which is as if the scene were before me and I heard of his disappointment from his own lips:

It was a warm summer night & there were few camp fires, & the weary soldiers were lying in groups, on the luxuriant grass of the beautiful meadows, discussing the events of the day, speculating on the morrow or watching that our horses did not straggle off while browsing. About 11 o'clock, a horseman came to summon me to Gen. Lee. I promptly mounted and, accompanied by the courier who brought the message, rode about two miles toward Gettysburg, to where half a dozen small tents, a little way from the road side, to our left, were pointed out as Gen. Lee's headquarters for the night. On inquiry I found that he was not there, but had gone to the quarters of Gen. Hill, about a half mile nearer to Gettysburg. When we reached the place, a single flickering candle, visible from the road, through the open front of a common wall tent, exposed to view Generals Lee & Hill, seated on camp stools, with a map spread upon their knees. Dismounting, I approached on foot. After exchanging the ordinary salutations, Gen. Lee directed me to go back to his headquarters, & wait for him. I did so, but he did not make his appearance until about 1 o'clock, when he came riding alone, at a slow walk, & evidently wrapped in profound thought.

When he arrived there was not even a sentinel on duty at his tent, & no one of his staff was awake. The moon was high in the clear sky, & the silent scene was unusually vivid. As he approached, & saw us lying on the grass under a tree, he spoke, reined in his jaded horse, and essayed to dismount. The effort to do so betrayed so much physical exhaustion that I hurriedly rose, & stepped forward to assist him but before I reached his side he had succeeded in alighting, & threw his arm across the saddle to rest, &, fixing his eyes upon the ground, leaned in silence & almost motionless upon his equally weary horse—the two forming a striking & never-to-be-forgotten group. The moon shone full upon his massive features, and revealed an expression of sadness that I had never seen before upon his face. Awed by his appearance, I waited for him to speak until the silence became embarrassing, when, to break it & change the silent current of his thoughts, I ventured to remark in a sympathetic tone, & in allusion to his great fatigue; "General, this has been a hard day on you." He looked up & replied mournfully, "Yes, it has been a sad, sad day to us," & immediately lapsed into his thoughtful mood & attitude. Being unwilling again to intrude upon his reflections, I said no more. After, perhaps, a minute or two, he suddenly straightened up, to his full height, & turning to me, with more animation & excitement of manner than I had ever seen in him before, for he was a man of wonderful equanimity, he said in a voice tremulous with emotion: "I never saw troops behave more magnificently than Pickett's division of Virginians did today, in that grand charge upon the enemy. And if they had been supported as they were to have been—but for some reason, not yet fully explained to me, were not—we would have held the position, & the day would have been ours." After a moment's pause he added in a loud voice, in a tone almost of agony, "Too bad! *Too bad*! *TOO BAD!*" I shall never forget his language, his manner, & his appearance of mental suffering. In a few moments all emotion was suppressed, & he spoke feelingly of several of his fallen & trusted officers; among others of Generals Armistead, Garnett, & Kemper of Pickett's division.[129]

Now let us inquire, 1st: What troops did Gen. Lee refer to, as those which he expected to support Pickett's charge, but which did not do so? 2nd: How came it to happen that they did not?

A number of writers have asserted that the troops referred to were Hood's & McLaws's divisions of Longstreet's corps, & I think that even some of Gen. Lee's staff officers have written letters indicating some thing of the same opinion. I have already referred briefly to this matter in my narrative. But besides the fact that Gen. Lee's own report speaks of having originally had that intention, but of afterward substituting other troops in their places, there remains the obvious difficulty, of withdrawing those troops from their positions in front of Round Top & putting them into the storming column, & the difficulty of holding the firing line of guns if this were done, as I have already told in my narrative.

Then, it must be remembered that the preparations for this charge were made deliberately, & under the observation of Gen. Lee himself, & of all his staff. From sunrise to 1:30 P.M. was nine hours, all devoted to this business, & within a few hundred acres of land. It seems to me impossible to believe that Gen. Lee did not know quite accurately the location of every brigade he had upon that battlefield, hours before the cannonade opened. Certainly he & his staff officers also were all about in my vicinity, during the morning, & if there was one thing they might be supposd to take an interest in, it would be in seeing that the troops which were to support the charge were in position to do it. Why else should they have been around there & what else had they of more importance to look after during all that time?

This consideration puts Hood & McLaws entirely out of the question, & shows that the only troops Gen. Lee could have expected to support the charge, were those who were at & about the point of departure of the storming column. Who were they? Wilcox's brigade (2,000) & Anderson's division, 6,000.[130] There can be no other answer.

There was, indeed, some early talk that Ewell's corps would make a simultaneous attack with Pickett's division, but the enemy forestalled that, at sunrise, by attacking Johnson's division in the lines they had gotten possession of the night before, as I have narrated. So that Gen. Lee could have expected nothing further after that from Ewell's corps. In fact, it never was possible to expect *much* from them, either of success, or even of simultaneous demonstration, on account of their unfortunate position, to which I have already referred in my narrative,[131] on account of the strength of the enemy's lines in their front & of the long & roundabout way of communicating.

Now, 2nd, we have the question why did not Anderson's division and Wilcox's brigade support the charge of Pickett's & Heth's divisions?

I will hardly attempt to answer that question exhaustively, or to apportion any blame among individuals. Accident, & the novelty of the situation, I am sure had much to do with it. We may call it by accident that these troops belonged to different corps. The storming column proper, of 9 brigades (Pickett 3, Pettigrew 4, Trimble 2) was distinctly put under Longstreet's control, though only three of the brigades were his own. But the five brigades of supports all belonged to A. P. Hill's corps, and I have never heard that Longstreet was charged with launching them into the battle. If they had been put under Longstreet's control, A. P. Hill would have been almost entirely overslaughed. He would have been left in command of but two brigades. Now whose duty was it to start those five brigades to Pickett's support? It may have been Wilcox & Anderson, or it may have been Hill, or it may have been Longstreet or it may have been Gen. Lee himself. I will not pretend to say, but I will designate whoever had that duty as X, for short, in this discussion. And I assert that X should have started every man of his supports before Pickett's division had advanced two hundred yards.

The situation was entirely a different one from any we had confronted in any of our previous aggressive battles. At Seven Pines, Gaines's Mill, Frazier's Farm, Malvern Hill, & Chancellorsville, we had attacked practically the enemy's whole fronts with our whole fronts, or that, at least, was the intention. Then, the enemy could not draw assistance, from the right & left, if he were broken anywhere; for each part of his front would have its own safety to look after.

It is plain that this difference, at once, demands consideration in the formation of this storming column. It must expect, at the very moment of its landing, to receive instantaneous & strong assaults upon both its flanks from troops who have no other enemy to occupy them, & are free even to swing out & enfilade them.

We had usually used two lines in our former assaults covering the enemy's entire front. Here the fire to be faced, the distance to be traversed, & the resistance to be encountered were all unusually great. Surely three lines would seem the least with which we should have attempted it. Well we had three lines, but *not full ones*. In the front line were 6 brigades, in the second line but 3, & in the third line 5. Now we have X in command of the 3rd line.

Surely, he should advance at the *same time that the first & second lines do, & keep close behind them.* There is no use in his advancing at all unless he share in the very shock & crisis of the assault. Really he would better have put some of his brigades in the 2nd line & filled it fuller than with only 3. Every man was bound to be needed & the sooner he arrived the better.

And the battle failed of being fought as Gen. Lee expected & wished, when Pickett's advance had traversed 400 yards, & Wilcox & Anderson were not moving under orders to close up on him & go with him to the bitter end.

Two further questions may be asked. If Anderson & Wilcox had been welded into the column from the first, & all 14 brigades launched together; or, in other words, if Pickett had had the support which Gen. Lee expected; would those five brigades have saved the day? That is a question upon which men will differ. Personally, I cannot feel confident of it, because of Gen. Meade's ability to use such an immense superiority of force. But some Confederates feel very sure about it, & the details of the fight by Pickett's division show that it was not defeated at all by what it first met in front, but was overwhelmed on the flanks & by reinforcements. It struck upon the front of two brigades of Gibbon's division, Hall's on our right, & Webb's on our left. This is Hall's account in his official report:[132]

> The perfect order & steady but rapid advance of the enemy called forth praise from our troops, but gave their line an appearance of being fearfully irresistible. The troops were pouring into their ranks a rapid & accurate fire when I saw that a portion of the line of Gen. Webb, on my right, had given way & many men were making to the rear as fast as possible, while the enemy was pouring over the rails that had been a slight cover for their troops. Having gained this apparent advantage the enemy seemed to turn again & re-engage my whole line. Going to the left I found two regiments, that could be spared from some command there, & endeavored to move them by the right flank to the break; but, coming under a warm fire, they crowded to the slight cover of the rail fence, mixing with the troops already there. Finding it impossible to draw them out & reform, & seeing no unengaged troops within reach, I was forced to order my own brigade back from the line, & move it by the flank under a heavy fire.
>
> The enemy was rapidly gaining a foothold; organisation was mostly lost in the confusion, commands were useless, while the disposition, on the part of the men, to fall back a pace or two each time to load, gave the line each time a retiring direction.

This is a plain confession that both Hall's & Webb's brigades were defeated, & were being driven, when their reinforcements saved them. Had five more Confederate brigades been then at hand we would certainly have stood some chances.

And that suggests the last question. Could we have had in that column any *further* supports than those five brigades?

I think so. Really, I see no reason why Ewell's whole corps could not have been drawn to the right, enough to spare fully two divisions, say 8 brigades more & three fourths of his artillery. And then, had the assault been delivered upon the bend of the fishhook, & all the artillery, of all three corps, handled as one mass, the heavier guns everywhere put to enfilading fire, & the lighter saved up to be used on the flanks as I had proposed to use Richardson's 9, we would have practically forged our storming column into a sort of armor piercing projectile, & could surely have driven its head a long ways into Meade's body, & stood a fair chance of precipitating a panic. What we did, under all our disadvantages, with only 9 brigades in the storming column, surely justifies sanguine anticipations of what might have been done by 22, at a more favorable locality, & with more artillery.

Finally, I again connect our failure in this battle with a deficiency of well trained staff officers, which I have often before noted. Not only did we greatly lack expert military engineers, but the general weakness of staff force had, I think, the effect of having many things done by verbal instructions which should be put in writing. For in written orders there is apt to be more attention to small details, such as may be overlooked in verbal. For instance, I believe that *nobody* was directly designated to launch Anderson's division to Pickett's support, & Wilcox was left to judge for himself. For surely no one would have neglected or disobeyed instructions so grossly had they known themselves charged with that duty. Had a written order given the details of that charge there could have been neither omission or misunderstanding on that important matter. There must have been either omission, misunderstanding or criminal disobedience. The probabilities are overwhelming that it was a misunderstanding somewhere.

CHICKAMAUGA

I think that the marches & battles, which I have yet to describe, can be told of much more briefly and simply than the campaign of Gettysburg. In no other battle of the whole war has so much seemed to be at stake, to the most of its historians; & in no other has a great Confederate victory seemed so long, as it were, trembling in the balance, & swayed by such slight events. The Comte de Paris,[1] & many other reputable writers speak of it as the crisis of the war, and a monument called the "High-water mark of the Rebellion" has been erected at the spot where Armistead fell, bearing the names of the principal commanders of regiments, brigades, &c. engaged in each army. I do not entirely agree in the opinion that it was the crisis of the war. I think equally as great, or greater, chances hung in the balance on Jun. 30th, 1862, & were lost by the inaction of the column under Stonewall Jackson; & again on June 15, 1864, & again lost, not in the shock of battle, but, as has yet to be told in due course, by 24 hours spent in camp, when the army should have been marching. But while Gettysburg remains the favorite theme of controversy, both of these events have largely escaped popular notice & comment.

For another reason, also, the narrative may, in future, be more rapid & simple. The severe fighting I have yet to describe, though bloody & prolonged, beyond almost all precedent, was mostly upon the defensive. Hence my guns usually fought from pits, or behind extempore breast works, & were distributed in smaller bodies, to defend our whole long lines, rather than massed for concentration upon some selected point of the enemy's. So I can tell no more of swift & fierce assaults, crowned with brilliant success, as on that glorious Sunday morning at Chancellorsville; or of prolonged struggles, like those of Gettysburg, whose desperation is told in the bloody list of casualties. The future fights are principally, now, to be of the Fredericksburg type, where the guns were protected, as far as possible, & saved for use against the enemy's infantry—where the best possible record to be made is merely that the enemy shall receive a quick and sanguinary repulse, & where the greatest technical skill will appear in the accomplishment of that result with the smallest list of casualties.

And, surely the good luck vouchsafed to me during the whole war—from first to last, & in small things as well as large—nowhere deserves more special & grateful recognition than for its having brought to me, in so short a time, & so unexpectedly, such rare and beautiful opportunities as I enjoyed at Marye's Hill, Chancellorsville, & Gettysburg. There are few days in my life, of which I would not sooner lose the memory, than those.

My Gettysburg chapter ended with our arrival near Orange C.H., Va., on Sunday, Aug. 2. I remember our camp as on a nice grassy hill, the site of an old residence, with no structure standing but an old cider press. We remained in that location for about five weeks, & I remember them as very busy, & very happy. Overhauling, refitting, & drilling were varied with some experiments on projectiles, fuses, &c., & I also devised & practised at a plan for raising our howitzers on skids, & getting a very nice mortar fire from them. And then there was an artillery board of officers, from all of the corps, for some technical purpose, I forget what, which met at my quarters, & brought some pleasant companionships. Among them I recall Lt. Col. Snowden Andrews, a nephew of the old Col. Andrews, of the 6th Infantry, with whom I had crossed the plains in 1858.

About a year before—at Cedar Mountain—Col. A. had been desperately wounded by a fragment of a shell which burst almost upon him & tore his side open. He was one of the few men who ever saw his own liver & survived. I remember also Alex Haskell as one of our most popular & frequent visitors, at this camp, & our special friendship dated from it.

But the dearest recollection of all is a furlough of five days, from Aug. 26th to 31st, which I got from Gen. Lee's headquarters, & spent at Mrs. Woolfolk's with my wife & little daughter.

A week after I came back, on the night of Sept. 8th, we received sudden orders to march the next day for Petersburg, Va., & then it was whispered that "Old Pete," as Longstreet was called, was ordered with his corps to Chattanooga to reinforce Bragg. This was practically the movement which was proposed by Longstreet in May & I have already sufficiently described its strategy. Now, Rosecrans[2] from near Nashville, was moving down upon Bragg, who was defending Chattanooga with a much inferior force, & we resorted to this movement in defense. So on Wed., Sep. 9th, the artillery board was unexpectedly dissolved by our breaking camp at an early hour, & marching for Louisa C.H., en route for Petersburg, Va., where we were to take the cars.

And, now, I quickly recognised a chance for a little strategy on my own account. Why should I march all that distance with my battalion, while my wife was at Milford, & the R.R. would take me from Milford to Petersburg in a few hours. On the road I went by Longstreet's hdqrs. & got permission, &, when we got to Louisa C.H. I turned over the battalion to Huger, & that very evening I gave my wife the surprise of another visit at Mrs. Woolfolk's. And I, as it were, just ravished from fate five more beautiful days; for I did not rejoin the battalion at Petersburg until Monday, Sep.3 14th. The Washington Artillery came with us, & all three divisions of infantry—Hood's, McLaws's, & Pickett's—but not other artillery, as it was supposed that we could get some battalions assigned to us out west, after we got there. But, for reasons I have never known, neither Pickett's division nor the Washington Artillery came beyond Petersburg. Both remained south of the James River all of that winter, & only rejoined the corps after we had fought, the next summer, from the Wilderness down to the vicinity of Richmond.

There was now but one line of railroad between Richmond & the South. The route through Lynchburg, Bristol, & Knoxville to Dalton & Chattanooga had been lost by the surrender of Cumberland Gap, & Burnside's advance from there upon Knoxville. This surrender was generally considered, at the time, to have been cowardly & without proper defence. A second route was being prepared by building some 40 miles4 of road, from Danville, Va., to Greensboro, No. Ca., but this was not completed until some time in 1864. So the only available line for all the immense tide of troops, travel, & freights, back & forth, between Virginia & the South, was the route via Weldon, Wilmington, Kingsville, Branchville, & Augusta, to Atlanta & beyond. In those days the Southern railroads were but lightly built & equipped, &, now, for two years they had been cut off from all sorts of supplies of railroad material but what their own small shops could produce. Naturally, therefore, the movement of our corps, considered in the light of modern railroading, was very slow. Precedence was given to the infantry—or at least to Hood's & McLaws's divisions. After all of them had been dispatched, my battalion was started. Our guns were mounted upon flat cars, the officers & men in box cars, & the horses in stock cars. When the weather was good, many from the box cars would swarm out on the flats among the guns & caissons. One night, a stock car door came open & some horses fell out, but, next morning, when they were missed, we sent some men back & the horses were finally recovered unhurt.

We left Petersburg on Thursday, Sep. 17th, but I have no record or recollection of the hour. We reached Wilmington, 240 miles,5 at 2 A.M. Sunday, [the] 20th. Here we had to unload, ferry across the Cape Fear River, & reload on the south side. At 2 P.M. that afternoon, we left, on the old Wilmington & Manchester Road, for Kingsville, S.C., 190 miles, & we arrived there at 6 P.M. on the 21st—28 hours' running time. It was on this road, during the night of the 20th, I think, that the horses fell out of the car. At Kingsville we took the South Ca. R.R. for Augusta, via Branchville, 140 miles. We did not change cars at Branchville, but they were not ready to take us on until 2 A.M. on Tuesday the 22nd. While waiting here, I heard, to my great disappointment, that we would be too late to take part in the great battle which was expected, for the telegraph operator in the Kingsville office told me it had been already fought on the 19th & 20th, at Chickamauga, & had proved to be a great victory. Hood, he told me, who had lost[6] his arm at Gettysburg, had now lost his leg. A part of the infantry of our corps, but only a part, had been engaged in the battle.

I will give a brief account of the battle presently, but will first finish my account of our journey. We reached Augusta at 2 P.M., Tuesday the 22nd— 12 hours, _____ miles.[7] Here again we changed cars, but were off at 7 P.M., & ran out to Belair, where we went upon a side track, & had to wait until daylight—why I do not remember. But we were off at a very early hour, & passing close by my old home at Washington we reached Atlanta, 172 miles, at 2 P.M. on the 24th.[8] Here my sister, Mrs. Hull, was keeping house, her husband being superintendent of the Atlanta & West Point Railroad. With all my staff we went there to such a good supper, & to spend, oh, such a delightful evening! I remember that Winthrop, & Colston both, refused brandy peaches, when handed, until they saw that knives & forks were provided to eat them with, instead of spoons, which they had been accustomed to see. At 4 A.M. on the 24th we left Atlanta, on the Western & Atlantic, & its crowded condition is told in our being 22 hours in making the 110 miles[9] to Ringgold, Geo., the terminus of train service. Our entire journey by rail had been about 852 miles in about 182 hours. Here we remained a day or two, getting fitted out with wagons, & quartermaster, commissary, & ordnance supplies, to get ourselves in the best shape; & here I can best tell what needs to be told about the battle of Chickamauga.

Rosecrans & Bragg were the opposing generals who had now, for more than a year, commanded the invading & the defending armies, on the important line of railroad from Louisville to Atlanta via Nashville & Chattanooga. Next to the Federal advance upon Richmond, this was the most dangerous & vital of all the Federal attacks.

A severe battle had been fought between the opposing armies at Murfreesboro, or Stone River, about 30 miles south of Nashville, from Dec. 31, '62, to Jan. 3, '63, but without decisive results. Bragg had captured [the] most guns & prisoners, but had finally withdrawn to Tullahoma, about 20 miles, leaving Murfreesboro to Rosecrans.[10]

In June, Rosecrans, with his superior forces, had been able to manouvre Bragg out of his lines & without any serious fighting the latter had fallen back to Chattanooga. And now, with about 70,000 men to Bragg's 40,000,

Rosecrans was coming to work Bragg out of Chattanooga, Burnside having already advanced through Cumberland Gap & taken Knoxville. That is why Longstreet was sent to reinforce Bragg, & he was bringing 10 brigades, about 14,000 men, & my battalion of artillery with 26 guns.

Now a larger army manouvers a smaller out of position by sending a part of its superior force to threaten its opponent's rear. The latter can only live for a few days if its supply trains are cut off; therefore it must fall back when its rear is seriously threatened. But in such manouvering the larger army is necessarily divided into two parts, & a skillful antagonist may find an opportunity to concentrate his whole force upon one of them & destroy it. Bragg's play then should have been to watch Rosecrans closely, & seize any such opportunity as might be offered. [Figure 24 appears here in the manuscript.]

Now it so happened on this occasion, that a splendid opportunity was offered to Bragg. Rosecrans sent his left flank, Crittenden's corps,[11] to cross the Tennessee above Chattanooga & threaten Ringgold. On his right he sent Thomas's & McCook's corps[12] via Trenton to threaten Lafayette. The last two corps got into a mountain valley called McLemore's Cove, just as Bragg's whole army was near it on its retreat from Chattanooga. Bragg discovered it, & promptly issued orders for its attack from three directions, from Dug Gap, Catlett's Gap, & directly up the cove. It takes an army with good discipline, a good staff, & all the qualities of a well organised machine to execute even a double attack efficiently. A triple attack is still harder. A whole day was lost, Sep. 9th, & Thomas found out that he had blundered into a dangerous place & safely withdrew. The fault was said to lie between Gen. Hindman[13] & Gen. D. H. Hill, but it rests primarily with Gen. Bragg who was present in person.[14]

Rosecrans then concentrated his whole army on the north side of Chickamauga Creek near Rossville. As his whole force was now united Bragg had nothing to gain by an immediate attack, & as his reinforcements from Virginia were now beginning to arrive he should certainly have remained on the defensive until they were all at hand. Even with them all his adversary would have about four men to his three,[15] & it was wretched play to bring on an offensive battle while five of Longstreet's splendid brigades & all of my 26 guns were not yet arrived. But that is exactly what Bragg did. On Sep. 15th he marched to attack Rosecrans wherever he could find him. On the 19th he crossed Chickamauga Creek & a partial but very severe engagement ensued. At the end he was successful driving back a part of the enemy's line & holding the field.

The supreme effort was then organised for the 20th. He put Gen. Polk in command of his right wing, & Longstreet of his left. Now Gen. Polk graduated at West Point with Prest. Davis about 1827, & went into the

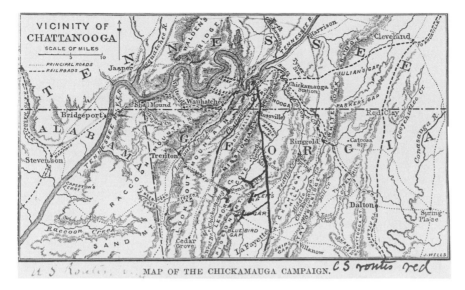

Figure 24. Vicinity of Chickamauga campaign

ministry about 1832. The Lord had made him a splendid bishop & a great & good man. So all our pious people with one consent & with secret conviction that the Lord would surely favor a bishop turned in & made him a lieut. gen., which the Lord had not. Had his corps marched from Corinth at the hour intended by Gen. Albert Sidney Johnston, the battle of Shiloh would have been fought just 24 hours earlier than it was. That battle was converted from a defeat of Gen. Grant, into a great victory for him, by the arrival of an army under Buell, which, the day before was 20 miles off.

Now, at Chickamauga, the attack on the 20th was to be begun by Gen. Polk, at dawn, & Longstreet was to take it up later. But it did not begin for four mortal hours after, or not until *about nine o'clock.* These four hours were diligently employed by the enemy in intrenching & strengthening their positions & the four hours less of daylight in the evening saved the enemy from a regular Bull Run panic.

I copy out of Pollard's "Lost Cause," page 450, a story which was universally current in the army when I arrived, & which is undoubtedly essentially true:[16]

> Lieut. Gen. Polk was ordered to assail the extreme right at day dawn on the 20th, & to take up the attack rapidly in succession to the left. The left wing was to await the attack by the right, take it up promptly when made, & the whole line was then to be pushed vigorously & persistently against the enemy throughout its extent.

At dawn Gen. Bragg was in his saddle, surrounded by his staff, eagerly listening for the sound of Polk's guns. The sun rose & was mounting the sky, & still there was no note of attack from the right wing. Bragg chafed with impatience, and at last dispatched one of his staff officers, Maj. Lee,[17] to ascertain the cause of Polk's delay, & urge him to a prompt & speedy movement. Gen. Polk, notwithstanding his clerical antecedents, was noted for his fondness for military ostentation, & carried a train of staff officers whose numbers & superb dress were the occasions of singular remark.

Maj. Lee found him seated at a comfortable breakfast, surrounded by brilliantly dressed officers, & delivered his message with military bluntness & brevity. Gen. Polk replied that he had ordered Hill to open the action, that he was waiting for him, & he added: "Do tell Gen. Bragg that my heart is overflowing with anxiety for the attack—overflowing with anxiety, Sir." Maj. Lee returned to the commanding general, & reported the reply literally. Bragg uttered a terrible exclamation in which Polk, Hill, & all his generals were included. "Maj. Lee," he cried, "ride along the line & order every captain to take his men instantly into action." In fifteen minutes the battle was joined, but three hours of valuable time had been lost in which Rosecrans was desperately busy in strengthening his position.

Pollard calls it three hours but it was really four or more, for the attack did not begin until nearly if not quite 9 A.M. Grant's favorite hour for attacking us during all of the next campaign was 4 A.M. or 4:30 A.M., & the attacks were as punctual to the minute, almost every time, as the starting of express railroad trains. Indeed, in all their method of distributing orders & managing the movements of troops the Federal Army of the Potomac was a beautiful military study.

When the action was finally joined, the fighting was very desperate & bloody, & our right flank was able to make no progress. But they pressed Thomas, who commanded Rosecrans's left wing so severely that reinforcements from their right had to be sent him.

In doing this a gap was made in front of Longstreet, who had already been pressing the enemy & was now about putting in his very utmost efforts. Longstreet's men found this gap, penetrated it, & in a very short while completely routed the enemy's whole right wing, swept it from the field, & sent it flying to Chattanooga in regular panic, carrying Gen. Rosecrans with it who was caught in the route. It practically ended his career as the commander of an army. The left wing, however, under Thomas, drew itself into a horseshoe, in a strong position, where it fought desperately until dark, when it managed to withdraw, leaving the entire field to the Confederates & losing a number of guns. Gen. Bragg had also left the field, before Thomas's position was taken, & only learned the final result next morning.

To give some picture of the details I will quote from Mr. C. A. Dana, asst. secy. of war, who was with Gen. Rosecrans, & also from our Gen. D. H. Hill, who was in Polk's corps. Mr. Dana writes in *McClure's Magazine,* Feb. '98, as follows:[18]

SEPTEMBER 20th AT CHICKAMAUGA

At daybreak we at headquarters were all up and on our horses ready to go with the commanding general to inspect our lines. We rode past McCook, Crittenden, and Thomas to the extreme left, Rosecrans giving, as he went, the orders he thought necessary to strengthen the several positions. The general intention of these orders was to close up on the left, where it was evident the attack would begin. We then rode back to the extreme right, Rosecrans stopping at each point to see if his orders had been obeyed. In several cases they had not been, and he made them more peremptory. When we found that McCook's line had been elongated so that it was a mere thread, Rosecrans was very angry, and sent for the general, rebuking him severely; although, as a matter of fact, General McCook's position had been taken under the written orders of the commander-in-chief, given the night before.

About half-past eight or nine o'clock the battle began again on the left, where Thomas was. At that time Rosecrans, with whom I always remained, was on the right, directing the movements of the troops there. I had not slept much for two nights, and as it was warm, I dismounted about noon, and giving my horse to my orderly, lay down on the grass and went to sleep. I was wakened by the most infernal noise I ever heard. Never in any battle I had witnessed was there such a discharge of cannon and musketry. I sat up on the grass, and the first thing I saw was General Rosecrans crossing himself—he was a very pious Catholic. "Hello," I said to myself, "if the general is crossing himself, we are in a desperate situation."

I was on my horse in a moment. I had no sooner collected my thoughts and looked around toward the front, where all this din came from, than I saw our lines break and melt away like leaves before the wind. Then the headquarters around me disappeared. The gray-backs came through with a rush, and soon the musket balls and the cannon shot began to reach the place where we stood. The whole right of the army had apparently been routed. My orderly stuck to me like a veteran, and we drew back for greater safety into the woods a little way. There I came upon General Porter (Captain Porter it was then) and Captain Drouillard[19]—an aide-de-camp infantry officer attached to General Rosecrans's staff—halting fugitives. They would halt a few of them, get them into some sort of a line, and make a beginning of order among them; and then there would come a few rounds of cannon shot through the treetops over their heads, and the men would break and run. I saw Porter and Drouillard plant themselves in front of a body of these stampeding men and command them to halt. One man charged with his bayonet, menacing Porter, but Porter held his ground, and the man gave in. That was the only case of real mutiny that I ever saw in the army, and it was under such circumstances that the man was excusable. The cause of all this disaster was the charge of the Confederates though a hiatus in our line, caused by the withdrawal of Wood's division,[20] under a misapprehension of orders, before its place could be filled.

I attempted to make my way from this point in the woods to Sheridan's division,[21] but when I reached the position where I knew it had been placed a little time before, I found it had been swept from the field. Not far away, however, I stumbled on a body of organized troops. This was a brigade of mounted riflemen under Colonel John T. Wilder, of Indiana.[22] "Mr. Dana," asked Colonel Wilder, "what is the situation?"

"I do not know," I said, "except that this end of the army has been routed. There is still heavy fighting on the left front, and our troops seem to be holding their ground there yet."

"Will you give me any orders?" he asked.

"I have no authority to give orders," I replied; "but if I were in your situation, I should go to the left, where Thomas is."

Then I turned my horse, and making my way over Missionary Ridge, struck the Chattanooga valley and rode to Chattanooga, twelve or fifteen miles away. Everything on the route was in the greatest disorder. The whole road was filled with flying soldiers, and here and there were piled up pieces of artillery, caissons, and baggage wagons. When I reached Chattanooga, a little before four o'clock, I found Rosecrans there. In the helter-skelter to the rear, he had escaped by the Rossville Road. He was expecting every moment that the enemy would arrive before the town, and was doing all he could to prepare to resist his entrance. Soon after I arrived, the two corps commanders, McCook and Crittenden, both came into Chattanooga.

The first thing I did on reaching the town was to telegraph to Mr. Stanton.[23] I had not sent him any telegrams in the morning, for I had been in the field with Rosecrans, and part of the time at some distance from the Widow Glenn's, where the operators were at work. The boys kept at their post there until the Confederates swept them out of the house. When they had to run, they went instruments and tools in hand, and as soon as out of reach of the enemy set up shop on a stump. It was not long before they were driven out of this. They next attempted to establish an office on the Rossville Road, but before they had succeeded in making connections, a battle was raging around them, and they had to retreat to Granger's[24] headquarters at Rossville.

Gen. D. H. Hill was at first in command of a division only, but at 3:30 P.M. Gen. Polk gave him command of the entire right wing, a very excellent selection for there was never a harder fighter than Gen. D. H. Hill. He writes as follows in [the] Century War Book:[25]

Bushrod Johnson's[26] three brigades in Longstreet's center were the first to fill the gap left by Wood's withdrawal from the Federal right; but the other five brigades under Hindman and Kershaw moved promptly into line as soon as space could be found for them, wheeled to the right, and engaged in the murderous flank attack. On they rushed, shouting, yelling, running over batteries, capturing trains, taking prisoners, seizing the headquarters of the Federal commander, at the Widow Glenn's, until they found themselves facing the new Federal line on Snodgrass Hill. Hindman had advanced a little later than the center, and had met great and immediate success. The brigades of Deas and Manigault[27] charged the breastworks at double-quick, rushed over them, drove Laiboldt's Federal brigade[28] of Sheridan's division off the field down the Rossville Road; then General Patton Anderson's[29] brigade of Hindman, having come into line, attacked and beat back the forces of Davis,[30] Sheridan, and Wilder, in their front, killed the hero and poet General Lytle,[31] took 1,100 prisoners, 27 pieces of artillery, commissary and ordnance trains, etc. Finding no more resistance on his front and left, Hindman wheeled to the right to assist the forces of the center. The divisions of Stewart,[32] Hood, Bushrod Johnson, and Hindman came together in front of the new stronghold of the Federals.

It was now 2:30 P.M. Longstreet, with his staff, was lunching on sweet-potatoes. A message came just then that the commanding general wished to see him. He found Bragg in rear of his lines, told him of the steady and satisfactory progress of the battle, that sixty pieces of artillery had been reported captured (though probably the number was overestimated), that many prisoners and stores had been taken, and that all was going well. He then asked for additional troops to hold the ground gained, while he pursued the two broken corps down the Dry Valley Road and cut off the retreat of Thomas. Bragg replied that there was no more fight in the troops of Polk's wing, that he could give Longstreet no reinforcements, and that his headquarters would be at Reed's Bridge. He seems not to have known that Cheatham's division and part of Liddell's[33] had not been in action that day.

Some of the severest fighting had yet to be done after 3 P.M. It probably never happened before for a great battle to be fought to its bloody conclusion with the commanders of each side away from the field of conflict. But the Federals were in the hands of the indomitable Thomas, and the Confederates were under their two heroic wing commanders, Longstreet and Polk. In the lull of the strife I went with a staff-officer to examine the ground on our left. One of Helm's wounded men had been overlooked, and was lying alone in the woods, his head partly supported by a tree. He was shockingly injured.[34]

Hindman and Bushrod Johnson organized a column of attack upon the front and rear of the stronghold of Thomas. It consisted of the brigades of Deas, Manigault, Gregg, Patton Anderson, and McNair.[35] Three of the brigades, Johnson says, had each but five hundred men, and the other two were not strong. Deas was on the north side of the gorge through which the Crawfish Road crosses, Manigault across the gorge and south, on the crest parallel to the Snodgrass Hill, where Thomas was. The other three brigades extended along the crest with their faces north, while the first two faced east. Kershaw, with his own and Humphreys's[36] brigade, was on the right of Anderson, and was to cooperate in the movement. It began at 3:30 P.M. A terrific contest ensued. The bayonet was used, and men were killed and wounded with clubbed muskets. A little after 4, the enemy was reinforced, and advanced, but was repulsed by Anderson and Kershaw.

General Bushrod Johnson claims that his men were surely, if slowly, gaining ground at all points, which must have made untenable the stronghold of Thomas. Relief was, however, to come to our men, so hotly engaged on the left, by the advance of the right. At 3 P.M. Forrest reported to me that a strong column was approaching from Rossville, which he was delaying all he could. From prisoners we soon learned that it was Granger's corps. We were apprehensive that a flank attack, by fresh troops, upon our exhausted and shattered ranks might prove fatal. Major-General Walker strongly advised falling back to the position of Cleburne,[37] but to this I would not consent, believing that it would invite attack, as we were in full view. Cheatham's fine division was sent to my assistance by the wing commander. . . .

Longstreet was determined to send Preston with his division of three brigades under Gracie, Trigg, and Kelly, aided by Robertson's brigade of Hood's division,[38] to carry the heights—the main point of defense. His troops were of the best material and had been in reserve all day; but brave, fresh, and strong as they were, it was with them alternate advance and retreat, until success was assured by a renewal of the fight on the right. At 3:30 P.M. General Polk sent an order to me to assume command of the attacking forces on the right and renew the assault. Owing to a delay in the adjustment of our lines, the advance did not begin until 4 o'clock. The men sprang to their arms with the utmost alacrity, though they had not heard of Longstreet's success, and they showed by their cheerfullness that there was plenty of "fight in them." Cleburne ran forward his batteries, some by hand, to within three hundred yards of the enemy's breastworks, pushed forward his infantry, and carried them. General J. K. Jackson,[39] of Cheatham's division, had a bloody struggle with the fortifications in his front, but had entered them when Cheatham with two more of his brigades, Maney's and Wright's,[40] came up. Breckinridge[41] and Walker met with but little opposition until the Chattanooga Road was passed, when their right was unable to overcome the forces covering the enemy's retreat. As we passed into the woods west of the road, it was reported to me that a line was advancing at right angles to ours. I rode to the left to ascertain whether they were foes or friends, and soon recognized General Buckner. The cheers that went up when the two wings met were such as I had never heard before, and shall never hear again.

Preston gained the heights a half hour later, capturing 1,000 prisoners and 4,500 stand of arms. But neither right nor left is entitled to the laurels of a complete triumph. It was the combined attack which, by weakening the enthusiasm of the brave warriors who had stood on the defense so long and so obstinately, won the day.

Thomas had received orders after Granger's arrival to retreat to Rossville, but, stout soldier as he was, he resolved to hold his ground until nightfall. An hour more of daylight would have insured his capture. Thomas had under him all the Federal army, except the six brigades which had been driven off by the left wing.

Whatever blunders each of us in authority committed before the battles of the 19th and 20th, and during their progress, the great blunder of all was that of not pursuing the enemy on the 21st. The day was spent in burying the dead and gathering up captured stores. Forrest, with his usual promptness, was early in the saddle, and saw that the retreat was a rout. Disorganized masses of men were hurrying to the rear; batteries of artillery were inextricably mixed with trains of wagons; disorder and confusion pervaded the broken ranks struggling to get on. Forrest sent back word to Bragg that "every hour was worth a thousand men." But the commander-in-chief did not know of the victory until the morning of the 21st, and then he did not order a pursuit. Rosecrans spent the day and the night of the 21st in hurrying his trains out of town. A breathing-space was allowed him; the panic among his troops subsided, and Chattanooga— the objective point of the campaign—was held.

I make a brief quotation also from Col. Thruston of the staff of Gen. McCook describing the route of the right wing in the Century War Book:[42]

When Longstreet struck the right, Rosecrans was near McCook and Crittenden. Seeing our line swept back, he hurried to Sheridan's force for aid. With staff and escort he recklessly strove to stem the tide. They attempted to pass to the left through a storm of canister and musketry, but were driven back.

All became confusion. No order could be heard above the tempest of battle. With a wild yell the Confederates swept on far to their left. They seemed everywhere victorious. Rosecrans was borne back in the retreat. Fugitives, wounded, caissons, escort, ambulances, thronged the narrow pathways. He concluded that our whole line had given way, that the day was lost, that the next stand must be made at Chattanooga. McCook and Crittenden, caught in the same tide of retreat, seeing only rout everywhere, shared the opinion of Rosecrans, and reported to him for instructions and cooperation.

[Figures 25 and 26 appear here in the manuscript.]

After reading these descriptions I think it seems very reasonable to suppose that even had Rosecrans only had four hours less of preparation in the morning, & Bragg four hours more of time in the afternoon a very important victory might have been won. And could 5 other brigades & my battalion of artillery have been there to help, it would seem to have been quite sure.

And the immense possibilities of the situation show the soundness of the strategy in sending troops from Virginia to help out pressure in Georgia. They show that it would, probably, have been best to have played that game in June instead of the Gettysburg campaign. They show that even after the Gettysburg campaign it would have been best to adopt it with at least two weeks' less delay. And they show that in the next campaign of 1864 such a movement would have offered, probably, the very best chance of defeating Sherman.

I have sometimes thought that one reason why this strategy was not oftener played was because each of our generals commanding an army was independent of all control except from the president, and each one was naturally always reluctant to give up troops to go elsewhere, & was apt to protest & say he would not be responsible for results. Had one *general*, like Gen. Lee, been commander in chief, with full authority to move troops back & forth, & go & come himself, it would have been a better working organisation. That, too, was what Mr. Davis tried to have arranged. He appointed Gen. Lee to that position in 1862. But Gen. Lee declined to assume the larger command without giving up that of the Army of Northern Virginia, & so the arrangement fell through until Feb. 1865. Then, after the fall of Wilmington, he consented to accept it, as will be told in due time. But then it was too late. The Confederacy was then in articulo mortis.

The casualties at Chickamauga are reported as follows:

	K[illed]	W[ounded]	M[issing]	Total	Generals Killed
CS	2,268	13,613	1,090	16,171	Deshler, Helm,
US	1,656	9,749	4,774	16,179	Lytle
Agg[regate]	3,924	23,352	5,864	32,350	

Figure 25. Gen. John Bell Hood

Figure 26. Lt. Gen. Nathan Bedford Forrest

The Confederate losses in killed & wounded were much the most severe, & were about 33% of their forces engaged, being 15,881. This resulted from their being the aggressors, & attacking the enemy within intrenchments with a pertinacity which would not be denied. The enemy's total killed & wounded were 11,405, only about 15% of their forces.

Gen. Jas. Deshler of Ala., who was killed, had made a special friend of me at West Point where he was a first class man when I was a plebe. He was a rather small but very well built, active, energetic, & fine looking fellow with very attractive manners & qualities. [Figure 27 appears here in the manuscript.]

Figure 27. Gen. Braxton Bragg

CHATTANOOGA
& KNOXVILLE

On Sunday, Sep. 27th, I left Huger to complete the equipment of the battalion, & I rode ahead to join Gen. Longstreet before Chattanooga, & acquaint myself with the topography in advance of the arrival of the battalion, so as to be more immediately useful. The distance from Ringgold was about 25 miles,[1] & my road took me directly through the battlefield, on which there still lay, unburied, a great many of the enemy's dead. I found Longstreet in camp, in a dense forest on the bank of Chattanooga Creek, close behind his lines. The enemy had been fortifying themselves, ever since the night succeeding the battle, in an intrenched camp just outside & around the town, its left flank resting upon the river above, & its right on the river below, & had already made his position an exceedingly strong one. There had been some Confederate outworks for him to start on, & these, with a few points naturally strong, he had quickly strengthened still further, & then connected all around with a continuous heavy breastwork. I was told, however, on arrival, that an early assault was to be made, so I put in all my time in reconnaissance, & as soon as the battalion arrived—on the 29th, I distributed them where I thought they would do the most good. I recall Moody's position, with his six 24 pr. howitzers, in a hollow to the left of the road to Rossville, where I put him on skids to give a mortar fire into a quite formidable fort, where that road entered the enemy's line.

By the way, I had now gotten all of my batteries uniformly armed. Woolfolk had four 20 pr. Parrott rifles; Jordan 4 U.S. 3 inch rifles; Parker 4 Parrott 10 prs.; Taylor 4 12 pr. Napoleons; & Ficklen 4 12 pr. howitzers.[2] But the assault was never made, for it was very wisely recognised that the position was too strong for it. We all exchanged a few shots, getting ranges, &c., & Capt. Moody, practising at his mortar fire, got a slight wound from the enemy's return fire, but there was nothing done of any consequence. In fact, my diary for the whole month of October has but three entries as follows:

Oct. 5th, Monday. Shelled Chattanooga
Oct. 10 to 12. Reconnaissance of Bridgeport
Oct. 30, Friday. Occupied Lookout Mountain & shelled everything daily
until Nov. 4th.

So I will record, first, my general recollections of a few camp happenings, & then I will resume the military narrative. At Longstreet's camp in the woods, at which I spent two nights before the battn. came up, was Mr. Vizetelly &, I think, also, Mr. Lawley. Vizetelly was an exceedingly fine looking & jolly Englishman, sent over as artist & correspondent for the *London Illustrated News*. He was really a man of rare fascination & accomplishments. He made great friends everywhere, but especially in Longstreet's corps, & we saw a great deal of him till near the close of the war. Mr. Lawley, who was generally with Mr. V, was correspondent of the *London Times*. He did not sing so many songs, & tell as many stories as Vizetelly, but his intelligence & character strongly impressed all who met him & made him welcome everywhere. He still lives & is, I believe, a member of Parliament. Poor Vizetelly was butchered by the Mahdi's troops in Egypt when they broke the British squares at _____ in _____ along with several other noted correspondents.[3] I remember two of Vizetelly's songs, "Tiddle-i-wink," and another composed by himself beginning:

> Twas in the Atlantic Ocean in the equinoctial gales
> A sailor he fell overboard, amid the sharks & whales.
> And in the midnight watch his ghost appeared unto me
> Saying I'm married to a mermaid in the bottom of the sea.
> (*Chorus*) Singing Rule Britannia! Britannia rule the waves
> Britons never, never, never will be slaves.

We encamped in the same woods with Longstreet for awhile, & there on Oct. 4th, I received a dispatch from Capt. Woolfolk, who was at his home, wounded. "Mother & twins all doing well." An earlier dispatch had been sent to me, telling me of the birth of the twins on the 21st of Sep., but the battle telegrams were then monopolising the wires & that message never did reach me.

After a while, we moved our camp over near the foot of Lookout Mountain, &, soon afterward, a tremendous freshet in the Tennessee River backed water up the creek for some miles, flooding its whole valley, which was wooded & several hundred yards wide. For some days we were practically cut off from the rest of our army, with two or three brigades of infantry. Rations among the infantry becoming scarce, some of them tore down an old cabin, & made a raft of the logs, & set out, through the woods, on a voyage to the other shore. After many hours they finally got back, too, with several boxes of hard tack & some bacon. Not long afterward some Georgia paper had a poetical account of it, which I have vainly tried to get a copy of, ever since. I can recall a few lines which will identify it if any old scrapbook has preserved it:

> I am a jolly Georgia boy, & do not care a dam.
> For our colonel, he detailed me, to build the boys a ram . . .
> We did not care for cut of jib, or streak of tarry coat,
> The only thing that puzzled us, was, would the dam thing float.
> . . . . . then the rumor spread
> . . . . had gone down with Benning's whole brigade,
> . . faint-hearted ones, the conscripts & recruits
> Forsook the bank, took to the fields & went to digging roots.

I remember that the reference to Benning's brigade was considered a good joke on their reduced ranks, which at this time, scarcely numbered 500 men.[4]

At this camp, I remember, one night just as I was going to sleep, particularly tired & sleepy, a courier from Gen. Bragg brought me a cipher dispatch captured from the enemy on its way up to Gen. Burnside at Knoxville; with the request that I would try & decipher it. It was a letter of 157 words all in a jumble beginning as follows:

> To Jaque Knoxville, Enemy the increasing they go period this as fortified
> into to some be it and Kingston direction you up cross numbers Wiley
> boy *Burton* & if will too in far strongly go ought surely free without your
> which it ought and between or are greatly for pontons front you we move
> as be stores you not to delay spare should least to probably us our
> preparing Stanton from you combinedly between to oppose fortune
> roanoke rapid we let possible speed if him that and your time a commu-
> nication can me at this news in so complete with the crossing keep move
> hear once more no from us open and McDowell julia five thousand ferry
> (114) the you must driven at them prisoners artillery men pieces wounded
> to Godwin relay horses in Lambs (131) of and yours truly quick killed
> Loss the over minds ten snow two deserters Bennet Gordon answer also
> with across day (152)

I had never seen a cipher of this character before, but it was very clear that it was simply a disarrangment of words, what may be called, for short, a jumble. Each correspondent, of course, had what was practically a list of the natural numbers, say from one up to 50, or whatever limit was used, taken in an agreed jumble, as for instance beginning 19, 3, 41, 22, &c. Then, the first word of the cipher would be the 19th of the genuine message, the 2nd cipher would be 3rd of message, the 3rd cipher would be 41st, &c.

Now, it was quite clear that if the jumble covered only 75 or 50 words or less, it would have been used twice or more times in ciphering 157 words. If it were used twice or three times, I could, by comparison & trial, probably decipher the whole business. But if the jumble was *not repeated,* I could never decipher it without getting another message in the same jumble in order to compare the two.

So my first task was to see if the jumble was repeated in the message. To do this, I first numbered all the words of the cipher, & then began to hunt for words which probably went together like "according to" "means of" "so that." First I picked out as many of such likely pairs as I could find. Then, I would take one of these pairs, & note how many words separated them in the cipher. Then I would go over the whole cipher message, & see if, any where else, the same interval separated two words which would possibly make sense. If I could find such a pair, the interval between these two pairs might be the size of the jumble. Without going into more detail, it is enough to say that I worked on it the whole live long night, but every test showed that the jumble was not repeated. I found one pair of words which certainly belonged together, "Lambs" & "ferry"—for there was a "Lamb's Ferry" on the Tennessee River. But it only made the demonstration absolute that the jumble was not repeated. I afterward found that the Federals made their jumbles by means of diagrams of rows & columns, writing up & down in different orders & then taking the words across; but the principles of jumbling are the same, however it is mechanically done. And the safety of the message depends on the jumble not being repeated. They also used some blind words to further confuse the cipher. This made, indeed, a most excellent cipher, quick & easy, both to write & to decipher, which is a very great advantage. But there is one objection to it, in that it required a book, & that book might get into wrong hands.

While on this subject of ciphers, it may be interesting to explain a cipher which I devised, & which was largely used by the Confederate War Department. It required no book or record, & was absolutely safe if properly used. At first, I did print, for convenience, a square card containing 26 rows & 26 in a row, the alphabet, in horizontal & vertical columns, beginning with each letter. Then, a key sentence was agreed upon, & when the message was written out, the key sentence was written under it, letter for letter, repeated as often as necessary. Then taking each letter of the message at the head of a vertical column & the key letter under it in a horizontal row the letter at the intersection gave the cipher letter to be transmitted.

The deciphering was done by first writing the key under the cipher, & finding the cipher letter in each key row & then the message letter at [the] top of its column. But, after a little practise, it was found that the card could be dispensed with, by the signal men, if they would learn, by heart, the number of each letter of the alphabet. Then writing the key under the message & adding together the numbers of the message letter & the key letter, & dropping one, the number of the cipher letter appeared & it could be at once written, & in a fifth of the time necessary to find it with a card. If the addition made more than 26, 26 was of course dropped.

Letter ciphers save books and are safe, but are slow & troublesome. On one occasion, a message sent in this cipher from President Davis to Gen. Dick Taylor⁵ fell into the hands of the enemy & was deciphered, & the key consequently discovered, by the ciphering officer very carelessly & stupidly putting in English enough of his message to enable the meaning of some cipher words to be very easily guessed. This, of course, disclosed the key & the whole message could be read.

And, now, in resuming my narrative, a little explanation of the military situation will make it all more clearly understood.

We had defeated the enemy in the field, but he had managed to take refuge at Chattanooga, & protect himself from assault by strong lines of fortification. Our problem was to compel him to quit those lines. If we could make him resume his retreat towards Bridgeport—his nearest railroad connection to Nashville & the North—we could hope to catch him at a disadvantage on the road, & perhaps convert his retreat into a disastrous panic. The first &, apparently, the most obvious way of running him out of his lines, was to shell him out. Our rifled guns, from one flank or the other, could throw their shells over nearly all the territory enclosed between the enemy's breast works & the river. Why could not we make their lives so miserable, & do such great damage with our shells, that they would be glad to clear out & try & get back to Bridgeport in spite of us?

The reason is that long range, random shelling is very far less effective than it is popularly supposed to be. A striking illustration afterward appeared at Petersburg where that whole city laid under Grant's immense force of artillery, from the middle of June 1864, to the end of March 1865, and even the women & children were not driven out of it. Briefly, while an aimed & accurate artillery fire can accomplish almost any result, a random, or an inaccurate one amounts to very little, except where it can enfilade lines. At Chattanooga, there was little chance of that, &, then, our rifled guns & ammunition were both comparatively inferior. At close quarters, we could hold our own very creditably, but when it came to extreme ranges, a considerable percentage of our rifle shell would tumble, or explode prematurely, or not explode at all. This made accurate shooting almost impossible. Yet, although no important results could be hoped for, Gen. Bragg ordered a general bombardment of the enemy's lines to be made on Oct. 5th; & it is that which is briefly referred to in the extract before given from my diary, "Shelled Chattanooga." My recollection is of firing slowly & carefully, most of the day, from selected positions, reaching from _____,⁶ a house on the slope of Lookout Mountain on our left, over to Missionary

Ridge on our right, & that the enemy's return fire was neither heavy or effective. We fired, mostly, at camps & wagon trains & we probably made some of them unhappy, but there was no result of importance to show.

So, when this plan of forcing the enemy to abandon Chattanooga failed, something else had to be tried. Gen. Longstreet conceived the idea of sending an expedition to capture Bridgeport itself, the enemy's railroad terminus & principal depot. In fact, I think, he had been constantly urging one or the other of several schemes to break up the enemy, on Gen. Bragg, but I only know of this one, for he sent me to make a secret reconnaissance of Bridgeport, & to report the most feasible plan of attacking it, & this expedition occupied me Oct. 10th, 11th, & 12th. A little description of the topography will help. Lookout Mountain rises at a steep angle from the bank of the Tennessee River, some three miles from Chattanooga, & runs S.W. some 30 or 40 miles with sides which, near the top, are almost like vertical walls. The top is a rolling table land sometimes a few hundred feet wide & sometimes a half mile. Around its base on the river, the Nashville & Chat. R.R. has blasted out its track, & a wagon road has also been opened, which crosses Lookout Creek on the western side & then runs up the valley to Trenton 20 miles.[7] I can still vividly remember the one visit to Lookout Mountain which I had made before my present experience on it. In 1850, when a school boy, I had spent two days at Chattanooga, with my teacher Mr. R. M. Wright. In company with a Mr. Dick Joiner, an old citizen of Wilke's Co. who lived across Fishing Creek from the Colley's and who had moved to Atlanta, we spent one day in exploring the remarkable cave under the mountain opposite whose mouth the railroad track passes, & another day on top of the mountain enjoying the view & listening to the remarkably reverberating echoes of the very extensive rock blasting then going on in the construction of the railroad.

We little imagined then the re-awakening of those echoes which would attend my next visit to that locality, but I always remembered them as old friends & listened for them & enjoyed them specially as such in all the fighting we did about Lookout. Parallel to Lookout & a mile or two off was Sand Mountain, somewhat similar in formation on its eastern edge, & its high opposing cliffs & the smaller irregular hills in between & across the river, would make each explosion roll & reverberate like thunder.

Lookout Mountain cuts off Dade County, Georgia, of which Trenton is the county town, from the rest of the state, & the mountain cannot be crossed by a vehicle within the limits of the state. But, near Chattanooga, a road to the top had been blasted out, & a summer hotel had been opened. On Sunday, Oct. 10th, I took that road to the top of the mountain, & then a road on the mountain plateau, which I followed until within three or four miles of Trenton. Here, a little path to the right led to the first break in the vertical cliff, where a steep & rocky ravine notched it with a narrow gully, &, by dismounting & leading my horse very carefully, I was able, at last, to get down into the valley & to a road which took me into Trenton. There was here part of one of our regiments of western cavalry. I am sorry to have forgotten its state & number, & the names of its principal officers, for they were nice fellows & our little trip together next day was in every way a pleasant one. I had orders for them to escort me over to Bridgeport for a reconnaissance, & I found them, as soon as I arrived, & made all arrangements to start at day break next morning. I spent the night at the little hotel in the village, which I walked around with much interest, for I had first heard of Trenton nearly 20 years before as the location of an awfully strict & severe boarding school for boys in that unhappy town which could only be reached through Alabama or Tennessee, & my father had held up to me, when I was about nine years old, the idea that I might be sent there if my deportment was unsatisfactory.

The next day we made our reconnaissance of Bridgeport, & returned, a delightful ride of about 40 miles[8] through a wild & rough, but very picturesque country. The military features of the situation at Bridgeport were as follows. The bridge by the railroad there [that] crossed the Tennessee River was burned. The enemy's camps, warehouses & railroad terminus, & a few little earthworks were upon the north side of the river, about opposite the middle of an island, mostly covered with wood, & about 3 miles long by a half mile wide.[9] A bridge of pontoon boats ran from the north shore to this island; a road came diagonally across it, & another pontoon bridge across the other channel brought the road out on the southern bank. Here, about 100 yards from the river, was a little stockade or block house, which was garrisoned by, perhaps, 100 men.

The situation seemed to me to give very fair chances for a surprise. If once the block house on the southern bank could be captured, or silenced, the three or four dozen ponton boats making the southern bridge would be easily cut loose & floated down the river under cover of the woods on the island, filled with our infantry & then rowing, down past the island, they could land on the northern shore, below the enemy's camps, & make a lodgment. Then the boats could be used as ferry boats to bring over a sufficient additional force to capture all that the enemy had at hand. The favorable features were the ponton boats in the exposed position, & the long wooded island screening our preparations to use them. The little block house was the only obstacle & that was not very serious.

I made a sketch of the whole environment & took it back to Chattanooga on the 12th to Gen. Longstreet. He seemed much pleased with the plan & took it to Gen. Bragg but there were some new developments nearer home & nothing ever came of it.

By the way, Gen. Bragg deserves a brief notice & this is as good a place as any to stop & give it. In Taylor's campaign in Mexico, Bragg had been prominent as a battery commander. He had graduated at West Point in 1834, &, when our war began, was still in the army a maj. in the artillery.[10] President Davis had a very high opinion of him and, not long after the death of Albert Sidney Johnston, Bragg practically succeeded him in the command of our principal western army—the one next in importance to Gen. Lee's. He had fought two severe battles at Murfreesboro on _____ & at Stone River on _____[11] before the Chickamauga campaign, both of them practically drawn battles. He was celebrated through all the Confederate armies as a stern disciplinarian. I recall the morning after the battalion joined me at Chattanooga, taking Huger & my staff to ride around the lines, we came upon one of Bragg's infantry divisions forming three sides of a hollow square. Some one asked what it meant, & I answered that, according to rumor, Bragg shot a man every day, & that this three sided formation seemed to indicate that this was his hour. And, sure enough, as we rode up, an adjutant came forward & read the proceedings of a court martial, only a few days before, upon a man who had deserted from one of our Tennessee regts. & had been just captured in a Federal regiment. And then the poor wretch, who had been standing near, in charge of a guard, was led out to the side of a newly dug grave, in a wheat stubble field, & placed in front of a firing party which stood, it seemed to me, thirty yards away. Their aim, however, was true enough, for, at their fire, he sank limp as a rag—a sergeant walked up, & gave a final shot as a coup de grace, & the burial detail came forward with their shovels, & the business was quickly over.

It is but fair however to Gen. Bragg to say that this was the only case I ever saw in his army, &, surely, if ever a man deserves shooting, it is one who takes service with the enemy. But I don't think Gen. Bragg inspired any enthusiasm in his men—certainly nothing to be compared with what I was accustomed to see in Virginia. And, to go a step further, he certainly never impressed me as a man of intellectual power—as a cool & clear thinker, at all. And to be entirely frank there were some who did not hesitate openly to say that he was simply muddle headed & especially that he never could understand a map, & that it was a spectacle to see him wrestle with one, with one finger painfully holding down his own position.

He had been noted in the old army, too, for his punctiliousness, & Gen. Dick Taylor told a story about his acting once, at a frontier post, as quartermaster, &, at [the] same time, as captain of his co.; &, that, as captain, he quarreled with himself as quartermaster, & called on the commanding officer to decide the point at issue.[12]

As it was now beginning to become apparent that our victory at Chickamauga would be a fruitless one, there began to spring up all over the South many evidences of great dissatisfaction with Gen. Bragg as the commander of the army; and, although our generals in the field kept their own counsel, I am sure that very few, if any of them, were sanguine of any success under his leadership.

But Gen. Bragg had one strong hold. He had the thorough confidence of President Davis, than whom no man was ever a more persistent friend, through evil report or good. Beside his friendship for Gen. Bragg, he had one other, equally noted; &, to be understood, the two should be mentioned together. The other was for the Confederate Commissary General Northrop.[13] He & Gen. Northrop had been cadets together at West Point, but both had resigned from the army afterward, Davis in 1836.[14] Northrop had studied medicine, and when the war began was a practising physician in Charleston. There seems to have been little reason to expect, from his training, that he possessed that power of organisation which would have made him an efficient commissary general, &, if popular report is to be accepted, he was conspicuously destitute of it from the very first. I knew nothing personally of him, & I used to half believe that the universal & chronic complaints must be founded on prejudice, or lack of appreciation of his difficulties. But, against that, it gradually appeared that although the Quartermaster's, the Ordnance, & the Medical Departments must surely have struggled with equal difficulties, yet against none of these was there any complaint at all, & each of those departments remained unchanged in management during all the last half of the war. But, at last, even Mr. Davis seems to have become convinced that Gen. Northrop's talents were not those of a commissary, &, during the last few months of the war, he was replaced by Gen. St. John,[15] a railroad engineer, who had built the Louisville & Cincinnati Railroad, & was especially noted for his executive ability & experience.

And, now, when the feeling against Gen. Bragg was rising & spreading on every hand, Mr. Davis paid a visit to the army & exercised his best influence to allay it there, &, after his return, he made some public addresses, calculated to have a similar effect upon the press throughout the country.

As will soon appear, however, he only succeeded in postponing Gen. Bragg's removal for a few weeks. For before the end of November the general received at Missionary Ridge the most complete, thorough, & disgraceful defeat which ever befell a Confederate army, & after that it was only possible [to] let him down easy, with a few weeks' command in winter quarters, & then Gen. Jos. E. Johnston replaced him.

But, even then, Mr. Davis found a soft place for him, & took him into the War Department as a sort of general adviser, & kept him there until the close of the war. Now, while we were having this dissatisfaction with our general, for having won only a fruitless victory, the feeling in the Federal army, & at the North, against some of their generals was much more intense. It was particularly directed against Gen. Rosecrans, & Genls. McCook & Crittenden commanding the 20th & 21st Army Corps. As I have already told, all three of these generals had retreated from the field clear into Chattanooga, while Thomas & a part of the army remained & fought until night.

And now, toward the middle of October, the Federal condition in Chattanooga was apparently becoming serious. The supplies they had on hand after the battle—about enough for ten days—& all they could gather in the country within their reach were exhausted, & they could now only supply themselves by wagon trains from Bridgeport. The most direct route, that on the south side of the river, via Wauhatchie & Shellmound—some 20 miles, was in our control. The next best, keeping on [the] north side of the river and about 40 miles long,[16] was at some places within sight & rifle range of the hills on the south side, & we had sent a brigade of infantry down on the spurs of Raccoon Mountain, who had blocked the road with dead mules, & driven the trains to take a still more roundabout & difficult road via _____,[17] some 55 miles. The roads, too, were already getting into fearful condition & it was plain that something must be done at an early day. It had not taken long to decide about McCook & Crittenden. Their two corps were consolidated into one & the command given to another officer, Gen. Granger, who had distinguished himself in the battle. Courts of inquiry, however, afterward, acquitted both of these officers of all blame. On Oct. 19 Gen. Rosecrans was transferred to St. Louis & Gen. Thomas was placed in command, & on Oct. 23rd Gen. Grant arrived, having been recently put in command of all of the armies in the West.

Meanwhile, too, Federal reinforcements were being hurried forward. Hooker was bringing two corps, the 11th & 12th, from Meade's army in Virginia, Sherman was bringing an army from Vicksburg, Hurlbut[18] was sending troops from Memphis, & even Burnside from Knoxville moved down toward London as if to threaten our rear.

The first intimation which we received that the enemy was taking courage & preparing to better his position was on the morning of Oct. 28th. [Figure 28 appears here in the manuscript.][19]

During the night he had floated down from Chattanooga the greater part of Hazen's brigade[20] loaded in pontoon boats & at dawn they surprised our pickets at Brown's Ferry in Lookout Valley, where they made a landing. A bridge was then soon constructed & a considerable force was brought over & intrenched with artillery, & supporting batteries were erected on the north side of [the] Tennessee River on a ridge in the narrow bend opposite Lookout, called Moccasin Bend from its shape like a foot. The batteries

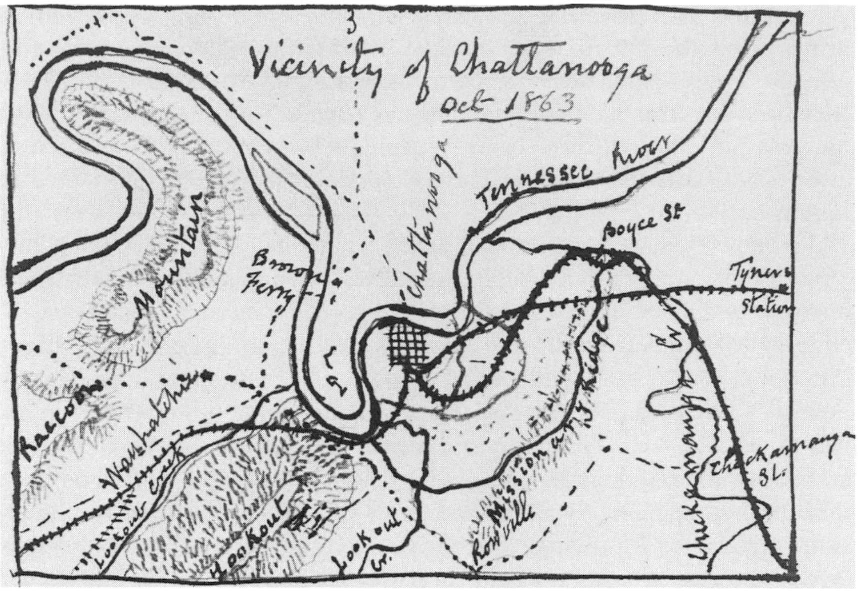

Figure 28. Vicinity of Chattanooga

here had very high parapets & deep embrasures to protect them from our greater elevations on the mountain. This move of the enemy's caused Hood's division, now under command of Gen. Jenkins of So. Ca., the ranking brigadier, to be brought around on the north west front of the mountain, & I spent much of my time on the mountain where I already had a rifle battery. And here on the afternoon of Oct. ____[21] we discovered the approach of a considerable body of the enemy, coming along the railroad track from Bridgeport. We had a signal station on the mountain, in communication with other stations on our line, one of which was at Gen. Bragg's headquarters; &, though I have now no recollection of doing it, I signalled the information to Gen. Bragg, for it seems that the Federals were at that time in possession of our alphabet, & could read all messages not sent in cipher, & I find the message given as follows in vol. ____ of the War Records.[22]

But though I cannot recall sending the message, I can recall, very vividly, the appearance of the marching columns coming down the valley, & the fun I had that afternoon with their advanced troops & my rifled guns which were up on the mountain. The range was too great to do them any very serious harm, but just far enough to give my gunners an excellent chance & excuse for an afternoon of target practice during which we put in a few very pretty shots, & had all the fun to ourselves, for they did not attempt to reply. A little before sundown, the main body, which seemed to be a division of three brigades, stopped & went into camp near Wauhatchie & about a mile beyond our range. Gen. Longstreet was on the mountain with us, with Gen. Jenkins, & it was at once determined to make a night attack upon the encampment.[23]

And now, after over forty days of idleness, during which the enemy was at their weakest & demoralized by lack of confidence in Gen. Rosecrans, when stronger & better men had taken hold, & had opened up shorter & better lines of communication, & when immense reinforcements had already begun to reach their camp, Gen. Bragg at last made up his mind to an offensive move. It would only have been about a second-class move to have made it forty days sooner & in ample force, but to make it, as it was now made, with the enemy rapidly getting ready to retake the offensive themselves, it does seem as remarkable a piece of strategy as the war produced. The move was to detach Longstreet with a certain force & to send him up to Knoxville (140 miles) to capture or drive off Burnside, who was there with the 9th Army Corps—about 15,000 men.[24] Immediately after the battle of Chickamauga it could have been safely attempted, & sufficient force could have been spared to make the task sure & easy, though it would have diminished the chances which Bragg had to ruin Rosecrans. As those chances proved of no value in his hands, it is a pity the enterprise was not then undertaken, for now the situation was very different. But even now it might probably have been safely done if Gen. Bragg had withdrawn his army from the immediate vicinity of Chattanooga, so that he could not be surprised, & taken a strong defensive position, & then sent a force overwhelming in proportion to Burnside's.

Gen. Longstreet urged this course upon Gen. Bragg, but he was unwilling to fall back, & had confidence in his breast works, & determined to hold them & stand the chances of repulsing any attack the enemy could make. And, at first, he would only allow Longstreet to take his own two divisions, Jenkins's & McLaws's, now about 15,000 men, though Wheeler was also to go along with three or four brigades of cavalry.[25] Later, he sent up after us two more brigades of infantry, Gracie's & Bushrod Johnson's, about 3,200 men, but they arrived too late to be of service.[26] The first intimation that I received of the movement was an order on Nov. 3rd to bring my whole battalion, which was now on top of Lookout, down that afternoon & to encamp near Rossville, & to come myself to Gen. Longstreet's headquarters for orders. It was late when the orders were received, & it was nearly nine at night when I reported at headquarters. Here I received news of our expedition, & was directed to march next morning to Tyner's Station where trains would be sent to meet us, & carry us as far as

Sweetwater, on the road to Knoxville, about ____ miles.²⁷ So the next morning we marched to Tyner's & encamped there, some of our infantry also coming up & encamping near us. Here too we were also joined by Leyden's battalion of artillery, which was assigned to us for this campaign, from among Bragg's artillery under Col. Hallonquist,²⁸ his chief of artillery. Leyden had four batteries of four guns each under _____.²⁹

We had only expected to remain at Tyner's Station for a day or two, but we were kept there until the afternoon of the 10th. My recollections of the place are only those of the struggle we had to get enough to eat, for no preparations had been made for any such delay. I made Charley mash up bullets & make shot for me, & I killed some rabbits & quail, & one wood cock, the first I had ever shot at. I fired at him, flying, three times, & apparently missed him each time, but ran back to camp for another load of shot, after noting where he lit, Charley being busy all the while at the camp chopping up the bullets. On my fourth approach, I suddenly discovered him squatting almost at my feet, his great liquid black eyes & beautiful smooth plumage making as exquisite a picture as I ever saw. He was too near to shoot, & I slowly & carefully drew the iron ramrod from the long Enfield musket I was using, & struck at him in his form. He was dead already. At my third shot, I had lodged a little slug in some artery, & he had died in his form without shutting his eyes or ruffling a feather.

But, in spite of all the game I could kill, our rations had about come to an end, when a fortunate event—for us—converted our last twenty-four hours at Tyner's from a fast into a feast, to which we were really even able to invite Gen. Longstreet & one of his staff at our last dinner. Close to our camp lived a woman who had several very fat, half-grown pigs. I had vainly tried to buy one, having only Confederate money to offer. By the way, a gold dollar, at that time, was worth about fifteen dollars in Confederate currency.³⁰ As we sat around our little breakfast table, in our tent, on the morning of the 9th, to about the very last half of a meal we could scrape up, an idea had occurred to me, & I said, "I wish an infantry man would kill one of that old woman's pigs & I could catch him at it." Some very few times in my life, I have wished something, apparently, very improbable, & immediately the thing wished has happened in a way that seems to indicate that nothing but the wish can have caused it. It is as if some fairy godmother had granted that every millionth wish should be at once fulfilled. And that wish seemed to be the millionth wish. For the words were hardly spoken when the explosion of a musket was heard in the edge of a wood, about 200 yards off across a meadow. From the head of the table, inside, I could see through the tent door two infantry men, one with a musket & the other was putting a pig in a bag. Frank Huger was at the foot of the table, at the door. My revolver hung on the tent pole by my chair. I reached it across to Huger, & said, "Run, Frank! The fellow with the bag, not the one with the gun."

Huger was off before any one else could get out of the tent. He chased the fellow into a brigade camp of infantry, & finally ran him into a tent & caught him, & brought him back, at the pistol's point, bag, pig, & all. Then I sent him, by a detail of my guard, with a note to his brigadier general, telling of his crime. But the pig & the bag stayed with me. Then I called on the old lady, & told her how lawless the soldiers were sometimes, in spite of all we could do, & that one of them had killed her pig. But I had had him caught & sent up for punishment & I would like to pay her for the pig & keep it. So she named her price—fifteen dollars I think it was,[31] & that glorious fat pig was honestly ours.

At last about 1 P.M. on Tuesday, Nov. 10th, a long train of flat cars arrived to take us. We loaded guns, caissons, harness, & ourselves & baggage, all on the flat cars. Our horses we sent by land with enough of the drivers to take care of them. The loading was troublesome, but by 3:00 P.M. we were off. Before we had gone very far the engine got out of wood. We stopped & cut up fence rails enough to go on, & we had this to do several times. As night came on it was quite cool, riding out on the flat cars, but we wrapped up in blankets & laid in under & among the guns, & managed to sleep with some comfort, arriving at Sweetwater about midnight & disembarking in the morning.

Here I left the battalion to wait for the arrival of the horses, & started off with Col. _____ Clarke,[32] of the engineers, to reconnoitre for a crossing of the French Broad near Loudon, where the railroad crossed, but the bridge was now burned. Clarke was a fine, clever fellow & had been assigned to Longstreet's staff as an engineer. We became great friends, &, through me, he also became afterward a great friend of Gen. Gilmer's, & Gilmer at one time had him, after the war, as superintendent of the Geo. Central R.R. He was finally killed by an accident in some little Jersey town near New York when about to take a train, along about 1889.

Clarke & I spent two days on the country & the roads about Loudon, & finally settled on making our crossing at Hough's Ferry a short distance below the burnt railroad bridge. [Figure 29 appears here in the manuscript.] The bank was high & concave on our side of the stream, & the R.R. track within a few hundred yards. Upon this track we could bring up our pontoon boats, which had been provided, & we planned to get a boat first carried down to the river quietly, some distance below the ferry, & to have a small force cross & come around in rear of the enemy's picket which was kept there & capture it.

The residents in all that East Tennessee country, at that time, were very much divided in their allegiance to the two contesting parties, & we learned

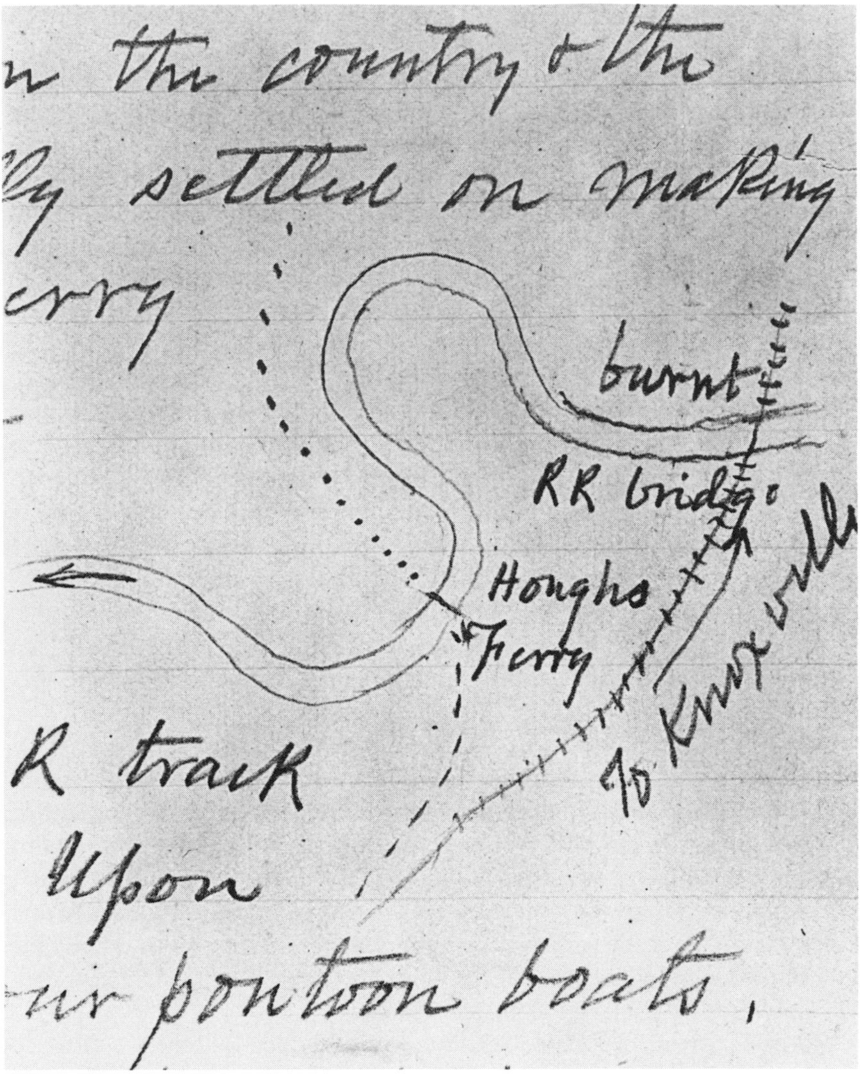

Figure 29. Vicinity of Hough's Ferry, Tennessee

that bushwhackers were abundant, & all strangers were regarded with suspicion. Once we knocked at the front door of a nice brick country house, evidently the home of well-to-do people. A little girl, about 8 years old, opened the door. Wishing to inquire something about the neighboring roads we asked, "Sissy, are any of the grown people at home?" She stepped back & surveyed us from head to foot, & answered our question with another: "What I wants to know is are you a Reb, or a Yank, or a bushwhack?"

Friday night the battalion came up. For two nights before we had found quarters with some citizen. An incident of this night, which I remember, is a thunder squall which came up just as we were going to sleep & blew the tent clear away from over us, & drenched everything we had. Only once beside in all my camping did I ever have such a calamity. In 1858 out on the Little Blue in Kansas a tornado took the tent from over Duane & myself, & gave us a drenching within two minutes.

The next night, Sat., Oct. 14th, we began at dark upon the pontoon bridge. I am sorry that I forget their names, but two very bright & clever young South Carolina captains, with their companies, first took a pontoon boat from the train & carried it through woods & rough ground down to the river, under my guidance, & then crossed with their companies & tried to capture the Federal picket, but they were not successful. They had gotten the alarm somehow, & all made their escape. I had some guns out on the bank in case we were molested, but no resistance was attempted. Clarke worked very hard & successfully, &, by soon after sunrise in the morning, the troops were able to pass, & the artillery & trains followed.

A small rear guard of the enemy's kept ahead of us, & made what delay they could; & we put out, ahead, a little advanced guard to keep them moving, under an officer with whom I then first became acquainted, but have been rather special friends with ever since; Lt. Col., afterward Gen. T. M. Logan.[33] Logan was slight, slender, blue eyed, youthful looking & with such delicate features that his college nickname, like "the gallant Pelham's," had been a girl's. Pelham's was Sally Pelham. Logan's was Molly Logan. He belonged, at this time, to the Hampton Legion infantry, but he was afterward transferred to the cavalry & promoted. I took a gun or two ahead of the column, to be able to promptly help Logan's sharpshooters on occasion, & then our column pushed forward. About three or four miles beyond the river we compelled the enemy to abandon a caisson, & we had several little skirmishes in which a few people were hurt. A considerable part of Burnside's forces had been in camp about Lenoir Station, & he was now falling back before us towards Knoxville. Had we had good maps of the country, we had it in our power to have cut off & captured a part of his troops, by pushing directly to Campbell's Station from our crossing; but, instead, we turned in towards Lenoir. Here we arrived too late to attack & during the night the enemy retreated.

Next day we overtook him at Campbell's Station in the afternoon, where he had taken a strong position, & posted a heavy artillery force. I was ordered to engage him with artillery in front while Jenkins's division turned his left flank by an advance under cover of a favorable ridge upon our right. Broad open meadows & the few houses making the so called station separated us, & I deployed a very pretty show of batteries, & opened up a slow duel, to try & hold the enemy until our infantry could get around his flank. But the scheme did not work. Before Jenkins could get his men into position the enemy discovered the movement, & withdrew their whole force so rapidly that we could not overtake it again that evening. The total casualties of the affair were on our side _____.34

I recall three things about the fight. First, was the pretty show the battalion made in the broad open meadows. Hardly any where else can I recall ground admitting so nice a display of the batteries in line advancing & firing. Next, was the bursting of one of Woolfolk's four 20 pr. Parrott rifles, at a moment when Gen. Longstreet & his staff happened to be quite near. Fragments whizzed about them but fortunately no one was hurt. The third was seeing a 20 lb. rifled shot from the enemy cut both arms & one leg off a man. He was kneeling behind a limber on his right knee, facing to the right, & was putting a fuze in a shell placed on the ground, & using both hands. This shot struck one of the wheel horses in the chest, ranged through the length of his body a little downward, wrecked the splinter bar of the limber, & passed just under the axle & struck this poor fellow's left leg above the knee, his left arm above the elbow & his right arm at or below it leaving all three only hanging by shreds. He was in one of the batteries of Leyden's battalion, & was still alive when carried off the field on a stretcher, but died from loss of blood soon after.

Our failure to catch the enemy on this occasion was afterwards attributed, by the friends of Gen. Jenkins, to Gen. Law, & I will suspend my narrative here for awhile to tell about the unfortunate jealousies which prevailed on this campaign between several most excellent officers. Hood's division was now without a maj. genl., Hood having lost an arm at Gettysburg & a leg at Chickamauga. Gen. Law was the ranking brigadier general left, of the brigades which had fought in all its recent battles. But Jenkins's big So. Ca. brigade, which had been kept below Petersburg for nine months, & which had had little fighting since Sharpsburg, was now attached to the division, & Jenkins ranked Law, & consequently took command of the division.

Law, naturally, thought that he had deserved promotion, & considered himself unjustly kept out of it. He would doubtless have made an excellent maj. genl., & no brigadier in the army had fought more bravely. He considered Gen. Longstreet responsible for the injustice being done him. At Campbell's Station it was charged that Law deliberately led his brigade, which was in front of the flanking column, where the enemy could & did discover the movement, & it was charged that he did it purposely to prevent Jenkins getting the credit of a success, & some of Law's company officers wrote letters supporting such charges.

Personally I know nothing about it, but I always had a very high appreciation both of Jenkins & Law. Both were exceptionally well educated, both had been in charge of military schools before the war,[35] & both were distinguished for personal bravery. I can say nothing more about the matter except that it was most unfortunate to have such a state of affairs in a division.

Besides this there was another difficulty brewing, of which I had not yet heard, but which had as well be mentioned here. Similar feelings of distrust to those entertained by Jenkins toward Law, were being felt by Gen. Longstreet himself toward Gen. McLaws. I have never learned when they began or how they arose, but they ended in the next two or three months in Gen. L.'s preferring charges & in Gen. McLaws being court martialled, all of which I will tell of in due course.[36]

And now I may take up my narrative. On Tuesday morning, Nov. 17th, we resumed our march, & found the enemy contesting our advance much more vigorously, as we now drew to the near vicinity of Knoxville. Logan's sharpshooters had to be reinforced, & a whole battery, also, brought forward to help, & with their aid, by noon, we came in sight of the lines around Knoxville, & during the afternoon we spread out to the right & left developing the situation. I encamped that night near the house of a man named Hazen, & I think we made that place our camp during the whole siege. It was some half mile to the left of the main road by which we approached. Gen. Longstreet stopped at a very nice house on that road, owned by a man named Armstrong, one of three brothers, or relatives, all of whom had houses between this first one & Knoxville.

The geography about Knoxville will be understood from the map.[37] The Confederates had partially fortified it while they held Cumberland Gap; &, particularly, they had partially built a considerable fort, with a bastioned front, a little north of this same main road from the west. This fort was indeed badly located for their purposes, but the Federals were hurried, & they made it not only a part, but an important angle of their defensive works, whence one line ran south toward the river, & another east, parallel to the river. This fort they afterward named Fort Sanders, for my former cadet friend "Dock Sanders," of meeting whom in San Francisco, at the breaking out of the war, & of whose fate at our next meeting I have already

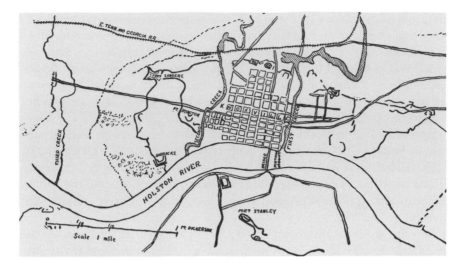

Figure 30. Siege of Knoxville

told in my narrative of those early days. We had parted there on the steamer in which I sailed, in warmest friendship, and promising to see each other soon down in Dixie. And now the meeting was about to occur, but not such as we had anticipated. For he had changed his politics & was now in command of a Federal brigade of cavalry. In fact I think we had been skirmishing with his brigade (he had very recently been promoted brigadier general) for several days, but I did not know that they were his troops we were fighting until I heard of his death.

On the morning of Wed., Nov. 18th, we started out to drive in all the enemy's pickets everywhere, so as to develop his main line, & be able to determine where was the most favorable point to attack it. We had no serious trouble anywhere except along the main road by which we had advanced. On that road, some 1,400 yards in front of their main line, Sanders's cavalry had dismounted & built a long breast work of fence rails, piled over three feet high & nearly as thick, behind which they ensconced themselves with their carbines.[38] The line was quite well located, on a sort of low ridge in open grass land, with a lone cedar tree or two marking it, & from the high range of hills behind it all the Federal line of battle could look on, & from the west & north our people also had some good views. Here these fellows held, & just would not quit for anything our skirmishers could do to them, and after some time had been wasted Gen. Longstreet directed me to move them with the artillery. Now, since we had gotten so far from all supplies, I had begun to get very stingy about ammunition, & I was very anxious to do this job with the least possible expenditure of it. So, before going in, I made a very close reconnaissance, & hit upon as pretty a little scheme for it as could be desired. I found a route by which I could carry a battery, without its being seen, up into the very yard of the second Armstrong house, which had been deserted by its occupants, & stood within less than 300 yards of the rail breast works. And then, close by—to the front & left, I found a low sort of swale in which I could hide a couple of regiments of infantry without the enemy's knowing it. Then I explained all to Gen. Longstreet & borrowed two So. Ca. regiments of infantry (the _____ & _____ of _____ brigade)39 & proceeded to organise a regular little surprise party to astonish the weak minds of our cavalry friends.

Taylor's battery of Napoleons was led through a series of hollows & ravines, & finally unlimbered right behind the Armstrong house, & loaded, ready to push out by hand at the word, & send solid shot through those rails. I felt confident that such a sudden & close opening, if I could make the rails begin to fly & kill a few men behind them, would rattle the enemy badly, & perhaps make many of them run off. But, at that close range, as soon as they sized us up, even a few cool men could kill my cannoneers very fast, so the infantry was sneaked into the swale to the left front ready to rise & charge with a yell at a signal at the right moment. Then, when all that was ready, some of Moody's 24 pr. howitzers came out in the open, about 800 yards off, to the north of the enemy's position, where they could throw shrapnel in the rear of it to annoy any supports or attempts to rally in the rear.

Moody's opening was the signal for Taylor. His guns were run out, carefully aimed & fired, & immediately we could see rails flying in the air, & we afterwards found men killed behind them struck by our solid shot. And, just as I had hoped, we could see the men deserting the breast work & running back in squads all along their line, while our guns piled in their work fast & furious. Within three minutes I gave the signal, & the infantry rose & charged with a yell. Meanwhile we could see the Federal officers running back & forth trying to rally the fugitives, & to keep steady those who had not run. Our men advanced handsomely until they were within 40 yards of the breast work, when, to my surprise & disgust, they halted, laid down in the line of battle & began firing. We had just had to stop firing our guns on account of their proximity. When I saw them stop I stamped & exclaimed, "My Lord! What did they do that for? They had it if they had gone on!"

Just then I heard an Irish gunner at the nearest gun say, "Faith! & there goes the captain!" Then I saw that Captain Winthrop, who was sitting on his horse near by, had immediately stuck in his spurs & was already nearly half way to the infantry. I can see him now, in a short, black, velveteen, shooting coat & corduroy trousers, with his rather short stout legs & high English seat in his saddle—his elbows square out & his sabre drawn— urging his horse almost into a run. But the officers of the infantry had already raised their men up, & the line was moving forward before Winthrop reached it. We could see some musketry from the rails, & some fugitives being brought back from the rear. Then Winthrop dashed through a little gap in our line & right up at the breast work. As he did so we could see several carbines, to the right & left, spit smoke obliquely up at him & he suddenly fell forward on his horse's neck, & the horse turned about in a curve & came back with him. He had gotten a bullet through the base of his neck tearing up the collar bone so that some inches of it had to be amputated out. Some years after the war, I found in a Northern newspaper a Federal account of this fight, which I saved & sent to England to Winthrop. It told of the charge & of the infantry lying down, & then about "a powerful rebel on a large white horse," galloping to the front & being shot down. Only the horse was not white, but dark bay to my recollection.

Meanwhile, our infantry made no further pause but went right into the rails & killed or captured all that were there. It was in this rallying his men that Sanders received a mortal wound, a shot through the stomach, as we were told by prisoners a few days afterward. He died within a day or two. I have no doubt that he & I actually saw each other often that day though not near enough for either to recognise the other. As soon as the rails were taken we limbered up Taylor's guns & went forward, & then we began to push the fugitives on into the Federal main line. Frank Huger & I went along with the skirmishers for quite a ways, & on that excursion I got myself an elegant India rubber poncho—Gen. Jackson not being along—& Frank & I had a successful little joke over it.

We would frequently, around our camp fires, talk about the luxuries we expected to capture in Knoxville, from Burnside's men & the army sutlers, such as cheese—sardines—champagne, &c. But I had always spoken of an India rubber poncho, & said that I knew that among so many thousand men as there were in Burnside's army some one would have had the good sense to realize that what would please me most would be a really fine poncho & that he would have one with him expressly for me. As we were advancing with the skirmishers I came upon a dead cavalry man who had slung over his shoulders a particularly nice looking poncho neatly rolled & tied. I called out to Frank who was about 20 yards to the left, "Frank! Here's that man I've been telling you about! Got my poncho! Here he is now!" Frank answered back, "Yes, Aleck! That's the very fellow! I always knew you were right about that!" A tall, lank South Carolinian had stopped to load his musket, & had the benefit of our conversation. I spoke to him very soberly, & said, "My friend that's my poncho on that dead Yankee there. Won't you please take it off him & give it to me." It was funny to see the puzzled look with which the man looked at me & at the Yankee, & seemed to debate how that could have happened. But he evidently concluded that as the yankee couldn't dispute my title, there was no reason why he should, & he rolled the fellow out of it & gave me the poncho. It was the very nicest one I ever had, & it lasted me till the end of the war, & for years after was a valuable article of house hold furniture in Columbia, S.C.

I have one other amusing recollection of the day. I had had given me, in May, a nice, half-grown, pointer puppy which was born in camp the winter before, & was raised in the army, & had never, even up to this time, been in a house, though he was now nearly a year old. When the fighting was all over, with Haskell & Huger, I rode back about a mile, to a nice, large, brick country house, where a hospital had been established, to see Winthrop. His collar bone had been resected, & the wound dressed, & he was in a room up stairs, at which, by the way, I was relieved, for I always kept away from the operating rooms with their instruments & loose pieces piled up, which are ugly things for soldiers to see or to think about. Buster, the dog went with us to the hospital. When we entered the house he followed, into the hall, without any difficulty. But when he saw us go up a staircase, he stood at the bottom & whined in great distress. Haskell went back & patted him, & encouraged him, & then he came up, as gingerly as an elephant, & evidently in great doubt how such rashness would terminate.

When he finally reached the second floor & found another broad, level hall, his relief & delight got the better of him. He raced around, & up & down, a time or two, & then, a window at one end being open, he took a flying leap through it. Fortunately he fell on some grass & received no serious injury, but we all, even Winthrop in his bandages, laughed ourselves sore over the idea of Buster's astonishment when he found himself falling through the air outside of the window.

Altogether, as memory looks back over the war, few days stand out in my recollection more vividly or brightly than this one. For, naturally, the success of the little private fight for the rail breastworks put us all in fine spirits, & we never doubted but that within a very few days we would have Burnside & all his people prisoners. And, oh I did wish so to have our people make Burnside ashamed of himself for something he had done a few months before. He had captured our cavalry general, John Morgan,[40] who had made a raid into Ohio, & he had had him confined in the Ohio State Penitentiary as a convict. That is, he had had him bathed, shaved, & dressed in convict's clothes, merely to try to degrade & mortify him. And, what is still more contemptible, he did not avow his object, but pretended that he could not keep Morgan *safely* anywhere but in the penitentiary. And that the bathing, shaving, & convict dress was not his doing, but the unfortunate accident of there being local regulations inside the penitentiary, which the warden had no authority to disregard. And, as if to brand this flimsy excuse moot publicly as a lie, the fates decreed that within a few months Morgan & many of his men escaped by night from the penitentiary, & through Ohio & Kentucky, safely into our lines in Tennessee.

The action was only not as mean and disgraceful as that by which Maj. Gen. Miles afterward made himself famous at Fortress Monroe—when he had the post blacksmith rivet irons on the limbs of poor, old Mr. Davis, upon the same contemptible pretense that it was necessary for his safe keeping—because Mr. Davis was the older, the more helpless, & the more dignified prisoner.[41] But, as far as his material permitted, Burnside had slurred his own character as a gentleman & his record as soldier. We would have been perfectly justified in committing an equal number of our prisoners, of equal rank, to a state penitentiary, but Mr. Davis himself, & all of our leading generals, were reluctant to inaugurate such a policy, & though I used to talk before Gen. Longstreet about Burnside's deserts, he would never contemplate any retaliation.

Our first care, now that we had the enemy driven into his permanent lines, was to erect lines of our own as a basis to operate from, & to prevent sorties, & for the next three or four days I was occupied in this. The map [Figure 30] will give a fair idea of the topography & the lines. It soon became apparent that the most favorable point for our attack was the old Confederate fort now renamed Fort Sanders, & I located all of my batteries, with that purpose, so as to enfilade its different fronts. And I also rigged up Fickling's howitzers on skids near the 3rd Armstrong house to give a mortar fire upon it. By Sunday I had everything in such shape that it was intended to attack Fort Sanders on Monday. But a very unfortunate thing, as it afterward turned out, happened that day. We had gotten hold, some how, of an old flat boat & some telegraph wire, & had made a little ferry across the river where our right flank rested upon it, & had put out scouts & pickets in the country on the other side of the river. And, by the way, we found the ferry useful for another purpose. We were very hard up for horse shoes—so much so, that all along the road, if horse or mule was killed or abandoned we had our rear guard equipped to take off the shoes & bring them along. And, now, the enemy in Knoxville were throwing all their dead animals in the river, &, every day, a half dozen or more of them would come floating down. Our little ferry boat enabled us to easily get the shoes off every one as it went by. Well, Maj. Fairfax of Gen. Longstreet's staff crossed this ferry, & went reconnoitering around in the hills on the other side, & came back Sunday afternoon very much excited. He had found a high hill from which one could look right down upon & enfilade a great deal of the enemy's line running from Fort Sanders to the river, & he gave such an account of it that

Gen. Longstreet ordered, at once, that I should take a battery over there the next day, & dig pits for it, & that the attack should be postponed until this could be done.

I did not like the idea much, but I could not help myself, for Fairfax was enthusiastic, & I had not been there, & the general thought well of it. My principal objection was that our rifled ammunition was poor & the range was far. It was slow also to get messages sent to regulate their fire, & I did not like to scatter batteries far. But I thought the delay would only be for a day or two & that the moral effect might be worth something so I made no protest.

And, Monday [the 23rd],[42] I started in person, early, with Parker's battery. It was slow work, ferrying & then making a road, & at the last carrying guns & ammunition by hand up places too steep & rough for horses, & we worked hard all day & all night & all the next day. But, late Tuesday afternoon, I came back & reported all ready to open fire at sunrise on Wed. [the] 25th. But now there was another delay. Gen. Longstreet told me that Bushrod Johnson, with his own & Gracie's brigades, had been sent to reinforce him, & would arrive Wed. afternoon. Naturally he determined to wait twenty-four hours to have such an important accession of strength. Johnson's division came in on time & all right, but our luck had turned now, & along with it came old Gen. Leadbetter. Leadbetter was one of the old captains of my old corps, the U.S. Engineers. He was from _____ and graduated at West Point in _____.[43] By education, experience, & position (he was now a general of engineers) he ought to have been as good a military field engineer as there was in either army. He had been stationed at Knoxville for months, & had himself built Fort Sanders. And now he had been sent up by Gen. Bragg, as a great favor to Longstreet, to advise him how he should attack. Naturally, Longstreet explained to Leadbetter that everything was ready for his attack at sunrise the next morning, & told how & where it was to be made. I can only judge what Leadbetter advised by the result. Late at night orders were sent postponing the attack. This was the third time & the fourth day. All this time the enemy were working, working, working, day & night.

Next morning Longstreet & Leadbetter started early on an expedition to our extreme left flank—away around to the north-east, or far side of Knoxville. Late in the afternoon, they returned and Gen. Longstreet ordered me to bring Parker's battery back from the other side of the river at once, & said that he & Gen. Leadbetter had found a more favorable place for attack, on our extreme left, & that the next day they would take the division commanders up there & show it to them. I never was more disgusted in my life. I couldn't say anything, because Longstreet said he had been there himself & seen the place where we could attack. But I had been there myself

& examined very carefully, more carefully than I believed that he & Leadbetter could have done—and I just knew there was no such place. Leadbetter evidently had no appreciation of ground. Longstreet had some, but was misled in some way I have never [been] able to understand. All I could do was to ask permission to go along with the party next day. Poor Capt. Parker had to bring down all his guns & ammunition—fortunately it was down hill this time—& to ferry over the whole business again, little by little in the little ferry boat. He did part that night & finished early the next day.

That was Friday, & early in the morning Longstreet & Leadbetter started with McLaws & Jenkins & Johnson & several of the brigade commanders & myself. And, near the left flank, we found Gen. Wheeler waiting for us with a brigade of cavalry. With this he drove in the enemy's pickets opposite our left, handling it very prettily, & enabled our party to make a thorough & complete examination of the whole ground. There never was a more complete fiasco than the attempt to find a favorable point for attack. Everywhere we saw near a mile of open level ground obstructed by a creek & artificial ponds, without cover anywhere, even for skirmishers, & all under fire of formidable breast works on commanding hills. It required no discussion, & even Leadbetter had not a word to say. When we had seen all there was to see, the party turned & came back to a point on our lines where we could get a good view of Fort Sanders. To understand the attack we afterward made on this fort, I attach a rough sketch of it on a larger scale.[44] One of the points about the fort which we were uncertain upon was the width & depth of the outer ditch. The enemy's picket line was only from 150 to 200 yards in front of the fort, where the valley of Second Creek began to fall away rapidly.[45] From where we stood, the parapet of one of the bastions was in relief against the sky. As we were looking we saw a soldier mount the parapet to come out across the ditch to the picket line. Longstreet exclaimed, & fixed his glasses on him, &, as he walked across the ditch, he said, "The ditch catches him to his waist." The ditch at that point afterward proved to be about five feet deep, & the man was probably using a plank crossing. But whatever the character of the ditch, the reasons pointing out this place as the most favorable for our attack were as follows.

In the first place, from the fort it was impossible to see into the rear half of the valley of Second Creek; & covered parts of this valley (or space sheltered from fire, dead space, as it is called) ran up, at one place, within 150 yards of the fort. The enemy maintained a line of rifle pits along the edge of this dead space, but, whenever we were ready, a quick dash would give us all of those rifle pits, & they would at once be used to shelter a very long line of our own sharpshooters, against their parapet & embrasures, at close range. Then our storming column could form under complete cover within 200 yards of the fort & would only have about that distance to advance under fire.

Then, in the second place, a faulty shape & position given to the lines of the fort accidentally made it that the ground over which our shortest line of approach lay was in what is called in fortification the "sector without fire" of the fort. It is found that soldiers firing over a parapet cannot effectively fire very obliquely, but only pretty square to the front. So the space, or sector, in front of a salient angle, which has only oblique fire over it is called "the sector without fire." To a certain extent it might be considered a dead space, but military engineers sharply distinguish these terms. A dead space is where the enemy cannot see at all, such as the space behind a hill. A sector without fire is exposed only to oblique fire, & our storming column's advance would be over such a space.

Now, in the third place it so happened that the enemy's long lines of battle, which ran from Fort Sanders, one to the east & one to the south, were so situated that neither of them could fire toward this space. Their sector without fire coincided with that of the fort's most exposed angle.

And in the fourth place, though this we only found out when we made the assault, within a stone's throw of the parapet there was a big limestone sink, making dead space in which several hundred men could stand—& the edge of it be lined with sharpshooters. Had Gen. Leadbetter had in him any conception of the value of peculiar features of the ground the existence of that remarkable circular sink would have cut such a figure in the character & value of that fort, that he would have never allowed the fort to be mentioned, in his presence, without telling about it. But he seemed to be demoralized after not finding the place he hunted for up above, & I cannot recall his making another suggestion or saying another word that day. But I have often wondered if it was not he who suggested to Longstreet, the next night, the sudden but absurd & fatal idea of converting his attack into a surprise, which I will soon have to tell about. Even if he did not originate it Longstreet would scarcely have made the change without consultation.

So the result of the reconnaissance was that everybody agreed that Fort Sanders was the place. We might have attacked on Saturday morning, if Longstreet had not been in such a hurry, the evening before, to bring Parker to our side of the river. Now he wanted him back on the south side. I was accordingly ordered to get him there as soon as possible, & we would try the attack Saturday afternoon. So we whirled in again on the little ferry with night work & by noon on Saturday I reported to Longstreet again all ready. And I admit that I was rather glad when, now, at the last minute, he decided to wait until sunrise on Sunday the 29th. For I thought we ought to have all day before us, when we once broke in, & then the weather was dark & drizzly, & Parker would have trouble in getting his ranges.

This was the plan for our attack.

First, our howitzers rigged as mortars were to open & have a reasonable time to practise & get their ranges, before any other shots were fired by anything else. Then the other batteries were to begin, very slowly & carefully, getting the range, & enfilading the main lines next to the fort. Then a big cloud of skirmishers was to make a rush, & take & occupy the enemy's rifle pits from the north of the fort through the west to the south, that the fort should be the centre of a concentrated fire of sharpshooters located around an entire semi circumference. Then all the guns & mortars should unite & fire rapidly, but carefully for about 20 minutes. Then the storming column should advance.

It seems to me that by such an attack we would have had that fort in our grip & have been able to keep down the little fire it was able to deliver at best, & that whatever obstacle the ditch might prove, it could then be deliberately examined, undertaken, & overcome, cutting little steps where needed. If our infantry once scaled the parapet the fort was ours. And the Federal lines became untenable when we held the fort.

And now I have to tell of the one thing I did, in this whole campaign, which I have regretted & blamed myself for ever since. A little before sundown that evening I left Longstreet's headquarters to return to my camp, across Second Creek. I had crossed the creek & gotten about a half mile on my road when I met Gen. Jenkins. He said, "Alexander, I want you to go back with me to Longstreet's. McLaws's troops are to form the storming column tomorrow, & I don't think McLaws has provided any ladders. I am going to urge Longstreet to order him to do so, for we don't know what we are going to find, & we ought to be well prepared in advance. I want you to go back with me & add your influence to mine."

Now there was a good deal of detail to be determined about the storming column, relating to its size, its tactical formation, its equipment, & its exact procedure, to all of which I had given but little thought, believing the infantry officers who would be in charge would be the most competent judges to decide them all. Now I at once realized that Jenkins's suggestion was a very important one, & that I ought to go back with him & help him urge it. But I was feeling unusually tired, the roads were wretched, & I was anxious to get home before dark. So I let sloth & fatigue prevail against the promptings of my conscience, & I said, "Jenkins, your influence will be enough. The matter is very simple & obvious. And if my opinion is of any weight you can tell the general that you met me & discussed it with me & that I asked you to say that I most heartily concur in your opinion."

Jenkins seemed disappointed, but went on, and my conscience began to reproach me at once. For in such matters as this every ounce of precaution possible to obtain should be had, even if it cost a ton of trouble. No one can ever tell what particular ounce will turn the scale. I consoled myself, however, thinking that in the morning there would still be time—even after the artillery began, to tear some stable to pieces if necessary & make ladders in an hour.

But I never dreamed that within a couple of hours Longstreet was going to change his mind, & completely alter the whole plan of attack. Had I gone on with Gen. Jenkins the chances are that some intimation of this new scheme would have been dropped & we might have shown its absurdities. For some of its features were crazy enough to have come out of Bedlam, & I will go to my grave believing that Leadbetter devised it & imposed it upon Longstreet, & he afterward preferred to accept the responsibility rather than plead that he had let himself be so taken in. I will give the orders, which we received about 8 o'clock that night, & every [one] can judge for himself if I speak of them fairly. They were short & simple. Instead of the attack by main force, & artillery, as planned for sunrise and after a good breakfast, an attempt would be made to surprise the fort a little before dawn. As a preliminary step, the enemy's rifle pits were to be attacked, captured, & occupied at 11 P.M. Then the assaulting troops would be formed at once in the rear of these pits, & held there all night but without fires. At the appointed hour in the morning a few shots from one of my batteries would be the signal for the infantry to assault the fort.

It should be noted that the legitimate occasion for resorting to a night surprise is when material disadvantages attend an attack by main force, & daylight. Here the very reverse obtained. It would have [been] impossible, I think, to find on the continent another earth work so advantageously situated for attack. No military engineer could ask for an easier task. It was like a one move problem in chess.

If a surprise were ever proper, it should have been tried a week before, for we had spent that much time, nearly, in building batteries & putting guns across the river which would now be of little or no use.

Again this surprise was carefully arranged not to be a surprise at all. The capture of their rifle pits, at 11 P.M., naturally put the enemy's whole army on guard all night, & the presence of our assaulting brigades so close to their works all night could not be concealed.

And lastly the cannon shots before dawn, as a signal to the brigades which had to advance, were equally signals to the enemy in the trenches to be ready to repel.

It resulted too from the sudden change of plan, & the short notice, that there was no special preparation of any part of the assaulting force as a storming column, with ladders, or guides, or special destination & instructions. The tactical formation was merely three brigades abreast in line of battle—just what it would have been in attacking a force in a wheat field!

I will not try to describe the disappointment in our camp at finding our whole part in the action suddenly cut down to firing the signal guns. We did not get much sleep, having to distribute the new orders everywhere, & all be on hand in the batteries by 4 A.M. And about 11 P.M. our sharpshooters rushed the enemy's pits, & captured them without the least difficulty & with but little loss. But, of course, it put the enemy on the "alert" & they not only fired quite a lot of canister around in the dark at the time, but they kept up turning loose a gun full of it at intervals all night long to show that they were ready for us.[46]

At the appointed hour I fired the signal guns from a battery near where we had had the fight with Sanders, putting in shells & sending them to burst over the enemy's line. Soon we heard a chorus of rebel yells break out & we knew our infantry was on the go. I put a few guns, which could shoot without firing over our infantry, to throwing shell just behind the fort to catch any reinforcements which might come up. Later that day, on flag of truce, I met an old cadet friend who had had to pass in that vicinity & whose overcoat was badly torn by a fragment of our shell & he described our fire as very remarkably accurate. Fort Sanders fired a few guns on the flanks & some musketry from her parapets, but no great amount even at first, & then it gradually grew less until it almost ceased entirely. All of us, looking on, supposed that we had captured the fort. We ceased all firing & limbered up some guns ready to advance them. By that time, it got light enough to see, & we could see our men coming back, walking slowly, & scarcely fired on at all. We were repulsed, but we knew the loss could not be very serious, and I felt sure that we would now renew the attack by main force & carry it. Gen. Jenkins, too, I was told had gone to Gen. Longstreet & begged to be allowed to try the fort with his division. It was a bright sunny day, & everything was favorable. But just as we were beginning to prepare for this, there came what was equivalent to a clap of thunder in a clear sky. Gen. Robt. Ransom arrived from the direction of Bristol, with a telegram from Prest. Davis informing Longstreet that Gen. Bragg had been routed on the 25th at Missionary Ridge, & was retreating toward Dalton. We were directed to abandon the siege of Knoxville & to make our way to join Bragg.

Even in spite of these orders it has seemed to me that Longstreet could & should have renewed his attack upon Burnside. Everything was ready, & six hours might have made Burnside a prisoner. The game was worth playing for. But Longstreet did not hesitate, so far as I know, but immediately prepared orders for trains to be started south, the troops to follow after dark.

Just at that juncture a flag of truce was sent in by Burnside, who proposed a cessation of hostilities until sundown, to allow us to remove our dead & wounded. Burnside, of course, was playing for time. His only salvation lay in what Grant could do for him, & every day increased the chances of

Grant's coming. But I think Longstreet should have interpreted Burnside's offer as showing nervousness, & should, all the more, have tried at once to take Fort Sanders by main force. But Longstreet accepted the flag of truce & our surgeons & litter bearers were sent up, around the fort & into the ditch, to bring out the poor fellows who were left dead or wounded on the ground. Our total casualties were _____.47

I will return to this assault from a convenient point of the narrative & give more details. During the prevalence of the truce I spent some time out in the neutral ground, observing all there was to see, & I met several old army acquaintances. Among them I recall Babcock, Babbitt, & Maj. Gen. Ferrero,48 now commanding one of Burnside's divisions, who used to come up to West Point in the summers to teach dancing.

During the day, there came further news involving another change of plan. A courier arrived from Bragg, bringing the news that Sherman had started from Chattanooga to come to Burnside's relief, & that we could not safely return by the way we came, but would have to make a detour through the mountains to the south west. This was something much easier said than done. There are few rougher or poorer countries than the mountain region we would have had to traverse, for about 200 miles. It would have been impossible to subsist either the men or the animals, even if practicable roads for artillery existed at this season of the year. Gen. Longstreet, during the next two or three days, held councils daily with the principal officers of infantry and cavalry, at which all possible routes were minutely inquired into, from parties having some local knowledge of them, & daily bulletins were also brought of Sherman's gradual approach. The unanimous conclusion was soon reached that it was extremely unwise to attempt to obey either the orders from Richmond or those from Gen. Bragg, that we should seek to rejoin the army of the latter. It was held to be the safest policy to keep up the siege of Knoxville & draw Sherman's army up there to its relief, but, at the last moment, to draw off towards Bristol where we would find a favorable country to winter in. I was present at all of the councils, &, when the above course was finally decided upon, I urged a renewal of the attack upon Fort Sanders. Gen. Longstreet readily agreed & I started to organise it in such a way that it could not fail, when, suddenly, on the morning of Dec. 4th, orders were issued to start our trains on the road towards Bristol, & that at dark the troops would leave their camp fires brightly burning, & would march after the trains. I have always believed, since, that the general consented to the scheme of renewing the attack merely to keep us amused, & did not really intend it. And I will not say that, considering our isolation, it was not the safest play.

During the day of the 4th (Friday) I took a small revenge on the enemy by distributing among them, here & there, some of the artillery ammunition I had been saving up so unnecessarily. I would have liked to have given them a genteel bombardment, but Gen. Longstreet thought that that might make them suspect our purpose to quit.

About sundown it began to rain cats & dogs. A couple of Moody's 24 pr. howitzers bellowed our last farewell, & sent two shells that made flashes, like lightening in the dark, where they exploded over the enemy's lines, & in five minutes more the last guns were limbered up & the column was in motion. Between the black dark & the pouring rain & the thick woods, generally bordering the road, progress was very slow, & we could do nothing but let our animals pick their own way.

When I was a small boy my father had a favorite anecdote which was often recalled on night marches during the war, & I had already introduced it into our mess. There was a celebrated country tavern upon one of the roads he used to travel, called "Moon's half-way house." It was a log house, with one large room for a guest chamber, having a big three cornered cupboard in one angle. Two travellers stopped one night who were very anxious to push on in the morning. About midnight both waked, & thought they heard it raining. One decided to get up & look out. After groping, for a while, for the wooden shutter to the window, he found & opened, by mistake, the door of the cupboard, & stuck his head inside of it thinking it was out of doors. "Well," said his comrade, "is it raining?" "No, it is not raining." "Well what does it look like?" The fellow in the cupboard gave several sniffs & said, "It's as black as hell and smells cheesey." We all declared that the night of Dec. 4th was the cheeseyest night the war had yet produced.

About ten o'clock we came upon Martin's brigade of cavalry,[49] bivouacing by the roadside, in readiness to act as our rear-guard in the morning. The men had fires by the road, kept up with fence rails in spite of the rain, &, a hundred yards back in the oak & hickory woods, Gen. Martin himself had a very large fire. I was riding with Gen. Longstreet's staff & we all rode up to Martin's fire.

After a little general conversation, Martin said, "Gen. Longstreet I caught a spy in our lines this afternoon. He was in Confederate uniform; but his underclothes are of Federal issue, & he had admitted that he belongs to the 8th Michigan Cavalry.[50] What shall I do with him?" Gen. Longstreet answered, "We usually hung them in Virginia." Gen. Martin called, "Sergeant! Sergeant!" A sergeant of couriers & a dozen men were around a separate fire about 20 yards off. The sergeant answered & came up, saluting, in a rubber poncho. "Sergeant, take that prisoner out & hang him." "General, I have not got any rope." "Hasn't Richards got a rope halter on his horse?" "Yes, Sir." "Borrow that." "Richards!" sang out the sergeant, turning toward the fire where the couriers and probably the prisoner were all together. "Yes, Sir," answered Richards from the fire. "Richards, I want that rope halter off your horse." "Yes, Sir," said Richards—"I'll get it for you." I was not sorry when Gen. Longstreet started to say good-bye to Martin & move on. The hanging bee was proceeding with uncomfortable rapidity for one who did not care to be a spectator. I never heard a word of the proceedings after we left, but, many years after the war I found in some war papers the following, which would indicate that Richards never got his halter back, but that the poor wretch was left hanging to be a warning to spies.[51]

That was a hard night's march. Not that the distance covered was great, but the killing feature is the perpetual halting & moving, & halting & moving, inseparable from either night marching or bad roads, & at its maximum when both fall together. It was quite cold too, & the officers were obliged to relax discipline, & let the men burn fence rails at will, whenever a regular rest was made. The men would set fire to the fences as they stood, at the angles where the rails crossed. In spite of the rain they seemed to have no trouble in starting fires in these corners, & during that night we frequently saw miles of fence on fire at a time. We marched all night, & until about 11 o'clock on Saturday, when we encamped at Blain's crossroads, 18 miles from Knoxville.

Here I bought a fine half grown pig, from a citizen, & I ran off some infantrymen who, in the afternoon, raided his pasture & killed two or three. One of these fellows, after getting off some distance, stopped & fired back, the ball passing in ten or twenty yards. I don't suppose he tried to hit me, but the shot was evidently fired to express his objection to being interfered with when he was after pork. On Sunday, Dec. 6th, we marched 15 miles, & encamped near Rutledge, where we laid over one day. I remember our trying to make "Big Hominy" by treating the corn to a bath in lye. But we never succeeded, then, in getting rid of the taste of the lye, & the hominy was more like soap. Tuesday, the 8th, we marched 17 miles & encamped near Mooresburg, & the next day we went 9 miles further, & camped within six miles of Rogersville, where we remained for several days.

While we were here, Gen. Longstreet learned that a force of the enemy had followed us, & were at Bean's Station some 15 miles in our rear, & he determined to turn back & attack them. Bean's Station is not upon the railroad, but on the old stage line, & it was a village of a rather large hotel, & perhaps twenty other houses in a well cultivated rolling valley.

On Monday [the] 14th, we made an early start & a rapid march back, & early in the afternoon struck the enemy's pickets, & soon after a strong skirmish line, & a battery. I advanced one to help Gracie's brigade & saw Gen. Gracie get a ball through his forearm. It seemed to be quite a painful wound, & there was a chill & numbness in the air which suggested that even light blows would hurt on such a day. We drove back the enemy's skirmishers & battery, & I discovered in advance a hill with an old grave-yard upon it, with a fine command of the enemy's whole position, & whence I could reach the main road in his rear by which he would retreat. I sent back for my whole battalion, & rushed it up right behind our skir-mishers, & crowned the hill a[t] just about sundown. But just as I was about to open Gen. Longstreet sent me word not to fire. He had sent Kershaw's brigade to turn the enemy's left flank & get in his rear, & he feared that my fire might interfere with Kershaw. I could see Kershaw skirmishing, & I could have helped him, & beside that have made a panic among the enemy's trains. It was one of the disappointments of my life not to have turned my whole battalion loose there that evening. Only the leading guns had fired a few shots when peremptory orders stopped us.

Next morning we found the enemy gone. We followed, & in a few miles found them in line of battle, in a new & strong position. We skirmished a little & developed it, & then waited till next morning to attack it in force, but in the morning they were gone.

I find in the War Records the following particulars about this affair.[52]

I made no entry in my diary from Dec. 16th to Dec. 22nd & cannot recall whether we moved camp or not. But on the 22nd we "forded the Holston River at Cobb's Ford" & encamped. And on Wednesday, the 23rd, being ordered to select a place for winter quarters, I found one & moved into one about halfway between Russellville & Morristown. It was on the southern & western slope of extensive hills, covered with a virgin forest of oak & hickory, & with a fine mountain stream close by, a few hundred yards east of the road between the two towns. A better site could not be desired, & the very next day every mess in the camp, our own included, began work on a hut, of some sort, according to its own ideas. I worked with the boys on our hut for two days, when a sudden & bold idea struck me. Longstreet was as good & kind & considerate to me as if he were my father. There was no prospect of any fighting for at least three months. I had a pair of twins at home which I had never seen. Wouldn't he let me go & see them? The next day I rode to headquarters, & came back the happiest man in the world, with sixty days' furlough in my pocket.

My wife was now at my father's in Washington, Georgia. I, at first, thought of riding across the mountains & going all the way on horse back. Joe Haskell, who also got a leave, took that method to go to his home near Abbeville. But I finally decided to ride to Bristol, & thence by rail to Richmond, & thence via Petersburg, Weldon, & Wilmington, the regular mail route. Capt. Parker also got a leave, & he & I started together on Monday, Dec. 28th. We had a little roughing it on the road, but got to

Bristol Thursday [the] 31st about sundown in time to catch the night train. It was bitter cold, & I remember that journey with a shudder, with its wretched & crowded cars, but little fire, & no eating houses, & it seems to me that we were at least a day & a half or two days in reaching Richmond. But I made no entries in my diary & cannot even fix the date of my arrrival at home, but it was probably about Wednesday [the] 6th. But I remember buying a raw sweet potato at a station & slicing & cooking it on the stove in the car. My poor wife had had a dreadful journey on her way south over the same route south of Richmond about a month before. She and her baggage, two nurses, three babies and all, would have been forever lost, scattered, dissipated, & starved, but for some gentleman of a Confederate surgeon, whose name she failed to get, but who assumed charge of her outfit & bossed it through its major difficulties. We are going to hunt him up in the next world if it takes a thousand years. I had come ahead of all letters & gave them a surprise at home. I reached the house a little after dark, when the family were at supper. They heard the front door open & footsteps in the long passage. Cynthia, the old Negro mammy who was waiting on the table said, "Lor, that walks like Mars Porter."[53]

14

SPRING OF 1864

A sixty day furlough contemplated from near its beginning looks so liberal that one may be easily tempted to extravagance with it. And that was what happened to me now. My father urged me to run down to Savannah for a few days, to visit my aunt & her husband, Maj. Porter.[1] My wife protested, but it seemed stingy to refuse even a very few days, & I consented, never dreaming that calamity was already loading up for me. I kept no record of exact dates, but early in Feb. I got back from the Savh. trip & received but a sad & tearful welcome. For, even when I had been in Sav., telegraphic orders had summoned me back to East Tennessee. Not for any active service—I would not have minded that, for if that were to go on, I would not willingly be absent from my men. But I was summoned as a witness in a court martial about to be held upon Gen. McLaws. Gen. Longstreet had preferred charges, which I will speak of more fully later, & had given in my name as a witness though really I knew little or nothing bearing upon the real merits of the case. When the telegram arrived, during my absence, my father & my wife not only did not forward it to me in Savh., but they agreed together that they would not tell me of it when I came. But as the time drew near to welcome me, with their guilty secret on their minds, my father broke down & had to admit that he could not keep it. He felt himself partly responsible for my going to Savh., & he could not be sure how I would feel about a failure to appear at the time & place ordered, & so I was informed of the dispatch. It was a dreadful blow to me—about three weeks of furlough cut off without warning, &, as I felt, for no earthly good.

However, there was nothing to do but to obey orders and after about the hardest farewell we had yet had to take—for we knew the coming summer would bring a severe campaign—I took the next train for Richmond. That was the one time of the war when I obeyed orders & have been sorry for it from that day to this. When I arrived in Richmond I learned that the meeting of the court martial had been postponed, & it was again postponed, & only took place long after my furlough expired. I might have had the whole of it at home. I have no record of the exact dates, but it was too late to return home, when I found out how it would be, & so I remained in Richmond where my sisters, Mrs. Gilmer & Mrs. Lawton, were keeping house for their husbands, who were at the head of the Engineering & Quartermaster Departments, & two of my brothers were also stationed, one in each of these offices.

Among the specially intimate friends whom I remember meeting during the two weeks or so that I stayed here were Tom Berry & Gen. Stuart. Berry was from Newnan, Geo., & was now colonel of [the] 61st Geo.[2] He had been distinguished & badly wounded, & had deserved promotion, but he could not help sometimes taking a little too much whiskey & that had always interfered with it. Mrs. Lawton took warm interest in him, & at one time, in fact I think during all the summer of 1864, hoped to have him both entirely reformed & promoted, but neither event ever happened, & I think we met on this occasion for the last time, for poor Tom died soon after the war. Gen. Stuart & I had both been desperate admirers of Miss Mary Lee[3] in former days, & we often joked each other about it. When I met him on this occasion he came into a photographic gallery, where I was waiting, with a lady on his arm wearing a veil. I rushed up to almost embrace him, as we had not met since Gettysburg. But he drew back & advanced the lady, saying, "An old friend of yours," & she held out her hand. I touched my hat & said, "I beg pardon. I have not the pleasure—" & then I recognized Miss Mary, whom I had last seen on a visit to Arlington in 1858. Stuart, always full of fun & humor, & especially so when in the society of ladies, was almost convulsed at my embarrassment, & thought it the best joke in the world, both upon Miss Mary & myself. We never met afterward without his making some reference to it. But it was not a great many times—poor fellow—for the last was to be under the next blooming of a Spottsylvania apple tree as I will soon have to tell.

I had been in Richmond perhaps a week when I was sent for one morning by Gen. Mackall,[4] of the Adjt. Genl's. Dept., who had a proposition for me which took my breath away. Gen. Jos. E. Johnston had relieved Gen. Bragg of the command of the army, now at Dalton, Geo., which was, during the coming campaign, to contest the advance of Sherman from Chattanooga. Johnston was now straining every nerve to reorganise this army, demoralised by its defeat at Missionary Ridge, & to equip it & get it into condition for the heavy work it would have to encounter. And he had especially reported that his artillery was in bad condition, & had applied to have me promoted & sent to him as his chief of arty. Gen. Mackall asked me if I desired the position. I really did desire it very much. I would have been very proud of the promotion, & I would have felt infinite interest &

enthusiasm at having a larger command & a greater field in the arm which I loved & believed in. And I had served upon Gen. Johnston's staff for ten months in '61 & '62 & had both confidence in him & affection for him, & I knew the personal relations would be as pleasant as they possibly could be. Now that I look back at it, I think there was really no reason whatever why I should not have accepted with delight & gone at once. But I had always set up a sort of extra military notion, that I would never express any preference for orders, but only a desire to be placed wherever the interests of the service demanded. I believe I have already told of one or two other applications which had been made for me & of my refusing to express any preference. But, with my present experience of life, I think a man should not be such a passive instrument in the hands of fate, but should use common sense & judgment in taking the path which seems most in accordance with his tastes & abilities.

So I answered Gen. Mackall, rather foolishly, as I now think, that I would express no preference & the department must do as they thought best. I was then told to go, but return next day. The next day I was told that Prest. Davis would wait a few days before deciding, as Gen. Lee would be in the city & it was wished to confer with him, as our corps was considered a part of his army. Gen. Lee came, & paid me the high compliment of refusing to let me go. Mr. Davis afterward told Mrs. Lawton that I was "one of a very few whom Gen. Lee would not give to anybody." But to compensate me for any disappointment, I was immediately promoted to the rank which the appointment would have given me—brig. gen. of arty. Gen. Johnston remonstrated, & considered himself so badly used that he published the correspondence in his "Narrative" after the war (see appendix page ____),[5] as an instance of the unfair treatment which, as he claimed, he always received from President Davis. Some years after the war I was told by Gen. B. D. Fry that Gen. Johnston had once written him that he had never made special application for but two officers by name, Fry & myself, & that both applications were refused.

I have already written that at the battle of Gettysburg a great opportunity was lost of using the artillery of Ewell's corps to enfilade many of the batteries which fired upon Pickett's charge, & that the fault of this lay primarily with Gen. Pendleton, Gen. Lee's chief of artillery. He was too old & had been too long out of army life to be thoroughly up to all the opportunities of his position. But I never knew that Gen. Lee himself fully appreciated it, until I read the correspondence which Gen. Johnston published. Gen. Lee sends Gen. Pendleton to inspect Johnston's artillery, & says that, "if he wishes, he may keep Gen. Pendleton as chief." But Gen. [Johnston] did not wish & finally took Col. Beckham, an extremely nice & gallant young fellow from near Harpers Ferry, Va., who had graduated at

West Point just before the war & who had made a fine reputation for gallantry as chief of Stuart's horse artillery. And poor Beckham lost his life at the battle of Franklin.[6]

I did not worry at not getting the position at the time though I really *had hoped* for it, & surely I have no cause to regret it now. For, even had I come through safely, & with all the possible credit to have been made in that unfortunate army, I feel now that nothing on earth could take the place of the memories of that last great campaign, & of Appomattox. There was no such spectacular fighting, but I would as soon lose Chancellorsville or Gettysburg from my record & recollections, as Wilderness, Spottsylvania, Cold Harbor, or Petersburg. And now I can claim the old Army of Northern Virginia—from Bull Run to Appomattox, & if ever that is mustered in the next world there will be no question where I belong.

It was Wed., Mar. 2nd, when, with my new commission in my pocket, I took the cars for East Tennessee. With me went Gen. Field, recently promoted maj. gen., & now sent to command Hood's old division to the great disappointment of both the rival brigadiers, Jenkins & Law. Longstreet's headquarters were now in Greeneville, but I cannot recall whether the cars ran that far or not. But my old battalion, when I arrived, was out on an expedition, & I immediately followed them, & joined them near a place called Ball's Bluff on Sat., Mar. 5th. I had as warm a welcome & as hearty congratulations, almost, as if I had arrived at home. For, indeed, the old battalion was, now, like a home to me, & I had a real affection for every officer & man in it. Everything was going on nicely. They had had some uncomfortable moving & marching to do though no fighting. Provisions & forage had been fairly well supplied, & the horses were in very good condition. Forage trains, however, always had to be guarded as there were no end of bushwhackers in the mountains. Particularly there was a set known as Kirk's men, who claimed to be regularly enlisted in the Federal army, who frequently raided our trains, &, when successful, generally took no prisoners but killed drivers & all.[7] One of Capt. Parker's sergeants was captured by them, but had the good fortune in some way to win the favor of one of their leaders, & after being a prisoner for two weeks, & seeing some very cruel performances, he was allowed to escape.

We remained near Ball's Bluff until Tuesday, Mar. 8th, & then marched back to Greeneville where we made headquarters on the premises of a Mrs. West. Until now Longstreet's corps had never had a permanent chief of artillery, or any proper organisation for the general supervision & care of its battalions. They were generally expected to procure all supplies from the nearest division quartermasters, commissaries, & surgeons, & each battalion largely rustled for itself in all things, on the march & in camp; & when the time for fighting came Gen. Longstreet would generally give me temporary charge as has been before told. Now all that was to be changed. I was to organise a regular staff & supervise all the artillery battalions, in camp & march as well as in action, just as a division commander would his brigades. For awhile, I kept with my old battalion mess, & I have no memorandum & cannot recall exactly when I separated. And I got together my different staff officers, one by one, & cannot fix the date when any one of them entered upon his duties. But I finally got together as efficient, & as delightful & congenial a staff as heart could wish, & we all went through together, to the end, with only increasing confidence in, & affection for each other.

My personal staff who messed & tented with me were Jos. Haskell, adjt.; Winthrop, inspector; & Willie Mason my aid.[8] He was my wife's youngest brother—was only 17 years of age, & was a private in Breathed's battery of horse artillery, in which he had distinguished himself for his coolness & gallantry, when I applied for him as my aid.[9] He was very young-looking, even for his age, & he became a sort of favorite with the infantry of the corps, who got to know him & would frequently call after him on the road, "There goes Lieutenant Willie." My quartermaster & my surgeon were both South Carolinians, Maj. John I. Middleton of Georgetown & Dr. William Post of Charleston. My commissary was Capt. _____ Franklin of Bedford Co., Virginia.[10] The duties of these gentlemen required their having separate establishments but we usually all encamped in the same vicinity.

Frank Huger was promoted colonel of my old battalion & Capt. Parker was promoted major. Haskell was succeeded as adjt. of the battalion by Jimmy Grattan of Richmond.[11]

There is very little to tell about our stay in Tennessee. A great deal of discussion was going on in Richmond, as to our entering upon an offensive campaign,[12] between the president & the different generals. Gen. Longstreet proposed our making one through Cumberland Gap, but our limited resources I think would have soon brought such a move to grief. And the immense preparations of the enemy in Virginia soon made it clear that our corps would undoubtedly have to rejoin Gen. Lee.

Meanwhile, about the middle of March, the enemy below us made some hostile demonstrations, & on Tuesday the 15th I moved the battalion to a place called Midway, & reconnoitered for defensive positions at two gaps, Bull's & Taylor's, in a little chain of young mountains in the vicinity. But the enemy did not come, &, on Sunday [the] 20th, we returned to Greeneville, & now I got quarters at a Mrs. Crawford's. About now McLaws's court martial was going on, & also that of the Miss. surgeon already told of in my account of Gettysburg. We now had in operation what I think was an improved system for court martials. Instead of detailing a lot of officers away from their duties to compose a court, three military judges were appointed for each corps, & they composed a permanent court—two making a quorum. The principal charges against McLaws were as follows:[13]

At last on Mar. 27th our anticipations were realized, & orders were received to march the next morning for Bristol. The roads were fair & the weather good, & the march was a regular little picnic. Our only trouble generally was in getting enough to eat for our personal mess. Not that our appetites were especially phenomenal for soldiers, but there had been some new regulations, which, under the guise of liberality, really oppressed us dreadfully, from now to the very end of the war.

Following the custom of the old U.S. Army, for the first two years, or thereabouts, of the war, officers were not *given* any rations, but were permitted to buy, at cost, from the commissary whatever they required. Provisions were now getting so scarce that this privilege could not be kept up, & became liable to abuse. In fact the full ration of meat had been nearly cut in half long before this period, & it was even further reduced afterward. So the Confederate Congress passed a law giving each officer a ration in kind, but taking away the privilege of purchasing any. But we had to have servants to care for our horses, & to cook, &c., & no way was provided for us to feed them, except by dividing our own reduced rations with them. The result of this was that we were in a chronic state of doubly short rations, & obliged to supplement what we could draw from the commissary with something from somewhere. Our first recourse was to buying from citizens in the vicinity of the army, but that was a very poor reliance. Every officer's mess which had servants was in the same fix, & the country was harried with darkeys out buying up everything to eat. And Confederate money was going down in value, so fast that the country people were getting more & more unwilling to sell provisions for it at any price. Eventually our mess managed to scrape along by having boxes sent to us from the South; not with cake, or poultry, or luxuries, but with good fat bacon & cow peas. Both Joe Haskell & I were fortunate in having parents living in a section remote from troops & camps, & on their own plantations. After we got back to Virginia we received such boxes very frequently, & they helped us wonderfully.

Then we struck upon another idea. When a commissary issued beef to a command the head was left as a perquisite to the soldier who acted as butcher, & we discovered that the butcher generally did not seem to value it highly. Possibly he had liver or some other perquisite he liked better. At any rate we rarely had any difficulty in cheating a butcher out of a whole beef's head for a little old Confederate dollar. And when a beef's head is skinned & chopped up & boiled all day, if one is in camp, or all night if he is on the march, it makes a big camp kettle nearly full of one of the most delightful

& richest stews in the world. And if any of it is left, by merely fishing out the big bones, all the meat jellies together solid when it is cold—much resembling a forced meat dish, which, in my young days, we knew as "Pompey's head," & it at once becomes one of those open questions upon which a man can never exactly make up his mind. Whether he likes it best hot for breakfast or supper, or cold, & cut into slices, & carried in the haversack for lunch along the road. But one thing about it seems to me strange enough to be recorded. I have never wanted any more since the war. All the other camp dishes which I enjoyed then are more than welcome when I come across them now. Pea soup, cornbread & good sweet bacon, blackberry dumpling, &c. have never lost their charm. But I have never hankered for a beef's head since the war though it was inferior to none of the others during it.

In another way, too, we added a great deal to our menu. I have already told of my using chopped up bullets to shoot a wood cock at Tyner's Station. We afterward tried melting lead & pouring it through fine holes, punched in tin, into a bucket of water. This produced things like commas having tails to them, only longer, but we made shift with them for a while, until our Ordnance Department, at Richmond, offered to exchange a bag of regular shot, which they imported through the blockade for the purpose, for 100 lbs. of lead. We could get plenty of lead, opening the enemy's shrapnel which failed to explode, &, at times, picking up musket balls about the trenches, &, during this year, our mess sent in 700 lbs. & got seven bags of shot. Meanwhile quail, rabbits, & squirrels seemed to have become more abundant while man was out gunning principally for his fellow man, & with our pointer, Buster, & some old captured rifled muskets, we very often managed to get a little game. I carried, too, an English revolver, with which I became quite expert. Winthrop had brought it from England with him, but insisted on presenting it to me on my making a remarkable scratch shot with it one day. After that any quail, squirrel, or rabbit which showed itself along our line of march was very apt to become our meat.[14]

These reminiscences of our days of scant rations recall a piece of dream-poetry which came to me during this East Tennessee experience, but I think it was just before I went on furlough. At any rate it was at a time when the commissary was issuing no meat & for some days the quartermaster had been out of horse feed. I can recall the camp—in a wood on a slope, but not the exact place or date. I had a nightmare, dreaming that a young lady insisted that I should write a piece of original poetry in her album. I protested that I had never made a rhyme in my life, but she still insisted. In my despair an inspiration came and I wrote this:

Confederate Rations
For a man, corn bread, so-so!
Any bacon? No! No!
For a horse
O!

It will not write out as pretty a triangle, with zero for the inverted apex, as it seemed to make in my dream where the top line seemed naturally the longest & the others tapered regularly, but it was a production entirely out of the line of my waking accomplishments.

One of the anticipations with which we set out upon our march from Greeneville was that we would be able to buy some poultry, butter, eggs, honey, &c., along the road, & on the very first day we struck what seemed a rare opportunity. We came to a large & prosperous looking farm, & in a meadow near the house we saw a flock of fully fifty peacocks. Surely they would sell us some of them. The lady of the house agreed very cheerfully—almost too cheerfully, I thought, unless she was unusually strong in her Confederate sympathies, to sell us just as many as we could catch. I forget the price, but it cut no figure, for the whole mess was excited over the idea of peacock for dinner. We got together all our darkeys, Frank Huger's Dick, Joe Haskell's Jim, & my Charley, & we all tied our horses & started for the peacocks, fully intending to have a least a dozen of them, and maybe two. But when we all charged down on them together, we were treated to a surprise. At first the peacocks ran a little as if to get out of our way & not interfere with what we were doing; but, when they once appreciated that we meant business & were after them, the whole flock rose in the air like wild turkeys—only more easily, & flew off to a great wood, a quarter of a mile away, & lit high up in the tallest oaks & pines.

Then we began to understand the cheerfulness with which the lady agreed to sell, without limit, all that we could catch. But having, as it were, taken the contract to catch some, we were ashamed to go & mount our horses & go off without any, & as I had my revolver, I felt no doubt of getting some of them. Unfortunately, only three barrels were loaded, & I had no more cartridges with me, nor had anyone else either pistol or cartridge. My first shot brought down a fine big bird. But the bullet had mangled part of the flesh, & an idea occurred to me to prevent that with the others by shooting at a leg. If I shot one leg off, I thought the bird would come to the ground, & then we could easily catch him. So I picked out another fine bird, & making a good shot, I broke one leg all to bits. But instead of falling, the bird rose above the very tops of the trees & lit again on the very tip of the highest tree in the woods. Then I had but one cartridge left, &, having crippled him, I would have to pay for him whether we got him or not. That English pistol, however, had a fatal knack for anything alive. It would often miss at inanimate targets, but it seemed to be a sort of hoo-doo for anything with life in it. It enfiladed the peacock from tail to neck, not hurting the meat at all, & he fell with a thud like a bag of shot. So we paid for our two peacocks with dignity, as if that was all we desired to buy & rode on.

We encamped that afternoon on the outskirts of Jonesboro (about ____ miles),[15] in a pasture belonging to a Confederate General _____ Jackson. It was said that early in the war he had been designated as Mudwall Jackson to distinguish him from Stonewall, but that, having some engagements with the enemy, he had stood the pressure so remarkably well, that already he had been promoted to be "Brickwall Jackson."[16] As soon as we got into camp the cook had put one of the peacocks on to boil in a camp kettle. When he thought it nearly done, he came to the tent & was fixing the table, when we heard a rumpus at the fire & our peacock was gone again. An old sow had raided us & knocked over the camp kettle & run off with the peacock in her mouth. It was a small job however to overhaul her & rescue the bird, somewhat bitten about the breast, indeed, but still all there, so we sat down to the table. And then came out what I think was the *real* reason why the lady had so many peacocks, & was so willing to sell them. They are so phenomenally tough that it is simply impossible to eat them. We once, when quite hard up, tried a hawk for dinner, but a hawk is a spring chicken, or a regular squab, to a peacock. The first trouble is to carve him.

But just as we fully realized that we were practically dinnerless, a servant came down from Gen. Jackson's house with an invitation to the whole mess to come up to supper. Except, possibly, the supper at Mrs. Hull's in Atlanta in September, this was the red letter & blue ribbon supper of the war. Nice hot breads, delightful butter, sausage, spare ribs, fat chickens, & two of the prettiest, & most cordial, & sweetest young women whom I ever met in my life, to grace the table. The oldest was married (Mrs. _____) & I can recall to this day the pretty chestnut bloom that tinged the reflexions in her hair & the light in her eyes & the color in her cheeks. The youngest Miss _____ Jackson was just as pretty—the boys even thought her more so, & both were so natural & so full of life & fun, & the old general was so warm & hospitable, that we felt at home at once. And we stayed very, very late & we came back to breakfast in the morning, & parted as good friends as if we had been neighbors all our lives. And I am sure too that the friendship was mutual, for about 1890, when I was living in Savannah, the old general passing through there hunted me up & paid me a visit.[17]

The next night we encamped near the ford of the Watauga River, at the house of a man named Devaux, where I think we bought some honey. And I think it was Mrs. Devaux who gave me a poetical aphorism the truth of which I have often seen confirmed since. She asked if I were married & then if I had any children. When I told her that I had three, she said that she had heard it said, "With one you can run. With two, it will do. With three, you must stay where you be."

On Wednesday evening we encamped at a place called Camp Ground, near the railroad bridge over the Holston River, & on Thursday [the] 31st we forded the river & marched into Bristol—in all ____ miles from Greeneville.[18]

Of our stay in Bristol, nearly two weeks, I can recall little. I remember vaguely that some troops, Georgians I believe, arriving there a few days before & being out of rations had tried to raid a commissary store house, & the guard had resisted & some were shot. And I recall going to the funeral of a young officer, a Maj. Quarterman or some such name,[19] who had died at home near there from wounds received in battle somewhere. The family sat on the front seats, & the preacher, a backwoods specimen, made the most of their presence, pointing out each to the audience & describing the affliction of the "bereaved father & the heart-broken mother & the weeping sister." He was an old preacher & could not talk without shouting half the time, & using the old sing-song inflections, & the funeral was the most gruesome I ever attended.

My diary says our quarters were at Mrs. Moon's. I can recall nothing of the locality, but I remember receiving much hospitality & kindness from a *very* charming family named _____.[20] We all became very intimate, & we took off with us when we left their very nice young son, who was only 16 years old, as a private in one of my batteries. He was crazy to enter the army, & his mother begged me to take him as a courier with me. The only way to do it was to enlist him, & then detail him as courier, which I did. And I may as well tell here that he made a capital little soldier, & we kept him with us to the end of the war.[21] Once we thought we had lost him. At Second Cold Harbor we heard a bullet hit him, & he doubled up & said something to the effect that he was shot through the body. But it turned out that the bullet had only pierced his canteen. The warm water ran out & ran down his leg, & he thought it was blood. It was a close call, but a miss is as good as a mile & I'm very glad that his mother got him back.

At noon on Tuesday, April 12th, we took the cars for Charlottesville, Virginia, & arrived there on Thursday. We encamped in the University grounds where we remained for a week. We found very pleasant neighbors in an old friend of Manassas days, Col. Morton Marye.[22] He had lost a leg and was on some staff duty; had quarters in one of the professor's houses, with his charming wife & an exceedingly attractive sister in law, Miss

Emily Voss. And I recall visiting Monticello on a horse back ride with Miss Emily. I also recall a very pleasant evening at a country house near the town where Mrs. _____ the hostess,[23] whom I had once met in Washington City before the war, sang "Castles in the Air"[24]—the first time that I had ever heard it.

WILDERNESS
& SPOTTSYLVANIA

On Friday, April 22nd, we marched down to a locality called Mechanicsville (though I never saw any ville about there) five miles S.W. of Gordonsville & encamped in some light open woods. I shall have a criticism to make presently upon the selection of our campground. We were now at last reunited with the beloved old Army of Northern Virginia, for Gen. Lee's headquarters were only 14 miles away—two miles beyond Orange C.H., & Ewell's corps & Hill's were in their winter quarters holding the line of the Rapidan. We had been absent seven months, but it seemed a year & every one, officers & men, felt a keen personal delight in the re-union with our old comrades, & in the command of Gen. Lee. We all knew of the tremendous preparations of the enemy, & of the enormous odds we would have to face, under their new general, who had beaten all our people in the West, & we knew that rivers of blood must be poured out in the struggle. But we were only anxious for it to begin. We wanted to see Grant introduced to Gen. Lee & the Army of Northern Virginia, & to let him have a smell of our powder. For we knew that we simply could never be driven off a battle field, & that whatever force Grant brought, his luck would have to accommodate itself to that fact.

While we had been away there had been no battle, but there had been an interesting little campaign called the Mine Run campaign & I will suspend my personal narrative here to outline its principal features.[1]

Lee honored our return to his command with a review. It was the first review held since the Shenandoah Valley after Sharpsburg in '62. Gen. Lee was not given to parades merely for show. Now, I am sure, he felt & reciprocated the stirrings of that deep affection in the hearts of his men inseparable from our return upon the eve of what all felt must be the struggle to a finish. It was the last review he ever held, and no one who was present could ever forget the occasion. It took place in a cleared valley, with extensive pastures, in which our two divisions of infantry, & our guns, could be massed.

It is over 40 years but I can see now the large square gate posts, without gate or fence, marking where a broad country road lead out of a tall oak wood upon an open knoll, in front of the centre of our long grey lines. And as the well-remembered figure of Lee upon Traveller—at the head of his staff, rides between the posts, & comes out upon the knoll, my bugle sounds a signal, & my old battalion thunders out a salute, & the general reins up his horse, & bares his good gray head, & looks at us & we shout & cry & wave our battleflags & look at him again. For sudden as a wind, a wave of sentiment,[2] such as can only come to large crowds in full sympathy, something alike what came a year later at Appomattox, seemed to sweep over the field. Each man seemed to feel the bond which held us all to Lee. There was no speaking, but the effect was that of a military sacrament, in which we pledged anew our lives. Dr. Boggs,[3] a chaplain in Jenkins's brigade, said to Col. Venable, Lee['s] aid, "Does it not make the general proud to see how these men love him?" Venable answered, "Not proud, it awes him." He rode along our lines, close enough to look in our faces. And then we marched in review & went back to our camps. When he next saw those two divisions of infantry, at sunrise on the 6th of May, as I will soon be telling, he was in the most desperate strait he had ever known. And they knew that he was glad to see them coming, & a whirlwind could scarcely have cleaned up & driven back the advancing & victorious enemy more quickly than they did it.

The narrative may now pause while I give a brief account of the forces of the two armies. In all other campaigns there had been, as it were, "intermissions for refreshment," after every great battle. The actual fighting had only lasted on one occasion, the Seven Days, before Richmond, as much as a week.[4] The armies would separate, pause, recruit, & replenish, then, one or the other would initiate new strategy to lead up to another collision. Now, from the 5th of May, when Lee & Grant met in the Wilderness, until the next 9th of April, the two armies were under each other's fire every day. The struggle was without pause for over eleven months.[5] Grant was undoubtedly a great commander. He was the first which the Army of the Potomac ever had who had the moral courage to fight his army for what it was worth. He was no intellectual genius, but he understood arithmetic. The blackamoor in Mother Goose says:

> What care I how black I be?
> Twenty pounds will marry me.
> If twenty won't, forty shall;
> For I'm my mother's bouncing gal![6]

Similarly Grant knew that if one hundred thousand men couldn't two hundred thousand might, & that three hundred thousand would make quite sure[7] to do it. That was the game which he deliberately set out to play.

Perhaps here is the best place to refer to his policy of stopping the exchange of prisoners, which had heretofore been made.[8] To be sure, in every exchange he always got a man for every one he gave up to us, but he evidently thought our men worth more than man for man. And I like & admire Gen. Grant so that I am sorry to have to say that in this matter, he made use of a "Yankee trick" which is doubtless politically justifiable, but which has always seemed to me below his usual dignity & directness of character. He did not wish it known that the policy of non-exchange was his own, but tried deliberately to put the onus upon us.[9] We had perhaps unwisely outlawed Butler[10] for some of his orders at New Orleans when he was in command there. Grant's trick was avowedly to make Butler[11] the commissioner of exchange in hopes that we would not communicate with him. When we swallowed our pride & offered exchanges, pretences were always found to evade them. Pains were also taken to exaggerate & advertise the sufferings of the prisoners we were compelled to guard & feed in great numbers, & to inflame a sentiment against us which yet smoulders. Even records showing less mortality among Federal prisoners than among Confederate have not brought any general appreciation of real facts. I cannot here go into the details, but, in spite of our lack of food & medicines, & of men to guard great camps of prisoners without enforcing rigid discipline, Federal prisoners were nowhere less humanely treated by us than were the Confederate prisoners by their jailers.

The campaign against us, then, was to be practically one of extermination—to reduce our numbers at all costs. It was to be conducted by four separate armies & as much of the navy as could be used in the James River. First, Grant had north of the Rapidan four corps, the 2nd, 5th, 6th, & 9th, with about 144,000 men & 274 guns. Beside these, a siege train of 106 heavy guns & mortars was being prepared, among which were 6 one hundred pounder rifles. This train came into service in May and June. Of the whole force, 16,000 were cavalry & they were now armed entirely with breechloading magazine carbines, which fully doubled their efficiency against ours, with only muzzleloaders. It was useless, too, for us to capture their guns, for we could not provide the brass cartridges required.

Second, in the Shenandoah Valley, Sigel[12] was preparing a force which was to advance up that valley to Staunton. It comprised about 15,000 men & 40 guns. Third, from West Va., Crook[13] also was to move upon Staunton by the way of Lewisburg & the Va. Central R.R., with a force of about 9,000 men & 24 guns.[14] When Crook & Sigel had united they were to move upon Lynchburg & thence upon Richmond. Fourth, Butler at Fortress Monroe & Yorktown was organising the Army of the James to move upon Richmond along the south bank of that river. He was to be assisted by five monitors & a large fleet of gunboats. A great number of ferry boats &

other river craft were collected to facilitate movements by water in every direction. His forces included two corps, the 10th & 18th, with Kautz's cavalry,[15] in all 37,370 men with 88 guns, of whom about 5,000 were cavalry.

Beside these four armies there were about 40,000 men[16] in & about Washington City & Maryland which within the first two months of the campaign sent forward large reinforcements. Beside these a constant stream of recruits was coming to every regiment by enlistments all over the North stimulated by bounties of a thousand dollars per man. But the term of enlistment of perhaps 15,000 effectives was to expire within 60 days. In addition to these forces Gen. Grant also drew the 19th Corps from New Orleans early in July, about 12,000.[17]

Our forces at the opening of the campaign were as follows. Lee had with him our corps, the 1st, less Pickett's division, about 10,000 men; Ewell's corps, the 2nd, about 17,000; & A. P. Hill's, the 3rd, about 22,000, with about 8,000 cavalry & 4,500 artillery—in all about 62,000 men & 224 guns.

To meet the armies of Sigel & Crook, Gen. Breckinridge was able to muster in the Valley & in Southwest Virginia about ten thousand cavalry, artillery, & mounted infantry with about 25 guns.

To meet the Army of the James, Gen. Beauregard was brought to Petersburg & from various points in the South there was collected about 22,000 infantry organised into four divisions & about 2,000 cavalry with about 50 guns. These included Pickett's division & one of Early's brigades.

Altogether Grant was directing upon Richmond about 227,000 men & 582 guns. His regiments would all be constantly recruited under the stimulus of large bounties & he would be aided by a large fleet of ironclads & gunboats. Lee would oppose this force with about 92,000 men & 300 guns. His regiments could only be recruited, as Grant expressed it, by "robbing the cradle or the grave," & his men who were taken prisoners were forever lost.[18]

Before entering upon [the] narrative I wish to say something about our location, Mechanicsville, to which our corps was assigned upon its arrival from Tennessee, & where it was allowed to remain until the campaign opened. Confederate history has heretofore passed over the matter in silence, as if it were one of no consequence. But I have always believed it to have been one of those small matters upon which, finally, hung very great & important events. I have never known why Mechanicsville was selected for our location, unless it were because of its offering good camping grounds, in the matters of wood, water, & grass. But the objection to it, which should have been fatal, was its distance from our probable battle-field. At a conference with his division commanders on May 2nd held on Clark's

Mountain, overlooking the Rapidan, Lee stated his belief that Grant would attempt to turn our right flank exactly as he did. But Mechanicsville was far behind our *left flank,* fully 33 miles in an air line & 43 by the roads we had to use from the first battlefield. Consequently the first day's battle was necessarily fought without our presence. The first day, naturally, offered us far the greatest chances. Grant's army was not all in hand, & had had no time to make breastworks. It was at a great disadvantage in the Wilderness & could not utilize its superiority in artillery. We had here the one rare chance of the whole campaign to involve it in a panic such as ruined Hooker on the same ground. That we would have stood fair chances will fully appear in the narrative of what we did accomplish, on the second day, when we did go in. And we might just as easily have been located where we would have been the first troops on the field, instead of the last.

Indeed in view of the great probabilities that Grant would move upon our right flank very early in May, it does not seem that there would have been any serious difficulty in having both Hill & Ewell out of their winter camps and extended a few miles in that direction & Longstreet's corps even as far down as Todd's Tavern. What proved a drawn battle when begun by three divisions reinforced by two more after six hours & by three more 18 hours later might have proved a decisive victory if fought by all eight from the beginning. I think this is but one more illustration of one of the inherent weaknesses of our army in its lack of an abundance of trained & professional soldiers in the staff corps to make constant studies of all matters of detail. The enemy were far ahead of [us] in that, & they owed their final success to the precision with which they combined some of their great movements, which are models of logistics—the science of moving armies.

And now we may hunt up our narrative again. When we went to Tennessee we left Cabell's & Henry's battalions of artillery behind us. They were still with the army & now rejoined us. Henry's was now commanded by Lt. Col. Jno. C. Haskell, who had been its major.[19] We had also brought Leyden's battalion with us & altogether I now had about 74 guns. Leyden resigned from ill health about this time or soon after or was transferred, & Maj. Wade Hampton Gibbes was sent to command the battalion in his place. I should also note that Gen. Kershaw had been made a maj. gen. & was now in command of McLaws's division.[20] He had been one of its most distinguished brigadiers & was of the highest type, both of a gentleman & a soldier.

On the morning of May 4th, one of our mess, Willie Mason I think, had returned from a day or so in Richmond, & had extravagantly brought up some fine fat roe shad for our mess. While it was being cooked for dinner the orders came. Grant was crossing the Rapidan below our right flank, & everything was ordered to hasten in that direction. I have described the thick Wilderness country in telling about Chancellorsville. Grant was crossing now at Germanna Ford & below, just where Hooker had crossed, & was marching through the Wilderness for the more open country beyond. Lee marched to strike him at the earliest possible moment by every road by which he could reach him. Ewell's corps took the old Turnpike, nearly parallel to the river & about 3 miles south of it. He started about 10 A.M. & he had about 18 miles to go. Hill's corps took the Plank Road about 2 miles south of the Turnpike. H. started about noon & had about 28 miles to go. Our corps, as I have before told, should have been where it could come in, promptly upon the Brock Road, & take in flank the forces fighting Hill & cut off those fighting Ewell. The Wilderness was our favorite fighting ground. The enemy's enormous force of artillery was there only in his way. Never was a better chance offered Gen. Lee, & never was a chance more quickly snapped at. But the one trouble was that we were so many miles away. It took longer for the orders to reach us, & we were only able to start about 4 P.M. with about 42 miles to go by the road used. It was 6 miles shorter by Orange Courthouse & the Plank Road, but we had to leave that road for Hill.

At four o'clock everything was on the road with orders to march all night, & until stopped on the road during the next day, only halting for such rest & feed as necessary to keep the horses from being broken down. Between midnight & daylight my staff & myself turned out into a wood & laid down under the trees & slept. Then the march was resumed & kept up until about 4 P.M. when the whole corps went into bivouac. We were then near Craig's Meeting house,[21] on the Catharpin Road, about 36 miles from Mechanicsville by the roads we had come. Just before we went into bivouac we passed a few bodies of Federal cavalrymen, freshly killed, showing that the enemy was, now, not very far away. We were ordered to cook, eat, & rest until 1 A.M., when we were again to march, having a very fair late risen moon—& our destination, I understood, was to be Todd's Tavern. But[22] my recollection is that before we started orders were received from Gen. Lee directing us to strike across to the Plank Road at Parker's Store & come in behind Hill's corps. At any rate[23] we took that route, and, at some place where there was a fork in the road, the leading division took the wrong road for a little ways & thus lost about its length in distance while the rear division lost none. It resulted that when we finally got out in the broad straight Plank Road at Parker's Store at daylight the heads of the two marching flanks were right abreast of each other, & the two sets of fours gave a front of 8 men to the column, which between dawn & sunrise came swinging fast down that road. I was at the front with Gen. Longstreet & the different battalions were some in & some behind the column.

And now I must let my story pause & tell what had taken place on May 4 & 5th. This was the 3rd campaign which the enemy had tried in the

Wilderness within 13 months. They, therefore, knew its geography & physical features & could form a very fair estimate of the difficulties they had to meet & the best ways of overcoming them. Their problem was to pass our flank & get between us & Richmond. Celerity was therefore a matter of prime importance to them. A careful study was made of the matter for weeks before hand, exact preparations were made & minute instructions prepared for every command. The hour of starting was fixed for midnight on the 3rd, & before that date the cavalry & pontoon trains were moved to the vicinity of the crossings selected, & guards were even placed over all the residents in the neighborhoods affected lest they should convey any information to us. The result of all their careful preparation was that within 18 hours after they started 120,000 men, with their artillery & fighting trains, had made a march of 20 miles & put themselves in selected positions, crossing a river on five pontoon bridges of their own building, & all in the face of the enemy & without mishap or interruption. They might easily have made five or six miles more, but purposely encamped for the night of the 4th in close order, for the Ninth Corps & the great bulk of their subsistence & ordnance trains were still behind.

This was really the most critical day of their whole enterprise, & to their great relief it closed without their seeing a Confederate. Gen. Grant said that his most serious apprehensions were removed now that so large a force was safely across. It might have been possible for Gen. Ewell to have come in contact with the Federal advance before sundown in the afternoon, but as the strength of a chain is only that of its weakest link, so the swiftness of a concentration of troops is only that of the approach of its most distant part. Ewell therefore was expressly ordered to go slowly down the pike, to permit A. P. Hill to get abreast of him in the Plank Road, on his right, & both were directed not to bring on a general engagement until Longstreet arrived. So Ewell encamped for the night of the 4th at Locust Grove, on the old Turnpike, five miles from Wilderness Tavern, which was about the centre of the Federal line & three miles from his battlefield of the next day. Hill's advance division, Heth's, encamped at Mine Run seven miles west of Parker's Store & 10 from his battlefield of the next day. But we—as has already been told—were at sun down but a few miles out from Gordonsville & near 30 miles away.

On the 5th both armies were in motion very early. Grant's forces were to move out towards the west—the direction from which our forces were expected, & to take a line of battle from Locust Grove on their right by Parker's Store to Shady Grove Church. They had not expected us to reach any of those localities before 10 A.M. at the earliest, because we had not done so on the Mine Run campaign in November. [Figure 31 appears here in the manuscript.]

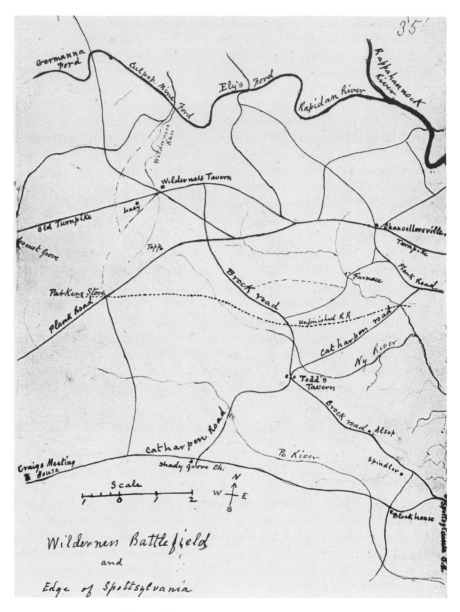

35

Germanna Ford
Culpep. Mine Ford
Ely's Ford
Rapidan River
Rappahannock River
Wilderness Run
Wilderness Tavern
Lacy
Old Turnpike
Locust Grove
Tapp
Chancellorsville
Turnpike
Plank Road
Furnace
Parker's Store
Plank Road
Brock road
Unfinished R.R.
Cat harpon road
Ny River
Todd's Tavern
Brock road. Alsop
Catharpen Road
Po River
Spindler
Craigs Meeting House
Shady Grove Ch.
Black house
Spottsylvania C.H.

Scale
1 0 1 2

N
W E
S

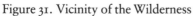

Wilderness Battlefield
and
Edge of Spottsylvania

Figure 31. Vicinity of the Wilderness

But now at 7 A.M. the 5th Corps met our 2nd Corps, Ewell's, within 2 miles of Wilderness Tavern. Ewell had his whole corps with him, all 3 divisions, about 17,000 men. Grant promptly appreciated that the rest of our army was not yet up & determined to overwhelm Ewell before they could arrive. So he at once turned on him the whole of the 5th Corps, about 26,000 men, & over one half of the 6th Corps, say 13,000 more. It did indeed seem that Ewell must prove easy fruit to these tremendous odds, for he had no intrenchments & no possible reinforcements, & he was strung out on the march. There was, too, in his vicinity a good deal of open ground in front of the Lacy house, giving the enemy chance of using a large force of artillery. It is not surprising that as their successive divisions deployed, & attacked Ewell from different directions, some of his brigades were, in the early part of the action, out-flanked & thrown into temporary confusion. The fighting did not become heavy until perhaps eleven o'clock[24] as it required time to get the troops into position through the woods, but from that hour until dark put an end to it Grant urged the fighting to the utmost. Fighting was his strong point & he made his headquarters near the Lacy house, where much of the fight with Ewell was under his own eye.[25] And dear, glorious, old, one-legged Ewell, with his bald head, & his big bright eyes, & his long nose (like a wood cock's as Dick Taylor said),[26] sat back & not only whipped everything that attacked him but he even sallied out on some rash ones & captured two guns & quite a lot of prisoners. In between the attacks & during the night he intrenched himself nicely. That was the first that Gen. Grant ever saw of the fighting of the Army of Northern Virginia, and, good soldier as he was I am sure that he must have admired it mightily.

Now we will see what happened with Hill. When he reached Parker's Store he found the enemy's cavalry there, but he drove them ahead of him, & followed them down the road. Meanwhile, Grant early in the morning, when he first discovered Ewell so close at hand, had halted Hancock, who was marching down the Brock Road, & recalled him to the Plank Road so as to have his whole force well in hand for whatever might happen. Also about 11 A.M. he had ordered the remainder of the 6th Corps to advance up the Plank Road so as to get on Ewell's flank.

As the latter already had enough to occupy him it was very well for him that about noon, Hill, driving the cavalry ahead of him, encountered the skirmishers of the smaller half of the 6th Corps, moving toward Ewell. Being under orders not to encourage fighting until Longstreet arrived, Hill halted & formed a line of battle but did not attack. He only had with him, at first, Heth's division, say 7,000 men, but Wilcox with about as many more were following close behind.[27] Grant was promptly notified of Heth's arrival. Knowing that Longstreet had to march from beyond Gordonsville, & could not possibly arrive that day, he became all the more earnest to destroy both Hill & Ewell before night. So the whole of the 2nd Corps, 28,000, & the smaller half of the 6th, about 11,000, were ordered to attack Hill's 14,000. But although urged to lose no time about it, so as to stand no chance of Longstreet's arrival, Gen. Hancock delayed for an hour or two to complete some intrenchments which had been already started by the 6th Corps, & by some of his own divisions, that morning, wishing to have something to fall back upon in case of disaster. This delay was doubtless of great importance to Hill, in enabling him to deploy & partially select his ground, & to utilize what logs he could pick up & place, so that his men could lie down behind them. The fact is that delay was awful bad play for the Federals. May 4th would have been *our day* if we had been there to utilize its opportunities. May 5th was Grant's day. Every hour of its daylight was to him a golden opportunity to crush an inferior enemy which had rashly ventured within his reach. May 6th was going to be anybody's day, after Longstreet arrived. Time would no longer cut any figure. And Grant seems to have fully appreciated the matter, himself, from the first, & to have urged his people to the utmost, but without getting more than half speed, sometimes, out of them.

Hancock's intrenchments did, indeed, prove very valuable on the 6th, but I firmly believe his stopping to build them lost him a victory on the 5th.

Hill's line of battle was square across the Plank Road, one brigade on its left, the other three on its right. On the left, just behind him, was a forty acre clearing[28] grown up in small pines & broom grass, & a small house, the Widow Tapp's. Poague's battalion of artillery took position here & Gen. Lee & Gen. Hill made their headquarters by it. It was about two miles from the Lacy house where Grant was.

During the delay Wilcox's division arrived & was posted on Hill's left flank & almost at right angles, extending back towards Ewell's battle, but with a gap between of near a mile.

At last, at 4:15 P.M., Hancock being at last all good & ready, the Assyrians came down like the wolf on the fold, on poor Heth. Hill very soon appreciated that the force attacking him was greater than he could long resist alone, & he recalled Wilcox from his left & brought him directly up to the support of Heth. There never was more desperate fighting than now ensued & continued until darkness put an end to it. The Wilderness hid our small numbers from the enemy & their great numbers from our men. When Wilcox's men came to Hill's support they, at first, passed in front, & made some attacks, but finally fell back pretty much into the same line. There they generally laid flat on the ground & fired through the thicket & the enemy failed whenever they attempted to advance in the face of that fire. But night did not terminate the fighting any sooner than Hill needed it. His men were exhausted, his ammunition low, his lines disarranged & ragged,

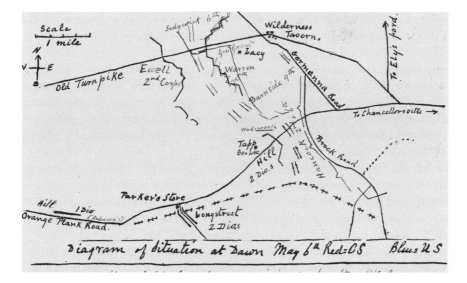

Figure 32. Battle of the Wilderness at dawn, 6 May 1864

sometimes disconnected, & sometimes facing in different directions. Fresh brigades of the enemy were making their way around him, & if Hancock could have recalled the daylight he had wasted, even the force he had at hand would probably have wrought disaster to the two gallant divisions in spite of their glorious resistance.

But besides this ruin impending on their front & right, a regular dead-fall was being set over them on their left. Gen. Warren, while fighting Ewell & hunting around his flank, had discovered Wilcox's division in its temporary location, & he also saw its withdrawal to go to Heth's assistance. He at once prepared a strong force to move in that direction & attack Heth in flank & rear, sending Wadsworth's whole division, & Baxter's brigade,[29] probably 8,000 men. Darkness overtook Wadsworth within a few hundred yards of Hill's flank, & his whole command bivouaced where they halted, ready to move on in the morning.

That was the state of affairs at dark & it was because of Hill's desperate condition that Gen. Lee sent orders to Longstreet to divert his march from Todd's Tavern, & to bring him down the Plank Road, even though Gen. Lee was not aware of the Wadsworth dead-fall, now ready to drop on Hill's left. [Figure 32 appears here in the manuscript.]

During the night Grant was joined by the 9th Corps, Burnside's, about 24,000 strong, including one division of Negroes. He ordered the three white divisions to the centre of his line; one to be held in reserve, & the other two to penetrate the gap of about a mile between Hill & Ewell.

During the night Hill's troops could hear noises indicating that the enemy were forming in the woods near at hand for an attack. But little could be done at night & in the darkness, either in rectifying their lines, or in making breastworks. Perhaps less was done than might have been, because the men expected to be relieved by Longstreet at or before daylight. And, surely, they deserved relief after their long march & four hours of such bloody fighting as they had done.

It is now dawn, 5 A.M. on Friday, May 6th, 1864. The opening movements in all campaigns are those most likely to present opportunities for one antagonist to catch the other in detail. As before stated May 4 was our best chance had we anticipated it & started a few days beforehand to prepare. But as we did not Grant had his innings on the 5th. He did not fail for lack of trying as is abundantly shown by the river of blood he shed, but the superb fighting of Hill & Ewell balked him. But even at 5 A.M. on the 6th he still had one hour left & one chance so good that it seems almost a certainty had he ventured it.

One of the reasons why he did not, & perhaps the principal one is that he had been deceived in some way by some false information. He believed that our absent division, Pickett's, had rejoined us & he therefore overestimated our strength & was uneasy about his left flank—on the Brock Road at the crossing of the unfinished railroad. Consequently he kept there idle this morning Barlow's division[30] & a large force of artillery. The railroad bed was a good road & would have brought them past our flank & into our rear, & given them opportunities too large to estimate. That they were all lost is a striking illustration of the great good which may be accomplished by one innocent little lie.

But, even without Barlow, it looked for awhile that morning as if the last hour of Heth & Wilcox had come. Grant had ordered his lines everywhere to assault at 5 A.M. At that time we were just about turning into the Plank Road at Parker's Store & very soon we began to hear from the front & left those grand roars of musketry & quick thunders of artillery which announce that the god or demon of war is about to hold one of his great carnivals.

As to what took place on the left, I can make a very short story of all the morning. Gen. Ewell was attacked by Sedgwick & Warren fiercely & frequently from 5 A.M. until about 11 A.M. He had improved his lines during the night, & gotten in more of his artillery, & he repelled every attack without any trouble & with severe loss to the enemy. By 11 o'clock all the fight was taken out of them, & Grant ordered them to give it up. But they were ordered to set to work & strengthen their own breastworks, so that a portion of their forces could be withdrawn & used elsewhere, & to help in this a brigade of engineer troops was sent to assist them.

But there is a very different story to tell of what happened to Hill's two divisions while we were marching the three miles, on the Plank Road, which separated us from them at dawn. Not only was the Wadsworth dead fall sprung upon their left flank at five o'clock, but their right flank was also far over lapped by Hancock's assaulting columns. The fight that they made was desperate, but it was not of long duration. The two extreme flanks, being taken in reverse, were soon rolled up toward the centre, & the men, appreciating that their position was no longer tenable, fell back from both sides into the Plank Road & came pouring past the Tapp house, & Gen. Lee & Poague's guns which were among the small pines. That was, I think the most critical moment which Gen. Lee's fortunes had yet known. Gen. McGowan afterward told me of an interview which he had with the general as he passed. Gen. Lee rode up to him & said, "My God! Gen. McGowan is this splendid brigade of yours running like a flock of *geese?*"

McGowan answered, "No, General! The men are not whipped. They just want a place to form and they are ready to fight as well as ever." And, indeed, the bearing of the men full confirmed McGowan's statement, that they were not whipped out of their positions, but only flanked out.

For now I may resume the narrative[31] & tell what I saw of the retreat of Heth's & Wilcox's divisions as I rode with Gen. Longstreet's staff at the head of our double column. When we still had, perhaps, a half mile to go I noted that we seemed to be passing some troops being marched in the opposite direction. Our two divisions, marching 8 abreast & file closers & mounted officers on the sides, nearly filled the road, & the troops going west were crowded to each side along the edge of the woods. But they went along nonchalantly & in such apparent order that I, & those about me, supposed them to be, perhaps, a reinforcement being sent to Ewell.

After awhile, we saw an excited officer[32] on horse back apparently trying to stop some of them. Jos. Haskell, who had the useful faculty of knowing every man whom he had ever seen before, said, "Major what's the matter. Are not those men being marched back?" "No! God damn 'em!" swore the major. "They are running!" They were, indeed, the men of Heth's & Wilcox's divisions, not running but now so mixed up as to be aware that they could be of no use until they had an opportunity to sort themselves out again into their respective commands. We could now tell too that the firing was approaching, particularly in the woods on the right flank, & as we approached the Tapp field, of small pines & broom grass, on the left, bullets began to whistle from the woods on the right, square across the road, & some also seemed to come directly from the front. Two or three guns among the pines (I could not see exactly how many) were firing square to their front. The head of our infantry column took the double quick, & soon after commands were shouted, "Forward into Line!" & Kershaw on the right & Field on the left began to form their leading brigades in line of battle. We had arrived in time but it was a pretty close call. In fact, there had now been three close calls. When Hill came & stopped Getty33 going for Ewell's flank; when night stopped Wadsworth on Hill's flank; & this, which was the closest of all, but the last, for now we were all up & united.

Field's leading brigade was Gregg's Texans, a very small brigade, only about 800 strong. It did not take them long to form line, &, as the bullets were now coming faster, they were ordered forward at once, while Benning's Georgians, the second brigade, began to form & Law's Alabamians with them. As the Texans started Gen. Lee rode up. They saw him & gave a cheer. The old man, with the light of battle in his eyes, & in the joy of seeing them arrive, rode up behind their line, following them in the charge. At once the men began to shout, "Lee, go back! Lee to the rear," & when he still rode on, a major took his horse by the bridle, & someone pointed out Gen. Longstreet to him, whom he had not yet seen, & he was in that way pulled off. The Texans caught the worst of it. They lost nearly half their men in a little while, & then Benning came to help them & then Law's Alabamians, and, meanwhile on the right of the road, Kershaw, who always looked like a gamecock, & now more so than ever, swarmed into the woods with his whole division. It was but a little after six o'clock when the terrific crashes of musketry, which began to burst out afresh in our front over the general roar of the morning, told Hancock & Meade & Grant that Longstreet had arrived. Hancock's advance was everywhere checked, & he sent for reinforcements. Everything possible was done to aid him. Sedgwick & Warren were ordered to push Ewell more fiercely. Burnside's two divisions, set to explore the gap between Hill & Ewell, & not yet engaged, were urged to hurry up & fight something. His reserve division, Stevenson's34 was sent direct to Hancock. Even Barlow, specially charged with protecting the left flank, was to come to the firing on our right, & Gen. Sheridan was ordered to administer a division of cavalry to our right flank.

Sedgwick & Warren only suffered more severely when they attacked Ewell harder. Burnside's people, in the centre, were so tangled in the woods, that they could get nowhere. Stevenson joined Hancock all right, & served with him the rest of the day. From the left two brigades were sent— but Barlow was uneasy over some false alarms, of our people being about to attack him right then & there. Gen. Stuart, indeed, did make some strong demonstrations with artillery & dismounted cavalry. And when Sheridan sent two brigades of cavalry, as ordered, Stuart repulsed them & they were recalled. Meanwhile, Anderson's div. of Hill's corps had joined us, some

8,000 men,³⁵ soon after our arrival, & they were placed mostly on our left of the road, over towards the gap still open between us & Ewell. This gap was finally closed, by the way, about noon by Heth's & Wilcox's divisions which had meanwhile been re-formed.

When I first met Gen. Lee after our arrival, he directed me to send back all the artillery with our column to Parker's Store, as there was no possibility of using it in the woods where we were fighting, & it would be in the way. I rode back, saw it all collected & properly placed, & then I returned & remained with Gen. Longstreet, to see all that went on. About 9 o'clock, Hancock having gotten his lines straightened & re-formed, & his reinforcements in hand, made another supreme effort, hoping, too, to have Burnside co-operate on his right. He put in about five whole divisions, & maintained the attack for about an hour & a half, but was repulsed every where, though we had, practically, then no breastworks, nor did we have to use all of the force we had at hand. About ten o'clock, Gen. Lee's chief engineer, Gen. M. L. Smith³⁶ reported that the enemy's left flank did not extend a great ways in the wood, & suggested a flank movement—something like Stonewall Jackson's movement upon Hooker on May 2nd, '63, only more quickly executed. Col. Moxley Sorrel, Gen. Longstreet's adjutant general who had been with Gen. Smith, was appointed to conduct it, & four brigades were assigned to it—Wofford's³⁷ & Anderson's Georgians, of our corps, & Mahone's Virginians & Davis's Mississippians & North Carolinians of Hill's corps, all under command of Gen. Mahone.

It was near 11 A.M. when they were fully started out, & about that time Gen. Longstreet directed me to go in person & find Gen. Stuart's cavalry, out on our right flank, & confer with him, & see if there was any opportunity for me to get a position for guns in that quarter. As I started on this errand I passed Jenkins's brigade halted in the road, & loading their muskets. I shook hands with Jenkins & said, "Old man, I hope you will win that next grade this morning." "Well," he said, turning toward his men, "we are going to fight for old South Carolina today, aren't we boys?" Through various old woods roads, I made my way to the right, & soon found Gen. Stuart. He took me all along his picket lines, but the country was generally thick & flat, & there was no chance. One incident I recall was our skirting an open field, with a pine thicket on the far side, say 200 yards off. Gen. Stuart thought that Federal pickets held the pines, & turning to a courier with him, said, "Ride out there & see if you can draw any fire." The courier had scarcely shown himself when there were several shots, & he came back with a bullet through his horse's nose. And it seemed as if the horse resented it, for he kept up a constant snorting & blowing blood on Stuart & myself as long as we were together.

Probably I was gone about two hours on this trip. As we regained the

Plank Road, on my return, we passed a tent which had just been pitched, & Jos. Haskell saw a surgeon there whom he knew, & stopped to speak to him. Soon he galloped after, & overtook me, with the news of the terrible calamity which had happened while we were away. Gen. Jenkins was dying in the tent at which Joe stopped, & Longstreet had been shot through the throat & was desperately—perhaps mortally wounded. And it was all done by our own men! By some strange fatality the flank movement, patterned after Jackson's of the year before in the same vicinity, had had the same brilliant success in routing the enemy in a panic, & the same melancholy termination, in the fall of the commander at the moment of pressing his advantage, by a volley from his own men.

This is what had happened. Sorrel conducted Mahone's force out to the unfinished railroad, lying there on the flank of each combatant, with a great opportunity for whoever would use it first. Mahone formed & charged [and] struck the enemy in flank. They were already about whipped out by the direct resistance they had met, & he rolled them up like a scroll. Those who made resistance only fared the worse for it in the end. Gen. Longstreet soon appreciated that he had the enemy "on the jump," & determined to press the panic to the utmost. The time was ripe for it & the opportunity far more favorable than the one presented to Jackson. In his case he had very little daylight left, & all the rest of Hooker's army was fresh, & had scarcely fired a shot. But here nearly the whole of Grant's army was already fought to a standstill.

At any rate Longstreet intended to play his hand for all it was worth, & to push the pursuit with his whole force. One of his best & largest brigades was still fresh, Jenkins's, & he put himself at its head, & pushed rapidly down the Plank Road. Kershaw was to follow & was riding with them concerting measures. Mahone's force was in the woods on their right in line nearly parallel to the Plank Road & scarcely a hundred yards off. They had been firing at retreating Federal commands not long before, but the firing had ceased. Suddenly a few shots were heard on the left or north of the road. A few scattered ones & then a volley came in reply from about a regiment of Mahone's. Jenkins's men were loaded & they faced & were about to answer it. Kershaw shouted, "Friends. They are friends," & all stopped & laid down.[38] [Figures 33 and 34 appear here in the manuscript.]

From the accounts of those who participated in this attack, experienced soldiers such as Gen. Mahone & others, & from details learned from prisoners, I have always believed that, but for Longstreet's fall, the panic which was fairly under way in Hancock's corps would have been extended & have resulted in Grant's being forced to retreat back across the Rapidan. The following extract is from Gen. Humphreys, Meade's chief of staff, & one of the greatest soldiers whom the war produced, on either side:[39]

Figure 33. Brig. Gen. Micah Jenkins

Gen. McAllister[40] found himself with a fire on his front, flank, & rear, under which his line broke, & fell back in confusion, to the intrench-ments on the Brock Road. The confusion extended to the adjoining troops. Gen. Hancock, whose bearing on the field had so powerful an influence on his command, endeavored to restore order, & reform his line of battle along the Orange Plank Road, retaining his right, as it was then, in front of Field & Anderson, but was unable to do so, owing to the great difficulty of adjusting lines under fire in such a dense forest, & to the partial disorganisation of the troops, most of whom had been engaged since five o'clock in the morning under heavy musketry fire. Consulting with Gen. Birney it was deemed advisable to withdraw to the breast-

Figure 34. Maj. Gen. Joseph Brevard Kershaw

works on the Brock Road, which was accomplished & the troops reformed in two lines of battle, on the ground from which they had advanced to the attack in the morning. The enemy pushed forward to within a few hundred yards of the breastworks but did not assault them.

Longstreet's fall seemed actually to paralyse our whole corps. When I returned from my trip to the flank, I was told that Gen. Field was in command, & it was said that the attack which Longstreet was about to make was going to be followed up. I don't recall seeing Gen. Lee about. I think he must have been on a visit to Ewell.

At any rate, nothing was done until about four o'clock, & then it seemed more like an apology for the attack that Longstreet was conducting, than anything really calculated to produce results. Only Field's & Anderson's divisions took part, & Law was absent from Field's, & Perry[41] from Anderson's. The enemy had now had several hours of rest & quiet. And yet, in spite of all that, & of their excellent intrenchments, & of some artillery that they had brought up, poor Jenkins's South Carolina boys, who had been loading their guns in the morning, & whom Longstreet was leading to the attack when he & Jenkins were shot, actually carried the breastworks in front of them & planted their colors & held them for quite a while, although no good was to be accomplished by it. They were led in this charge by my great personal friend, Gen. Bratton,[42] who succeeded Jenkins in their command. This attack ought *never, never* to have been made. It was sending a boy on a man's errand. It was wasting good soldiers whom we could not spare. It was discouraging pluck & spirit by setting it an impossible task. During the morning the woods had taken fire, & on part of the enemy's line the log breastworks were actually blazing when the attack was made. On the 5th, they had caught fire on Ewell's front, & some 200 of the Federal wounded were burned & smothered in them.

I must go back a few hours to tell that Burnside's two divisions, which started out at 5 A.M., & got tangled in the woods, did finally, at 2 P.M., find Law's & Perry's brigades, & had a temporary success with them. But Wofford's brigade came to their help, & turned the tables completely, & recovered the original Confederate line. And, finally, Ewell ended the day by letting Gen. Gordon undertake a flanking expedition which he had planned & which he carried out so successfully as to capture two brigadiers, Generals Shaler & Seymour[43] & about 1,000 prisoners—& created great temporary excitement among the enemy. So Ewell's corps carried off the honors of the engagement, in the capture of guns & prisoners.

The casualties are given as follows. Those of the Confederates are only estimates as no exact reports exist.

	Killed	Wounded	Missing	Total
US	2,246	12,037	3,383	17,666
CS	1,956	10,444		12,400

Beside Gen. Jenkins we had killed Gen. J. M. Jones & L. A. Stafford, both in Ewell's corps in the early part of the fighting. Wounded we had Generals Longstreet, Pegram, Benning, & Perry. The Federals had killed Genls. Wadsworth [and] Hays & wounded Gens. Carroll [and] Baxter.[44] [Figure 35 appears here in the manuscript.]

To return, now, to more personal narrative of May 7th. As I was still forbidden to bring up any guns, during the afternoon I had nothing to do but to keep near the corps headquarters in readiness for anything which might turn up. The only incident of that afternoon, which I recall, was the

Figure 35. Lt. Gen. Richard Heron Anderson

seeing in the woods, a little ways north of the Plank Road, the Federal Maj.
Gen. Wadsworth lying mortally wounded under the screen of a rubber
blanket held up by some muskets. He had been shot through the brain &
was unconscious, but was alive, & had gotten his finger on the trigger of
one of the muskets & was picking & playing with it. The next day, Gen.
R. H. Anderson—who was A. P. Hill's senior maj. general, was sent to our
corps as its commander, pro. tem., until Longstreet's recovery & return to
duty. This did not occur until the next December. The bullet struck in the
front of his throat & passed out in the back of the neck. It cut the nerves

which controlled the right arm, & afterward Gen. Longstreet had no use of that arm & carried it in a sling.[45]

Gen. Dick Anderson was as pleasant a commander to serve under as could be wished, & was a sturdy & reliable fighter. He had been one of our division commanders before the 3rd Corps was organised, so we were no strangers to him. As I think of him, my memory harks back to the first time I ever saw him. About the end of August 1858, Duane & I, with 60 sappers, were marching back from Utah & encamped one night on a stream, the Big Sandy, about fifty miles west of the South Pass of the Rocky Mountains.[46] We had no idea of any white man being within some hundreds of miles, when about sunset we heard the faint notes of a bugle from about 2 miles down the stream. I rode down to investigate & found in camp Capt. Dick Anderson, of the 2nd Dragoons, & his company—about 40 men—on their way out to Utah. I had known of him, for my classmate, Tom Berry, had served with him & had often mentioned him in his letters. And particularly he had told me of their once having for breakfast a fried rattlesnake & some boiled nettles for greens.

On the 7th, Saturday, it was evident that both parties were intrenched & that neither would attack. There was no movement, & nothing but sharpshooting. I remember extensive fires in the woods, & rumors that more of the enemy's wounded, who had not been all found & removed by our people, & some, perhaps, between the lines, were burned in them. Toward sundown our corps received orders to march at night for Spottsylvania C.H. Gen. Grant was preparing to do the same thing, & had put his trains in motion at 3 P.M., in order to have the roads clear for his troops at 8. It is probable that our cavalry saw some of these trains & reported some movement as on foot, & Gen. Lee could easily guess the rest.

In this renewed effort to get past our flank, Grant gave us further experience of his qualities as a general. Both Burnside & Hooker had given up their campaigns, & recrossed the river, after less severe & bloody repulses than Grant had received in the Wilderness. But he, without hesitation, made all his arrangements on the 7th to give us the slip at night, & let us find him established on our flank, & practically between us & Richmond in the morning. That was his little game, & not a bad one. Fortunately, Gen. Lee correctly anticipated it, & the night was devoted to a foot race. Grant had a slight advantage in distance, say 12 to our 15 miles; & a more material one in having the initiative. While Gen. Lee could venture to draw Longstreet's corps out of its intrenchments, & start it in the race soon after nightfall, the other two corps had to hold the lines until morning to see whether the movement was a feint, a partial movement, or an entire one. Consequently, our corps could not possibly expect any reinforcements during the greater part of the first day. We only had two divisions, & those weakened by the losses of the Wilderness, & Grant would practically have a whole day to picnic with us as he saw fit & no one to interrupt him.

We had one single advantage in the race. On the Brock Road, from Todd's Tavern to Spottsylvania, was Fitz Lee's division of cavalry. Grant would have to drive that before him. At Todd's Tavern he had two divisions of cavalry, Gregg's & Merritt's.[47] Merritt's was sent in front, on the Brock Road, to drive Fitz Lee. Gregg was ordered to move down the Catharpin Road to Corbin's Bridge, to intercept any movement on our part. Gregg was opposed by Hampton's division of cavalry on the Catharpin Road; and, aided by the darkness, both Hampton & Fitz Lee were successful in entirely defeating the Federal generals in the execution of their orders. Fitz Lee had cut down trees, & blockaded the roads, & defended the blockades so well that the task of opening the road had to wait for daylight, & for Warren's corps of infantry. And, on the Catharpin Road, Gregg proved unable to make Hampton yield at all, & the infantry of our corps passed within little more than a mile of Todd's Tavern, unmolested & unobserved.

This excellent work of Hampton & Fitz Lee with their divisions enabled our corps to win the race. The cavalry, by the way, had been having some very sharp fighting in this vicinity for two days; and on the 7th poor Charley Collins was killed, commanding his regt., the _____ Va.[48] He was superb & admirable, both in person & character, & universally popular. His body fell into the enemy's hands & was recognized & buried by one of his West Point class mates.

Our infantry left their trenches about 10 P.M. & marched by a country road from near their right flank. I brought down the artillery from Parker's Store by the Shady Grove Church Road, &, about day break, we joined the infantry near the Po River, & halted for an hour to rest & eat a little breakfast, for we expected this to be our busy day. For already the racket of the cavalry about 2 miles on our left could be heard & it indicated that a great many people were bound for Spottsylvania that morning beside ourselves. The Federals in fact were sure that they had won the race. Mr. Dana, the assistant sec. of war, who was with Grant at the time, wrote of it afterward:

> I remember distinctly the sensation in the ranks when the rumor first went around that our position was south of Lee's. It was the morning of May 8th. The night before, the army had made a forced march on Spottsylvania C. H. There was no indication, the next morning that Lee had moved in any direction. As the army began to realize that we were moving south, and, at that moment, were probably much nearer Richmond than was our enemy, the spirits of officers & men rose to the highest pitch of animation. On every hand I heard the cry, "On to Richmond."[49]

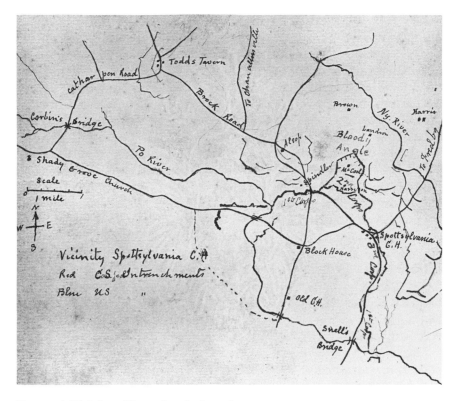

Figure 36. Vicinity of Spotsylvania Courthouse

[Figure 36 appears here in the manuscript.]

The little rest & breakfast, which we took at dawn, had been almost necessary for men & animals after the night march, but it about exhausted all the margin we had to spare in winning the race; for it was nearly 8 o'clock when the head of our column reached a crossroad where stood a peculiar looking house of squared logs, called the Blockhouse. It was a mile & a half from the court house, by the straight forward road, & a mile to the Brock Road by the road to the left. Why it was built, & why called Blockhouse, I was much too busy to find out. Here we met pressing appeals for help from each of the roads. From Spottsylvania C.H., Rosser's brigade[50] of cavalry reported itself as being driven off by Wilson's division,[51] coming in from towards Fredericksburg. And from the junction of the cross road with the Brock Road, near the house of a man named Spindler, Fitz Lee reported himself as being heavily pressed by Warren's corps of infantry, and a severe and increasing musketry fire told that the situation was growing critical. Kershaw's division was in front, & it at once turned the two leading brigades, Kershaw's & Humphreys's, to the left to the aid of Fitz Lee. The other two, Wofford & Bryan,[52] were sent ahead to the aid of Rosser. Haskell's battalion of artillery was the first I could get, & that was taken rapidly to help Kershaw & Humphreys. Lee's cavalry had some very slight rail breast works on the edge of a pine thicket, overlooking a large cleared area, & the two brigades of infantry relieved the cavalrymen behind the rails. The latter were then at once taken to the rear by Fitz Lee, & carried to the help of Rosser.

Kershaw & Humphreys had just gotten into position when they were charged by the 3 brigades of Robinson's divn. of the 5th Corps.[53] Each brigade was formed in column of regiments. Two brigades formed the front line, & the 3rd brigade followed in rear as a reserve. Warren had told them, the prisoners said, that there was only cavalry in their front, who had no bayonets, & could not stand close quarters. And accordingly they actually did come up to the rail breastworks, & there was a regular melee & bayonet fight, but, though their numbers were probably double ours, they were repulsed leaving the ground blue with their dead, and Gen. Robinson himself was severely wounded. Haskell's battalion got in fine work with its guns upon this charge, but lost an excellent captain killed, Capt. _____ Potts[54] of No. Ca.

Meanwhile, Anderson ordered Field's division to go to Kershaw's support, & his line of battle to be extended in both directions. This gave me such busy & promiscuous occupation in examining & selecting ground, distributing batteries, & having them intrench themselves in the intervals when they were not firing, that I have little more than a general recollection of the other events of the day. But it was a day of solid, hard fighting, as might be anticipated, when our two weak divisions were holding back all the force that Grant was able to bring into play against us, & we had to intrench ourselves the best we could in the intervals of his repeated attacks. The two brigades sent ahead were fortunately able to return about noon.[55] It happened that Sheridan had recalled Wilson's divn., about the same time that Rosser got his reinforcements, so that Wilson made little resistance, & Spottsylvania became ours. Warren, at first, followed up Robinson's charge with an attack by his other three divisions, but, by the time they advanced, Field's divn. had been gotten into line, &, for all the enemy's immense superiority in force, they were only able to make lodgments from 200 to 500 yards distant in our front, where they would begin at once to intrench & whence they would keep up tremendous fire on our lines. I found the position of the rail breastworks left by the cavalry, on the edge of the pine thicket, a beautiful place to locate my whole old battalion in a mass, having a fine sweep over fairly open grounds. The others I had to scatter more or less on the lines & in rear.

About noon, Warren called for Sedgwick's corps, the 6th, to come to his assistance, &, a little later, Meade ordered Sedgwick & Warren to unite in an immediate & vigorous attack. It was finally made, but made near sundown, and was not much more vigorous than it had been immediate. But it was made with a wider front, there being more troops in it; & thus, a part of Wright's division[56] overlapped our line & came around our right flank. It was another close call, but again luck was on our side. Good old Ewell had just arrived, after an awfully long, hot, dusty march around by Parker's Store. He was just arriving, in fact, when these intruders ran into him, & Rodes's division drove them back, & then Ewell extended our line & intrenched.

There remains one personal incident in my recollections of the day. I happened to become thirsty, along towards noon, while passing in rear of our infantry line of battle, here drawn up across a meadow, & I rode up to it & asked for a drink of water. A captain took off his canteen and handed it to me, & I took a good drink. Our party had attracted [the] attention of a Federal battery, & they fired a beautiful volley at us. It came just as I handed the canteen back to the captain. Three shells exploded together, just short of us & a little high, at what seemed to be the exact spot to ruin us. The whirring & whizzing of the fragments filled the air, & they tore up turf all around. One piece tore the sleeve half off the arm of the captain, as he took his canteen. But no one in the infantry ranks, & neither man or horse of our party, was touched except my old Dixie. With a loud spat, a piece about 2 inches square struck her in the neck, about a foot behind her ear. She gave a squeal, unlike anything I ever before heard from a horse; though I have heard it said that horses which have been badly wounded once will always squeal if they are hit a second time. She reared up, too, on her hind legs, until I feared she would fall backwards on me. I tried to fling myself off, & fall far & clear, but somehow I could not get off at all. Something seemed to be holding me on. Presently, I discovered that the strap of my field glass, which passed across my breast, had been caught in the high pommel of my saddle when she reared up, & it was holding me to the pommel. Quickly bringing a strain on that strap I broke it, & then threw myself clear.

Dixie then came on all fours and ran around promiscuously for a while, while I looked about hunting in the ragweeds for my fieldglass. After some delay I discovered it caught on the pommel of the saddle. Winthrop called out, "General! She's mortally wounded. Shall I put her out of her misery?" I believed she was mortally wounded, for while I was held down by the strap I could see the big hole in her neck & blood flying so, that I thought a large artery was cut. So I said, "Yes! You may as well." Winthrop drew his revolver & commenced riding after Dixie to get a fair shot at her brain, when an idea occurred to me, & I said, "Hold on, Winthrop. I guess she will live to carry her own saddle to the wagon train & save our packing it." That saved Dixie's life, for she not only lived to carry her saddle to the train, but on examination we found the wound only a flesh wound—no important artery cut, & in six weeks she was all well again.

The fighting lasted until dark &, during it, I think I brought into action about every gun I had, either on the line or from positions whence we could fire over our line. At night we made a headquarters bivouac near the Blockhouse. The guns on the line had put in their leisure moments in digging so industriously that they nearly all had fair cover, & meanwhile they had suffered but little in spite of the heavy fire they had given & taken.[57]

Monday the 9th proved to be comparatively a quiet day. Grant wished to give his men a little rest & to bring up his whole force, & let them intrench themselves in our front, so as to have something to hold on to in case of disaster when they assaulted us. Gen. Lee was not averse either to letting his men have a little rest, & a chance to improve their trenches & parapets.

In this connection should be noted the great advantages which the Federals had over us in the matter of intrenching. Not only were their greatly superior numbers abundantly supplied with axes, picks, & shovels, but they had a large brigade of engineer troops especially instructed & expert at all such work, which was kept steadily engaged at it during the whole campaign, from the beginning in the Wilderness until the fall of Petersburg. These two thousand to twenty-five hundred expert picks, shovels, & axes, under engineer officers & non-commissioned officers of experience, were practically worth almost another corps to Grant's army in the quantity & quality of intrenchments they were able to turn out. Our supply of intrenching tools was wretchedly inadequate. Not one fourth of what it should have been, if so much, among the infantry, & they very commonly resorted to loosening up the ground with their bayonets, & throwing it with their tin cups. The many leagues & leagues of trenches with which our army scarred the country, from the Rapidan to Petersburg, in this campaign, all represent extra work, under immense difficulties & disadvantages, of the thin grey ranks which fought off Grant's legions by day & worked by night.

Another reason why Gen. Lee may well have approved a rest on the 9th was that our 3rd Corps was still behind. It had been held all day on the 8th in our Wilderness lines covering the movement of our trains. It left on the morning of the 9th, & reached us in the afternoon. Mahone's division was put on Field's left, where Hancock threatened to turn our left flank. The other two, Heth & Wilcox, went on Ewell's right & in front of the court house.

Today, the enemy, while making no regular assaults, pressed our lines heavily with skirmishers endeavoring to locate them & find the weak spots.

Sharpshooting, consequently, was hot all day long, & the guns on both sides also put into it constantly. One of our sharpshooters, probably from the position of my old battalion, killed Gen. Sedgwick commanding the 6th Corps—an excellent officer. Gen. Wright succeeded him. One of our couriers was killed by a cannon shot in the pines behind the battalion. As indicating the accuracy of the artillery at our close range, Huger had two of Moody's 24 pr. brass howitzers hit in the muzzle, though neither was disabled. A 12 pr. solid shot actually went down the bore of one, after knocking its mouth some what askew. Frank Huger loaded the ball in one of Taylor's Napoleons & fired it back, as, he said, it seemed to know the road. Huger, today, called my attention to the number of Federal wounded still alive, lying out between the lines, among those shot down in yesterday's assaults. They could be heard to call out for water, & seen to move & to throw up their hands, & one in particular would sometimes sit up. For Grant to ask a flag of truce to remove them would be a serious confession of having been repulsed. And we could not let men come to get them & have the chance to spy into our lines. So there was nothing left for those men but to die there. At night some of Huger's men ventured out to one or two of the nearest to give them water, but it was very dangerous to do this even at night, & in daylight it would have been fatal. And it even is a question whether it was charity to give them water, when it probably only prolonged their sufferings.

I have already referred to Hancock's demonstrations upon our left flank, & to Mahone's being put to the left of Field. He threw up breastworks during the night of the 9th, overlooking the Blockhouse bridge over the Po, for Hancock during the afternoon had built three pontoon bridges up above & at night had 3 of his divisions across, & in a very threatening position. The Confederate breast works shown on the map [Figure 36] west of the Po were not built at that time nor was any infantry on the west side.

This brings us to the morning of the 10th. It was a great, an immense piece of luck for us, that Hancock had made his move across the Po late in the afternoon, giving us the night to make preparation to meet him. Early on the 10th Gen. Lee had Heth's division brought back from Spottsylvania & taken down the road past the Blockhouse, by the old court house, across the Po & then turned to the right to go up & take Hancock in flank. It was a very bold proposition to send this lone division to meet so large a force, & one so easily reinforced, but fortune favors the brave & luck was still with us. The line which had been taken up by Ewell's corps was over some difficult ground & had some bad location on it. I will explain more fully about it later but for the present it is enough to say that Warren had discovered some of this bad location[58] (not the worst of it as yet, however) & Grant had decided on making a great assault upon it with an overwhelming force. That is what saved us west of the Po. Hancock was ordered to come himself, in order to command in the attack, & to bring two of the three divisions on the west side of the river. That only left Barlow's division opposite to Heth, who was also assisted by Hampton's cavalry. But Barlow standing on the defensive, & having still a superior force to Heth, was making a very successful fight, when Meade, hearing of the attack on him, ordered him withdrawn. About this time, too, the woods caught fire in his rear & probably from our shells, for our guns on Field's left took an active part in the affair, & Barlow finally fell back under such pressure from Heth & Hampton & the fire & our guns on his flank & the fire in the woods that he lost a piece of artillery & many men & some of his wounded were burned. Heth's division also suffered sharply & Gen. H. H. Walker[59] lost a foot. After this action Heth's division built the intrenchments on the west side shown on the map [Figure 36]. And, after Barlow got across, Hancock's guns, as if specially mad with us for what we had done, duelled with us sharply for quite a while.

And now I must explain about the bad location of Ewell's line of intrenchments. On the first day, when we began fighting about Spindler's house, I personally extended the infantry line to the right very nearly due east. Off to the north was some favorable ground for the Federals to put their batteries, but, to take it in, made lines which could be enfiladed & had large dead spaces close in front. But when Ewell's corps came to be located, the engineers decided to take in that ground anyhow. To protect from enfilade fire they proposed to make traverses. To guard against assaults from out of the dead spaces they proposed to put abattis. And so they made the big salient shown on the map [Figure 36], a mile long & half a mile wide. Their abattis & traverses, on which they relied to cure the defects of such a line, are all very good when one has time & means to make them complete & in first class shape. But with our limited means, several days would have been required to build properly the three miles of parapets & three miles of abattis necessary to be constructed. Even after it was built a fatal objection would exist in its extra length of 2 miles, because those extra miles would have to be kept manned with men & guns which might be of infinite value elsewhere either for attack or defense. I think therefore by all the rules of military science we must pronounce these lines a great mistake although they were consented to, if they were not adopted by Gen. Lee's chief engineer Gen. M. L. Smith, who was a West Pointer & an ex-officer of the U.S. Engineers & a veteran of Mexico & recently distinguished in the defence of Vicksburg.

However, so far as the fighting upon the 10th is concerned, it was the existence of these defective lines that probably saved us—as has been told—for they induced Meade to recall Hancock from a position which might have ruined us.

And now I come to tell of the grand assault in the afternoon of the 10th. All the morning the sharpshooters & skirmishers were pecking at the lines everywhere, & getting themselves as close up as possible, while the troops were being massed at the proper places for the assault—which it was at first intended to make at 5 P.M. But Warren thought the opportunity so favorable that he got permission to make his part of it about four o'clock. He atttacked the lower west face of Ewell's long salient with 7 brigades & he felt so sure of success that he put on full uniform to honor the occasion. He had but a short distance to go under fire—attacking from a large dead space. An abattis was in process of construction, but it was too incomplete to be of much value & some few of his troops actually gained our parapets, but his repulse was prompt, bloody, & decided. He struck with heaviest force on Ramseur's[60] N.C. brig. of Rodes's division. There were never, anywhere, two better fighters than Rodes & Ramseur or two more attractive men. Both of them, poor fellows, were killed in the Valley in the fall. Ramseur's brigade did especially good work this afternoon. The next part of the general attack was postponed until 6 P.M. by delay in getting the troops ready, though a heavy cannonade preceded it for over a half hour. This was an attack upon the apex of Ewell's angle by Upton with three brigades, & Mott's division with two.[61] Mott's approach on Upton's left was over ground we could see, & our fire on Mott broke him up & prevented his coming at all near. But Upton had only 200 yards to go under fire. He had his men formed in four lines, the abattis was again incomplete, & by sheer weight of numbers they stormed over the parapet & captured about 1,000 men of Doles's Georgia brigade.[62] But Gordon's division was in reserve & fell upon Upton & drove him out & back to his lines with heavy loss & in short order.

Gen. Hancock, who was to command the joint assault, but who went back across the Po to see Barlow withdraw under difficulties, as before narrated, only got back about the time of Warren's repulse, say at 5:30. At 7 P.M. he made a fresh attack with a mixed command for fresh troops, some half dozen or more brigades, but only accomplished another repulse. A Federal Gen. Rice[63] was killed in Warren's attack & Maj. Gen. Stevenson of Burnside's corps was killed in a reconnaissance on our right flank in front of Hill's lines during the afternoon.

Wednesday, May 11, was again a day of bitter sharpshooting & angry artillery practice, all along the lines, while plans were being formed in the Federal councils for another & better managed attack upon what every general among them said was our weak spot—the "Bloody Angle."

Meanwhile, during the day, Grant made some casual movements which cut a great figure in determining the result, when his attack came to be made. One was to move Burnside (who was close in front of Spottsylvania C.H.) a little further back, & then he moved again to his right so as to be near the position whence he was to take his part in the assault the next morning. More or less of these movements were seen & reported to Gen. Lee. Another casual movement, also reported to him, was the movement of a brigade of infantry sent on a scout back towards Todd's Tavern. Gen. Lee took these movements as preparations upon Gen. Grant's part for another foot-race, & as they were both directed toward our left, he rather anticipated that the effort would be to turn over left flank. Consequently he sent orders during the afternoon through Gen. Pendleton to each chief of artillery to withdraw, at night fall, all of his guns which were on lines close to the enemy, so that if it should become necessary to march suddenly during the night there would be no delay, & no noise which the enemy might hear in our getting the guns out. This proved to be a most unfortunate order, as will be set forth presently. On such little things do great events often turn.

In the trenches today Huger again showed me a few wounded men, yet alive out between the lines. The fellow who could sit up still did so occasionally. The others only showed life by sometimes moving their arms, as if trying to keep flies from their wounds. It was a sight to move one's heart, but it was beyond our power to remedy.

I should have mentioned, on the 9th, my going to Spottsylvania C.H. for some purpose & meeting Gen. Stuart, & sitting under an apple tree with him & having our last interview. He told me that Sheridan had gone on a grand raid toward Richmond & that his cavalry was partly in pursuit & part trying to head him off, & that he himself was starting presently to join the latter body. He was in his usual high spirits & cheerful mood & of course we laughed over our Richmond interview. Poor fellow, he was mortally wounded at Yellow Tavern, 6 miles from Richmond, two days afterward & died in Richmond on the _____.[64] In him we lost a soldier whose qualities were as rare & high as his personal character was admirable & attractive. Of all our officers who did not rise to command independent armies, I have always believed that Stuart & Gen. Hampton were the fittest. Fortunately we had Hampton to succeed Stuart & his life has been spared & prolonged so that a younger generation has been able to see this fine specimen of the type of the older.

A little before sundown I received the written orders, before mentioned, to withdraw at dusk the guns on the lines close to the enemy. As the order stated its object—to have the artillery prepared for a swift & silent movement during the night, should one prove necessary—I ventured to accomplish that purpose without a strict compliance with its terms, which would have left our lines seriously weakened against any sudden surprise. I visited every battery & had its ammunition chests mounted (they were always dismounted in the trenches) & the carriages so placed & roads so opened that we could withdraw everything easily & without noise, but, at the same time our guns still remained in position.

In both the other corps the order was literally executed, & among the guns withdrawn were 20 pieces[65] which were posted in the "Bloody Angle" lines that Grant was preparing a supreme effort against at dawn on the morrow. And with Grant dawn meant dawn—not 9 A.M. as with Gen. Polk at Chickamauga. The program was to be as follows. Hancock was to mass four divisions, comprising 11 brigades, for a direct assault upon the angle at dawn. The 6th Corps, on his right, should hold its trenches with one division, & the other two divisions, composed of 8 brigades, should be ready to assist Hancock's battle. On Hancock's left the three white divisions of Burnside's corps, 6 brigades, were also to make an attack at dawn upon the lines of our 3rd Corps.

Warren's whole corps, the 5th, which was in the trenches opposite our corps, was ordered to press us closely, & assault us if we sent any reinforcements to the other corps.

All the details were carefully studied out, & the formation adopted for Hancock's storming column is worthy of note. In telling of the battle of Gettysburg I spoke of the formation of Pickett's column, as being too light to encounter the numbers it would meet. It was two lines of battle separated by an interval of 200 yards, & followed by a third line at a still greater distance. In other words, our column was three ranks or six men deep, but covering at least 400 yards from the leading pair to the rear pair.

A part of the ground over which Hancock had to advance was wooded. For the woods he adopted four lines, or 8 men deep, but separated by intervals not exactly given, but apparently very short. Probably his column was 150 yards from front-to-rear. But where the advance was unobstructed, he massed four brigades in two lines of regimental masses. Each regiment of 10 companies formed a close column of two companies front & five companies deep. So his formation was like this:

This column was 20 men deep & from front-to-rear there was probably less than 100 yards. The question at once arises, how such a column would support artillery fire which would be very destructive in such masses. Their advance had to be made over about the same ground that Mott tried to advance over on the afternoon of the 10th, & he was repulsed apparently by artillery alone.

To be sure, darkness was expected to hide their approach until they were quite near. But it would be very instructive to know what 20 well served guns could do with such a column even within the space of 150 yards. And this column was heard coming at least 400 yards. But that can never be known, for our 20 guns withdrawn, as has been told, the night before, were not there in time to try the experiment. Possibly we may find out in the next world but we will never know in this. Events fell out as follows.

It rained hard early in the night, & the morning was dark & threatening—so dark that Hancock delayed starting from four until 4:35, when there was light to see to walk. During the night, Gen. Johnson, whose division held the lines about to be assailed, had learned from his pickets & scouts of the massing of troops in his front, & had his men on the alert & had sent & asked to have his artillery sent back to him. It was ordered to rejoin him at daylight.

The first notice which he had of the attack was a cheer set up by the assailants when still several hundred yards off & not visible. Then his pickets fired, & his line of battle opened, but the great blue wave could not be stopped by that; the abattis existed[66] on[ly] in name & embryo, [and] was overrun by weight of numbers, & they swarmed over his[67] parapet everywhere, overwhelming the thin lines which fought them with the bayonet, & capturing the whole 20 guns coming in at a gallop, only the two leading ones being able to unlimber & fire one shot each. All this from Lee see[ing] some movements & being misled. Gen. Johnson himself, one of his brigadiers, Gen. Steuart,[68] & nearly 4,000 men were also captured.

It was the noise of this assault that opened the day for us on Thursday the 12th. It was soon followed by the roar of Burnside's attack upon the 3rd Corps, &, as if it were a signal for him, Gen. Warren's artillery opened upon our lines, & his skirmishers & sharpshooters everywhere joined in. Our guns & sharpshooters answered, & Warren was not encouraged to make any attack. Soon a message came to me that Gen. Lee wished me to send him a battalion of artillery. I soon got together Cabell's, which could be best spared, from towards our left & sent him off at a gallop. He remained all day & rendered excellent & very effective service.[69]

Gen. Lee's position for a while was very critical. Indeed it is hard to understand why & how the enemy failed to ruin us after having made such an important capture of position, & men, & guns with their ammunition, ready for use against their former owners, & with such a large force already inside our works & flushed with victory.

It is only to be accounted for, I think, by that wonderful morale of the Army of Northern Virginia which even its remnants had not lost when they surrendered at Appomattox Court House. The capture of Johnson's division left Ewell with only two others, Gordon's & Rodes's, not over 9,000 men, now taken in flank & confronted by Hancock, perhaps the best of the Federal generals, with at least 20,000 men.[70] Yet in the space of two hours, without any reinforcements, Gordon's division of 3 brigades, which had been in reserve, with the help of Daniel's & Ramseur's brigades of Rodes's division had attacked the enemy, & not only checked their advance, but had driven them back to the parapets over which they had come, & had actually recaptured some of the guns, though they were unable to bring them away, as the horses were all killed. As Gordon was preparing for his attack, near the Harrison house, Gen. Lee started, as he had done at the Wilderness, to accompany the charge, and as was done there the men called to him to go back, & his bridle was taken hold of & he was induced to stop.[71]

By seven o'clock the enemy had entirely abandoned the area within our parapets, except for a short distance on our left, where they were sheltered by some traverses, & we had worked up behind other traverses so as to be very near them. Meanwhile, too, Burnside's attack upon the 3rd Corps had had a small preliminary success converted into a failure. Potter's division[72] had captured some intrenchments from Lane's brigade & two guns. But Lane rallied, &, helped by Scales[73] & Thomas of Wilcox's division, he recaptured both guns & lines. Under urgent orders from Grant, Burnside made repeated attacks, but meeting with no success his troops were gradually drawn to their right to connect with Hancock & reinforce him. Grant was now determined to conquer by main force, & there ensued a struggle more desperate, bloody, & prolonged than any other which took place in the war. I cannot go into its details but will give only its outlines.

As soon as Grant heard that Hancock was attacked & checked, Wright was ordered to reinforce Hancock with the 8 brigades which he had ready for the purpose. Warren also was ordered to assault the lines of our corps, which Grant thought must have sent reinforcement to Ewell. Warren accordingly assaulted our lines about 10 A.M. Of course we were ready for him & he was repulsed. Meanwhile Grant had sent for the last division of the 6th Corps (Ricketts with 2 brigades) & had also sent them to Hancock. When Warren reported his repulse & that our corps was in its trenches, he was ordered to send first Cutler's division,[74] & afterward also Griffin's, of 3 brigades each. Thus 16 additional brigades were sent to help the 11 which had first attacked the angle, beside the reinforcement from Burnside's corps which at last joined them on the left. And at last Grant even ordered Warren to bring still another division, leaving only one in the lines in our front. But this last order was countermanded before execution. Hancock also brought guns & used them over the captured parapets & posted guns & coehorn mortars at neighboring points outside, whence they could fire over the heads of his own men & on our positions.

To meet all these reinforcements Gen. Lee could send nothing until he had first thoroughly disposed of Burnside's attack. Then he was able to send 3 brigades, Perrin, Harris,75 & McGowan. Also a little later Gen. Gordon made what proved a valuable suggestion. He suspected that Burnside was leaving only skirmishers in his trenches & was closing in to Hancock's assistance. He proposed an attack upon the trenches where he suspected the skirmishers. It was made with Lane's & Weisiger's76 brigades & was effective as a diversion & called back a portion of Burnside's troops. Late in the afternoon, also, when it was seen that Warren had weakened his force opposite the 1st Corps, Humphreys's & Bryan's brigades were sent to Ewell but I think were not engaged.

It had rained a great deal during the day & toward night it rained more heavily, but the struggle over the parapets & traverses went on incessantly all day, &, though it slacked off after dark, it did not finally cease until 3 A.M. At that time our troops were withdrawn to a new line in rear cutting off the whole of the bad salient. I can give the best idea of the character of the terrific struggle which had gone on over those parapets & traverses in rain & mud & light & darkness for over 18 hours by a few short extracts.

Brig. Gen. Grant, commanding a Vermont brigade, wrote:

> It was not only a desperate struggle, it was a hand to hand fight. Nothing but the piled up logs or breastworks separated the combatants. Our men would reach over the logs & fire into the faces of the enemy, would stab over with their bayonets; many were shot & stabbed through the crevices & holes between the logs; men mounted the works, &, with muskets rapidly handed them, kept up a continuous fire until they were shot down, when others would take their place & continue the deadly work. . . . It was there that the somewhat celebrated tree was cut off by bullets, there that the brush & logs were cut to pieces & whipped into basket stuff . . . there that the rebel ditches & cross sections were filled with dead men several deep. . . . I was at the angle next day. The sight was terrible & sickening, much worse than at Bloody Lane—Antietam. There a great many dead man were lying in the road & across the rails of the torn down fences, & out in the cornfield, but they were not piled up several deep & their flesh was not so torn & mangled as at the angle.77

Mr. Dana, asst. sec. of war, wrote:

> All around us the underbrush & trees had been riddled & burnt. The ground was thick with dead & wounded men among whom the relief corps was at work. The earth, which was soft from the heavy rains we had been having before & during the battle, had been trampled by the fighting of thousands of men until it was soft, like thin hasty pudding. Beyond the fence against which we leaned lay a great pool of this mud, its surface as smooth as that of a pond. As we stood there looking silently down at it, of a sudden the leg of a man was lifted up from the pool & the mud dripped off his boot. It was so unexpected, so horrible, that for a moment we were stunned. Then we pulled ourselves together & called to some soldiers near by to rescue the owner of the leg. They pulled him out, with but little trouble, & discovered that he was not dead only wounded. He was taken to the hospital where he got well I believe.[78]

Gen. McGowan says:

> Our men lay on one side of the breastwork the enemy on the other. In many cases men were pulled over. . . . The trenches on the right in the bloody angle had to be cleared of the dead more than once. An oak tree, 22 inches in diameter in rear of the brigade was cut down by musket balls & fell about 12 o'clock Thursday night injuring several men in the 1st So. Ca. Regt.[79]

Gen. Humphreys, who was Meade's chief of staff during this campaign & who has written an admirable history of it, writes about this action:

> It has been said that the continuance of this desperate contest at the apex of the salient, on the part of Gen. Lee, was an unnecessary sacrifice of troops he could ill afford to spare; but in fact he could not withdraw them during daylight without the risk of serious disaster, & Meade continued to press against him there with the hope of bringing about the withdrawal & disaster.[80]

I would say, in addition, that we required time to prepare the cut off line into which we withdrew. It would not have been prudent to fall back to that line without some preliminary intrenchment there. And, against all the adverse criticism which can ever be made upon our originally taking such a line, it must always be remembered that its very defects caused Hancock to be recalled from an attack which might easily have proven far more disastrous to us than the Bloody Angle did.

Gen. Humphreys estimates the Federal losses on the 12th [to be] 6,020 killed & wounded, & 800 captured. Our killed & wounded he puts between 4,000 & 5,000 & near 4,000 captured. It was especially a bloody day among our generals. Two were killed—Daniel of No. Ca. & Perrin of

So. Ca.; & four severely wounded—Walker, Ramseur, R. D. Johnston,[81] & McGowan; & two captured—Edward Johnson & Steuart. The Federals had three generals wounded—Wright, Webb, & Carroll.[82]

As might have been expected, Friday the 13th was an off day, after the great struggle of the 12th. The only record in my note book is of skirmishing & sharpshooting—but I recall one incident of my usual trip through the lines. Huger had gotten much interested in the particular wounded man who sometimes sat up, out between the two lines of battle. Today he had seen him trying to knock himself in the head with the butt of a musket—raising it up & letting it fall on him. It hardly seemed possible that a man could really give himself a fatal blow in that way, but through the glass he now seemed to be dead.

The next day, Sat. [the] 14th, in the early morning, the sharpshooters were rather unusually active, but as the morning waxed their fire waned. At last it died out, & then we sent a skirmish line to investigate, & they found all the lines in our front vacated. We felt like boys out of school. For a little while the strain would be off. We could walk & sit outside the trenches, & shells stopped coming around. Frank Huger & I rode out to see his wounded man. The poor fellow had already been stripped by some one who wanted his clothes & his body was notable for beautiful tatooing all over arms & chest, principally in patriotic patterns of eagles, flags, &c. Then we rode on with great interest to look over the enemies' lines & batteries, which we had been fighting all the week.

We hurried our inspection, however, for we anticipated orders at any moment to march. For, of course, Warren's corps was off to make trouble for us elsewhere. The fact was, though we did not then know it, that, but for the heavy rain which fell on the 12th, we would have heard of the trouble long before we discovered that Warren had gone. Grant had, only on the 11th, telegraphed to Washington his famous dispatch that he would fight it out on that line if it took all the summer, & he was losing as little time as possible between the fights. And on the 13th he devised an attack which would have had a very fair chance of taking us quite by surprise, had he been able to make it. Warren had really moved at dark on the 13th, under orders to pass in rear of the rest of the army & extend its left flank, & at 4 A.M. on the 14th the whole army was to attack us simultaneously. Of course Warren's sudden arrival on our extreme right, where we had as yet no breast works, would give opportunities of out flanking us & taking us in reverse, which might prove serious. From this danger we were unconsciously delivered by the darkness and the mud. In spite of well considered precautions, of numerous fires, & men posted all along the line of march, the rain & darkness & difficulties triumphed. The head of his column very nearly arrived in time but the rear of it was so scattered & tired out that the whole attack had to be abandoned.

That evening Gen. Lee moved one of our divisions, Field's, over to the right flank, & Grant's opportunity was now lost. The rest of the corps, however, remained all the next day on the left, & then at night received orders to follow Field to the extreme right. Our orders were received about 10 P.M., just as we had gotten asleep; & we marched at 11 P.M. At daylight we extended our line of battle to the Po at Snell's Bridge & began to intrench. We had, here, open ground in front & a very pretty line. I put Haskell's whole battalion on the south side, where they could enfilade all approaches. The only trouble was that we made these lines too good—so good that the enemy never attacked them.

I find, by the way, a curious comment upon the character of our intrenchments in this campaign by Gen. Humphreys, whose special training was as a military engineer. In writing of the Confederate casualties he says—"Excepting on those days, and at those parts of the field noted in the narrative, they must have been much fewer in number than our own, since they remained on the defensive under the cover of intrenchments entangled in their front in a manner unknown to European warfare, &, indeed, in a manner new to warfare in this country."[83]

The character of our works I think was but the natural outcome of the conditions under which they were constructed. These have been already referred to. The Federal works were built with intrenching tools, labor, & skilled supervision in abundance. Ours were built, principally, with bayonets & tin cups, every man for himself. Only if we remained many days in the same lines, were we able to connect them up & make room to move about. It was not choice but necessity, & the hard fighting which our infantry put up was rather in spite of such mud-pie works than on account of them. A strong evidence of their incomplete character is to be found in the fact that the abattis we succeeded in getting built was never enough even to delay the Federal storming columns a minute, so far as I can find any record. [Figures 37, 38, and 39 appear here in the manuscript.]

Our corps remained in these intrenchments, with our right at Snell's Bridge, from Monday morning the 16th until the night of Saturday the 21st, without any occurrences worthy of note. It was but a labor of love to daily put fine touches on our batteries & trenches & it seemed a great pity when we finally had to go off & leave them unutilised. But there were two severe engagements in the meanwhile on our left which deserve notice.

First, Gen. Grant adopted what seemed a very fair piece of strategy, suggested by two of his best generals, Humphreys & Wright. His army had now swung around us, about 90 degrees to our right, & thus brought our

Figure 37. Maj. Gen. Stephen Dodson Ramseur

corps around as has been told. He put in three whole days, fortifying his new lines & demonstrating in various ways out to our right, as if he had lost all interest in the old lines about the Bloody Angle & beyond.

Then during the night of the 17th, leaving only the 5th Corps in his new intrenchments, the 2nd & the 6th were marched around during the night to the Bloody Angle lines where these two corps formed to give us another 4 A.M. surprise. Burnside, too, on their left was to attack with them, & Warren from the new works was to help with a powerful artillery fire, & to be prepared to take the offensive. It was a well laid plan, but Gen. Lee was not caught napping. Hancock, Wright, & Burnside were all repulsed so easily & decidedly that they reported against any further attack & the effort was abandoned. These assaults do not seem to have been very determined, as Gen. Humphreys reports the wounded on this date as only 552 & estimates about 125 killed.

This would have ended the battle of Spottsylvania, but for a movement of Gen. Lee's on the next day, Thursday the 19th. Gen. Ewell, who made it,

Figure 38. Maj. Gen. Edward Johnson

speaks of it as only a reconnaissance, but there was evidently a great deal of aggressiveness mixed up with it. Gen. Grant's right flank was now east of the Ny River, near the house of Harris, shown on the map [Figure 36], close to the Fredbg. road. He had recently received from Washington Tyler's division[84] of 8,000 men & some other reinforcements. Tyler & some other troops were encamped near the Harris house. On the 19th, Gen. Ewell's infantry, now reduced to about 6,000 men, made a long detour by roads impassable to artillery, & about half past five o'clock in the afternoon it showed up in Tyler's vicinity & it immediately attacked him. This looks to me exceedingly like a repetition of the Stonewall Jackson movement around Hooker's flank, only in much less force. It might have proved quite serious

Figure 39. Lt. Gen. Wade Hampton

however, had it not been discovered before its attack & preparations made to meet it. Its only chance lay in making a surprise as Jackson did. Its attack was at first successful, but its force was too small to make front long against the reinforcements which rapidly came to Tyler's assistance. Indeed, being without artillery it is wonderful that Ewell was able to escape complete annihilation. But by a display of good fighting which seemed able to rise to meet the occasion he fought off all comers until after dark & then withdrew with the loss of about 1,000 men, of whom about 400 were captured. Gen. Humphreys estimates the Federal loss at about 1,300, killed & wounded.

That was the end of the battle of Spottsylvania, & before entering upon Grant's next movement I will give the casualties of the two armies in the following table.[85] The Confederate casualties were never formally reported & tabulated. The campaign work was so incessant & pressing from now until the surrender, that but few reports were made, &, meanwhile the officers who should have made very many were killed. So the Confederate figures all through this campaign must be understood to be largely made up from partial returns & estimates made on various circumstantial indications. There are, also, often conflicting statements as to the Federal losses. I shall not bother to give authority or to seek to reach exact accuracy, in either case, but will adopt any estimate which seems substantially correct & is vouched for by what seems careful & impartial authority.

Casualties: Battles of the Wilderness & Spottsylvania,
May 5 to May 20th '64

Battle	Force	Killed	Woun.	Missing	Total
Wilderness	CS	2,000	6,000	3,400	11,400
	US	2,246	12,037	3,383	17,666
	Total				
Spotts.	CS				
	US	2,725	13,413	2,258	18,396
	Total				
Both	CS				
	US	4,971	25,450	5,641	36,062
Aggreg.					

C.S. genls. killed: Jones, Stafford, Jenkins, Stuart, Perrin, Daniel
[C.S. genls.] wounded: Longstreet, Pegram, Benning, Perry, Hill (?),[86] Hays, Ramseur, Johnston, R. D., Walker, W. W., Walker, H. H., McGowan, Walker, J. A.
U.S. [genls.] killed: Hays, Wadsworth, Sedgwick, Rice, Stephenson
[U.S. genls.] wounded: Carroll, Getty, Baxter, Robinson, Morris, Wright, Webb
Genls. captured: Shaler, Seymour, Johnson, Steuart

Gen. Humphreys closes his account of these two battles with the following remarks. Before I saw them I had already written something quite to the same effect, but yet I will also quote Humphreys:

This account of the operation shows in what manner the contest between the two armies was carried on. The marching was done chiefly at night, & the contact was so close as to require constant vigilance day & night & allow but little time for sleep. The firing was incessant—the fatigue, the loss of sleep, the watchfulness, taxed severely the powers of endurance of both officers & men. Usually, in military operations, the opposing armies come together, fight a battle, & separate again, the strain lasting only a few days. In a siege, it is only a small part of the opposing troops that are close together. But with these two armies it was different. From the 5th of May 1864 to the 9th of April 1865 they were in constant close contact, with rare intervals of brief comparative repose.[87]

16

NORTH ANNA
& DRURY'S BLUFF

With the failure of Grant's second assault upon the Confederate lines in rear of the Bloody Angle on May 18th, he lost all hope of any further successful attack on Lee's Spottsylvania intrenchments & resorted to try a piece of strategy, by which he hoped to bring on a battle in the open. He set a trap. He decided to send Hancock's corps off some twenty miles around Lee's right flank, in hopes that Lee would be tempted to make a dash at & try to destroy it while isolated. But he, meanwhile, would be so fully prepared that he could fall upon Lee before Lee could harm Hancock.

Hancock was accordingly prepared to move on the night of the 19th but Early's affair that afternoon led to the delay of a day. On Friday night Hancock started, & on Saturday, the 21st, Gen. Lee learned through his cavalry that Hancock was in position at Milford Station, where he had been ordered to act as a lure. But Gen. Lee does not seem to have been tempted at all. He could not remain at Spottsylvania, for Hancock's movement had the merit of being a turning operation if it did not act as a trap. But about 30 miles in Lee's rear was the very important position of Hanover Junction behind the North Anna River. Had Grant originally started his movement as a *race for the North Anna,* having the initiative, he might easily have won it. But Hancock's delay, while acting as a bait, enabled Gen. Lee to seize the advantage, which he was quick to do. By midday of the 21st Ewell's corps was started for Hanover Junction. Our corps started at dark, & Hill's corps took a parallel road on the west.

We marched all night, the weather being pleasant, & the roads good. I recall being impressed with the unusual silence of the ranks as they marched. There was none of the usual joking & chaffing among the men though all were in good humor. But they were serious & created the impression of being on serious business. We struck into the Telegraph Road, which went right by my old winter camps of 1862 at Mt. Carmel Church. I rode by Squire Wortham's to greet the good old man & his wife, whom I then saw for the last time. Some of my pleasantest recollections of the world are of our stay in their home. They were very cordial & glad to see me, but they were very much depressed by the idea that their house would soon be left within the Federal lines. About the least they could expect would be to lose all their poultry & live stock, & to have all their fences burned. But they had no where else to go, and they might at least protect the house from being burned by remaining in it.

At about 2 P.M., Sunday [the] 22nd, we reached Hanover Junction & went into camp a little north of it, near a nice looking farm house of a Mr. Cox[1] on a little knoll. Our march had been about 30 miles in about 18 hours. I saw a few chickens about the farm house & tried to buy them, but the owner thought Confederate money no temptation & said that he had but few & he wanted them for seed.

The next morning, Monday [the] 23rd, we were lying quietly in camp when suddenly the fire of a battery was opened from the opposite bank of the North Anna about a mile away & shells began to land about promiscuously. The enemy had followed us up much more closely than we seemed to expect, & he announced himself as if he was in a hurry & meant business. I quickly ran Parker's rifle battery—now commanded by his former 1st lieut. & a fine officer, J. Wilcox Brown,[2] up on the knoll by the farm house, & began to return the fire of the Federal battery. One of their shells struck the farm house, & the owner & his family, [named] Miller,[3] who were already somewhat scared up, swarmed out like bees & fled as fast as they could run—man, wife, & daughters. I just happened to see them in time & I shouted after, "I say, won't you sell me those chickens now?" He shouted back, "Yes, pay me next time you see me." So Willie Mason & Winthrop & Joe & I chased down the chickens & caught the last one of them, & Willie tied them on his saddle & took them to camp. Meanwhile, Gen. Anderson felt uneasy for two regiments which he had left on the north side of the North Anna River, one[4] at a small breastwork at the end of the R.R. bridge, & another at the end of the Telegraph Road bridge. So I ran several batteries down to the river to help those two little establishments. But though we had a sharp little duel across the river with the Federal batteries, we could do little to help our friends, because trees & hills & ravines were so fixed that we could not see the ground over which both of them were approached & captured with most of the men in them.[5]

During the afternoon I had a very narrow escape. Between the Telegraph Road & the R.R. on the bluff over the valley of the stream, was a large two story & basement, square, brick house, belonging to Parson Fox, whom we had known at Mr. Wortham's & who wrote to congratulate me on the birth of the twins, that I now had "a King in his cradle & a queen to salute you." Our batteries were distributed along the bluffs both above & below, &

Gen. Anderson & his staff had stopped in the yard behind this brick house. I joined them, & being tired sat down on the sill of a closed basement window, several couriers standing just in front of me & holding horses. Just then a shell cut off about ten feet of a chimney top which there ran up in the wall. I could not jump clear of the bricks as they began to fall for the couriers & horses were in the way, but as quick as a cat jumped on the sill, about a foot above the ground, & flattened my back against the window. The recess was scarcely four inches deep, & the avalanch[e] of bricks fell so close to me that when they were done falling the slope of the pile completely covered my feet & ankles, which were badly bruised. Two couriers lay in the pile, one of them killed. There are a number of places on that line of R.R. from Richmond to Fredericksburg which I always like to look at out of the car windows as I go by, even to this day, & Parson Fox's house is one of them. For I would not like to have been killed by bricks.

I have another recollection of the evening & an amusing one. While we had been dueling with the enemy's guns Gen. Lee had had some of the engineers looking for a line of battle for our corps, & they did not agree whether we should form in front or in rear of a sort of flat swamp about a half mile back from the river. A little before sundown the gen. sent me to look over both lines & then make him a report at his headquarters near Hanover Junction. It was dusk when I got there, and a regular little council was held under a big, lone oak tree in a forty acre clearing. All around us troops were going into bivouac for the night. Men loaded with bunches of canteens, which rattled as they walked, were wandering about inquiring for wells & springs & streams. Company cooks were kindling their fires & impatient mules were braying for their suppers. The air was still & it was one of those evenings when all sounds are distinct & far-reaching. Gen. Lee sat on a big root, his back against the tree, with some of his own staff around & some three or four engineers, among whom I remember Sam Johnston & Proctor Smith.[6] Those who wanted the line in front of the swamp were invited to explain why, & then those who preferred to have the swamp in front. Gen. Lee heard the arguments, which were all brief & to the point, for all night would be needed to distribute troops & artillery, & prepare for the assault at day break, which we fully expected. Then Gen. Lee decided that the line should have the swamp in front, & began giving details about the location of troops.

Just then a teamster began to remonstrate with a mule, some hundred yards or more across the clearing. His remarks were as audible as if he had been under the tree with us. "Get around there you damned infernal long-eared son of a jackass," & a tremendous whack emphasized the injunction. Gen. Lee could stand anything better than having an animal maltreated. He hesitated a moment in his speech & gave that peculiar little shake of his head which he used when he was worried, & which we used to call snapping at his ear. But the misunderstanding between the man & the mule only seemed to widen. I won't try to repeat his lurid language, for I could not do it justice, & only a pile driver could describe the whacks which accompanied his volley of oaths. Gen. Lee stopped his discourse, snapped at his ear a time or two, & then shouted out in a tone which I thought would scare anybody, "What are you beating that mule for?" But the teamster evidently thought only that some one was guying him, for assuming a sort of Georgia cracker whine in his voice, he sung out, "Is this any of you-r-r mule?" It was an awful moment. Not one of us dared to crack a smile. The general snapped at his ear again a time or two, & then apparently determined to finish with us first, before making good his claim to the mule. I have no doubt that he did this as soon as we were gone and to the teamster's entire satisfaction, but I never heard any particulars.

I & my staff were busy all night putting the guns in position with the troops, & fortifying as much as could be done before daylight for we fully expected to receive one of Grant's interesting 4 A.M. calls. But he did not come; neither this morning nor any other morning as long as we held those lines. It was decidedly another case of our making them too good. They wanted to attack us. They crossed the river for that purpose and for that they built themselves a strong line, about 800 yards from ours, to fall back into if defeated. And their engineers & their generals looked at our beautiful lines with longing eyes for several days. But they always shook their heads & said it would not do. This little map gives the whole location & also shows the houses of Squire Wortham & Parson Fox & of Mr. Lowry, who sold his chickens. [Figure 40 appears here in the manuscript.]

The left flank of the 3rd Corps rested on Little River. Their line was short & good only it had to have traverses against enfilade fire from across [the] North Anna. Our holding a half mile of river made the Federal line very bad. To go from one of their flanks to the other, one must cross the river twice. We had the interior lines, & had our forces been near equality with theirs Gen. Lee would have endeavored to improve the occasion by attacking their left wing. But Grant was cautious, & never exposed himself outside of intrenchments. There was much sharpshooting & artillery practice, but only one affair approaching an engagement. In the afternoon of the 23rd, Warren's corps crossed the river above Hill's corps & moved down & was forming to attack, when Hill took the initiative, & advanced & attacked Warren. At first he routed Cutler's division, but Warren's artillery & other infantry restored the battle & Hill lost a few hundred prisoners. The casualties were probably about equal, perhaps 1,500 on each side. With our corps nothing took place except sharpshooting and artillery practice.

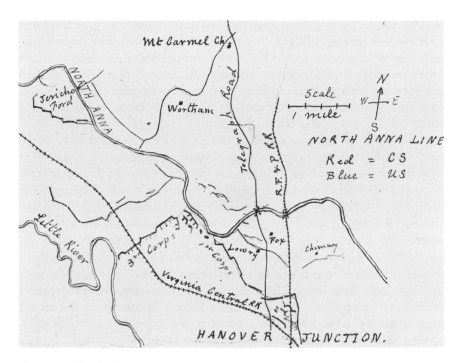

Figure 40. North Anna lines

Capt. John Donnell Smith,[7] of my old battalion, had an escape from a very skillful marksman which was unique. The shooting, at the time, was so light that it seemed to be all done by one man. But, though 800 yards off, his shots were all so close that Capt. Smith with his field glasses mounted the parapet to try & locate him, & treat him to a rifled shell. While looking for him, the fellow fired & smashed one barrel of the glasses at Smith's eye. Fortunately, both his head & eye escaped severe injury.

Grant's whole casualties while in these lines were about 570 killed & 2,100 wounded. Ours were estimated at about 300 killed & 1,500 wounded.

Before taking up Grant's next movement we must pause to tell briefly of the fortunes of the two flank movements set on foot simultaneously with Grant's direct advance[8] upon Richmond, Sigel's up the Shenandoah Valley, & Butler's up the James—for their fortunes will soon begin to influence events with us.

Sigel's story is short & inglorious. Gen. Breckinridge was sent to oppose him, with such troops as could be spared from other quarters, & gave him a decisive defeat at New Market on May 15th. Breckinridge's force was

_____. Sigel's was _____. And the casualties were _____.⁹ Sigel was afterward succeeded by Hunter who renewed the advance; but, meanwhile, Gen. Lee in his pressing need for men to supply his great losses in battle called on Gen. Breckinridge to join him at Hanover Junction with two brigades of infantry, about 2,500 men. Gen. Breckinridge came in person with these reinforcements, arriving at Hanover Junction by rail on May 20th.

Now let us turn to Butler's expedition. As before stated it comprised the 10th & 18th Corps & Kautz's cavalry—about 39,000 men, 5 monitors, a large fleet of gunboats, another of transports & ferry boats, & a great store of bridge material. As a blind, most of the infantry were assembled at Yorktown & Gloucester Point, to mislead us as to their real point of attack. On the same day that Grant moved, May 4th, Butler also embarked his infantry, & descended the York River & ascended the James. By the morning of the 6th he had disembarked without opposition at Bermuda Hundreds. Meanwhile, Kautz's cavalry had moved by land from Suffolk, with orders to burn three important bridges on the railroad between Petersburg & Weldon, which would cut off the arrival of reinforcements at Petersburg from all points south. Kautz was successful in burning two of the bridges, & then united with Butler at City Point on the 10th.

The movement, so far, had been eminently successful. The Confederates indeed were making every possible preparation to meet Butler's expedition, wherever it might strike, but the preparations were at least a week behind the need for them. When Butler landed, the available infantry for the defence of Richmond & Petersburg was scarcely 6,000 men, which were necessarily divided. Petersburg was close at his hand & had the smallest force & must have fallen an easy prey to a vigorous attack. But Butler, first, kindly made us a present of four days while he fortified a line of intrenchments, from the James at Trent's Reach to the Appomattox at Port Walthall. Here, by a short line of a mile & a half, he was able to make a little Gibraltar of a considerable territory in the angle between the two rivers, about which I will have more to say hereafter. The possession of that territory ultimately determined the possession of Petersburg, but during all those days, & probably for several more, Petersburg itself might have been had for the asking.

The Confederate preparations consisted in summoning Gen. Beauregard from Charleston with some of his troops & scattered commands from all along the coast & as far south as Florida. In that way Beauregard would have an army of about 19,000 infantry & from 2,000 to 3,000 cavalry. A few trains only of this infantry had arrived when Kautz burned the two bridges, on [the] 7th & 8th, & those in the rear were detained for some days by that means. Only on the 12th did Butler start out from his intrenchments to advance towards Drury's Bluff & Richmond.

By this time Beauregard was getting his force in hand. The night of the 15th found the two armies facing each other just below Drury's Bluff & Beauregard giving orders to take the aggressive & attack Butler at dawn on the 16th. Butler had sent his cavalry on a raid, & left his Negro division at City Point, & had left also some 3,000 men in his line of intrenchments & a division under Ames,[10] at Walthall Junction on the railroad, to look out for any advance from Petersburg. This gave him about 22,000 infantry in the field. Beauregard had about 19,000 but about 4,500 of them were at Petersburg, under Gen. Whiting—as was also most of his cavalry.

His plan of battle was to attack Butler at dawn in front, & especially to have his left so extended as to turn Butler's right. Meanwhile, Whiting was to come out from Petersburg & to attack in rear, coming toward the heaviest firing. This plan violates an axiom of war, which declares it practically impossible to combine simultaneous attacks by armies or parts of armies from opposite directions. We could not do it at Gettysburg, though our wings were much nearer than here. Indeed, Prest. Davis states in his book that he disapproved of this feature of Beauregard's plan, & ordered that Whiting be brought around & united with the other divisions during the night before the attack.[11] But it was not done. Perhaps there was another reason which weighed with Mr. Davis, & not improperly. None of the histories have ever mentioned it, but it was as notorious in the Confederacy, almost, as the fact of the battle. Poor Whiting was a very hard drinker, & no one who knew him could but fear & wonder how he would acquit himself, off alone with his division.

That I will tell about presently. There was one other weak point in Beauregard's orders. No military axiom yet condemns it, but it is high time that one did. The sound of the firing was to be to Whiting a signal & a direction. He declared that he never heard any firing at all—though it was only 6 miles off, & was heavy, both of infantry & artillery, for many hours. This is but one more instance of similar cases before referred to—at Seven Pines, Chickamauga, & others still to be noted, where the sound of battle has sometimes scarcely seemed to carry at all in some direction. At dawn on the 16th Beauregard attacked. The enemy had intrenched themselves everywhere, & the battle was hot & bloody. His left gained some successes but could not push them. His right also got some ground & captured five guns & five colors. But to rout such a large force of veteran troops from intrenchments was plainly a task beyond the power of Beauregard's force in hand. For the long hoped for sound of Whiting's guns was never heard, though he fought his men until late in the afternoon—& sent many messages by roundabout roads to urge Whiting forward. And, meanwhile, Butler fell slowly back, and at night was safe inside his little Gibraltar lines again; retiring under cover of a heavy rainstorm which stopped Beauregard's pursuit.

What would have happened had Whiting advanced, & fought as our Confederate troops were usually counted on to do, it might be rash to try & say. He would have had to whip Ames's 5,000 men first, with his 4,500. If he succeeded in that the rest would have been comparatively easy. The excuse given to the world was that false rumors of Federal troops, about to attack Petersburg from the other side, had paralyzed Whiting's movements. But Whiting's friends said that the real reason of his failure was that he was afraid of getting drunk, & therefore did not touch any liquor, & his nerves, accustomed to have a stimulant, were upset by the lack of it.

At any rate he had done mischief enough & was relieved, at his own request, I believe, & sent to Wilmington, N.C., where he was mortally wounded in the attack on Fort Fisher in Feb. 1865. It is said that he never forgave himself for this failure & that he purposely exposed himself & sought his fate. He was a graduate of West Point & an officer of the old U.S. Engr. Corps—& a pleasant & brilliant man socially.

When the news of the battle of Drury's Bluff reached Generals Lee & Grant the same idea seemed to occur to each, simultaneously—to draw reinforcements from that vicinity. Lee at once had Pickett's division sent to rejoin our corps, & Lewis's brigade,[12] & perhaps a stray regiment, which belonged to Ewell's corps, were also returned. Pickett came to us, at Hanover Junction, with about 5,000 men. Lewis brought about 1,200. So with the 2,500 brought by Breckinridge we received about 9,000 reinforcements against losses up to date of about 25,000.[13] Gen. Grant, seemingly disgusted with Butler's peformance, ordered him to retain only troops enough to hold his lines, & to send all the rest to join his own army. Butler sent him Gen. W. F. Smith,[14] with a corps of 16,000 men, made up of two divisions of the 10th Corps & one of the 18th. They joined Grant about May 30th. When Gen. Lee got nearer Richmond, on his next move, he also had Hoke's[15] division sent him by Beauregard, about 6,000 men, in time for our next battle as will be told. The casualties at Drury's Bluff were:

	Killed	Wounded	Missing	Total
CS	354	1,610	220	2,184
US	390	1,721	1,390	3,501
[Total]	749	3,331	2,610	5,685

On the North Anna the casualties were:

	Killed	Wounded	Missing	Total
CS	304	1,513	200	2,017
US	223	1,460	290	1,973

17

TOTOPOTOMOY
& COLD HARBOR

On the 26th of May, Gen. Grant was satisfied that Lee's lines were impregnable to assault & he decided to change the scene of action and to bring on another foot race with its possibilities. Sheridan's cavalry had now rejoined the army after an absence, on his great raid, from the 8th to the 24th. This raid, by the way, accomplished little real harm to us except in the killing of Gen. Stuart. Possibly, the absence of the cavalry may have influenced Grant, on his move from Spottsylvania, to try the trap for us, which I described, instead of a foot race, which would have given him much better chances. But, however that may be, the absence of his cavalry certainly promoted our ability to make a rapid march, & to again throw ourselves across his path. So this raid should be classed, I think, as another example of bad play; like Pleasonton's raid at Chancellorsville & Stuart's at Gettysburg. [Figure 41 appears here in the manuscript.]

The move decided upon now was to turn our left flank, by crossing the Pamunkey River at Hanovertown. The rough sketch map shows the two lines at Hanover Junction from which both armies started and the positions near Totopotomoy Creek to which they went; Lee again placing himself across Grant's road to Richmond. Grant had the longest road, but he was always able to send his cavalry with the ponton trains practically a day ahead, & to start his infantry at dark, so as to get in a good 12 hours' march before we knew what was going on. In this case Grant's cavalry marched at noon on the 26th with the bridge trains. His infantry followed at dark & in the afternoon of the 28th he had taken position on the south side of the Pamunkey & intrenched it considerably, in case Lee attempted to attack him while crossing.

On Friday the 27th we discovered the enemy gone, & got ourselves in motion to the rear as fast as possible. We encamped that night at a place called Half Sink after a march of about 15 miles.[1] The next morning we went via Atlee's to Hundley's Corner, where lines were being extended &

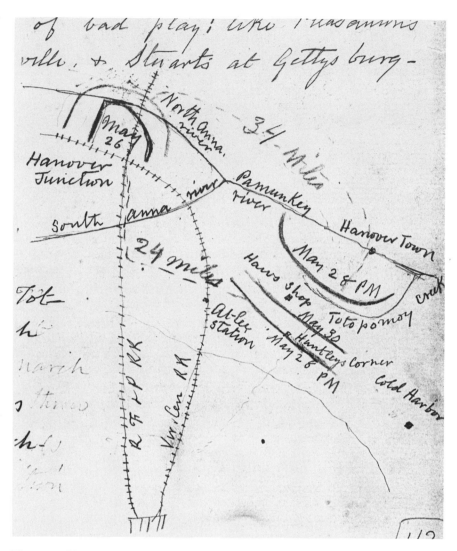

Figure 41. Hanover Junction to Totopotomoy Creek

intrenched by all three of our corps. The day was marked by a very severe fight between our cavalry & the enemy's, at Haw's Shop, in between the armies. It lasted all day & was practically a drawn battle, although at the end of the day the enemy held most of the field. I have already referred to the fact that their cavalry was all armed with magazine breech loaders which doubled their efficiency in action. The conservative Ordnance Department, however, still said they would get out of order & waste ammunition, and except for a few brigades they managed to keep them out of the hands of the infantry. There they might have ended the war two years sooner. Even those in the hands of the cavalry will be found to have decided many important events.

On this march I must note that good old Gen. Ewell had to give up the command of the 2nd Corps, from illness, to Gen. Early; & Gen. Ewell never resumed its command. Early proved himself a remarkable corps commander. His greatest quality perhaps was the fearlessness with which he fought against all odds & discouragements. Yet no man in the army, in any corps, but loved & still loves the name & memory of good old Ewell or that did not see him leave with regret. He was afterward put in charge of the local forces organised in Richmond among department clerks, &c. On Sunday, May 29, Grant advanced his whole line to find where we were & how we were fixed. It was a slow process in some places owing to swamps & woods, & faster in others, & a good deal of skirmishing resulted in spots. On Monday the 30th the process was continued, & two of my battalions, Cabell's & Huger's, came in for some smart affairs.

Nor did Gen. Lee leave the aggressive entirely to the enemy. He was, if possible, more on the alert than ever for some chance, or some weak spot to strike. I happened to see an instance. Some half mile in front of where our line crossed the Old Church Road, stood Bethesda Church, a locality which I remembered well from May '62, when Gen. Johnston sent me with the engineers on a reconnaissance to select a line of battle north of [the] Chickahominy. We could see the church dimly in the woods from our line, &, about noon, when I happened to go there to see Gen. Lee on some matter, for this was not a part of the line of our corps, he & Gen. Early were noting the appearance of about a brigade of the enemy near the church. Their coming there was to be expected, for they were extending in that direction from their right. It was clear that Bethesda Church would be soon in the very midst of their intrenchments. But these fellows were not yet intrenched. Gen. Lee struck at them like lightning. He said to Gen. Early, "Send out a brigade & see if those people are in force." The chances were ten to one that they were in force, considering the locality, but Pegram's brigade was quickly sent out to attack them. It was commanded (Pegram [was] absent wounded) by a special friend of mine, a splendid, young fellow Ed Willis,[2] of Savannah, Geo. He had just been promoted to brig. gen., but his commission was not yet made out. I hated to see him start, for I felt sure he would wake up a big hornet's nest. He whipped out the brigade we had seen in short order, & pursued them fiercely—to our left. Then he ran into some artillery, & several other brigades attacked him, & he was driven back with severe loss. And poor Willis was mortally wounded & two of his colonels, Terrill & Watkins[3] were killed. Gen. Lee was personally very fond of Willis, and I used to wonder if he ever reproached himself for having made this attack. But a general would not be fit [to] command an army who was not alert to seize occasions, & who shrank from paying the price it costs to try them.

When the enemy closed up on our lines the cavalry went out on the flanks—particularly on our right flank about Cold Harbor—where a number of very sharp encounters took place on the 30th & 31st. On one of these days Col. A. C. Haskell received a very severe wound. On the 31st Grant pressed still closer along our lines every where, & the sharpshooting was constant but he did not assault. Gen. Smith with the reinforcements from Butler, before told about, were now close at hand. And, on our side, Hoke's division, from Beauregard, had also moved out to Gen. Lee's help, & was near Cold Harbor. Each general felt inclined to improve the opportunity & to make a stroke.

And so it came about that Gen. Grant planned an attack upon our right flank, for the morning of June 1st, through Cold Harbor; & Gen. Lee planned an attack upon Grant's left flank for the very same time & place.

At Cold Harbor, Sheridan had constructed some intrenchments on the 31st & had successfully supported a severe attack in them about sundown. But he knew of the proximity of Hoke's division, & after dark he started to retreat. Orders however soon reached him to return, & to hold the position at all hazards. He spent the night in strengthening his works & filled them with his dismounted men with their magazine carbines, ready for an attack in the morning, which he expected Hoke to make.

Gen. Grant's plan was to have two corps, the 6th under Wright & the 18th under Smith, brought around to Cold Harbor during the night, where they would crush Hoke's division at dawn, & could then destroy in detail any reinforcements which Lee might send to aid him. It was for this that Sheridan was instructed to hold the position at all hazards.

Lee did not yet know that Butler had sent any troops to Grant. His plan was that our corps should move by night to the vicinity of Cold Harbor, where it was to unite with Hoke's division, & first crush Sheridan's cavalry. Then it was to wheel around to the left, & come down on the flank & rear of Grant's whole fortified line. Once fairly started, success might mean the driving of Grant back to the Pamunkey. And surely it looked easy for our whole corps aided by Hoke's division & some of our own cavalry, to clean up Sheridan in very short order & start. After that we would have open fighting for we would take all breastworks in flank.

Cold Harbor is shown on the [map (Figure 41)]. It was about three miles beyond our right flank. Our corps was near the middle of our line, & had to draw out & pass in rear of Ewell's. The whole march could only have been some 8 or 9 miles & yet my recollection of it is as a march taking up, practically, the whole night. Nor can I even recall any special halt for breakfast. But I can recall dust & darkness & unusually silent ranks, & also the great anticipations of what we might accomplish, once started in the enemy's rear—which we talked of during the night. And now to tell of the performance.

We arrived in front of Cold Harbor, & formed line of battle, & connected with Hoke, by about sunrise. That is we connected with him theoretically, but practically there was some 200 or more yards' interval between his left & our right. Had Gen. Grant's plans been carried out, about this time we would have been attacked by the two corps he had sent to crush Hoke.

But this morning luck seemed to be on our side & a great opportunity was offered us. Neither of the two corps, which Grant had ordered to be there at dawn, were within miles of the place. Wright's 6th Corps was so delayed by the difficulties of night marching that it was ten o'clock before the head of his long scattered column arrived & 2 P.M. before it was all up. Smith's corps had been sent some miles wrong by a case of heterophemy, some one writing Newcastle Ferry where Cold Harbor was intended. Smith's corps did not get into its position until 6 P.M.

So we had all the time we needed to work our own sweet will upon Sheridan, & if we had once gobbled him the other corps, in their scattered condition, should have been easy prey.

And the reason why we did not destroy Sheridan was solely & entirely because he had magazine guns. We attacked him twice with two brigades of infantry each time, & both times they were repulsed by the fire of the breech loaders from the breastworks. In one of these assaults, Col. Keitt[4] of So. Ca. was killed. He had just brought on a new regiment of near a thousand men, which had never before been under fire. Perhaps more vigor might have been put into our offensive, by employing heavier columns & longer lines at first, & by hurrying up our movements, had Gen. Anderson known the exact situation. But after our skirmishers discovered the arrival of infantry reinforcements, all idea of the offensive was abandoned, & the men were set to work intrenching the line of battle pretty much where they stood. Indeed they had begun to do that while waiting, even when we still expected to advance. I recall seeing a man digging with his bayonet & tin cup, while most of his comrades were lying down awaiting orders, & he suddenly dropped on his hands & knees gasping dreadfully for breath. A hole in the back of his soiled, grey shirt showed where a stray bullet had gone in his lungs. I had never before realized exactly what knocking the breath out of one means, and it made an impression on me. Hoke's command was not engaged at all this morning. The best manoeuvre would perhaps have been at the very first to send this division around Sheridan's left flank at sunrise & threaten his rear & his dismounts.

I do not recall seeing Gen. Lee with our corps during the morning.

Whether Hoke was under Gen. Anderson's command I do not know. But after it was determined to give up our brilliant hopes of sweeping Grant's rear, we were ordered to close up gaps & begin immediately to intrench ourselves. And all the rest of the army, which we had left three miles behind us, was directed to stretch & extend itself to connect with us, and to abandon the extreme left flank, from opposite which the Federals had now withdrawn most of their troops.

In carrying out the order to close upon Hoke's division one blunder was made which afterward proved serious. Between our right & Hoke's left a swampy thicket, along a small stream, was allowed to make a gap of perhaps fifty yards between Hoke & Kershaw's divs. It was a country generally flat, with many small clearings, & thin woods, & scattered pines. No long ranges, but favorable to cross fires & smooth bore ricochet firing—& I put in position every gun I had. The general direction of our line was unusually straight, which gave these cross fires sweep through the thin woods much further than we could see, but my men were instructed to fire at the sound of assaults & where possible even to get out in front of the breast works to do so. Although the men had marched all night they worked industriously all day, & it was well for them that they did, for a powerful storming column was being formed in the old fields & pines, about 1,200 yards off, to come & test them that very afternoon. Different formations were used in the two corps & they are interesting as examples.

Smith's three divisions were in columns of brigades. In Wright's three each brigade was in column of regiments. So Smith's attack was made with an average of 6 men deep & Wright's about 8.

Our single line was only 2 deep, & had no reserves or reinforcements. Their force was very much greater than ours, and, moreover, from the way in which it was massed, its attack had to be borne by but little more than one half of our line. We had had the advantage of a few hours' work at intrenching, but though the men had worked well they had been on the road all night, & were very tired & had accomplished scarcely more than a good beginning. This rough sketch will illustrate the formation: [Figure 42 appears here in the manuscript.]

We were scarcely expecting an attack so late in the evening when, at six o'clock, a sharp increase of fire on our skirmish line, & presently the skirmishers running in, caused a sudden cessation of our digging & every one stood to his arms. Soon a perfect tornado of fire broke out in front of Hoke & Kershaw, & every thing on their lines turned loose in reply, guns & musketry.

Some of our guns, too, from Pickett's front were able to put in very effective cross fires. Everywhere the enemy suffered severely, & were driven back promptly & decidedly, except at the 50 yards gap between Hoke &

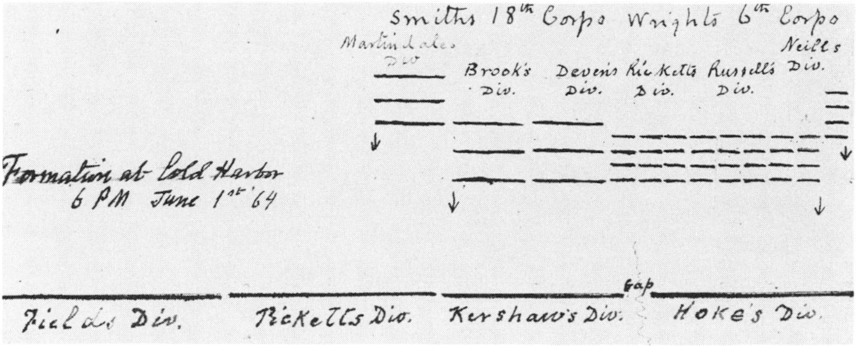

Figure 42. Federal formation for assault at Cold Harbor

Kershaw, through which flowed a small stream, bordered with woods & thicket. The enemy's dense column filled this wood, which sheltered them from our view entirely, & they penetrated the gap, & suddenly appeared on the flanks of the brigades on each side. Here they captured about 500 prisoners & a little of each adjacent end of breastwork. As Pickett & Field were not directly attacked Hunton's[5] brigade was sent from Pickett to reinforce Hoke, & Gregg's brigade from Field to help Kershaw. These brigades recovered a portion, but not quite all of the captured lines & took a number of prisoners. They then made a horse shoe connection between the two lines around the gap—& intrenched it during the night. [Figures 43 and 44 appear here in the manuscript.]

In this assault the 6th Corps lost about 1,200 killed & wounded & the 18th Corps lost about 1,000. When Gen. Grant heard of this partial success of the assault at Cold Harbor, he prepared at once to treat it as the thin edge of his wedge, which only needed to be driven home, to rend our lines apart. So he immediately ordered that Hancock's whole corps should be brought around to Cold Harbor during the night, & put to reinforce Wright, & then that the whole army everywhere should make a general & simultaneous assault as early as possible. Hancock was brought around, but arrived so exhausted by the night march, in the heat & dust, that the attack was deferred until 5 P.M. And, later, to give the men some rest, it was again deferred to Grant's favorite hour, 4:30 A.M. on the 3rd.

On our part of the line, Thursday, Jun. 2nd, passed quietly, except for very severe sharp shooting & a great deal of artillery practice. I was ordered to do a large amount of this during the day, to keep the enemy occupied while Gen. Early made an attack, of which I will tell later.[6] So I not only fired constantly on the enemy's lines in our front, but, where their lines were not close, as in front of Field, I took guns out in front to annoy them all I could.

Figure 43. Lt. Gen. Jubal Anderson Early

In the intervals, & at night, we improved our intrenchments, which as yet were mere little ditches that a calf might run over. As soon as Gen. Lee discovered that Hancock had been removed during the night, he at once ordered Breckinridge's division & Wilcox's & Mahone's divisions of Hill's corps to transfer to our extreme right & prolong the line of Hoke's division to the Chickahominy.

And having been disappointed in our attack by the right flank on the 1st he now ordered Early with Heth's division of Hill's corps & Rodes's &

Figure 44. Maj. Gen. John Brown Gordon

Gordon's of his own to swing around across Hancock's abandoned intrenchments, &, forming at right angles to our former lines, to sweep down on the flanks of Warren & Burnside, who were still in front of him. It was a quick bold move, &, had there been more troops to give it force, it might have produced important results. But after some preliminary successes & capturing a number of prisoners, & some very hard fighting, in which Gen. Doles of Georgia, a very gallant officer in Rodes's division, was killed, he was able to make no substantial advance. He remained all night, however, in his new position & intrenched.

Grant's orders provided for an assault at dawn on Friday, June 3, with every pound of force he could bring into play. Gen. Lee had the Chickahominy River close in his rear. If he could be routed there would be a chance to destroy him before he could get across. Hill & Breckinridge, on Lee's right, had had but little opportunity to intrench, & so had Early. Even our 1st Corps intrenchments were still very slight. A reinforcement of 3,000 infantry & 2,000 cavalry under Gen. Cesnola,7 had just arrived from Port Royal, S.C. Some of them, perhaps, were scarcely in very efficient condition, but they were all sent to join Gen. Wilson's division of cavalry upon our left, & this also was directed to attack Early in flank & rear while Warren & Burnside attacked him in front. The only part of the whole Federal army not ordered to take part in the action was the cavalry under Gen. Sheridan, which was along the lower Chickahominy & separated by that stream from any opposing force.

No long description of the battle is necessary. Of course it came off punctually to the minute, for, among Gen. Grant's great & rare qualities, was his ability to start his fights on schedule time. And, I may almost say, of course we repulsed him everywhere, for it was still true, as Stonewall Jackson had said, that "they always failed to drive us from our positions." The Army of Northern Virginia, in that respect, will be seen to have been like the "One Horse Shay." We held together wonderfully until the very end of all things came at once. As the attack had been on the largest possible scale, naturally, the repulse was unusually bloody & severe. The losses were especially heavy among regimental officers, who are the leaders in such affairs.

The grand roar of the battle coming upon the stillness of the early dawn was something terrific to hear. The whole strength of both armies was being put forth against each other, at once, more completely than ever before or afterward. The rolling & thundering crashes of musketry, the quick, incessant booming of the guns, & the mingled yells & cheers at times heard amid it all, gave a wonderful sense of the tremendous concentration of power, & of the skill & courage here pitted against it in a contest to the death. Richmond heard the roar, but heard it calmly. Hearts fluttered for the sake of husbands & sons who were in the conflict, & houses were opened for the wounded

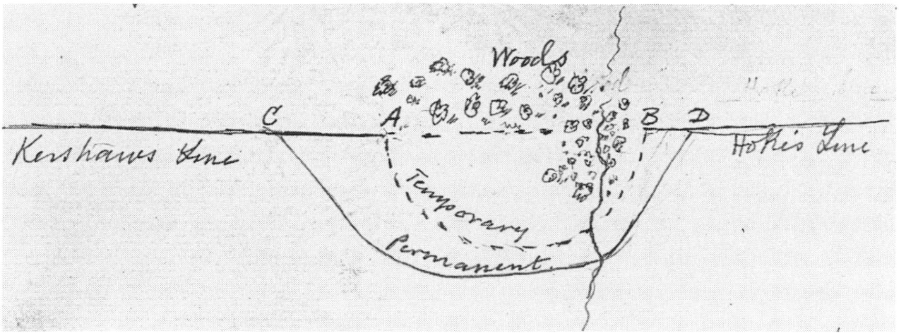

Figure 45. Confederate horseshoe at Cold Harbor

who would soon begin to arrive, but Richmond believed in the Army of Northern Va. as the army believed in itself & in its commander.

Such tremendous efforts could not be maintained in full vigor very long. In an hour practically the heavy fighting was all over. At a single place, only, had the enemy gained a temporary foothold. On our far right[8] in Hill's front there was a piece of bad location of our line, allowing a dead space in front to come up within forty to eighty yards, & there had been no time to provide abattis. Here Barlow's division of the 2nd Corps ran over a small piece of our line & after a sharp fight captured 200 prisoners & had temporary possession of 3 guns.

But adjacent troops were quickly brought to the rescue & the guns recaptured & the intruders driven out, themselves losing a number of prisoners. Finegan's brigade was prominent in the recapture.[9] The part of the line where the efforts of the enemy were most concentrated & prolonged, & where their loss was much heaviest, was on the front of our corps, in the little horse shoe built around the break between Kershaw & Hoke on the first. A temporary horse shoe had been taken up that night & was held all day on the 2nd; but a better line meanwhile was selected, a trifle in rear, & it was intrenched on the 2nd & the troops were withdrawn into it just before the Federal assault was made. A rough sketch will illustrate. [Figure 45 appears here in the manuscript.]

All day on the 2nd a Napoleon gun of Cabell's battalion had been maintained at the angle (A) where the temporary line left Kershaw's original line. It kept up a constant fire on the enemy in the trenches which they had succeeded in retaining & in new ones they were building close by in the wood.

To keep it supplied with ammunition, boxes were brought up to the line at a convenient point some distance to the left, & the cartridges were passed from hand to hand, down the infantry ranks, until they reached the gun—

the men singing sailor ditties as they passed them along. The night of the 2nd was rainy, but in the rain the men could hear noises and muffled commands close by in the woods, & knew that a daylight assault was being prepared. When all was ready at the new line in their rear, whispered instructions were given, and in dead silence the gun was slowly dragged back by hand, & was located at the new angle, & double shotted with canister, & trained upon the trench from which it had been removed. Now, too, it had neighbors, & a fresh supply of ammunition was provided. Objects were only half visible in the early dawn when the Federal columns set up their cheers & swarmed through the wood & over & into the vacated trenches, whence they were surprised to receive no fire.

Then we turned loose on them, everything, infantry & artillery, canister, shot, & shell. I think that at no point in the war, except at the Bloody Angle, were the woods so torn up by fire or the dead left so thickly strewn over the ground as in the centre of that horseshoe.

With any other commander which the Army of the Potomac had ever had, that first hour's fighting would have ended all offensive operations for the day—for it had suffered in that time nearly as heavy casualties as Burnside or Hooker had suffered in their whole campaigns at Fredericksburg & Chancellorsville. But Grant was of a different temper. Orders to renew the assaults were immediately sent every where. At some places they were obeyed, but with less spirit than at first, & were more easily repulsed. At other places excuses were made that certain artillery cross fires must first be gotten under, before the troops in question could be advanced. About 7 A.M. Gen. Grant authorized Gen. Meade to suspend the attack whenever he felt certain that it would fail. But Meade continued to press his corps commanders to renew their assaults. The following extract from Gen. Humphreys will give an idea of the situation. Describing the fighting of the 18th Corps he says:[10]

> Gen. Martindale[11] was ordered to keep his column covered as much as possible, & to move only when Brooks[12] moved. Hearing the firing in front of the 6th Corps, he mistook it for Brooks, & made three gallant assaults with Stannard's brigade but was repulsed each time. This brought so severe a cross fire upon Brooks, who was forming his column for attack, that he was ordered to keep his men under shelter until it was over. The fire from the right came a part of the enemy's works against which no part of our attack was directed, & Gen. Smith was unable to keep it down with his artillery. (This was evidently from Huger's battalion on our left.)[13] Reporting the condition in his front, Gen. Smith said that his troops were very much cut up, & that he had no hope of being able to carry the works in his front, unless the 6th Corps could relieve him from the galling fire on his left flank.

To this Gen. Meade replied, (8 A.M.) that Gen. Wright had been ordered to assault without reference to his, Gen. Smith's, advance; & that he, Gen. Smith, must continue his assaults without reference to Gen. Wright, who, but a short time before, had reported that his assault was waiting for Gen. Smith's.

To this Gen. Smith replied, giving special reasons why 8 of his 9 brigades could not attack, but said that the 10th would attack if more artillery were first concentrated on Huger so as to silence him. More artillery was sent for, but, meanwhile, at 1:30 P.M., orders were issued suspending all further offensive operations. In Swinton's history of the Army of the Potomac, a somewhat different account is given. It is not in conflict with Humphreys's, but it goes further, & states that the men would not obey orders to charge again, although orders were given them. Swinton is not considered a friendly historian to Gen. Grant, but I have never seen this statement contradicted, as would doubtless be done bitterly were it not very near the truth. Swinton writes as follows:

> The action was decided, as I have said, in an incredibly brief time in the the morning's assault. But, rapidly as the result was reached, it was *decisive*; for the consciousness of every man pronounced further assault hopeless. The troops went forward as far as the example of their officers could carry them; nor was it possible to urge them beyond; for there they knew lay only death, without even the chance of victory. The completeness with which this judgment had been reached by the whole army was strikingly illustrated by an incident that occurred during the forenoon. Some hours after the failure of the first assault, General Meade sent instructions to each corps-commander to renew the attack without reference to the troops on his right or left. The order was issued through these officers to their subordinate commanders, and from them descended through the wonted channels; but no man stirred, and the immobile lines pronounced a verdict, silent, yet emphatic, against further slaughter. The loss on the Union side in this sanguinary action was over thirteen thousand, while on the part of the Confederates, it is doubtful whether it reached that many hundreds.[14]

There can be no doubt that the temper, as it were, of Grant's army had been impaired by the fighting & losses of the last 30 days. Among every one thousand men, there is a certain percent who have initiative, courage, & are leaders; a larger percentage who will make sturdy followers only, & a residue who are shirkers. In assaulting breastworks, & particularly in assaults which fail, the leaders are thinned out & the shirkers are most apt to survive. The same thing, of course, happened in our own army, but to a much less extent for we assaulted less. And then our constant success in repulsing assaults partly repaired this loss by increase of the general morale.

At dusk in the evening heavy firing of musketry & artillery broke out at two or three points, & after awhile died out again. Each side believed it had been attacked & had repulsed an assault. The actual fact was that each side was putting out pickets for the night, & had drawn each other's heavy fire in false alarm. I have not mentioned them generally[15] & I kept no notes of them, but frequently, throughout the campaign when the lines of battle were close there would be during the night false alarms & heavy firing of artillery & musketry on both sides. But there was never, I believe, any real night attack anywhere.

We now entered upon eight days of life in the trenches, which I think were almost the eight days of greatest hardship that the army ever endured. Before giving any description from our side I will quote Gen. Humphreys on the conditions in the Federal army, who had men, labor, tools, provisions, clothing, shoes, & medicines in profusion where we were stinted to the barest necessities in all. He says:

> The daily skirmishing during this time was sharp & caused severe loss in some divisions; during the nights there was heavy artillery firing, & sometimes heavy musketry. The labor in making the approaches & strengthening the intrenchments was hard. The men in the advanced part of the lines, which were some miles in length, had to lie close in narrow trenches with no water except a little to drink, & that of the worst kind, being from surface drainage; they were exposed to great heat during the day; they had but little sleep; their cooking was of the rudest character. For over a month the army had had no vegetables & the beef used was from cattle exhausted by a long march through a country scantily provided with forage. Dead horses & mules & offal were scattered over the country, & between the lines were many dead bodies of both parties lying unburied in a burning sun. The country was low & marshy in character. The exhausting effect of all this began to show itself & sickness of malarial character increased largely. Every effort was made to correct this; large quantities of vegetables were brought up to the army, & a more stringent police enforced. . . . At the close of the day, on June 3rd, there were many of our wounded lying between the lines, & very near the enemy's intrenchments, completely covered by the fire of his pickets & sharpshooters. But our men made extraordinary efforts by night to get in their wounded comrades, & so far succeeded that very few were left. There were many dead of both sides lying there unburied, and Gen. Grant proposed an arrangement with Gen. Lee for bringing in the wounded, & burying the dead. This proposition was made on the afternoon of the 5th, but no cessation of hostilities took place for the purpose until the afternoon of the 7th, when a truce was agreed upon from 6 to 8 in the evening. Very few wounded were collected . Of those not brought in at night by their comrades, the greater number had died of their wounds & exposure. The dead were buried where they lay.[16]

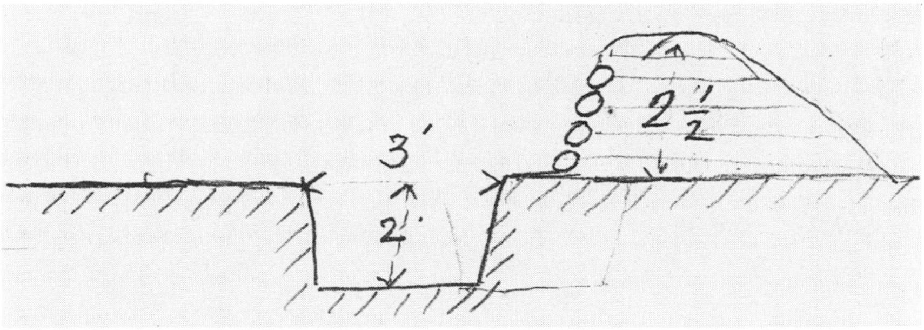

Figure 46. Cross section of works at Cold Harbor

During two weeks in these lines the Federal surgeon-general McParlin[17] reported 3,000 sick sent to Northern hospitals. The feature of the country which was responsible for the greatest part of the misery of the Cold Harbor lines was its flatness. There was no cover from the fire of the enemy, in rear of our parapets, except in the ditch itself. That kept the men crowded together & in constrained positions all day long. Our average ditches would not exceed 3 feet wide & 2 feet deep, with the parapet two & a half feet high. [Figure 46 appears here in the manuscript.] They would answer fairly well for men to kneel on the berm & load & fire from. But when two ranks of men had to occupy them day & night, in rain & shine, for days at a time it is hard to exaggerate the weary discomfort of it.

The Federals built for themselves many zig zag covered approaches leading to the rear. We had no spare labor for that, & had to confine ourselves to a few natural approaches—averaging one in a mile perhaps, where some ravine or hollow would permit one to come in from the rear unseen by the enemy's sharpshooters. Provisions & ammunition were usually brought in for the next day and the dead were removed under cover of night. Orders during the day would be carried to one of the entrance points & thence passed from hand to hand to their destination.

Sharpshooters, with logs & sand bags, made little loop holes over the parapet through which they watched the opposing lines. If one caught a glimpse of an enemy any where, he would sight carefully at that spot, & watch with his finger on the trigger to see if like causes would not presently cause another glimpse to be given at the same place. If it did he had only to press his trigger. In that way they would soon locate places where regimental trenches did not unite, or when men would try to go out for water, & several marksmen would then train on every such spot.

All along these lines I had my guns distributed, and, visiting them, I spent a large part of my time going back & forth through the trenches. That, at the best, meant my bending nearly double, so as to keep my head below the level of the parapet, & then stepping carefully over & between the men as they laid & sat in the ditch, usually half asleep. That was bad enough, but in the heat of the day it was far worse. Then the baking down of the summer sun became so intolerable that the line of men would canopy the whole trench with their blankets. Four men would reverse their muskets & stick the bayonets deep in the ground, for four corner posts, & let the hammers of the muskets pinch down on the four corners of a blanket. This would hold the blanket spread about three feet above the bottom of the ditch, & under it the four men would shelter from the sun & doze & sleep. Imagine how thick four men with canteens, blankets, & haversacks must lie to one single blanket, conceive that vermin were plentifully distributed in the army, conceive all the nuisances attendant upon great & crowded aggregations of humanity, & conceive that every once in a while a sick or freshly killed or wounded comrade is to be cared for, & you begin to have a mental picture of the Cold Harbor trenches.

To pass when the blankets were spread I would have to literally crawl under every blanket & over every set of fours. I cannot give a[n] idea of what it must all have been to every body, officers & men, better than by the details of the following personal incident which occurred a few days after the battle.

One morning, just before starting on a tour of the trenches, I visited the paymaster & drew my pay for the month of May. As brig. gen. it was $301.00 and it was paid in $20.00 notes, of what we called "New Issue"— bright, pink bills, fresh from the printing press & the signing room, where about 400 girls were kept busy signing them for the various officials whose names they bore. I put this beautiful money, at that time worth about $25.00 gold,[18] in a large envelope, & put it in my breast pocket, & started my trip through the trenches on the left flank, sending my horse to meet me at the furthest outlet on our right flank, some 2 miles off. About half way through I found I had lost my envelope. I knew at once how. The breast pocket was a trifle shallow. At three places I had passed were little gaps, where the trenches of adjoining regiments[19] did not unite. The enemy's sharpshooters soon discovered such places by seeing men exposed in passing, & they laid & watched them with fingers on triggers.[20] To get by, it was usual to stoop very low, & then dash across, literally as one would dash through fire. I knew that at one of these stooping dashes my envelope had fallen from my shallow breast pocket but before it had hit the ground I was too far off to hear it. So I stopped awhile, at Gen. Gregg's headquarters, to make an effort to recover it. I wrote on a piece of paper a notice about as follows: "Gen. Alexander has dropped an envelope containing a few personal letters, and $301.00 in currency. Whoever finds it is authorized to retain $20 as

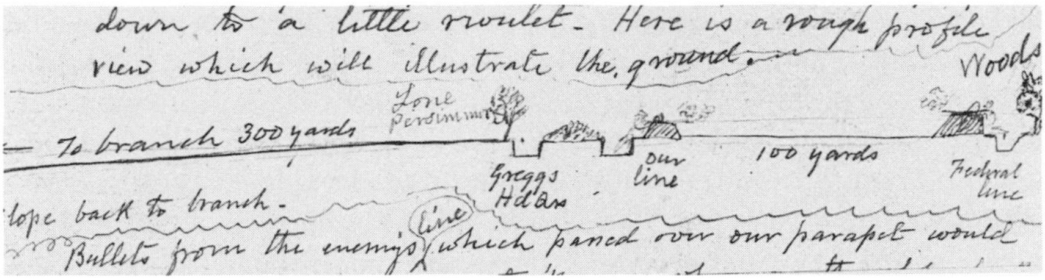

Figure 47. Approach to General Gregg's headquarters at Cold Harbor

reward, & will please pass the envelope, along the line, back to Gen. Gregg's headquarters."

I split the end of a short stick, which would serve as a handle, & stuck the open paper in the split so that it could be easily read. Then I put it in the trenches to be read, and passed back from hand to hand until it found the envelope. Then I went on in my rounds, which occupied the greater part of the day. But I usually finished up these rounds in time, afterward, to ride to some creek & take a bath.

The next day I was occupied at something else & did not go through the trenches, but about noon passing in rear of Gen. Gregg's headquarters I decided to try a direct approach from the rear & see if he had heard from my lost envelope. The headquarters consisted of a hole in the ground about 3 feet deep & about 8 by 4 in dimensions. It was located about twenty feet in rear of our main line trench, which was here only about 150 yards from the Federal line, on the edge of a wood. A persimmon tree by the side of the hole gave it a little shade in the middle of the day, and a little narrow trench from one end led obliquely into the infantry line in front. But I had noticed that not far in rear began a very, very gentle slope, for about 300 yards down to a little rivulet. Here is a rough profile view which will illustrate the ground: [Figure 47 appears here in the manuscript.]

Bullets from the enemy's line which passed over our parapet would naturally curve down & strike somewhere on the slope back to the branch, & any person walking up that slope would run the risk of such random bullets. But that risk was very slight The real danger would begin when his head became visible, over the top of our parapet, to the Federal sharpshooters. By stooping very low a man might approach apparently within fifty yards of the headquarters. To be safe beyond that point he would have to get on his hands & knees, & perhaps even to be flat & crawl for the last part of the distance. I left my horse at the little rivulet with my staff & walked up the slope. Every one of my staff begged to be allowed to go for me, but I would not trust any of the young fellows to use the caution necessary, & to turn back if, on near inspection, the approach proved to be too hazardous. Within 100 yards of the tree I began to stoop & got within 50 when I stopped awhile to rest & decide whether to crawl the balance or to risk a dash. It was so hot in the sun I decided on the dash. Then bending as low & running as fast as could be combined, I made the dash successfully, not being fired at that I was aware of, & I jumped headlong into the hole. I landed between two dead Texans, each shot through the head, & a third one, alive & well, was squatted in one corner. He did not change his attitude, but smiled & said sociably, "By Gosh! You has to be mighty careful how you shows a head around here, or they'll get you certain! Thars two they got already this morning!" "Yes," said I, "I see. But where's Gen. Gregg's headquarters?" "Oh! he moved last night down thar somewhar nigh that little branch. You go thar & hunt. You'll find him." It would have been safer for me to crawl out, but I had come in safely, & after resting awhile & recovering my breath & muscles, I decided on a flying retreat & made it safely. And I found Gen. Gregg's headquarters, & he had my money for me, all right, less the $20.00 reward. My story has proved longer than I expected when I began to tell it, but it gives a better idea of the trenches than I could accomplish by description alone.

And while on the subject of the sharpshooting I will mention one incident illustrating its severity. Every night each gun was ordered to be double shotted with canister, ready for instant use in case of a night attack. One of Cabell's Napoleons had had its wheels so cut & torn by bullets one evening that it was thought best to put on new ones. This was done, & the breech of the gun was elevated & 37 musket balls fell out, which had gone down its muzzle during the day.[21]

My note book makes brief mention of a few special incidents only. On the 4th another battalion of artillery commanded by Floyd King[22] was assigned to me & put in position. It had served with us for awhile in West Virginia in the spring, & had later served with Breckinridge in the Valley & had come with the infantry he brought. I was also put in charge of all the artillery on Hoke's lines, & on the 5th made my first trip through them. They were worse lines to traverse than ours, with frequent breaks between regiments, & I passed several men freshly killed or wounded. When I reached the exreme right flank, the trench ended in a light, sandy, open field, the enemy's line about 300 yards off—the colonel commanding the last regiment advised me either to wait until night or to return the way I came. But I saw a breast work about 100 yards in rear, Colquitt's brigade in reserve, I was told. I made a dash for that & jumped its parapet & fell in the ditch, out of breath, & almost on Gen. Colquitt of Georgia, whom I thus met for the first time with scarcely breath to introduce myself.

I have notes of some special cannonades, by Haskell's battalion on the

4th, Huger's on the 5th, & Hardaway's[23] on the 7th. Gen. Lee was anxious to take the offensive & both on the 6th & 7th had Early out in the woods trying to find ways to get at Grant's right flank, but without success. Hardaway's battalion was advanced in front of our left flank & used to aid the last of these attempts. At a few close points the enemy seemed disposed to regular siege operations, & I rigged howitzers on skids, for use as mortars, at two points, & I also got my friend, Col. Gorgas,[24] chief of [the] Ordnance Bureau, to get up an iron coehorn mortar, a 12 pounder, for me, & to put two dozen under immediate construction. The mortars recall a curious experience of the enormous differences in the audibility of guns in different conditions of even calm air. Our camp was some 1,200 yards in rear of our lines. One calm, smoky evening at sundown, shells from the enemy's guns fell around us, but no sound of the guns could be heard. They were about a mile away. A few nights later our howitzers, rigged as mortars, opened, using scarcely two ounces of powder. At our camp the reports, which we never expected to hear at all, sounded so heavy that we were sure that the enemy were replying to us with 10 inch seacoast mortars & 120 lb. shell.

Sunday, Jun. 12th, I have noted as largely spent in sharpshooting among Gregg's Texans. I felt it desirable to learn all the tricks of the sharpshooter's trade. I very much doubt that I hit any one. It was not shooting at a whole man, but generally at only an edge, or corner, exposed for a few seconds from behind some obstacle. If any larger fraction, it was jumping across some gap & harder to hit than a snipe.

Meanwhile some important events were occurring up in the Valley. Hunter, who had succeeded Sigel, had advanced up the Valley after Breckinridge had come to reinforce Gen. Lee. On Jun. 5th he with a force of about 12,000 had defeated Jones's, Vaughn's, & Imboden's brigades[25] of cavalry & mounted infantry, about 5,000 men, at Piedmont near Staunton, capturing 1,500 prisoners. In this battle, my old friend & class mate, Dick Brewer of Maryland was killed—col. of the _____[26] Regt. of cavy. On hearing of this disaster Gen. Breckinridge was sent back to the Valley.

Later Gen. Lee heard of Hunter's uniting with Crook & Averell at Staunton on Jun. 8th & marching via Lexington to destroy Lynchburg with now about 20,000 men. There was but one way to save it—he must risk detaching an entire corps & sending it after Hunter. Early's was designated, & on the 12th it drew out of the Cold Harbor lines & marched at 3 A.M. of the 13th to pursue Hunter. Breckinridge had gone ahead to Lynchburg.

Meanwhile, [on] Jun. 5th Gen. Sheridan, with two divisions of cavalry, had been started on an important raid. He was to go to Charlottesville destroying the railroad bridges all the way, to unite with Hunter & to bring Hunter back with him to join Grant's army. Hampton pursued Sheridan with two of his divisions & some very desperate cavalry fighting took place June 11th & 12th in the vicinity of Trevilian's Station. Each claimed a victory but Sheridan's expedition turned back & crossing the North Anna it retreated to the White House. Hampton followed but had to keep south of the river having no pontons. From White House, Sheridan tried to strike across & join Butler, but Hampton again struck him & drove him to the shelter of the gunboats at Douthard's Landing on the James near the site of Grant's crossing. Here ferry boats brought them across on June 26 & 27th, Grant being already across, as has yet to be told.

Grant's total losses in the two weeks between the Pamunkey & the Chickahominy were reported by his chief surgeon McParlin as about 1,920 killed, 10,345 wounded, 1,864 missing. Total 14,129. Probably at least a half of this loss took place on the 3rd. Gen. Lee's loss on that day was very slight, & has been generally estimated at about 1,700. His total losses in the two weeks were about 4,500.

The Confederates lost Gen. Doles killed & Col. Willis, who had actually been promoted but the commission not issued, & they had wounded Genls. Law, Kirkland,[27] Lane, & Finegan. The Federals lost Gen. McKeen[28] killed & Gen. Tyler wounded.

PASSAGE OF JAMES RIVER

I have dwelt somewhat upon the battle of Cold Harbor & the situation after it, because I think we have now reached the most interesting point in the whole military history of the Confederacy.

Perhaps the South never had any real chance of success in the war, from the very first. Perhaps, the only real crisis of the war was the day she ventured to undertake it—the day on which she decided to fire the first gun at Fort Sumter, rather than to risk the enemy's effort to reinforce it. But I prefer to believe that in the long struggle there were other crises after this. That as in a game of chess more than one crisis may be passed through, so in the game of war. The last must be the one par excellence, and it is of that I now have to tell.

When the South entered upon war with a power so immensely her superior in men & money, & all the wealth of modern resources in machinery and transportation appliances by land & sea, she could entertain but one single hope of final success. That was, that the desperation of her resistance would finally exact from her adversary such a price in blood & treasure as to exhaust the enthusiasm of its population for the objects of the war. We could not hope to *conquer* her. Our one chance was to wear her out.

If therefore there was ever any "High Tide" of the Confederacy it was when the enthusiasm of the North for the war was at "low tide." If there was ever any "Crisis," it was when fresh disaster was averted, & some success gained which stimulated anew the hopes of the North. Tried by these tests it seems to me that the pause after the battle of Cold Harbor was our last, & perhaps our highest tide. Also that Grant's next move, risking but escaping another great disaster, & gaining a strategic position of controlling value was the last crisis of the war.

First let us note briefly the main features of the military situation. A competent military critic might, indeed, confidently predict Grant's final success, from his wonderful pertinacity, & his confidence in himself, and his arithmetical methods, & the tireless persistence with which he kept his great war machine, day & night, at the highest pressure to be gotten out of men.

But to the average citizen what was the situation? Though having odds, practically two to one in his favor, in three terrific battles within a month, he had been always thwarted, & had lost about 50,000 men. And he was no nearer Richmond at the end than his ships might have landed him at the beginning, without loss of a man. He was, indeed, consuming the Southern male population, but beside the cost of over two million dollars a day, he was paying more than man for man in Northern blood.

In Georgia, Sherman, with over 100,000 men against Johnston's 45,000, had advanced as far as Kennesaw Mountain, near Marietta, but had gained no advantage over Johnston, and had fought no serious battle. Johnston's strength & position were improved as he drew near to Atlanta, which our Engineer Bureau, under Gen. Gilmer, had wisely intrenched before hand; while Sherman's communications became more difficult.

Nowhere were the Federal armies accomplishing any success of importance, &, in Virginia, it looked as if their greatest army was being wrecked. And by the general sentiment of both parties it was in Virginia that the issue was to be settled.

Now, let us see what evidences there are—if any—that the tide of Northern enthusiasm was running low. I will first quote from Swinton because he states the matter so very emphatically & succinctly. But I must say beforehand that he is considered by many at the North as hostile & unreliable. He writes of the period now under consideration as follows:[1]

> War is sustained quite as much by the moral energy of a people as by its material resources, and the former must be active to bring out and make available the latter. It has not unfrequently occurred that, with abundant resources, a nation has failed in war by the sapping of the animating principle in the minds of its citizens. For armies are things visible and formal, circumscribed by time and space; but the soul of war is a power unseen, bound up with the interests, convictions, passions of men. Now, so gloomy was the military outlook after the action on the Chickahominy, and to such a degree by consequence had the moral spring of the public mind become relaxed, that there was at this time great danger of a collapse of the war. The history of this conflict truthfully written will show this. *The archives of the State Department, when one day made public, will show how deeply the Government was affected by the want of military success, and to what resolutions the Executive had in consequence come.*[2] Had not success elsewhere come to brighten the horizon, it would have been difficult to have raised new forces to recruit the Army of the Potomac, which, shaken in its structure, its valor quenched in blood, and

thousands of its ablest officers killed and wounded, was the Army of the Potomac no more.

Of the condition of General Lee's army at the same time he says:

> The Confederates, elated at the skillful manner in which they had constantly been thrust between Richmond and the Union army, and conscious of the terrible price in blood they had exacted from the latter, were in high spirit, and the *morale* of Lee's army was never better than after the battle of Cold Harbor.[3]

Now within our limits I cannot go deeply or at length into the state of public sentiment at the period but there are a few facts which briefly stated may be considered as barometers of the public mind. One of these is the price of gold in New York. Another is the value of U.S. bonds. Others are the falling off in the enlistments of volunteers, the difficulties enforcing the draft and the bounties paid to procure recruits. Still another will appear in the activity, the hopes, & the platform, perhaps, of the opposition party, the Democrats, for the approaching election in Nov. The following table will show the principal fluctuation in the prices of gold & of U.S. bonds.[4]

We now come to explain Grant's next move, & to show how, in its execution, he avoided another disaster, & gained a strategic position of such controlling value that the fall of Richmond, and with it of the Confederacy, was, after that, only a question of a few moves more or less.

In my account of the situation in 1862, when McClellan's army took refuge on the James River below the Appomattox, I spoke of the strategic advantages to the enemy of a position astraddle of the James River. If Petersburg were captured, Richmond could no longer be held, more than a few days, at the utmost. An enemy astraddle of the James could threaten alternately, with his whole force, Petersburg on the south bank, or Richmond on the north. This would force the Confederates to so divide their forces, & so extend their lines, that they must finally be weakened to the breaking point. The enemy would have what are called the interior lines & we the exterior, which are necessarily longer. And as his force was enormously in excess of ours we have the weaker party on the longer line, a situation sure to prove fatal in the end. The inevitable way in which that result must work out will appear very clearly in the final events of the war— as we come to their narration. [Figure 48 appears here in the manuscript.]

The map on this page shows the relative positions of Cold Harbor, Richmond, & Petersburg, & the James, Chickahominy, & Appomattox Rivers,[5] with an out of scale sketch of [the] York River & the lower James.

I have already told of Butler's occupation of the ground in between the James & Appomattox, & of his converting it into a small Gibraltar, by a short line of intrenchments where the two rivers bend toward each other, at

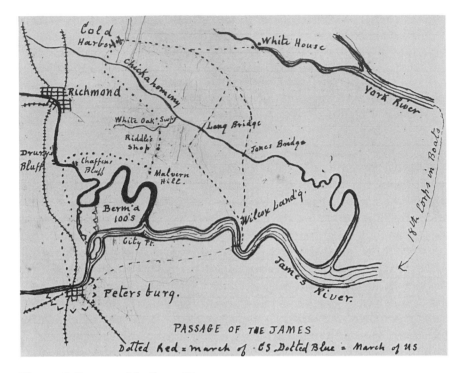

Figure 48. Passage of the James River

a point about three miles above their junction. The position is called Bermuda Hundreds; &, being surrounded on the north, east, & south by the rivers, bearing iron clads & gun boats, it was unassailable. Also, by means of ponton bridges, it commanded the opposite shores of both rivers. Note, too, that it is almost directly in line between Richmond & Petersburg, & the strategic value of the position becomes apparent.

It is as if, on a chessboard, one's adversary had established a pawn on one's king's bishop's pawn's square, checking his king & threatening his back row & all his vitals.

Grant's army was now only a few miles away, & on its next move would certainly endeavor, somewhere, to make connection with Butler. When he had once accomplished that, he would soon become unassailable.

It was of immense, of vital importance to Gen. Lee to strike his hardest blow in the progress of Grant's next move.

His most obvious move was to seek the connection with Butler between Deep Bottom & City Point. This would have been the shortest, & this was evidently the move which Gen. Lee anticipated he would make. And this movement was also recommended too to Gen. Grant from Washington City by Gen. Halleck.

But Grant had devised a piece of strategy all his own, which seems to me the most brilliant stroke in all the Federal campaigns of the whole war. It was, by somewhat roundabout roads, but entirely out of our observation, to precipitate his whole army upon Petersburg,[6] which was held by scarcely 6,000 men. If he succeeded in capturing it a speedy evacuation of Richmond would follow, & he would be in position to make the retreat a disastrous one.

Not only was this strategy brilliant in conception, for which all the credit, I believe, belongs to Gen. Grant, but the orders & the details of such a rapid movement of so mighty an army, with all its immense trains & its artillery, across two rivers, on its own ponton bridges, make it also the most brilliant piece of logistics of the war. For this, of course, the credit is largely due to the large, competent, & well-trained Federal staff & engineers.

On Saturday, June 11th, Grant withdrew Warren's 5th Corps to the rear, from Cold Harbor, & moved it some 10 miles toward where it was to cross the Chickahominy at Long's Bridge the next night. At dark on the 12th his whole army was in motion. Smith's 18th Corps marched back to White House on the Pamunkey, where it took transports in the morning, &, going down the York & up the James, it was landed during the night of Tuesday, June 14, on the south side of the Appomattox River, where Butler's ponton bridges crossed near the left of his line.

Here they were joined by Kautz's cavalry, 2,400, & Hincks's colored division,[7] 3,700, making with their 10,000 infantry a little over 16,000 men, who were ordered to march at dawn on Wed. [the] 15th to attack Petersburg. And here we will leave them for awhile, & follow the rest of the army. All the bridges over the Chickahominy had been burned long before, but Grant's engineers soon after midnight of the 12th had double ponton bridges at the Long Bridge site & Warren's corps moved across & took a position advanced toward Riddell's Shop to cover the passage of the other troops & intrenched themselves. The 2nd Corps followed the 5th across & marched on to Wilcox's Landing on the James. The 6th & 9th Corps crossed at Jones's Bridge 5 miles lower down & marched to the same place.

The 2nd Corps reached Wilcox's at 6 P.M. on Mon. [the] 13th after a march of about thirty miles. The 5th Corps, having successfully covered the passage arrived at noon of the 14th, & the 6th & 9th Corps, whose marches had been ten to 15 miles longer, also arrived during this day. A ponton bridge was being prepared, but, without waiting for it, the transports & ferry boats which had handled the 18th Corps now came & ferried Hancock's corps across the James during the 14th. He was ordered to march early on the 15th to the vicinity of Petersburg, by the most direct route—about 16 miles.

At 4 P.M. on the 14th the engineers began to lay the pontoon bridge—the greatest bridge of boats since the time of Xerxes. It was 2,100 feet long, the river from 70 to 90 feet deep in the channel, with strong currents & a four foot rise & fall of tide. A draw was provided for the passage of vessels. The bridge was finished at midnight, & artillery & trains immediately began to pour over it, while the ferry boats continued to carry over the infantry. This was kept up all day of the 15th & 16th. By the night of the 16th the last trains were over, when the bridge was removed. As fast as the different corps were united on the south side they moved forward to Petersburg.

Now it is time to return to Cold Harbor & take up our own movements on Monday morning, Jun. 13, when we waked & found the enemy gone. We were now only two corps; ours, under Anderson, & A. P. Hill's; Early having started after Hunter but the night before. Our corps at that time was about 12,000 strong & Hill's probably about 11,000.[8]

I don't think Grant's movement was anticipated, nor was it discovered until after daylight. But by eight o'clock, I think, we were all in motion to cross the Chickahominy. Hoke's division, which was considered as a part of Beauregard's army, was directed to go to Drury's Bluff on the James where we had a ponton bridge, some ten or 12 miles from Cold Harbor. Our corps & Hill's by 3 P.M. were stretched along a line from White Oak Swamp to Malvern Hill by Riddell's Shop. Our skirmishers here soon developed the skirmishers of Warren's 5th Corps opposite Hill on our left, & cavalry in front of us. Hill had something of an affair at his end, the enemy reporting a loss, for the afternoon, of 300 killed & wounded. On our flank, it looked, for awhile, as if we were about to make a strong attack; but we did not. I never knew why, & about sundown we went quietly into bivouac.

This was the first of three critical days, when the result of Grant's strategy was in the balance, & success or disaster depended upon our movements. The sending of Hoke's division to Drury's Bluff was exactly right—as far as it went. It would only have been better had he been sent as much further towards Petersburg as he could march.

We could only successfully oppose Grant's movement in two ways. First, by having an adequate force in the Petersburg intrenchments to meet him on his arrival there. Second, by taking advantage of the isolated position of the 5th Corps, on the afternoon of the 13th, & crushing it. The only trouble about that was that we were entirely ignorant of the fact that it was isolated. On the contrary, by a well devised piece of strategy (the suggestion of Gen. Humphreys), Warren's corps had taken up its line so near to Riddell's Shop as to give us the idea that it was the advance corps of Grant's whole army pushing toward Richmond on the road from Long Bridge. It is not sure, either, that we had daylight enough left, after we found it, to have accomplished a great deal, as it was partly intrenched & its numbers were probably nearly equal to ours.⁹

Gen. Lee's view of the affair we had with it is given in a telegram to Gen. Beauregard, which he sent on the 17th: "Warren's Corps, the 5th, crossed Chickahominy at Long Bridge on 13th, was driven from Riddell's Shop by Hill, leaving many dead & prisoners in our hands. That night it marched to Westover. . . . Have not heard from it since."¹⁰

The next day was Tuesday, Jun. 14th, the second day of our three days' grace. Had we marched at any hour of the day there was ample time for us to reach the Petersburg intrenchments, say 28 miles, before the foremost of Grant's troops. These intrenchments had been built by Gen. Gilmer, chief engineer, in 1862, with a thorough appreciation of the strategic value of the city. They occupied a line ten miles in length, two miles outside of the city, & reached from the river above to the river below. They consisted of detached redans, with platforms for artillery, connected by infantry parapets averaging 4½ feet high covering a road in their rear. All timber in front, for a half mile or more, was leveled to give full play to the guns.¹¹

We lay quiet in camp all day on the 14th. I cannot recall any hunting for best lines of battle, or positions for batteries, or anything, but just hanging about headquarters & waiting for developments. Warren's corps had gone, & it would seem that that event might have aroused suspicion of something unusual.

Meanwhile, too, Gen. Beauregard had not only begun to telegraph his belief that the enemy were preparing an attack upon Petersburg, but he sent a member of his staff, Major Paul,¹² to personally interview Gen. Lee, & ask for strong reinforcements. The one, vivid personal reminiscence which I have of this day is of watching, from a little distance, the interview of this officer with Gen. Lee, in a little grassy field on the north of the road.

I could not hear the conversation, but I was told of his errand, & Gen. Lee's air & attitude seemed to me so suggestive of hostility that I drew a mental inference that he, for some cause, disliked either the message or the messenger, or perhaps both. And I imagined a new military precept, to be taught in the schools, that "personae gratas" should always be selected for messengers who are sent with verbal communications.

But whatever reply Gen. Lee made to Gen. Beauregard's message, our corps received orders during the evening of the 14th to march next morning for the ponton bridge over the James, between Drury's & Chaffin's Bluffs. Accordingly, about sunrise, Wed., Jun. 15th, some of the brigades were already on the road, & all of my battalions were ready to file into their places in the column, when there came sudden orders from Gen. Lee to suspend the movement, on account of some demonstrations by the Federal cavalry in our front below Malvern Hill. The brigades were halted & the men sat down by the road side. I did not dare to unhitch, although I would have liked to let my horses graze, but I thought that whatever orders came would be rush orders so I would not risk it.

This was our last day of grace & very nearly our last hour. At 7 P.M. that afteroon the Federals would assault our Petersburg intrenchments, which were 25 miles away, & were nearly destitute of troops. Could our single corps march behind those admirable breast works, & our veteran artillery unlimber their guns on those platforms, even at the very last moment, the repulse of the enemy could not fail to be far more complete & disastrous than it was at Cold Harbor.

For Cold Harbor was but an accidental field, held by scratch works made in a few hours. But here would have been a field skillfully chosen & fortified and prepared long in advance. For the Confederacy to succeed, it would not be enough merely to keep Grant from taking Petersburg. It was requisite to repeat the bloody blow given at Cold Harbor. Few generals, receiving such an one, would so soon expose themselves to another, but Grant's personal equation was such as to give us that rare chance. His undaunted confidence & pertinacity led him to hurl his whole army, corps after corps, for three days against those beautiful Petersburg lines. And Gen. Lee did not have a soldier there to meet him! Grant had gotten away from *US* completely & was fighting *Beauregard*. The Army of Northern Virginia had lost him, & was sucking its thumbs by the roadside 25 miles away, & wondering where he could be!!!

That was the time & place, the day & the hour, when the last hope of the Confederacy died down & flickered out. The last flicker was about 8 A.M. Wednesday, Jun. 15th, 1864, between Malvern Hill & Riddell's Shop. It was not in the crash & excitement of battle; it was in the weary waiting in the road, with all accoutrements on, & the men wondering whether the halt is for minutes or hours.

In this case it was for all day. The whole morning passed & still at noon no further orders had been received. About that time, my staff made our boys kindle a little fire, & get out a frying pan to broil some bacon for lunch. About the time it was started a courier came along with a note to Gen. Lee from our cavalry officer in front who, in the morning, had first reported the enemy's demonstration. Gen. Anderson read the note before sending it on to Gen. Lee. It stated that the demonstration had proved to be only a reconnaissance, & that the troops making it had now retired down the Peninsula.

It was in fact a final look at our lines, merely to see if we were still there, taken by Chapman's brigade of Wilson's cavalry division,[13] just before moving to cross the ponton bridge at Wilcox's Landing. I have often wondered if they laughed when they saw us. When I saw that note I felt sure that orders would soon come to resume our march, & we very hastily finished our cooking & got the frying pan back into the wagon. But no orders came, and after a long time troops & artillery all returned to their bivouacs of the night before, where the narrative must leave them for awhile, they having, unfortunately, no part to play in the important events about to happen— though the nearest to them of all of Gen. Lee's army.

Chapman's reconnaissance, it may be noted, cut no real figure in determining our failure to arrive at Petersburg before 7 P.M., for our orders had been to halt at Drury's when we got there. The root of the matter was in Gen. Lee's disbelief that Grant had crossed the James. Had we marched on, the only difference would have been that our time of grace would have expired at Drury's Bluff, about noon, instead of at Malvern Hill early in the morning.

But either on the night of the 14th or this morning of the 15th, Gen. Lee had yielded to Gen. Beauregard's urgent representations so far as to give one order, the effect of which, aided by some lucky accidents for us in the Federal camp, was destined to rob Grant of very much of the prize so nearly in his reach. That order directed Hoke's division, already at Drury's Bluff & considered, too, strictly a part of Beauregard's army, to march to Petersburg. Had the division been started a few hours earlier & given time to occupy the breast works before 7 P.M., it would at least have extended our day of grace for 24 hours or more. It arrived too late to accomplish that, but its arrival delayed Grant's capture of Petersburg for over 9 months. But no less force than our whole corps in addition, and the greater part, too, of Hill's could & should have been present to improve our opportunity to the full & win a great victory. When it is seen what was done by two divisions something larger may reasonably be expected of eight.

And now we may return to the Federal camps, whence Gen. Smith is to march at dawn, with his 16,000 men to attack the Petersburg intrenchments; & Gen. Hancock to march "as early as possible" with his 20,000 men to support. Smith had only about 6 miles to go, Hancock about 16.

Fate, that morning, was playing large stakes upon trifling events at several points. While our corps was halted by the roadside at Malvern Hill, & Hoke's division was somehow losing precious hours about Drury's Bluff, Gen. Hancock's corps was playing hide & seek for three days' rations which ought to have been delivered to him. He finally marched at 10:30 A.M. without them—having then & there lost the hours which would have given him Petersburg that afternoon.

Perhaps Smith moved with superfluous caution & slowness, but the event is very instructive as to the time necessary to approach, reconnoitre & attack a hostile line. He moved against a force greatly his inferior, & had, in his advance, Kautz's cavalry, who knew the topography, having taken principal part in an attack made by Butler's orders on Jun. 9th. Yet he consumed 14 hours between his start & his final assault.

This attack of Butler's on Jun. 9, by the way, deserves a brief notice. It seems to me a flaw in Grant's otherwise perfect strategy, to have allowed it to be made. It proved a fiasco, as enterprises under Butler's charge so often did. And it alarmed Beauregard, & caused him to increase his garrison & his vigilance, & to plan in advance the effective measures he afterward resorted to when in extremity.

His original garrison had been only Wise's brigade of infantry, 2,400 strong; Sturdivant's light battery,[14] 4 guns; about 25 guns of position in the principal redans; & about 300 reserves, old men & boys, citizens, not uniformed & armed generally with inferior weapons. But on Jun. 9th less than 200 of these reserves, led by Gen. R. E. Colston, one of our wounded veteran generals, & Col. F. H. Archer,[15] a veteran of Mexico, had repulsed three front attacks of Spear's brigade[16] of cavalry, armed with breech loaders; & had only been routed after artillery had been brought against them, & both flanks turned, & personal fighting with bayonets & butts of guns.

Many were killed, wounded, & captured, &, of the experiences of the captured ones, I shall have something to tell when I come to the 20th of October.

The good fight put up by these nice old gentlemen and their grandsons undoubtedly saved the town. Gillmore,[17] with 3,000 infantry, was confronting Wise, & was waiting for Kautz to turn Wise's flank. Kautz was so long coming that Gillmore gave him up and went back home. Meanwhile, too, Dearing's brigade of cavalry & Graham's battery[18] arrived, & Kautz had no chance but to follow Gillmore.

After that, Dearing's cavalry, about 2,000 men, were added to the garrison.[19] As the intrenchments covered 10 miles the cavalry were necessary to observe the portion which the single brigade of infantry could not cover, & also to scout out in front, & give timely warning of the approach of the enemy. Very few of them were available to actually man the breast works.

Until Gen. Lee, on the 14th or 15th, returned Hoke's division to Beauregard's control, as already told, the latter had under his direct orders, beside the two brigades at Petersburg, only Bushrod Johnson's division, about 7,000 men, who confronted Butler's 10,000 infantry in the opposing intrenchments across the Bermuda Hundreds neck.

Gen. Beauregard had more about him of what I would call military technique than any of our Confederate generals. He was very particular in the observance of all military routines, traditions, & methods, in keeping up scouting & secret service & in requiring reports & preserving office records. His records of the siege of Charleston, preserved by his special care

& published by his surviving chief engineer, Maj. Johnson, would do credit to the staff of any European nation, and form the most admirable & valuable military narrative which the war produced.[20] And the defence of Petersburg which Beauregard was now about to make, is a rare model of beautiful, exact & ship-shape play on the part of the commander, worthily backed by skillful administration in every department & by superb fighting in his troops. He was particularly fortunate in his chief engineer, Col. D. B. Harris, who was my special personal friend since the days of Manassas, when I was myself on the general's staff with him. Gen. B. had appreciated him & kept him as chief engineer wherever he went. He was a graduate of West Point, of the class of 1833,[21] but had resigned & been a railroad engineer in Virginia for many years. He was the very type of everything brave & modest & gentle, of indefatigable energy, & of most excellent engineering judgment & skill. I had not met him for nearly three years, until we were at Petersburg together for a short while during which I took great pleasure in him. Then he returned to Charleston, where he soon after took yellow fever & died. As did also another old comrade of Manassas days, Pliny Bryan, whom Beauregard had kept on secret service, & who had been blowing up Federal steamboats on the St. Johns River in Florida.[22]

Gen. Beauregard's department charged with getting intelligence of the enemy's movements kept a close watch upon the James River, & their reports of special activity there had made him suspect Gen. Grant's plan soon after its execution began. We have seen his staff officer sent for a personal interview with Gen. Lee on the 14th.

Now on the 15th Gen. Beauregard had Hoke's division, say 5,000 men, marching to him from Drury's Bluff. And lest they should prove insufficient, he determined also to withdraw Johnson's 7,000 from the Bermuda Hundreds lines. That would be leaving Butler free to destroy the railroad between Richmond & Petersburg, but was a less evil than the loss of Petersburg, & Gen. Lee would be able to drive him back. And Gen. B. notified both Gen. Lee & the War Dept. in Richmond of his resolution.

He had, about two miles in front of his intrenchments, one of the regulation devices for delaying an approaching enemy, about a regiment of Dearing's cavalry,[23] dismounted, with a light battery, all covered by some rifle pits & light works. The event fully justified the venture, while illustrating its risks. One of the guns was captured, but some very precious time was gained by the fight they made & the delay their presence there caused.

By noon however the infantry were deploying in front of the left of our intrenchments, while Kautz's cavalry went about four miles further, & began to make demonstrations to draw us in that direction. The infantry were to make the real assault. Wise's single brigade, with a part of Dearing's dismounted, had to be stretched out nearly three miles to face the enemy's three divisions numbering over 13,000. But they & the artillery kept up a sharp fire on the enemy's efforts to reconnoitre & deploy, & usually broke them up & drove them back. In this way they consumed most of the afternoon. At last, however, their very thin musketry fire disclosed to Gen. Smith that they were little more than a skirmish line, and, about five o'clock, he decided to cannonade heavily, & then to charge with a cloud of skirmishers, against which our artillery fire could accomplish little. He was one hour in preparing his lines & was ready at 6. Had he gone ahead at that hour the chances are that he would have gotten Petersburg. But his chief of artillery had taken all the artillery horses to water, & he lost another hour, during which night & Hoke's division were both drawing near. Tall oaks from little acorns grow. At last, at 7 P.M., all delays were over & the charge was made. Smith's device was eminently successful. Our artillery would not fire at the skirmishers at all. They reserved their fire for the storming columns which they expected to follow. The skirmishers over ran & captured two redans, Nos. 5 & 6 counting from the river, at a salient where the line crossed the railroad to City Point, capturing about 250 prisoners & 4 guns.

One division was then sent to the right & one to the left to take the other redans in flank & rear. Martindale's division sent to the right accomplished nothing. But Hincks's colored division, sent to the left, in a couple of hours got possession of 5 more redans, Nos. 7 to 11, with 12 more guns in them. [Figure 49 appears here in the manuscript.]

Kautz with his 2,400 cavalry had been making his demonstrations all the afternoon opposite Redans 27 & 28, & he should now have converted them into a real attack. If he had done so it would be a reflection upon him not to say that he would have taken the city. But the last hour of delay had exhausted his patience, just as his own delay on the 9th had exhausted Gillmore's, & when Smith attacked Kautz was on his way home.

It was at this time about 3 days before full moon, & the nights were generally bright.

The head of Gen. Hancock's column had arrived, & halted a mile in rear of Smith's line, a half hour before his assault was made. At 9 o'clock, he requested Gen. Hancock to relieve his troops, which Hancock did by 11 P.M. One might suppose that Hancock's troops were in as much need of rest as Smith's. Very naturally there was afterward a great deal of criticism of Gen. Smith for letting the prize of Petersburg slip through his fingers. His excuse was that he knew that reinforcements were arriving in Petersburg at dark, & that he thought it safest to make sure of what he had secured. And he laid upon Hancock responsibility for doing nothing with his own troops either before 9 o'clock or after. An angry controversy resulted. Certainly

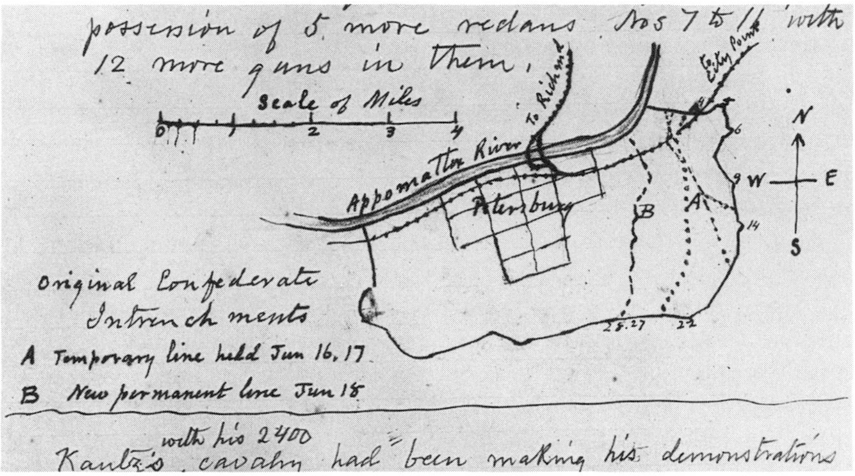

Figure 49. Original Confederate intrenchments at Petersburg

there were few indications of ambition or enterprise, or even of confidence, on the part of either of them or of Gen. Kautz.

Hoke's division arrived at Petersburg just too late to take part in repelling the assault, but it took up a line, throwing out the mile & a half of captured line from Redans 5 to 11 inclusive, & spent the rest of the night in intrenching itself. Meanwhile, too, Gen. Beauregard called for Johnson's division, from the Bermuda Hundreds lines, as he had advised that he would do, & he promptly notified Gen. Lee & the War Department. He ordered them, however, to leave Gracie's brigade & about a thousand men, to keep the enemy, if possible, from finding out the movement. Unfortunately, a vigilant officer in charge of the Federal picket line—a Col. Greeley[24] of [the] 10th Con., heard unusual noises about 10 P.M., &, crawling on hands & knees up near our lines, he found out that our troops were being withdrawn. He listened to the movement for a long time. He did not report it to Gen. Terry,[25] division commander, until three o'clock, &, fortunately for us, about as little use was made of the information as possible. But at daylight Gracie's scattered men were run off & some captured & Terry occupied our lines.

Johnson's division reached Petersburg by daybreak on Thursday [the] 16th & was at once put into the lines, where Gen. Beauregard had now united his whole force of about 14,000 infantry. These manned his intrenchments from the river out to about Redan 22. All west of that, fully five miles, were vacant. Grant had ordered no general attack on [the] 16th until 6 P.M., to allow time for the arrival of more of his troops. Yet there were strong reconnaissances by Hancock's troops in the morning, one of which captured Redan 12. The 9th Corps arrived about 11 A.M., giving now over 50,000 troops on the ground. At 6 P.M. a grand assault was made, & desperate fighting continued till long after dark. The enemy captured Redan 4 on our left, & Redans 13 & 14 on the right, but were unable to push their advantages any further.

At dawn on the 17th, however, a very neat & well managed affair by Potter's division of the 9th Corps got possession of Redans 15 & 16, near the Shand house, with 4 guns and 600 prisoners. The operation was a surprise at early dawn, the Federals' favorite time. The division had been quietly brought within 100 yards, in a ravine, during the night, & advanced with empty guns & by whispered orders. They found our men sound asleep with their guns in their hands. One of our gunners alone was awake, & saw them, & discharged his cannon, which was the only shot fired.

But here, too, the enemy was unable to push his advantage. The 5th Corps had now arrived & a division of the 6th, the other two divisions of the latter having gone to Butler at Bermuda Hundreds. Grant must now have had near 75,000 men at hand. The fighting was continuous & severe all day. Parts of our line were taken & retaken, but when the struggle finally ceased, which it did not do until near midnight, our lines were practically intact, & Beauregard & what were left of his splendid little force had covered themselves with glory. For they had successfully stood off Grant's whole army for three days. They have still a good many hours to spend in the trenches, but before another general assault comes, our corps will be on hand, & after three days of such a strain they may well ask for a rest.

We will now go back to the night of the 15th, Wednesday, when we returned to our old bivouacs, after being kept in the road ready to march most of the day. At 2 A.M. on [the] 16th Gen. Lee received a dispatch from Gen. Beauregard telling of Smith's attack in the afternoon, & his partial success, &, also, that Johnson's division was being withdrawn from the Bermuda Hundreds lines. On this, Pickett's division was ordered to march immediately to Drury's Bluff, & Gen. Lee seems also to have removed his own headquarters there at the same time. All the rest of Longstreet's corps, & our headquarters moved at daylight. We crossed at Drury's Bluff & were ordered to proceed to [the] vicinity of Bermuda Hundreds, following Pickett, to find out what Butler was doing & to drive him back into his intrenchments. Kershaw's division was, however, halted & kept at Drury's Bluff. About 11 A.M. we found Butler tearing up the railroad track between Richmond and Petersburg. We drove him from that, & gradually worked up opposite Johnson's abandoned intrenchments, with a little scattered skirmishing. At about 6 P.M. Pickett's division attacked them, & gained the greater part of the intrenchments with such ease that I entirely credit the statement of Federal officers, who were there, that Butler had ordered a withdrawal.

The next day, Friday the 17th, while Beauregard's people are having their third and severest day, only 12 miles away from us, we were quietly fixing ourselves up in the Bermuda lines. Gen. Lee visited us, & I cannot recall hearing the sound of the Petersburg fighting or receiving any information about it.

The enemy still held opposite to us some ground that we wished to get, to improve our line & our picket posts, & Lee, after slight hesitation as I recollect, consented that it should be taken by assault.

The assault was made, & seemed to be easily successful. They reported taking even more than it was originally designed to take. Pickett's division was put to hold this line of intrenchment, & they held it without change for many months. For artillery I put in both my own old battn. & Cabell's— about 44 guns, so they were well supplied with artillery.

During the night of the 17th two important events happened. First, in Petersburg Gen. Beauregard abandoned entirely the lines in which he had fought so stubbornly & well on the 16th & 17th & fell back to a new & shorter line which had been selected & marked out by Col. Harris, averaging over a half mile further back, & nearly a mile in rear of the original breast works on the east. The delicate task of withdrawing the troops & locating them in their new positions was successfully accomplished without the enemy's knowledge soon after midnight & they set to work to intrench themselves as rapidly as possible. For they had good reason to expect one of Grant's daylight calls with all the force he could muster, early on the morning of the 18th.

The other event took place in Gen. Lee's tent near Drury's Bluff at 3:30 A.M. on the 18th, where he was finally convinced that Grant & all of his army were in front of Petersburg.

It seems hard now, in the after light of exact knowledge, to understand why Gen. Lee was so slow to believe that Grant had gone to Petersburg. For Beauregard had continued to keep him informed about the fighting, & to beg for reinforcements. I can only suggest that he underestimated the enemy's facilities for crossing, & over estimated the time that would be required for them to do it.

Some of the telegrams which he sent to Gen. Beauregard were as follows:[26]

Jun. 16 10:30 A.M. "I do not know the position of Grant's army and cannot strip the north bank of troops."

Jun. 16 4 P.M. "The transports you mention have probably returned Butler's troops. Has Grant been seen crossing James now?"

Jun. 17 12 M. "Until I can get more definite information of Grant's movements I do not think it prudent to draw more troops to this side of river."

Jun. 17 [4:30] P.M. "I have no information of Grant's crossing James River, but upon your report have ordered troops up to Chaffin's Bluff."

At 3:30 P.M. on the 17th Gen. Lee had telegraphed W. H. F. Lee, commanding a division of cavalry at Malvern Hill, to push out & ascertain where the enemy were & to inform Gen. Hill. At 4:30 P.M. he wired Gen. Hill that Beauregard reported the enemy as crossing the river, & if Hill had no contradictory information he was directed to march his corps to Chaffin's Bluff.[27]

Later during the evening, Kershaw's division, which had been halted at Drury's Bluff on the morning of the 16th, was ordered to march to Bermuda Hundreds, & its orders were subsequently extended to continue their march to Petersburg.

Probably the occasion of Kershaw's movement was the following dispatch sent by Beauregard to Gen. Lee at 6:40 P.M. on the 17th:

> The increasing number of the enemy in my front, & inadequacy of my force to defend the already much too extended lines, will compel me to fall within a shorter one, which I will attempt tonight. This I shall hold as long as practicable, but without reinforcements, I may have to evacuate the city very shortly.
>
> In that event I shall retire in the direction of Drury's Bluff, defending the crossing of the Appomattox River & Swift Creek.[28]

The fighting on Gen. Beauregard's lines lasted more than four hours after his sending this last dispatch. But when it was over & the transfer of his troops to their new lines was fairly under way, having been begun as soon as possible after the fighting ceased, Beauregard began to take more radical measures to convince Gen. Lee of the situation. He sent three of his staff officers, one after the other, within a couple of hours, with messages about the prisoners whom he had captured from three different corps of the Federal army, & with such details as seemed to be convincing. The first messenger was his aid Col. A. R. Chisolm, who interviewed Gen. Lee lying on the ground in his tent, between 1 & 2:00 A.M. on the 18th. Gen. Lee was very placid & heard all the messages, but still said he thought Gen. Beauregard was mistaken in supposing that any large part of Grant's army had crossed the James. But he said that Kershaw's division was already under orders to Petersburg & that he himself would come there in the morning. Chisolm had to leave with only that satisfaction.

He was soon followed by Col. Alfred Roman,[29] but Col. R. had to leave his messages as Gen. Lee's staff would not disturb him again. About 3:00

A.M. Col. Roman was followed by Maj. Giles B. Cooke,[30] who insisted upon an interview & who brought details (statements by prisoners, &c.) which when laid before Gen. Lee thoroughly satisfied him that Grant's whole army was across. The following telegrams, which he sent immediately will indicate his change of mind:

> Jun. 18th 3:30 A.M. "Superintendent R.&P. Railroad—Can trains run to Petersburg? If so send all cars available to Rice's turn-out. If they cannot run through can any be sent from Petersburg to the point where the road is broken? It is important to get troops to Petersburg without delay."

> To Gen. Early, Lynchburg. "Grant is in front of Petersburg. Will be opposed there. Strike as quick as you can & if circumstances authorise carry out the original plan or move upon Petersburg without delay."[31]

At the same time orders were sent to Gen. Anderson for Field's division & the headquarters of our corps to go at once to Petersburg following Kershaw. The latter arrived there about 7:30 A.M. & the rest of us about 9. A. P. Hill's corps was ordered to follow us from Chaffin's Bluff & it arrived during the afternoon.

Immediately upon arrivals Kershaw's & Field's divisions were put in the trenches to relieve, as far as possible, Beauregard's exhausted men. Grant had, indeed, ordered an attack upon them in full force at 4:00 A.M. The 2nd, 5th, & 9th Corps, probably 50,000 men, were to assault in strong columns, the other two corps being held in support. Punctually at the hour the columns advanced, but found deserted the trenches which had been so desperately defended the day before, with only the Federal dead scattered thickly over the approaches in front, & our own dead abundantly strewn within them.

A few prisoners or deserters were picked up, & from them Meade learned that Beauregard's whole force had been only two divisions, & that now it was hastily trying to build a new line of breastworks a half mile or so in rear. This information was communicated to all the corps commanders, who were ordered to press forward vigorously & overwhelm our lines in their unfinished condition.

Indeed it would seem that an army could hardly ask for a more favorable chance than was here presented to destroy the worn out remainder of Beauregard's gallant little force. They could not now have exceeded 10,000 men, & the reinforcements coming, Kershaw & Field, were scarcely 5,000 each, & they were three & five hours away.[32] The little which was accomplished during the whole day is strong evidence of the inefficient condition to which the Federal army was now reduced. At first, a great deal of time was lost in driving back our skirmishes & advanced guards, & in the different corps waiting on each other in an effort to assault simultaneously. At last Gen. Meade himself fixed upon 12:00 o'clock as the hour, & ordered all to assault then. But the 2nd Corps assaulted alone, & was repulsed with severe loss in two attempts. The other two corps had not been able to work themselves into position, from which they thought assault practicable. Then Gen. Meade, finding it impossible to attain simultaneous action, ordered each one to assault as soon as it could, regardless of its neighbors, with full force & at all hazards.

Thus spurred & driven by Meade, each of the three corps, late in the afternoon, not together, but not very far apart in time, went through the motions, as it were, of making an assault. On our right parts of the 5th Corps, & on our left parts of the 2nd Corps made some show of fighting & took some little punishment.

The 9th Corps had in its front the weakest part of our whole line, a piece of bad location with a great dead space close in front, of which there will be much to tell hereafter, but it accomplished no more than to drive out our skirmishers, & to occupy this dead space. On our extreme left, too, a division of the 18th Corps captured a skirmish line, but attempted nothing more. None of the Federal corps brought from the South or West ever rivalled the fighting of the old corps of the Army of the Potomac.[33]

On the whole, we did not recognize the fighting on the 18th as intended to be, at all; a first class battle,[34] with full power in play. I think our soldiers, & our generals alike, considered it as only a day of demonstrations & reconnaissances, intended only to establish the enemy in close quarters with us.

It was necessary to wait until night before Beauregard's artillery could be withdrawn & that of our corps substituted for it. Of all the moonlight nights which I can remember I recall that Saturday night as perhaps the most brilliant & beautiful. The weather was exceedingly dry, the air perfectly calm, the dust rose with every movement & hung in the air, the whole landscape was bathed & saturated in silver, & sounds were unusually distinct & seemed to be alive & to travel, travel everywhere.

It was not a night for sleep in the trenches. There was a great deal to be done, everywhere, to improve & strengthen them, & every man was personally interested in working at his immediate location. And then, in spite of all our pains, the drawing out of the old batteries & the approach of the new would be attended with sounds & white clouds of dust; & the enemy would think we were coming to attack them, & there would come great crashes of musketry & volleys of artillery at random from their lines. Then our infantry would imagine themselves attacked, & they would respond in like fashion for some minutes, & the fire would run along to the right & left for perhaps a half a mile. And then, gradually, it would subside for a while to break out somewhere else. I was accompanied in it all by a Maj. Branch, who had been acting as Gen. Beauregard's chief of artillery & with whom I became very friendly & intimate. He was an excellent officer & a fine fellow, but was afterwards killed.[35]

So by Sunday morning, Jun. 19th, Gen. Lee's army was again fully established in its trenches in front of Grant and a new chapter of the campaign was now about to begin.

In brief review of the last, it must be said that Grant had successfully deceived us as to his whereabouts for several days & thus escaped having piled upon him within two weeks the odium of a second defeat, more bloody, more signal, & more undeniable, even, than that at Cold Harbor. Such a defeat would have cast a baleful back-light even on Wilderness & Chancellorsville, & must have exercised strong influence on the depression at the North which at that time was at the maximum state which it ever attained.

But, by his successful strategy, he not only escaped this sure & certain defeat, upon which he was rushing (for if Beauregard alone checked him what would Lee & Beauregard together have done?) but he was able to claim a substantial victory in his lodgment a mile within the Petersburg fortifications. This in itself was enough to tinge his whole campaign with success & change the direction of the current at the North.

The position which he had now secured, & the character of the military operations he now contemplated, removed all risk of any serious future catastrophe, however bold we might be, or however desperately we might fight. We were sure to be soon worn out. It was now only a question of a few moves more or less.

Of this period the future historian will doubtless write that by all the rules of war & of statecraft the time had now fully arrived for President Davis to open negotiations for peace. Now was the time to save his people the most of blood, of treasure, & of political rights. The last chance of winning independence, if it ever existed, *had* now expired, & all rules must condemn the hopeless shedding of blood.

It is, indeed, a fact that both the army and the people at that time would have been very loth to recognize that the cause was hopeless. In the army, I am sure, such an idea was undreamed of. Gen. Lee's influence could doubtless have secured acquiescence in it, for his influence had no bounds; but nothing short of that would. He would not have opposed any policy adopted by President Davis; so the matter was really entirely within the president's power. And, perhaps, by a peace he might have saved the South five hundred, or even a thousand million dollars, & doubtless also some thousands of lives. But there is this to be said. In every war there are two prizes fought for. 1st, the political principle in question. With us this was the right of secession. 2nd, military reputation in the eyes of the world & of posterity. This involves the respect in which a nation & a generation is held.

We lost the first prize, & the more utterly it was lost the better for us & all concerned. Without detraction from our adversaries' merits, but rather enhancing them, we gained the second prize by courage & constancy which could only be fully brought out & exemplified under extreme tests. Was it not best that we endured these extreme tests to the bitter end? And is not that end the only proper & dignified & worthy end to a struggle based as ours was not upon dollars or property but upon principle? And I am sure that, as to the army, any end but the last ditch would have seemed to them a breach of faith with the dead we had left on every battlefield.

The losses in this campaign are shown in the table below, which also sums up the losses of the whole campaign from the Rapidan to Petersburg; which was practically one battle lasting 45 days:[36]

		Killed	Woun.	Missing	Total	Generals K	W	C
Petersburg	CS	500	2,200	2,000	4,700			
Jun. 13–18	US	1,298	7,474	1,814	10,586	1		
	Total							
Campaign	CS				37,500	8	15	2
May 5 to Jun. 18th	US	8,412	44,629	9,609	62,750	6	8	4
	Total				100,250			
Bermuda Lines	CS				3,000		3	1
May 5 to Jun. 18	US				4,500			1
	Total				5,685		3	2
Battle at	CS	124	582	500	1,204			
Trevilians	US	85	490	570	1,145			
Jun. 11, 12	Total	209	1,072	1,070	2,349			
Grand Agg.	CS				42,000	8	18	3
May 5 [to] Jun. 18	US				68,395	6	9	3
	Total				109,000	14	27	6

SIEGE OF PETERSBURG

My first few days in the trenches in front of Petersburg were very busy ones. The intrenchments occupied by our corps were on the new line taken up by Col. Harris the night before our arrival, & consequently were as yet of but slight profile & much like what the Cold Harbor trenches had been. And the hostile disposition animating both sides seemed, if possible, even aggravated. The daily entry in my note book for six days—from the 19th to the 24th, was, "Severe sharpshooting and artillery practise, without intermission, day or night."

Most of these days I spent in the trenches supervising the constant work of getting the batteries into proper shape, with little magazines & with good communications. At one point on our line, already referred to in the last chapter, our location was very bad. A deep valley or ravine in front, through which flowed a small brook, gave a large sheltered or dead space, which came up within a hundred yards of a small redan on our main line. There the enemy promptly built a strong line of rifle pits, all along the edge of the dead space with elaborate loop holes & head logs to protect their sharpshooters, & they maintained from it a close & accurate fire on all parts of our line near them. An incident will illustrate the situation there. Gen. Stevens,[1] who was now Gen. Lee's chief engineer, wished to study the enemy's line closely, & as it was impossible to look over the parapet, & dangerous even to look through a loop hole, he decided to try a mirror. Keeping his head below the level of the parapet, he cautiously stuck up one end of a small glass, held at such an angle as to reflect the enemy's parapet down to his eye. In a minute a bullet smashed the glass in his hands & the marksman in the Federal trenches shouted out to him, "Set it up again, Johnny!"

This place was afterward called Elliott's Salient, as it was on the part of the trenches held by Elliott's S.C. brigade.[2] At this time, too, the enemy were bringing into use 60 mortars ranging in size from 24 pr. coehorns up to 10 inch or 120 pounders, manned by expert artillerists of Abbot's heavy artillery regiment of 1,700 men.[3] Gen. Humphreys writes of it as follows:

> The enemy suffered severely for the first few days when the mortars were opened on them at Petersburg. Having no mortars with which to reply, & no bomb-proofs for cover, & yet being compelled by the proximity of the main lines to keep their own fully manned, in order to guard against assault, the effect upon their troops was depressing. As soon as the enemy could obtain mortars they placed them in position, & from that time to the evacuation the mortar fire was frequent & severe though Col. Abbot's gunners retained their advantage of greater precision of fire.[4]

Upon that I would remark that the heavier mortars are always more accurate. Most of ours were only 12 prs., which I had fortunately gotten Col. Gorgas to start to build for me about two weeks before. But though at a disadvantage against the enemy's heavier metal we always held our own with them to the end. Beside his 60 mortars, Abbot also manned a tremendous battery of forty 30 pr. rifles, & six 100 pr. rifles, against which we could only oppose our ordinary light field pieces. But we were so used to fighting odds that we took it as a matter of course in all branches, & only built up our parapets thicker & let his big guns shoot.

We soon got our lines at most places in such shape that we did not fear any assault, but meanwhile this mortar firing had commenced & that added immensely to the work in the trenches. Every man needed a little bombproof to sleep in at night, & to dodge into in the day when the mortar shells were coming. They soon honey combed the rear side of the trenches with all sorts of little caves & cellars in which all sorts of individual ingenuity was displayed in the arrangement of these sleeping & dodging places.

We could see that the Federals too were working like beavers, & every morning there appeared fresh piles & lines of red dirt thrown up during the night all along their front. These I studied with great attention for I believed they portended regular siege operations about to be begun.

One siege operation, indeed, was tried a little later, as will be told, but Grant's plan included really nothing of that sort & was calculated to accomplish much quicker & larger results.

It was briefly this. He practically constructed two systems of works. In front an offensive one of trenches & redans, pressed as closely as could be to ours, & from which we were perpetually observed & threatened with assault, should we weaken our garrison. In rear, a defensive system of strong enclosed forts, connected with each other by good parapets with ditches & effective abattis. In these a small force might be safely left to defend itself for days, while the greater part of the army could be free & foot loose to operate upon either of Lee's flanks.

It is easy to see how that policy would enable him to utilize the advantages of his interior position. One fourth of his army, or less, could at any time securely hold his lines & continue to threaten Petersburg, while all the remainder, with his cavalry to help, could undertake operations upon Richmond, or upon the railroads which were absolutely necessary for its support. A surer move to utilize his fatal advantage in position could not be suggested. The "Little Gibraltar" which had been inaugurated by Butler's expedition was now to be extended. First it was to encircle Petersburg & afterward we shall see it stretched out toward Richmond.

While this sure, but somewhat slow process, was being securely inaugurated, Grant was still aggressive & very hopeful of hastening results by striking immediately at the railroads to Weldon & Lynchburg which ran south & west from Petersburg. He first sent Wilson, with his own & Kautz's divisions of cavalry,[5] together about 5,500 men with 12 guns, on a great raid against the Lynchburg & the Danville railroads. Wilson started at 2 A.M. Jun. 22nd. He struck the Lynchburg Road thirty miles east of Burkeville, &, though promptly & persistently followed by W. H. F. Lee's division, he tore up that road to Burkeville, which he burned. Then he turned and followed the Danville Road, tearing it up for 30 miles south to Staunton River. Here a force of county militia, in some earthworks with a little artillery, successfully defended the bridge against all of Wilson's force, &, being pressed in rear by Lee, Wilson made a large circuit to the east & started to rejoin Grant before Petersburg. Unfortunately for him, Gen. Hampton with the two divisions of cavalry which had been following up Sheridan now rejoined Gen. Lee in time to intercept Wilson on the Weldon Railroad on Jun. 28th & to give him a sharp defeat. He finally reached the Federal lines on July 2nd by roundabout roads having lost 1,500 men, all 12 guns, & his whole wagon train either burnt or captured.

Meanwhile, also, on June 22nd, the same day on which Wilson started on his raid, the 2nd & 6th Corps were stretched out on the Federal left, with the intent of reaching the Weldon Railroad, & perhaps even the Lynchburg. A. P. Hill was sent to meet this movement with three divisions.

With Wilcox's division he annoyed & obstructed the advance of the 6th Corps so that it failed to reach the Weldon Road by about a mile & a half. With Mahone's & Bushrod Johnson's divisions he struck the 2nd Corps on the flank & rolled it up, capturing 1,700 prisoners & four guns.[6] Mahone's men told a good story about the captured guns. The infantrymen who got them turned them on the fugitives, but made some very poor shots. A captured Federal gunner, who was looking on, could not contain his professional disgust, at seeing his pet gun used so unskillfully, & at last broke out—"My God! don't you men know any more about a gun than that? Here, why don't you do the thing like this?" And with that he turned the elevating screw and aimed a shot which went exactly where it was wanted. But, although from this affair we bore off the prestige of victory & prisoners & guns, Grant meanwhile had yet extended his lines about a mile & a half to the westward, compelling us also to extend our lines equally.

About this time some important events were happening near Lynchburg, at which we must glance.

I have told how Gen. Breckinridge, with his small infantry force of some 2,500 men, & later, on Jun. 13th, Early with the 2nd Corps, about 9,000 men, had been sent to meet Hunter & Averell whose united forces, some 16,000 men, were advancing on Lynchburg.[7] Early & Breckinridge got to Lynchburg ahead of the Federals, who, learning of their presence, were afraid either to attack or to retreat by the way they came. After skirmishing around for a day or two, Hunter having 600 killed & wounded & Early 200, on Jun. 19th Hunter struck out due west across the mountains for the Kanawha River. Early could not pursue him, nor could Hunter hope by that route to get to Washington City for some weeks. This left Early without any immediate antagonist.

I have already given Gen. Lee's dispatch to Gen. Early on Jun. 18th—either to "carry out the original plan" or to "come to Petersburg." This original plan had been given Gen. Early before he left Cold Harbor, & it was that he should practise upon the well known but very absurd apprehensions of the Federal executive & War Department for the safety of Washington.

It is worthwhile to let the narrative pause & speak of this, for the actual state almost of terror into which they seemed to be thrown by every threat of a Confederate attack was one of the strangest phenomena of the war.

Immediately after the Bull Run scare in 1861 the Federal engineers had gone to work deliberately to make Washington into a Gibraltar. Beside the protection afforded it by the great river & the armed vessels which it floated, the city was surrounded, about 4 miles out,[8] by a cordon of works which are thus described by Gen. Barnard:

> Every prominent point, at intervals of eight hundred to one thousand yards, was occupied by an inclosed field-fort; every important approach or depression of ground, unseen from the forts, swept by a battery for field-guns; and the whole connected by rifle-trenches which were in fact lines of infantry parapets, furnishing emplacement for two ranks of men, and affording covered communication along the line, while roads were opened wherever necessary, so that troops and artillery could be moved rapidly from one point of the immense periphery to another, or under cover, from point to point along the line. The counterscarps were surrounded by abatis; bomb-proofs were provided in nearly all the forts; all

guns not solely intended for distant fire placed in embrasures and well traversed. All commanding points on which an enemy would be likely to concentrate artillery to overpower that of one or two of our forts or batteries were subjected not only to the fire, direct and cross, of many points along the line, but also from heavy rifled guns from distant points unattainable by the enemy's field-guns. With all these developments, the lines certainly approximated to the maximum degree of strength which can be attained from unrevetted earthworks. Inadequately manned as they were, the fortifications compelled at least a concentration and an arraying of force on the part of the assailants, and thus gave time for the arrival of succor.[9]

Permanent garrisons of artillery were maintained to man the numerous heavy guns, & from the city of Washington there were always Veteran Reserves, volunteers, &c. available to swell the garrison to near 20,000 men to guard against a sudden surprise.

Yet, in 1862, as has been before told, McClellan was recalled from the James as soon as Gen. Lee, at Gordonsville, threatened an advance toward Washington; &, always afterward, it was made a condition of every Federal campaign that their army should always be between us & Washington. It was that condition which controlled Grant in making his campaign overland instead of by water, at the expense of 50,000 men. Really the Federals ought to have left the gates wide open, & encouraged us to come & attempt surprises against such a strong position. We would have been gnawing at a file, & could only have broken our teeth.

And now it was finally decided by Gen. Early, to whom Gen. Lee left it, to try this scare upon the Federals once more, & on Jun. 23rd Gen. Early started from Lynchburg to make a demonstration upon Washington City itself. I had as well anticipate here & tell briefly the result of his raid.

A small army of about 12,000 men under Gen. Wallace was collected to oppose Early but he defeated it at the Monocacy River on July 9 & drove it toward Baltimore. Federal casualties 669, Confederate 400. About noon on the 11th his advanced guard was fired on by the artillery in the Federal lines about Washington. He demonstrated in their front until the evening of the 12th, looking in vain for some opportunity to attack. But his infantry, by fighting & marching, was now reduced to 8,000 muskets, & the Washington garrison had been reinforced by the 6th Corps sent from Grant's army, & the 19th Corps just arrived from New Orleans. One division of the 6th Corps had been under Wallace at Monocacy. The 19th Corps was intended to join Grant at Petersburg but Early's move diverted it. Swinton writes, however, that such was the fright in Washington & the pressure brought to bear upon Grant to come with his whole army, that it "required all of Grant's moral courage to resist it."[10]

Early then fell back to the Valley near Winchester, where he was followed by the 6th & 19th Corps.

Playing him, therefore, against Washington accomplished nothing but to reduce Grant by those two corps, while Lee was himself reduced by but one. But as that still left 5 corps at Petersburg, the 2nd, 5th, 9th, 10th, & 18th, against our 2 there was really no advantage in it.

I have always thought that there was a much better play than the sending of Early on the raid to Washington. That play was purely bluff. We had seen enough of Grant already to judge that he was *not* easily bluffed. As to Early's really taking Washington with his little force, the very idea was absurd.

But if Early had been sent to reinforce Johnston above Atlanta, it would not have been bluff at all, but the very strongest play on the whole military board.

Then every man sent might have counted for his full weight in a decisive struggle with Sherman, &, if it proved successful, then Early might return bringing a large part of Johnston's army with him to reinforce Lee. As between Grant's army & Sherman's, we held the interior lines, & first class play would have required that we should utilize our one single advantage.

Before resuming my personal narrative the following quotations from Gen. Early & from Gen. Gibbon briefly reviewing the effects of the campaign on their respective commands are interesting as illustrating conditions which prevailed to a greater or less extent everywhere. Gen. Early wrote of his corps on Jun. 12th, that of 12 brigadier generals in his corps on May 5,[11]

> only one now remained in command of his brigade. Two, Gordon & Ramseur, had been made maj. genls. One, Steuart, had been captured, five, Pegram,[12] Hays, Ramseur, Walker, & Johnston had been severely wounded, and four, Stafford, Jones, Daniel, & Doles had been killed in action. Constant exposures to the weather, a limited supply of provisions & two weeks' service in the swamps north of the Chickahominy had told on the health of the men. Divisions were not stronger than brigades ought to have been, nor brigades than regiments.

Some six weeks later than this, Gen. Gibbon, who commanded the 2nd Divn. of the Federal 2nd Corps, wrote of his division that it had entered on the campaign, May 3rd, with 6,799 officers & men, & that it had received as reinforcements up to July 31st, 4,263, making a total of 11,062. Of these 5,075 had been killed or wounded. Among the casualties were 9 to officers at the time acting in command of brigades, & 40 to officers commanding regiments.

These figures indicate also what a stream of fresh men was constantly pouring into Grant's army to make good his losses. But although they were generally distributed through the old regiments, where they were associated with the veteran troops, Gen. Humphreys's account, after this period, several times complains that the behavior of troops was badly affected by the great number of new men among them. Gen. Humphreys gives the following account of the weather at this period:

> The weather had become oppressively hot. No rain fell from the 3rd of June to the 19th of July, a period of 47 days. There was no surface water; the springs, the marshes, the ponds, even streams of some magnitude were dry. The dust was several inches thick upon the roads & bare plains, & the passage of troops or trains over them raised great clouds of fine dust. Any movement of the troops occasioned severe suffering among them. But the surface soil was porous, & at no great depth below it were strata of clay where there was abundance of cool water that did not prove unhealthy; and the troops, whenever they halted, at once sunk wells.[13]

Having glanced over all these side issues, we may now return to my personal experiences in the lines about Petersburg. Our corps occupied about the right-hand half of our intrenchments before the town, with Field's & Kershaw's divisions.

As one of our divisions, Pickett's, held the Bermuda front I was also directed to take charge of the artillery defense of the whole line from the Appomattox to the James, including the batteries at Drury's & Chaffin's Bluffs. To keep back the enemy's fleet we had already begun the installment of a heavy battery of about ten or twelve seacoast guns at the Howlett house, on the left flank of our Bermuda lines. Another smaller battery, manned by sailors from our little gunboats, was also created some two miles above the Howlett house. These batteries quite frequently had long range duels with the enemy's monitors & other vessels, but these never attempted to pass the batteries. For we had torpedoes in the river beside, and early in May we had blown up an enterprising gunboat, the *Commodore Jones*, destroying half of her crew.

I only visited these lines once however during the month of June, for the situation in front of Petersburg occupied my whole attention. I received my first installment of mortars, 12 of them, on June 24th & had them in action on the 25th. I had recently had put under my command a Captain Lamkin,[14] an enthusiastic artillerist, & a fine, big, handsome fellow, with a big company from Bedford County, Va., but without any guns. Until we could get guns somehow, I had armed his 120 men with muskets & made special sharpshooters of them; but now I put the whole company in training with the mortars, which we set to firing at the big forts we could see going up everywhere and at the strong rifle pits in front of the Elliott Salient. I

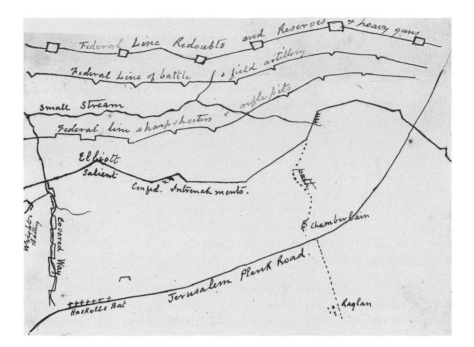

Figure 50. Lines at Petersburg, including the Elliott Salient

have already referred to this place as very badly located. It was, indeed, a worse location than that of the "Bloody Angle" at Spottsylvania; for here the great dead space came up closer—within 100 yards. The rough sketch shown below will give a fair idea of the situation. As the ground sloped toward the enemy, all the ground between our line & the Jerusalem Plank Road was exposed to their view & fire from their lines on the far side of the little stream. [Figure 50 appears here in the manuscript.]

For this reason it was impossible to approach our line from the rear except at two points. On our left was a ravine with a small stream in it, & in this we constructed a regular trench which made a covered way. Some two thirds of a mile to the right a path was found, winding among some shallow hollows, which was also covered from the enemy's observation. Within 3 or 4 days after the coming of our corps, it was noticed that the sharpshooters' fire, in front of the other corps to our left, was slackening & also that on our extreme right. We were always willing to encourage a truce of that sort, & gradually, one was instituted all along the line except at the Elliott Salient. Here the popping of the muskets rather seemed to increase, & for several hundred yards on each side there was always more or less of it. This satisfied me very soon that something was going on there and that the next attempt of the Federals would be made at that point, & I began at once to prepare for it. About 800 yards in rear of the salient, the Jerusalem Plank Road was sunken about five feet below the ordinary surface, offering a beautiful place for an ambuscade of artillery & infantry. Here I put 14 of Haskell's guns, & the other four in an earthwork out in front to sweep a sort of hollow out to the right. Out near the path I put two guns under Lt. Chamberlayne to enfilade our own trenches if the enemy ever got in them, & to take in flank any advance from them.

And then I found a beautiful place for a whole battery to give the same sort of flanking fire which had been so effective at Cold Harbor—a random fire, which did not directly see the enemy (& consequently he could not reply to it) but every shot from which would come bouncing & skipping along, exactly parallel to the front of his brigades, killing bunches when they hit & demoralizing the troops by their very direction even when they went clear. The map [Figure 50] shows the battery near the end of the path. It could see little or nothing in front, little knolls in front on each side of the winding creek cutting off the direct view down the course of the stream, but every shot fired over them would rake the dead space in front of Elliott's Salient. To keep the gunners from trying to shoot at what they could see to their right, & confine their fire exclusively to raking the front of the salient,[15] where the heart of the fight would be, I ordered the captain, a big old countryman named Davidson[16] of Leyden's old battalion, now commanded by Maj. W. H. Gibbes, to build high & narrow embrasures for his guns which could see no where else.

Next morning his embrasures saw too far to the right, & to make an impression on him, I had them torn down & threatened to arrest him if they did it again. And I charged him in case of any sudden battle firing, by day or night, in that direction, to fire rapidly every round he had of shot, shell, shrapnel, & canister, elevated for about 1,000 yards, right straight down the valley, & let them go where they would. It was near about the very prettiest artillery position I saw in the whole war.[17]

Beside these three special positions, I already had a battery of four guns under Cap. _____ of Maj. Gibbes's battalion[18] in a smaller salient about 200 yards to the right of the Elliott Salient. I had the two left guns of this battery well traversed & their embrasures specially shaped to give a raking fire along the right flank of the Elliott while the guns themselves should be protected from direct fire anywhere. At that close range their canister fire would be very effective.

Beside these precautions I also sent to Richmond to have a large lot of hand grenades made, of a pattern which Gen. Rains[19] had recently devised. [Figure 51 appears here in the manuscript.] They were thin, iron shells, about the size of a goose egg, filled with powder & with a sensitive paper *devised. They were thin, iron shells, about the size of a goose egg, filled with powder & with a sensitive paper percussion fuze in the front end, & a two foot strap, or strong cord, to the rear end. A man could swing one of these & throw it 60 yards, & they would burst wherever they struck — I sent for these, believing that the enemy were preparing to make a regular siege approach, upon Elliott's Salient, with a Sap-roller, that is great cylinder of basket work, stuffed full of fascines so as to be bullet proof. It is about five feet high, as it lies on its side, & twelve feet long, and a man kneeling behind it starts a narrow trench, or sap, & rolls the roller ahead of him foot by foot as he digs his trench forward Throwing the dirt on the side toward* Sap Roller

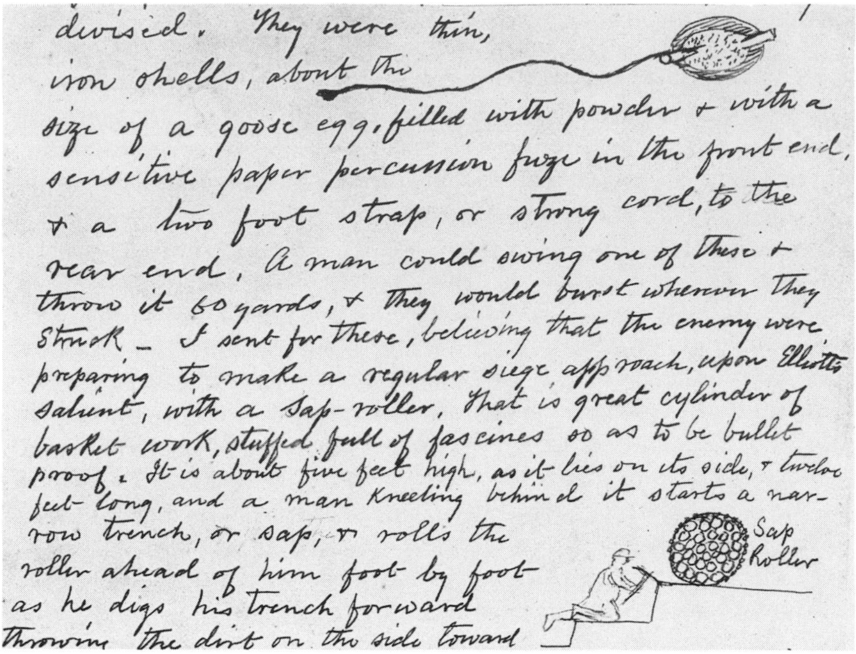

Figures 51 and 52. Confederate hand grenade; Sap roller

percussion fuze in the front end, & a two foot strap, or strong cord, to the rear end. A man could swing one of these & throw it 60 yards, & they would burst wherever they struck. I sent for these, believing that the enemy were preparing to make a regular siege approach, upon Elliott's Salient, with a sap-roller. That is [a] great cylinder of basket work, stuffed full of fascines so as to be bullet proof. It is about five feet high, as it lies on its side, & twelve feet long, and a man kneeling behind it starts [Figure 52 appears here in the manuscript] a narrow trench, or sap, & rolls the roller ahead of him foot by foot as he digs his trench forward throwing the dirt on the side toward the enemy—close behind him a string of other diggers widen & deepen the trench to whatever is needed.

And in the latter days of June, every morning early I went down to Elliott's Salient expecting to see a Federal sap roller started toward it. And behind it I thought would be my old friend Duane, with whom I went to Utah in 1858, he being now Meade's chief engineer.[20] Going backward & forwards in the trenches so much, & always having a fondness for target practice, I sometimes stopped & did a little sharpshooting. On Jun. 29 I made a remarkably good shot. I was in the trenches, a little to the left of the path, & I saw a man walking from the enemy's middle line back to the rear line in a direction straight from me. I was in DuBose's Georgia brigade,[21] & I said, "Look at that fellow! Lend me a gun & let me try him." I fixed the sight at 800 yards, took a very careful aim & fired. The man fell & the men around me, looking over [the] parapet gave a little hurrah at the shot. I think he was shot through a leg, for he did not lie there, but managed to scramble over a parapet which he had nearly reached when I shot. I only hope he got as nice a furlough from his wound as I got from one received very near the same spot the next day.

When I started out on Wed., Jun. 30th, for the Elliott Salient, I felt certain that the sap-roller must surely appear that morning, for now there had been ample time for all possible preparations. But again there was none. No fresh dirt now anywhere in that vicinity, but only that vicious sharpshooting & mortar firing. I loitered about & studied their lines every where for a long time, & then suddenly a light broke in on me. They were coming, but it was not above ground or it would show. But they were coming underground. They were mining us! As soon as the idea occurred to me it solved all the mysteries & everything in the whole situation confirmed it. I was as sure of it as if I had seen the mine. I determined to go at once to Gen. Lee's headquarters & tell him about it.

So I started back along the trenches to the path, my horse being left at the Raglan house. When nearly to the path I concluded to cut across the ridge to the right & save distance. It exposed me, but here the sharpshooting was not very much. As I crossed the little rising ground I stopped a moment, & turning around took a general view over the enemy's position. From one of their far lines came the faint pop of a rifle, & then the whiz of the bullet. It tipped the hard ground in front & rising struck me in the shoulder, going under the bone & lodging in the muscle behind. It numbed all my left arm but gave no real pain. At first I stood still, not wanting the marksman to know that he had hit me, but a very brief pause suggested that he was too good a shot to give a second chance to, so I walked on down the hill & was soon under cover.

Then it suddenly came over me, "I'll get a furlough!" I don't know that I ever had a more blissful moment. I had never realized before how badly I wanted one. For over a week I had been having chills & fever every alternate day. My eyes & skin were as yellow as a pumpkin from an attack of jaundice, & incipient scurvy, for lack of fresh vegetables, was already making all my gums sore. When I came to Chamberlain's battery, as the wound still bled freely, I got him to send a gunner with me, lest I should get too weak to reach my horse, but I needed no help.

My camp was among some large pines, not far back, & there I laid under a pine, on a nice pair of new white blankets I had been allowed to buy out of an importation through the blockade by the state of Geo. for Georgia troops. Then I took my lunch from my pocket & ate it—two thick camp biscuits, each with a slice of fat bacon in it, while I waited for the doctor, Dorsey Cullen,[22] who was chief surgeon of our corps.

He congratulated me on the bullet's narrowly missing both artery & joint, gave me chloroform & enlarged the wound to get his forceps in, & extracted the ball. It was a calibre .58 which had struck a little sideways & slightly flattened, with the impression of the cross threads of my coat stamped in the lead as if done with a steel die.

That afternoon I obtained a furlough, & next morning I went to Gen. Lee's headquarters, before taking the train for Richmond later in the day, in order to report my conviction that the enemy were mining the Elliott Salient. Gen. Lee had gone off somewhere on a long ride, & I made my report to his aid Col. Venable. In Venable's tent, at the time, was Mr. Lawley, the correspondent of the *London Times,* whom I have before mentioned as at Longstreet's camp near Chattanooga in Sep. '63. Lawley was much interested in my report, & asked how long a gallery the enemy would have to run to get underneath us. I said, about 500 feet. Lawley said they could not ventilate so long a gallery. That the longest military mine ever run was at Delhi, & that about 400 feet was the limit that could be ventilated. I answered that in the Federal ranks were plenty of coal miners who had ventilated galleries in coal mines miles under ground, & that they were up to devices to which 500 feet would be only child's play. The history of the Mine which is still to be told will show that the Mine was originally suggested & then constructed entirely by one of these coal miners, & that work on it had only been begun four days when I guessed its existence.

I remained in Richmond, with my sisters, Mrs. Lawton & Mrs. Gilmer, until July 4th on account of the 30 mile gap in the railroad connection, south from Burkeville, which had been caused by Wilson's raid, & was not yet repaired. But on July 4th a train of quartermaster's wagons would leave Burkeville & go around the gap, & Gen. Lawton would give me a pass on a wagon. Gen. John Preston,[23] chief of the Conscript Bureau, & a very pretty young lady under his charge, Miss Kate Crawford, also had wagon passes by that train, &, what was better, they had invitations to spend the night, which had to be passed on the road, at a very nice & comfortable farm house, & they got that invitation extended to me also.

That wagon ride was no picnic, some forty rough wagons in a string, & ordered to keep together, & roads deep in dust & never worked since the war began. I had my left arm fixed in a sling, to keep the shoulder from working, & after a brief enjoyment of the heat & dust & jolting under the wagon cover, I preferred to walk, which I could easily do faster than the wagons. Quite a lot of wounded men who were able to walk were making their way along with the train, & I accidentally got into conversation with one who proved to be Ed Calhoun, a brother of my sister in law Ida Calhoun.[24]

He was in the cavalry, & in one of the recent battles had received a remarkable wound. He was dismounted & lying down firing, when he was shot from the upper story of a house. The ball struck him about in the centre of his forehead, & ranged downward & lodged in the roof of his mouth, part of the bullet projecting into his mouth; but it was so firmly held by the bone that the surgeons could not move it. I think it remained there for a number of years, and was finally extracted long after the war.

About noon on July 5th, we took the cars on the far side of the break. I kept no notes of my journey, after this time, until I arrived at Barnett on the Georgia Railroad, the junction of the Washington branch, about 10 P.M. on the 9th, & I regret it as they would have helped give an idea of the condition of our railroad service. But I was four days & ten hours in going about 475 miles. I think every night was spent in the cars or at railroad stations but one in Columbia, where I had a hospitable welcome at Dr. Gibbs's house, which was burnt by Sherman the next February.

At that time every train from Virginia was loaded, day after day[25] with the aftermath of so many bloody battles, by the wounded & the maimed, sent off from the hospitals in Virginia as soon as they could travel, in order to make room for fresh arrivals. And the women & girls of every town, & of every way side station however small, were organised into bands, who awaited the arrival of every train, by day or by night, however much behind time it might be.

They then went through every train to see if anything could be done for the comfort of any sick or wounded soldier, with food or flowers or medicine or sympathy. They would dress the wounds of the wounded, & feed the hungry, & if nothing more could be done they would stay by the sickest & the weakest, & at least fan them during the long stops that the trains then made everywhere. There were no luxuries, there was not even ice; & the coffee was only parched corn, & the tea was sassafras. But the flowers & the sympathy were genuine enough, & nobody in the community ate chickens or eggs or fruit except what the sick & wounded could not consume.

At Barnett the station agent gave me a bed Saturday night & a breakfast Sunday morning, & then I started out at once on foot, as there was no Sunday train, having about 17 miles to go. I found that I had to rest often & I had only made about 5 miles by 11 o'clock, when I stopped at a nice looking farm house near the track to get some water. The white family had gone to church & only the Negro house servants were there, but they insisted that I should wait for the family's return & have dinner with them, saying their master would be angry with them if they allowed me to go on.

When I feared that I could not reach Washington by night, the Negro foreman assured me that his master would lend me a horse, & that he could guide me to a ford in Little River & put me on a good road. This induced me to wait, & never in my life have I met more hospitable people than that family proved to be. Nor have I eaten many dinners as good as theirs of chicken & a profusion of all summer vegetables.[26] After dinner I took the horse & forded the river, & about dark I reached home, surprising the family; for none of my telegrams had reached them, the wires having been down since Wilson's raid. They had only seen in an Augusta paper that I had been wounded but was doing well. My furlough was for 30 days but as the wound healed slowly it was extended 15 more to Aug. 15th, & thus I was away from Petersburg when the enemy exploded his mine at dawn on July 30th.

This is the history of the Mine, which was the only real siege operation in the so called siege of Petersburg. Grant expected quicker results from other methods, but this, meanwhile, having been prepared by the enthusiasm of a coal miner who appreciated the rare facilities which the ground presented for such an operation, he finally saw the great opportunity it offered to strike a fatal blow & put his whole strength [in] it.

Lt. Col. Henry Pleasants,[27] of the 48th Pa. Regt., in the 9th Corps, was the practical mining engineer who saw how easy it would be to run a horizontal gallery under the Elliott Salient from the valley behind their rifle pits. He offered to do it all by himself with his own regiment, & he got the permission of his corps commander, Gen. Burnside, to try it. It seems that the regular Engineer Corps shared the views about it which were expressed to me by Mr. Lawley, for Col. Pleasants says:

> General Burnside told me that Gen. Meade & Maj. Duane, chief engineer of the Army of the Potomac, said the thing could not be done— that it was all claptrap & nonsense; that such a length of mine had never been excavated in military operations, & could not be, I would either get the men smothered for want of air or crushed by the falling of the earth— or the enemy would find it out & it would amount to nothing.[28]

So Col. Pleasants had no assistance & few facilities in doing his work, but he persevered at it & in less than a month had it practically finished. His device for ventilating his gallery, which was 511 feet long, was so simple & pretty that I make a sketch of it. The entrance to the gallery was through an airtight bulk head, with a door also air tight & usually kept closed. A little way inside a fire place was excavated on the side with a chimney up through the hill. A long air box or ventilating flue ran through the bulk head & along on the floor to the far end of the gallery. [Figure 53 appears here in the manuscript.] Now, a little fire being kindled in the fire place, the chimney will begin to draw. Air will flow through the air box & flue, to supply this

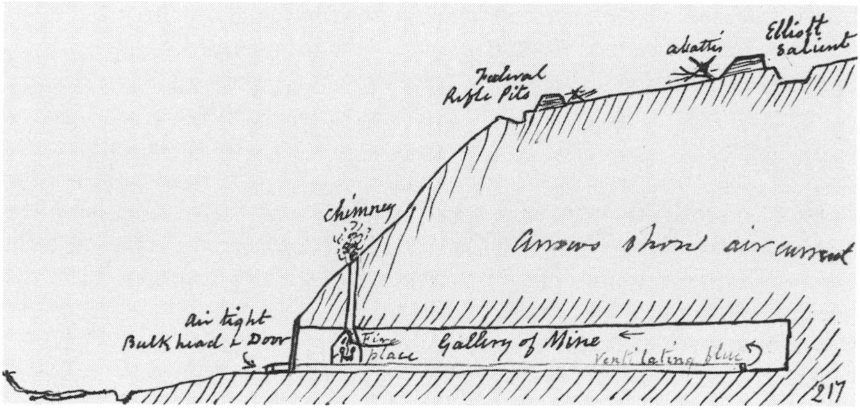

Figure 53. Cross section of Federal Mine at Petersburg

draft, & thus fresh air is always being delivered at the far end of the gallery, whence it flows back to the fire place & up the chimney. There is scarcely any limit to the distance which may be ventilated by this device.

When the gallery was directly under our works branches were run out to the right & left, each near 40 feet long, and in these were put 8 charges of powder of 1,000 lbs. each. Col. Pleasants asked for 14,000 pounds, but Gen. Meade decided that this amount was sufficient. Fuzes connected all the charges, & gallery & branches were then filled with bags of earth, to tamp all solid & prevent any of the force of the explosion coming back through the gallery. The powder was about 20 feet[29] beneath the surface of the ground at our lines.

And now we may leave the mine, & see what has been taking place above ground. When I went upon my furlough, at my suggestion Col. Frank Huger was sent for from the Bermuda lines & he came to Petersburg & lived with my staff & took my duties during my absence. Gen. Lee seems to me to have only about one half believed my report that the enemy were mining. At least he took only about one half the precautions which I think he would have taken had he known it certainly. He ordered our engineers to start a countermine, but he took no steps to build an interior line, which is the ordinary countermove to a mine. Often too a part of the garrison is withdrawn from the point threatened & kept in the interior line—close at hand but removed from danger.

Gen. Humphreys writes:

> Gen. Burnside had reason to believe that the enemy had not discovered his mine. His mining work however, had not escaped detection by them

> & Gen. Beauregard at first directed countermining, but abandoned it, &
> threw up intrenchments at the gorge of the salient against which the
> mining was apparently directed. Batteries of 8 & 10 inch mortars were
> also established by him to give a front & cross fire on the points
> threatened.[30]

There is surely some mistake here. Counter-mining was going on at the
moment of the explosion. I never before heard of any gorge intrenchment,
nor does any appear nor any 8 or 10 inch mortar fire, in any account of the
fighting which I have ever heard or seen.

I never knew who supervised our counter-mining operation, or any of the
details as to the cause of the delays, but they were badly planned & were so
slowly executed that the Mine was finished & exploded before our mines
ever reached a state of usefulness. [Figure 54 appears here in the manuscript.] What we did was to sink two shafts, B & C, at the two flanks of
the salient, intending to connect them with a listening gallery to run like a
horseshoe around in front. That would have been excellent if we had had
time to complete it. But the danger point was in front of the center & we
were too slow getting to it. The two shafts had been sunk & the galleries
started, but neither had pushed far enough forward to hear the enemy at
work before they had the Mine completed & loaded. When the explosion
took place one of the shafts was buried under the falling debris, but the
other had been started so far away that it was uninjured, & some of our
miners were actually at work within it at the moment. They came out
uninjured, & were taken prisoners & ordered to the rear, but in the confusion they escaped into our own lines. The other shaft was fortunately
unoccupied. We should have sunk a single shaft, as quickly as possible, at
the salient angle, & have pushed out a listening gallery toward the enemy
until we could hear him at work. Then we should have exploded what is
called a camonflet, or smothered mine, which would have crushed in his
gallery upon him. He would probably have abandoned the effort upon that,
& upon seeing interior intrenchments being thrown up in rear of the
salient.

The most important work done on our side during the month of July, in
preparation for the defense of this position, was the erection of a four gun
battery about 350 yards to its left, across the covered way ravine, & in a
little secondary hollow where it was entirely sheltered from the enemy's
observation. It was able to flank & sweep the salient & its approaches from
the left even better than Chamberlayne could from the right. This battery
was on Gen. Beauregard's front and, I understood, was located by instructions from Gen. Gilmer, chief engineer, who took a very close interest in all
the Petersburg operations. It was occupied by Wright's battery of Coit's

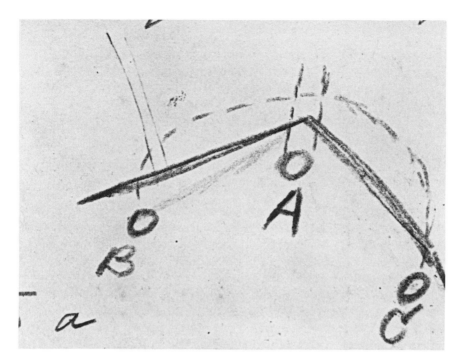

Figure 54. Sketch of Confederate counter-mines at Petersburg

battalion, to which also belonged Pegram's battery which was posted in the Elliott Salient itself.[31]

No extension of his lines & no aggressive operations were undertaken by Grant during the greater part of July. The results of his dash at the Weldon Road on June 22nd & of Wilson's cavalry raid had been disappointing. Early in July he had had to send off the 6th Corps to Washington City to oppose Early. So the greater part of the month was devoted to strengthening his system of intrenchments, as already described. Moreover, as the days passed, it became clear that, in spite of all the predictions of his failure, Col. Pleasants would soon have a great mine located under the Elliott Salient, & only needing the lighting of a match to blow it into the air. The great physical & moral effect to be expected from that, & the favorable features of the ground for an assault, finally led to a concentration of every possible effort to make it a success. Careful study was made from tall signal towers, erected in the enemy's lines, of every pile of dirt visible in ours, &, wherever it seemed to have any reference or relation to the defence of the salient, a great concentration, not only of siege & field artillery was prepared against it, but also a special one of heavy mortar fire.

Gen. Humphreys, on this subject, writes as follows:

> The siege & field artillery of our forces had been put in position to keep down both the front & flank fire of the enemy wherever we might attack their intrenchments, &, on Burnside's front, great care was taken to establish it so as to keep down their fire upon the flanks of our columns of attack against the Elliott Salient & to keep back their reinforcements. . . .
>
> Upon the explosion of the mine, the artillery of all kinds in battery was to open upon those points of the enemy's works whose fire covered the ground over which our columns must move.[32]

The force of artillery so employed he afterward gives as "heavy guns & mortars, eighty-one in all, & about the same number of field guns."[33] Not only, too, was every ounce of main force to be put forth in the effort, but strategy was to lend its powerful[34] aid in weakening our forces in Petersburg at the time of the attempt.

At Deep Bottom, Butler maintained two ponton bridges to the north side of the James, with part of the 10th Corps on that side under cover of his gunboats & iron clads. Of course, we had to maintain a moderate force in observation, & we had it located along the line of Bailey's Creek. Grant could come & go between that locality and his lines around Petersburg, by a march of 12 miles. We could only get there by a march of about 20 miles, which we could only begin to prepare for after we found out Grant's movement. [Figure 55 appears here in the manuscript.]

On the afternoon of July 26th, Gen. Hancock, with the 2nd Corps, about 20,000 infantry, & Sheridan with two divisions of cavalry, about 5,000, marched from near Petersburg for Deep Bottom. They were to be aided by the 10th Corps & endeavor to surprise or to turn our position, &, if successful, to make a dash upon Richmond itself. Sheridan, with the cavalry, was at least expected to cut the railroads leading north from Richmond.

The whole force crossed the bridges during the night & moved forward at dawn, Tuesday [the] 27th. Our advanced forces, on the east of Bailey's Creek, were driven back, & four 20 pr. Parrott rifles, too heavy for their teams, were captured.

But in some way Gen. Lee had information of, or had guessed Grant's movement, & two divisions, Wilcox's & Kershaw's, had arrived from Petersburg in time to extend our lines, so that Hancock was unable to turn them. Indeed, Kershaw took the offensive against Sheridan's cavalry, but met a sharp repulse from a dismounted line using their breech loading carbines—not the first occasion of the sort, where we have had to note the great value of the breech loader. Gen. Lee seems to have considered this movement of Hancock's a very dangerous one, for, during this day and the

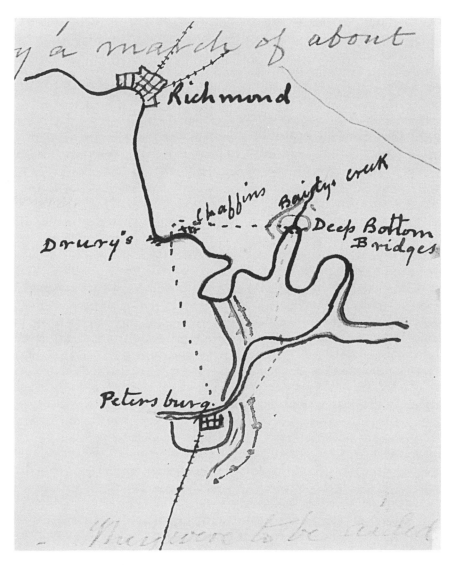

Figure 55. Vicinity of Deep Bottom, Virginia

next, he brought over from Petersburg two more divisions of infantry, Heth's & Field's, & two of cavalry, Fitz Lee's & W. H. F. Lee's. That left in all the Petersburg lines only three divisions of infantry, Hoke's, Johnson's, & Mahone's, instead of the seven which usually garrisoned them. At dark on the 29th, the 2nd Corps & Sheridan's cavalry recrossed the ponton bridges & marched back to Petersburg & were easily in their assigned positions in the lines ready for the explosion of the Mine at 3:30 A.M. on the 30th, leaving our 6 divisions at Deep Bottom with their thumbs to suck.

With the complete success of his strategy in thus denuding Petersburg of so great a proportion of its garrison, it would seem that Grant might now assuredly count upon an easy victory. Every possible provision & precaution seems to have been made, & taken in advance, in the preparatory orders given. On the explosion of the Mine the tremendous artillery, prepared to crush our few batteries in its vicinity, were to open upon them. The 9th Corps was to pass over the gap made by the explosion & advance toward the town, supported by the 5th Corps on its left & the 18th Corps on its right, & the 2nd in its rear. Meanwhile, Sheridan, on the extreme left with his whole Cavalry Corps, was to hunt any weak places on our right clear to the river whence we might draw troops to meet the pressure in the centre. Strong pioneer parties, equipped for removing abattis & for opening passages for artillery, were with every body of troops, depots of intrenching tools were made close at hand in accessible places, & abundant supplies of gabions, sand bags, fascines, &c. were provided, as well as engineer officers to accompany all columns. Even ponton trains were at hand in case of success to promptly bridge the Appomattox River in pursuit of our fugitives. And personal instructions were given emphasizing the value of celerity.

I think I can give a clearer idea of the fight by first describing, very briefly, how all this tremendous force & these elaborate preparations came to naught, & then at leisure I can go into details.

The primary cause of the failure, I think, was in the over-fought, or fought-out condition of the Federal army, to which I have before alluded. Everything else was to follow the lead of the 9th Corps. Part of this corps got into the crater made by the explosion (where they had no business going at all) & into the trenches close adjoining, but they were not able to make any advance beyond them toward the town. Many efforts were made but they were feeble for the force that was available, & all were soon repulsed. This early halt in the advance of the 9th Corps brought everything else to a stand still except that the Federal artillery continued to rain a furious fire on our lines in vain efforts to silence the batteries which bore upon the Crater, Wright's, Chamberlayne's, & Haskell's.[35] Thus, the whole Federal force stood blockaded from dawn until about ten o'clock, & no one found a way to raise the blockade. Then, Gen. Meade, conceiving that the opportunity had passed, ordered all offensive operations to cease.

Yet there were, necessarily, many weak places in our long lines (about nine miles in all) now held by only three divisions, of whom about one division was held near the salient. And this, too, was known to Meade at 6 A.M., from prisoners captured, who told that our force at Deep Bottom had not returned.

Meanwhile, by robbing our lines elsewhere, we gradually got three brigades in hand, & took the offensive against the Federals in the Crater, & vicinity, who could not get back to their own lines except under our fire. About 2 P.M., Gen. Mahone charged them with part of Johnson's division and Weisiger's, Sanders's,[36] & Wright's brigades, of his own. He captured 1,100 in the Crater including two brigade commanders, Gen. Bartlett & Col. Graham,[37] besides killing a great many, especially of the Negroes, not only in the melee in the Crater, but among the fugitives who tried to escape.

That was the battle as a whole, & now we may take up interesting details. A Federal court of inquiry afterward found several prominent Federal officers guilty of varied degrees of misconduct. Gen. Burnside himself was guilty of neglect of orders. Gen. Ledlie, commanding the leading division of the 9th Corps, & Gen. Ferrero commanding the colored division were both pronounced guilty of cowardice, staying in bomb proofs & not going with their divisions. Gen. Willcox, another division commander of that corps, was guilty of lack of energy & Col. Bliss commanding a brigade was convicted of staying behind with a small part of it which was not engaged.[38]

Indeed there was a striking absence of general officers from the front, & the opinion of the court ends with the following remarkable sentence:

> Without intending to convey the impression that there was any disinclination on the part of the commanders of the supports to heartily cooperate in the attack, on the 30th day of July, the Court express their opinion that explicit orders should have been given, assigning one officer to the command of all the troops intended to engage in the assault, when the Commanding General was not present in person to witness the operations.[39]

From all accounts there seem to have been two opinions held as to where the blame of the failure should lie. Some were disposed to place it upon the higher officers, & some upon the subordinate officers & the troops themselves. Gen. Humphreys writes of it as follows:

> The principal facts being known it was apparent that the assault failed from mismanagement & misbehaviour on the part of several of the chief actors, unless, indeed, which I believe, the troops were in such condition that the best management, the best handling, & the best leading would have been lost upon them. This, in brief, was the opinion of the Court.[40]

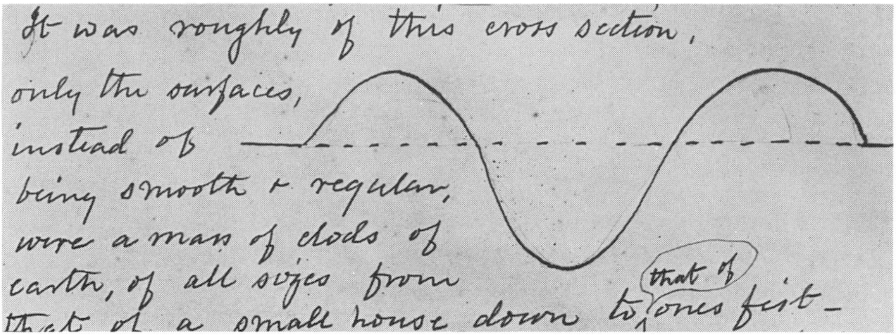

It was roughly of this cross section, only the surfaces, instead of being smooth & regular, were a mass of clods of earth, of all sizes from that of a small house down to that of one's fist—

Figure 56. Cross section of the Crater at Petersburg

Burnside, Ledlie, & Ferrero all disappear from the records of the 9th Corps very soon after this affair.

The explosion of the Mine was set for 3:30 A.M. But the first effort was a failure owing to a defect in the fuse, at a splicing in the gallery; outside of the tamping, however, where it could be easily gotten at. After some delay a Sergeant Reese[41] ventured to explore, & then a new splice was made & the Mine was finally fired at 4:40 A.M. Our men were entirely unprepared & were generally asleep. The crater made was about 200 feet long, 70 feet wide, & about 25 feet deep.[42] It was roughly of this cross section, [Figure 56 appears here in the manuscript] only the surfaces, instead of being smooth & regular, were a mass of clods of earth, of all sizes from that of a small house down to that of one's fist. In Elder's oil painting of the Battle of the Crater[43] he shows quite accurately one large clod lodged on the crest, which remained a feature of the locality for many months.

By the explosion, the 18th South Carolina Regt. & Pegram's battery were entirely destroyed, & about one half, perhaps, of the 23rd So. Ca. Some were blown in the air & fell with the debris, & some sleeping in their little bomb proofs were buried by it, perhaps still alive. Some in the debris escaped severe injury, & were dug out & taken prisoners by the enemy.

A story was told of one of these, an Irishman, who was completely stunned for awhile, &, when he recovered his senses, found himself in a mixed party of Federal & Confederates without knowing exactly what had happened. So he nudged a comrade & asked, "I say, Byes! Have we tuk them or have they tuk us?" [Figures 57 and 58 appear here in the manuscript.]

The following description of the explosion is given by Maj. W. H. Powell, U.S.A.:[44]

> I returned immediately, and just as I arrived in rear of the First Division the mine was sprung. It was a magnificent spectacle, and as the mass of

Figure 57. Explosion of the Mine at Petersburg

Figure 58. Approach to the Crater from southeast of the mouth of the Mine

earth went up into the air, carrying with it men, guns, carriages, and timbers, and spread out like an immense cloud as it reached its altitude, so close were the Union lines that the mass appeared as if it would descend immediately upon the troops waiting to make the charge. This caused them to break and scatter to the rear, and about ten minutes were consumed in re-forming for the attack.

(Immediately following the explosion the heavy guns along the line opened a severe fire.)

Not much was lost by this delay, however, as it took nearly that time for the cloud of dust to pass off. The order was then given for the advance. As no part of the Union line of breastworks had been removed (which would have been an arduous as well as hazardous undertaking), the troops clambered over them as best they could. This in itself broke the ranks, and they did not stop to reform, but pushed ahead toward the crater, about 130 yards distant, the debris from the explosion having covered up the abattis and *cheavaux-de-frise* in front of the enemy's works.

Little did these men anticipate what they would see upon arriving there: an enormous hole in the ground about 30 feet deep, 60 feet wide, and 170 feet long, filled with dust, great blocks of clay, guns, broken carriages, projecting timbers, and men buried in various ways—some up to their necks, others to their waists, and some with only their feet and legs protruding from the earth. One of these near me was pulled out, and proved to be a second lieutenant of the battery which had been blown up. The fresh air revived him, and he was soon able to walk and talk. He was very grateful and said that he was asleep when the explosion took place, and only awoke to find himself wriggling up in the air; then a few seconds afterward he felt himself descending, and soon lost consciousness.

The whole scene of the explosion struck every one dumb with astonishment as we arrived at the crest of the debris. It was impossible for the troops of the Second Brigade to move forward in line, as they had advanced; and, owing to the broken state they were in, every man crowding up to look into the hole, and being pressed by the First Brigade, which was immediately in rear, it was equally impossible to move by the flank, by any command, around the crater. Before the brigade commanders could realize the situation, the two brigades became inextricably mixed, in the desire to look into the hole.

However, Colonel Marshall[45] yelled to the Second Brigade to move forward, and the men did so, jumping, sliding, and tumbling into the hole, over the debris of material, and dead and dying men, and huge blocks of solid clay. They were followed by General Bartlett's brigade. Up on the other side of the crater they climbed, and while a detachment stopped to place two of the dismounted guns of the battery in position on the enemy's side of the crest of the crater, a portion of the leading brigade passed over the crest and attempted to reform. In doing so members of these regiments were killed by musket-shots from the rear, fired by the Confederates who were still occupying the traverses and intrenchments to the right and left of the crater. These men had been awakened by the noise and shock of the explosion, and during the interval before the attack had recovered their equanimity, and when the Union troops attempted to reform on the enemy's side of the crater, they had faced about and delivered a fire into the backs of our men. This coming so unexpectedly caused the forming line to fall back into the crater.

Had General Burnside's original plan, providing that two regiments should sweep down inside the enemy's line to the right and left of the crater, been sanctioned, the brigades of Colonel Marshall and General Bartlett could and would have reformed and moved on to Cemetery Hill before the enemy realized fully what was intended; but the occupation of the trenches to the right and left by the enemy prevented re-formation, and there being no division, corps, or army commander present to give orders to other troops to clear the trenches, a formation under fire from the rear was something no troops could accomplish.

After falling back into the crater a partial formation was made by General Bartlett and Colonel Marshall with some of their troops, but owing to the precipitous walls the men could find no footing except by facing inward, digging their heels into the earth, and throwing their backs against the side of the crater, or squatting in a half-sitting, half-standing posture, and some of the men were shot even there by the fire from the enemy in the traverses. It was at this juncture that Colonel Marshall requested me to go to General Ledlie and explain the condition of affairs, which he knew that I had seen and understood perfectly well. This I did immediately.

While the above was taking place the enemy had not been idle. He had brought a battery from his left to bear upon the position, and as I started on my errand the crest of the crater was being swept with canister. Special attention was given to this battery by our artillery, but for some reason or other the enemy's guns could not be silenced. Passing to the Union lines under this storm of canister, I found General Ledlie and a part of his staff ensconced in a protected angle of the works. I gave him Colonel Marshall's message, explained to him the situation, and Colonel Marshall's reasons for not being able to move forward. General Ledlie then directed me to return at once and say to Colonel Marshall and General Bartlett that it was General Burnside's order that they should move forward immediately. This message was delivered. But the firing on the crater now was incessant, and it was as heavy a fire of canister as was ever poured continuously upon a single objective point. It was as utterly impracticable to re-form a brigade in that crater as it would be to marshal bees into line after upsetting the hive; and equally as impracticable to re-form outside of the crater, under the severe fire in front and rear, as it would be to hold a dress parade in front of a charging enemy. . . .

There was no means of getting food or water to them, for which they were suffering. The midsummer sun caused waves of moisture produced by the exhalation from this mass to raise above the crater. Wounded men died there begging piteously for water, and soldiers extended their tongues to dampen their parched lips until their tongues seemed to hang from their mouths. Finally, the enemy, having taken advantage of our inactivity to mass his troops, was seen to emerge from the swale between the hill on which the crater was situated and that of the cemetery. On account of this depression they could not be seen by our artillery, and hence no guns were brought to bear upon them. The only place where they could be observed was from the crater. But there was no serviceable artillery there, and no infantry force sufficiently organized to offer resistance when the enemy's column pressed forward. All in the crater who could possibly hang on by their elbows and toes lay flat against its conical wall and delivered their fire; but not more than a hundred men at a time could get into position, and these were only armed with muzzle-loading guns, and in order to re-load they were compelled to face about and place their backs against the wall.

The enemy's guns suddenly ceased their long-continued and uninterrupted fire on the crater, and the advancing column charged in the face of feeble resistance offered by the Union troops. At this stage they were perceived by our artillery, which opened a murderous fire, but too late. Over the crest and into the crater they poured, and a hand-to-hand conflict ensued. It was of short duration, however; crowded as our troops were, and without organization, resistance was vain. Many men were bayoneted at that time—some probably that would not have been, except for the excitement of battle. About 87 officers and 1,652 men of the Ninth Corps were captured, the remainder retiring to our own lines, to which the enemy did not attempt to advance. Among the captured was General William F. Bartlett. Earlier in the war he had lost a leg, which he replaced with one of cork. While he was standing in the crater, a shot was heard to strike with the peculiar thud known to those who have been in action, and the general was seen to totter and fall. A number of officers and men immediately lifted him, when he cried out, "Put me any place where I can sit down." "But you are wounded, General, aren't you?" was the inquiry. "My leg is shattered all to pieces," said he. "Then you can't sit up," they urged; "you'll have to lie down." "Oh, no!" exclaimed the general, *"it's only my cork leg that's shattered!"*

[Figure 59 appears here in the manuscript.]

I was told, by one who witnessed it, that Gen. Bartlett produced a sensation among our troops when the prisoners were brought out of the Crater. He came using two muskets as crutches, muzzles down & the butts under his arms, & the fragments of the cork leg dangling. One of our men was overheard to remark, "By God! there's a plucky Yankee! One leg shot off & look at him hoofing it along on the stump!"

Strange to say, our people seem not to have noted any of the enemy's preparations or heard any unusual noises during the night. Naturally the explosion, awaking them with its tremendous concussion & smoke & dust, followed as it was by the fire of 160 guns, created consternation in the

Figure 59. *The Battle of the Crater* by Elder

trenches in[46] all of that vicinity. But in a very few minutes the officers began to realize what had happened & to rise to the occasion. Gen. Elliott himself took prompt & well considered action, & began to form a line of battle in rear of the Crater, which, he rightly judged, would soon be charged. While forming this line he received a severe wound, but he was succeeded in command by Col F. W. McMaster,[47] who soon formed part of the brigade in a swale in rear of the Crater—in time to open fire on the enemy when they attempted to come out from the Crater & form on our side of it.

From that time until about half past eight o'clock, say for three hours and a half, there were no reinforcements, & no force to hold the enemy into the Crater, but these, with the adjoining troops on the two flanks (Ransom's brigade[48] on the left & Wise's on the right) and the batteries of artillery which have been before described. The enemy seems never to have discovered Haskell's guns, in the sunken part of the Jerusalem Plank Road, until they opened upon their men trying to form outside of the Crater. Then they supposed them to be fresh batteries, just brought up for the purpose, & turned a heavy fire on them both of mortars & siege guns. The road, however, gave very fair protection & Haskell was always able to maintain his fire upon their infantry when it would endeavor to come out. They told me an incident of one of the attempted charges by the Negro troops, of which I give further details presently. Their line started to advance fairly well, but the fire soon proved too hot, & it broke & scattered wildly. One

Negro, with his musket at a support arms, seemed to be dazed, or lost, & ran straight for the guns, which were firing canister rapidly. He escaped being hit, & ran up to the Jerusalem Road & jumped down into it between two of the guns. One of the gunners drew the trail handspike from his piece & knocked him in the head with it.

In fact there were, comparatively, very few Negro prisoners taken that day. It was the first occasion on which any of the Army of Northern Virginia came in contact with Negro troops, & the general feeling of the men toward their employment was very bitter. The sympathy of the North for John Brown's memory was taken for proof of a desire that our slaves should rise in a servile insurrection & massacre throughout the South, & the enlistment of Negro troops was regarded as advertisement of that desire & encouragement of the idea to the Negro.

That made the fighting on this occasion exceedingly fierce & bitter on the part of our men, not only toward the Negroes themselves, but sometimes even to the whites along with them. Note Maj. Powell's remarks about the use of the bayonet on the charge upon the Crater.

Some of the Negro prisoners, who were originally allowed to surrender by some soldiers, were afterward shot by others, & there was, without doubt, a great deal of unnecessary killing of them.

Col. Frank Huger told me of his being recognized by one, lying mortally wounded near the edge of the Crater. He heard a voice call "Mass Frank," & recognized a barber who used to shave him in Norfolk four years before. The poor fellow said, "Please, Mass Frank, can I have some old greasy water what they been washing dishes in? I don't want no good water but just old greasy water they are going to throw away." Frank gave him water, but his wound was one for which nothing could be done.

The fighting of the Negro troops seems to have been about as good as that of most of the white troops. Gen. Thomas, commanding one of their brigades, writes as follows of the first charge he attempted:[49]

> Among the officers, the first to fall was the gallant Fessenden of the 23rd Regiment. Ayers and Woodruff of the 31st dropped within a few yards of Fessenden, Ayers being killed, and Woodruff mortally wounded. Liscomb of the 23rd then fell to rise no more; and then Hackhiser of the 28th and Flint and Aiken of the 29th. Major Rockwood of the 19th then mounted the crest and fell back dead, with a cheer on his lips.[50] Nor were these all; for at that time hundreds of heroes "carved in ebony" fell. These black men commanded the admiration and respect of every beholder.
>
> The most advantageous point for the purpose, about eight hundred feet from the crater, having been reached, we leaped from the works and endeavored to make a rush for the crest. Captain Marshal L. Dempcy, and Lieutenant Christopher Pennell, of my staff, and four white orderlies

with the brigade guidon accompanied me, closely followed by Lieutenant-Colonel Ross, leading the 31st Regiment. At the instant of leaving the works Ross was shot down; the next officer in rank, Captain Wright, was shot as he stooped over him.[51] The men were largely without leaders, and their organization was destroyed. Two of my four orderlies were wounded: one, flag in hand; the remaining two sought shelter when Lieutenant Pennell, rescuing the guidon, hastened down the line outside the pits. With his sword uplifted in his right hand and the banner in his left, he sought to call out the men along the whole line of the parapet. In a moment, a musketry fire was focused upon him, whirling him round and round several times before he fell. Of commanding figure, his bravery was so conspicuous that, according to Colonel Weld's[52] testimony, a number of his (Weld's) men were shot because, spell-bound, they forgot their own shelter in watching this superb boy, who was an only child of an old Massachusetts clergyman, and to me as Jonathan was to David.

The men of the 31st making the charge were being mowed down like grass, with no hope of any one reaching the crest, so I ordered them to scatter and run back. The fire was such that Captain Dempcy and myself were the only officers who returned, unharmed, of those who left the works for that charge.

Later, with another portion of his brigade to help, not in his first charge, Gen. Thomas was ordered to charge again, & thus describes his effort:[53]

We managed to make the charge, however, Colonel Bross of the 29th leading. The 31st had been so shattered, was so diminished, so largely without officers, that I got what was left of them out of the way of the charging column as much as possible. This column met the same fate in one respect as the former. As I gave the order, Lieutenant-Colonel John A. Bross, taking the flag into his own hands, was the first man to leap from the works into the valley of death below. He had attired himself in full uniform, evidently with the intent of inspiring his men. He had hardly reached the ground outside the works before he fell to rise no more. He was conspicuous and magnificent in his gallantry. The black men followed into the jaws of death, and advanced until met by a charge in force from the Confederate lines.

I lost in all 36 officers and 877 men—total, 913. The 23rd Regiment entered the charge with eighteen officers, it came out with seven. The 28th entered with eleven officers, and came out with four. The 31st had but two officers for duty that night.

[Figure 60 appears here in the manuscript.]

This second charge described by Thomas was the last of several efforts made meanwhile by other commands & it produced one important result. A material change had just taken place in our lines.[54]

Figure 60. Confederate lines as reconstructed at the Crater

Soon after 6 A.M. Gen. Lee had arrived at the Gee house, on the Jerusa-lem Plank Road, close by Haskell's guns, & within 500 yards of the Crater. From the windows of this house a view could be had of the whole field, & Gen. Beauregard was already there. A. P. Hill had been there, & had gone off to the right to send up batteries & troops to be taken from points not so immediately threatened. Genls. Lee & Beauregard viewed the fighting from this near point during its whole progress, & I do not know of any battle in the whole war where the commanding general occupied a point of such danger. It was the very point aimed at by all the Federal charges, it was under their view & musketry fire from the Crater, & it was about the centre of convergence of the 80 siege guns & 80 field guns especially placed for this attack. Early in June, when Haskell's battalion was first placed there, he had one or more men killed or wounded every day by the stray bullets fired by the Federal sharpshooters, which passed over our parapet at the salient, & struck about here. He had even asked permission to move his camp a short distance away to one side, but I objected, saying, that whenever he was needed in that position it would be an emergency where minutes would be invaluable, & he must live in instantaneous readiness.

About 8 A.M. Gen. Mahone arrived, followed by two of his brigades, Weisiger's Virginians & Wright's Georgians. They were conducted by ravines & hollows hiding them from view, having been drawn from the intrenchments on the far right by spreading out very thin the rest of the division. They were now led down the covered way ravine & joined the remains of Elliott's brigade & began to extend their line across the Crater-front, in the swale or depression before mentioned, which hid them from the view of the enemy's artillery. But as the presence of such great numbers of the enemy's troops became more apparent, orders were sent also for Sanders's Alabama brigade, leaving only Harris's Mississippi & Finegan's Florida to hold the lines held that morning by all five brigades.

Up to this time the troops originally in the lines near the Crater had been able to repel all the charges & attempts to form ouside of the Crater by their fire, aided by the artillery, but they had been far too few to attempt any counter-charge. Nor, indeed, did the small accession of about 2,000 men justify it even now. But it happened that the second charge attempted by the colored division, & briefly described above by Gen. Thomas, came to be made just as Weisiger's men had formed along with McMaster's Carolinians. The sight of the Negro troops inflamed them, & without waiting for the Georgians who were coming up, the whole line charged to meet the Negroes. The latter recognised the coming of the Day of Wrath, & turned & fled. And they did not even stop when they got back under shelter of the captured breastworks, but only communicated the alarm to those sheltering themselves there, & not only did the whole lot stampede back to the Federal lines, but they took with them the greater part of two white divisions, one of the 9th Corps & one of the 18th.

Gen. Humphreys writes of this:[55]

> Weisiger's brigade, with some of Elliott's advanced against them, charged & drove them back in confusion, the whole division rising from the ground & running in wild disorder back to our intrenchments, carrying with them many of Potter's troops, both of Turner's brigades[56] & most of the men lying around & in rear of the crater. . . . This attack left the enemy in possession of nearly all their intrenchments on our right of the crater.

It had a more important effect even than that. It decided the day, which was still easily anybody's battle. The 2nd & 5th Corps & the cavalry had not been engaged, & we had nearly five miles of line on our right held by not over 3,000 men. And it was not yet 10 A.M. But when the result of that charge was known all offensive movements were suspended, except that Gen. Sheridan was directed to reconnoiter our right, & "to be governed by circumstances." He did not seem to find any spot which he thought weak— Gen. Humphreys says that these orders were given by Gen. Meade, with Gen. Grant's concurrence. No where else in his account does Gen. Humphreys imply Gen. Grant's presence, & the opinion of the court of inquiry which has been quoted would seem to imply that neither Genls. Grant or Meade were in close observation of the fighting.

Warren was about undertaking the offensive upon our right of the Mine, & particularly the silencing of our two guns which swept the approaches to the Crater upon that flank with their close canister fire, when the orders suspending offensive operations stopped him.

Those two guns & Wright's four guns over on our left gave fearful trouble to the enemy all that day. All of their accounts speak of it, & special efforts to silence them were called for and made by concentrations of artillery & mortar fire on them, but without success. Wright's battery indeed was located out of their view, but Gibbes's two guns were a part of our main front line & in quite a prominent location—Gen. Humphreys speaks of them as in a ravine, but the position was really on a knoll & their only protection was their own parapets & traverses. For perhaps an hour after the explosion, under the heavy fire of the enemy's guns, this battery was silent, the officer in charge of it becoming demoralized. But, by that time, Maj. Gibbes arrived at the battery & took command himself, & it opened an effective fire. Col. Huger & all of my staff, Haskell, Winthrop, & Willie Mason, joined him there soon afterward, & all helped man the guns: the lieutenant in command & many of the men having disappeared. Gibbes was presently severely wounded, by a bullet through the neck, but Huger & my staff remained there, & kept up the fire until the end of the action. In the pauses they even got rifles & acted as sharp shooters at individual officers & men seeking to pass back & forth. After the battle charges were preferred against the lieutenant (Otey)[57] who had acted badly. He was convicted of cowardice & sentenced to death, and had all arrangements made to shoot him when he was pardoned by President Davis, of which I have since been very glad. For the strain of that position, that morning, was very severe upon men of little experience in action.

When the news of the battle reached me, the point that I was most anxious of all to hear about was how many rounds of ammunition my old Captain Davidson fired, enfilading the valley in front.[58] It was one of my great disappointments to learn that he fired only between 20 & 30. He excused himself, saying that he couldn't see any result, & that he believed the enemy were all in the Crater. But the real reason was the tremendous fire the enemy turned upon him, both of mortars & heavy guns. They could not hurt him, materially, but that battalion to which he belonged, recently put under command of Maj. Gibbes, was not seasoned to battle like the battalions of the Army of Northern Virginia, and Huger & Gibbes & all of my staff were too busily occupied, at what was then the point of greatest danger, to leave it, or scarcely even to think of anything else. Perhaps it is as well. Had Davidson fired vigorously, it might have precipitated Warren's assault, & it would, at least, have been better made than that of the 9th Corps. All's well that ends well.

I was also anxious to know if the hand grenades were used, as they might very well have been, about the Crater. They had been made, & had arrived from Richmond, but had not been brought out to the lines & distributed.

Our little coehorn mortars, however, had proved very serviceable. John Haskell had taken one down very near to the Crater, & thrown shells inside, the explosion of which would sometimes throw up fragments that were taken to be limbs of persons blown up by them. It was reported to have been a fragment of one of Haskell's shells which wounded Gen. Bartlett's cork leg.

The success of Gen. Mahone's first charge with Weisiger's brigade was such as to encourage the making [of] a second one about an hour later, but on this occasion there were none of the enemy in front to pursue & the troops making this one extended so far toward our right that they came under the view & fire of the Federal artillery which compelled them to seek cover.

But they continued to work up toward the Crater through the trenches, & to keep a hot fire upon its crest, & every person who sought to reach it or to leave it had to run the gauntlet both of canister & musketry fire from both flanks.

At length, Sanders's brigade having arrived, about two o'clock a charge was made upon & into the Crater itself, which was really able to make no resistance worthy of the name & the battle was ended.

The casualties of the day are given by the Federal tabular statement of the Medical Department as follows:

	Killed	Wounded	Missing	Total	General Officers K	W	Cap
C.S.	400	600	200	1,200	2		
U.S.	419	1,679	1,910	4,008			1
Aggregate	819	2,279	2,110	5,208			

The two Confederate generals wounded were Elliott & Weisiger. The only Federal general wounded was Gen. Bartlett in his cork leg, he being also captured. The total loss in Elliott's brigade including those killed by the explosion was 677. Burnside's colored division's losses were reported [as] killed 176, wounded 688, missing 801. Total 1,665—out of a total of perhaps 5,000.[59] Many of the missing were killed.

Gen. Meade reported his casualties at 4,400 killed, wounded, & missing. He reported capturing from us 246 prisoners & two colors.

Gen. Humphreys gives the strength of the two armies in the Petersburg & Bermuda Hundreds lines just before this battle as follows—not including troops in [the] Shenandoah Valley. The Federal armies comprised 61,993 infantry (enlisted men present for duty equipped) in 17 divisions, & 12,180 cavalry in 4 divisions. Of Confederates there were 39,295 effective infantry in 8 divisions & 8,436 cavalry in 3 divisions.

FALL OF 1864

While I was at home on furlough an event took place in Georgia, to which I must refer, for, if a last nail was needed in the Confederate coffin, it was now supplied. The credit of it is due, I have always understood, to our Georgia Governor Joseph E. Brown & our senator, the eloquent Benjamin H. Hill.[1] By political arts & pressure, in which they were both adept, they forced Prest. Davis to relieve Gen. Jos. E. Johnston from the command of the army in front of Sherman at Atlanta.

Gen. Johnston always believed that Prest. Davis was unfriendly & prejudiced against him, & that, in this case, he required little urging. But Genls. Gilmer & Lawton told me of discussions in the cabinet which conveyed to them a very different impression. Brown & Hill, in the plenitude of their military wisdom, declared that Johnston was no general, because he had not stopped Sherman's advance. Mr. Davis had answered, "If Johnston is not a general we have none in the Confederacy. Show me a general to put in his place."[2]

But day after day & week after week the pressure was kept up, & at last Mr. Davis was led to give a conditional promise. It had been charged that Johnston would surrender Georgia without a fight, & Pres. Davis undertook to get from Johnston some expression of satisfactory intentions, and promised to remove him if he failed to give it. Accordingly, he asked Johnston for some statement of his plans. Johnston answered, very curtly, that being confronted by a largely superior force his plans would be governed by the enemy's movements. He had long believed himself unfairly treated by Mr. Davis and he doubtless knew of this attack upon him.[3] Being high strung & sensitive, he seemed to disdain to make any apology or defence. When the removal finally came, what took place he told as follows:[4]

On July 17th we learned that the whole Federal army had crossed the Chattahoochee; and late in the evening, while Colonel Presstman[5] was receiving from me instructions for the next day, I received the following telegram of that date:

"Lieutenant-General J. B. Hood has been commissioned to the temporary rank of general under the late law of Congress. I am directed by the Secretary of War to inform you that, as you have failed to arrest the advance of the enemy to the vicinity of Atlanta, and express no confidence that you can defeat or repel him, you are hereby relieved from the command of the Army and Department of Tennessee, which you will immediately turn over to General Hood.

S. COOPER, Adjutant and Inspector-General."

Orders transferring the command of the army to General Hood were written and published immediately, and next morning I replied to the telegram of the Secretary of War:

"Your despatch of yesterday received and obeyed—command of the Army and Department of Tennessee has been transferred to General Hood. As to the alleged cause of my removal, I assert that Sherman's army is much stronger, compared with that of Tennessee, than Grant's compared with that of Northern Virginia. Yet the enemy has been compelled to advance much more slowly to the vicinity of Atlanta than to that of Richmond and Petersburg, and penetrated much deeper into Virginia than into Georgia. Confident language by a military commander is not usually regarded as evidence of competence."

As before said that was the last nail in the coffin. Mr. Davis drove it under the political pressure of Brown & Hill, & perhaps others; but he, of course, cannot plead the baby act, & must be held responsible. But it ought to teach the South for all time to distrust eloquence & beware of politicians. Before Hood was promoted to replace Johnston the command was tendered to Hardee, & also to Gen. Gilmer, but both declined it. Later, I will tell briefly how Hood lost his army, & Johnston had his vindication & revenge, by being recalled to command in the last gasps of the Confederacy.

I[6] was at home on furlough just four weeks & started back to Virginia on Monday, August 8th. I probably stayed a day or two in Richmond, for I only rejoined my headquarters in Petersburg on Aug. 15th. I found affairs on the lines very much as I had left them, except that the enemy were no longer either trying to mine us, or to advance their trenches any nearer. And on the Bermuda Hundreds front, & on the flanks about Petersburg, too, there was little or no sharpshooting.

But in the vicinity of the Crater, & all along in the center for, perhaps, two miles, the lines were just infested with sharpshooting, mortar firing, & artillery practise, all day & more or less all night. The 9th Army Corps, which was opposite our corps, had reported an average loss of 36 men a day by this business, on about one mile front, for nearly six weeks before the explosion of the Mine. These figures serve to give an idea of what this sort of fighting amounts to. Our own losses are not known, as official reports could not be kept up under the incessant strain in which we lived, but doubtless they were from one half to two thirds as great [as] the enemy's. We had fewer men exposed than they, but their trenches were materially better than ours, & they had more ammunition & more guns than we, & did much more artillery firing.

The siege had now settled down to the arithmetical process of killing us off little by little, & the slow but sure one of compelling us to lengthen our lines until they became too weak to hold. These processes were now to be kept up without intermission for eight months.

Gen. Humphreys writes of the situation, early in August, as follows:

> Between this time & the month of March, 1865, several movements of portions of the Army of the Potomac & the Army of the James were made to the right & to the left, which resulted in the extension of our lines of intrenchments in both directions, & caused a corresponding extension of the Confederate intrenchments on our left, & their occupation in stronger force of their intrenchments on the north bank of the James. By this process their lines finally became so thinly manned, when the last movement to our left was made, in March 1865, as to be vulnerable at one or two points, where some of the obstructions in their front had been, in a great measure, destroyed by the necessities of the winter. These flank movements had not only that general object of Confederate extension in view, but other special objects also, which were important at the time, & which were to a greater or less extent accomplished.[7]

In other words, now for 8 months there were to be no more direct attacks upon our lines in front, but a succession of efforts, first around one of our flanks, & then around the other. Could Grant successfully turn either our game was up at once. Around our right flank lay the only lines of railroad by which we could get provisions; around our left flank lay Richmond itself open to this entrance. With the short interior line & the initiative, he could always surprise us to a certain extent, & he could swing his force from one flank to the other without our knowledge. Even when we defeated him in his immediate purpose (as we did—almost miraculously, it would seem— for eight long months), yet there was always a bloody price to pay, from our diminishing numbers, for every temporary success, & there always remained more intrenchments to build and to man. I will not attempt to go into the details of these different affairs, nearly every one of which involved heavy & desperate fighting by one or more of our brigades or divisions, though none of them are known to history as battles, & few are even remembered as skirmishes. Yet the casualties in any one of them frequently exceeded all our casualties in the late Spanish war.

I will only note the principal ones, briefly, & will give the casualties when I can find them stated. The Federal losses were generally reported, but our own rarely, for reasons before explained.

One of these operations upon our flanks was in progress on Aug. 15th, the day of my return from furlough. A few days before that Lee had sent Kershaw's division of our corps up to the Valley to reinforce Early. By all the rules of the game of war, it seems to me that if we could spare a division to go anywhere, we should have sent it to help out Hood in front of Atlanta. Early's original demonstration against Washington City as I have already said may, perhaps, be justified on account of the excessive sensitiveness of the enemy under such threats. But now the chance to surprise Washington was gone forever, & there was no reasonable hope of Early's accomplishing any valuable result with any force we could possibly send him. It seems to me, therefore, whatever was the case beforehand, that now, after the middle of July, our policy should have been to play our two armies at Petersburg & Atlanta more like parts of a single whole; to have them partially concentrate alternately at one point or the other, wherever opportunity offered for a blow. Grant was not easily vulnerable in his position, but Sherman was, & could Lee have left Beauregard at Petersburg after the Mine, & gone in person to Hood with even Early's full corps, an effective blow might possibly have been given to Sherman, & the troops returned before Grant could accomplish any great harm. It was, indeed, very late in the game, but Mr. Lincoln's position was critical, also, with the election approaching. And as long as we fought, we would have stood most chances had we tried to utilize our interior lines. I will recur to this subject again when I come to tell of Hood's campaign—these remarks being only apropos to Gen. Lee's feeling strong enough, after his victory of the Crater, to send Kershaw to the Valley. At the same time, too, he sent Field's division over to our extreme left flank, near Deep Bottom, on the north side of the James, & he sent Wilcox's division to Chaffin's Bluff. Grant had several tall signal towers in his lines, opposite Petersburg & at Bermuda Hundreds, whence our lines & all the roads in sight were watched & studied. From these towers, & perhaps from deserters, he knew that three divisions had moved, & he thought all had been sent to the Valley.

Believing, then, that Lee's whole force was reduced to five divisions, he planned a strong movement around our left flank at Deep Bottom, striking at Richmond itself. It was to be made by two corps of infantry, the 2nd & 10th, & Gregg's division of cavalry. Instead of marching the 2nd Corps over to Deep Bottom, an effort was made to mislead our spies & scouts & make them think that that corps had been sent to the Valley. It was marched to City Point & embarked upon transports, which left in the middle of the night, taking them, however, up to Deep Bottom where they united with the cavalry & the 10th Corps. This was Sunday morning, Aug. 14th. Fortunately, Field's division was already on hand to oppose them, &, though they surprised & captured four guns, they were held at bay while Wilcox's division came from Drury's Bluff. Gen. Lee also sent from Petersburg Mahone's division of infantry & two divisions of cavalry, Hampton's & W. H. F. Lee's, which began to arrive on the 15th. There was some sharp fighting on the 14th and 16th, though Gen. Hancock complains that his men did not respond to the leadership of the officers on some occasions, which he attributes to the numbers of new recruits in the ranks. On the 16th, in a cavalry affair we lost an excellent officer, Gen. Chambliss,[8] killed. Meanwhile Gen. Grant, by the 17th, had discovered his mistake in supposing that three corps had gone to the Valley. Also, he found from his signal towers that only three divisions of infantry & one brigade of cavalry were opposed to him south of the Appomattox. So he immediately ordered Hancock to send back one division of the 2nd Corps, Mott's, to relieve the 9th Corps in the trenches. Meanwhile, the 5th Corps at daylight on the 18th, with a brigade of cavalry to help, was to pass our left flank & strike at the Weldon R.R.; & the 9th Corps was to follow & reinforce them, as soon as relieved from the trenches by Mott. Meanwhile also, Hancock, with the rest of his force on the north side was to remain there to threaten us.

Thus, on the 18th, Grant was threatening both our flanks at once, with near about 2 corps on each. On our left we had 3 divisions of infantry & we took the aggressive, but found the enemy intrenched & still in superior force. On our right, Heth with Davis's & Walker's brigades attacked Ayres's division & rolled it up, but then had to retreat before superior forces. Hancock remained at Deep Bottom, skirmishing & demonstrating, until the night of the 20th, but on the night of the 18th Gen. Lee withdrew Mahone's & W. H. F. Lee's divisions & sent them back to Petersburg.

On the 19th, Mahone with three of his brigades joined Heth with his two above named, & the five assaulted the 5th & 9th Corps, which were intrenching themselves about the Weldon Road. They had a decided success at first & captured many prisoners; but eventually the enemy made good & held his intrenchments. During these two days Warren's casualties were 926 killed & wounded & 2,910 missing. Our killed & wounded were probably as many, but we lost few prisoners. The Federal Gen. Hayes was captured, & our Gen. Clingman[9] was wounded.

The casualties in the Federal forces engaged on the north side of the James, from the 14th to the 20th, were 321 killed, 1,840 wounded, 625 missing; total 2,786. Aggregate on both flanks 6,622.

During all of this fighting on the flanks I remained in Petersburg, for the infantry in our intrenchments was then reduced to a mere skirmish line, &

unusual vigilance and activity was enjoined upon the artillery, lest the enemy should suspect our weakness & seek to take advantage of it.

My diary notes that at 2 A.M. on the morning of the 18th, & again at the same hour on the 19th, Gen. Lee ordered me to open a brisk fire from all of my guns upon the enemy's lines for about a half hour, the idea probably being to make them fear an attack, & prevent their sending troops to the flanks. On Sunday, Aug. 21st, Wilcox's & Hampton's divs. having returned from the north side, Gen. Lee determined upon another serious effort to dislodge the enemy from the Weldon Road. Hill's entire corps, & part of Hoke's division & W. H. F. Lee's cavalry, were all concentrated against them. Gen. Lee went also in person & I accompanied him, taking with me a reserve battalion of artillery. Meanwhile, our guns on the lines were to cannonade, & endeavor to prevent reinforcements going to the enemy's left. The plan was to break the enemy's line at some point & then roll it up. It involved assaulting him in his breastworks, where he had been located for two or three days, in a flat country & light soil, where it was very easy to fortify. Two attempts were made, & both were bloody & entire failures, with probably a thousand killed & wounded, & 500 captured, the enemy only losing about 300. Among our killed was Gen. Sanders of Ala., a most excellent officer.

Hagood's[10] brigade at one time, close up to the enemy's works, found itself taken in flank & nearly surrounded. A great [number] of the men called out "Surrender! Surrender!" & the enemy ceased firing upon them, & some of their officers came forward to receive them as prisoners. But Gen. Hagood, who had not authorized any surrender, shouted to his men to resume their fire, & opened fire himself with his pistol. Some did resume & some did not; most of the prisoners lost being in that brigade.[11] The reserve battalion of artillery, which I took down, was not engaged & my principal recollection of the day is that it was my chill day & it was one of intense heat; & one side of me in the sun would be burning while the other, in the shade, shook with a cold ague.

The next little disturbance was also on Gen. Lee's initiative, & was a much more successful venture. Although we could no longer bring trains into Petersburg over the Weldon Road, we could bring them up within a day's drive by wagons, passing around the Federal left. To prevent this Grant sent Hancock with two divisions of infantry, Miles's & Gibbon's, & Gregg's division of cavalry, with instructions to tear up about thirteen miles of the railroad track. They had accomplished about half their work on the morning of Thursday, Aug. 25th, when they were interrupted by Gen. A. P. Hill with seven of his own brigades & Anderson's brigade of Field's div., & Gen. Hampton with his cavalry. This time the enemy had only some inferior breastworks, built along the railroad, in June, by troops sent to reinforce Wilson's cavalry on its return from its raid. Hancock occupied these works, & started to strengthen them. Hill however was able to attack him successfully & compel his withdrawal. Hancock reported 610 killed & wounded & 1,762 missing, total 2,372. He complains, in his report, of unsatisfactory behavior by a portion of his troops. A. P. Hill reported a total loss of 720, mostly killed & wounded. He reported the capture of 12 colors, 9 guns, 10 caissons, 2,150 prisoners & 3,100 small arms.

This affair was followed by a full month's rest. Perhaps its moral effect contributed to bring this about.

Meanwhile both sides were busily at work upon their recently extended lines, & all the new batteries, redoubts, &c., which they involved. The only hostilities were along our old front in the vicinity of the Mine, where small arms, mortars, & guns were as active as ever. I made very few notes in my diary during this period & those that were made do not now recall any event of interest. But the following reminiscence of one of my captains, recently told in a Virginia newspaper, will at least give an idea of life along the lines, & the spirit of the times.[12]

I recall, about this period, also, that Grant shelled the city of Petersburg more frequently & severely than ever before, sometimes by day & sometimes by night, both with guns & with mortars. But the casualties were remarkably few, & the damage done was but trifling. Nearly every house had a bomb proof in the yard, or cellar, & the citizens got accustomed to the shells in a surprising way. I have seen ladies walking the streets, & on their front porches, when, about once in ten minutes, a shell would fall somewhere.

Toward the end of Sept., Gen. Grant had completed his double lines out to the Weldon Road, & had opportunity to rest his men & drill his new recruits into shape, & he was now ready for a new move on a large scale. Little complaint about the behavior of his troops appears after this rest. At this time the most tempting opportunity to attack was offered him on the north bank of the James. To make it clear I attach a map [Figure 61] showing the defences of Richmond on that side.

The principal feature of the defense is the line of breastworks, about eleven miles long, stretching from Chaffin's Bluff on the James to the Chickahominy near New Bridge. This was called the Exterior Line, but the greater portion of it—say the 7 miles north of the New Market road—was simply the abandoned trenches of the campaign of 1862, much washed by rains, destitute even of gun platforms, & of abattis & of any garrison except a picket line.

Inside of this line, & generally within one or two miles of the city, an Interior Line encircled it from the river below to the river above. This line was intended as a defense against cavalry raids, as were, also, about a dozen interior small forts on the edges of the city, which were built during the first year of the war. All of these interior lines were garrisoned with permanent batteries of stationary artillery, & they were also manned, on emergency, by two brigades of Local Defense infantry, organised from the city militia & clerks & employees of the governmental departments; the whole being under the command of Gen. Ewell.

And as the heavy batteries at Chaffin's Bluff, & the ponton bridge maintained there, had become in the past year points of vital importance, a Spur Line of intrenchments had been extended south, from the Interior Line down to the Exterior Line, so as to embrace Chaffin's Bluff & the Osborne Pike, the principal road to it.

This Spur Line joined the Exterior Line at a considerable open work called Battery Harrison; & another notable point on it was Fort Gilmer, about a mile north of Battery Harrison. Both of these works mounted stationary artillery. Fort Gilmer was an enclosed work, & its ditches were deep enough to form obstacles though they were not swept with fire.

But none of these lines were provided with abattis in front, to delay an assaulting column under fire. This is absolutely essential, where the defense are armed only with muzzle loading guns, against any well conducted charge by superior numbers. [Figure 61 appears here in the manuscript.]

This was abundantly shown, if proof of it were necessary, by the capture of Battery Harrison, of which I have soon to tell. It seems to me, therefore, that a great opportunity was now open to Grant to strike a blow on the north side of the James. Had he put his whole strength into it, I believe that Richmond would have been his immediate prize. But he made the mistake of striking upon both flanks at the same time, & neither blow was heavy enough to accomplish any important result. He extended his lines, of course, & that process, slow but sure, would win in the end. But as a military problem, his play here should have been to strike at Richmond with fifty thousand men, whose presence on the north side Lee could not know until they swarmed over his exterior line.

What actually occurred was as follows. On Sep. 28th Meade's army, in front of Petersburg, executed some movements carefully contrived that we should discover them, but should think that they were intended to be concealed; & that they indicated an attack upon our extreme right. This was to lead us,[13] if possible, to draw some of our troops from the north side, & to be slow to reinforce it when the trouble broke out there.

It seems, however, to have entirely failed to have any effect in either way. Gen. Lee, at that time, had on the north side only four brigades of infantry, Benning's, Law's, Gregg's, & Fulton's,[14] about 5,000 men; & Gary's brigade of cavalry, about 1,000. The infantry held the advanced position near

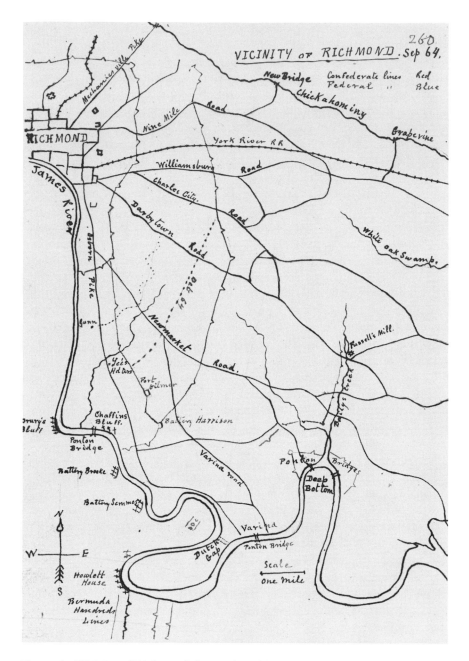

Figure 61. Vicinity of Richmond, September 1864

Deep Bottom, along Bailey's Creek, & from thence back to Chaffin's Bluff, while the cavalry picketed all roads. These lines, at Bailey's Creek, it will be remembered, had completely blocked Gen. Hancock's attempted advances from Deep Bottom upon two occasions, July 27th & Aug. 14th. Now, however, they were to be very easily turned by the secret construction of a new bridge at Varina, at dark on the 28th. Over this bridge, & the upper bridge at Deep Bottom, there passed, during the same night, about 15,000 infantry under Genls. Ord of the 18th Corps & Birney of the 10th,[15] & about 4,000 cavalry under Kautz. By 7:30 A.M. on Thursday, Sep. 29th, Ord on the left was before Battery Harrison. It & a small part of [the] adjacent lines was defended by Fulton's brigade of Johnson's division, about 1,000 strong. It was assaulted by 4,000 men, &, though well defended, it was overrun for lack of abattis & was captured on the first effort. The loss of the assailants was 594, about 15 per cent. Gen. Burnham[16] was killed, & two officers succeeding him were successively wounded. Sixteen guns were captured & a number of prisoners, including Lt. Col. _____ in command.[17]

Encouraged by this success the enemy now endeavored to spread to the left & right, & to capture Chaffin's Bluff. Ord's unexpected advance from Varina had compelled the troops from the vicinity of Bailey's Creek to come in by roundabout routes through the woods & our defence was at first scattered & weak in infantry, and Ord captured six more guns in adjacent lunettes. But, fortunately, one of my battalions of artillery, Hardaway's, was near, & after the fall of Battery Harrison it took position inside of our lines where it covered the rear of the Bluff, & prevented also any extension toward Richmond. It did excellent service & suffered severely in men & horses. Our little gunboats, also, under Admiral Semmes, lying in the river below the ponton bridge, protected the right flank of the line, which extended to the river below the Bluff, so that the enemy were held within comparatively narrow limits. Gen. Ord himself was severely wounded in this fighting. Gen. Grant was also upon the ground. News of this assault was promptly telegraphed to Gen. Lee at Petersburg, who not only took the quickest possible measures to reinforce, but who set out in person for the scene. Gen. Pickett was wired to dispatch four regiments, at once, under Col. Montague[18] from the Howlett house. Field's two brigades which were at Petersburg, Bratton's & Anderson's, were brought over, by rail, to the nearest point to the ponton bridge, & marched from there; and Hoke with three of his own brigades, Kirkland's, Clingman's, & Colquitt's, & Scales's of Wilcox's division, all marched over. I was also ordered to come in person, & to bring as many batteries as could be spared from other points.

Meanwhile, Gen. Birney's command advanced upon the New Market Road, driving in our pickets & taking our Exterior Line where it crossed that road and was practically without any garrison. Thence, some of his troops were pushed over to attack Fort Gilmer & the lines in its vicinity—but the attack failed every where. The best of it was made by Birney's colored brigade, which was directed upon Fort Gilmer. There was only a picket line of infantry in the fort at the time, and along the neighboring Spur Line intrenchments, & the guns in the fort, some six or eight, were better adapted for distant than for a close defence. So, without much loss, the colored troops made a rush & jumped into the large ditch, some eight to ten feet deep, around the fort. Once in the ditch they were comparatively safe from fire, most of the ditch being dead space. At first they made some effort to scale the parapet. A large Negro helped by his comrades got upon the berm & mounted the exterior slope. He was shot & fell back in the ditch, & his comrades were heard to exclaim, "Dar now! Dey done kill Corporal Dick! Corporal Dick was best man in de rigimint!" News spread along the line, on both flanks, that Negro troops were corralled in [the] Fort Gilmer ditch, & many of the Texans & Georgians, who had never met them before, came running into the fort & asking for "a chance to shoot a nigger." Meanwhile the artillerists lighted shells & rolled them over the parapets to explode in the ditch, & the infantry mounted the parapets to fire into the crowd, & nearly every man in the ditch was finally killed or captured, the majority being killed. After that all colored troops were known in our corps as the "Corporal Dicks." The loss of the brigade which made this charge was 434 on the 29th & 30th. Probably 400 of it was in this charge.

There was no serious fighting after the assault on Fort Gilmer. Kautz's cavalry was on the Darbytown Road, abreast of the infantry, but was not engaged. As the enemy reasonably anticipated that Gen. Lee would make an effort to recapture Battery Harrison, a large force was put to work to close its rear, & to strengthen it in every way to resist an assault. And at 2 P.M. on the 30th we did assault it with five brigades—Law's, Anderson's, Bratton's, Clingman's, & Colquitt's. I preceded the assault with a cannonade, from our right, so as to interfere least with the advance of the infantry from the centre & left. But the enemy was now thoroughly protected & well prepared, & his trenches full of men, & the assault failed with severe losses. In Bratton's brigade the losses were 377 out of 1,294, nearly 30 per cent. I can find no report of losses in other commands, but they were probably not so severe as this. My recollection is that by some misunderstanding the whole attacking force was not simultaneously engaged. It was, however, almost a hopeless task to try & drive superior forces from works so strong as these now were.

The enemy now prepared to hold the position permanently, & intrenched themselves in a line extending back to the James River near Dutch

Gap. Gen. Lee now made his headquarters for some weeks at a house on the Osborne Pike, near Cornelius Creek, & Gen. Anderson also came over with the headquarters of our corps. That, of course, brought over my own headquarters, & we established a camp near Mrs. Gunn's house on the Pike, & we remained there until the final break up in April '65.

We return now to Petersburg, to show what Grant accomplished by the simultaneous effort upon his left flank. On the morning of the 29th the whole Army of the Potomac was under arms at 4 A.M., & dispositions were made to leave small garrisons in the enclosed forts, & to withdraw, if necessary, the great bulk of the army for use elsewhere. Nevertheless, no movement was made during this whole day, Gen. Grant hoping that the pressure on the north side would lead Gen. Lee to draw still more troops from Petersburg. On Friday the 30th, however, two divisions of the 5th Corps, & two of the 9th, were sent to attack our right flank. They struck & captured some temporary works on the Squirrel Level Road, taking one gun & a few prisoners, & then advanced toward a line of works which we were constructing to cover the Boydton Plank Road. Gen. Beauregard had at this time returned south, & Gen. A. P. Hill was in command in Petersburg. He had withdrawn Heth's & Wilcox's divisions from his trenches, & with them he advanced to meet the Federal line and assaulted it. He struck the two divisions of the 9th Corps & drove them back in confusion, with a loss of 485 in killed & wounded & a large number of prisoners. On the next day, Oct. 1st, Mott's division of the 2nd Corps came to reinforce the four already on the ground. On Oct. 2nd they advanced to within about a mile of our lines, & established under our artillery fire a well intrenched position, shown on the map with the date. Our line meanwhile was now being extended to rest on Hatcher's Run below Burgess's Mill. The total casualties reported by the Federals in this operation were 661 killed & wounded, 1,348 missing, total 2,009. [Figure 62 appears here in the manuscript.]

The next active hostilities occurred upon the north side of the James, where Gen. Lee was not content to permit the enemy to continue to occupy Fort Harrison, as it was now called, without another effort to dislodge them. On the afternoon of Thurs., Oct. 6th, I was ordered to send two battalions of artillery across to the Darbytown Road, with Field's & Hoke's divisions, which were to go across & bivouac on that road that night, in order to make an advance at daylight upon the enemy's flank. Late in the afternoon I called at Gen. Lee's headquarters, & had an interview with him as to the proposed operation. To get across to the Darbytown Road it was necessary to take a cross road from the Osborne Pike opposite the Gunn house, near which I was encamped, about 100 yards from the pike, in a pine thicket. The general told me that he would start at 2 A.M. & that I could

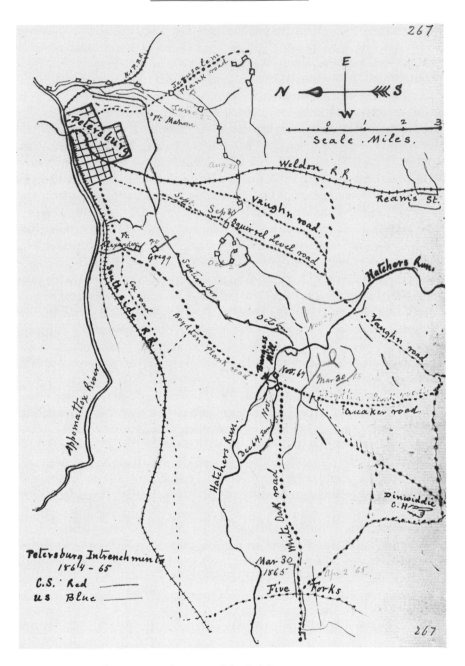

Figure 62. Petersburg intrenchments, 1864–65 (1)

join him as he passed my camp. Accordingly we were up at one, & at half past had finished breakfast, & I was smoking a cigarette by the fire & Charley had just brought up my horse, when Col. Venable rode up. "Aleck," he said, "Come on! The Old Man is out here waiting for you & mad enough to bite nails." "Why," said I; "it's only half past one, & he told me he would start at two. I'm all ready though, & would have been out in a little while anyhow." And by that time I was on my horse, & my staff, too, mounting we started for the road. "Yes," said Venable, "two o'clock was the hour he told us all last night, but now he swears he said one. And he scolded every body & started off all alone, & with scarcely any breakfast, because nothing was ready. I overtook him & the rest of the staff are coming along as fast as they can get their horses."

By that time we were at the road, where Gen. Lee was sitting on old Traveller waiting for me, & three or four dark figures near were either staff or couriers. I remember the conversation very vividly. "Good morning, General Alexander. I had hoped to find you waiting in the road for me on my arrival." This was said with the very utmost stiffness & formality. "Yes, Sir! I was all ready & might have been here just as well, but you told me last night that you'd start at two o'clock, & it's not near that yet, so I did not hurry." Which I said as good-naturedly & blandly as I knew how. "One o'clock was the hour, Sir, at which I said I would start!" This was said with a very severe emphasis.

"I misunderstood you then, General, I thought you said two." "One o'clock, Sir, was the hour!" This was so emphatic that I concluded to let him have the last word, & I said no more. Then he went on, "Well, Sir, have you gotten a guide who can direct us on the best crossroads to reach the Darbytown Road?" That attack took me by surprise, for in the afternoon no word had been said to imply that any guide would be needed; & moreover he himself, & his staff & couriers, in daily communication with the cavalry & with every detachment in the army, naturally knew the roads better than those occupied entirely in the lines of a single corps. So I had tacitly expected that one of his staff or couriers would guide, & had given the matter no thought. So I said, "No, General, as the subject was not mentioned I supposed no guide would be needed, & I would only have to follow you." "Well, Sir, when I was a young man & had a march to make in the morning, I never went to bed until I had procured some citizen of the neighborhood who could conduct me." I felt like telling him that all the citizens of the neighborhood, strong enough to carry a musket, had been conscripted, but I did not dare to, so I said, "It will be easy enough to follow the road which the infantry took this afternoon, for at every cross roads we can tell by feeling in the road if it has been trodden smooth by a column, & that will take us to them, anyhow."

He could not gainsay that proposition, so he dropped me saying, "Well, we will have to make the best of it. Col. Venable, will you ride ahead then &

guide us." Now, unluckily for poor Venable, he was conversing with one of the belated staff, & did not hear his name called. Gen. Lee paused for a moment, & no one immediately appearing, he called to one of his couriers, named Evans[19] if I recollect aright, & said, "Evans, I will have to ask you to act upon my staff today, for my officers are all disappointing me. Will you ride ahead & guide us." Meanwhile, some one had told Venable that the general had called him, & he spurred forward just in time to hear it all, & to be sent back, while Evans took the lead. Poor Venable was deeply mortified, but for my part, I did not mind it a row of pins, for I knew that I had not deserved it, & it was only that something had upset the remarkable control of his temper which the general usually preserved. It was the one time, in all the war, when I saw him apparently harsh & cross. And before the morning was over he became particularly & especially gracious & good natured to me, & to every one else about him—except poor Venable. Venable told me afterward that for two weeks the general never addressed him except officially. Then he gradually resumed his former kindness. Col. V. was a man of high type in intellect & character—a professor of mathematics in the University of Va. both before & after the war, & a valuable & efficient staff officer.

Before the general's temper cleared, however, this morning, it demanded one other victim. He was found in a little old Frenchman who had a small, white cottage about 100 yards from the road we were traversing. We had gone about a mile & without any trouble, easily following the infantry by feeling the surface of the road, & we had passed one fork in the road a quarter of a mile back, but when he discovered this cottage Gen. Lee insisted on going up to it. Some of the staff banged at the door & roused the occupant, & Gen. Lee said, "Bring him here." It was quite a cool fall morning, but they trotted out, in a long night shirt & bare legs & feet a little old Frenchman, as was plain from his broken English. As he came up Gen. Lee, without one word of explanation, & in quite a stern voice said, "Ought I to have taken that right hand road back yonder?" The old man answered, "Ah, may be so, yes; may be so no. Vere bouts you vant to go?" "Well you just come along here with me & show me," said the general; I was immensely amused at the idea that perhaps he had gotten this "citizen of the neighborhood" for a guide just to show me how I should do it in future, but I kept the joke strictly to myself. And we took that old fellow in his bare feet & legs & night shirt about a quarter of a mile down the road before the general would let him go back. And we had no trouble anywhere, & joined the infantry on the Darbytown Road in ample time & to spare.

For Gen. Kautz, with 1,700 cavalry with their breech loading carbines, & 12 guns, was holding our exterior line of breastworks where it crossed the Darbytown Road; & our strategy was merely to amuse him with a skirmish line, after daylight, until Gary's brigade of cavalry, going out by one of the roads farther to our left, could get in his rear. Our little game was worked so successfully that when at last we moved on Kautz with a force which he respected & retreated before, Gary fell on him & captured 8 of his nice guns. Our two divisions of infantry, & my two battalions of artillery then turned to the right, skirmishing & advancing down the breast works toward the New Market Road, meeting increased resistance, for the 10th Corps of infantry had been sent out to support Kautz & to meet our advance. At last we developed them occupying a line of intrenchment facing our advance, & with several batteries of artillery in position, & Gen. Lee ordered them to be assaulted. There was here a considerable stretch of open & level country & it gave me the only opportunity I ever had, in action, to use that beautiful manoeuvre in artillery drill of "Fire advancing by half battery." One half of a battery stands & fires, while the second half advances a short distance, when it also halts & opens fire. At its first shot, the first half stops firing, limbers up, & then at a gallop itself passes the second & takes a still more advanced position & opens. So they go, alternately, one half always firing & the other advancing.

I advanced in this way a long line of batteries for about a half mile across the plain, & lined them up in easy range of the 10th Corps line, all under Gen. Lee's eye, who was now in the pleasantest mood in the world, & while Field's & Hoke's infantry were taking positions whence they were to charge the enemy. I largely silenced the enemy's fire, having more guns at work than he, & just as the infantry rose for the charge we blew up one of the enemy's caissons, which raised a general hurrah along our line, & I felt sure we were about to smash them. But the event rapidly disappointed my sanguine expectations. In the first place only Field's line of infantry rose & charged. Hoke's line on his right never moved. I never knew why. I had understood it was to be a general & desperate attack. Hoke's advance would have been over ground more exposed & wider than Field's, but it would not have struck troops armed with breech loaders as Field's did. It would seem that the attack should have been by both or neither.

Two of the infantry brigades opposed to Field were armed with Spencer magazine rifles. In front, they had put out a strong skirmish line with orders to await our charge, &, on its approach, to empty their magazines at it & then to run back into the breast works & rejoin the line of battle before reloading. Field's men were moving forward handsomely, & still cheering, when this skirmish line opened fire & discharged their seven shots apiece in less than a minute. It made quite a hot volley, & gave the idea of a considerable force. It plainly shook up our advancing line of battle, which dropped men here & there all along, but which gathered itself & with fresh cheers & fresh impetus threw itself forward. And then the Federal line of battle opened on them with a roar which told its own story of its deadly power.

Our line hardly seemed to last a minute before it became a confused mass of fugitives back to cover. Good General Gregg, who had led the Texans through many a bloody scene, was dead on the field, & my special friend, grand old Gen. Bratton was very severely wounded. The time had been wonderfully short but our losses are estimated to have been nearly a thousand men killed & wounded.

This ended the fight & after gathering up our wounded we were marched back within our lines. The Federal losses were reported as in Kautz's cavalry 72 killed & wounded & 202 missing.

Col. John Haskell (the one armed) comdg. one of my artillery battalions, & Aleck Haskell, his brother, comdg. the 7th S.C. Cavalry of Gary's brigade, each had remarkably narrow escapes. John was riding a tall & beautiful horse, with a head & eye more like a deer's than I have ever seen on any other horse before or since. When we started our fire, advancing, he sent that horse to the rear, & mounted, instead, a small & ordinary battery horse. During the fight a musket ball struck him at the top of his forehead, exactly in the centre. It split the scalp & scraped the bone of the skull for nearly six inches & passed on. Had his horse been a half inch taller he would have been instantly killed. He did not leave the field, however.

Aleck's wound was much more serious.[20] At the head of a part of his regiment, he had charged a Federal squadron & broken it, & led a pursuit in a melee down a road, through the woods far in the Federal rear, emptying two revolvers & using his long, straight, & sharpened Austrian sabre freely in the general mix up. Then, sending his command back by the road they came, he, with two men, started on a road leading toward our infantry fight, where he wished to report to Gen. Lee some observations he had made of the enemy's position.

On his way he came unexpectedly, in the road, upon Gen. Kautz with a number of staff & couriers. Hoping to cut his way through, Haskell shouted "Charge," & rode at them, firing with his revolver. He had fired twice & wounded two men, when he was struck in the eye by a ball from a carbine, & fell from his horse. One of his men was also shot, the other then turning into the woods & escaping. He heard the man who shot him say, "I killed him. I killed the general!" The orders for the day were taken from his breast pocket & read, while a surgeon dismounted & examined his wound & pronounced him dying. Kautz said, "Can you do nothing for him?" "No, he would die at once on any effort to remove him." "Leave a man to watch him & we will send an ambulance for him." He was conscious, & heard all, & then felt his sword, spurs, watch, & two rings on his fingers being removed. As the last ring was being removed, he tried to prevent it, & said, "What are you doing?" The man answered, "We are not robbing you, Colonel. Your things will be preserved & returned to you when you are well."

At the end of the charge he had captured the headquarters wagon of the 1st N.Y. Mounted Rifles, driven by an Irishman who only surrendered after Haskell had threatened him with his sabre, unless he surrendered before Haskell counted three. When he had counted two Pat said, "And do you mane it?" "I do." "Well thin I surrender." Haskell had ordered him to take that road & drive into our lines, but he had first met Gen. Kautz & staff, who had taken charge of him. As he lay on the ground now, he saw Pat approaching, folding up a blanket. He raised Haskell's head & put the blanket under it saying, "Colonel, you were after me with yer ould sabre this morning, but you are dying now & we are all brothers thin, an I'll do what I can to make you comfortable." Haskell has always believed that this raising his head by that blanket saved his life, & he tried hard after the war to find Pat, but in vain, for he had been mustered out & gone west.

He now laid there for some time & exchanged a few words with his man (Sergeant _____)[21] who had been shot with him, & who soon died. After an hour or two he heard motion in the woods, &, looking, saw a Confederate infantryman. It was one of a party of scouts on the left flank of Field's division. He raised his arm to attract notice & that he might show the Confederate braid on his sleeve. The man looked, jumped behind a tree, leveled his musket & fired. Haskell supposes he fired on the Federal who was watching him, but could not see as his face was turned in [the] opposite direction. He then came up & was joined by two or three others; they found who Haskell was, & sent & got one of Field's ambulances, & he was taken into our own lines & carried to Richmond. When he was placed in the ambulance he fainted. On the road the mules ran away with the ambulance, bouncing the driver off, but they ran into a brigade of infantry & were stopped without harm. Haskell went through a long spell of brain fever & when, after many weeks, he slowly recovered he had to almost learn to speak over again, words having lost their meanings to him as in aphasia. He resumed command of his regiment about Feb. 1865 & had to be introduced, over, to all his officers. For more than a year after it his former life was forgotten & came back little by little, & he always spoke of it as "the time I was killed."

A day or so after the battle, Gen. Kautz sent in a flag of truce to ask for the body of a Maj. _____[22] which had fallen into our hands, & he sent by the same flag Haskell's watch, spurs, & one of his rings. The other ring, Haskell particularly prized & tried to trace it after the war, but failed.

In 1876, however, the man who had shot him sent a letter to the *Charleston News,* saying that he had a ring taken from a Col. Haskell killed in 1864 which he wished to restore to the family if any one could identify it. Of course identification was easily made & the ring recovered.

FALL & WINTER
OF 1864 & '65

At the time of the affair of Oct. 7th, the intrenchments below Richmond, whose plan seems very simple when seen on a map, were really not marked down upon any of the maps which we had. There were, moreover, more or less of scattered shorter lines in many places, all of which helped to confuse one's ideas on the subject very much. I became impressed with this during the fight on the 7th, & on Sunday the 9th I did some exploring of the lines, & then rode into Richmond & spent some hours with Gen. Gilmer, in marking out what then existed upon a map. This at once suggested to me the great need for a line to run from the Spur Line, somewhere near Fort Gilmer, across to strike our old Exterior Line near the Charles City Road, whence the old lines, clear to the Chickahominy, could be easily restored. So I got the proposition on a map which I at once took back to Gen. Lee's headquarters. The general approved the idea, & orders were sent to the engineers that very night & work was begun the next morning. That was the beginning of the most beautiful line of intrenchments which I saw during the whole war. We were, of course, many weeks, & even months in completing them, but they were a pride & delight when finished, & it seemed a great pity that the enemy would never test their qualities. They were less broken by salients than any other lines we ever built, but were in long sweeps, each one carefully arranged for artillery to enfilade all assaults, & for the easiest & swiftest shifting of troops to right & left. A third feature was the abattis in front, & a fourth was some mantlet or screen protection for gunners in loading & aiming artillery.

We were none too soon, either, in beginning to construct this line, for on Thursday, Oct. 13th, Gen. Butler made a reconnaissance in force upon the Darbytown Road, where he found us hard at work. At one point, where the work was least advanced & no abattis constructed, Pond's brigade, of Ames's division,[1] of the 10th Corps assaulted us but was easily repulsed. Some of Haskell's guns were here located in some unfinished breastworks,

& had some loose ammunition out on the ground near. The musketry fire of the infantry exploded a cartridge which lit the fuse of a shell. A little North Carolina corporal picked up the shell & threw it in a mud puddle & extinguished it.

I have dotted the course of this line of intrenchments we were now building on the map [Figure 61] & I give another map showing the new line & also the Federal intrenchments. [Figure 63 appears here in the manuscript.]

My command now embraced all the artillery between the James & the Appomattox Rivers, as well as that on the 11 miles north of the James, across to the Chickahominy, about 24 miles in all. From Petersburg to the Bermuda Hundreds lines was about four miles, held by a picket line of infantry, & isolated batteries down to Swift Creek. From there to the Howlett house batteries was five miles, held by Pickett's division of infantry & Huger's & Cabell's battalions of artillery. Thence to Drury's & Chaffin's Bluffs was four miles more, held by isolated heavy batteries, which often exchanged shots with the enemy's vessels across Dutch Gap, & in the river below Howlett's. We had, also, some electric torpedoes located in this portion of the river, to be fired from concealed stations on the shore, & they were also assigned to my command for unity of control in case of a serious attack by the enemy's fleet, which we always anticipated but which never came. For some months Butler had had a large force at work digging a canal across the Dutch Gap, which would let his fleet turn the Howlett house batteries, and among my commands upon that part of the line was a mortar battery, located in a large wood about 600 yards from the canal under charge of _____.² It was the duty of this battery to throw mortar shells into the canal at all hours of the day & night.

About this time, there arose some trouble between the Confederate & Federal authorities about the treatment of prisoners. I believe it was claimed by them that we had put Negro prisoners to work upon intrenchments where they were exposed to fire. If that is true it was unjustifiable but I do not think it true. At least I never saw or heard of such a thing in our army. Our men had sometimes shot Negro troops when they could & would have taken prisoners if they had been white, but so far as I know once delivered to the provost guard they were treated as white prisoners. But, at any rate, as a measure of retaliation Butler selected a lot of the good old citizen militia of Petersburg, whom he had captured in June, & placed them, about the middle of October, in the Dutch Gap Canal, where they would be exposed to our mortar shells. I am under the impression that our people retaliated by sending Federal officers to Charleston, to be placed under the Federal bombardment of that city; & they replied to that by taking a lot of our men to Morris Island, which was under our guns, but I am not sure that these Charleston incidents were part of this Dutch Gap affair.³

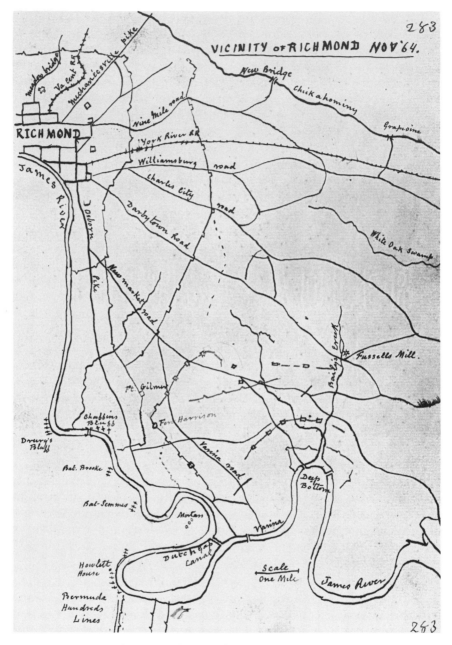

Figure 63. Vicinity of Richmond, November 1864

But, at any rate, the Petersburg party were placed in the Dutch Gap Canal, & then a committee of them was allowed to come, under a flag of truce, to visit Gen. Lee, pledging themselves to return. I never knew what their proposition to him was, nor his reply, but I chanced to see the delegation start back. This was Thursday, Oct. 20th, & it seemed to be by no means a cheerful procession. And soon after, I was sent for by the general. I never, but on one other occasion, saw him seem so worried. That was on the Potomac, after Gettysburg, when a freshet prevented our crossing, & Meade's army came up with us, as I believe was mentioned in my account of that period. He told me of our men being held in the canal under our fire, & said that he feared seeming to flinch from such an issue, lest the enemy should next come charging our breastworks, & driving our women & children before them to check our fire. So he directed me to go in person to the mortar battery, & to prevent the possibility of any one's thinking that we were shrinking from the issue, not only by doubling the frequency of our shells, but specially, also, by trying to improve their accuracy. He told me especially to watch the gunners who aimed the mortars, lest their sympathies should interfere with their duties, & to try to make them appreciate the importance of making it hotter in the Dutch Gap Canal than it had ever been before. And it seemed really to relieve his mind when he found me to concur very cordially, as if he had feared lest I might wink at a little bad aiming. After that interview I could understand the depression which seemed to prevail in the Petersburg procession, as it started back to Dutch Gap—only about 6 miles away. And as they marched down on the north side, I crossed the bridge & rode down to the mortar battery on the south side to prepare a warm reception for them. And I could not but smile to think how welcome they would be to their comrades, with the news they would bring & the practical demonstration of its truth which would soon follow.

I did my best, & we kept up the increased fire for some days, & then gradually fell back to the normal, & after a while, I forget how long though, the good old gentlemen were taken away. And, strange to say, I don't think one of them was ever hit, nor do I think any one on either side was hit at Charleston, in the retaliation camps. In the Dutch Gap they were allowed to dodge as much as they could, & even, I believe, to dig holes & bomb-proofs.

While on the subject of Butler's canal I may say that he was never able to open it so that any vessel could pass. But after the war freshets scoured it out, & it now makes the regular channel for navigation.

On Oct. 19th we had all been delighted by Gen. Longstreet's return to the command of the corps, from which he had been absent since May 6th, on account of his terrible wound through the throat at [the] Wilder-

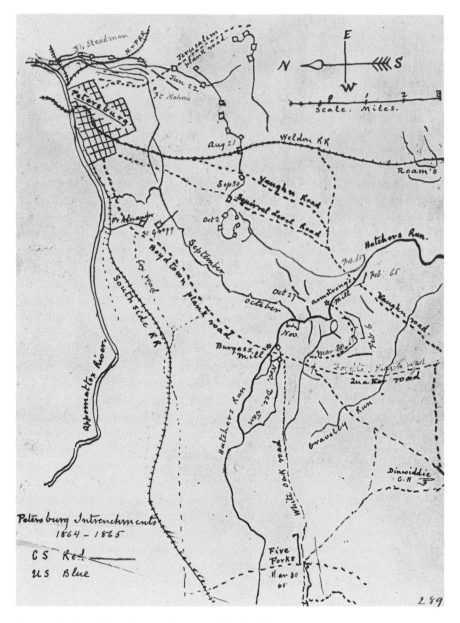

Figure 64. Petersburg intrenchments, 1864–65 (2)

ness. Not that we loved good old Dick Anderson less, either; for he had been everything that heart could wish, & had won both the love & confidence of all, for the brave, simple minded & earnest soldier that he was. Longstreet still wore his right arm in a sling, for the nerves controlling it had been severed in his neck, & it was entirely useless.

On Oct. 27th Gen. Grant again attempted our flanks; & again, I think, made the mistake of not concentrating more force in a single blow.

On his left he sent out Hancock with 10,000 infantry of the 2nd Corps, Warren with 11,000 of the 5th, Parke4 with 11,000 of the 9th, & Gregg with 3,000 cavalry, 35,000 in all. Gen. Humphreys states that more infantry could have been easily taken from the intrenchments, & attributes their failure to the fact this was not done.

The force used by Butler on the north side is not stated, but, as his Army of the James was about 30,000 strong, & his intrenchments were easily held with small forces, he probably had at least 18,000 in his demonstration. Gen. Lee had at this time about 35,000 infantry, say 10,000 north of the James, holding 11 miles of line, 5,000 at Bermuda Hundreds holding 5 miles, & 20,000 at Petersburg holding to Hatcher's Run, about 10 miles of line. For convenience of reference I attach another map of the Petersburg lines. [Figure 64 appears here in the manuscript.]

We will first follow the movement against our right flank, which rested on Hatcher's Run, about a mile below the Burgess's Mill, where the Boydton Plank Road crosses this creek. No works at that time existed upon the right bank of the creek, & our intrenchments on the left bank were scarcely completed. At dawn on Oct. 27th, Parke & Warren advanced upon these works, but, finding them too strong to assault, they began to intrench & skirmish, while waiting for Hancock to turn them. Hancock, at daylight, crossed Hatcher's Run by the Vaughn Road, & thence he moved by the Quaker Road to the Boydton Plank Road near Burgess's Mill. Meanwhile, also, Warren sent about 5,000 men, under Crawford,5 to cross at Armstrong's Mill & sweep up the right bank of the creek & take our intrenchments on the left bank in flank.

This plan seems simple & sound, & the forces seem adequate. And the prize of success was great. Could Hancock cross at Burgess's Mill, the three Federal corps would unite, & our whole line as far back as Fort Gregg would be lost, doubtless with many prisoners. Petersburg would be invested from the river below to the river above, & would not long be held.

But small mistakes often change events materially, in military affairs. Warren's corps proved to be pratically paralysed by being on the wrong side of Hatcher's Run. Had it accompanied Hancock their combined force would have been irresistible. Even the 5,000 sent over to him under

Crawford would probably have made him so, but they became partially lost & entangled in the swamps, & never reached him. Not waiting for Crawford, however, in the afternoon Hancock had forced his way up very near to the Burgess bridge, & about four o'clock was in the very act of assaulting it, when, in the very nick of time, he was interrupted. Mahone, with 3 brigades, had crossed the run & moved through the woods & now struck Hancock on his right just as the advance of his assaulting force had crossed the bridge, & captured a gun on the far side. At first Mahone was successful, routing Pierce's brigade,[6] which he struck, & capturing some guns. But he soon found himself in a hornet's nest. While he faced south to meet two brigades attacking him from that side, the three or four brigades which had been about to cross the bridge attacked him in rear, & he was glad to escape, losing the guns he had captured & two colors & several hundred prisoners; though he still brought off 3 colors & 400 prisoners. This attack, however, had broken up the enemy's advance. That night they retreated in a heavy rain, leaving us 250 of their wounded on the field & in temporary hospitals.

The losses in Hancock's & Warren's corps were reported at 1,068 killed & wounded & 673 missing; total 1,741. There were probably some losses also in the 9th Corps & in the cavalry.

We may now return to affairs on the north side of the James. A good part of Gen. Ewell's Local Defence troops had been brought forward & now garrisoned the right of our line, from the river to near Fort Gilmer, being under the immediate command of Gen. Custis Lee.[7] Then Hoke's & Field's divisions held the line to the Charles City Road (see map [Figure 63]). Beyond that, Gary's brigade of cavalry were in observation. On the morning of Oct. 27th Butler pushed a skirmish line up in our front, from the New Market to the Charles City Road, supported by Gen. Terry & a portion of the 10th Corps; while Weitzel,[8] with a considerable force from the 18th Corps, by a circuitous route, marched to surprise our line at the crossings of the Williamsburg Road & the York River Railroad. Gen. Longstreet soon noted that Terry's skirmishers were merely demonstrating, & suspected an attempt to surprise our left, & he ordered Field's division to extend itself in that direction. They did so, some of our artillery going along also, & were just in time to meet Gen. Weitzel's attack. It was quickly repulsed with a number of killed & wounded, & a half dozen colors left on the ground. Farther to our left, two guns supported by some of Gary's dismounted men were captured, & held for a short while, when Gary charged & recaptured them. About 4 P.M. Gen. Terry pressed his demonstration in front of the new part of our line, but soon found out its qualities & retired. So, during the whole of that black & rainy night great columns of defeated troops were floundering back home through mud & darkness on each flank of Grant's army, and many a poor wounded fellow lay out in the weather. Had all his force been concentrated on either one flank the result might have been very different. In this affair Gen. Humphreys gives Butler's losses as 516 killed & wounded, & 587 missing; total 1,103. Longstreet reports only 64 killed, wounded, & missing—our troops having the protection of the intrench-ments except where Gary recovered the guns.

As this affair ended the active operations of the year we will briefly review what had happened in the Valley & also in Georgia since July. Quite early in August Gen. Sheridan had been sent to the Valley to command the forces concentrated to crush Gen. Early; & two divisions of the Federal cavalry from Grant's army, Wilson's & Torbert's,[9] had been sent with him. Gen. Lee had sent Kershaw's division of infantry, as has already been told, & he also sent Fitz Lee's division of cavalry. But the preponderance of force against Early was very great, & the breech-loading carbines of the enemy's heavy cavalry force enormously increased their advantages; so that from nearly every encounter Early had to retire worsted. But his skill and cour-age always saved him from great disaster & his pertinacity kept him still in the field, and still threatening the enemy's flank. Thus they felt it necessary to retain there the whole force which they had collected, until the season for active operations was over. There were very many minor affairs, during the fall, & two notable battles. At Winchester, on Sep. 19th, Early was defeated in a very desperate fight which lasted all day. His force was about _____ & his losses about 5,500. Among them were our two very promising & admi-rable young Major Generals Rodes & Ramseur & Brig. Gen. Godwin. Sheridan's forces were about _____ & his losses 4,873.[10] This battle was very largely won by the cavalry with their breech loaders.

After this battle Early was pursued to Staunton, Va., but he again ad-vanced, & on October 19th he surprised & utterly routed most of Sher-idan's army at Cedar Creek. But his victory was not followed up, & his men were somewhat demoralized by the plunder of the enemy's camps. And Sheridan, who had been absent, returning in the nick of time & rallying his fugitives was able with his superior numbers to give Early another crushing defeat.

The forces engaged & the losses are reported as follows:

Early's force was _____
[Early's] losses were 4,200
Sheridan's force was _____
[Sheridan's] losses [were] 5,995.[11]

Kershaw's division was recalled from the Valley early in November & rejoined our corps on the north side of the James. About December 1st Gen. Grant recalled the 6th Corps, Gen. Wright's, to Petersburg and also brought down a new division, Harris's of the Army of West Virginia, which was added to Butler's Army of the James.[12] Gen. Lee, on this, brought back also the 2nd Corps, now reduced to about 10,000 men, which was placed under command of Gen. Gordon. Gen. Early remained still commanding a small force of infantry & cavalry about Staunton, which were necessary to protect the railroads & towns from raids.

Now let us take a bird's eye view of events in Georgia. I have already told of the fatal success of Gov. Jos. E. Brown & Senator Benjamin Hill in inducing Mr. Davis to replace Gen. Johnston by Gen. Hood on July 18th. Mr. Davis, before acting, had telegraphed to Gen. Lee, at Petersburg, asking his views upon the proposed change, & Gen. Lee had answered that, while Hood was capable & deserving, he thought a change would be unwise. In spite of his disapproval, however, it took place. Hood was put in command in order to fight. Within ten days, he made three attacks upon different parts of Sherman's lines: on the 20th, the 22nd, & the 28th. His total losses, in the three actions, were about 18,000 men; one half of them on the 22nd, which was the most severe and important.[13] In this battle, on our side was killed good old Gen. W. H. T. Walker, of Geo., one of my old commandants at West Point; & whose frail, thin body had survived desperate wounds from Seminole rifle bullets, & from Mexican grapeshot. On the Federal side, fell my special friend, Gen. McPherson, who had done his best, in San Francisco in 1861, to persuade me to "keep out of it." He rode upon an advancing line of our skirmishers, &, being summoned to halt, spurred his horse & tried to escape. Poor fellow, he was as lovable a gentleman as he was a fine soldier.

Whether these three days of battle satisfied Gov. Brown & Senator Hill that Hood's army could not meet Sherman's in equal battle, I do not know. But it did satisfy Gen. Hood & all of his principal officers of that fact, & after that the army stuck to its breastworks. After Sherman had intrenched himself sufficiently, he moved several corps around behind Hood, to Jonesboro, & cut off his line of supplies. This compelled Hood to evacuate Atlanta, & Sherman occupied it on Sep. 2nd. He was guilty of most unnecessary, unusual, & unjustifiable cruelty, in ordering the non-combatant population to vacate the town—which he afterwards largely burnt. Hood, meanwhile, looked on from some twenty or thirty miles away, but could do nothing. During Sept. Mr. Davis visited Hood &, in speeches afterward, perhaps incautiously promised to bring much trouble on Sherman's communications. And on Oct. 1st Hood started with his whole army, passed Sherman's right, & got on the railroad in his rear. Sherman at once started after him with all his force. Hood tore up some forty miles of road at different points, but the most important ones, having taken warning, Sherman had fortified & garrisoned so heavily that they successfully resisted

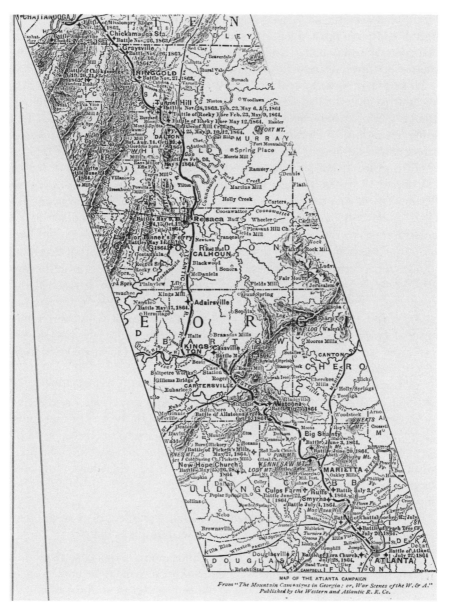

Figure 65. North central Georgia

Hood's hurried attacks. After going so far north as Dalton, & not daring to fight Sherman in pitched battle, he turned off into Alabama & halted near Gadsden. Sherman halted over in Georgia, at Gaylesville, & observed him. [Figure 65 appears here in the manuscript.]

Hood was in something of a quandry. His army was in that condition that he and his principal officers were all agreed that any movement which would be construed by his men to be a retreat would result in disaster. After some hesitation, he decided on the desperate alternative, in view of his resources, of dashing at Nashville. He not only believed it possible that he could capture it, but he even proposed to go into Kentucky & threaten Cincinnati, & then to march through Cumberland Gap & down to Petersburg, & enable Lee to destroy Grant & march upon Washington City. It was truly a cheerful & refreshing scheme to contemplate at the present stage of our affairs!! On Oct. 21st, Gen. Beauregard, who had recently joined Hood & had discussed his plan with him, authorized him, though apparently with some hesitation, to attempt its execution. His army was promptly put in motion on Oct. 22nd. On Nov. 1st it reached the Tennessee River at Tuscumbia. When Sherman saw this move he sent two of his six corps, say 15,000 each, to Thomas at Nashville, & with his remaining four corps returned to Atlanta whence he marched on Nov. 12th, for Savannah, unopposed except by a few cavalry pickets. He carried with him 68,000 men & 65 guns.

At Tuscumbia Hood was delayed for nearly 3 weeks by bad weather & to accumulate supplies which he had hoped would have met him, & he attributes all of the disasters which later befell him to the loss of that time. There is no doubt that this delay was of grave injury to his chances, & of very great value to the Federals in their preparations to meet him. The final result could not now have been changed, but Hood might have had some temporary brilliant successes which would have given him high rank in popular esteem.

During this delay the inaugurated campaign was anew discussed. Gen. Beauregard was still present & Gen. Hood writes of it as follows:

> General Sherman was still in the neighborhood of Rome, and the question arose as to whether we should take trains and return to Georgia to oppose his movements south, or endeavor to execute the projected operations into Tennessee and Kentucky. I adhered to the conviction I had held at Lafayette, and Gadsden, and a second time desired General Beauregard to consult the corps commanders, together with other officers, in regard to the effect a return to Georgia would produce upon the army. I also urged the consideration that Thomas would immediately overrun Alabama, if we marched to confront Sherman. I had fixedly determined, unless withheld by Beauregard or the authorities at Rich-

Figure 66. Maj. Gen. Patrick Ronayne Cleburne

mond, to proceed, as soon as supplies were received, to the execution of the plan submitted at Gadsden.

At this juncture I was advised of the President's opposition to the campaign into Tennessee previous to a defeat of Sherman in battle. The President was evidently under the impression that the army should have been equal to battle by the time it had reached the Alabama line, and was averse to my going into Tennessee. He was not, as were General Beauregard and myself, acquainted with its true condition. Therefore, a high regard for his views notwithstanding, I continued firm in the belief that the only means to checkmate Sherman, and cooperate with General Lee to save the Confederacy, lay in speedy success in Tennessee and Kentucky, and in my ability finally to attack Grant in rear with my entire force.[14]

[Figure 66 appears here in the manuscript.]

On Nov. 20th Hood was at last in motion toward Nashville, & in a few days was in close contact with Thomas's troops which were being drawn in for concentration. It was Hood's game, of course, by quick movement to try & cut off and beat portions of them in detail. And the story has been generally told ever since that, near Spring Hill, on the night of Nov. 29th, Hood had cut off a large part of Schofield's army,[15] which would have been easily captured but for very shameful negligence ascribed to Gen. Cheatham, who was said to have been improperly absent from his division & to have permitted the enemy to march past him in the night within a few hundred feet, which they did without interruption.

Perhaps it was in his disappointment at this narrow escape of Schofield's, which certainly took place on the 29th,[16] that led Hood into fighting the fatal battle of Franklin the next afternoon. Schofield had taken a very strong position to let his trains get ahead, but at night he would vacate it himself. Hood however decided to attack it in the afternoon. The country in that part of Tennessee is well cleared & cultivated, & good positions are abundant. But this position was peculiarly good, & defended by 26 guns & ample infantry, well intrenched, while the assailants would be under full fire for a mile.

There is no assault in military history, of which I have ever heard, that equals this in the loss of the generals engaged upon the side of the assailants. Five were killed, three severely wounded & one captured within the enemy's works. The following extract from an account by Col. Stone, a Federal staff officer, will give an idea of the desperate character of the fighting:[17]

> Where there was nothing to hinder the Union fire, the muskets of Stile's and Casement's brigades[18] made fearful havoc; while the batteries at the railroad-cut plowed furrows through the ranks of the advancing foe. Time after time they came up to the very works, but they never crossed them except as prisoners. More than one color-bearer was shot down on the parapet. It is impossible to exaggerate the fierce energy with which the Confederate soldiers, that short November afternoon, threw themselves against the works, fighting with what seemed the very madness of despair. There was not a breath of wind, and the dense smoke settled down upon the field, so that, after the first assault, it was impossible to see at any distance. Through this blinding medium, assault after assault was made, several of the Union officers declaring in their reports that their lines received as many as thirteen distinct attacks.
>
> Between the gin-house and the Columbia Pike the fighting was fiercest, and the Confederate losses the greatest. Here fell most of the Confederate generals, who, that fateful afternoon, madly gave up their lives; Adams of Stewart's corps—his horse astride the works, and himself within a few

Figure 67. Battlefield at Franklin from General Cheatham's headquarters

feet of them. Cockrell and Quarles, of the same corps, were severely wounded. In Cheatham's corps, Cleburne and Granbury were killed near the pike. On the west of the pike Strahl and Gist were killed, and Brown was severely wounded. General G. W. Gordon was captured by Opdycke's brigade, inside the works.[19]

Hood's losses are given as 6,252; the Federal losses as 2,326. This battle lost Hood his last chance of the campaign. It was not only the men & the ammunition gone, but the blow to the morale of the troops to find that even the most desperate valor may be in vain, & the lack of the leadership of those nine veteran generals. The field was an open one & its character was plain beforehand. And, on principle, Hood should have avoided all dangerous or unprofitable combats, & saved every ounce of strength & spirit for the crisis. [Figure 67 appears here in the manuscript.] This came at Nashville on Dec. 16th. Thomas with 36,000 attacked Hood with about 20,000, & defeated him & utterly routed him. Hood's losses are given as 15,000, & Thomas's 3,057. Hood was on the defensive, & in earth works. Had his men fought as they did at Franklin he might have easily given Thomas a very bloody defeat. But Franklin took the temper out of Hood's army even worse than Cold Harbor did from Grant's, for the proportion of veteran generals[20] killed was so much greater. Imagine those 6,000 men slain at Franklin & those 9 generals fighting behind breast works, & it is not easy to imagine them defeated. And so Cheatham's absence & negligence knocked over the Spring Hill brick, & that probably brought on the

Franklin brick-fall, & that knocked over the Nashville bricks, which was the end of Hood's army.[21]

The remnants, with great hardship & suffering but with a devotion & courage all the more admirable, retreated to Tupelo, Mississippi. Later some were brought east, I believe, & again served under Gen. Johnston in North Carolina at the wind up.

The months of November & December were spent in finishing our breast works & putting the fine touches on them. At all of my batteries, for instance, I built lookout loopholes, for use when the parapet was under a close fire of musketry; & little magazines were built for the ammunition. I made but few memoranda of the dates in my note book, & those few recall very little. Thus:

"Sat. Oct. 29 False alarm A.M."
"Tues. Nov. 15 Rode over to Petersburg."
"Thurs. [Nov.] 17 Picket took skirmish line of enemy."

I can recall nothing of either of these incidents.

"Mon. Dec. 5. Target firing at Chaffin's Bluff." I had put Maj. W. H. Gibbes in command of the Bluff, after his recovery from his severe wound at the Crater July 30th, & we had target practise to let his gunners get ranges on the river, & to test his ammunition. His powder was bad & fresh had to be provided. I also got a Lt. Wilkinson[22] assigned to me, to make some experiments with some seacoast mortars there. I tried to improve their accuracy by firing at 60° elevations instead of 45°. And for use in mortars I got the Ordnance Department to try & get me up powder with uniform cubical or hexagonal grains large enough to be counted, as to graduate the charges by counting grains. But the powder factory never got my powder finished in time to be tried.

On Wed., Dec. 7th, I have a note of a fight with the gunboats at Howlett's, & a telegram from Gen. Lee to go there, but I can recall nothing of it.

On Sat., Dec. 10th, my book says, "We make a demonstration on the Charles City Road." I recall of that only that we were advancing down this road before daylight, & as I rode along with a column of infantry I overheard one of the men say to a comrade, "I reckon we will get some Corporal Dicks before we get back today." But I don't think we got any. Also, I recollect being asked by Gen. Lee about this time to try if [it] were possible to see any of the enemy's ponton bridges from any trees within our lines, & I picked out the tallest pine on the highest ground, in the best location, & had cleats nailed on the tree, & climbed with my glasses to the smallest limb at the top which would bear me, but none of the bridges were where they could be seen.

I also made one attempt to cut down one of the enemy's tall signal towers, at a mile range nearly, with Captain Parker's light rifles, but our ammunition was not reliable enough for such nice work, & we gave it up after a short trial.

And then, on Sat., Jan. 7, '65, I had a rare piece of good luck. I had been down on Pickett's lines & at the Howlett house batteries, & was riding about in the afternoon with Maj. _____ Smith[23] of Mobile, who commanded these batteries. He was, by the way, an exceedingly attractive fellow, remarkably intelligent, highly cultivated, refined, brave, genial, & handsome. I thought him one of the most valuable officers in our army. And on the retreat, in the very last days, he was killed by a volley fired in the night, by his own men, under a false alarm. This afternoon he was riding a perfectly superb bay mare, as fat as a seal, as pretty as a picture, & as full of life & play as a kitten. We were going down a slope where the men had cut off all the trees, &, somehow, my old Dixie stumbled over a stump, & it being down hill, she fell, throwing me over her head. As I lit on the ground, trying to catch myself, Smith's mare wheeled somehow & kicked with both feet, planting them a little below my left shoulder blade. It knocked me several feet & broke at least one rib. As I got the blow I thought of the poor fellow I had seen shot through the lungs at Cold Harbor, for the breath was knocked out of me. I just laid on the ground gasping, as he had done, horribly; & loud enough to be heard a hundred yards. Smith jumped off & held up my head, & presently saw some one whom he sent for a litter, & four men shouldered me & carried me to Frank Huger's, where I stayed for several days before I could go back to my camp.

Meanwhile, the excuse was too good to be lost, & I applied for a furlough. As soon as I could safely travel, on Tuesday, Jan. 17th, [I] started home. Thursday night I was in Columbia & went to a sort of fair or bazaar, where I bought for my children a pound box of French candy which had run the blockade. I paid $80.00 for it in Confederate money, or about $1.50 gold. I left on Friday morning for Augusta, with a haversack full of the nicest biscuit, I think, that I ever saw—two days' rations of them. I regret them yet, for I only had one lunch out of them before I was waked up from a doze, & found our car rolling down a bank. It at last stopped bottom up in a shallow creek, but the water two feet deep in the top, I climbed out of the window all right, & never noticed that in rolling over I had rolled out of the haversack strap some how, & I never saw it or biscuit again. Fortunately the rolling did not hurt my loose rib, & I got home safely Saturday night.

My furlough was for 30 days but before it expired some matters had occurred which must be told.

I have already written that, by all the rules of state craft, the Confederate government (the executive & the Senate) should have opened negotiations for peace some months before. For at that time we had been in better

position to secure concessions than we ever could have reasonably hoped to
be again. Since then our position had been growing steadily worse. It would
seem, too, that the defeat of the Democrats, & the re-election of Mr. Lincoln
in November, might well have been generally recognised as the very funeral of
our last chances. But, strange as it now seems to look back upon, our eyes
were blinded utterly—at least my own & those of my associates, & we cared
not a straw whom the Federals elected, & confidently expected final success
to come, some how. And that was the general sentiment in the army. I can
only account for it in the generally religious character of our people. They
believed in a God who overruled all human affairs, & who in the end brought
the right to prevail. They *knew* they were right, & there they were! It was
only waiting on God, a little more or less. As one old chaplain, in the army,
used to pray, He would surely come down, after a while, & "take a proper
view of this situation," & then we would be all right.

Well at last, as it really seemed, by Providential interposition, & not by
any initiative of our own a meeting was arranged at Fortress Monroe, early
in Feb. 1865, to discuss terms of peace. It was brought about by a[n] Hon.
Montgomery Blair, &c.[24] He came to Richmond in January, of his own
notion but by Mr. Lincoln's consent, & at last, with some little difficulty, it
was arranged that a commission composed of Vice Prest. Stephens, Judge
Campbell, & R. M. T. Hunter,[25] should meet President Lincoln & Secretary Seward at Fortress Monroe on Feb. 9th. All the other crises of the war
seem to me to be vague & shadowy figures & of uncertain proportions, as
compared with the sitting of this conference. For, practically, a proposition
was here made to the South, & rejected, which seems absolutely incredible
when one reflects that she was then within 60 days of an unconditional
surrender! Not from any sudden or unforeseen calamity, either. But from
the natural & ordinary operation of forces playing on the side of all men, &
only waiting for the winter to pass to produce their inevitable results.

At that date, Feb. 9th, Mr. Lincoln practically offered the South four
hundred million dollars as compensation for the slaves set free, & any other
reasonable political conditions they might choose to name, if she would
return to the Union. But our committee was under instructions. The president & cabinet had absolutely forbidden our delegates to accept any terms,
or even to consider any, short of our independence. That was the one thing
Mr. Lincoln would not grant. He said to the commission, "Let me write the
one word 'Union' at the head of a sheet, & you can fill in the rest of the
treaty to suit yourselves." He took Mr. Stephens to one side, & said that it
had always seemed to him as only just to the South that the nation should
pay for the slaves set free, and that he would recommend to Congress the
payment of four hundred millions dollars & believed that it would be
granted.[26]

I have seen in a newspaper a denial by Judge Reagan of Texas that an offer of four hundred millions was ever really made. As Judge Reagan was one of the Confederate cabinet, he doubtless felt his judgment impugned by the non-acceptance of such an offer.[27] Technically, perhaps, it may be denied, because it was never reduced to writing & formally submitted. But that was only because, being first informally suggested to Mr. Stephens, it appeared that it could not possibly be accepted. But from other evidence which I have seen recorded it was really always a desire of Mr. Lincoln's to eventually pay the South for the slaves set free as a matter of justice and as other nations have always done. Indeed, I will have an incident to narrate in connection with the surrender, which has always made me believe that, had Mr. Lincoln not been assassinated, some compensation would have been made, even after that date.

So I put it down as a fact beyond all question, that 60 days before the surrender we were practically offered four hundred million dollars, & any reasonable political rights we might ask, if we would peaceably return to the Union!

The future historian may greatly condemn the rejection of such terms by our executive, particularly when the pitiable condition is considered to which we were reduced by unconditional surrender, & by Negro suffrage, & all the iniquities of Reconstruction under the passions engendered by the assassination. But it must never be forgotten that our executive simply carried out the wishes of our army & of the people at that time. We were not "whipped." We were fighting for *Rights,* & we would have scorned the idea of parting with them for money.

Which is all admirable enough, but the trouble was that we were struggling against changes which the advance of the world in railroads & steamboats & telegraphs, in science & knowledge and commerce, &, in short, in civilization, had rendered inevitable.

And as our cause was thus foredoomed to failure, perhaps the most fitting obsequies which could be wished for it, by those who loved it, were those afterward performed at Appomattox.

I cannot give a better brief statement of our condition, at this period, than by the following quotation from Gen. Humphreys:

> The winter of 1864–65 was one of unusual severity, making the picket duty in front of the intrenchments very severe. It was especially so to the Confederate troops, with their threadbare insufficient clothing, and meager food, chiefly cornbread made of the coarsest meal. Meat they had but little of, and their Subsistence Department was actually importing it from abroad. Of coffee, tea, & sugar they had none, except in the hospitals. It is stated that at a secret session of the Confederate Congress the condition of the Confederacy as to subsistence was declared to be:

"That there was not meat in the Southern Confederacy for the armies
it had in the field.
That there was not in Virginia either meat or bread enough for the
armies within her limits.
That the supply of bread for those armies, to be obtained from other
places, depended absolutely upon keeping open the railroad connections of the south.
That the meat must be obtained from abroad through a seaport.
That the transportation was not now adequate, from whatever
cause, to meet the necessary demands of the service.
That the supply of fresh meat to Gen. Lee's army was precarious."

To this Gen. Humphreys adds, "The condition of the deserters, who
constantly came into our lines during the winter, appeared to prove that
there was no exaggeration in this statement."[28]

It was of this period that the story was told of the half-frozen Confederate picket, who sat on a stump & took stock of his nearly bare feet & thin
& ragged clothes & empty haversack, & exclaimed, "Well, damn me if
ever I love another *Country!*" The quotation above by Gen. Humphreys is
from a secret report made by the Subsistence Department. At the same
time secret reports were called from all the departments, and all told
similar stories. The Quartermaster Department was on the verge of exhaustion of all supplies of forage & its only chance to get clothing, or such
supplies as were needed to keep the worn out railroads even passable,
were through blockade running. The Medical Department had always
only lived from hand to mouth, through the blockade. And the Ordnance
Department, which had already cut up the last turpentine still in the South
to make percussion caps from the copper, was now dependent upon the
blockade runners for them, as well as for many other essentials. And,
about the middle of February, Wilmington was captured & all possible
blockade running was ended. Briefly, had not the poem of the deacon's
One-horse Shay been written some years before, it might well be supposed
to have been suggested by the condition of the Confederacy at this time.
Every part had done its duty & lasted its time. And now everything was
ready to go to smash all at once!

Sherman had taken Savannah Dec. 21st, 1864, & he remained there
about a month. He then crossed the Savannah River & moved toward
Columbia. This compelled our immediate evacuation of Charleston, lest
our whole garrison there should be cut off & captured. And thus it happened, also, that when the end of my furlough approached, the railroad
between Augusta and Columbia had been destroyed & I had to seek
another route by which to return to Richmond. I started on Monday, Feb.
13th, riding to Abbeville, S.C., & taking James, the carriage driver, with me

to bring back my horse. I spent that night at Ed Calhoun's on Little River, the same one whom I had met on the road in July, with the bullet lodged in the roof of his mouth. Tuesday I went on to Abbeville, to the hotel, & started James back home. Wednesday I took the cars & went as far as Alston. From that point to Columbia a terrible freshet had destroyed the railroad, & passengers going toward Virginia walked or rode across to Winnsboro. The only accommodation at Alston was a small room in the railroad station, where I slept, as well as I could, on a bare floor, without blanket or cover, or pillow except my valise, with about a dozen other passengers. Among them was Vice-President Stephens, who came in from the Winnsboro side on his way to Georgia, having recently returned from Fortress Monroe. He was a great friend of my father's, & he talked to me freely of the conference. I, of course, heartily approved our standing out boldly for independence, & he did not gainsay my ideas. But I could perceive that he was in a very discouraged frame of mind. He was always a believer that the war would prove disastrous to us.

On Thursday [the] 16th, I got my little hand valise in a wagon, & walked across to Winnsboro, about 24 miles. Here I spent part of the night at a little hotel, & then managed, with much trouble, to get on one of three or four trains of refugees, & prisoners, & I don't know what all else, that had been run out of Columbia at the approach of Sherman's army. Of course there were guards on the trains to see that every man had a pass. My pass was my furlough paper from Lee's headquarters. But the trouble in taking trains now was to find even standing room on them. When I lost my haversack of biscuits, as already told, it was because after getting out of the car window I hurried so after the train, which was stopped 100 yards ahead, lest there should not be standing room for all in the remaining cars. We only reached Charlotte, say 80 miles, next afternoon, & again had to stay all night. At the hotel, in view of my rank, I was favored with supper & permission to sleep in the parlor, where there was a carpet, with at least fifty other occupants, men & women, the whole floor being literally covered. Among them was a whole girls' school which had run off from Sherman somewhere; & one of the party, either a pupil or a very young teacher, had a husband in the army, who, somehow, turned up there, & they had a very affectionate meeting. Then they got two rocking chairs in which they spent the night laughing & talking to each other all night, though in somewhat subdued tones so that the crowd could sleep—at least a little. For that carpet was very thin and the snoring in that room that night was something phenomenal.

That was the night of Friday, Feb. 17th, the night in which Sherman burned Columbia. He officially stated that it was burned by fires set by Hampton's men. When the willful falsity of this statement was fully established, some years afterward, Sherman admitted it, but said that he made it as a war measure—to destroy Hampton's popularity in So. Ca.![29]

The whole incident was utterly discreditable. I cannot conceive of Gen. Grant, for instance, as either winking at the unnecessary burning of a city, or of making a false statement about it afterward.

Although it is only 280 miles from Charlotte to Richmond I was another night on the road, only reaching Richmond Sunday, Feb. 19th.

Early in February there had been another of those numerous affairs below Petersburg on our right flank. Grant had found that we were still hauling supplies from the Weldon Road & had sent a force to destroy it for forty miles south, & had a heavy force, to guard their rear, on the south side of Hatcher's Run. Gen. Lee had sent parts of Hill's & Gordon's corps down to attack them & there were several sharp fights in the neighborhood of Gravelly Run, without material advantage on either side (see map [Figure 64]). The Federal losses here were reported as 1,320 killed & wounded & 154 missing. Ours are not reported.

Among the killed, unfortunately, was our brilliant Gen. John Pegram, now commanding a division. In this connection, too, I must note the death of Gen. Gracie, killed Dec. 2nd in the trenches around Petersburg by a chance shot. Pegram & Gracie were classmates at West Point, first class men when I was a plebe. Both had done superb fighting throughout the whole campaign now to be killed, as it were, almost by accident at its close.

After my return my time & thoughts were largely taken up with the river. The lines held by our infantry and field artillery I now considered inpregnable; but I feared an earnest effort in the river by the enemy's monitors & gunboats when spring freshets gave abundant water. The only notes which I made of this period relate to conferences with Admiral Semmes on these matters, & to preparations to increase our torpedoes in the river, & to turn loose in the river torpedoes which would explode by contact, & let them float down toward the enemy various estimated distances & then have them automatically anchor themselves under water. I proposed to do this on a scale which would breed a torpedo panic, if possible, and make the enemy believe there were more torpedoes in the river than there were catfish. And so the time passed until the end of March with only one hostile incident.

This was an incident very characteristic of Gen. Lee for it seems to me one of the greatest instances of audacity which the war produced. It was nothing less than an attempt to surprize & seize Fort Stedman, one of Grant's specially prepared forts, near the right of his line around Petersburg (see map [Figure 64]). Having taken that fort an effort was to be made to roll up Grant's line to the right, while forces should also be sent to the left to destroy the ponton bridges over the Appomattox & to burn wharves, storehouses, &c. at City Point.

A great compliment was paid Gen. Gordon in selecting him to command this assault. Indeed I think the very idea of the scheme is, in itself, an immense compliment to our whole army, that Gen. Lee believed it equal to such an undertaking.

It was made at 4:30 A.M., Saturday, March 25th, & it was at first successful. We captured Fort Stedman & some adjoining batteries, but we wasted valuable time and lost a lot of men in hunting for some works in the rear, which did not exist, but which we supposed to be there & to be of vital importance. The hour of the attack had also been delayed by accidents to trains bringing up troops. So daylight found the plan only half executed & the Federal troops & batteries swarmed upon it. The few who got back, of all those sent forward to execute the plan, had to run the gauntlet of a terrible fire. Meanwhile, at several points along the intrenchments, the Federals, believing our lines to be thinly manned, attacked them vigorously. They were repulsed everywhere from our main lines, but at two points they took & held our picket lines, which proved of fatal advantage to them when the final struggle came on—a week later.

In all of this fighting our losses were about 4,000 & the Federals' about 2,000.

I have not mentioned our winter quarters, which we fixed up in the fall & lived in very comfortably all winter. We had a wall tent about ten by eight, with a fly. On the sides & rear we placed logs on each other for about two & a half feet high, & banked dirt outside. One half of the doorway was filled with a mud & stick chimney, whose fireplace faced inside. The other half was the entrance with its door flap. With a good fire we could always be comfortable. Late in March Winthrop took a leave of absence, & had not returned when we started on the retreat, so we saw him no more. After the surrender he left the country, going to South America, where he married a pretty English girl in Buenos Aires, whom he took home to England.

Just before I went on furlough in January I remember buying a pair of boots, at a great bargain, from a shoemaker who had made them on order, but his customer was an officer who by some fortune of war did not come for them. And so the shoemaker offered them to me, he said, for $200 less than his regular price or for only $500. And as one of my friends had recently paid $700 for a pair, & the boots were a good fit I thought myself very lucky to save that much money on a single pair of boots.

One day, during the last week in March, I made another little financial transaction by some strange and sudden inspiration which could only have come from unconscious cerebratim, or some "sub-ego" whose mental operations were not my own. My boy Charley had been hired, in 1861, from a gentleman, Jno. Carr, who lived up in Loudoun County, Va. His home was generally in the Federal lines, & I never saw him but once. In 1862 he came to Richmond & I paid him Charley's hire up to date, & suggested that in future he should draw on me at a bank in Richmond where I kept an account.

After that I was always careful to keep that account good, at least for Charley's accumulated wages. But the gentleman had never drawn, & now over two & a half years' wages & some margin had accumulated in the bank. On this day, Joe Haskell had mounted & started to ride to town when that remarkable inspiration suddenly overcame me. I called him back & gave him a check to draw my whole balance, & buy gold for me with it. It was near seven hundred dollars, and in the afternoon he brought me a ten dollar gold piece which it just sufficed to purchase. I put it in my pocket, & carried it to the surrender. And, to close the incident, I may say here that I gave it to Charley when I took my final farewell of him after that event.

Early in the year a change had been made by Mr. Davis in the head of our Subsistence Department. Gen. Northrop was replaced by Gen. St. John. I believe I have before referred to the general dissatisfaction with Northrop, from early in the war, & the tenacity with which Mr. Davis supported him. If he had supported Gen. Johnston with such firmness, Brown & Hill would have kicked in vain. St. John was a man of remarkable executive ability, & almost miraculously conjured up from somewhere about three million rations, which he accumulated in reserve depots in Richmond, Lynchburg, Danville, & Greensboro—say enough for 50,000 men for 60 days. An illustration of the popular feeling in the matter of feeding the army is found in the loan made to the Confederate government by the Virginia legislature & executive, in the month of March. Nearly every bank in Richmond had in its vaults some gold, which was carefully hoarded against the bank's obligations. The state volunteered to get a large amount of the gold from some of these banks & to lend it to the Confederacy, to be used, however, solely to subsist troops in Virginia. The state got it from the banks by giving state obligations, which the banks were willing to accept as less difficult & hazardous to protect & preserve in case the city was captured. The gold, about three hundred thousand dollars, was turned over to a special commissary in the last days of March.

I shall tell later of a personal adventure connected with this money at home in Georgia after the surrender.

One other subject must be referred to in endeavoring to give an idea of the general situation at this period. The condition of the country at large was one of almost as great deprivation & suffering as that of the army itself; & in many localities even of much greater. North Carolina, South Carolina, & Georgia had been over-run by Sherman's army carrying off many of the Negroes & most of the stock & destroying all accumulations of provisions which they could not use, & often burning barns & dwellings & all implements of agriculture. I have heard of instances where women & children had no food for days but corn which they were able to pick up where the enemy's cavalry had fed their horses on the ground. The other Southern states had not been so generally over run, but in all there had been many districts more or less ravaged by raids & marches. Naturally, the wives & mothers left at home wrote longingly for the return of the husbands & sons who were in the ranks in Virginia. And, naturally, many of them could not resist these appeals, & deserted in order to return & care for their families. Col. Walter H. Taylor, in his "Four Years with Lee," says that during the last 30 days before Petersburg "the loss to the army by desertion averaged a hundred men a day." And he writes as follows:

> The condition of affairs throughout the South at that period was truly deplorable. Hundreds of letters addressed to soldiers were intercepted, & sent to army headquarters, in which mothers, wives, & sisters told of their inability to respond to the appeals of hungry children for bread, or to provide proper care & remedies for the sick, &, in the name of all that was dear, appealed to the men to come home, & rescue them from the ills which they suffered & the starvation which threatened them. Surely never was devotion to one's country & to one's duty more sorely tested than was the case with the soldier's of Lee's army during the last year of the war.[30]

APPOMATTOX

Before rolling up the curtain on the last scene of the great game we have been following through four bloody years, let us glance briefly at the pieces on the board.

Gen. Humphreys estimates Gen. Lee's whole available force on the last days of March as 46,000 infantry, 5,000 artillery, & 6,000 cavalry. Col. Walter H. Taylor estimates the effective infantry at not more than 33,000. The difference lies principally in Taylor's allowance of 3,000 for desertions since Feb. 28th, the date of the last monthly return, & in not including Ewell's Local Defence brigades, Wise's brigade, Rosser's cavalry & some Richmond & Danville R.R. defence troops, which did not belong to the Army of Northern Virginia, but which were serving with or near it & took part in the retreat.[1]

From his left flank near the Chickahominy to his right flank at Burgess's Mill on Hatcher's Run was thirty seven miles by the shortest roads. There were, within these limits, fully thirty miles of parapet to be defended & liable to assault at any time on very brief warning. Along the railroads to the south small intrenchments & garrisons were required at all important bridges, & considerable [prov]ost[2] guards in Richmond & Petersburg. I am satisfied that 40,000 infantry would be an extreme limit for those holding the thirty miles of parapet, or say an average of 1,300 muskets to the mile. With muzzle loading guns that is too small allowance, even for good works. At some points, also, we had weakened our abattis to procure firewood in very cold weather.

Gen. Humphreys gives Grant's effective force as 101,000 infantry, 9,000 artillery with 369 field guns, & 15,000 cavalry. Total 125,000. The report of the secretary of war to the 39th Congress gives Grant's strength, at this time, as 162,239. The difference is that Gen. Humphreys counts only those who appear on the line of battle, which is correct. The sec. of war's report includes teamsters & detailed men of all sorts who do not fight.[3]

When Sherman started north from Savannah it was clear that a very serious situation must soon be confronted, for there was no army between him and Grant. So, at last, something was done which had far better have been done more than two years before. Gen. Lee was made commander in chief of all the armies of the Confederacy. His first act, on Feb. 23, was to assign Gen. Jos. E. Johnston to the command in North Carolina (it is not said whether Brown & Hill protested); & to endeavor to concentrate under him a force which might at least delay Sherman. Mr. Davis had sent Gen. Bragg to Wilmington, in January, with Hoke's division in a vain effort to prevent its capture. Wilmington fell on Feb. 22nd, & its garrison retreated & joined Gen. Johnston, as did, also, Gen. Hardee with the troops which had formerly held Savannah and Charleston. The remnants too of Hood's army were hurried across from Miss. & Ala., & by the middle of March Gen. Johnston had collected perhaps 25,000 men. He had two sharp affairs with Sherman's advance at Averasboro & Bentonville but of course could not prevent him from going where he pleased. Sherman was marching for Goldsboro, where there already awaited him the force which had captured Wilmington. This consisted of the Army of the Ohio under Schofield, brought east after the destruction of Hood in December, & Gen. Terry with 8,000 infantry detached in January from the Army of the James.[4]

Sherman arrived at Goldsboro & united all these forces in his own command on Feb. 25th. His whole force was now about 100,000 men.

On Feb. 27th he visited Gen. Grant at City Point, where joint operations were concerted. Now, in the game of war, when two weaker armies are confronted by two stronger, their sole salvation is by [a] prompt & sudden move to unite & throw themselves on one of the stronger & try & destroy it. When the armies are separated as far as Virginia & Georgia that strategy may not seem so obvious. But now it was so very plain that Gen. Grant was in constant apprehension that when he waked some morning he would find Lee gone. Had he reflected on it a bit he need not have worried himself.

Gen. Lee did indeed want to go. Not only that, he had planned with Prest. Davis that they all would go, & go soon. But what they planned was an orderly & decent retreat, taking with them, or sending ahead, stores & supplies & many things in Richmond without which our army could not long keep the field. *And no such retreat as that was ever practicable.* If it were attempted the whole city would have known it in 12 hours & Grant in 24. Secrecy would have been impossible. No retreat was ever possible except an abandonment—a flight, such as actually took place; with such destruction of supplies & resources, & such moral effect as would itself have been fatal to any long resistance.

It has been sometimes said that if Gen. Lee had been allowed to do so, he would have evacuated Richmond & Petersburg at some time in 1864, &

marched rapidly to Georgia to unite with Johnston or Hood & destroy Sherman. He might very well have sent help on some occasions as I have already suggested more than once. But I do not at all believe he would ever have evacuated Richmond. Apart from the military value of the morale which would have been lost by such a step, was the strategic value of the position as a railroad centre5 & head of navigation, & the enormous value of the Tredegar Iron Works & the Richmond Arsenal & all the stores & factories & machinery & skilled labor concentrated there, which could never be moved. Civilized armies cannot fight like savages without bases of supply. Should they try it their fighting would at once degenerate even below the value of the fighting of savages.

Doubtless Gen. Lee often felt, & perhaps expressed himself, as embarrassed by the defence of Richmond, but it was inexorable necessity, military & political, which compelled it. The Federals, too, were similarly embarrassed by the defence of Washington, & with far less cause. After Richmond fell there was nothing left to fight for but honor, & that would have been the case, probably, at any time in the war, certainly in the last two years. So though it was planned that Gen. Lee should evacuate Richmond, the enormous & really impossible preliminary detail was always deferring the date, & would have kept on doing so all the summer.

Meanwhile, Grant intended to take no chances, & his army was thoroughly organised & equipped for rapid motion & only waited his nod. On the 27th of February he had recalled Gen. Sheridan, his best general, from Winchester, with two divisions of his excellent cavalry, with their breech-loading carbines. These divisions, on their march, had destroyed the railroads from Staunton to Lynchburg & Gordonsville, & also the James River Canal,6 & had finally arrived before Petersburg on Mar. 27th. The very next day Grant gave the nod & the whole business was in motion.

This time Grant avoided two great mistakes, one of which he had made at least twice in the fall. The other was the mistake which lost Chancellorsville to Hooker, &, perhaps, Gettysburg to Lee.

First: this time he concentrated his whole force in a single blow from his left, instead of dividing it, & striking on both flanks at the same time. It is a good general who shows himself able to learn from experience, & Grant had learned.

The second error he came very near falling into; to wit, sending his cavalry off on a raid after railroads, &c. instead of keeping it for the battle. He had practically given Sheridan orders for such a raid, but he recalled them, & Sheridan's presence & personality changed incipient disaster into victory.

I will not go into details but only outline what took place. Grant left but two divisions of infantry at Bermuda Hundreds & one division north of the

James. This left him about 90,000 infantry & 15,000 cavalry to use against the Petersburg lines. On March the 29th the first collision occurred when their advance approached our left, intending to envelope it. If there ever was a general who was a past master in the art of stretching a thin line & of audacious aggressiveness, under cover of woods & bushes, against a superior enemy in motion, it was Gen. Lee. And in A. P. Hill, Heth, Mahone, Wilcox, Johnson, & his Petersburg army generally, he had assistants who were veterans as hard as nails & thoroughly at home in their business.

But, at last, the conditions had become too severe for all their resources; & the Federals, too, had learned from much experience the danger of leaving any gaps in their lines, & now had men enough to meet all demands.

On the 30th, Wilcox's division on the north, & Heth's on the south of Hatcher's Run had sharp affairs with the approaching Federals, whom they went out to attack in some cases but were finally driven back within their lines. The Federal losses for this day were 1,780; ours perhaps 1,200. Meanwhile Pickett with 6,600 infantry, & Fitz Lee with 5,700 cavalry, were brought up to be used in a flank attack. They were sent out on the 31st &, going by Five Forks, they struck Sheridan's cavalry & drove it back in some confusion nearly to Dinwiddie Court House, some four miles. Night ended the fighting, with Pickett so far advanced that he would have been taken in rear & cut off by Warren's corps had he waited till morning. Accordingly he fell back during the night & took position in the morning at Five Forks, four miles from our right at Burgess's Mill. Here he intrenched himself as well as the time and scarcity of tools permitted. But his halting here was a fatal mistake. He was four miles from where any other troops could help him or he could help them. He should never, never, never have stopped until he connected with our right flank. The final result, as I've sometimes said before, would have been the same, but our game would have been correctly played to the end. As it was he gave himself to be Sheridan's meat, & Sheridan was general enough to see it at a glance, & to take him in. Nothing could be easier! He merely deployed in his front a force fully equal to Pickett's, while he turned his left flank with Warren's whole corps of infantry, about 15,000 men. It is the old standard move for such opportunities. Naturally, that was the end of Pickett's division, though he himself escaped. The cavalry also lost heavily in prisoners, but being on the right flank of the infantry, more of them got away.

I have before noted some occasions when the noise of severe engagements both with musketry and artillery has been entirely inaudible, even two miles away. This action was another instance of it. Probably 35,000 men were engaged, and artillery on both sides. About a mile & a quarter in rear was Hatcher's Run. Gen. Humphreys writes: "A singular circumstance connected with this battle is the fact that Gen. Pickett was all of this time, & until near the close of the action, on the north side of Hatcher's Run where he had heard no sound of the engagement, nor had he received any information concerning it."[7]

At another point he refers to it again & ascribes it to the density of the woods. That doubtless had influence, but I once saw a similar occurrence at Fredericksburg where there were no woods.

The battle was fought between four & six P.M. The Federals claimed 4,500 prisoners, 13 colors, & six guns. The Fifth Corps lost only 634 men. Among them was Gen. Winthrop,[8] killed. Although the action was a complete victory, after it was over Gen. Warren was removed from the command of the 5th Corps by Gen. Sheridan. Some personal misunderstanding was the occasion, for a court of inquiry afterward acquitted him of fault or mismanagement, & no Federal corps commander had a higher personal reputation for courage, enterprise, or good judgment.

When Gen. Grant heard, at 9 P.M., of Sheridan's success he was satisfied that he now had Lee's lines stretched & strained to a point where strong assaults, at spots selected for some element of weakness, would break them. The time had come therefore to renew assaults, after an intermission of 8 months, since the occasion of the Mine.

With his usual promptness, the 2nd Corps, which was near him, south of Hatcher's Run, was ordered to immediately feel of the works in its front, while the other corps, stretching back to & around Petersburg, were ordered to cannonade our lines during the night &, at the favorite hour, 4 A.M., to assault the soft spots, of which each corps commander had already been for three days making a study. The midnight attack by the 2nd Corps waked a very heavy musketry and artillery fire & proved a failure. But the 4 A.M. assaults, in deep & heavy columns, were able to overrun our thin lines in two places. The new lines built in September—the commencement of the long stretch parallel to the Boydton Plank Road—were taken by Genls. Wright & Ord & everything from there to our right was cut off & fell. Near the Jerusalem Plank Road Gen. Parke got in & took about eight hundred yards of our line, but then Gen. Gordon was able to prevent his going further.

At dawn on the morning of Sunday, April 2nd, Gen. Lee was waked by the noise of the tremendous fighting, & very soon the news of the capture of the lines, at the points described, was brought him. Gen. A. P. Hill was also aroused by the noise, & mounting his horse started to the scene. Near the Boydton Road he met the skirmishers of the already successful enemy, & was shot. Poor fellow, he was an ideal soldier & deserved a better fate.[9] As a handsome young lieut. of artillery on coast survey duty, he had cut out many competitors for the favor of Miss Nellie Marcy, the greatest army belle of all the traditions. But he was afterward cut out himself by Gen. McClellan.

In this connection, also, I must note the death of a specially splendid & popular artillery officer, Col. Willie Pegram, a brother of Gen. John Pegram, killed Feb. 6. He belonged to the 3rd Corps but was equally well known & loved & admired in all. He too was killed at Five Forks in one of these last affairs.[10]

It was immediately clear to Gen. Lee that both Petersburg & Richmond must be evacuated. The only thing he could hope to do was to try & hold the enemy out of the town until night, to let his trains get a start upon the roads. To help in this he telegraphed Gen. Longstreet to come over in person, & to bring Field's division from our side of the James. Trains were sent to meet them & they were hurried over. It would seem an almost impossible feat for the broken fragments of our small army to stay[11] the victorious swarms of our enemies, but it was done. Never did the superb morale of our men shine out more beautifully than on that long day when they stood at bay in their fragments of lines before four times their numbers.

As an illustration of their temper I will quote briefly from Gen. Humphreys's account of the Federal assaults upon two forts, Fort Gregg, & one which he calls Fort Whitworth, from its being near the Whitworth house. But Gen. Lee's engineers did me the honor to name that fort after me, & it appears on all the Confederate maps as Fort Alexander, a compliment of which I am proud. The forts were entirely isolated, 1,000 yards in front of our main line & separated by a creek. Gen. Humphreys writes:[12]

> Gen. Wilcox says the 200 infantry in Fort Gregg was composed of detachments from Thomas's (Geo.) and Lane's (N.C.) brigades of Hill's corps and Harris's (Miss.) brig. of Gordon's corps. There were 2 guns in Gregg, 3 in Whitworth. Harris's brigade formed the garrison of the latter work.
>
> As soon as Ord's & Wright's commands arrived before these works, Foster's div.[13] of Gibbon's corps was ordered to charge them, & moved forward steadily, under artillery & musketry fire, to find Fort Gregg surrounded by a deep, wide ditch, partially filled with water, & flanked by fire from the right & left. Turner's 1st & 2nd Brigades were now pushed up as supports while his 3rd Brig., Harris's,[14] assailed Fort Whitworth. The enemy, Gibbon says, made a desperate resistance, & it was not until Fort Gregg was nearly surrounded, & his men had succeeded in climbing upon the parapet under a murderous fire, that the place was finally taken by the last of several determined dashes with the bayonet. Harris, & a portion of the 1st Division, he says, carried Fort Whitworth at the same time. Gen. Wilcox says the troops were ordered to retire from this work to prevent further sacrifice.

Gibbon says of the assault on Fort Gregg that it was one of the most desperate of the war, that 55 of the enemy were found dead inside the fort, while his own loss during the day, most of which occurred around these two works, was 10 officers & 112 men killed & 27 officers & 565 men wounded, making a total loss of 714.

Pollard's *Lost Cause* gives the following account: [15]

In rear of the line of works captured by the enemy were batteries Alexander & Gregg. . . . After getting in order the enemy moved on these works—on Fort Alexander first, taking it with a rush, although the gunners stood to their guns to the last & fired their last shot while the Federal troops were on the parapet. In Fort Gregg there was a small & mixed garrison. Capt. Chew[16] of the 4th Maryland battery of artillery was in command of the work. There was added to his battery two 3 inch rifles & 30 men, a body of men known in the vulgar parlance of soldiers as "Walker's Mules," dismounted drivers to whom were given muskets. . . . Having run over Fort Alexander, the enemy moved on Fort Gregg with cheers. Confidently, in beautiful lines, & in all the majesty of overpowering numbers did the Federal troops advance upon the devoted work. They had got within fifty yards & not the flash of a single rifle had yet defied them. The painful thought passed through the minds of their comrades who watched in the distance that the garrison was about to surrender. But instead of a white flag there was a white puff of smoke; & artillery & infantry simultaneously opened on the confident assailants, who staggering & reeling under the death dealing volley at last gave way & retreated in masses under cover.

A loud & wild cheer rang out from the Confederate lines & was answered in excellent tones by the heroic little garrison in Fort Gregg. But reinforcements were hastening from the lines of the enemy. There were none to send to the succour of the garrison. Every Confederate soldier was needed at his post, & no reserves were at hand. As the enemy came up again in battle array the troops moved forward in serried ranks & soon the fort was canopied in smoke. It seemed that by mutual consent the conflict ceased on other parts of the line while both sides stood silent & anxious spectators of the struggle at the fort. As the smoke lifts it is seen that the Federals have reached the ditch. Those in the distance could descry lines of blue uniforms swarming up the sides of the work; & as the foremost reached the top they reeled & fell upon their comrades below. Once, twice, & thrice they reached the top, only to be repulsed, & yet they persevered while the guns in the embrasures continued to fire in rapid succession. Presently the sound of artillery ceased & the Federals mounted the work & poured a rapid fire on the defenders within. Many of the garrison, unwilling to surrender, used their bayonets & clubbed their guns in an unequal struggle. But such resistance could be of but short duration. . . . The event had been marked by heroic self-immolation. Of the 250 men who defended the fort there were not more than 30 survivors; and to the illumined story of the Army of Northern Virginia, Fort Gregg gave a fitting conclusion, an ornament of glory that well clasped the record of its deeds.

The news of what had happened at Petersburg was taken to Mr. Davis in church in Richmond Sunday morning. He at once left church to arrange for the removal of the personnel & the most important archives of the government & the news spread like wild fire through the city. Richmond was going to be evacuated practically at the point of the bayonet, the only way in which it could ever have been done.

And now I may take up a little of my personal story. I have already told of my ambition to fill the waters of the James as full of torpedoes as they were of catfish. I had just gotten a lot of torpedoes delivered on the bank of the river, in the woods, & left my camp very early on Sunday, April 2nd, & spent the entire day down there, in having them filled & capped & made ready for the water that night. Towards sundown I rode back to camp to get dinner, & then I proposed to come back & spend the night in seeing the torpedoes launched. Only the servants were at camp, when I arrived, who told me that a message had been left for me to come to Gen. Kershaw's headquarters. They had heard some rumors of trouble at Petersburg, but nothing very definite. I hurried to Kershaw's, who was in command in Longstreet's absence. There I found my staff waiting for me, and heard the news, & received the orders which had only come late in the afternoon for the evacuation that night. My commands were scattered from 9 miles to the left to 15 miles to the right & all had to be given instructions. All the heavy batteries, the mortars, and the garrisons of Drury's & Chaffin's Bluffs were to spike their guns, take their muskets with which most were already provided, form as infantry & report to Gen. Ewell, whose Local Defense troops would cross at the ponton bridge & march for Amelia C.H.; being joined also by the sailors from our little fleet.

All the light batteries had simply to limber up in light marching order, & were to move through Richmond, where, at the entrance to Mayo's Bridge, I would see each battery pass & give final instructions. To promptly distribute these orders they were divided out among my staff & couriers & I had to take some of them myself, & we all started out from Kershaw's. When I got back to camp, about ten P.M., our darkies had packed every thing & our wagon was ready to move. I was disappointed, for I had brought back from furlough a nice new uniform suit, & I had planned to put it on & also to get out my sword, which I usually kept in the wagon &

only carried a pistol. But now it was impossible to get anything, without much time & trouble, so I decided to wait until we made a camp somewhere. And I rode into Richmond, where I had a margin of two or three hours before the batteries[17] would begin to pass.

I first called briefly on my brothers & Genls. Gilmer & Lawton. Their families had already gone, or were about to go on board trains for Danville. But they had horses & were to ride in a party with Gen. Breckinridge & some others. Finally I went to Mrs. Webb's house—my sister-in-law who was matron of the officers' hospital near by. This was a general rendezvous for a great many officers & the house was full. And Mrs. Webb's kitchen was cooking a steady stream of biscuits & meat in shape to take in one's hands & eat, or to pack in one's pockets & haversack, & every man was both eating & packing all he could carry. For once, & suddenly, provisions were plentiful; for with the morning the enemy would come in & all the stores in the store houses would be theirs. So Dr. Read,[18] the surgeon in charge, had given Mrs. Webb an ambulance load from the hospital stores, to tide her over what might happen for a few days, & she was in imminent danger, I feared, of having all consumed before breakfast. All of the men were in good spirits & taking it as a matter of course that in a short while we would be coming back, but the ladies, who would all be left alone at dawn, were nervous & depressed. Poor Mrs. Gibbes, whose husband had been at Chaffin's Bluff, had been sharing his quarters with him, & now found herself suddenly bundled up to town by night, to be left in the Federal lines in the morning. Her husband could not even accompany her to town, having to march with Ewell's command. She was very tearful and begged me to "take care of him for her." Mrs. Field was also there, Gen. F. having gone to Petersburg early that morning. She proposed to go to Fredericksburg on a last train, starting at daylight.

About two o'clock I had to go to my station at the bridge. Every private house in the city, & public ones as well, were open & lit up, & the streets swarmed like bee hives. A provost guard on Main Street was emptying barrels of liquor in the gutters, but I noticed no drunken men. A little later I heard that there had been some attempts to loot stores on Main St. & some men had been shot. And I also heard that the provost guard had hung one looter to a lamp post & left his body hanging. Soon after I took my post at the entrance to the bridge, I saw an old woman with a wheel barrow, loaded with a bale of blankets, coming from the Danville freight depot near by. She opened a cellar door & rolled them down, & returned for another. I followed her & found that extensive depot wide open, partially lit up, & filled with goods which had evidently come through the blockade. All was deserted, except for the old woman & perhaps two or three stragglers.

I walked about & helped myself to three things. First, I took[19] a fine

English bridle. Next a nice, thick, felt contrivance to put under a saddle in place of a horse blanket. Last I looked over a big pile of beautiful English bacon-sides & picked out the biggest & the prettiest. I threw away Dixie's old bridle & horse blanket & rigged her up in the new, & I hung my side of bacon to my saddle until some chance occurred for me to get it taken on the the wagon. It proved our very salvation in the next two or three days, for we had left camp with very little on hand. The old woman worked well & steadily at her blanket business, & she seemed to pack her cellar full of bales. But I fear they did her little service, for I believe all that portion of the city was burned during the next day. A canal here runs parallel to the river and was crossed by a covered through bridge.[20] Beyond that some few hundred feet began the long bridge across the river. Some extensive fires had been burning in the city for some time, particularly up toward the Tredegar Works & the arsenal; & towards daylight we heard terrific explosions at Chaffin's Bluff, where our gunboats were all burned & blown up.

Soon after daylight I noted canal boats on fire in the canal, & at last one of them either drifted, or in some mysterious way got directly under the bridge. One of my batteries was still behind, but presently, when flames began to rise through all the cracks in the floor, with my staff we spurred across lest we should be cut off. Some soldiers, however, in the nick of time, managed to push the burning boat out, & presently my last battery came along & then we all crossed. It was after sunrise of a bright morning when from the Manchester high grounds we turned to take our last look at the old city for which we had fought so long & so hard. It was a sad, a terrible & a solemn sight. I don't know that any moment in the whole war impressed me more deeply with all its stern realities than this. The whole river front seemed to be in flames, amid which occasional heavy explosions were heard, & the black smoke spreading & hanging over the city seemed to be full of dreadful portents. I rode on with a distinctly heavy heart & with a peculiar sort of feeling of orphanage.

After a while, I recall meeting Col. Walter Taylor & Col. John Saunders[21] & hearing that Col. Taylor had married Col. Saunders's sister the night before. And that reminded me that the day, April 3rd, was the 5th anniversary of my own wedding, Saunders having been one of my groomsmen.

The roads were very bad & we got along slowly. It was after dark when we stopped to bivouac for the night in some tall pine woods near a country church 24 miles from Richmond, known as Tomahawk. I had barely eaten a little supper when orders came for me to join some engineers, Col. Clarke,[22] I think, was one, & go on ahead about 20 miles to the Danville Railroad bridge over the Appomattox River. We were to find wagon roads by which it could be reached & to do whatever was necessary to enable the artillery & trains to cross the river on it. We were travelling all night long in darkness & mud, waking up people in houses to ask directions, & I was so sleepy & tired that it was a very forlorn night. But we did what we were sent to do, & everything followed us & crossed on the deck of the overhead railroad bridge. Not far beyond the bridge we went into camp, & here I was the recipient of some courtesy which I have always since considered as a great calamity. We camped about sundown in sight of a very nice looking farm house, about a quarter mile off. It proved to be the home of some ladies, near relatives of our Confederate Gen. Sam Jones. The ladies found out that it was my camp, & sent & insisted that I should come up & take supper. I did not want to, a bit, for I had now not had a wink of sleep, & been but little off my horse for three days & two nights. But it seemed ungracious to refuse, & they were old army people, & so I went. I had intended to unpack the wagon & get my sword & new uniform, but when I got back from supper I was so overwhelmed with fatigue & sleep that I concluded to put it [off] to the next camp. Alas! The next camp never came! I may get that sword & uniform in the next world; I will if I can; but I can never get them in this, for Custer burned our wagon.

On Wed., Apr. 5th, we were off at dawn, & soon after sunrise halted at Amelia C.H. Somehow I was found out by one of the family, & taken to a large house full of nice and pretty girls, named Smith, who said they were cousins of my wife's & who gave me cousinly welcomes & a Virginia breakfast equally rare & delightful. They were refugees from Alexandria, & it seemed to me little short of a miracle the lots of nice things they managed to have on that breakfast table; eggs, chicken, butter, & more kinds of bread & waffles & such things than I could count. Gen. Lee was at Amelia, & here the troops who came from Petersburg united with ours from Richmond. We should have gotten rations here, but in all the crash we had come through many plans had been sure to miscarry, & the plan to have rations here for us had been one of them.

We stopped at Amelia all the morning reorganizing commands, & waiting for the rear to close up. As the number of guns with the army was now out of proportion to our greatly reduced force of infantry & it would be difficult to feed so many horses, I was directed to take only certain of the best equipped battalions & batteries, & all the surplus was placed [under] command of Gen. R. L. Walker, chief of arty. of Hill's corps, who was ordered to march direct to Lynchburg with them by roads leading off to our right. The destination of the rest of the army at this time was Danville.

In organising my new artillery command, I needed another field officer and I got Maj. Gibbes taken from Ewell's corps, & assigned to me. This was fortunate for him, for Ewell, next day, was badly cut up & then captured at Sailor's Creek, & all who were thus taken prisoners were held for some time; while those who got to Appomattox & surrendered were released.

About 1 P.M., having as it were stripped to fighting trim, we took the road for Jetersville, where it was understood that Sheridan with his cavalry was across our path, & Gen. Lee intended to attack him. I rode with him & his staff & Gen. Longstreet, & we were not long in coming to where our skirmish line was already engaged. I never saw Gen. Lee seem so anxious to bring on a battle in my life as he seemed this afternoon; but a conference with Gen. W. H. F. Lee in command of the cavalry in our front seemed to disappoint him greatly.

Lee reported that Sheridan had been reinforced by two infantry corps who were intrenching, & that force was more than we could venture to attack.

That blocked our direct road to Danville. But Gen. Lee hoped that by a rapid all night march he might pass Grant's flank & yet get ahead of him. So Longstreet's corps with Mahone's division now attached to it turned square to our right & struck out for Rice's Station on the Lynchburg railroad, west of Burkeville Junction, where we were ordered to take a line of battle & keep off the enemy while the rest of the army could go past.

I should have stated before that our mess had been increased a few days before the evacuation by Jos. Haskell's brother Lewis,[23] a well grown young fellow of about 17, who came on to be a soldier, the 7th of that family of brothers. Then, Doctor Read, from the officers' hospital in Richmond, had joined us, & also Captain Webb[24] from a quartermaster's office.

And this afternoon we were almost entirely out of provisions. Starting on this new road seemed to offer an opportunity to get something, & I hastened to dispatch our darkies out as foragers. They were lucky enough to buy two hens. They were told to kill them & pick them as they rode along, & have them ready to cook whenever we halted. Our wagon from Amelia C.H. had been sent by a different road. Our route took us by Amelia Springs, a large hotel building, and here I remember meeting Col. Aleck Haskell with his regiment of cavalry. Here, also, I was delighted to meet the party from Richmond in which were Genls. Lawton & Gilmer. Gen. Longstreet joined their party; we all rode together until about 3 A.M., which ride was the one bright spot in the retreat. A young moon behind thin clouds gave some light, &, as we were ahead of all trains & artillery, the roads were comparatively good. We passed about midnight through a dark & silent little collection of houses called Deatonsville, & about three o'clock, being very near Rice's Station, Gen. Longstreet stopped at a nice looking house, among shade trees, to get a little rest. My party & I went off from the road to the edge of a wood near by, where we soon had our hens boiling, while we laid down & got an hour or two of sleep.

At dawn we wrestled with the hens, which were so dreadfully tough we pronounced them roosters in disguise, and then rode on to Rice's Station. Here I at once selected a line of battle to cover the road, and as troops & artillery came up they were formed upon it & everybody put to work to strengthen it as much as was possible. Toward midday the enemy appeared & skirmished with us, but they were not in force & ventured nothing serious. Gen. Lee was with us very early, & I remember his getting very impatient & worried because the troops we were expecting to come up & pass us did not appear. As we expected to be there all day, I dispatched my servant Charley to hunt up our wagon, on one of the roads to our right, & see if he could scare up something to eat & bring to us. I had had him riding my extra horse, Meg, & keeping near me all the while, & some one had given him to carry a haversack containing our headquarters' flag. In the afternoon Charley came back, but without rations & without the flag. He had just found the train, when it was charged by a brigade of Federal cavalry, Custer's, I believe. Charley, on Meg, fled across a field, & declared that he was pursued &, being afraid they would hang him if they caught him carrying one of our flags, he threw the haversack off as he fled!

The whole train was burned in the road. In fact Grant had broken into our line of march, both with cavalry & infantry, & had played great havoc. Half of my own splendid old battalion of artillery under Huger, for instance, had been captured. At Amelia it had been divided, and this half had just crossed a street, & the two leading guns had reached the top of a long ascent of bad road, when Custer's brigade was seen charging down upon them. These two guns quickly unlimbered & fired two rounds each of canister, when Custer's men were in between them, cutting & shooting at the men & calling on them to surrender. Capt. O. B. Taylor, the leading captain, swore he would not surrender and tried to fire again, & was shot dead. Col. Huger, dismounted, shot with his revolver the horse of a corporal who charged him, & with another shot laid open [the] cheek of a major who was following the corporal. Then he attempted to run for the bushes. But another fellow rode up & held a carbine to his head & said, "Surrender, damn you!" & he surrendered. Custer & Huger had been great friends & class mates, & Custer made him ride along all day, & sleep with him that night, & treated him very nicely. The major whom he had shot came to see him, with his face sewed up & bandaged, & expressed his sincere thanks for a glorious furlough he was about to enjoy.

But trains, & even battalions, were small captures compared with some others which happened during the day. When the enemy in the morning discovered our movement, three corps of infantry and the greater part of Sheridan's cavalry was thrown against our marching flank whose rear was

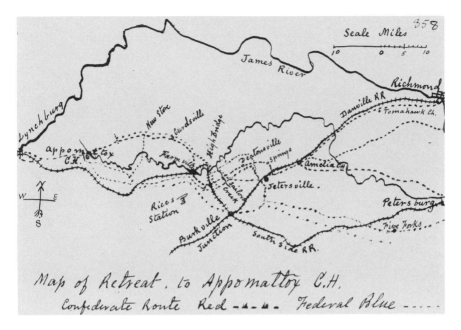

Figure 68. Retreat to Appomattox

still behind Deatonsville. At Sailor's Creek, Ewell's command was practically annihilated. His men were unused to marching & camping, & now
the heavy roads & the lack of food & sleep had reduced his original force
from about 6,000 to 3,600. These made a desperate fight, but were surrounded & badly cut up, & all captured but about 200.[25] [Figures 68 and
69 appear here in the manuscript.]

Gen. Anderson, who had in his command the remnants of Pickett's div.
& Johnson's divn., was also involved in this disaster and lost about 2,600.
Six of our generals were captured—Ewell, Custis Lee, Kershaw, Dubose,
Hunton, & Corse.[26]

Gordon's corps had also severe running fighting all day, & lost probably
2,000 men. A notable affair occurred near the High Bridge. On the 5th a
light body of 600 men under Gen. Theodore Read of Ord's staff[27] had been
sent ahead by Gen. Ord to burn the bridges on the Appomattox. Gen.
Dearing's brigade was sent in pursuit of it, & a very desperate fight occurred. Read & his next in command, Col. Washburn of [the] 5th Mass.
were both killed. Dearing, Col. Boston of _____ & Maj. Thomson of
_____ were also killed.[28] The Federal forces being greatly outnumbered
were all killed or captured. With us Dearing was noted for his gallantry, his
fine athletic figure & his attractive personality. We heard similar things said

Figure 69. *With Fate against Them* by Gilbert Gaul

about Gen. Read from Federal sources, and there was also a rumor that the two had known each other well before the war.

With Longstreet, at Rice's, the day wore on rather quietly, the skirmishing increasing in the afternoon, when two of Ord's divisions of infantry, under Gibbon, deployed in front of us but did not attack. Meanwhile, about one o'clock, Gen. Lee had gone to the rear to see what was the matter, & after some time had sent for Mahone's division. He had found the rear only a mass of fugitives which could not have resisted a squadron of cavalry, & Mahone's division was needed to cover their retreat. He came back about sundown, & at dark we turned our positions over to a cavalry rear guard, & now we marched for Farmville. We had given up the road to Danville, & Lynchburg was now our objective. The very first day's experience in the presence of the enemy had demonstrated that it was a military impossibility for us to retreat with trains at that season of the year. Practically all our trains were already destroyed except the few wagons of ammunition, cooking utensils, &c. which marched with the troops. If we had had only pack animals, possibly a good portion might have gotten by, but packing is an art that requires equipment & experts which we did not possess.

The night of the 3rd had been forlorn but this night was actively wretched. I was 8 hours in riding the 6 miles to Farmville. The road was one sea of mud through which men, horses, ambulances, artillery, & cavalry splashed & floundered & stopped in the darkness & splashed & floundered & stopped again. And if it was that to me on horseback what must it have been to the poor fellows on foot loaded with muskets, blankets, & ammunition, & worn with continuous marching & digging & lack of food. Our dog Buster, who has been mentioned before, born & bred in the army, & always before able to locate the artillery of the 1st Corps with ease, in all sorts of night marchings & mixes up, lost us during this night, & we never got him again.

About sunrise we passed through Farmville. Here we got three or four days' rations—our ordinary reduced rations I mean, not the U.S. ration. And here to my surprise I found the column crossing the Appomattox again, getting back on the north side; from which we had crossed, on the 4th, on the railroad bridge. I went across, & about a half mile on the other side, stopped & put our servants to cooking some of our new rations.

While that was going on, Gen. Lee sent for me. He had halted in a field near by, & meanwhile we could see the enemy's cavalry coming, over the far hills across the river, & now I knew that we had *had* to cross, because we were pressed too closely and were practically headed off. Gen. Lee had two orders for me. First, he ordered me to take charge of the two bridges at Farmville & burn them. I was to set them on fire, not too soon, which would cut off some of our people, but not too late, which would permit the enemy to rush in & save them. Then I was told that this very thing had happened at a road bridge, near the High Bridge on the railroad, a few miles below; & the gen. took his map from his breast pocket & opened it to show me where a force crossing there would strike our line of march, some four miles ahead.

It was the first sight I had had of a map since we left Richmond, & I scanned it eagerly to see our general situation. The most direct & shortest road to Lynchburg from Farmville did not cross the river as we had done, but kept up the south side near the railroad. The road we were on bent up & then back, & was evidently longer, finally recrossing the headwaters of the river & rejoining the straighter road at Appomattox Court House. I pointed to that place, & said it looked as if there we might have [the] most trouble.

The gen. said, "I don't know if this map is accurate, & I would like to question some citizen of the country about it. Can you find me one?" I had seen a very intelligent looking gentleman that morning at a house near by. I sent one of my staff & soon had him present. He looked at the map & pronounced it entirely correct. The gen. said, "Well there is time enough to think about that. Go now & attend to these matters here." I sent, if I recollect aright, Poague's & Haskell's battalions to take position & be prepared to protect the point four miles beyond, & then with all my staff I went to inspect the bridges & prepare them for burning. There were two, a railroad and county bridge. The railroad bridge was a through bridge, uncovered & difficult to kindle. It was not being used & I took no chances on it, but started a fire at once. The county bridge, over which our troops were still coming, occasionally & in squads, was a covered through bridge. The whole art of a quick, sure burn lies in the kindling. It ought to be very good & plenty of it. We had a lot of trouble in finding stuff suitable for kindling, but at last we got it well primed, & then I left my aid, "Lieut. Willie" Mason, to fire it on my giving a signal with my revolver from a near by knoll whence I could watch the enemy's approach.

From there I could see large forces of cavalry deploying, & before long they became engaged with a small rear guard of cavalry we had left in the town. To my surprise these did not fall back toward the bridge, where I was waiting for them to cross & wanted them too to defend the fire if necessary; but they fell back toward the upper end of the town.

By the time I realized this, the enemy's skirmishers were very close to the bridge. I gave the signal & Willie fired the priming & ran across & the bridge was soon in flames from one end to the other. But there was little margin & had the enemy rushed a heavy force up at double quick, they might have saved it.

As soon as the bridge was burned, I hastened on to where the artillery had been sent. They had taken good positions & were supported by Mahone's division & part of Field's, & they were left there to protect the road until the rear of the column had passed. They were attacked in the afternoon by Miles's division, but repulsed it, & Mahone even captured two hundred or more prisoners & two regimental guidons. Our cavalry retreated up the river because they knew of a ford, though a very poor one. They got across all right, but Gregg's division[29] of cavalry followed them, after a while, & came across also. I happened to be passing, in the afternoon, the junction of a road from that ford, when I heard a cheer, &, looking across some fields to my left, I saw coming a cavalry charge. There were no troops near—only some wagons & ambulances. I turned into a field on the right, intending to get cover in some woods beyond. But I had scarcely gone 50 yards when I heard the rebel yell, & saw our cavalry strike Gregg on the flank. They broke him all up, & drove him back, & Gen. Gregg himself was captured with quite a few of his men. Indeed the spirit with which our men fought, whenever they had the slightest chance, was something wonderful. It just seemed as if they had gotten into a certain habit of fighting, which they could not change, although they were now beginning to foresee the inevitable end.

I had intimations of this for the first time, today, Friday the 7th. Our men sometimes ventured to call out good natured remarks after their officers when the latter were passing them; and today I heard called after me on several occasions, by the cannoneers of batteries, remarks like this: "Don't surrender no ammunition!" "Let us shoot up this ammunition first if we got to surrender!" "You been making us save ammunition all this war, but we did not save it to surrender." It was very plain that the prospect of being surrendered had suddenly become a topic of general conversation. Indeed, no man who looked at our situation on a map, or who understood the geography of the country, could fail to see that Gen. Grant now had us completely in a trap. He had stood upon the hills at Farmville that morning & watched the last of our column go in. We were now in a sort of jug shaped peninsula between the James River & the Appomattox, & there was but one outlet, the neck of the jug at Appomattox C.H., and to that Grant had the shortest road!

And that Gen. Grant himself so appreciated the situation is clear from the following note, which he wrote that afternoon from Farmville & sent to Gen. Lee by flag of truce. It was a good note & a generous act to send it.[30]

April 7, 1865

> General. The events of the last week must convince you of the hope-lessness of further resistance on the part of the Army of Northern Virginia, in this struggle. I feel that it is so, & regard it as my duty to shift from myself the responsibility of any further effusion of blood by asking of you the surrender of that portion of the Confederate States Army known as the Army of Northern Virginia.
>
> U. S. Grant, Lt. Genl.

To this Gen. Lee replied about 8 P.M.:

April 7, 1865

> General, I have received your note of this date. Though not entertaining the opinion you express on the hopelessness of further resistance on the part of the Army of Northern Virginia, I reciprocate your desire to avoid useless effusion of blood, & therefore, before considering your proposition, ask the terms you will offer on condition of its surrender.
>
> R. E. Lee, Genl.

As this note had to be taken around by High Bridge, & roundabout roads, to reach Grant he only received it next morning. Meanwhile the march of our tired column was pushed all night & all the next day. It was the third consecutive night of marching, & I was at last scarcely able to keep from falling off my horse for sleep. So with my staff I left the column & went a quarter of a mile, or more, off to our right through old broom grass & second growth pines, by cloudy moonlight, until we found a secluded nook by an old worn fence, & there we all laid down & slept for three or four hours. It was necessary to hide out, or our horses would have been stolen while we slept. Cases occurred where officers, seated by the road side, holding their horses by the bridles, had them stolen while they dozed; the thief cutting the bridle & leaving a piece in the officer's hand.

Saturday the 8th was the first quiet day of the march, since leaving Amelia. Until now the sound of musketry & the boom of occasional guns could always be heard in some direction. But today's march was free from any flank attack, & we had such a start of the 2nd Corps under Gen. Humphreys, which was following right behind us, that there was but little heard from the rear. The reason of this fatal quiet was that we were safe in between the two rivers, & the troops which would otherwise have been attacking our flanks as we marched were hurrying along to get to the neck of the jug first & head us off.

Sometime during the 7th & 8th an incident happened which was told me by Gen. Pendleton in the afternoon of the 8th. There had been a sort of conference between a number of our principal generals over the situation. They had agreed that a speedy surrender was inevitable. They also thought it desirable that they should first suggest the necessity to Gen. Lee, that the blame or odium, if any, might be laid upon them instead of upon him. Then the question arose, who should go to Gen. Lee & tell him. Longstreet was not present at the conference, & it was agreed that Gen. Pendleton should see Longstreet & get him, as next in command to Gen. Lee, to take the message. But Longstreet, being approached, refused. As Pendleton told it to me, Longstreet said his corps were still able to whip four times their numbers, & as long as that was so he should never suggest a surrender. That he was there to back Lee up, not to pull him down. Then Gen. Pendleton, as the delegate of the conference, went himself to Gen. Lee & told his story. It had evidently been very coldly received. He said that Gen. Lee had answered him that there were too many men there with arms in their hands to think of laying them down.[31]

From this, & from other minor details I believe that Gen. Lee took no one into his confidence as to his intentions, or as to his correspondence with Gen. Grant; preferring, as his hand became the harder to play, to play it more & more alone.

During the afternoon of the 8th he received Gen. Grant's reply to his letter of the night before, as follows:

April 8th, 1865

General R. E. Lee, Commanding C.S.A.
    Your note of last evening in reply to mine of the same date, asking the conditions on which I will accept the surrender of the Army of Northern

Figure 70. Capture of Ewell's Corps, 6 April 1865

Virginia, is just received. In reply I would say that, peace being my great desire, there is but one condition I would insist upon,—namely, that the men and officers surrendered shall be disqualified for taking up arms against the Government of the United States until properly exchanged. I will meet you, or will designate officers to meet any officers you may name for the same purpose, at any point agreeable to you, for the purpose of arranging definitely the terms upon which the surrender of the Army of Northern Virginia will be received.

U. S. Grant,
Lieutenant General[32]

[Figure 70 appears here in the manuscript.]

To this note Gen. Lee replied as follows:

April 8th

General, I received at a late hour your note of today. I did not intend to propose the surrender of the Army of Northern Virginia, but to ask the terms of your proposition. To be frank, I do not think the emergency has arisen to call for the surrender of this army; but, as the restoration of peace should be the sole object of all, I desire to know whether your proposals would lead to that end. I cannot therefore meet you with a view to surrender the Army of Northern Va., but, as far as your proposal may affect the Confederate States forces under my command, & tend to the restoration of peace, I should be pleased to meet you at 10 A.M. tomorrow on the old stage road to Richmond between the picket lines of the two armies.

R. E. Lee, Genl.

I must say that I think this letter somewhat difficult to understand, & I could easily imagine Gen. Grant taking it only for a ruse to gain time. But yet, early next morning, as I will presently tell, & before any reply had been received, Gen. Lee told me of the proposed meeting at 10 A.M. & that he would then surrender the army, & the very terms of the surrender which were those of Grant's last note. Indeed, he seemed to consider that he had closed with Grant on Grant's terms. I attribute the references to the "Confederate States forces under his command" & to the "restoration of peace" to a desire in some way to include all the other Confederate armies in the surrender, he having only a few weeks before been placed in command of them all for the first time since 1862. In that year he was in command for awhile, but himself insisted upon being relieved either of that or of the Army of Northern Virginia, being unwilling to hold both.33

On the march again today my artillery men several times called out: "Don't let's surrender any ammunition." The horses today began to fail in some of the batteries, & we had to abandon some caissons & perhaps one or two guns. But at last we were allowed to camp at sundown & have one solid night of sleep, the first I had had for exactly one week.

On Sunday the 9th we were up at dawn, and soon after sunrise, having travelled already some two miles, we came upon Gen. Lee, halted at the road side at the top of a rise, the road having there woods on the left & open ground on the right. It was within two miles of Appomattox C.H.; & already musketry & artillery were briskly at work there. We too halted & dismounted. I had not seen the gen., to speak with, since we talked over the map on the 7th. As I came up he called to me, & walking off to a clean oak log from which the bark had been recently stripped, he sat down & said, "Well here we are at Appomattox, & there seems to be a considerable force in front of us. Now, what shall we have to do today?" I answered that if he saw any chance to cut our way through I would answer for the artillery making as good a fight as they ever had made34 in all their lives. And I told him how they had called after me, along the road, not to surrender any ammunition. He said the trouble was in lack of infantry. That there were only two divisions left, Field's & Mahone's, which had not been worn to frazzles, & these divisions mustered too small a force to meet the force which seemed to be already in front of us.

Now for several days there had been a good deal going on in my head. It would be wrong to call it thought; as will appear if I pause for a moment & tell my conclusions upon a single point. For about a year now there had been no exchange of prisoners. So, to me either capture or surrender meant going to prison for an indefinite period, maybe for years, & with all sorts of hardships & persecutions.

So I had made up my mind that if ever a white flag was raised I would take to the bushes. And, somehow, I would manage to get out of the country & would go to Brazil. Brazil was just going to war with Paraguay, & I could doubtless get a place in their artillery, if only captain or lieutenant of a battery, & then I would send for my wife & children. And, judging from the map, then for once I would be on the winning side.[35]

So, when the general said in effect that it was impossible to cut our way out, I was glad of the unexpected opportunity, & spoke from the fullness of my heart as follows:

> Well, Sir, then we have only two alternatives to choose from. We must either surrender; or, the army may be ordered to scatter in the woods & bushes & either to rally upon Gen. Johnston in North Carolina, or to make their way, each man to his own state, with his arms, & to report to his governor.
>
> This last course is the one which seems to me to offer us much the best chances.

"Well," said Gen. Lee, "what would you hope to accomplish by that?" "Well, Sir,"[36] I said,

> If there is *any* hope for the Confederacy it is in *delay.* For if the Army of Northern Va. surrenders every other army will surrender as fast as the news reaches it. For it is the morale of this army which has supported the whole Confederacy.[37] And Grant if necessary could move successively on each with 100,000 men & they would go like a row of bricks.[38] If there is any hope of help from *abroad,* we stand the chances by delay. But if the news of the surrender of this army crosses the water it ends every possible chance from there. Meanwhile, the one thing left us now to fight for is to try & get some sort of *terms*; not to be absolutely helpless, & at the mercy of the enemy. The Confederacy will never be recognised in a treaty, & never can get *terms,* but there have been intimations that the states might be recognized. That Vance might make peace for North Carolina, & Brown for Georgia. That is why I suggest sending the men to their states instead of to Johnston, that the governors may make some sort of show and get some sort of terms.

"But General," I said at the last; & now I was wound up to a pitch of feeling I could scarcely control:

> if there is *no* hope, & no terms possible, & if this is just the end,[39] & the wreck of all things; there is still one thing that the men who have fought under you for four years now have the right to ask you. You don't care for military fame & glory, but we are proud of your name & record & the record of this army. We want to leave it to our children. Its last hour has come and a little blood more or less now makes no difference. And the men that have fought under you for four years have got the right

to ask you to spare us the mortification of having you ask Grant for terms & have him reply "Unconditional Surrender." They call him that: U. S. Unconditional Surrender Grant. General, spare us the mortification of having you receive that reply.

Usually I stood very much in awe of Gen. Lee but now I was wrought up & words came to me as never before. And as I made my points they seemed to me unanswerable. And at the end when I made, on top of all my good logic, an appeal that I knew the soldier in him must respond to I believed firmly that I had him, & he would do it.

He had listened very patiently until I finished & then he said, "If I took your suggestion & ordered the army to disperse how many do you suppose would get away?" I answered: "Two thirds of us, I think would get away. We would scatter like rabbits & partridges in the woods, & they could not scatter so to catch us."

He said:

There are here only about 15,000 men with muskets. Suppose two thirds, say 10,000, got away. Divided among the states their numbers would be too insignificant to accomplish the least good. Yes! The surrender of this army is the end of the Confederacy. As for foreign help I've never believed we could gain our independence except by our own arms. If I ordered the men to go to Gen. Johnston few would go. Their homes have been overrun by the enemy & their families need them badly. We have now simply to look the fact in the face that the Confederacy has failed.

And as Christian men, Gen. Alexander, you & I have no right to think for one moment of our personal feelings or affairs. We must consider only the effect which our action will have upon the country at large.

Suppose I should take your suggestion & order the army to disperse & make their way to their homes. The men would have no rations & they would be under no discipline. They are already demoralized by four years of war. They would have to plunder & rob to procure subsistence. The country would be full of lawless bands in every part, & a state of society would ensue from which it would take the country years to recover. Then the enemy's cavalry would pursue in the hopes of catching the principal officers, & wherever they went there would be fresh rapine & destruction.

And as for myself, while you young men might afford to go to bushwhacking, the only proper & dignified course for me would be to surrender myself & take the consequences of my actions.

But it is still early in the spring, & if the men can be quietly & quickly returned to their homes there is time to plant crops & begin to repair the ravages of the war. That is what I must now try to bring about. I expect to meet Gen. Grant at ten this morning in rear of the army & to surrender this army to him.

"But," he said, with a faint sort of smile, and with sympathy in his look & tone, for when he had said surrender the tears would swell in my eyes in spite of all I could do, "I can tell you for your comfort that Gen. Grant will not demand unconditional surrender. He will give us as honorable terms as we have right to ask or expect. The men can go to their homes & will only be bound not to fight again until exchanged."

Then I thought I had never half known before what a big heart & brain our general had. I was so ashamed of having proposed to him such a foolish and wild cat scheme as my suggestion had been that I felt like begging him to forget that he had ever heard it. And not only did my own little plan, of running away if ever I saw a white flag, vanish into thin air, but nothing could now have induced me to miss the opportunity of contributing by presence, example, & every means in my power to carrying out the general's wishes in every respect. It seemed now an inestimable privilege[40] to serve under him to the very last moment, & that no scene in the whole life of the Army of Northern Virginia would be more honorable than the one which was now to close its record.

About this time Gen. Wise rode up & wished to see the general, & I left him & hurried to communicate my information to some of my artillery officers who had also planned skipping from the white flag. Of course no one would run off who knew that he would be allowed to go home after the surrender, & my news stopped several parties already made up to go.

Meanwhile Gordon's fight in the front was growing hotter. The advance of the army was stopped, & as the rear of our long column had marched at dawn it was now closing itself up. Artillery, ambulances, & ammunition wagons parked near the road & infantry was collected toward the front.

And about eight o'clock an incident happened which amused me in spite of the depressing surroundings.

Two guns from a Federal battery were captured in the fighting in front, complete with all their horses, & brought back to me to be added to my command. The idea seemed positively ridiculous that men who were about to be surrendered were actually still capturing guns from their opponents.

This battery from which they were captured was _____ & the captors were _____ under Gen. Fitz Lee.[41] When they came up with their fat horses, each with his pretty red saddle blanket & nice equipments, and bags of corn & oats on the caissons, it formed such a contrast to our forlorn & starving teams that I was actually ashamed to have our animals see it.

It gave me an opportunity for a little joke on Capt. Lamkin which I could not resist. I have mentioned before big Captain Lamkin, & his big company of over a hundred men, who came to me in June & who were put in charge of many coehorn mortars which they served admirably during all the siege of Petersburg & at Fort Harrison. He was really a fine officer & the company a good one.[42] On the evacuation, as his mortars had to be left I made him take his muskets again; but instead of putting them in with Ewell's infantry I brought them along with Haskell's artillery for sharp-shooters. But Lamkin's ambition in life seemed to be to show us all how he could fight with field guns & on the retreat he never saw me without getting a fresh promise of the first battery I could scrape up for him. So now I lost no time in turning over the new captures to Lamkin in solemn fulfil[l]ment of my promise. He took them, but he did not seem to appreciate it as any favor. And in the afternoon the former owners came & took them away again.

About this time the pressure upon Gordon at the village had become so heavy that his line was falling back & he sent urgent requests for reinforcements. On this Gen. Longstreet directed me to select a line of battle upon which Gen. Gordon's force could fall back, & to form upon that line the whole force of infantry & artillery that could be mustered. This occupied me busily for two or three hours. The country was open, which was favorable; for we had more guns in proportion than infantry. I found a very fair line & made a very good show upon it, putting in every fragment of every command in the army, except the rear guard under Field. So that when Gordon united, our whole available force except [the] rear guard was in one unit.

Meanwhile, about 8:30 A.M., Gen. Lee started to the rear to meet Gen. Grant. He passed through our rear guard & advanced nearly a mile down the road when he was met by Col. Whittier[43] of Meade's staff, who bore the following reply to Gen. Lee's letter of the day before:

April 9th, 1865

General: Your note of yesterday is received. I have no authority to treat on the subject of peace. The meeting proposed for 10 A.M. to-day could lead to no good. I will state, however, that I am equally desirous for peace with yourself, and the whole North entertains the same feeling. The terms upon which peace can be had are well understood. By the South laying down their arms, they would hasten that most desirable event, save thousands of human lives, and hundreds of millions of property not yet destroyed. Seriously hoping that all our difficulties may be settled without the loss of another life, I subscribe myself, etc.,

U. S. Grant, Lieutenant-General.

General R. E. Lee.

Figure 71. Village of Appomattox Court House—McLean House on right

To this Gen. Lee immediately replied as follows:

April 9th, 1865

General: I received your note of this morning on the picket-line,
whither I had come to meet you and ascertain definitely what terms were
embraced in your proposal of yesterday with reference to the surrender of
this army. I now ask an interview, in accordance with the offer contained
in your letter of yesterday, for that purpose.

R. E. Lee, General

Lieutenant-General U. S. Grant.[44]

[Figure 71 appears here in the manuscript.]

Just as Gen. Lee was dictating this letter to Col. Marshall, John Haskell
came around a near bend in the road, riding at very utmost speed, & only
able to check his horse & halt some fifty yards beyond. Not long after Gen.
Lee had started to the rear, Gen. Fitz Lee,[45] commanding the cavalry, had
imagined that he had found an unguarded outlet through which the whole
army could escape, & he sent word of it to Longstreet. Haskell always had
the prettiest horse in the army, & he was now riding a mare that was
remarkable both for swiftness & beauty. Gen. Longstreet told him of Fitz
Lee's report, & that Gen. Lee had gone to the rear to surrender the army;
& told him "to kill his horse if necessary but to overtake Gen. Lee, & tell
him of the chance to escape."

When Haskell passed Gen. Lee, as has been described, the latter stopped
dictating his letter, & advanced to meet Haskell & said, "What is it? What
is it?" Then, before Haskell could reply, he noticed the condition of the
mare & said, "Oh, you have killed your beautiful mare! What did you do it
for?"

Haskell explained his errand & Gen. Lee asked a few questions, but apparently considered the matter of no consequence; & then completed his letter & dispatched it by Col. Whittier. And, presently, another messenger from Gen. Longstreet came to say that Gen. Fitz Lee had found himself mistaken.

Gen. Lee now waited by the roadside for a reply to his last letter. But it happened this morning that Gen. Grant was for several hours practically inaccessible, & not only was the surrender, which might have been made at 10 A.M., postponed until 3 P.M., but there was great danger meanwhile of unnecessary & bloody fighting on both flanks of the armies, by his officers who had received no orders authorizing truces. He had spent the night at Curdsville (see map [Figure 68]) & about 8 A.M. had left the road we were upon, &, at New Store, had taken a cross road which led across the river into the road by which Sheridan had gotten ahead of us to Appomattox; & now he would next be communicated with at that point.

About 10:30 A.M., Gen. Humphreys at the head of the 2nd & 6th Corps approached the place where Gen. Lee was waiting at the roadside. One of his aides, with a white flag, requested Gen. Humphreys to stop his advance; explaining the circumstances, which, indeed, Gen. Humphreys already knew. But in the absence of explicit orders from Gen. Grant he refused to halt. And when the head of his column was within 100 yards Gen. Lee decided to return to our front near Appomattox & to await Grant's reply from that direction. Humphreys then advanced until he came in contact with our rear guard under Field.[46] As they could retreat no further they had now intrenched themselves as well as they could, & were ready to sell their lives as dearly as possible. The two big Federal corps were formed to assault them, the 2nd on the left & the 6th on the right; about 30,000 men against about 3,000. A terrible & useless slaughter was on [the] very verge of beginning, when Gen. Meade fortunately arrived upon the ground & granted a truce for an hour. Afterward he seems to have extended it informally for he did not assault.

Meanwhile, at the front, during Gen. Lee's absence in the rear, Gen. Longstreet had suggested to Gen. Gordon that he should send in a flag of truce to the Federal officers in his front & ask for a cessation of hostilities; as it was useless to be killing each other upon one flank, while the generals were making peace on the other. Gen. Gordon asked Maj. R. M. Sims[47] of Longstreet's staff, who brought him the message, to take the flag, & begged him not to let our own men see the flag start. Sims's baggage consisted of a towel & a toothbrush. The two skirmish lines were firing at each other across a field of some four hundred yards, & he edged out into that field without displaying his towel until our men would not see it, though in great danger of being shot meanwhile. Then he waved it to the enemy & galloped in. He struck Custer's brigade & was taken to Custer, who sent him on to Sheridan. Sheridan at first made some difficulty. Genls. Gordon and Wilcox came forward & met him, & finally Gen. Ord was consulted, who says: "As I knew that a surrender had been called for, & terms asked for & made known, I knew this second request meant acceptance, and the bugles were sounded to halt."[48]

Meanwhile, soon after Custer had forwarded Sims to Sheridan, the bold idea struck him of trying to secure a surrender to himself & Gen. Sheridan. So, with only an orderly, he rode up to our line on which the firing had just ceased. Some rough fellows got around his orderly & proposed to trade boots, when Custer recognised Maj. Gibbes, who was in command of the artillery which had just been engaged there. Custer & Gibbes had been classmates at West Point & he called to Gibbes & asked to be taken to the officer in command. He was taken to Gen. Longstreet, from whom he demanded a surrender. Longstreet explained that Lee was in communication with Gen. Grant upon that matter. Custer said, "Well, Sheridan & I are independent here today, & unless you surrender immediately we are going to pitch in." Longstreet answered, "Pitch in as much as you like," & turning to one of his staff said, "Take this gentleman & conduct him back to his lines, & he may consider himself lucky to get back safely after his impertinent errand." Custer went back apparently crest fallen, & the episode seems to have been very little known for years after.[49]

I was still forming our line of battle when the flag was sent & the firing ceased. Shortly after the last shot I saw a body of Federal cavalry, about a mile off, moving rapidly around our left flank. Doubtless the news of the flag had not yet reached them. On any ordinary occasion I should probably have fired a shot at them, but under the influence of Gen. Lee's talk that morning all desire to shoot had gone, & I might have been fired at & never returned it.

When Gen. Lee came back from the rear, say about 11 o'clock, he passed through our line of battle & came out into a little apple orchard perhaps 100 yards in front of the line & on the right of the road

A very plain little wooden house, which seemed recently deserted, was at the far edge of the orchard. The place belonged to one of the Sweeneys, celebrated as banjo players, before the war, all over the Union.[50] Here the general stood for some minutes, receiving & sending messages. When the last messenger left him he said, "I would like to sit down. Is there any place where I can sit near here?"

He spoke to no one in particular & I was the only person near enough to hear the remark. About half way to the road stood one of the apple trees with more leaves out than its neighbors, & already two or three couriers, attracted by its shade, were squatted under it holding their horses. I asked them to remove their horses, & to bring some rails from the fence by the roadside. With a dozen or more rails we fixed up a comfortable seat, & the general sat down & invited me to sit also. I did for a few minutes—long enough to roll a cigarette, & then went off to some smouldering ashes near by for a light, & thus launched myself back, as it were, into my native element.

But Gen. Lee sat there for about three hours, nearly, if not quite, until Col. Babcock,[51] of Gen. Grant's staff, came to accompany him to the village. He was in plain view of quite a long stretch of our line of battle on which the troops stood at rest all day, the officers generally out in front, and doubtless, during the day, the idea occurred to many of his old soldiers who were soon to scatter & never see him again to have a piece of that tree as a memento of the day. To myself, I am sorry to say the idea did not occur until too late. My staff & I bivouaced in that orchard that night, & made it our headquarters until we broke up on the 12th. The tree was cut down on the 10th & its remotest roots dug up on the 11th & I never thought to get a piece until too late. I have never since seen a piece & I have only heard of one. My sister Mrs. Gilmer, making her way to Georgia in an ambulance, got in conversation on the road, somewhere in South Carolina, with a soldier from Texas who had been at the surrender, & he showed her a piece of the apple tree which he was taking home.

I think it must have been about two o'clock when Col. Babcock, on a seal fat bay, rode up with a note from Gen. Grant saying that he was on his way to Appomattox C.H. Gen. Horace Porter has written that Babcock reported finding Gen. Lee lying down on a blanket under a tree by the roadside, & he may have gone to another tree to take a rest, leaving Longstreet under his original tree.[52] At any rate Longstreet, as Gen. Lee left to go with Babcock, said to him: "General, if he does not give us good terms come back & let us fight it out"—to which Gen. Lee is not said to have made any reply.

I sat a little ways off on a grassy knoll, with my staff, & watched them ride to the village, and a great feeling of strangeness came over me. It was as if I had suddenly died & waked up in an entirely new & different world. All my life, hitherto had been absorbed in military affairs & military ideas. Now I was suddenly converted into a civilian with a wife & family to support, & military occupation of any sort was forbidden me. There are no words to tell how forlorn & blank the future looked to me. I could not imagine myself making a living in any civil occupation, & I could see no resource but to set out for Brazil. It was a decidedly blue afternoon, as I sat there on the grass & waited for Gen. Lee to come back. And I remembered that it was four years to an hour since I had started from old Fort Steilacoom to take my part in the war, & practically ended the happy & prosperous old army life which had lain before me. [Figure 72 appears here in the manuscript.]

Figure 72. Appomattox Courthouse

It was about half past four o'clock when we saw the general on old Traveller, & Col. Marshall, who had alone accompanied him, appear in the road returning; still about a half mile off. A strong desire seized me to have the men do *something,* to indicate to the general that our affection for him was even deeper than in the days of greatest victory & prosperity.

Ordinary cheering seemed inappropriate, so I quickly sent & had Col. Jno. Haskell, & all the artillery officers near, bring their men & form them along the roadside, with orders to uncover their heads, but in silence, as the general passed.

But the infantry line, being at rest & noting us artillerists at something, swarmed down to see. And thus, as the general came up, our few hundred artillery were swallowed up in a mob of infantry, & some one started to cheer, & then, of course, all joined in.

And Gen. Lee stopped & spoke a few words. It was I believe only the second time that he ever spoke to a crowd. The first occasion was when a crowd at a station had called him from the train, as he went from Washington City to Richmond to enter the service of Virginia at the breaking out of the war. He advised them to go to their homes & prepare for a bloody & desperate struggle.

Now, he told the men in a few words that he had done his best for them & advised them to go home & become as good citizens as they had been soldiers. As he spoke a wave of emotion seemed to strike the crowd & a great many men were weeping, & many pressed to shake his hand & to try

& express in some way the feelings which shook every heart. As he passed on toward his camp he stopped & spoke to me for a moment & told me that Gen. Grant had very generously agreed that our soldiers could keep their private horses, which would enable them to plant crops before it was too late. This seemed to be a very special gratification to him. Indeed Gen. Grant's conduct toward us in the whole matter is worthy of the very highest praise & indicates a great & broad & generous mind. *For all time it will be a good thing for the whole United States, that of all the Federal generals it fell to Grant to receive the surrender of Lee.*

The terms of the surrender were drawn up by Gen. Grant himself in a brief note rapidly written, & all the details as afterward carried out seem to me a remarkable model of practical simplicity. This is Gen. Grant's letter, which, being accepted by Gen. Lee in a brief note, then became the contract of surrender:

Appomattox Ct.H., Va., April 9th, 1865

General R. E. Lee, Commanding C.S.A.

General: In accordance with the substance of my letter to you of the 8th inst., I propose to receive the surrender of the Army of Northern Virginia on the following terms, to wit: Rolls of all the officers and men to be made in duplicate, one copy to be given to an officer to be designated by me, the other to be retained by such officer or officers as you may designate. The officers to give their individual paroles not to take up arms against the Government of the United States until properly [exchanged], and each company or regimental commander to sign a like parole for the men of their commands. The arms, artillery, and public property to be parked, and stacked, and turned over to the officers appointed by me to receive them. This will not embrace the side-arms of the officers, nor their private horses or baggage. This done, each officer and man will be allowed to return to his home, not to be disturbed by the United States authorities so long as they observe their paroles, and the laws in force where they may reside.

Very respectfully,
U. S. Grant, Lieutenant-General[53]

I've always been particularly impressed with the last sentence, which in such few & simple & unobjectionable words, practically gave an amnesty to every surrendered soldier for all political offences. The subject had not been discussed, nor referred to in any way. Nor did there seem, at that time, any likelihood that there would ever be any vindictive desire to hang or punish our prominent men for treason. Nor would there have been had Mr. Lincoln lived. But after his death there came a time when even Gen. Lee's blood was specially thirsted for, and when this provision enabled Gen. Grant to protect him even against President Johnson & with him every paroled soldier in the South. For the terms given by Gen. Grant were followed in the surrender of all the other armies. Gen. Horace Porter has told me personally of President Johnson's insisting that "the hanging should begin," & of Gen. Grant's threatening to resign from the command of the army if the protection he had promised to the surrendered were violated in a single instance.54

On the morning of the 10th, Gen. Grant rode to our lines where he was met by Gen. Lee, & a friendly conference took place. Gen. Grant asked if Gen. Lee thought the example of his surrender would be followed by the other armies, without additional bloodshed. Gen. Lee thought that it would. Gen. Grant suggested that Lee should go to North Carolina and confer with President Davis, & endeavor to promote the prompt advent of peace. But Gen. Lee did not feel authorized to thus intrude upon the functions of President Davis. I think there is no doubt that Mr. Davis would have considered it a great intrusion. But, fortunately, the generals of each of our other armies recognized the situation readily; & each one surrendered his army soon after the news reached him: Johnston in North Carolina on April 2[6], Dick Taylor in Miss. on May 4th, & Kirby Smith in the Trans Miss. on May 26th.55

Gen. Grant started for Washington City at noon on Monday the 10th. Gen. Lee started for Richmond early on the 11th. I was detained until the 12th with all the details attending the parole of my men, & turning over all of the artillery to Gen. Gibbon, who was appointed to receive it. That would have been a sad ceremony to me any how, but it was made doubly more so56 by the sad fate of my poor faithful horses, already worked down to only skin & bone before the surrender. The Federals were able to give us rations for our men, but nothing for our horses. I had arranged to form all our guns on the road early Tuesday morning, & did so, making over half a mile of column. There we left them to the Federals, & on Wednesday, when I saw them last, there they were still standing—or lying, for many were down & many were dead from starvation. It was a pitiable sight. [Figure 73 and 74 appear here in the manuscript.]

It was arranged to give each paroled person a parole signed by one of his commanding officers, & also a copy of an order issued from Grant's headquarters referring to these papers & validating them as paroles. My parole was signed by Gen. Pendleton as Gen. Lee's chief of artillery, & as I have preserved it & also the order spoken of I copy them both & also Gen. Lee's farewell order.57 [Figure 75 and 76 appear here in the manuscript.]

I had to ride into the village two or three times on some matters of detail, & on the first occasion of going to the house in which the surrender had

Figure 73. The Surrender at Appomattox

Figure 74. General Lee and Colonel Marshall leaving McLean House after surrender

Figure 75. General Lee's return to his lines after surrender

Figure 76. McLean House, Appomattox Court House

taken place, & which was still the headquarters, I was surprised to meet Maj. Wilmer McLean, whom I mentioned in my narrative of Bull Run. He had married an aunt of my wife's, and his house on Bull Run had been Gen. Beauregard's head quarters during the affair at Blackburn's Ford, July 18th, 1861—the very first collision between the hostile armies in Va., the action being fought upon his lands. I had been intimate with himself & his family as long as the army was in that vicinity, but I had not seen him now for over two years. Said I, "Why, hello, McLean! What are you doing here?" He answered, "By Heavens, Alexander, what are *you* doing here?" He then went on & told me that his place on Bull Run had been so ravaged & torn up by the constant passage of armies that it became impossible to live there; & he had at last sold out & moved to Appomattox C.H., nearly 200 miles, as a secluded spot where he could hope never to see a soldier. And then he pointed out his wrecked fences & trampled fields, over which infantry, artillery, & cavalry had contended on the 9th, & the headquarters in his yard & house & asked what I thought of that for luck. It was certainly a very remarkable coincidence. The first hostile shot I ever saw strike, went through his kitchen. The last gun was fired on his land and the surrender took place in his parlor; nearly four years of time & 200 miles of space intervening.

Of course I met at the Federal headquarters many old army friends & acquaintances & the courtesy, consideration, & good will of every one of them was shown in every way possible. Indeed, Gen. Grant's spirit of kindness seemed to imbue his whole army down to the private soldiers & the teamsters one met upon the roads, who would turn out into the mud for any Confederate officer, & salute him with a better grace & courtesy, doubtless, than they sometimes showed to their own officers.

Among those whom I met was one of my class-mates named Warner[58] from Pa. We had never been in the least intimate as cadets, running in different circles entirely, & I doubt whether in the four years either of us was ever in the other's room. But Warner called me to one side, & said:

> Aleck, I guess you fellows haven't much money about you but Confederate, just now, & in your present situation it may be a little inconvenient. And you know our pay has been raised & we have just got greenbacks to burn. And I've just drawn several months' pay & I will really be very much obliged to you if you will let me lend you two or three hundred dollars, that you may return, if you insist upon it, sometime in the future, but if never it would be only the more grateful to me.

That touched me very deeply, coming from one to whom I had really no special relations at all; but it is only a fair sample of the spirit that breathed everywhere, & which I believe would have animated the North every where but for the assassination of Lincoln.

I did not accept Warner's generous offer, however, because I had just borrowed $200 in gold from Maj. W. H. Gibbes. He had been great friends of a Mr. Cameron of Petersburg, in whose house he lay while recovering from his severe wound received at the Mine. Cameron was a British subject & was largely interested in blockade-running & he gave Gibbes a chance to send out a bale of cotton, the profit on which was about $400 gold, & Gibbes had recently received it.[59]

I was making all my preparations for Brazil. The Haskells were going to ride home to Abbeville, S.C., from Appomattox, & it would have been very nice to go with them & then on to Washington, Georgia. I have regretted a thousand times since that I did not. But I feared that if I once got down to Georgia I could not get off from there, either to go to Brazil, or to find out anything about it. So I decided to go first from Appomattox C.H. to Washington City & [call] on the Brazilian minister. If he would send me to Brazil I would put myself in his hands. So I had borrowed $200.00 gold from Gibbes, & I had also gotten letters from Gen. Lee & Gen. Longstreet & Gen. Pendleton, endorsing me as a good artillerist.[60] So now, my men all paroled, my guns turned over to our captors, & money & letters in my pocket, I was ready to start.

The Federals had opened the railroad from City Point on the James via Petersburg to Burkeville, & I was invited to join a mixed party of Federals & Confederates who were to set out about 9 A.M. on the 12th for Burkeville. We spent the last night in the apple orchard and Wed. morning, Apr. 12th, marked the final breaking up & separation of my dearly beloved staff and the remnant of my battalion and of battery commanders.

I will not attempt to describe it. Just imagine yourself parting from your very dearest friends, after years of common danger & hardship; & now, in common disaster, saying farewell and separating apparently forever to face unknown futures. For I thought it possible that in a few weeks I might be actually fighting down in Paraguay.

Charley was very anxious to accompany me; & would have gone anywhere on earth, but I gave him the ten dollars in gold which his accumulated hire had bought, as has already been told, & bade him good by, for it would have been impossible to take him.

The Haskells agreed to take along my horses, Dixie & Meg; & to send them over to Washington for me to my wife, & also to take a letter which I wrote telling her all about it. The mails had been very slow & I had had no letter from her now for over three weeks. To take me to Burkeville I had reserved a battery sergeant's horse which I would turn over at that place to the Federal quartermaster. And so at 9 A.M. on Wed., April 12th, I set out from Appomattox C.H. to seek my fortune again in the "wide, wide world."

Two other Confederates, Gen. Gordon & Gen. Wilcox, were in the party, & also Senator E. B. Washburne of Illinois.[61] I had known him personally when on duty with Major A. J. Myer, introducing the wig-wag signals, he being on the military committee of the Senate. Beside these, there were several Federal officers whose names I am sorry I cannot recall; for they were all very nice fellows. Then there was an escort of some thirty troopers, for there were said to be lawless gangs about & it was unsafe for small parties of either side to meet them.

I only recall one special incident of this ride. Senator Washburne was exceedingly pleasant & courteous to us Confederates, & riding at one time with Gen. Wilcox & myself, he asked us if we thought the other Confederate armies would try to prolong the war. We thought not; & then we asked him what was Mr. Lincoln going to do with us, & on what terms he proposed to reconstruct the Union. Mr. Washburne answered quite nearly in these exact words:

> When the news came of the evacuation of Richmond I called on Mr.
> Lincoln to congratulate him, & I had quite a conversation with him upon
> that very subject. It would not be proper for me to repeat all that he told
> me of what he proposed to do. But I am going to make you a prediction.
> Within a year, Mr. Lincoln will be as popular at the South as he is at the
> North, and the whole world will be surprised at the liberality of the terms
> upon which he will have reconstructed the Union.

These words, & Mr. Washburne's manner impressed us both so much that we soon got together alone, & discussed them over again, & tried to guess what they could exactly mean. We agreed that they meant money to the South in some way, & most probably in compensation for the emancipation of her slaves.

Without going into it farther here I am confident, from all I have learned since, that that is really what Sen. Washburne meant, & that had Mr. Lincoln lived the South would certainly have received payment in some shape.[62]

It was after dark that night when we reached Farmville & went to the Federal head quarters. The officer in command was a handsome & exceedingly nice, young General Curtin, a son of the Governor of Pa.[63] He took care of the whole party for the night, & took me actually to share his own pallet with him, & gave us all a good breakfast in the morning.

About noon on the 13th we got to Burkeville. Here I turned over my horse to the Federal quartermaster, who was very anxious to pay me for him as if he were my private property, but, of course, I positively refused.

About dusk I boarded a train for City Point, which was jammed & packed with men & had no lights in the cars. It did not start for an hour, & while it waited some one came to the door of the car I was in & called

"Alexander." Not supposing it meant for me I made no reply. Then, "Is Gen. Alexander of the Confederate army here?" On this I spoke, & up rushed Gen. A. S. Webb, who had been an intimate friend at West Point in the old times. Regardless of the crowd he threw his arms about my neck, & hugged me saying, "I've got you at last. I've been trying to get you for four years & now I have got you." Then we got in a corner behind the door, & he produced from one pocket a candle & a tumbler, & from another a bottle of whiskey, & we renewed old friendship & discussed places where we had fought each other—particularly Pickett's charge at Gettysburg— until the train left. His brigade had been at the very brunt of our assault.

I was all night on that train, & all next day getting up to Richmond by boat. I went to Mrs. Webb's house in Richmond & stayed there until Monday, April 17th. Gen. Lee was staying in the city with his family, who had remained during the evacuation & the fire, & I called & spent an evening with them, all of his daughters being at home. Gen. Lee did not at all sympathise with my plan of going to Brazil.

Gen. Ord was in the city, & in command of it. I called on him to get a permit to go to Washington City, & found him very cordial & pleasant & glad to hear of Lawton & Gilmer, who were intimate with him in cadet days.

Sunday evening I first heard on the streets rumors of the assassination of Prest. Lincoln. I did not believe it & went to Gen. Ord's after supper to ask if it could be true. Gen. Ord confirmed it & advised me not to got to Washington City. But I did not know exactly what else I could do & decided to risk it. I left on Mon. morning in a boat which went down the James & up the Potomac, & landed me in Washn. on Tuesday the 18th.

I had no sooner landed than I felt it in the atmosphere that I was in the wrong place. The streets swarmed like beehives. The president's body was lying in the White House to be viewed, & the column, four deep, forming & marching past reached a half mile up Pa. Avenue.

Little was yet known of the plot which resulted in the murder, & it was naturally ascribed to Confederates in general. And somehow Mr. Davis, Mr. Clay, & others were supposed to be connected with it & rewards of $100,000 each were offered for their capture. The passion & excitement of the crowds were so great that anyone on the street, recognised merely as a Confederate, would have been instantly mobbed & lynched. In Richmond I had gotten a citizen coat & pants, & I wore a U.S. army private's overcoat, only dyed black instead of in its original blue. But, to a close observer, such a coat would seem particularly suspicious. However, being there I went to see the Brazilian minister. He read my letters & told me that if I should go to Brazil he had no doubt I could secure a commission in the Brazilian army, but he had no authority to speak on the matter or to send any one, nor any means to use to that end. Possibly, he said, the consul in N.Y. might render aid. He said that, I am sure, just to get rid of me. He seemed to be actually afraid lest my being in his house might bring a mob on him.

His suggestion of the consul in New York determined me to leave Washington on the train at 5 P.M. that afternoon. On the street I met my old friend Major—now Gen. Myer, chief signal officer. He was very cordial & took me to his house to lunch with Mrs. Myer. After leaving them I went to the office of Gen. Augur,[64] commanding in the city, to get my pass made good to N.Y.

Augur's adjt. was Col. Jos. Taylor,[65] one of my most special & intimate friends. As I walked up to his desk, he stared at me & said, "Great God! Alexander, what are you doing here?" "I am trying to get away," I said, "& I'll do it quick if you'll fix me these papers." "Well," said he, "old fellow, you had better. Yesterday a company of cavalry brought in your Confederate General Payne, who had surrendered up at Leesburg, & the crowd started after him to hang him. It was all the soldiers could do to stop them long enough for us to run Payne out the back way & put him in a hack & take him to the Old Capital Prison where we have him now, locked up for his own safety."[66]

On looking at my papers Taylor decided to send me to Grant's office, which he did, with a soldier to conduct me; & there my pass was fixed by some subordinate & I saw no one whom I knew. Then I went by the old National Hotel for my hand baggage, left there in the morning, & took a street car to the B.&O. Railway station. I knew the city was swarming with detectives, amateur & regular, all stimulated by the enormous rewards offered for every one connected with the murder plot; and, as I got out of the street car, I spotted one of them standing on the side walk & evidently sizing up the people coming to take the train.

My dyed soldier's overcoat & my $500 Richmond boots, with my pants tucked inside, evidently took his eye, & he turned down the side walk so as to be abreast of me as I reached it. I tried to shake him, as if casually, by long quick strides across the muddy street; but he was also quick. So, on the side walk, I came down to a very leisurely gait to let him pass. But he also slowed down as he drew along side of me & said, "Good evening, Sir." "Good evening," said I with a blandness which would have turned Ah Sin[67] green with envy. "Going to Baltimore?" said he. "Yes," said I; & butter, in my mouth, would have thought itself in a refrigerator. "So am I," said he. "Ah?" said I, with an accent of utterly indifferent good nature, plainer than the nose on most people's faces. "Yes," said he, "seems to be a big crowd"—as we entered the big waiting room. I grunted a polite "Um Hoo," & we joined in the swarm of hundreds pressing into the funnel shaped space before the ticket seller's window. I was awfully scared. During all the war my favorite nightmare had been to dream of being in the Federal lines & in danger of arrest as a spy; & now, here was a situation very like it. But I continued to play my hand with a coolness & nonchalance that seemed to me really inspired. It was a pushing crowd & presently some man pushed to get between me & my friend. I *apparently* resisted but I let him in. And I played that game so carefully & so well that when we came near the neck of the funnel he was some three or four files ahead of me. But I heard him say, "Ticket to Baltimore," & the agent answered, "This is [the] New York train. No Baltimore tickets sold until this train has gone. Pass on please." He motioned to me & tried to speak, but I was looking another way & he was squeezed along. As my turn came I had my money ready & said "N.Y." in a low tone, got my ticket, & shot through the train gate a little ways ahead, & hid myself in the most distant & darkest corner I could find in a long train of about a dozen coaches. I saw my friend no more, the train starting in a short while.

I was in N.Y. from Wed. [the] 19th to Sunday the 23rd. The Brazilian consul could do no more for me than the minister, & I, perforce, dropped the whole business & at once became crazy to get home. The steamer *Arago* sailed on Sunday for Hilton Head & I got passage on her, going to army hdqrs. for my pass, & to Gen. Van Vliet,[68] quartermaster, for my transportation. Van Vliet had been stationed in Sav. before the war, & knew all my family & was very nice.

The government gave me transportation as a prisoner of war & it was a government transport, but required me to feed myself. As it takes very little to feed me at sea, usually, I just laid in some cheese & crackers. I stayed at the old Brandeth House, in Canal St., on the European plan; & spent no money, not absolutely necessary, except for *one thing*! My poor wife had had an awful time for clothes during the war. Now I went into Stewarts, & I got the last ounce of stuff I could carry to take to her. The cream of it all was a whole piece of New York Mills shirting, for which I paid if [I] recollect aright 60 cents a yard in greenbacks. Then I got some soft pretty gray stuff called pongee, & some beautiful dark thing with fine red stripes for two dresses & a lot of little things. Never in all my life, before or since, did I so enjoy the spending of money. Nobody need ever try to duplicate that pleasure, either, for it can't be done except under those particular conditions, & they can never return.

We reached Hilton Head on Wed., April 26th, & next day I went on to Savannah on a river steamer. Gen. Q. A. Gillmore, who had been [an] instructor at West Point in my day, was in command here & was nice to me as everybody was. My notes also record the names of Gen. Jeffers & Gen. de Trobriand[69] but without any particulars & I cannot recall any. I stayed in Savannah with my old Uncle Major Porter, until Sunday, April 30th, but it was because of an accident. I was wildly impatient to get home, not only to see my family, from whom I had not heard since the middle of March, but I was also particularly & specially anxious to meet President Davis, who I knew must soon pass through the town.

I was exceedingly anxious to repeat to him my conversation with Gen. Lee on the morning of the surrender. Gen. Lee had said that, even if younger men went to bushwhacking, the only dignified & proper course for his years & position would be to surrender himself, & take the consequences of his actions. Now it was already plain to every one that the war could not be prolonged. There would not even be bushwhacking, & it seemed to me that a surrender of himself would have been the best & most dignified course for Mr. Davis. And on top of that situation had come the assassination of Lincoln, & the accusation that Mr. Davis was accessory, & the offer of $100,000 reward for his capture. That seemed to me to offer him a peculiarly favorable opportunity to surrender himself upon that charge, & deny that he was either an assassin or fugitive, & demand a trial. It seemed to me that it would be a dignified & honorable outcome from a very awkward & embarrassing situation; & one which the whole South would be proud to see him adopt. For, as he stood, he must soon become either a captive or a fugitive with chances ten to one that it would be a captive, hampered as he was with a family.

From Savannah it was necessary to go by horseback, or private conveyance, some 90 miles to Waynesboro, whence there was [a] railroad to Augusta, & thence to Washington. But horses & mules & buggies in all that region were very few & very far between. So I thought myself very lucky to strike in Savannah a Col. Lawton Singleton, a relative of Gen. Lawton's, who had gotten a buggy & would start on Saturday, the 29th, for his home, 55 miles on the way. And he readily promised to take me that far, & to forward me the balance of the way.

Major Porter, who was now 76 years of age but in remarkable health & vigor, was president of the Bank of the State of Georgia, & had managed for me my few little financial affairs all during the war. And as some men are born great mathematicians, & some poets & some orators, &c., so was he born, & so he always lived & died God & Nature's ideal & example of what a *trustee* should be. He did not have a speculative bone in his body or hair on his head. He did not pretend to understand any finance except dividend paying investments, at fair rates, and reinvestments of the income. Every cent in his care belonging to another person was a fetich, entitled to worship by book entries & vouchers, and as careful watching & nursing as a human infant, sure so to grow to large proportions. And all his statements & reports with their fine, firm figures, were the very embodiment of conscientious exactitude. And now he brought me the little bundle of securities he had had in his vaults for me & the paper on which the minutest transaction was noted. He had rigidly carried out the instructions which I had given him in every matter *but one!* I will tell what they were merely to illustrate what desperate idiocy my mind had been capable of accepting as logic & common sense.

I wrote to my uncle early in the war, "I am risking life in support of the Confederacy. If it fails my life may be lost in the failure & certainly distress will be upon me. So I ought to support it with my whole strength; that is with my money as well as with my services. Ergo, invest every cent I have in Confederate govt. bonds."

Well, he never pretended to understand logic, & so he simply carried out my instructions so far as all dividends were concerned, & some outside investments which came in of themselves. But he delayed to sell a block of Southwestern Railroad stock which I had sent him. Well, after about a year I wrote again, "Why don't you sell that stock & put it in Confederate bonds? I ought to be helping the Confederacy & I am not doing it as much as I can." But he had one rule which he would not violate for any instructions, & answered, "Your stock is advancing, last year it was par, now it is 200. I can't sell while it is advancing." In about another year I wrote again. But now it was $500, & still going up. And so it went on to the end of the war, when a single share would have easily brought $10,000 in Confederate bonds, for this railroad stock was really worth about par in gold.

And now at the end of the war he handed me back the stock which his simple financial common sense had so barely rescued from my insanity, & without which I would not now have had a single dollar in the world.

With equal particularity, also, he handed me about $20,000 in Confederate notes & bonds, the proceeds of the investments in which my instructions had been followed, with a beautiful statement which testified the scrupulous care bestowed even upon every Confederate cent.

On Saturday morning, April 29th, I started in the buggy with Col. Singleton, but our progress was very brief. At the edge of the town the road ran between the high Central Railroad embankment on one side, & a fence on the other. A dead mule lay at the foot of the embankment. Our animal took fright at it, & whirled around, breaking our shafts to splinters. I could have cried with vexation. We could not get another buggy until the next day. I was hampered somewhat by being a guest in the matter & could not drive & push & kick as I might otherwise have done, if it had been a matter of business only. So on Sunday the 30th we made a fresh start. The roads were heavy with sand & we only accomplished 36 miles, putting up for the night at "Uncle Billy Moore's," a very nice country place where they took in travellers.

The next day we reached Col. Singleton's to dinner, 18 miles. His wife was a remarkably pretty & accomplished young woman, with a lot of children too; & their hospitality would by no means let me press on in the afternoon as I wished. Even the next day they were reluctant to let me go; but at last took me on about 18 miles more, to a Mr. Jno. M. Miller's, who could get me into Waynesboro in time for the train on Wednesday by an early start. That landed me in Augusta Wednesday night. And on Thursday morning, May 4th,[70] I took the train for Washington, & arrived, at last, about noon.

But I heard on the train that I was too late to see Mr. Davis. He had arrived with his party in Washington at 10 A.M. the day before. Some of his cabinet were already there, & others came with him. The last cabinet meeting had been held in the afternoon in the old bank building of which my father had been cashier during my youth. At that meeting he parted with his cabinet & elected to become a fugitive. He left the town that night, May 3rd, at ten o'clock, with a single attendant; & followed his family, who had arrived on Apr. 30th & left on May 1st. He was captured with them near Irwinville on the morning of May 10th.[71] I have always believed, and I believe today, that if I could have seen him in Washington he would have elected to surrender himself. I had later news of the situation at the North than any one else, & I had, by chance, Gen. Lee's expressed opinion as to the only proper & dignified course for himself, which would apply with even more force to President Davis. It has always been & always will be one of the disappointments of my life that I was too late to see him. It *might* have changed for the better many subsequent events.

But the dead mule was lying on the Central Railroad embankment at Savannah.

With a darkey carrying my valise, stuffed with my New York Mills & pongee & other purchases at Stewarts, I started from the railroad depot, where I had landed, for my father's house. Nearly the whole family was now collected there by the military & political events which happened for a while to center upon the town. The Haskells had sent over my horse & my letter from Appomattox, telling of my plans, & I was supposed by all to be en route to Brazil.

Passing through the public square, I accidentally met Gen. Lawton, the first one from whom I could learn any personal news. He turned & walked with me home telling me of all that had happened. I had a little daughter born on April 7th[72] & my wife was still very weak & ill.

But although she thought me far on my road to Brazil, she knew the rush of my feet up the stairs the moment that she heard it, & as I opened the door she was in the middle of the room advancing to meet me.

NOTES

Abbreviations

Alexander Papers SHC   Edward Porter Alexander Papers, Southern Historical Collection, Wilson Library, University of North Carolina, Chapel Hill.

B&L   Johnson, Robert Underwood, and Clarence Clough Buel, eds. *Battles and Leaders of the Civil War.* 4 vols. New York, 1887–88.

EPA   Edward Porter Alexander.

Military Memoirs   Alexander, Edward Porter. *Military Memoirs of a Confederate: A Critical Narrative.* New York, 1907.

OR   U.S. War Department. *The War of the Rebellion: A Compilation of the Official Records of the Union and Confederate Armies.* 127 vols., index, and atlas. Washington, D.C., 1880–1901.

SHC   Southern Historical Collection, Wilson Library, University of North Carolina, Chapel Hill.

SHSP   Jones, J. William, et al., eds. *Southern Historical Society Papers.* 52 vols. 1876–1959. Reprint, with 2-vol. index. New York, 1977–80.

Introduction

1. This quotation is on p. 519 below.

2. The first edition was published by Charles Scribner's Sons of New York.

3. Theodore Roosevelt to EPA, 16 July 1907, William A. Dunning to Frederic Bancroft, 31 May 1907, folders 67, 66, Alexander Papers SHC; excerpt from a review in *Army and Navy Journal* quoted in an ad for *Military Memoirs* in *Confederate Veteran* 15 (June 1907): third page of advertisements inside the front cover.

4. Douglas Southall Freeman, *Lee's Lieutenants: A Study in Command,* 3 vols. (New York, 1942–44), 3:809; Richard Barksdale Harwell, *In Tall Cotton: The 200 Most Important Confederate Books for the Reader, Researcher and Collector* (Austin, Tex., 1978), p. 1; introduction by T. Harry Williams in a reprint of E. P. Alexander, *Military Memoirs of a Confederate,* ed. T. Harry Williams (Bloomington, Ind., 1962), p. xxxv.

5. Introduction by Maury Klein in a reprint of E. P. Alexander, *Military Memoirs of a Confederate: A Critical Narrative* (Dayton, Ohio, 1977), p. 1. For an example of the criticism leveled at EPA by southerners offended by his impartiality, see *Confederate Veteran* 23 (June 1915): 252.

6. Williams reprint of *Military Memoirs,* p. xxxiv; Douglas Southall Freeman, *The South to Posterity: An Introduction to the Writing of Confederate History* (1939; reprint, Wendell, N.C., 1983), p. 178.

7. Alexander considered a number of titles for his reminiscences, including "Fighting for the Lost Cause," "Fighting for the Confederacy," "Fighting Under the Conquered Banner," "How the Cause was Lost," "What Became of the Lost Cause," "Fighting Under Lee & Longstreet," "Personal Recollections of the Civil War," and "Military Experiences in the Civil War." He wrote "Personal Recollections of the War 1861–1865" at the top of the first page of his manuscript, then crossed it out and substituted "Fighting for the Confederacy." For the list of potential titles, see manuscript vol. 26, Alexander Papers SHC; for the first page with the change of titles, see manuscript vol. 27, Alexander Papers SHC.

8. The original draft of *Fighting for the Confederacy* is in manuscript vols. 27–35, 39, 40, 42–47, 49–52, Alexander Papers SHC.

9. Robert K. Krick to Iris Tillman Hill, 15 Nov. 1984, copy in possession of the editor.

10. Henry Kyd Douglas, *I Rode with Stonewall: The War Reminiscences of the Youngest Member of Jackson's Staff,* ed. Fletcher M. Green (Chapel Hill, 1940); Jedediah Hotchkiss, *Make Me a Map of the Valley: The Civil War Journal of Stonewall Jackson's Topographer,* ed. Archie P. McDonald (Dallas, 1973).

11. EPA to Thomas Jewett Goree, 24 Apr. 1868, in Langston James Goree V, ed., *The Thomas Jewett Goree Letters: Volume 1, The Civil War Correspondence* (Bryan, Tex., 1981), pp. 281–82. Longstreet optimistically estimated that EPA could complete the task in "a three month vacation." By the time he wrote Goree, EPA had already given two years of his spare time to the project and "hardly made a beginning."

12. See *SHSP* for EPA's "The 'Seven Days Battles'" (1:61–76); "Letter from General E. P. Alexander, late Chief of Artillery First Corps, A. N. V." (4:97–111); "Sketch of Longstreet's Division. Winter of 1861–62" (9:512–18); "Sketch of Longstreet's Division—Yorktown and Williamsburg" (10:32–45); "The Battle of Fredericksburg. Paper No. 1" (10:382–92); "The Battle of Fredericksburg. Paper No. 2—(Conclusion.)" (10:445–64); and "Confederate Artillery Service" (11:98–113). See also *B&L* for EPA's "The Great Charge and Artillery Fighting at Gettysburg" and "Longstreet at Knoxville" (3:357–68, 745–51). During these same years, EPA also published *Railway Practice* (New York, 1887), *On Various Railroad Questions* (Louisville, 1881), and *Catteral Ratteral Doggeral* (New York, 1890), a satirical account of an ambitious rat. Later publications on the war included "Lee at Appomattox" (*Century Illustrated Monthly Magazine* 63 [1902]: 921–31); "The Battle of Bull Run" (*Scribner's Magazine* 41 [1907]: 80–94); and "Grant's Conduct of the Wilderness Campaign" (*Annual Report of the American Historical Association* 1 [1908]: 226–34).

13. Robert Underwood Johnson, *Remembered Yesterdays* (Boston, 1929), p. 197. The second "lovable man" was Union artillerist Henry Jackson Hunt.

14. On the background of EPA's relationship with Cleveland and his appointment as arbitrator, see Maury Klein, *Edward Porter Alexander* (Athens, Ga., 1971), pp. 201–3.

15. EPA to Bettie Mason Alexander, 3 June, 29 July 1897, EPA to Bessie Alexander Ficklen, 28 July, 2 Aug. 1897, folder 39, Alexander Papers SHC.

16. EPA to Frederick M. Colston, 7 Apr. 1898, 26 Apr., 8 Aug. 1899, folder 16, Campbell-Colston Papers, SHC; EPA to Louise Alexander Gilmer, 2 July, 2 Oct. 1899, folder 4, Minis Family Papers, SHC.

17. See John B. Gordon, *Reminiscences of the Civil War* (New York, 1903). A superb soldier during the war, Gordon wrote in a floridly romantic style and tailored his narrative to foster good relations between the North and South.

18. These items are in manuscript vols. 8, 9-A, and 9-B, Alexander Papers SHC. See chapter 11, p. 221 below for EPA's description of the diary covering the last two years of the war.

19. EPA's little reference collection definitely included Andrew A. Humphreys, *The Virginia Campaign of '64 and '65: The Army of the Potomac and the Army of the James* (New York, 1883); William Swinton, *Campaigns of the Army of the Potomac: A Critical History of Operations in Virginia, Maryland and Pennsylvania, from the Commencement to the Close of the War, 1861-5* (New York, 1866); Alfred Roman, *The Military Operations of General Beauregard in the War Between the States, 1861 to 1865: Including a Brief Personal Sketch and a Narrative of His Services in the War with Mexico, 1846-8,* 2 vols. (New York, 1884); Edward A. Pollard, *The Lost Cause: A New Southern History of the War of the Confederates* (New York, 1866); parts 4 and 7 of Charles A. Dana's "Recollections of Men and Events of the Civil War," *McClure's Magazine* 10 (February 1898), 11 (May 1898); and unnamed issues of the *SHSP* and *Confederate Veteran.*

20. See for example EPA to Frederick M. Colston, 26 Apr., 13 June, 8 Aug. 1899, folder 16, Campbell-Colston Papers, SHC; EPA to Bettie Mason Alexander, 30 Aug. addendum to letter of 27 Aug. 1899, folder 47, Alexander Papers SHC. Colston was EPA's most frequent correspondent.

21. EPA to Bettie Mason Alexander, 13 Feb., 17 June 1898, 6 Feb. (with addenda for 7, 10 Feb.), 13 Aug. 1899, folders 43, 44, 45, 47, Alexander Papers SHC; EPA to Bessie Alexander Ficklen, 2 Mar., 13 June 1898, folder 2, John Rose Ficklen Papers, SHC.

22. EPA to Bessie Alexander Ficklen, 20 May 1898, EPA to Bettie Mason Alexander, 17 June 1898, folder 44, Alexander Papers SHC. Fitzhugh Lee and Joseph Wheeler, both of whom had served as major generals of cavalry in the Confederate army, were appointed to that same rank in the U.S. Volunteers on 4 May 1898. Thomas L. Rosser, another former Confederate cavalryman, was made a brigadier general on 10 June 1898.

23. EPA to Bettie Mason Alexander, 6 Feb., 22, 28 May 1899, folders 45, 46, Alexander Papers SHC; EPA to Frederick M. Colston, 8 Aug. 1899, folder 16, Campbell-Colston Papers, SHC.

24. EPA to Bettie Mason Alexander, 27 July 1899, folder 46, Alexander Papers SHC.

25. EPA to Bettie Mason Alexander, 27 Aug. (with addenda for 30, 31 Aug.), 1 Oct. 1899, folder 47, Alexander Papers SHC; EPA to Louise Alexander Gilmer, 2 Oct. 1899, folder 4, Minis Family Papers, SHC.

26. On Alexander's trip home and the death of his wife, see Klein, *Alexander,* 210-13. The signing of the boundary agreement did not take place until the summer of 1900. For a long description of that event, see EPA to his children, 24 July 1900, in Marion Alexander Boggs, ed., *The Alexander Letters, 1787-1900* (1910; reprint, Athens, Ga., 1980), pp. 366-70.

27. Klein, *Alexander,* p. 214; EPA to William Mason Alexander, 26 Sept. 1900, folder 49, Alexander Papers SHC.

28. EPA to My Dear Hal, 20 Aug. 1901, folder 51, Alexander Papers SHC.

29. On EPA and the historians, see Klein, *Alexander,* pp. 220-21. Drafts of the

chapters on Gettysburg in *Military Memoirs* sent to Bancroft for his suggestions are in manuscript vols. 36–38, Alexander Papers SHC.

30. Quotations are from the printed description of the Edward Porter Alexander Papers, Collection #7, prepared by Dr. Carolyn Wallace and dated 13 Jan. 1960.

31. Williams reprint of *Military Memoirs,* pp. xxxiii, xli n. 32.

32. James I. Robertson, Jr., "The War in Words," *Civil War Times Illustrated* 14 (Oct. 1975): 44.

33. Klein, *Alexander,* p. 251 n. 16; Klein reprint of *Military Memoirs,* pp. 7–10.

34. Bessie Ficklen's ledgers are in manuscript vols. 27–28, the others in manuscript vols. 41 and 48, Alexander Papers SHC.

35. EPA to Well dem dear little daughters, 6 Feb. 1899, EPA to Bettie Mason Alexander, 28 May 1899, folders 45, 46, Alexander Papers SHC.

Chapter 1

1. EPA's reference is to the division of sentiment in Georgia in the wake of the Compromise of 1850. Robert Augustus Toombs supported the compromise, while Lucius Jeremiah Gartrell opposed it. Both men subsequently became generals in the Confederate army and members of the Confederate Congress.

2. G. D. percussion caps were a French brand notable for their weak ignition and high rate of misfires. Some users insisted that "their trade name 'G. D.' was but the abbreviation of a well-known profanity." See Ned H. Roberts, *The Muzzle-Loading Cap Lock Rifle,* 4th ed. (York, Pa., 1978), pp. 84–86.

3. The boys involved in this episode were James Hester (son of Simeon Hester, a farmer who lived near Washington), Benjamin Kappell (who lived with his mother, Dianah Kappell), and Charles Atwood Alexander, the older of EPA's two younger brothers.

4. Alexander Robert Lawton and Jeremy Francis Gilmer were married to EPA's older sisters, Sarah Gilbert Alexander and Louisa Frederika Alexander. Lawton served as a brigadier general, and Gilmer as a major general in the Confederate army.

5. William Robertson Boggs became a brigadier general in the Confederate army.

6. Russell M. Wright, EPA's principal instructor, was in his early thirties when he moved to Washington. The *Washington Chronicle* of 14 March 1898 described him as a "distinguished educator" who "about 50 years ago came here at the instance of Mr. Adam Alexander, and taught school in Washington for thirteen years."

7. James M. Dyson was a 38-year-old farmer in 1850. Dempsey Carroll Colley, born twelve years before EPA, was a soldier in the 61st Georgia Infantry when he was killed on 13 December 1862 at the battle of Fredericksburg. Henry Francis Andrews and Garnett Andrews were sons of Judge Garnett Andrews, a leading citizen of Washington who held $20,000 in real property in 1850. Wylie Hill DuBose and James Rembert DuBose, Jr., were sons of James Rembert DuBose, Sr., whose substantial holdings included more than $25,000 in real property in 1850; Wylie, a member of the 61st Georgia Infantry, was mortally wounded on 29 June 1862.

8. EPA was born into one of the most prominent families of Georgia. The marriage of his father, Adam Leopold Alexander (1803–82), and his mother, Sarah Hillhouse Gilbert (1805–55), had united important seaboard and upcountry clans. In 1850, Adam L. Alexander's real property in and around Washington exceeded $25,000, and the "home place," where EPA spent most of his boyhood, was a substantial establishment with

fifty-five slaves. On the Alexander family, see Marion Alexander Boggs, ed., *The Alexander Letters, 1787–1900* (1910; reprint, Athens, Ga., 1980).

9. EPA first wrote "small rifle."

10. EPA first identified the washerwoman as Hannah.

11. *Uncle Tom's Cabin, or, Life among the Lowly* (Boston,1852) by Harriet Beecher Stowe was the most influential antislavery publication in American history. Adams's *A South-Side View of Slavery; or, Three Months at the South, in 1854* (Boston, 1854) went through three printings within a year. At the end of the first volume of EPA's reminiscences, Mary Clifford Alexander Hull added the following passage about Adams: "Dr. Adams's first book was *A South-side View of Slavery*. But afterwards he published another called 'The Sable Cloud,' & that opens with a letter from Sister H. to Mother, telling of the death of the child of her cook (Cora) & how she & he went to the cem. to select a lot to bury it. Father & M. were North & Dr. A. went to N.Y. to see them. He was shown this letter, not supposing it would be considered anything unusual. But after his return home he wrote & begged to be given the letter with permission to use it as he pleased—& he opens his book with it. He wrote that after a visit to A. R. L.'s in Sav. in '54. She died in Nov. '54. M. C. H."

12. EPA's roommates were Robert Houston Anderson of Georgia; Richard Kidder Meade of Virginia; Thomas J. Berry; Richard Henry Brewer; Edward E. Burnet; Lawrence Kip, who was born in New York and appointed from California (his father was Episcopal bishop William Ingraham Kip); and Charles Hale Morgan. EPA's maternal grandmother was Sarah Hillhouse, whose parents moved from Connecticut to Washington, Georgia, in 1787.

13. Mary Clifford Alexander, the youngest of EPA's four older sisters.

14. John Reuben Church of Georgia resigned from the U.S. Army in 1860 and later served in the Confederate artillery.

15. EPA's roll call included Manning Marius Kimmel (Mo.), Paul Jones Quattlebaum (S.C.), Ira Wallace Claflin (born in Vt. and appointed from Iowa—for some reason, EPA placed his name among both sergts. and privates), Benjamin F. Sloan (S.C.), Jonathan Bacon (Tex.), Guilford Dudley Bailey (N.Y.), William Butler Beck (Pa.), Thomas J. Berry (Ga.), John M. Bevill (Ky.), Richard Henry Brewer (Md.), Warren W. Chamberlain (N.Y.), Theodore W. M. Coontz (Va.), George Alfred Cunningham (Mass.), Herbert Merton Enos (N.Y.), Samuel Wragg Ferguson (S.C.), Wade Hampton Gibbes (S.C.), John C. Gilmer (N.C.), George Waller Holt (Ala.), Edward Robie Hopkins (N.Y.), Brayton C. Ives (N.Y.), Robert Cobb Kennedy (La.), John Marshall Kerr (N.C.), Fitzhugh Lee (Va.), Lorenzo Lorain (Pa.), Charles D. Lyon (born in Pa. and appointed from D.C.) or Hylan Benton Lyon (Ky.), Walter McFarland (N.Y.), John Sappington Marmaduke (Mo.), Anson Mills (born in Ind. and appointed from Texas), Lyman Mishler (Pa.), Charles Hale Morgan (N.Y.), Leroy Napier (Ga.), Henry C. Parker (La.), Stephen Dodson Ramseur (N.C.), Alanson Merwin Randol (N.Y.), William Wallace Ricketts (Pa.), DeWitt Clinton Rugg (Ind.), William Price Sanders (born in Ky. and appointed from Miss.), Alfred Theophilus Smith (born in Mo. and appointed from Ill.), Charles Bryant Stivers (Ky.), John Jay Sweet (Ill.), James M. Tabor (Miss.), George Daley Talbot (Mo.), Joseph Hancock Taylor (born in Ky. and appointed from Md.), Bryan Morel Thomas (Ga.), George Washington Vanderbilt (N.Y.), Robert White (Tenn.), and John Benson Williams (Mich.) or Solomon Williams (N.C.). The Cadet Record Cards in the United States Military Academy Archives list no Laramie or Johnson during EPA's tenure at West Point. Photographs of a number of the men on EPA's roll call are in

William C. Davis and the editors of Time-Life Books, *Brother Against Brother: The War Begins* (Alexandria, Va., 1983), pp. 142–45.

16. For a full account of Kennedy's activities and death, see Nat Brandt, *The Man Who Tried to Burn New York* (Syracuse, 1986). The officer at Fort Lafayette from whom Kennedy requested a drink was Lt. Col. Martin Burke.

17. Thomas Gregory Baylor of Virginia remained in the U.S. Army during the Civil War and was breveted major, lieutenant colonel, and colonel during Sherman's campaign through Georgia and the Carolinas.

18. Col. Albert Sidney Johnston of the 2nd Cavalry, a native of Kentucky, became the second-ranking general in the Confederate army and was killed at Shiloh. Brigham Young, a Vermonter who succeeded Joseph Smith as head of the Mormons, was the first territorial governor of Utah; in 1857 President James Buchanan replaced Young with Alfred Cumming of Georgia, who served until Abraham Lincoln's inauguration in 1861.

19. James Chatham Duane of New York eventually rose to the rank of brigadier general and in 1886 became chief of engineers in the U.S. Army.

20. George Andrews, a graduate of West Point in 1823 and veteran of the Seminole Wars, retired from the army in 1862.

21. Lewis Addison Armistead was a native of North Carolina; Richard Brooke Garnett and George Edward Pickett were both Virginians.

22. James Lawrence Corley of South Carolina became a lieutenant colonel in the Confederate army.

23. John T. Magruder of Virginia.

24. Francis Theodore Bryan of North Carolina.

25. John Charles Frémont, who won fame as an explorer in the antebellum years, ran as the first Republican presidential candidate in 1856 and had a checkered career as a major general in the Union army during the Civil War.

26. Colonel of the 1st Cavalry in the late 1850s, Edwin Vose Sumner later served as a major general in the Army of the Potomac.

27. Spotted Tail was a member of the Brule Teton Sioux, a tribe that lived on the far western plains.

28. One of EPA's children wrote the following in the margin below this sentence: "Father gave an Indian, who asked him for an American name, the name 'Puddin' Head.'"

29. In the margin opposite this sentence, someone wrote: "B.A.F. took down another version told the children." B.A.F. was Bessie Alexander Ficklen, EPA's eldest child.

30. On 17 May 1858 about 1,000 warriors from several northern tribes attacked a column of 6 officers and 158 men commanded by Maj. Edward Jenner Steptoe of the 9th Infantry, killing six and wounding twelve. On the prelude and aftermath of this episode, see chapter 9 of Robert M. Utley, *Frontiersmen in Blue: The United States Army and the Indian, 1848–1865* (New York, 1967).

31. George Wright, a Vermonter, was colonel of the 9th Infantry in the late 1850s. During the Civil War he commanded the Department of the Pacific.

32. Professor of Civil and Military Engineering and the Art (later Science) of War, Dennis Hart Mahan was the preeminent member of the faculty at West Point in the late antebellum years.

33. John Cunningham Kelton of Pennsylvania.

34. Albert James Myer, a New Yorker, became chief signal officer of the U.S. Army and retired as a brigadier general in 1880.

35. Joseph Gilbert Totten of Connecticut, a colonel at the time he reviewed Myer's system of signals, was chief of engineers in the U.S. Army from 1838 until his death in 1864; Benjamin Huger of South Carolina was a major of ordnance who subsequently became a Confederate major general; Robert Edward Lee was lieutenant colonel of the 2nd Cavalry in the late 1850s.

36. EPA's first wife was Bettie Mason, a Virginian from King George County whom he first met in the summer of 1859. His affectionate name for her was "Miss Teen." She died in 1900, and in October 1901 EPA married Mary Mason, Bettie Mason Alexander's niece.

37. Henry Lane Kendrick, a native of New Hampshire, was Professor of Chemistry, Mineralogy, and Geology at West Point from 1857 to 1880.

38. A second lieutenant of engineers in 1860, Henry Martyn Robert remained in that branch of the service, retiring in 1901 as brigadier general and chief engineer of the army.

39. A body created to investigate obstacles to navigation on the stretch of the Columbia River at The Dalles, where imposing rock formations made portaging necessary.

40. EPA left a blank space at the bottom of this page for a footnote listing other participants in his wedding; however, all he wrote was "Our other bridesmaids and groomsmen were as follows:"

41. Henry Wager Halleck of New York, later one of the principal Union generals during the Civil War.

42. Thomas Lincoln Casey was a New Yorker who became the army's chief of engineers in 1888.

43. A native of New York, Robert W. Weir was Professor of Drawing at West Point from 1846 to 1876.

44. Silas Casey of Rhode Island served as a Federal major general during the Civil War and compiled and edited *Infantry Tactics,* the standard manual in the Union army.

45. EPA added the next two sentences in another ink in the margin.

46. The officers of the 9th Infantry mentioned by EPA include Thomas Cooper English of Pennsylvania, David Bell McKibbin of Pennsylvania, Abraham C. Myers of South Carolina, Daniel Kendig of Pennsylvania, Abraham B. Ragan of Georgia, Joseph Bullock Brown of New York, John Vansant of Virginia, and Anthony Heger, a native of Austria who lived in Pennsylvania. Lewis Cass Hunt of Wisconsin and Robert Nicholson Scott of Tennessee, whom the Casey daughters married, were officers in the 4th Infantry.

47. Lt. Charles M. Fauntleroy, who subsequently served as a lieutenant in the Confederate navy.

48. These Indians lived in the region of the Stikine River, which traverses southern Alaska.

49. Fauntleroy's father was Col. Thomas Turner Fauntleroy of the 1st Dragoons, who resigned in May 1861 and served from 18 May to 8 Oct. 1861 as brigadier general of Virginia Volunteers. See "Diary of Captain Robert E. Park, Twelfth Alabama Regiment," *SHSP,* 2:78, and ibid., "Confederate Register," pp. 40–41. The Navy Register contains no midshipman named Barron for the years 1855-61. Only three officers named Barron, all of whom were Virginians, served in the navy before the Civil War—Commodore James Barron, who killed Stephen Decatur in a duel in 1820 and died in 1851; his brother, Captain Samuel Barron, who died in 1810; and Samuel Barron's son Samuel, who was dismissed from the navy as a captain in May 1861 and subsequently held that rank in the Confederate navy. The second Samuel Barron also had a son named Samuel, who held no appointment in the U.S. Navy but was a lieutenant in the Confederate navy.

It is possible this youngest Samuel Barron was aboard the *Massachusetts* in some capacity (his father was stationed at the Mare Island Navy Yard near San Francisco when war broke out) and that EPA mistakenly thought him a son rather than a nephew of James Barron. See Edward W. Callahan, ed., *List of Officers of the Navy of the United States and of the Marine Corps from 1775 to 1900* (New York, 1901), pp. 43, 190, 621-32.

50. The eleven states of the Confederacy seceded on the following dates: South Carolina, 20 Dec. 1860; Mississippi, 9 Jan. 1861; Florida, 10 Jan. 1861; Alabama, 11 Jan. 1861; Georgia, 19 Jan. 1861; Louisiana, 26 Jan. 1861; Texas, 1 Feb. 1861; Virginia, 17 Apr. 1861; Arkansas, 6 May 1861; Tennessee, 7 May 1861; and North Carolina, 20 May 1861.

51. A sea island off the coast of South Carolina, which EPA owned and where he lived for a time after the death of Bettie Mason Alexander.

52. EPA probably bought a copy of the first American edition of English novelist and detective writer Wilkie Collins's *The Woman in White,* which was published in New York in 1860.

53. James Birdseye McPherson of Ohio.

54. EPA crossed out this sentence and wrote "No" in the margin.

55. EPA crossed out the next seven words.

56. EPA crossed out the remainder of this paragraph.

57. McPherson was killed in the battle of Atlanta on 22 July 1864.

58. EPA wrote the following above this sentence: "Yes you would. It was duty & the place where duty calls you is the safest."

59. Lloyd Tevis and James Ben Ali Haggin, both Kentuckians, were married respectively to Susan G. Sanders and Elizabeth Sanders.

60. Ambrose Everett Burnside, a native of Indiana, saw wide service as a Union major general during the Civil War, including a stint in East Tennessee in 1863 that EPA discusses at length in chapter 13.

61. James Longstreet, born in South Carolina, became the senior corps commander in the Confederate army. Because EPA served under him for most of the war, Longstreet occupies an important place in these reminiscences.

62. The Confederate bombardment began on 12 Apr. 1861; the Federal garrison surrendered on 14 Apr. 1861.

63. A proslavery Kentuckian married to a Georgian, Robert Anderson stayed in the U.S. Army and achieved the rank of brigadier general.

64. Secretary of State William Henry Seward.

65. The question of which side provoked the hostilities at Fort Sumter has spawned a large literature. Two excellent treatments are Kenneth M. Stampp, *And the War Came: The North and the Secession Crisis 1860-61* (Baton Rouge, 1950), and Richard N. Current, *Lincoln and the First Shot* (New York, 1963). A prosouthern interpretation is John S. Tilley, *Lincoln Takes Command* (Chapel Hill, 1941).

66. EPA crossed out this sentence.

67. EPA wrote and crossed out "April 20th" and "May 1st" for dates of departure; he gave no date of arrival in Panama.

68. A native of Canada, James Henry Rion made his antebellum home in South Carolina and during the Civil War attained the rank of lieutenant colonel in command of South Carolina troops.

69. A number of former Confederate officers served abroad after the war, many of them in Egypt. On this subject, see Willam B. Hesseltine and Hazel C. Wolf, *The Blue and Gray on the Nile* (Chicago, 1961).

70. Alexander Cheves Haskell, who figures prominently in these reminiscences, married Alice Van Yeveren Alexander, EPA's youngest sister.

71. Ephraim Elmer Ellsworth of New York won fame before the Civil War as the organizer of the Chicago Zouaves, a crack drill unit. He later raised and took to Washington in May 1861 the Fire Zouaves (11th New York), the regiment to which EPA refers.

72. James W. Jackson was innkeeper at the Marshall House in Alexandria, where he shot Ellsworth.

73. Lord John Russell was British foreign secretary in the spring of 1861.

74. A Kentuckian and veteran of the Mexican War, Simon Bolivar Buckner was a captain in the prewar U.S. Army and became a lieutenant general in the Confederate army.

75. Gustavus Woodson Smith of Kentucky fought in Mexico, taught at West Point before the war, and subsequently served as a Confederate major general and secretary of war.

76. A Kentuckian who became a brigadier general in the Confederate army, Benjamin Hardin Helm was married to Emily Todd, Mary Todd Lincoln's half sister.

77. Leroy Pope Walker of Alabama was secretary of war under Jefferson Davis from 16 Feb. to 16 Sept. 1861.

78. George Gilmer Hull, husband of EPA's sister Mary Clifford Alexander.

79. The younger siblings who greeted EPA in Washington, Georgia, were James Hillhouse Alexander, Marion Brackett Alexander, and Alice Van Yeveren Alexander.

Chapter 2

1. Robert Selden Garnett, a Virginian and cousin of Richard Brooke Garnett, was killed in the engagement at Corrick's Ford on 13 July 1861.

2. William Felix Alexander, the fifth child and oldest son in the family.

3. Joseph Eggleston Johnston of Virginia was the fourth-ranking officer in the Confederate army and commanded a force in the lower Shenandoah Valley.

4. Pierre Gustave Toutant Beauregard, fifth-ranking officer in the Confederate army and a native of Louisiana, commanded the southern army near Manassas Junction, Virginia.

5. Samuel Wragg Ferguson of South Carolina left Beauregard's staff after the battle of Shiloh and subsequently became a brigadier general.

6. Francis Asbury Shoup of Indiana, who rose to the rank of brigadier general in the Confederate army.

7. EPA's fellow staff officers were Thomas Jordan of Virginia, who rose to the rank of brigadier general; William Porcher Miles; James Chesnut, Jr., husband of the famous diarist Mary Boykin Chesnut and later a brigadier general; Alexander Robert Chisolm; Robert Little Brodie of South Carolina; and William Lewis Cabell ("Old Tige") of Virginia, who became a brigadier general and fought in the Trans-Mississippi theater.

8. Brig. Gen. (later Maj. Gen.) David Rumph "Neighbor" Jones of South Carolina.

9. Skipwith Wilmer became a lieutenant and signal officer to Gen. John B. Gordon in July 1864; James Hardeman Stuart, a private in Co. K, 18th Mississippi Infantry in 1861 and later a captain and signal officer to Gen. James E. B. Stuart, was killed at Second Manassas.

10. EPA habitually misspelled Meg Merrilies, sometimes dropping one r and other times adding an extra l; it is not known whether he or the original owner named the animal after the old gypsy woman in Sir Walter Scott's *Guy Mannering; or The Astrologer* (first published in 1815).

11. EPA crossed out the next six words.

12. A brigadier general when he was wounded at Second Manassas, Charles William Field of Kentucky was a major general when the war ended. EPA's first child was Bessie Mason Alexander, born 10 Nov. 1861.

13. EPA misspelled Wilmer McLean's name on this map.

14. Nathan Bedford Forrest, a Tennessean, often is credited with the aphorism that the way to win battles was to "git thar fustest with the mostest men." If he did say something to this effect, he almost certainly employed grammar similar to that in EPA's version.

15. Robert Patterson, a native of Ireland and resident of Pennsylvania, was major general of the Pennsylvania Volunteers and head of the Military Departments of Pennsylvania, Delaware, Maryland, and Washington, D.C.; Irvin McDowell of Ohio commanded the principal Federal army in Virginia; Maj. Gen. (later Lt. Gen.) Theophilus Hunter Holmes of North Carolina served for most of the war in the Trans-Mississippi. In *Military Memoirs,* p. 16, EPA estimated the various strengths as follows: Johnston, 11,000; Patterson, 15,000; Beauregard, 22,000; and McDowell, 35,000. These totals are in line with modern scholarship. He made no mention of Holmes, who had about 3,000 men at Fredericksburg.

16. EPA crossed out the next four words.

17. EPA crossed out the next six paragraphs.

18. Charles H. Tompkins of the 2nd U.S. Cavalry. For his report of the action, see *OR,* 2:60–61.

19. Capt. John Quincy Marr of the Warrenton Rifles (Co. K, 17th Virginia Infantry). For the Confederate side of this affair, see *OR,* 2:61–64.

20. Maxcy Gregg, later a brigadier general, commanded the 1st South Carolina Infantry; Delaware Kemper of Virginia led a battery from Alexandria. Gregg's report of the skirmish is in *OR,* 2:128–30.

21. Brig. Gen. (later Maj. Gen.) Robert Cumming Schenck of Ohio. His report is in *OR,* 2:126–28.

22. EPA first estimated the distance to be 600 yards.

23. The skirmish at Big Bethel took place on 10 June 1861 between the forces of Maj. Gen. Benjamin Franklin Butler, a politician from New Hampshire who became a very controversial figure during the war, and Col. (later Maj. Gen.) John Bankhead Magruder of Virginia. Butler lost seventy-six men, Magruder just eight; their reports are in *OR,* 2:77–103.

24. John Trout Greble, a Pennsylvanian, was a lieutenant in the 2nd Artillery.

25. John W. French of Connecticut was chaplain and Professor of Ethics at the Academy.

26. Theodore Winthrop's books, all published posthumously, included the novels *Cecil Dreeme* (1861) and *John Brent* (1862), together with *The Canoe and the Saddle* (1863) and *Life in the Open Air* (1863).

27. Daniel Harvey Hill of North Carolina, who was colonel of the 1st North Carolina Volunteers at Big Bethel and later became a major general.

28. Henry L. Wyatt was a private in Co. A.

29. Colonel of the 3rd U.S. Cavalry and commander of the Federal 2nd Division at

First Manassas, David Hunter later became a major general. See *OR*, 2:382–87 for the reports on his unit at Manassas. EPA first identified the officer who brought up the Zouaves as William Buel Franklin.

30. Daniel Tyler of Connecticut was brigadier general of Connecticut Volunteers in July 1861.

31. EPA crossed out this sentence.

32. Lt. Samuel Nicoll Benjamin, a New Yorker, took part in the action at Blackburn's Ford as a member of Capt. Romeyn B. Ayres's Co. E, 5th U.S. Artillery.

33. EPA's use of these names for the armies in July 1861 is anachronistic. The Federal army commanded by McDowell did not become known as the Army of the Potomac until later in the summer of 1861; the Confederate army commanded first by Beauregard and then by J. E. Johnston was generally called the Army of the Potomac until the late spring of 1862, when it became known as the Army of Northern Virginia.

34. A native of Pennsylvania who was reared in North Carolina and had three brothers in the Confederate army, John Gibbon was a major general commanding the Federal XXIV Corps at Appomattox.

35. For the reports on the Washington Artillery, see *OR*, 2:465–69.

36. In *Military Memoirs,* p. 25, EPA gives the casualties as sixty-eight killed and wounded for the Confederates and eighty-three killed, wounded, and missing for the Federals.

37. Mustered out on 11 Aug. 1861, Tyler was appointed brigadier general of U.S. Volunteers in March 1862 and served until 6 Apr. 1864.

38. Johnston's staff officer was Lt. James Barroll Washington; Wade Hampton of South Carolina was widely considered to be one of the strongest officers in the Confederacy. On Hampton's strength, see Manly Wade Wellman, *Giant in Gray: A Biography of Wade Hampton of South Carolina* (New York, 1949), p. 39.

39. Heros Von Borcke was a Prussian officer who served on Confederate Gen. J. E. B. Stuart's staff in 1862–63. Six feet four inches tall and muscular, he reputedly carried the largest sword in the southern army.

40. Richard Stoddert Ewell of Virginia, a brigadier general at First Manassas and later a lieutenant general commanding the Second Corps in the Army of Northern Virginia.

41. Col. (later Brig. Gen.) Nathan George "Shanks" Evans, a South Carolinian, commanded a small brigade at First Manassas.

42. EPA first placed the time at 7:00 A.M.

43. On EPA's signal to Evans, see also "The First Signal Message. It Was Sent at Bull Run by Gen. E. P. Alexander, C.S.A.," in *The National Tribune,* 8 Jan. 1903.

44. EPA first wrote "Gen. Franklin" here, then added "or Hunter" in the right margin (see note 29 above).

45. Johnston's report that notes the roles of EPA, Gen. Barnard Elliott Bee of South Carolina, Col. Francis Stebbins Bartow of Georgia, and Thomas Jonathan "Stonewall" Jackson of Virginia is in *OR*, 2:470–79; Beauregard's report mentioning EPA is in ibid., pp. 484–504.

46. Casualties (killed and wounded only) for these regiments are given in *OR*, 2:570, as 153 for the 7th Georgia and 200 for the 8th Georgia.

47. William Tecumseh Sherman of Ohio, who was a brigadier general of volunteers at First Manassas.

48. Col. Robert Taylor Preston, a Virginian, and his 28th Virginia were in Col. (later Brig. Gen.) Philip St. George Cocke's brigade.

49. EPA first wrote "nine o'clock."

50. EPA crossed out the next six words.

51. William Henry Chase Whiting of Mississippi was a major at First Manassas and later a major general.

52. Brig. Gen. (later Gen.) Edmund Kirby Smith of Florida, who subsequently commanded the Trans-Mississippi Department.

53. Capt. Charles Griffin of the 5th U.S. Artillery, an Ohioan, who rose to the rank of major general by the close of the war.

54. EPA crossed out the rest of this sentence.

55. Virginian James Lawson Kemper, colonel of the 7th Virginia Infantry at First Manassas and later a major general.

56. Delaware Kemper and the Alexandria (Virginia) Artillery.

57. Joseph Brevard Kershaw of South Carolina, colonel of the 2nd South Carolina Infantry at First Manassas and subsequently a major general.

58. Ellerbe Boggan Crawford Cash, a native of North Carolina, whose unit was the 8th South Carolina Infantry.

59. Cash killed William McCreight Shannon on 5 July 1880; Shannon had organized a company of the 7th South Carolina Cavalry during the war.

60. Cash evidently had heard that Sen. Lafayette Sabine Foster of Connecticut was also on the field.

61. A Republican congressman from New York, Alfred Ely told of his experiences in *Journal of Alfred Ely, A Prisoner of War in Richmond* (New York, 1862).

62. Lt. Presley O. Craig of the 2nd U.S. Artillery was the son of Col. Henry Knox Craig. EPA wrote in the margin opposite the anecdote about Craig: "No. Near Blackburn's Ford." Craig was killed near Blackburn's Ford rather than at Cub Run Bridge.

63. EPA first wrote "fully for over a day."

64. EPA offered no estimate in *Military Memoirs* of the number of troops immediately available for pursuit, probably because it was impossible when he wrote, as it is now, to determine the figure with any precision. One careful student estimates that about 17,000 of Johnston's and Beauregard's soldiers did most of the fighting on the southern side during battle. William C. Davis, *Battle at Bull Run: A History of the First Major Campaign of the Civil War* (Garden City, 1977), pp. 245–46.

65. Brig. Gen. Milledge Luke Bonham of South Carolina.

66. EPA first wrote "line—a small force [of]."

67. EPA crossed out the rest of this paragraph.

68. Judith Carter Henry, whose house stood at the center of the fighting on Henry House Hill.

69. Capt. James Brewerton Ricketts of the 1st U.S. Artillery, a New Yorker who became a major general.

70. Maj. Chatham Roberdeau Wheat, a native of Virginia who lived in Tennessee for many years and was associated with Louisiana before and during the war.

71. Robert Clinton Hill, whose eyes EPA first described as blue.

72. EPA first wrote "between 9 & 10 o'clock."

73. EPA crossed out the rest of this paragraph.

74. EPA crossed out the rest of this paragraph.

75. Col. (later Maj. Gen.) James Ewell Brown "Jeb" Stuart of Virginia, who commanded the 1st Virginia Cavalry at First Manassas.

76. EPA left a blank space here, at the top of which he wrote, "The following mis-

cellaneous items may be of interest." After the blank space he began his account of events during the fall and winter following Manassas.

Chapter 3

1. Samuel Jones, a Virginian, replaced Braxton Bragg as commander at Pensacola, Florida, and eventually became a major general.

2. Francis John Thomas of Virginia.

3. EPA added this sentence in another ink.

4. George Duffey was associated with the Virginia volunteer forces for twenty years before the war and, according to his own testimony, rose to the rank of lieutenant colonel of artillery. However, R. E. Lee spoke of him as "Major Duffey" of Alexandria in endorsing his application for a commission in April 1862, and EPA always called him "Major Duffey," which suggests it was not widely known that he had been a lieutenant colonel. He served without formal appointment in the Confederate army until 20 May 1862, when he received a commission as lieutenant; his captaincy came on 23 Dec. 1862, and it was at that rank that he surrendered at Appomattox. See Compiled Service Records of Confederate Generals and Staff Officers, Microcopy 331, National Archives and Records Service.

5. EPA crossed out the words in parentheses. Duffey used no middle initial; however, in 1928 a woman claiming to be a descendant asked for the service record of a major of artillery named George Hurd Duffey, and the 1850 census for Alexandria listed a George H. Duffey.

6. Clement Carrington McPhail later served as an ordnance officer in North Carolina. Thomas Mann Randolph Talcott, who first served as an aide-de-camp to Lee and eventually rose to the rank of colonel of engineers, was the son of Lee's old friend Col. Andrew Talcott (also an engineer) and Harriet Randolph Hackley Talcott. Harriet Talcott was a striking woman whom Lee called "The Beautiful Talcott."

7. Capt. (later Maj.) William Norris had served on the staff of John Bankhead Magruder in May and June 1862.

8. John Lane was the son of Joseph Lane, former senator from Oregon and a staunch friend of the South. His command was Battery E of the Sumter (Georgia) Battalion of artillery. Robert Garlick Hill Kean, head of the Confederate Bureau of War, mentioned the experiment with rockets in his diary entry for 29 Oct. 1861: "The rocket stand was tried yesterday. The inventor, Captain Duffy, says it acted well. The fragments are lying about the ordnance yard. It was blown to atoms by a rocket bursting in it; he says the rocket was too old and defective and that it is a success. I could improve on his contrivance a good deal I think." Edward Younger, ed., *Inside the Confederate Government: The Diary of Robert Garlick Hill Kean* (New York, 1957), p. 14.

9. James Ryder Randall, a native of Baltimore teaching at Poydras College in Louisiana, wrote the poem on 23 Apr. 1861 after learning that a friend had been killed in the clash between the 6th Massachusetts Infantry and citizens of Baltimore on 19 Apr. 1861.

10. The Carys, who were cousins of Constance Cary (Mrs. Burton Harrison), set the poem to the music of "Lauriger Horatius," which had almost exactly the same tune as "Tannenbaum, O Tannenbaum." See Richard B. Harwell, *Confederate Music* (Chapel Hill, 1950), pp. 52–54, and Mrs. Harrison, *Recollections Grave and Gay* (New York, 1911), pp. 57–60.

11. In the battle of Ball's Bluff, which took place on 21 Oct. 1861 on the west bank of the Potomac River near Leesburg, Virginia, Col. Edward Dickinson Baker led a portion of Brig. Gen. Charles Pomeroy Stone's Federal division against a small Confederate force under Col. (later Brig. Gen.) Nathan G. "Shanks" Evans. Walter Hanson Jenifer of Maryland commanded the 8th Virginia Cavalry in the action. The death of Baker, a close friend of Abraham Lincoln, caused wide political repercussions. On the battle and its aftermath, see Kim Bernard Holien, *Battle at Ball's Bluff* (Orange, Va., 1985).

12. Appreciative of EPA's assistance on the works, Hill asserted in January 1862 that he required more help: "I need another Engineer who has tact at governing men & making them work. Can such an officer be sent here? The Fort will be finished at present rates in about seven years. . . . Any effort of yours to send us an *energetic* Engineer and to forward guns *promptly* will be most gratefully appreciated." Transcript of D. H. Hill to EPA, 4 Jan. 1862, Petersburg National Battlefield.

13. The doctors probably were Talcott Eliason, surgeon of the 1st Virginia Cavalry, and Augustine Smith Mason; the engineer was Capt. William Alexander Eliason, a native of Washington, D.C.

14. Here EPA presumably wanted the reader to see the location of Dr. Marsteller's house.

15. This is the end of the first of the two ledger books in which EPA wrote the opening chapters of *Fighting for the Confederacy*. The second ledger book begins under the heading "Fall & Winter after Bull Run continued." Pasted in the manuscript at this point are two clippings—one is from the *New York Tribune* of 30 May 1897 noting EPA's diplomatic errand to Nicaragua; the other, a *Baltimore Sun* obituary for EPA's close friend Frank Huger, was reprinted on 14 June 1897 in an unnamed newspaper. Opposite the opening page of the second ledger book EPA wrote: "'Is that a Man?' said the Lion. 'No,' said the Fox, 'but it used to be.' Grimm"; and "Which sayin lies in the happlication of it. Capt. Cuttler."

16. EPA wrote "Ravenel" above this line in another ink.

17. This text is from an undated and unidentified clipping EPA pasted in the manuscript. Edward Pliny Bryan died in service in Sept. 1864 as a captain in the Signal Corps.

18. Rose O'Neal Greenhow, a native of Washington, D.C.

19. Maj. Gen. George Brinton McClellan of Pennsylvania, who commanded the Army of the Potomac.

20. In early 1862 Federal officers interrogated Mrs. Morris and examined her papers, reporting that as Augusta Heath Morris she had married John Francis Mason in Paris on 20 Jan. 1854. The officers reported further that she went by the names of Mrs. Morris, Mrs. Mason, and Miss Ada. M. Hewitt. While incarcerated in Old Capitol Prison, Mrs. Morris wrote to "Dr. J. F. Mason" in care of Maj. Thomas Grimké Rhett, a South Carolinian serving as Johnston's assistant adjutant general. See *OR*, ser. 2, 2:1346–51.

21. No Dr. Wyman appears in *OR* among the names of those arrested as Confederate spies in late 1861 and early 1862. Mrs. Morris mentioned a Mr. Wycoff, who passed information to General Johnston. *OR*, ser. 2, 2:1350.

22. For documents relating to these arrests, see *OR*, ser. 2, 2:561–77 (Greenhow), 1315–21 (Baxley), and 1346–51 (Morris).

23. Lt. Col. (later Col.) Thomas Taylor Munford of Virginia, whose regiment was the 2nd Virginia Cavalry.

24. Lt. Gen. Winfield Scott, a Virginian, was general-in-chief of the U.S. Army until his retirement on 31 Oct. 1861.

25. In *Military Memoirs,* p. 59, EPA gives no figures for the fall of 1861, but states that in late February 1862 McClellan had 185,420 men and Johnston 47,617. These estimates include southern troops near Fredericksburg and Federals and Confederates in the Shenandoah Valley. Johnston's total was probably nearer 53,000.

26. EPA wrote "S or H" in the margin opposite Rhett's name, where he left space for a middle initial; Rhett's middle name was Grimké, and EPA may have confused him with Col. Thomas Smith Rhett, another South Carolinian, who served in the Confederate artillery. Both Rhetts had been officers in the prewar U.S. Army.

27. EPA's comrades on Johnston's staff were Arthur Pendleton Mason, a Virginian who later served on the staffs of R. E. Lee and John Bell Hood; James Barroll Washington; Archibald H. Cole; James Lawrence Corley of South Carolina; Robert Granderson Cole of Virginia; Samuel Choppin, later a medical officer on the staffs of P. G. T. Beauregard and Earl Van Dorn; and Robert Little Brodie of South Carolina.

28. Alexander Cheves Haskell, John Cheves Haskell, and Joseph Cheves Haskell. On this remarkable family, see Louise Haskell Daly, *Alexander Cheves Haskell: The Portrait of a Man* (Norwood, Mass., 1934) and John Haskell, *The Haskell Memoirs: The Personal Narrative of a Confederate Officer,* ed. Gilbert E. Govan and James W. Livingood (New York, 1960).

29. Maj. (later Brig. Gen.) Walter Husted Stevens, a New Yorker who fought for the Confederacy.

30. William Felix Alexander, the fifth child and oldest son.

31. In the margin opposite this sentence EPA wrote, "Was this told in Vol. I."

32. In the margin below this sentence EPA wrote, "Wasn't it Michigan. What did it lose." He may have been referring to the action on 6 Apr. of the 5th Wisconsin, which, together with the 6th Maine, crossed a dam and made a temporary lodgement in the Confederate line. See *OR,* 11:308–10. More probably, he meant the action of 16 Apr. at Dam No. 1 involving the 3rd Vermont, which he mentioned in *Military Memoirs,* p. 65.

33. "The Half Way house" appears in very faint writing above this part of the text.

34. Lt. Orlando G. Wagner, who was two years behind EPA at West Point.

35. Thomas Kinloch Fauntleroy, who began the war as a member of Co. D, 1st Virginia Cavalry.

36. Dr. Gaines's house, called Powhite, was situated on a knoll a short distance below the mill on Powhite Creek.

37. In *Military Memoirs,* p. 66, EPA states that the column averaged less than one mile per hour on this march but gives no mileage.

38. EPA crossed out the next seven words.

39. Adm. Raphael Semmes was a native of Maryland.

40. After the contest, Semmes accused Capt. John A. Winslow of the *Kearsarge* of "cheating" by secretly converting his vessel into an ironclad.

41. James Dunwody Bulloch, *The Secret Service of the Confederate States in Europe; or, How the Confederate Cruisers Were Equipped,* 2 vols. (New York, 1884); John Johnson, *The Defense of Charleston Harbor, Including Fort Sumter and the Adjacent Islands, 1863–1865* (Charleston, 1890).

42. John Anthony Gardner Davis; the assassination took place in November 1840.

43. Paul Jones Semmes was mortally wounded at Gettysburg on 2 July and died on 10 July. His superior was Maj. Gen. Lafayette McLaws, a fellow Georgian.

44. EPA incorrectly wrote the 5th in his manuscript.

45. Weems commanded the 10th Georgia.

46. EPA wrote "put in facts" and left a small blank space here. See Longstreet's report in *OR,* 11, pt. 1:566, for details about the captured Federal guns.

47. Brig. Gen. (later Maj. Gen.) Winfield Scott Hancock of Pennsylvania, whose command was the 1st Brigade of the 2nd Division of the IV Corps. See *OR,* 11, pt. 1:533–43 for Hancock's long report.

48. EPA wrote "some detail" and left a small blank space here. Hill's report is in *OR,* 11, pt. 1:601–6.

49. Benjamin Stoddert Ewell was president of William & Mary in 1854–61 and 1865–88; during the war he served as a colonel on the staff of Joseph E. Johnston.

50. This allusion is to the engagement of Eltham's Landing on 7 May—not 6 May as EPA states—in which some of Gustavus Woodson Smith's troops attacked Federals under William B. Franklin. Brig. Gen. (later Gen.) John Bell Hood, a native of Kentucky, played a conspicuous role in the fight.

51. EPA first wrote "Charles City Court House"; the distance from Barhamsville to New Kent Court House was probably between eleven and twelve miles.

52. At the top of this page EPA wrote, "4th skirmish, 5th Battle Wmsburg, 6th Eltham's Landing."

53. EPA left a blank page for a map of Seven Pines but did not include one; the map in the text [Figure 12] is from *Military Memoirs,* p. 76.

54. Johnston planned to fight on 4 Apr., but delays prevented his opening the battle until 6 Apr.

55. Maj. Gen. (later Lt. Gen.) Leonidas Polk, a native of North Carolina.

56. Maj. Gen. Don Carlos Buell of Ohio, commander of the Army of the Ohio.

57. For a harsher view of Longstreet's failure at Seven Pines, see chapter 5 of H. J. Eckenrode and Bryan Conrad's *James Longstreet: Lee's War Horse* (1936; reprint, Chapel Hill, 1986).

58. EPA crossed out the first four words of this sentence.

59. For the official reports see *OR,* 11, pt. 1:933–35 (Johnston), 939–41 (Longstreet), 943–46 (D. H. Hill), 989–94 (Smith). See also Gustavus Woodson Smith, *The Battle of Seven Pines* (New York, 1891).

60. Col. Guilford Dudley Bailey of the 1st New York Artillery.

61. EPA first wrote that communications were cut off for "at least 36 hours."

62. EPA wrote "How many" opposite this sentence. Sumner's II Corps had 17,412 men present for duty on 31 May.

63. W. H. C. Whiting commanded a division made up of his own brigade and those of John Bell Hood and Wade Hampton.

64. EPA first wrote that the shell "knocked" Johnston to the ground.

65. EPA wrote this sentence at the bottom of the page and indicated with an asterisk where it should be inserted.

66. The members of Lee's staff were Maj. (later Lt. Col.) Walter Herron Taylor, Maj. (later Lt. Col.) Charles Marshall, Col. (later Brig. Gen.) Armistead Lindsey Long, and Maj. (later Lt. Col.) Charles Scott Venable, all of Virginia.

67. Col. Joseph Christmas Ives, who was married to Cora Semmes, sister of Confederate senator Thomas Jenkins Semmes of Louisiana. Ives served on R. E. Lee's staff before becoming an aide to Jefferson Davis.

68. John Buchanan Floyd of Virginia, former governor of his state (1848–52) and secretary of war under James Buchanan (1857–60), and Henry A. Wise of Virginia,

former member of Congress and governor of Virginia (1856–60), were brigadier generals.

69. John Moncure Daniel, a native of Virginia, was widely known for the unbridled invective he often employed as editor of the *Examiner* 1847–53 and 1861–65.

70. Brig. Gen. (later Maj. Gen.) Fitz John Porter of New Hampshire commanded the Federal V Corps.

71. Maj. Gen. Joseph Hooker of Massachusetts, commander of the Army of the Potomac in the spring and early summer of 1863.

Chapter 4

1. EPA did not include a map; the maps in this chapter are taken from *Military Memoirs*, pp. 120 (Figure 13) and 126 (Figure 14).

2. Maj. Gen. Nathaniel Prentiss Banks of Massachusetts commanded the Department of the Shenandoah.

3. Jackson defeated Banks at the battle of First Winchester on 25 May 1862.

4. McDowell sent Irish-born Brig. Gen. James Shields and the 1st Division of the Department of the Rappahannock to reinforce Banks. Frémont commanded the Mountain Department.

5. Jackson defeated Frémont's force at Cross Keys on 8 June and Shields's at Port Republic on 9 June.

6. EPA left two blank pages for the order and one for a map; the order is in *OR, 11*, pt. 2:498–99. EPA reproduced part of it in *Military Memoirs*, p. 113.

7. Maj. Gen. (later Lt. Gen.) Ambrose Powell Hill of Virginia, who commanded the six-brigade Light Division.

8. See Fitzhugh Lee, *General Lee* (New York, 1894), chapters 8 and 12. Lee was R. E. Lee's nephew and a major general of cavalry.

9. At the end of the second ledger book, among other miscellaneous notes, EPA included the following testimony on this question: "Letter from Walter Taylor, Aug. 26, 1902, says 'Jackson's army was at Frederick's Hall on Jun. 22, 1862. . . . Old Jack was one day behind time—. . . . Nothing was said of it in a general way, although there was quiet talk of it at the time, because we were so elated at raising the siege & there was no disposition to find fault.'"

10. EPA deleted the rest of this sentence.

11. Throughout the remainder of his reminiscences EPA quotes from various articles that first appeared in *The Century Magazine* and later were collected in *B&L*. In Greytown, EPA had a one-volume abridgement entitled *Battles and Leaders of the Civil War: The Century War Book, People's Pictorial Edition* (New York, 1894), which he called "The Century War Book." His transcriptions invariably differ from the originals in matters of punctuation. This quotation is from D. H. Hill, "McClellan's Change of Base and Malvern Hill," *B&L*, 2:388–89.

12. Hill quoted from Robert Lewis Dabney, *Life and Campaigns of Lieut.-Gen. Thomas J. Jackson, (Stonewall Jackson.)* (New York, 1866), p. 466. Below this quotation EPA wrote, "Maj. Dabney had been upon Jackson's staff."

13. Hill, "McClellan's Change of Base," p. 389.

14. Ibid. (quotation by Hill). EPA left a blank space, at the top of which he

wrote, "leave for Franklin's account"; he doubtless meant to quote from William Buel Franklin, "Rear-Guard Fighting During the Change of Base," *B&L*, 2:366–82. Brig. Gen. (later Maj. Gen.) Franklin, a Pennsylvanian, commanded the VI Corps during the Seven Days.

15. This distance cannot be given with any precision because it is not clear what part of Jackson's journey EPA meant to include in the total.

16. EPA wrote "Extracts from reports of hour of march" at the bottom of the page and left a blank space. For the reports, see *OR*, 11, pt. 2:552 (Jackson), 562 (Whiting), 605 (Ewell).

17. In *Military Memoirs*, p. 116, EPA states that Jackson faced a march of fifteen to sixteen miles from Ashland to the enemy's position.

18. EPA replaced "practically" with "almost."

19. EPA crossed out the next two words.

20. EPA crossed out the rest of the sentence.

21. Brig. Gen. Roswell Sabine Ripley was a native of Ohio who married into a Charleston, South Carolina, family. His brigade contained the 1st and 3rd North Carolina and 44th and 48th Georgia infantries; the 1st North Carolina and 44th Georgia suffered severely in this assault. Ripley's report is in *OR*, 11, pt. 2:647–48.

22. EPA left a blank space but added no details. The various reports are in *OR*, 11, pt. 2.

23. EPA first began this sentence, "During the night Fitz John retired."

24. Lt. Henry C. Heise of Co. C, 1st South Carolina Infantry. See *OR*, 11, pt. 2:847, 861.

25. Fitz John Porter, "Hanover Court House and Gaines's Mill," *B&L*, 2:331, 333.

26. Brig. Gen. (later Maj. Gen.) Henry Warner Slocum of New York commanded the 1st Division in the VI Corps; Brig. Gen. (later Maj. Gen.) William Henry French of Maryland commanded the 3rd Brigade of the 1st Division in the II Corps; Brig. Gen. Thomas Francis Meagher, a native of Ireland, led the 2nd Brigade of the 1st Division of the II Corps.

27. Porter, "Gaines's Mill," pp. 336–37.

28. Capt. Augustus P. Martin of Battery C, Massachusetts Light Artillery, and Brig. Gen. (later Maj. Gen.) George Webb Morell, commander of the 1st Division of the V Corps.

29. Hill, "McClellan's Change of Base," p. 395.

30. EPA put a question mark opposite this sentence—perhaps because he failed to mention David R. Jones's division.

31. Brig. Gen. William Nelson Pendleton of Virginia, chief of artillery in Lee's army.

32. William E. Birkhimer, *Historical Sketch of the Organization, Administration, Materiel and Tactics of the Artillery, United States Army* (Washington, D.C., 1884), p. 84.

33. Brig. Gen. Charles Sidney Winder, a Marylander in charge of the Stonewall Brigade, led Jackson's division while Jackson exercised wing command. In *Military Memoirs*, p. 134, EPA places Jackson's strength at about 25,000.

34. EPA first wrote "passed in rear of all the rest of our army."

35. Hill, "McClellan's Change of Base," pp. 383, 385.

36. Maj. Gen. Samuel Peter Heintzelman of Pennsylvania commanded the Federal III Corps.

37. EPA substituted "immediately" for "promptly."

38. Col. (later Brig. Gen.) Micah Jenkins of South Carolina left his Palmetto Sharp-

shooters to lead Brig. Gen. (later Lt. Gen.) Richard Heron Anderson's brigade; the latter took Longstreet's division while Longstreet exercised wing command.

39. Brig. Gen. George Archibald McCall's division of Pennsylvania Reserves was in the Federal V Corps; Brig. Gen. (later Maj. Gen.) Cadmus Marcellus Wilcox, an Alabamian, and Brig. Gen. (later Maj. Gen.) Charles William Field, a native of Kentucky, commanded brigades respectively in Longstreet's and A. P. Hill's divisions.

40. EPA left a space here and wrote "for details" in the margin.

41. EPA first wrote "6 batteries comprising some 28 guns."

42. EPA substituted "several" for "many."

43. EPA first wrote, "one or two others went."

44. EPA substituted "rich" for "great" and "seemed easily possible" for "was within reach" in this sentence.

45. EPA first wrote "at this moment perhaps."

46. William Swinton, *Campaigns of the Army of the Potomac: A Critical History of Operations in Virginia, Maryland and Pennsylvania, from the Commencement to the Close of the War 1861–5* (New York, 1866).

47. EPA crossed out the rest of this sentence.

48. EPA crossed out the last two words of this sentence.

49. Fitz John Porter, "The Battle of Malvern Hill," *B&L,* 2:409.

50. EPA crossed out "such" and the last twelve words of this sentence.

51. Hill, "McClellan's Change of Base," pp. 390–91.

52. Pendleton's report is in *OR,* 11, pt. 2:533–37.

53. Porter, "Malvern Hill," p. 421.

54. William J. Johnson was a Virginian who served from 1861 to 1864 under J. E. B. Stuart, most of the time as a commissary officer.

55. Porter, "Malvern Hill," pp. 416–17, 419.

56. Brig. Gen. (later Maj. Gen.) Darius Nash Couch of New York, commander of the 1st Division of the IV Corps.

57. EPA crossed out the next three words.

58. EPA first began this sentence with "Next morning the enemy were gone of course," crossed it out, and used nearly the same language in the second paragraph below.

59. Brig. Gen. George Burgwyn Anderson of North Carolina, Brig. Gen. (later Maj. Gen.) Robert Emmett Rodes of Virginia, Brig. Gen. Samuel Garland, Jr., of Virginia, and Col. (later Brig. Gen.) Alfred Holt Colquitt of Georgia.

60. Hill, "McClellan's Change of Base," p. 394.

61. Brig. Gen. (later Maj. Gen.) William Mahone of Virginia, Brig. Gen. (later Maj. Gen.) Ambrose Ransom "Rans" Wright of Georgia, Col. (later Brig. Gen.) William Barksdale of Tennessee (but long associated with Mississippi), Brig. Gen. (later Maj. Gen.) Robert Ransom, Jr., of North Carolina, Brig. Gen. Howell Cobb of Georgia, and Brig. Gen. George Thomas "Tige" Anderson of Georgia.

62. EPA left a space here, at the top of which he wrote, "Leave for any further details, captured guns &c." See chapter 9 of *Military Memoirs* for more information on the fighting of 1 July.

63. EPA's reference is to the action on 3 July at Evelington Heights. On this controversy, see Douglas Southall Freeman, *Lee's Lieutenants: A Study In Command,* 3 vols. (New York, 1942–44), 1:639–43.

64. For background on the use of balloons, see Frederick Stansbury Haydon, *Aero-*

nautics in the Union and Confederate Armies, with a Survey of Military Aeronautics Prior to 1861 (Baltimore, 1941).

65. EPA substituted "copies" for "these codes."

66. James Deshler was a brigadier general when he was killed on 20 Sept. 1863.

67. Lt. (later Comdr.) Hunter Davidson, who subsequently played a prominent role in placing torpedoes (mines) in the James River below Richmond. See his "Electrical Torpedoes as a System of Defence," *SHSP*, 2:1–6.

68. There is no formal report in the OR of EPA's activities with the balloon. For the report of the commander of the *Maratanza*, which mentions EPA's balloon, see U.S. Naval War Records Office, *Official Records of the Union and Confederate Navies in the War of the Rebellion*, 30 vols. (Washington, D.C., 1894–1922), 7:543. Albert J. Myer, EPA's old mentor, humorously recounted the episode involving the capture of the *Teaser* in a letter to his wife: "Major Alexander was on board and had to swim ashore to escape—He had with him a balloon made of ladies silk dresses which we captured. He wept on reaching shore & exclaimed 'What will the ladies say?'" Myer to Mrs. Myer, 17 July 1862, Albert J. Myer Papers, Division of Manuscripts, Library of Congress (quoted in E. P. Alexander, *Military Memoirs of a Confederate*, ed. T. Harry Williams [Bloomington, Ind., 1962], p. 626, note for pp. 172–73).

69. EPA did not attach the letter.

70. John Bell Hood, *Advance and Retreat: Personal Experiences in the United States & Confederate States Armies* (1880; reprint, Bloomington, Ind., 1959), pp. 28–29.

71. EPA first wrote "Baltimore"; Wheat was born in Alexandria.

72. The Regiment of Voltigeurs and Foot Riflemen was organized in 1847 for service in the war with Mexico.

73. During the 1850s, William Walker of Tennessee led filibustering expeditions into Lower California, Sonora, and Nicaragua. Wheat accompanied Walker to Nicaragua.

74. On Wheat and the Louisiana troops in Virginia, see Terry L. Jones, *Lee's Tigers: The Louisiana Infantry in the Army of Northern Virginia* (Baton Rouge, 1987).

75. EPA was mistaken here—Wheat was six feet, four inches tall.

76. Brig. Gen. Gilbert Moxley Sorrel of Georgia.

77. Sorrel did not mention the conversation with Wheat in his *Recollections of a Confederate Staff Officer* (1905; reprint, Jackson, Tenn., 1958). Jones, *Lee's Tigers*, p. 104, asserts that Wheat was killed instantly and made no dramatic last statement. Following this paragraph EPA wrote "The strength & the casualties of the two armies I give from" and "guns captured &c.," but he supplied no figures (on p. 194 of the second ledger book he made a few notes relating to casualties). In *Military Memoirs*, p. 174, he places Confederate killed, wounded, and missing during the Seven Days at 20,168 and Federal killed and wounded at 9,796. McClellan also lost 6,053 missing.

78. The Seven Days began with a minor engagement on 25 June at Oak Grove or King's School House and progressed through Mechanicsville (also known as Beaver Dam Creek and Ellerson's Mill) on 26 June, Gaines's Mill (also known as First Cold Harbor) on 27 June, skirmishing at Garnett's and Golding's Farms on 28 June, Savage Station on 29 June, Frayser's Farm (also known as Glendale or White Oak Swamp) on 30 June, and Malvern Hill on 1 July.

79. EPA first wrote "a brigade or two" and added a marginal note to "find out." Magruder reported that Kershaw's and Semmes's brigades, together with two regiments of Barksdale's, bore the brunt of the fighting. *OR*, 11, pt. 2:664–66.

80. EPA crossed out the rest of this sentence.

Chapter 5

1. EPA placed an asterisk here and wrote at the bottom of the page, "I forgot to leave space. See page 190 [of the second ledger book]." His transcription of the order, which is in *OR*, 11, pt. 3:634, is not exact.

2. A month after Malvern Hill, Confederate chief of ordnance Josiah Gorgas wrote EPA that there were "still large quantities of Ord- and other stores lying about on the battle fields." Gorgas directed EPA to have the ordnance officer from each division request details from various regiments to comb the fields for useful material, including the *"scattered cartridges"* that had been dropped by both armies. "I pray your earnest attention to this," concluded Gorgas, "not a cartridge should be lost which can be saved." Transcript of Josiah Gorgas to EPA, 1 Aug. 1862, Petersburg National Battlefield.

3. Maj. Gen. John Pope, a native of Kentucky, commanded the new Army of Virginia.

4. James William Abert of New Jersey, who advanced from second lieutenant to captain of topographical engineers between 1847 and 1861.

5. Capt. George H. Derby of Massachusetts, an officer in the topographical engineers, published satirical pieces in newspapers and magazines under the pen name John Phoenix. His stories were collected in *Phoenixiana* (1856) and *The Squibob Papers* (1865).

6. EPA apparently credited "Hope Told a Flattering Tale" to Dublin-born Thomas Moore (1779–1852), a prolific writer and collector of songs who was considered the national bard of Ireland in his day. In fact, Giovanni Paisiello composed the music for his opera *La Molinara* (1793), and Peter Pindar (John Wolcott) wrote the lyrics.

7. EPA first wrote "by flowing artesian wells."

8. Pope's General Orders No. 1 was a straightforward announcement that he had taken command of the soldiers under Frémont, Banks, and McDowell. EPA probably had in mind Pope's address to his officers and men dated 14 July 1862, which included the bombastic statement, "I have come to you from the West, where we have always seen the backs of our enemies; from an army whose business it has been to seek the adversary and to beat him when he was found; whose policy has been attack and not defense." For both documents, see *OR*, 12, pt. 3:436–37, 473–74.

9. EPA replaced "point out" with "state briefly."

10. EPA crossed out the rest of this sentence. Halleck's book was *Elements of Military Art and Science* (New York, 1846).

11. EPA first wrote "hold the centre of a considerable circle & compel the enemy to occupy a large part of the circumference he would possess."

12. EPA crossed out "most excellent" and "of all others in the United States" in this sentence.

13. For a good discussion of this subject, see chapters 7–8 of Herman Hattaway and Archer Jones, *How the North Won: A Military History of the Civil War* (Urbana, Ill., 1983).

14. EPA wrote "Greytown, Nicaragua" in the margin opposite this passage.

15. EPA first estimated 40,000 without breaking down the total by Federal army; he later wrote the individual strengths above each commander's name and changed the number to 47,000.

16. Here EPA crossed out "& a division, Cox's, from the Kanawha" and wrote above it "not until after battle."

17. EPA crossed out "anyway."

18. Maj. (later Lt. Col.) Richard Snowden Andrews, a native of Washington, D.C., was with the 1st Maryland Light Artillery.

19. Brig. Gen. (later Maj. Gen.) John George Walker of Missouri.

20. James Longstreet, "Our March Against Pope," *B&L,* 2:515.

21. Brig. Gen. William Booth Taliaferro of Virginia.

22. EPA placed the totals for brigades and batteries at the bottom of the page and marked them for insertion at some point in this sentence.

23. Brig. Gen. Beverly Holcombe Robertson of Virginia.

24. EPA first wrote "pushed on & before night."

25. EPA first gave the distance as thirty miles.

26. EPA first wrote "sure that Jackson would be his meat."

27. EPA replaced "2nd" with "3rd." Longstreet began his march on the afternoon of 26 Aug., and the head of his column reached Thoroughfare Gap about 3 P.M. on 28 Aug. The movement thus consisted of about two days of marching spread over three calendar days.

28. Brig. Gen. George William Taylor, a native of New Jersey commanding the 1st New Jersey Brigade.

29. EPA first wrote 800 yards.

30. It is also possible that Hill went to Centreville because Jackson failed to tell him that he was concentrating his divisions at Groveton. This paragraph marks the end of the second ledger book of reminiscences. On the last two pages EPA wrote miscellaneous names and troop strengths.

31. EPA first began this sentence "There is perhaps room for criticism of Jackson's."

32. EPA placed a question mark in the margin opposite this line. Pope's army consisted of Sigel's I Corps (three divisions and one independent brigade), McDowell's III Corps (three divisions), Heintzelman's III Corps of the Army of the Potomac (two divisions), Porter's V Corps of the Army of the Potomac (two divisions), and Reno's IX Corps (two divisions). See John Hennessy, *Historical Report on the Troop Movements for the Second Battle of Manassas, August 28 Through August 30, 1862* (Denver, 1985), pp. 525–36.

33. Brig. Gen. Rufus King of New York commanded the 1st Division of McDowell's III Corps.

34. EPA placed a question mark in the margin opposite this line. It is unlikely that on the evening of 28 Aug. even the men on Jackson's right heard anything from Thoroughfare Gap, which was roughly ten miles away. John H. Worsham of the 21st Virginia Infantry later wrote that the first news of Longstreet's arrival swept through Jackson's ranks on the afternoon of 29 Aug.: "This put new life into Jackson's men, who had heard nothing of Longstreet." Worsham, *One of Jackson's Foot Cavalry* (1912; reprint, Jackson, Tenn., 1964), p. 78.

35. Maj. Gen. Jesse Lee Reno of Ohio, who led the IX Corps while Ambrose E. Burnside exercised wing command.

36. Brig. Gen. (later Maj. Gen.) John Fulton Reynolds, a Pennsylvanian, commanded a division of Pennsylvania Reserves attached to the III Corps.

37. Brig. Gen. William Edward Starke of Virginia took command of Jackson's division when W. B. Taliaferro was wounded at Groveton on 28 Aug. Col. (later Brig. Gen.) Leroy Augustus Stafford of Louisiana replaced Starke at the head of the brigade.

38. Col. (later Lt. Gen.) Stephen Dill Lee of South Carolina commanded the battalion; Maj. Delaware Kemper was his subordinate.

39. EPA left a blank page for this information but supplied no figures. In *Military Memoirs,* p. 219, he gives the casualties as 9,112 for Lee and 14,462 for Pope.

40. EPA crossed out the next two words.

41. EPA crossed out this sentence.

Chapter 6

1. George B. McClellan, "From the Peninsula to Antietam," *B&L,* 2:549–50.

2. John Cunningham Kelton of Pennsylvania was McClellan's assistant adjutant general.

3. EPA first wrote Sept. 5.

4. Early American editions of Sir Samuel Ferguson's *Father Tom and the Pope; or, A Night at the Vatican* were published in Baltimore (1858) and Philadelphia (1861); "Caricature and Caricaturists" was in *Harper's New Monthly Magazine* 24 (April 1862): 586–607.

5. John Greenleaf Whittier published "Barbara Frietchie" in *In War Time, and Other Poems* (Boston, 1864).

6. Capt. (later Maj.) William Watts Parker of Virginia was a physician before and after the war. For an excellent study of his unit, see Robert K. Krick, *Parker's Virginia Battery C.S.A.* (Berryville, Va., 1975).

7. EPA deleted this sentence.

8. The fighting discussed here and in the following two paragraphs was the battle of South Mountain, which included action at Crampton's, Fox's, and Turner's gaps. EPA was at Turner's Gap.

9. EPA's "old tower" was a stone monument built by the citizens of Boonsboro, Maryland, in the 1820s to honor George Washington. Already in ruins in September 1862, it was rebuilt in the 1880s and again in the 1930s and currently is maintained by the state of Maryland.

10. EPA first wrote "6th" here. The VI Corps was engaged at Crampton's Gap, south of the position at Turner's Gap whence EPA watched the I Corps deploy.

11. Capt. (later Maj.) John Lane of Georgia. See chapter 3, note 8, above.

12. The 13th Pennsylvania Reserves under Col. Hugh W. McNeil.

13. Samuel Garland, Jr., was killed at Fox's Gap.

14. Col. Benjamin Franklin "Grimes" Davis, a native of Alabama who remained loyal to the Union, commanded the 8th New York Cavalry (EPA first identified this officer as Gen. Gregg).

15. EPA first wrote "captured some small & unimportant train which was following us."

16. Col. Dixon Stansbury Miles of Maryland.

17. EPA first wrote "Ewell's division under Lawton."

18. EPA first wrote "forty guns."

19. EPA crossed out "perhaps."

20. EPA first wrote "about 80,000."

21. EPA wrote "1 or 2" in the margin.

22. EPA crossed out a sentence here that read: "Across on [the] Maryland side the road turned up the towpath, between [the] canal & [the] river, & went back opposite the town before the canal could be crossed, the only bridge being there." In the margin opposite this sentence he wrote "No! Canal was bridged near ford before retreat."

23. On John Brown and Dr. Mason, see Oswald Garrison Villard, *John Brown, 1800–1859: A Biography Fifty Years After* (Boston, 1910), pp. 489, 495. According to Villard's evidence, Mason insisted that Brown was not seriously wounded.

24. EPA crossed out the rest of this paragraph.

25. EPA first began this sentence "So getting my orders from Gen. Lee in a hurry."

26. EPA first wrote "10 miles."

27. EPA replaced "a few men" with "Thomas's brigade." Col. (later Brig. Gen.) Edward Lloyd Thomas of Georgia and his men missed the battle of Antietam because of their duty in Harpers Ferry.

28. The original ending for this sentence was: "ammunition for some four pounders, or light [illegible] pieces of some sort, which helped make up the total of forty pieces surrendered in all."

29. EPA crossed out the next three sentences.

30. Maj. Gen. Ambrose Everett Burnside, a native of Indiana, commander of the IX Corps (and temporarily in charge of the I Corps as well at Antietam).

31. Maj. Gen. Joseph King Fenno Mansfield of Connecticut.

32. Brig. Gen. (later Maj. Gen.) Alfred Pleasonton, a native of Washington, D.C., commanded a division of cavalry.

33. James Longstreet, "The Invasion of Maryland," *B&L*, 2:668–70.

34. Col. (later Brig. Gen.) John Rogers Cooke, a native of Missouri.

35. EPA wrote in the margin opposite this sentence "Read his report." Pendleton's report is in *OR*, 19, pt. 1:829–35.

36. EPA crossed out "no" and replaced it with "a very small." Pendleton had under his command about 300 infantrymen.

37. EPA left a blank space but provided no figures. In *Military Memoirs*, pp. 273–75, he gives Lee's losses for the entire Maryland campaign as 13,609 and McClellan's as 27,767 (including 12,347 captured at Harpers Ferry).

38. Confederate generals killed or mortally wounded included Samuel Garland, Jr., George B. Anderson, William E. Starke, and Lawrence O'Bryan Branch; those wounded were Richard H. Anderson, Robert Toombs, Ambrose R. Wright, Roswell S. Ripley, and Alexander R. Lawton.

Chapter 7

1. Viscount Garnet Joseph Wolseley, a lieutenant colonel in the British army, was ordered to Canada at the time of the *Trent* affair in 1861 and subsequently made his way to the Confederacy. For Wolseley's writings about his time with the Confederate army, see *The American Civil War: An English View,* ed. James A. Rawley (Charlottesville, 1964).

2. Belle Boyd, a native of Virginia, spent some time in Old Capitol Prison as a result of her activities.

3. EPA first wrote "of no value."

4. Dixon Barnes was described by one witness as a "quiet gentleman with a long white beard." EPA's friend A. C. Haskell wrote of Daniel Heyward Hamilton: "The Brigade had no confidence in him, for he had never shown any capacity." See Robert K. Krick, *Lee's Colonels: A Biographical Register of the Field Officers of the Army of Northern Virginia,* 2nd ed. (Dayton, Ohio, 1984), pp. 40, 149.

5. Brig. Gens. Lawrence O'Bryan Branch of North Carolina and James Jay Archer of Maryland.

6. George V. Moody of the Madison Light Artillery (a hybrid battery that included men from both Louisiana and Mississippi, and accordingly sometimes was identified as from one or the other of those states), Tyler Calhoun Jordan of the Bedford (Virginia) Artillery, and Pichegru Woolfolk, Jr., of the Ashland (Virginia) Artillery.

7. EPA replaced "him" with "S. D. Lee."

8. EPA crossed out "every where."

9. Lt. Col. Briscoe Gerard Baldwin of Virginia, who graduated from the Virginia Military Institute in 1848 and lived in Texas after the war. See *Confederate Veteran*, 8:370, for an obituary.

10. EPA crossed out "my nominee."

11. EPA's batteries and their commanders, in addition to those given in note 6 above, were: the Brooks (South Carolina) Light Artillery of Andrew Burnet Rhett, John Lewis Eubank's Virginia Light Artillery (Bath Battery), and William Watts Parker's Company Virginia Light Artillery (see chapter 6, note 6).

12. On 27 Apr. 1870, during a trial that attracted a packed house, the gallery in the Virginia Supreme Court chambers in the State Capitol collapsed, killing 63 and injuring more than 250. For an account of the disaster, see W. Asbury Christian, *Richmond: Her Past and Present* (Richmond, 1912), pp. 315–20.

13. Dwight Lyman Moody of Massachusetts, among the most famous nineteenth-century American evangelists, was a missionary in Chicago in 1860.

14. Lt. George E. Saville of Virginia, whom Parker commended for bravery at Gettysburg, died in April 1864 following a brief illness.

15. Osmond B. Taylor took command of the battery after Eubank resigned on 28 Mar. 1863. EPA was mistaken in thinking Eubank subsequently served in the Confederate Congress; Eubank did serve two terms in the Virginia Senate after the war, which might explain EPA's confusion.

16. Maj. Gen. George Armstrong Custer of Ohio, who commanded the 3rd Division of P. H. Sheridan's Cavalry Corps during the Appomattox campaign.

17. Stephen Capers Gilbert and William W. Fickling were South Carolinians. On the problem of finding a successor to Rhett, see Robert K. Krick, *Parker's Virginia Battery, C.S.A.* (Berryville, Va., 1975), pp. 109, 367 n. 2, which argues that the difficulty arose because EPA did not trust the ranking officer in the battery.

18. John Donnell Smith had served originally in Thomas Jefferson Page's Magruder (Virginia) Light Artillery.

19. EPA crossed out the rest of this sentence.

20. J. R. C. Lewis of Virginia, who early in 1863 requested duty "more congenial with his former service" (the marines) and was transferred to the Department of the Gulf. See *OR,* 25, pt. 2:640.

21. EPA's low rank in the fall of 1862 probably dictated that his adjutant was a lieutenant of artillery; Lieutenant Smith might have been Tucker H. Smith of the Fluvanna (Virginia) Artillery, who was relieved of duty with his battery on 4 Oct. 1862 and later returned to it, suggesting a possible stint as a staff officer.

22. Henry Vincent Gray and Aristides Monteiro were Virginians. Gray also saw service with the 13th Louisiana, 21st Mississippi, and at hospitals in Richmond (see *Confederate Veteran*, 18:455, for a sketch of him); Monteiro later served with John S.

Mosby and wrote *War Reminiscences, by the Surgeon of Mosby's Command* (Richmond, 1890).

23. Poindexter was listed as a first lieutenant on the roll of Moody's battery when it surrendered at Appomattox. See "Paroles of the Army of Northern Virginia . . . Surrendered at Appomattox C.H., Va., April 9, 1865," *SHSP*, 15:13, 51.

Chapter 8

1. Lee knew Burnside was moving toward Fredericksburg by the afternoon of 17 Nov. See *OR*, 21:1016.

2. The George Guest House was located two miles west of Fredericksburg on the south side of the Orange Turnpike/Plank Road, where it stood until 1985 when it was razed to make way for a shopping center.

3. John L. Marye's substantial house, called Brompton, stood atop Marye's Heights just west of Fredericksburg; it remains there today, having undergone only slight architectural changes. John L. Stansbury's home, also known as Snowden, was located north of Brompton on Marye's Heights; fire destroyed it in 1926. J. Horace Lacy's house was Chatham, situated immediately east of Fredericksburg on Stafford Heights; now owned by the National Park Service, it serves as headquarters for Fredericksburg and Spotsylvania National Military Park.

4. Capt. (later Lt. Col.) Samuel Richards Johnston of Virginia.

5. Maj. Gen. George Edward Pickett of Virginia.

6. James Birge Walton had commanded the Washington Artillery, the oldest military organization in the state of Louisiana, since 1857. EPA erred in describing the Washington Artillery as containing three companies; at Fredericksburg and throughout most of the war it had four companies (plus a fifth that served in the West).

7. In "The Battle of Fredericksburg," *B&L*, 3:79, Longstreet recounted the following exchange with EPA: "General E. P. Alexander . . . had been placing the guns, and in going over the field with him before the battle, I noticed an idle cannon. I suggested that he place it so as to aid in covering the plain in front of Marye's Hill. He answered: 'General, we cover that ground now so well that we will comb it as with a fine-tooth comb. A chicken could not live on that field when we open on it.'"

8. EPA first wrote "three." Barksdale's regiments were the 13th, 17th, 18th, and 21st Mississippi.

9. See Darius N. Couch, "Sumner's 'Right Grand Division,'" *B&L*, 3:108–9. Contrary to EPA's statement, two civilians were killed by the shelling.

10. EPA crossed out "single."

11. The Confederates were also prepared to fire into Fredericksburg. Longstreet ordered EPA to get "the bearing and range of the streets of the town. The enemy passing through them will give you an opportunity to rake him which you will of course take." Typescript of an unsigned note from Longstreet's assistant adjutant general (probably Gilbert Moxley Sorrel) to EPA, 11 Dec. 1862, Petersburg National Battlefield. EPA did not mention these instructions in his report of the battle, which is in *OR*, 21:575–77.

12. EPA crossed out this sentence and wrote at the bottom of the page: "PS I have come to doubt the truth of this incident which was told me at the time by Roy Mason, himself, but I never heard it mentioned again by *any one*. It is inherently exceedingly improbable. Some of the 7 would only have been wounded."

13. EPA left a small blank space here in which he wrote, "Get temperatures record from Weather Bureau." The Georgetown, D.C., weather station, some fifty miles north of Fredericksburg, recorded lows of twenty-four degrees on 11 Dec., twenty-eight degrees on 12 Dec., thirty-four degrees on 13 Dec., and forty degrees on 14 Dec. (the readings were taken at 7:00 A.M.).

14. The map of the battlefield at Fredericksburg (Figure 20) is from *Military Memoirs*, p. 301.

15. Maj. (posthumous Lt. Col.) John Pelham of Alabama commanded Pelham's Battery of Horse Artillery.

16. EPA wrote "(See appendix page ____)" but failed to include the text of Lee's dispatch. See Lee to Secretary of War James A. Seddon, 14 Dec. 1862, in *OR*, 21:546.

17. Pelham was killed in the cavalry action at Kelly's Ford on 17 Mar. 1863.

18. EPA crossed out "very."

19. Maj. Gen. George Gordon Meade, born in Spain and appointed to West Point from Pennsylvania, commanded the 3rd Division of the I Corps.

20. Brig. Gen. (later Maj. Gen.) David Bell Birney, a native of Alabama, commanded the 1st Division of the III Corps; Gibbon led the 2nd Division of the I Corps.

21. Brig. Gen. Thomas Reade Rootes Cobb of Georgia.

22. EPA placed a question mark in the margin opposite this passage. The brigades were not in a single line along the foot of the hill. See McLaws's report in *OR*, 21:578–82.

23. Capt. Victor Maurin's Donaldsonville (Louisiana) Battery was one of four attached to R. H. Anderson's division; Col. Henry Coalter Cabell's battalion of four batteries was attached to McLaws's division.

24. EPA wrote in the margin, "Put in a footnote about Franklin, Tenn., & fact no Federal generals killed"—an allusion to the assaults mounted by the Army of Tennessee against entrenched Federal defenders at the battle of Franklin on 30 Nov. 1864. See note 37 below.

25. EPA first wrote "a hundred yards."

26. EPA wrote in the margin, "Get report & give abstract." For Meagher's report, see *OR*, 21:240–46.

27. John Walter Fairfax of Virginia, Longstreet's assistant adjutant general.

28. Brig. Gen. (later Maj. Gen.) Andrew Atkinson Humphreys of Pennsylvania, who commanded the 3rd Division of the V Corps.

29. EPA placed an asterisk here and added the next five sentences on a separate page. The quotation is in Couch, "Sumner's 'Right Grand Division,'" p. 115.

30. Brig. Gen. (later Maj. Gen.) George Washington Getty, a native of Washington, D.C., who commanded the 3rd Division of the IX Corps.

31. James A. Logwood, whom EPA mentioned in his report of the battle.

32. Couch, "Sumner's 'Right Grand Division,'" p. 116.

33. The brick tanyard that occupied so much of EPA's attention straddled what is now the intersection of William and Littlepage streets in Fredericksburg.

34. John Worthington Ames, "In Front of the Stone Wall at Fredericksburg," *B&L*, 3:122–25. A captain with the 11th U.S. Infantry at Fredericksburg, Ames was later a brevet brigadier general.

35. In *Military Memoirs*, p. 313, EPA breaks down the losses for each army into three parts—Federal left attack, 3,415 Confederate and 4,447 Federal; Federal center skirmish, 305 Confederate and 383 Federal; Federal right attack, 1,589 Confederate and 7,817 Federal. Total 5,309 Confederate and 12,647 Federal. Confederate losses by category

were 595 killed, 4,061 wounded, and 653 missing. Confederate Brig. Gen. T. R. R. Cobb was killed, Brig. Gen. Maxcy Gregg mortally wounded, and Brig. Gens. William Dorsey Pender of North Carolina and John Rogers Cooke wounded.

36. Using EPA's figures from *Military Memoirs* (combining the Federal casualties from their right and center), the totals are 4,447 on Jackson's front and 8,200 on Longstreet's. Federal Brig. Gen. Conrad Feger Jackson of Pennsylvania was killed and Brig. Gen. George Dashiell Bayard of New York mortally wounded.

37. At Franklin, approximately 20,000 Confederate infantry attacked across nearly two miles of open ground against a greater number of entrenched Federals supported by ample artillery. Southern casualties were 1,750 killed, 4,500 wounded, and 702 taken prisoner—more than one-third of their total strength. Six Confederate generals were killed or mortally wounded, another 5 wounded, and 1 captured. See James Lee McDonough and Thomas L. Connelly, *Five Tragic Hours: The Battle of Franklin* (Knoxville, 1983).

38. Capt. Edward P. Lawton.

39. John Reuben Thompson of Virginia, a poet and editor of the *Southern Literary Messenger* and other publications, humorously dedicated "Richmond is a Hard Road to Travel" to Ambrose E. Burnside.

40. Phoebe Yates Pember was a matron at Chimborazo Hospital in Richmond. Her *A Southern Woman's Story: Life in Confederate Richmond* (1879; reprint, Jackson, Tenn., 1959) is one of the classic personal accounts of the war.

Chapter 9

1. Chesterfield Station.

2. George W. Hobson of the Amherst (Virginia) Artillery was killed on 9 July 1864 at the battle of the Monocacy.

3. Bessie Mason Alexander; Pendleton was an Episcopal priest.

4. EPA placed an asterisk here and added the next six sentences at the bottom of the page.

5. EPA crossed out "stray."

6. On 29 Apr. 1863 the secretary of war instructed Longstreet to rejoin Lee, and by 12 May Longstreet had established his headquarters near Fredericksburg. See *OR*, 18:1057.

7. James Howard.

8. William Wilson, whose real name was Daniel Cavenaugh.

9. A tobacco warehouse converted for use as a prison.

10. Capt. (later Maj.) Henry Edward Young.

11. EPA crossed out the next four words.

12. For a brief article on this episode, see Robert K. Krick, "The Confederate Deserter: 'D' on the Hip," *Virginia Country's Civil War Vol. III* (Middleburg, Va., 1985).

13. John Brown Gordon of Georgia, who subsequently became a major general.

Chapter 10

1. EPA first began this sentence "On one of the last days of April 1863."

2. Maj. Gen. John Sedgwick of New Hampshire, whose own command was the VI Corps.

3. EPA first wrote "the 30th."

4. When EPA corrected the date above (see note 3), he neglected to make a similar change here, where he left "the 30th."

5. EPA first wrote "4 A.M."

6. This sentence originally continued as follows: "& we encamped in the vicinity that night, & studied out all the secrets of the ground that afternoon & the next morning until about noon." EPA crossed out this passage and wrote in the margin, "No, it was May 1st & that very morning Lee & Jackson came up & we advanced that afternoon."

7. EPA crossed out the next eight sentences.

8. EPA wrote in the margin, "Was it exactly there?" His guns were a short distance west of the point where the roads diverged.

9. The Orange Turnpike, which ran from Fredericksburg to Orange Court House, and the newer Orange Plank Road, which roughly paralleled the Pike a short distance to the south.

10. EPA wrote J. Wilcox Brown but meant Lt. John Thompson Brown (no relation to Col. John Thompson Brown, another Virginia artillerist).

11. EPA crossed out the next fifteen words.

12. Col. (later Lt. Gen.) Nelson Appleton Miles of Massachusetts, who commanded the 61st New York Infantry at Chancellorsville.

13. EPA first began this paragraph with the following sentence fragment: "We encamped that night very close to Genls. Lee & Jackson, who encamped together, & I can recall vividly seeing them sitting."

14. EPA first wrote "ten miles." The actual distance was about twelve miles.

15. Stapleton Crutchfield ranked first in the graduating class of 1855 at the Virginia Military Institute and later taught mathematics there, thus making him both student and colleague of Jackson.

16. EPA is confused here—Jackson continued past the Plank Road to the Turnpike, astride which he formed for his assault. His consultation with Fitzhugh Lee had convinced him to proceed to the Turnpike. See Fitzhugh Lee, "Chancellorsville—Address of General Fitzhugh Lee before the Virginia Division, A.N.V. Association, October 29, 1879," *SHSP*, 7:571–72.

17. Maj. Gen. George Stoneman of New York.

18. Brig. Gen. Raleigh Edward Colston, a native of France.

19. EPA first wrote "a little after five o'clock." Most accounts place the time at about 5:15 P.M.

20. Maj. Gen. Oliver Otis Howard of Maine.

21. Alfred Pleasonton, "The Successes and Failures of Chancellorsville," *B&L*, 3:179. Pleasonton's writings are highly unreliable, a fact of which EPA was almost certainly unaware. EPA's acceptance of Pleasonton's account of the action at Hazel Grove on May 2 was a major error.

22. Capt. James Keith Boswell of Virginia, Jackson's chief engineer, and William E. Cunliffe of Mississippi.

23. Robert Eggleston Wilbourn of Mississippi, whose detailed account of the episode is in *SHSP*, 6:266–75.

24. EPA crossed out the rest of this sentence and the next seven sentences.

25. Benjamin Watkins Leigh, whose account of Jackson's wounding is in *SHSP*, 6:230–34.

26. EPA relied heavily on Smith's "Stonewall Jackson's Last Battle," *B&L*, 3:203–14.

27. Reuben Lindsay Walker of Virginia, later a brigadier general, commanded the artillery attached to A. P. Hill's division.

28. EPA first wrote "cut our man's left leg off at the knee seemingly as cleanly as an axe could have done & then."

29. EPA quoted the last two lines of the final quatrain of Robert Southey's ballad, "The King of the Crocodiles: Part II." See *The Poetical Works of Robert Southey* (New York, 1839), p. 457.

30. EPA wrote at the bottom of the page, "Tell which corps." Federal casualties were: I Corps, 299; II Corps, 1,925; III Corps, 4,119; V Corps, 700; VI Corps, 4,610; XI Corps, 2,412; and XII Corps, 2,824.

31. EPA wrote below this sentence, "Was Hooker drunk?" On this much-debated question, see Walter H. Hebert, *Fighting Joe Hooker* (Indianapolis, 1944), p. 225. Unpublished testimony suggests that Hooker had been drinking. Washington Augustus Roebling, a staff officer present at Chancellorsville with Hooker (and later the builder of the Brooklyn Bridge), wrote privately that Hooker was drunk. Robert Goldthwaite Carter, a soldier who walked sentry outside Hooker's tent, also insisted that the general was drunk. In his copy of Theodore A. Dodge's *The Campaign of Chancellorsville* (Boston, 1881), Carter wrote that Lee's division of forces at Chancellorsville "would and ought to have proved a disastrous one but for Hooker's whiskey soaked brain." Some of Carter's other marginalia described "a prolonged debauch," "maudlin" behavior brought on by drinking, and "an over drunken brain." For this information on Roebling and Carter, the editor is indebted to Robert K. Krick, chief historian of the Fredericksburg and Spotsylvania National Military Park. Carter also accused Hooker of drunkenness in his *Four Brothers in Blue* (1913; reprint, Austin, 1979), pp. 271–72.

32. EPA wrote J. Wilcox Brown but meant Col. John Thompson Brown, who commanded a battalion of six batteries in the Second Corps artillery reserve (see note 10 above).

33. EPA crossed out the rest of this sentence.

34. EPA first wrote "slowly done."

35. EPA crossed out the next three words.

36. EPA crossed out the rest of this sentence.

37. EPA crossed out the next three words.

38. EPA first gave the Federal casualties as 1,955 killed, 11,160 wounded, 11,311 missing—total 25,027 (his addition was off by 401). Below his table he wrote, "&c. put in Lee & my battalion &c." In *Military Memoirs*, pp. 360–61, he gives Lee's casualties as 1,683 killed, 9,277 wounded, and 2,196 missing—total 13,156; his battalion losses as 6 killed, 35 wounded, and 21 missing—total 62. On the next page of the manuscript he left a large space in which he wrote, "woods catching fire & burning wounded." The woods caught fire at several places during the battle, adding to the horror of the scene. See, for example, David Gregg McIntosh, "The Campaign of Chancellorsville," *SHSP*, 40:89.

Chapter 11

1. EPA placed an asterisk here but provided no further text. For Longstreet's discussion of this question, see his "Lee's Invasion of Pennsylvania," *B&L*, 3:244–49.

2. EPA crossed out the rest of this paragraph. The fullest treatment of the controversy surrounding Longstreet's role in the Gettysburg campaign is in William Garrett Piston,

Lee's Tarnished Lieutenant: James Longstreet and His Place in Southern History (Athens, Ga., 1987).

3. The twins were Edward Porter II and Lucy Roy Alexander.

4. Lt. James Woolfolk and Sergt. Edmund T. Woolfolk were in the Ashland Artillery (Edmund had been in the 30th Virginia Infantry until 13 Oct. 1862); Lt. (later Capt.) Clarence L. Woolfolk, whose unit was the 47th Virginia Infantry, was killed in action on 3 June 1864.

5. Maj. Mathis Winston Henry of Kentucky.

6. EPA placed question marks in the margin opposite "8 miles" and "8,000 men." Stuart's cavalry numbered slightly more than 9,500.

7. Benjamin Franklin Davis, a native of Alabama, who commanded the 8th New York Cavalry.

8. Henry Coalter Cabell of Virginia.

9. Maj. (later Brig. Gen.) James Dearing of Virginia.

10. EPA placed a question mark in the margin opposite "9." William Miller Owen's *In Camp and Battle with the Washington Artillery of New Orleans* (1885; reprint, Gaithersburg, Md., n.d. [1983]), p. 249, states that Walton's battalion had 10 guns.

11. At some point EPA showed this chapter to John Donnell Smith, formerly captain of the Bedford (Virginia) Light Artillery, who wrote the following in the margin here: "This man was given in my charge at Millwood, and I delivered him to the provost guard of Pickett's division as it descended the western slope of Snicker's Gap. J. D. Smith."

12. Maj. Gen. Robert Huston Milroy of Indiana, who commanded a small Federal force in the Lower Shenandoah Valley.

13. Perhaps a joking reference to Maj. John Alexander Harman, Stonewall Jackson's profane and widely known quartermaster.

14. EPA left a space here in which he wrote, "Get some details of Pickett's movements." For details on Pickett's march from Culpeper to Gettysburg, see James Dearing's report in *OR*, 27, pt. 2:387–88 (Dearing's battalion accompanied Pickett's division).

15. The commanders left behind by Stuart were Beverly H. Robertson, Brig. Gen. William Edmondson "Grumble" Jones of Virginia, Brig. Gen. Albert Gallatin Jenkins, a native of what is now West Virginia, and Lt. Col. Elijah Viers White of Maryland.

16. Lee's reports of the campaign are in *OR*, 27, pt. 2:305–11 and 313–25 (see especially pp. 306–7, 316). Stuart's report is in ibid., pp. 687–710. On Stuart's receiving permission from Lee to make his swing around the Army of the Potomac, EPA almost certainly relied upon John S. Mosby, "The Confederate Cavalry in the Gettysburg Campaign," *B&L*, 3:251–52.

17. A derisive comment many an infantryman made to passing cavalrymen. See Douglas Southall Freeman, *Lee's Lieutenants: A Study in Command,* 3 vols. (New York, 1942–44), 3:4–5, for an amusing example.

18. EPA crossed out the next three words.

19. EPA's quotation of the passage in Owen, *Washington Artillery,* p. 241 is not exact.

20. EPA placed a question mark in the margin opposite "five miles." The distance was nearly double his estimate.

21. EPA wrote above this sentence, "Heywood or Seabrook?"; however, there was no officer of either name in Rhett's battery. The commissioned officers for the war—other than Rhett, Fickling, and Gilbert—were Lts. William Elliott and J. F. Moorer and 2nd Lts. Edmund H. O'Neil and Edward L. Purse.

22. John Donnell Smith wrote in the margin opposite this passage, "The corre-

spondence between Capts. Woolfolk & Moody was shown to me by the former during the midday halt of the battalion before reaching the battlefield. J.D.S."

23. EPA wrote this sentence in the margin. Meade assumed control of the Army of the Potomac at 3:00 A.M. on 28 June. That morning the Federal corps were marching to concentrate at Frederick, Maryland, and were positioned as follows: I, III, and XI Corps near Middletown, Maryland (less than ten miles west of Frederick); II Corps near Barnesville, Maryland (nearly twenty miles south of Frederick); VI Corps near Poolesville, Maryland (some five miles behind the II Corps); XII Corps between Knoxville and Jefferson, Maryland (less than fifteen miles southwest of Frederick); and the V Corps near Frederick. Depending on the route, it was another thirty-five miles or more from Frederick to Gettysburg.

24. Maj. Gen. Henry Heth of Virginia.

25. Maj. Gen William Dorsey Pender of North Carolina.

26. EPA placed a question mark in the margin opposite this sentence. A. P. Hill did not anticipate serious trouble. See his report in *OR*, 27, pt. 2:606–7.

27. Brig. Gen. John Buford, a native of Kentucky, commanded the 1st Division of the Cavalry Corps.

28. EPA placed question marks in the margin opposite these figures. Buford had just under 3,000 men; the I Corps had about 9,400 and the XI (not XII) Corps about 9,600.

29. Heth and Pender had about 15,000 men between them and outnumbered the Federal I Corps, which was in their front.

30. EPA placed a question mark opposite this sentence. The brigade of Brig. Gen. Joseph Robert Davis of Mississippi suffered heavily, though there are no exact returns for the fight on 1 July.

31. EPA placed a question mark in the margin opposite this figure. Rodes's division numbered just more than 8,000 men, which together with Heth's and Pender's outnumbered the Federal I and XI Corps.

32. Brig. Gen. Alfred Iverson, Jr., of Georgia.

33. EPA placed a question mark in the margin opposite this sentence, which contains no apparent error.

34. EPA placed a question mark opposite these figures. The Confederates captured 3,655 Federals.

35. EPA placed a question mark in the margin opposite "some 2 miles." The distance is about two and one-half miles.

36. EPA placed a question mark in the margin opposite "some 2,000 yards." This distance is impossible to state with precision because EPA does not give a clear southeastern terminus.

37. EPA placed a question mark opposite "4½ miles." The actual Federal line covered about 3½ miles.

38. EPA placed a question mark in the margin opposite this sentence. Erasures suggest that he made corrections (Howard left Col. Orlando Smith's brigade and Capt. Michael Wiedrich's battery on the hill).

39. Maj. Gen. Edward "Allegheny" Johnson of Virginia.

40. See *OR*, 27, pt. 2:308. EPA's transcription is not precise.

41. EPA was correct in doubting that such an order was issued. For a full discussion of the alleged "sunrise attack order," see Harry W. Pfanz, *Gettysburg—The Second Day* (Chapel Hill, 1987).

42. EPA crossed out the next two words.

43. EPA placed a question mark in the margin opposite "15 miles."

44. Walton did feel "overslaughed," and in the postwar years jealously insisted that he had been First Corps chief of artillery at Gettysburg. See "Letter from Colonel J. B. Walton," *SHSP*, 5:47–52, and "Letter from General Longstreet," ibid., pp. 52–53.

45. EPA's detour turned right, not left, beyond any reasonable doubt. See Pfanz, *Gettysburg—The Second Day*, pp. 117–18.

46. EPA placed a question mark opposite this sentence.

47. Maj. Gen. Gouverneur Kemble Warren of New York was chief engineer in the Army of the Potomac.

48. Brig. Gen. Evander McIvor Law of South Carolina.

49. EPA left a large space here, at the top of which he wrote, "find how much was due to this & then finish discussion"; however, he added nothing more on this subject. Longstreet's report in *OR*, 27, pt. 2:358, mentions the wait for Law but no request that Lee allow it; Lee's report in ibid., pp. 318–19, does not mention the wait for Law to come up. Longstreet first claimed that he received permission from Lee to delay the attack until Law arrived in "The Campaign of Gettysburg," a piece published on 3 Nov. 1877 in the *Philadelphia Weekly Times* and subsequently reprinted as "Lee in Pennsylvania" in *The Annals of the War, Written by Leading Participants North and South* (Philadelphia, 1879), pp. 414–46, and in *SHSP*, 5:54–85.

50. Willoughby Run.

51. EPA crossed out this sentence.

52. On this subject, see Richard A. Sauers, "Gettysburg: The Meade-Sickles Controversy," *Civil War History* 26 (September 1980): 197–217.

53. EPA placed a question mark in the margin opposite "500 yards."

54. EPA placed a question mark in the margin opposite the last part of this sentence—probably because of his estimate of 500 yards. In *Military Memoirs*, p. 395, he gives the ranges at the Peach Orchard as "generally between 500 and 700 yards."

55. EPA first wrote "about 75 men."

56. Henry J. Hunt, "The Second Day at Gettysburg," *B&L*, 3:310.

57. EPA placed a question mark in the margin opposite "1,000 yards." This estimate is probably too low.

58. EPA placed a question mark in the margin opposite this sentence. Law did succeed Hood; Hood did not lose his arm, though it was crippled.

59. Joseph B. Kershaw, "Kershaw's Brigade at Gettysburg," *B&L*, 3:335.

60. John Russell Young, a prominent journalist of the nineteenth century, was among the most popular northern war correspondents. EPA placed question marks in the margin opposite Captain Young's name here and below. The guide almost certainly was Jesse Bowman Young, a veteran of the battle who lived in or near Gettysburg for many years after the war and studied the battle and battlefield intensively. See his *The Battle of Gettysburg: A Comprehensive Narrative* (New York, 1913), pp. 3–5.

61. EPA placed a question mark in the margin opposite this passage. Erasures suggest that he made corrections.

62. Brig. Gen. (later Maj. Gen.) Thomas Howard Ruger of New York commanded the 1st Division of the XII Corps at Gettysburg.

63. EPA placed a question mark in the margin opposite this sentence. Erasures suggest that he made corrections (Heth's and Pender's divisions were not heavily engaged on 2 July).

64. See *OR* 27, pt. 2:351–52. EPA's transcription is not precise; he intended to include

---

also an excerpt in which Pendleton described sixty-two guns deployed "in a sweeping curve of about a mile."

65. EPA crossed out the next five words.

66. Maj. Gen. Daniel Butterfield of New York, Meade's chief of staff at Gettysburg, who later became a bitter enemy of his former commander.

67. Dahlgren, a native of New York, was the son of Adm. John Adolph Bernard Dahlgren and an aide-de-camp to Meade.

68. Maj. (later Lt. Col.) Charles Richardson, a Virginian, commanded nine guns of Col. John J. Garnett's battalion of the Third Corps on 2–3 July.

69. EPA did not mention a Catlett in his report of the battle (see *OR*, 27, pt. 2:429–31). Arthur C. Catlett was a private in the Bedford Artillery—the only man bearing that surname in any of the six batteries in EPA's battalion.

70. EPA mistakenly began this sentence with "Do," which has been deleted.

71. EPA's reference probably was to Thomas W. Osborn, "The Artillery at Gettysburg," *Philadelphia Weekly Times,* 31 May 1879.

72. EPA placed a question mark in the margin opposite "1,400 yards."

73. EPA first wrote "not less favorable."

74. Brig. Gen. James Johnston Pettigrew of North Carolina.

75. Henry H. Carlton of the Troup (Georgia) Battery.

76. Lt. (later Capt.) Frederick Morgan Colston of Maryland.

77. The exchange of messages between EPA and Longstreet relating to the assault on 3 July, together with EPA's later notes to Pickett (all with slight variations of punctuation and spelling), are also in "Letter from General E. P. Alexander, late Chief of Artillery First Corps, A. N. V.," *SHSP,* 4:97–111; E. Porter Alexander, "The Great Charge and Artillery Fighting at Gettysburg," *B&L,* 3:357–68; and *Military Memoirs,* pp. 421–23.

78. EPA first began this sentence, "I was talking at the moment to Gen. A. R. Wright of Ga. when."

79. EPA crossed out "infernal."

80. Maj. Gen. Isaac Ridgeway Trimble, a native of Virginia long identified with Maryland, commanded a part of Pender's division because the latter had been wounded.

81. Wilcox's brigade was in R. H. Anderson's division.

82. EPA placed a question mark in the margin opposite these numbers. Though figures for individual commands vary somewhat from those given by EPA, Edwin B. Coddington's careful *The Gettysburg Campaign: A Study in Command* (New York, 1968), pp. 462, 777 n. 114, places the strength of the attacking column at "about 13,500"—almost exactly the same as EPA's estimate.

83. Brig. Gen. (later Maj. Gen.) John White Geary of Pennsylvania, who commanded the 2nd Division of the XII Corps.

84. Henry J. Hunt, "The Third Day at Gettysburg," *B&L,* 3:371–73.

85. EPA first wrote "or more or less."

86. EPA crossed out the last two words of this sentence.

87. Col. (later Brig. Gen.) Birkett Davenport Fry, a native of what is now West Virginia, commanded Archer's brigade after the latter's capture on 1 July.

88. EPA left a space, at the top of which he wrote, "Quote account Webb's battery's losing 27 horses out of 36 in ten minutes." See EPA, "The Great Charge," p. 364.

89. Hunt, "Third Day at Gettysburg," pp. 374–75.

90. Capt. (later Maj.) Henry Harrison Bingham of Pennsylvania.

91. Capt. (later Lt. Col.) Robert Hughes Fitzhugh (Battery K, 1st New York), Capt.

Gulian Verplanck Weir (Battery A, 5th U.S.), Lt. William Wheeler (13th New York Independent), Lt. Augustin N. Parsons (Battery A, 1st New Jersey), Lt. T. Frederick Brown (Battery B, 1st Rhode Island), Capt. William A. Arnold (Battery A, 1st Rhode Island), and Capt. Andrew Cowan (1st New York Independent).

92. Lt. (later Capt.) Benjamin Franklin Rittenhouse (Battery D, 5th U.S.).

93. Capt. (later Brevet Brig. Gen.) John Gardner Hazard, who commanded the artillery brigade of the II Corps.

94. Most accounts state that the bombardment lasted until about 3:00 P.M., when the southern infantry came into view. EPA's estimate of 2:00 P.M. is so much earlier that it is difficult to explain the discrepancy. He admits to looking at his watch for the last time at 1:35 P.M.; however, even the excitement and anxieties of events preceding the assault should not have caused him to lose track of an entire hour.

95. EPA placed question marks in the margin opposite these distances.

96. Brig. Gen. (later Brevet Maj. Gen.) George Jerrison Stannard of Vermont commanded the 3rd Brigade of the 3rd Division of the I Corps.

97. Edmund Rice, "Repelling Lee's Last Blow at Gettysburg," *B&L,* 3:387–90. At Gettysburg, Rice was a major with the 19th Massachusetts Infantry.

98. EPA added the sentence in parentheses.

99. Brig. Gen. (later Maj. Gen.) Alexander Stewart Webb of New York, whose command was the 2nd Brigade of the 2nd Division of the II Corps.

100. Brig. Gen. William Harrow, a native of Kentucky, who led the 1st Brigade of the 2nd Division of the II Corps.

101. EPA crossed out the next three words.

102. The pseudonym of Henry Wheeler Shaw, a nineteenth-century humorist.

103. Lt. Col. Arthur James Lyon Fremantle.

104. Fremantle published an account of his adventures in the Confederacy entitled *Three Months in the Southern States: April–June, 1863* (New York, 1864); other editions were published in London in 1863 and Mobile, Ala., in 1864. Justly famous and often quoted, it was reprinted with an introduction by Walter Lord as *The Fremantle Diary: Being the Journal of Lieutenant Colonel Arthur James Lyon Fremantle, Coldstream Guards, on His Three Months in the Southern States* (Boston, 1954).

105. For Fremantle's comments, see Lord, *Fremantle Diary,* pp. 214–15.

106. EPA crossed out the rest of this sentence.

107. EPA crossed out the next two words.

108. EPA crossed out these first five words.

109. EPA placed a question mark opposite this sentence.

110. EPA crossed out the next two words.

111. Winthrop's unit had been the 22nd Regiment Foot.

112. EPA crossed out the rest of this paragraph.

113. Brig. Gen. (later Maj. Gen.) Hugh Judson Kilpatrick of New Jersey commanded the 3rd Division of the Cavalry Corps.

114. Brig. Gen. John Daniel Imboden of Virginia.

115. EPA crossed out this sentence. ·

116. EPA left a space here, at the top of which he wrote, "some detail about Pettigrew." Pettigrew was wounded in the stomach just before midnight on 13 July. Surgeons thought a move would kill him and recommended that he be left behind so Federal doctors could care for him; however, Pettigrew insisted on accompanying the army. Transported twenty-two miles southward to Bunker Hill, he died there on 17 July. R. E.

Lee remarked that "The Army has lost a brave soldier and the Confederacy an accomplished officer." See Freeman, *Lee's Lieutenants,* 3:192–93, and *OR,* 27, pt. 3:1016.

117. EPA placed a question mark in the margin opposite this sentence. Erasures suggest that he made corrections.

118. EPA placed a question mark in the margin opposite this sentence.

119. Capt. William Thomson Haskell of the 1st South Carolina Volunteers (Provisional Army) was killed at Gettysburg; Charles Thomson Haskell, Jr., of the 1st South Carolina Regular Infantry (3rd Artillery) and Capt. Langdon Cheves were killed 10 July 1863 at Morris Island, South Carolina. See Louise Haskell Daly, *Alexander Cheves Haskell: The Portrait of a Man* (Norwood, Mass., 1934), pp. 105–7, and *OR,* 28, pt. 1:370–71.

120. EPA placed a question mark in the margin opposite "Wilcox's division." Brig. Gen. Samuel McGowan of South Carolina commanded a brigade in Pender's division.

121. EPA crossed out a sentence fragment here that reads, "Gen. Lee of course appreciated."

122. EPA crossed out the rest of this sentence.

123. This could have been John S. Pendleton, who died ca. 1881.

124. The battle of Chickamauga on 19–20 Sept. 1863, with combined casualties of more than 34,500, was the second bloodiest engagement of the war. The highest single day's casualty list came at Antietam, where more than 23,000 men fell on 17 Sept. 1862.

125. EPA drew a table with all Confederate divisions, the artillery of each corps, and his own battalion, but he gave no figures.

126. EPA first wrote "who ever lived may be profitably analysed by the results, and the search for valuable rules & principles [erasure] record of their moves," then substituted "who ever lived would be but little interesting."

127. EPA crossed out the rest of this sentence.

128. Alexander, "The Great Charge," p. 367. EPA's transcription here is not exact.

129. John D. Imboden, "The Confederate Retreat from Gettysburg," *B&L,* 3:420–21.

130. EPA placed a question mark in the margin opposite this sentence.

131. EPA crossed out the rest of this sentence.

132. Col. Norman Jonathan Hall, a native of New York, commanded the 3rd Brigade of the 2nd Division of the II Corps. His report is in *OR,* 27, pt. 1:435–41.

Chapter 12

1. Louis Philippe Albert d' Orleans, a French nobleman who served on George B. McClellan's staff and subsequently wrote a massive study of the war entitled *History of the Civil War in America,* 4 vols. (Philadelphia, 1876–88); the chapters on Gettysburg were extracted and published as *The Battle of Gettysburg, from the History of the Civil War in America* (Philadelphia, c. 1886).

2. Maj. Gen. William Starke Rosecrans of Ohio, commanding the Federal Army of the Cumberland.

3. EPA first wrote "Aug."

4. EPA placed a question mark in the margin opposite "some 40 miles."

5. EPA placed a question mark in the margin opposite "240 miles."

6. EPA placed a question mark here. At Chickamauga, Hood's arm was still in a sling from the wound at Gettysburg.

7. EPA made no estimate of this mileage.

8. EPA placed a question mark in the margin opposite this mileage and time.

9. EPA placed a question mark in the margin opposite this mileage and time.

10. EPA placed question marks opposite "30 miles" and "20 miles."

11. Maj. Gen. Thomas Leonidas Crittenden, a native of Kentucky, commanded the Federal XXI Corps.

12. Maj. Gens. George Henry Thomas of Virginia and Alexander McDowell McCook of Ohio commanded respectively the Federal XIV and XX Corps.

13. Maj. Gen. Thomas Carmichael Hindman of Tennessee led a division in Leonidas Polk's corps.

14. EPA left a space here, at the top of which he wrote, "some details from reports." For the Confederate reports, see *OR,* 30, pt. 2:23–25 (Bragg), pp. 136–47 (Hill), pp. 292–99, 302 (Hindman).

15. Bragg actually outnumbered Rosecrans at Chickamauga 66,000 to 58,000—a rare instance in which a southern army held the advantage on a major battlefield.

16. Edward A. Pollard, *The Lost Cause: A New Southern History of the War of the Confederates* (New York, 1866), p. 450.

17. Pollok B. Lee, Bragg's assistant adjutant general.

18. Charles Anderson Dana, a native of New Hampshire, was especially close to U. S. Grant and W. T. Sherman. EPA pasted the clipping from Dana's "Reminiscences of Men and Events of the Civil War, Part IV," *McClure's Magazine* 10 (February 1898): 352–53, in his manuscript (a portrait of Union general George H. Thomas, which is part of the clipping, has not been reproduced). Dana also published his memoirs as *Recollections of the Civil War, With the Leaders at Washington and in the Field in the Sixties* (New York, 1898); the quotation about Chickamauga is on pp. 114–15.

19. Horace Porter of Pennsylvania, chief of ordnance, and James Pierre Drouillard of Ohio.

20. Brig. Gen. (later Maj. Gen.) Thomas John Wood of Kentucky commanded the 1st Division of the XXI Corps.

21. Maj. Gen. Philip Henry Sheridan, a native of New York, commanded the 3rd Division of the XX Corps.

22. John Thomas Wilder commanded the 1st Brigade of Mounted Infantry.

23. Secretary of War Edwin McMasters Stanton of Ohio.

24. Maj. Gen. Gordon Granger of New York, commander of the Federal Reserve Corps.

25. Daniel Harvey Hill, "Chickamauga—The Great Battle of the West," *B&L,* 3:658–62. EPA pasted the article in his manuscript and wrote to the side of it, "Did not Polk then withdraw? I think so. If not where was he & at what?" Three illustrations of the battlefield included in Hill's article have not been reproduced.

26. Brig. Gen. (later Maj. Gen.) Bushrod Rust Johnson, a native of Ohio.

27. Brig. Gens. Zachariah Cantey Deas and Arthur Middleton Manigault, both of South Carolina, commanded brigades in Hindman's division.

28. Col. Bernard Laiboldt, commander of the 2nd Brigade of Sheridan's division.

29. Brig. Gen. (later Maj. Gen.) James Patton Anderson of Tennessee.

30. Brig. Gen. Jefferson Columbus Davis of Kentucky led the 1st Division of the XX Corps.

31. Brig. Gen. William Haines Lytle of Ohio, commander of the 1st Brigade in Sheridan's division.

32. Maj. Gen. (later Lt. Gen.) Alexander Peter Stewart of Tennessee.

33. Maj. Gen. Benjamin Franklin Cheatham of Tennessee and Brig. Gen. St. John Richardson Liddell of Mississippi.

34. D. H. Hill placed the following footnote at this point in his article: "He belonged to Von Zinken's regiment, of New Orleans, composed of French, Germans, and Irish. I said to him: 'My poor fellow, you are badly hurt. What regiment do you belong to?' He replied: 'The Fifth Confederit, and a dommed good regiment it is.' The answer, though almost ludicrous, touched me as illustrating the *esprit de corps* of the soldier—his pride in and his affection for his command. Colonel Von Zinken told me afterward that one of his desperately wounded Irishmen cried out to his comrades, 'Charge them, boys; they have cha-ase (cheese) in their haversacks.' Poor Pat, he has fought courageously in every land in quarrels not his own.—D.H.H."

35. Brig. Gens. John Gregg of Alabama and Evander McNair of North Carolina, whose brigades were in Bushrod Johnson's division.

36. Brig. Gen. Benjamin Grubb Humphreys of Mississippi commanded a brigade in McLaws's division.

37. Maj. Gen. William Henry Talbot Walker of Georgia commanded Bragg's Reserve Corps; Maj. Gen. Patrick Ronayne Cleburne, a native of Ireland, led a division in Hill's corps.

38. Brig. Gen. William Preston of Kentucky, Brig. Gen. Archibald Gracie, Jr., a native of New York, Col. Robert C. Trigg of Virginia, Brig. Gen. John Herbert Kelly of Alabama, and Brig. Gen. Jerome Bonaparte Robertson, who was born in Kentucky but spent his entire adult life in Texas and led a brigade of Texans.

39. Brig. Gen. John King Jackson of Georgia.

40. Brig. Gens. George Earl Maney and Marcus Joseph Wright of Tennessee.

41. Maj. Gen. (later Secretary of War) John Cabell Breckinridge of Kentucky, whose division was in Hill's corps.

42. EPA pasted in his manuscript an excerpt from Lt. Col. Gates Phillips Thruston's article "The Crisis at Chickamauga," *B&L,* 3:663–65.

Chapter 13

1. EPA placed a question mark in the margin opposite "25 miles."

2. EPA placed a question mark in the margin opposite this sentence.

3. Francis C. Lawley, who had crossed the Potomac with Colonel Wolseley in September 1862, represented the *London Times;* Frank Vizetelly was an artist for the *Illustrated London News* who subsequently covered other wars and probably was killed in November 1883 at Kashgil in the Sudan (his exact fate is unknown). For examples of their coverage of the war, see William Stanley Hoole, *Lawley Covers the Confederacy* (Tuscaloosa, Ala., 1964) and Hoole, *Vizetelly Covers the Confederacy* (Tuscaloosa, Ala., 1957).

4. EPA placed a question mark in the margin opposite "500 men." Brig. Gen. Henry Lewis Benning of Georgia commanded a brigade in Hood's division.

5. Maj. Gen. (later Lt. Gen.) Richard Taylor of Louisiana, the son of President Zachary Taylor.

6. Probably the house of Robert Cravens.

7. EPA placed question marks in the margin opposite the distances, heights, and widths in this discussion of topography.

8. EPA placed a question mark in the margin opposite "40 miles."

9. EPA placed a question mark in the margin opposite the end of this sentence.

10. Bragg graduated in the class of 1837; he had risen to the rank of captain (brevet lieutenant colonel) when he resigned from the army in January 1856 to become a planter in Louisiana.

11. The battle of Murfreesboro or Stones River was fought 31 Dec. 1862 and 2 Jan. 1863; EPA treated these as separate engagements.

12. Ulysses S. Grant also related this probably apocryphal anecdote about Bragg in *Personal Memoirs of U. S. Grant,* 2 vols. (New York, 1885), 2:86–87.

13. Col. Lucius Bellinger Northrop of South Carolina was appointed brigadier general by Jefferson Davis but never confirmed by the Senate.

14. Davis and Northrop were not, as was widely believed in the Confederacy, close friends from their days at West Point. Davis graduated in the class of 1828 and resigned in 1835; Northrop graduated in the class of 1831 and was dropped from the service in January 1848. As senator from Mississippi, Davis did help win reinstatement for Northrop in August 1848. See Charles L. Dufour, *Nine Men in Gray* (Garden City, 1963), pp. 199–202.

15. Brig. Gen. Isaac Munroe St. John of Georgia.

16. EPA placed question marks in the margin opposite "20 miles" and "40 miles."

17. The Federal supply route followed a road from Bridgeport up the Sequatchie Valley to an intersection with the Anderson Road, which ran southeast into Chattanooga.

18. Maj. Gen. Stephen Augustus Hurlbut, a native of South Carolina, who commanded the Federal XVI Corps.

19. EPA placed a question mark in the margin opposite "Oct. 28th"; the action described below actually took place on 27 Oct. A "the" left before "Oct. 28th" has been deleted.

20. Brig. Gen. (later Maj. Gen.) William Babcock Hazen of Vermont commanded the 2nd Brigade of the 3rd Division of the IV Corps.

21. EPA is describing his activities on the afternoon of 28 Oct.

22. EPA left space here for the message, in which he wrote, "Not uncommon to read each other's messages"; a search of *OR* turned up no such document.

23. EPA left a large space here, in which he wrote, "Describe the fight &c. to Nov. 4th." See *Military Memoirs,* pp. 467–73, for an account of the engagement at Wauhatchie.

24. EPA placed a question mark in the margin opposite "15,000 men." Burnside had about 20,000 soldiers in Knoxville and another 5,000 under his command at Cumberland Gap and elsewhere in East Tennessee.

25. EPA placed a question mark in the margin opposite this sentence. Maj. Gen. Joseph Wheeler of Georgia commanded Bragg's cavalry.

26. EPA placed a question mark in the margin opposite this sentence; "about 3,200 men" was inserted later.

27. EPA placed a question mark in the margin opposite "Sweetwater." The distance by railroad was fifty-five to sixty miles.

28. Maj. Austin Leyden and Lt. Col. James Henry Hallonquist.

29. EPA placed a question mark in the margin opposite this sentence. Leyden's battalion consisted of three Georgia batteries under Capts. Tyler M. Peeples, Andrew M. Wolihin, and Billington W. York. EPA left a space here, in which he wrote, "Our fellows got along well &c."

30. EPA placed a question mark in the margin opposite this sentence.

31. EPA placed a question mark in the margin opposite this sentence.

32. Maj. (later Col.) John J. Clarke, an engineer on James Longstreet's staff in 1863–64.

33. Thomas Muldrup Logan of South Carolina.

34. EPA left space for but did not give the casualties. Gen. Jenkins reported a loss of 22 killed and 152 wounded. *OR,* 31, pt. 1:527.

35. EPA placed a question mark in the margin opposite this sentence. Jenkins helped organize and then taught at the King's Mountain Military School at Yorkville, South Carolina; Law was among the founders and faculty at the Military High School at Tuskegee, Alabama. Both were graduates of the South Carolina Military Academy, in 1854 and 1856 respectively.

36. EPA wrote underneath this sentence, "Was one charge based on Campbell's Station?" Longstreet's charges against McLaws, which are set forth in *OR,* 31, pt. 1:503–5, related to events of 28–29 Nov. 1863.

37. EPA left space for a map but did not provide one. The map in the text (Figure 30) is from *Military Memoirs,* p. 482.

38. EPA placed a question mark in the margin opposite "1,400 yards." Sanders commanded the 1st Division of the Cavalry Corps in the Army of the Ohio.

39. EPA undoubtedly "borrowed" two of Joseph B. Kershaw's five regiments, which were the 2nd, 3rd, 7th, 8th, and 15th South Carolina. Reports in *OR,* 31, pt. 1:477–80 (EPA), pp. 508–17 (the five regimental commanders), do not make clear which regiments EPA used. B. Augustus Dickert's *History of Kershaw's Brigade, with Complete Roll of Companies, Biographical Sketches, Incidents, Anecdotes, Etc.* (1899; reprint, Dayton, Ohio, 1976), pp. 306–7, makes clear that the regiments were the 2nd and 3rd South Carolina.

40. Brig. Gen. John Hunt Morgan, a native of Alabama strongly associated with Kentucky.

41. On Davis's imprisonment, see Edward K. Eckert, *"Fiction Distorting Fact": Prison Life, Annotated by Jefferson Davis* (Macon, Ga., 1987), esp. pp. xi–lxiv.

42. EPA mistakenly wrote "25th."

43. Brig. Gen. Danville Leadbetter, a native of Maine, graduated from West Point in the class of 1836.

44. EPA provided no sketch.

45. EPA placed a question mark in the margin opposite "Second Creek." He meant Third Creek, which ran across the front of the fort; Second Creek ran behind the fort.

46. EPA left a blank page here for a map.

47. In *Military Memoirs,* p. 492, EPA gives the casualties as 129 killed, 458 wounded, and 226 missing.

48. Lt. Col. Orville Elias Babcock, assistant inspector general of the IX Corps (beside whose name EPA placed a question mark); Edward Ferrero, commander of the 1st Division of the IX Corps; and perhaps Lawrence Sprague Babbitt, a lieutenant of ordnance who was a cadet at West Point while EPA taught there (Babbitt does not appear in any of the Federal reports of the Knoxville campaign).

49. EPA placed question marks in the margin opposite Martin's name in this paragraph and wrote "Divn.?" Maj. Gen. William Thompson Martin commanded all of Longstreet's cavalry, which consisted of four small divisions.

50. EPA placed a question mark in the margin opposite "8th Michigan Cavalry."

51. EPA left a space here, in which he wrote, "find it & put it in here."

52. EPA left a space here, in which he wrote, "Particulars about Bean's Station." EPA's report, in *OR*, 31, pt. 1:480, gives the following account of his part in the engagement: "On the 14th, my battalion accompanied the infantry in the march and attack upon the enemy at Bean's Station, Parker's and Taylor's batteries in front, the others in the middle of the column. The intense cold and high wind unfortunately delayed the march, nearly freezing the ragged and shoeless drivers. Parker's and Taylor's batteries were engaged, and advanced with the foremost infantry, and sustained the fight alone until sundown, when, the other batteries arriving (all had marched 16 miles that day), I advanced Moody's, Parker's, and Taylor's batteries within 400 yards of the enemy's line of battle. Darkness, and the advance of Kershaw's brigade upon the enemy's left flank coming near our line of fire, alone prevented our making a heavy slaughter of the enemy. During the night they retreated, and have avoided all subsequent efforts to engage them."

53. EPA left a space, in which he wrote, "And now we will take the narrative back to the assault upon Fort Sanders in order to give some interesting & instructive details of that unfortunate affair."

Chapter 14

1. Anthony Porter, who oversaw all of EPA's financial affairs during the war.

2. EPA placed a question mark after "61st Geo." Thomas J. Berry was lieutenant colonel of the 60th Georgia.

3. Mary Custis Lee was the eldest of R. E. Lee's daughters. EPA delivered an address at West Point on 9 June 1902 in which he stated that it was well the Confederacy failed. In the audience were other former Confederates, including James Longstreet. When Mary Custis Lee read of the speech, she wrote EPA "a severe reproof for . . . having delivered it in the presence of Longstreet who had abused her father; & at West Point where there is no memorial of Gen Lee." Postscript to an EPA note dated June ? 1902, folder 53, Alexander Papers SHC.

4. Brig. Gen. William Whann Mackall of Maryland.

5. Joseph E. Johnston, *Narrative of Military Operations* (1874; reprint, Bloomington, Ind., 1959), pp. 288–89, 570.

6. EPA wrote "or was it Shoup?" above Beckham's name and placed question marks opposite "graduated at West Point" and "Franklin." Col. Robert Franklin Beckham of Virginia, a graduate of West Point in the class of 1859, transferred from the Army of Northern Virginia to the Army of Tennessee in late spring 1864 to command the artillery in John Bell Hood's corps. He subsequently became chief of artillery when Hood took over the Army of Tennessee and was killed near Columbia on 29 Nov. 1864. Brig. Gen. Francis Asbury Shoup served as Johnston's chief of artillery during the Atlanta campaign and later was Hood's chief of staff.

7. George W. Kirk was a Tennessean who entered Federal service as captain of Company D, 5th East Tennessee Cavalry (later the 8th Tennessee Cavalry) in June 1863. He subsequently recruited bushwhackers, Confederate deserters, and Union sympathizers for the 3rd North Carolina Mounted Infantry, of which he was made colonel in March 1865. Labeled a guerrilla by his Confederate opponents, Kirk conducted operations throughout East Tennessee and western North Carolina.

8. EPA wrote "Colston?" in the margin opposite this part of the sentence. William T.

Mason joined EPA's staff in March 1864; Capt. Frederick Morgan Colston was ordnance officer in EPA's battalion May–September 1864.

9. EPA placed a question mark in the margin opposite this sentence. Capt. (later Maj.) James Breathed was a native of Maryland who commanded the 1st Stuart Horse Artillery.

10. John Izard Middleton, Jr., William M. Post, and Jacob H. Franklin, who later was promoted to major.

11. Lt. James F. Grattan. EPA left a space here, in which he wrote, "In case I wish to say any more about staff & such little details. Was Colston my ordnance offr. or did he stay with battn." Frederick Morgan Colston was ordnance officer in EPA's battalion until September 1864, when he was commissioned captain of artillery on ordnance duty and assigned to assist Briscoe G. Baldwin, Lee's chief of ordnance. See Colston's "Recollections of the Last Months in the Army of Northern Virginia," *SHSP,* 38:1.

12. EPA erased the rest of this sentence.

13. EPA left a blank page here, at the top of which he wrote, "McLaws court martial," and at the bottom of which he wrote, "But though he wins Kershaw gets his division." See *OR,* 31, pt. 1:487–88 for some of EPA's testimony before the court martial.

14. EPA labeled the next two paragraphs a footnote, although they appear in sequence in the text.

15. EPA gave no mileage; the distance between Greeneville and Jonesboro was slightly more than twenty miles.

16. Most sources identify Brig. Gen. William Lowther Jackson, a native of Virginia (now West Virginia) and second cousin of Stonewall Jackson, as "Mudwall" Jackson. See, for examples, Ezra J. Warner, *Generals in Gray,* 3rd printing (Baton Rouge, 1965), pp. 153–54; and John A. McNeil, "The Imboden Raid and Its Effects," *SHSP,* 34:300–303 (a confident explanation of how W. L. Jackson acquired the nickname "Mudwall"). However, it is clear that EPA stayed in a field belonging to Brig. Gen. Alfred Eugene Jackson, a native of Tennessee also sometimes called "Mudwall" Jackson. For A. E. Jackson's claim to the sobriquet, see "A Modern Horatius," *SHSP,* 21:295, and Warner, *Generals in Gray,* 1st printing (Baton Rouge, 1959), pp. 148–49. A. E. Jackson was stationed in East Tennessee in the spring of 1864 and made his home in Jonesboro after the war; W. L. Jackson was serving in West Virginia and thus could not have been present at Jonesboro when EPA stopped there. Finally, EPA refers to "the old general" in describing Jackson— A. E. Jackson was fifty-seven years old in the spring of 1864, and W. L. Jackson just thirty-nine.

17. A. E. Jackson died in Jonesboro in October 1889.

18. EPA made no estimate of this mileage, but it was probably between fifty and sixty miles.

19. No Quarterman appears in the 1860 Tennessee census; EPA may have confused the death of a Tennessee major with that of Col. Joseph Quarterman, a planter from EPA's region.

20. EPA placed a question mark in the margin opposite this blank and wrote, "Ask Joe Haskell."

21. EPA placed a question mark in the margin opposite this sentence.

22. Morton Marye was lieutenant colonel of the 17th Virginia Infantry when he was badly wounded at Second Manassas. He retired from the service as a colonel on 8 July 1864.

23. EPA offered no other clue to this woman's identity.

24. "Castles in the Air" (or "The Bonnie, Bonnie Bairn") was written by James Ballantine of Scotland (1808–1877).

Chapter 15

1. EPA wrote "omit" in the margin opposite these first two paragraphs and left two blank pages under the heading "Mine Run Campaign." On Meade's attempt to force Lee back from the Rapidan River in late November 1863, see Martin F. Graham and George F. Skoch, *Mine Run: A Campaign of Lost Opportunities* (Lynchburg, Va., 1988).

2. EPA crossed out the next eleven words. A number of erasures suggest that the description of Lee's review of the First Corps underwent considerable revision.

3. William E. Boggs of the 6th South Carolina.

4. EPA crossed out this sentence.

5. EPA crossed out the next three sentences.

6. On this rhyme, see Iona and Peter Opie, *The Oxford Dictionary of Nursery Rhymes* (London, 1973), pp. 86–87 (where the text is the same except "gal" is "girl"). Because of its racist overtones, the rhyme does not appear in modern American editions of Mother Goose.

7. EPA crossed out the rest of this sentence and the next sentence.

8. EPA crossed out the next two sentences.

9. EPA crossed out "of non exchange" and "deliberately" in this sentence.

10. EPA crossed out the rest of this sentence.

11. EPA crossed out this opening and changed it to "Grant made Butler the commissioner."

12. Maj. Gen. Franz Sigel, a native of Baden, Germany, commanded the Department of West Virginia.

13. Brig. Gen. (later Maj. Gen.) George Crook of Ohio commanded the 2nd Division of the Department of West Virginia, together with other units assigned to him for this operation.

14. EPA placed question marks in the margin opposite the figures for Sigel's and Crook's forces. Erasures suggest that he made corrections (Crook had some 8,500 men, and Sigel about 9,000 and 28 guns).

15. Brig. Gen. August Valentine Kautz, a native of Baden, Germany.

16. EPA placed a question mark in the margin opposite "40,000 men."

17. EPA left a small blank space here and wrote at the bottom of the page "64,000," "9,000," and "before the fourth we had to send force to meet Sherman."

18. EPA wrote "Omit this page" above the next two paragraphs.

19. EPA crossed out the next two sentences. Leyden's battalion does not appear on the 4 May 1864 roster of artillery with the Army of Northern Virginia printed in *OR*, 36, pt. 1:1036–39. In June 1864 Leyden was serving under John D. Imboden near Lynchburg. Wade Hampton Gibbes took command of the 13th Battalion Virginia Light Artillery in April 1864. John C. Haskell had contemplated leaving the Army of Northern Virginia during the winter of 1863–64. In late January 1864, EPA had written Lt. Gen. W. J. Hardee that Haskell wanted a change of location "for sufficient reason but too long to specify." "I do not know any officer," stated EPA of his good friend, "whom I could more confidently & conscientiously recommend for any Arty command—even to the position

of Chf of Arty of a Corps." Haskell's promotion to lieutenant colonel and assignment to Henry's battalion made it possible for EPA to retain him as a subordinate. Typescript of EPA to W. J. Hardee, 27 Jan. 1864, Petersburg National Battlefield.

20. EPA wrote "Kershaw & Field" in the margin opposite this sentence.

21. EPA first began this sentence, "As well as I can locate the spot we were then at Richard's Shop."

22. EPA crossed out the next four words.

23. EPA crossed out "at any rate."

24. EPA placed a question mark opposite "eleven o'clock." The action increased sharply after about 10:30 A.M., and the heaviest Federal assaults began in the early afternoon.

25. Grant's headquarters were northeast of Ellwood, the summer residence of J. Horace Lacy that stood about one-half mile southwest of the point where the Orange Turnpike joined the Orange Plank Road (see note 3 in chapter 8 for a reference to Chatham, Lacy's principal residence).

26. See Richard Taylor, *Destruction and Reconstruction* (1879; reprint, New York, 1955), p. 36.

27. EPA placed a question mark in the margin opposite "7,000 men." Heth had fewer than 6,500 men.

28. EPA placed a question mark in the margin opposite "forty acre clearing." The cleared area on the Tapp farm consisted of a twenty-acre rectangle around the house, another twenty-eight acres extending to the northwest, and an eight-acre parcel extending northeast. EPA's reference probably is to the twenty-acre field surrounding the house.

29. Brig. Gen. James Samuel Wadsworth commanded the 4th Division of the V Corps; Brig. Gen. Henry Baxter led the 2nd Brigade of the 2nd Division of the V Corps.

30. Brig Gen. (later Maj. Gen.) Francis Channing Barlow, a native of New York, commanded the 1st Division of the II Corps.

31. Deleted from this part of the sentence is "suspended on page 34"—EPA's reference to the pagination in the manuscript.

32. EPA crossed out the next three words.

33. Brig. Gen. (later Maj. Gen.) George Washington Getty, a native of Washington, D.C., whose command was the 2nd Division of the VI Corps.

34. Brig. Gen. Thomas Greely Stevenson of Massachusetts, commander of the 1st Division of the IX Corps.

35. EPA placed a question mark in the margin opposite "8,000 men." Anderson actually had fewer than 6,500.

36. Maj. Gen. Martin Luther Smith, a native of New York.

37. Brig. Gen. William Tatum Wofford of Georgia.

38. EPA left a space here in which he wrote, "Give names of others killed &c." Also mortally wounded were Capt. Alfred English Doby, aide-de-camp to Kershaw, and Marcus Baum, one of Kershaw's orderlies. Pasted in the manuscript at the bottom of this page is the engraving of Micah Jenkins from *B&L*, 4:125, above which EPA wrote "good picture."

39. Andrew A. Humphreys, *The Virginia Campaign of '64 and '65: The Army of the Potomac and the Army of the James* (New York, 1883), pp. 43–44.

40. Col. (later Brevet Brig. Gen.) Robert McAllister of Pennsylvania, who commanded the 1st Brigade of the 4th Division of the II Corps.

41. Brig. Gen. Edward Aylesworth Perry, a native of Massachusetts.

42. John Bratton of South Carolina was made a brigadier general to rank from 6 May 1864.

43. Brig. Gens. Alexander Shaler of Connecticut, commander of the 4th Brigade of the 1st Division of the VI Corps, and Truman Seymour of Vermont, whose unit was the 2nd Brigade of the 3rd Division of the VI Corps.

44. EPA crossed out this reckoning of casualties and referred his readers to the larger table at the end of the chapter.

45. EPA questioned the date of Longstreet's return to duty and left a space here, in which he wrote, "Partics. about Longstreet's arm." Longstreet rejoined Lee's army on 19 Oct. 1864, despite the fact that his arm remained largely paralyzed.

46. EPA placed question marks in the margin opposite "the Big Sandy" and "fifty miles." "The Big Sandy" is written in a different ink than the rest of the sentence.

47. Brig. Gen. David McMurtrie Gregg, a Pennsylvanian, led the 2nd Division, and Brig. Gen. (later Maj. Gen.) Wesley Merritt, a native of New York, led the Reserve Brigade of the Cavalry Corps.

48. Col. Charles Read Collins, a native of Pennsylvania, commanded the 15th Virginia Cavalry.

49. Charles Anderson Dana, "Reminiscences of Men and Events of the Civil War, Part VII," *McClure's Magazine* 11 (May 1898): 30; see also Dana, *Recollections of the Civil War, With the Leaders at Washington and in the Field in the Sixties* (New York, 1898), p. 194.

50. Brig. Gen. (later Maj. Gen.) Thomas Lafayette Rosser's brigade was in Hampton's division.

51. Brig. Gen. (later Maj. Gen.) James Harrison Wilson of Illinois commanded the 3rd Division of the Cavalry Corps.

52. Brig. Gen. Goode Bryan of Georgia.

53. Brig. Gen. John Cleveland Robinson of New York led the 2nd Division of the V Corps.

54. John R. Potts of the Branch (North Carolina) Battery.

55. EPA placed a question mark after "noon."

56. Maj. Gen. Horatio Gouverneur Wright of Connecticut commanded the 1st Division of the VI Corps.

57. At the end of this sentence EPA wrote, "Burroughs killed &c. next page" and left a blank page. Lt. Dent Burroughs of Moody's battery was killed on 12 May at Spotsylvania.

58. EPA crossed out the next eight words.

59. Brig. Gen. Henry Harrison Walker of Virginia.

60. Brig. Gen. (later Maj. Gen.) Stephen Dodson Ramseur of North Carolina.

61. Col. (later Brig. Gen.) Emory Upton, a New Yorker, commanded the 2nd Brigade of the 1st Division of the VI Corps; Brig. Gen. (later Maj. Gen.) Gershom Mott of New Jersey led the 4th Division of the II Corps.

62. Brig. Gen. George Pierce Doles of Georgia, whose brigade was in Rodes's division.

63. Brig. Gen. James Clay Rice of Massachusetts, commanding the 2nd Brigade of the 4th Division of the V Corps.

64. Stuart died on 12 May 1864.

65. EPA wrote in the margin here, "Page 12 Cutshaw 8"—Maj. Richard Channing Moore Page's battalion lost 12 guns and Maj. Wilfred Emory Cutshaw's battalion lost 8 (all Second Corps cannon).

66. EPA crossed out the next five words.

67. Above this part of the sentence EPA wrote, "Guns said in Century book 12 Page & 8 Cutshaw." See G. Norton Galloway, "Hand-to-Hand Fighting at Spotsylvania," *B&L*, 4:171.

68. Brig. Gen. George Hume Steuart of Maryland.

69. EPA left a space here, in which he wrote "Detail about Cabell." For mention of Cabell's work on 12 May, see *OR*, 36, pt. 1:1045, 1087.

70. EPA crossed out the rest of this paragraph and wrote in the margin, "This is all an error. It never happened." What prompted him to do this is a mystery, as most of what he mentions in this passage took place. See, for example, Douglas Southall Freeman, *Lee's Lieutenants: A Study in Command,* 3 vols. (New York, 1942–44), 3:404–9, and Gary W. Gallagher, *Stephen Dodson Ramseur: Lee's Gallant General* (Chapel Hill, 1985), pp. 107–11.

71. EPA left a space below this sentence, in which he wrote, "Further details about this?" On the "Lee to the Rear" incident at Spotsylvania, see Douglas Southall Freeman, *R. E. Lee: A Biography,* 4 vols. (New York, 1934–36), 3:316–21.

72. Brig. Gen. (later Maj. Gen.) Robert Brown Potter of New York led the 2nd Division of the IX Corps.

73. Brig. Gen. Alfred Moore Scales of North Carolina.

74. Brig. Gen. Lysander Cutler, a native of Massachusetts, commanded the 4th Division of the V Corps after Wadsworth's death in the Wilderness.

75. Brig. Gens. Abner Monroe Perrin of South Carolina and Nathaniel Harrison Harris of Mississippi, whose brigades were in R. H. Anderson's division (commanded by Mahone while Anderson had charge of the First Corps).

76. Col. (later Brig. Gen.) David Addison Weisiger of Virginia, who was given Mahone's brigade when the latter replaced R. H. Anderson in divisional command.

77. Brig. Gen. Lewis Addison Grant of Vermont, commander of the 2nd Brigade of the 2nd Division of the VI Corps, as quoted in Humphreys, *Virginia Campaign of '64 and '65,* pp. 99–100.

78. Dana, "Reminiscences Part VII," *McClure's Magazine* 11 (May 1898): 31; see also Dana, *Recollections of the Civil War,* p. 197.

79. See *OR*, 36, pt. 1:1094. EPA left another page here for additional accounts of the Bloody Angle. One of the best is in Varina Davis Brown, *A Colonel at Gettysburg and Spotsylvania* (Columbia, S.C., 1931), pp. 92–139, 246–302.

80. Humphreys, *Virginia Campaign of '64 and '65,* p. 104.

81. Brig. Gen. Robert Daniel Johnston of North Carolina, whose brigade was in Rodes's division.

82. Col. (later Brig. Gen.) Samuel Sprigg Carroll, a native of the District of Columbia, commanded the 3rd Brigade of the 2nd Division of the II Corps.

83. Humphreys, *Virginia Campaign of '64 and '65,* p. 117.

84. Brig. Gen. Robert Ogden Tyler of New York, whose division joined the II Corps.

85. EPA wrote "will be found in general table for the campaign" above the end of this sentence.

86. A. P. Hill was ill rather than wounded. Jubal Early commanded the Third Corps 8–21 May 1864.

87. Humphreys, *Virginia Campaign of '64 and '65,* pp. 117–18.

Chapter 16

1. EPA identified the farmer as Cox here, as Miller in a second reference, and as Lowry in a third reference.

2. EPA placed a question mark in the margin opposite Brown's name. He was again confusing J. Wilcox Brown, the ordnance officer, with John Thompson Brown, the artillerist who served under Parker (see chapter 10, note 10).

3. EPA added "Miller" in a different ink.

4. EPA added "each" after "one"; it has been deleted to make the sentence read correctly.

5. The action EPA describes centered on the earthwork near the Telegraph Road Bridge (better known as Fox's Bridge). The regiment in the work was the 2nd South Carolina. The 3rd and 7th South Carolina and the 3rd South Carolina Battalion were also north of the river, but only the 2nd South Carolina suffered notably in the Federal assault.

6. Lt. Col. William Proctor Smith of Virginia, who served on Lee's staff as an engineer from the summer of 1863 through the Petersburg campaign.

7. Smith commanded the Bedford (Virginia) Light Artillery.

8. EPA crossed out the next two words.

9. Breckinridge suffered 531 casualties out of 4,087 engaged, and Sigel 841 of 6,275. For a careful discussion of losses on both sides, see William C. Davis, *The Battle of New Market* (Garden City, 1975), pp. 198–201.

10. Brig. Gen. Adelbert Ames of Maine commanded the 3rd Division of the X Corps.

11. Jefferson Davis, *The Rise and Fall of the Confederate Government*, 2 vols. (1881; reprint, New York, 1958), 2:512.

12. Brig. Gen. William Gaston Lewis of North Carolina, whose brigade joined S. D. Ramseur's division (formerly Jubal A. Early's).

13. Here EPA refers the reader to the table of casualties at the end of chapter 15.

14. Maj. Gen. William Farrar Smith of Vermont.

15. Maj. Gen. Robert Frederick Hoke of North Carolina.

Chapter 17

1. EPA placed a question mark in the margin opposite "15 miles."

2. Col. Edward S. Willis (he did use his middle initial), a native of Georgia whose regiment was the 12th Georgia, was acting commander of Pegram's brigade.

3. Col. James Barbour Terrill (promoted to brigadier general the day after he was killed) and Lt. Col. Thomas H. Watkins, both Virginians, commanded respectively the 13th and 52nd Virginia.

4. Col. Laurence Massillon Keitt, a former member of the Provisional Confederate Congress, commanded the 20th South Carolina.

5. Brig. Gen. Eppa Hunton of Virginia.

6. EPA first wrote "amount of this all day," and "while Gen. Ewell" in this sentence.

7. Andrew A. Humphreys, *The Virginia Campaign of '64 and '65: The Army of the Potomac and the Army of the James* (New York, 1883), p. 180 n. 1, quotes Wilson as reporting on the morning of 3 June that "Col. Cesnola's" command was on its way. Louis P. Di Cesnola was colonel of the 4th New York Cavalry.

8. EPA first wrote "far left."

9. EPA placed a question mark in the margin opposite "losing a number of prisoners." Brig. Gen. Joseph Finegan, a native of Ireland, commanded a Florida brigade in Mahone's division.

10. Humphreys, *Virginia Campaign of '64 and '65,* p. 186.

11. Brig. Gen. John Henry Martindale of New York led the 2nd Division of the XVIII Corps.

12. Brig. Gen. William Thomas Harbaugh Brooks, an Ohioan, led the 1st Division of the XVIII Corps.

13. EPA added the material in parentheses.

14. William Swinton, *Campaigns of the Army of the Potomac: A Critical History of Operations in Virginia, Maryland and Pennsylvania, from the Commencement to the Close of the War, 1861–5* (New York, 1866), p. 487.

15. EPA crossed out the next seven words.

16. Humphreys, *Virginia Campaign of '64 and '65,* pp. 190–92.

17. Maj. (later Col.) Thomas Andrew McParlin of Maryland. His report covering the operations at Cold Harbor is in *OR,* 36, pt. 1:209–26.

18. EPA placed a question mark in the margin opposite "$25.00 gold."

19. EPA first wrote "adjoining commands."

20. EPA crossed out this sentence.

21. EPA left a space here, in which he wrote, "Tell of the killing of Capt. McCarthy (?)." Capt. Edward Stephens McCarthy, who commanded the 1st Richmond Howitzers in Cabell's battalion, was killed on 4 June 1864.

22. Lt. Col. John Floyd King, a native of Georgia, led the 13th Battalion Virginia Artillery.

23. Lt. Col. Robert Archelaus Hardaway of Georgia commanded a battalion in the Second Corps.

24. Col. (later Brig. Gen.) Josiah Gorgas, a native of Pennsylvania.

25. Brig. Gen. John Crawford Vaughn, a Tennessean, and Imboden were under the overall command of W. E. "Grumble" Jones, who was killed in the engagement.

26. Maj. Richard Henry Brewer at various times commanded a battalion of Alabama cavalry and the 8th Confederate Cavalry (also called the 2nd Alabama and Mississippi Cavalry Regiment), neither of which was at the battle of Piedmont. Marshall M. Brice's *Conquest of a Valley* (Charlottesville, 1965), p. 37, states that Brewer led a mixed "command of infantry" that included a "130-man battalion of niter miners."

27. Brig. Gen. William Whedbee Kirkland of North Carolina, who commanded a brigade in Heth's division.

28. Col. H. Boyd McKeen, who commanded the 1st Brigade of the 2nd Division of the II Corps after A. S. Webb was wounded at Spotsylvania.

Chapter 18

1. EPA put in parentheses "Army of Potomac. 1st Edition, p. 494." The quotation, which is typewritten in the manuscript, is in William Swinton, *Campaigns of the Army of the Potomac: A Critical History of Operations in Virginia, Maryland and Pennsylvania, from the Commencement to the Close of the War, 1861–5* (New York, 1866), pp. 494–95.

2. EPA underlined this passage, put it in parentheses, and wrote in the margin, "What is in parenthesis is a foot note."

3. Swinton, *Army of the Potomac,* p. 492 (this quotation is typewritten in the manuscript).

4. EPA provided no table but wrote "5 pages for data about draft bounties, politics, &c." He left the five pages blank. See *Military Memoirs,* pp. 545–46 for a table and a brief discussion of politics and bounties.

5. EPA crossed out the rest of this sentence.

6. EPA first wrote "whole army suddenly upon Petersburg."

7. Brig. Gen. Edward Winslow Hincks of Maine commanded the 3rd Division of the XVIII Corps.

8. EPA placed question marks in the margin opposite these estimates. After an examination of Confederate records in the U.S. War Department, Walter H. Taylor gave the strengths as 14,058 (First Corps) and 15,530 (Third Corps) in *Four Years with General Lee* (1877; reprint, Bloomington, Ind., 1962), p. 177.

9. EPA placed a question mark in the margin opposite the end of this sentence.

10. See *OR,* 40, pt. 2:664–65.

11. EPA left a space here, in which he wrote, "How many guns? about 20 to 25."

12. Col. Samuel B. Paul, whose account of his interview with Lee is in Alfred Roman, *The Military Operations of General Beauregard in the War Between the States, 1861 to 1865,* 2 vols. (New York, 1884), 2: 579–81.

13. Brig. Gen. George H. Chapman of Massachusetts commanded the 2nd Brigade in Wilson's 3rd Division.

14. Capt. Nathaniel A. Sturdivant commanded Company A (2nd) of the 12th Battalion Virginia Light Artillery.

15. Lt. Col. Fletcher Harris Archer, a Virginian, of the 3rd Battalion Virginia Reserves.

16. Col. Samuel Perkins Spear, a native of Massachusetts, whose command was the 2nd Brigade of Kautz's division of cavalry.

17. Maj. Gen. Quincy Adams Gillmore of Ohio commanded the X Corps until 17 June 1864, when he was relieved at his own request.

18. Capt. Edward Graham led the Petersburg (Virginia) Horse Artillery.

19. EPA wrote "perhaps arty.?" in the margin opposite this sentence.

20. See chapter 3, note 41, for the bibliographical information on Johnson's book.

21. EPA placed a question mark in the margin opposite "class of 1833." Harris ranked seventh in the graduating class of 1833.

22. EPA circled this sentence and wrote "Foot note" in the margin opposite it.

23. EPA placed a question mark in the margin opposite this sentence. At 9:30 A.M. on 15 June, Beauregard reported that "General Dearing, from south side of Appomattox, reports enemy have attacked my outposts in force." *OR,* 40, pt. 2:655.

24. Maj. (later Col.) Edwin Seneca Greeley, a native of New Hampshire.

25. Brig. Gen. Alfred Howe Terry of Connecticut, who led the 1st Division of the X Corps, was given temporary command of the corps 14–21 June 1864.

26. See *OR,* 40, pt. 2:659, 664–65. EPA quoted from P. G. T. Beauregard, "Four Days of Battle at Petersburg," *B&L,* 4:541–42.

27. Maj. Gen. William Henry Fitzhugh "Rooney" Lee of Virginia, R. E. Lee's second son, commanded a division of Stuart's cavalry. Lee's messages are in *OR,* 40, pt. 2:662–63, and Beauregard, "Four Days of Battle," p. 542.

28. This message is in neither *OR* nor Beauregard's "Four Days of Battle"; EPA probably found it in Roman, *Beauregard*, 2:234–35.

29. Lt. Col. Alfred Roman of Louisiana was Beauregard's inspector general and after the war his authorized biographer.

30. Giles Buckner Cooke of Virginia was assistant adjutant general to Beauregard and later served in the same capacity on R. E. Lee's staff.

31. See *OR,* 40, pt. 2:667–68.

32. EPA placed question marks in the margin opposite these figures. In *Military Memoirs,* p. 557, EPA gave Beauregard's strength as 14,000; Walter Taylor, *Four Years,* p. 177, estimated that on 30 June Field's division numbered 4,757, and Kershaw's 4,517.

33. EPA crossed out this sentence.

34. EPA crossed out the next five words.

35. Lt. Col. James Read Branch of Virginia, who commanded a battalion of four batteries, was subsequently wounded near Plymouth, North Carolina, but survived the war.

36. EPA never completed this table, which shows evidence of considerable revision.

Chapter 19

1. Col. (later Brig. Gen.) Walter Husted Stevens, a native of New York.

2. Brig. Gen. Stephen Elliott, Jr., a South Carolinian, commanded a brigade in Bushrod Johnson's division.

3. Col. Henry Larcom Abbot of Massachusetts commanded the 1st Connecticut Heavy Artillery.

4. Andrew A. Humphreys, *The Virginia Campaign of '64 and '65: The Army of the Potomac and the Army of the James* (New York, 1883), p. 247 n. 1.

5. EPA revised this part of the sentence and inadvertently left an "of" in front of "Kautz's."

6. EPA wrote "omit" in the margin opposite the next five sentences.

7. EPA placed question marks in the margin opposite these figures. Hunter had slightly more than 18,000 men; Early between 8,000 and 9,000; and Breckinridge between 2,500 and 3,200 infantry. Also on the Confederate side at Lynchburg were some cavalry under Imboden and McCausland that had fought at Piedmont, and a few reserves and invalids.

8. EPA placed a question mark in the margin opposite "about 4 miles out." In most places, the distance from Washington to the surrounding works was less than four miles.

9. EPA pasted a clipping of Barnard's description in the manuscript. See Jubal A. Early, "Early's March to Washington in 1864," *B&L,* 4:498 n marked by an anchor (this is an excerpt from Early's *A Memoir of the Last Year of the War for Independence in the Confederate States of America* [Lynchburg, Va., 1867], and other editions).

10. William Swinton, *Campaigns of the Army of the Potomac: A Critical History of Operations in Virginia, Maryland and Pennsylvania, from the Commencement to the Close of the War, 1861–5* (New York, 1866), p. 528 (the quotation is not verbatim). EPA left a space here in which he wrote, "Hunt War Records for telegrams for foot note." For a sampling of these telegrams between Grant and Halleck and Grant and Lincoln, see *OR,* 37, pt. 2:58–60, 79–80, 98, 118–20, 133–35, 155–59.

11. See Early, *Memoir of Last Year,* pp. 40–41.

12. Brig. Gen. John Pegram of Virginia.

13. Humphreys, *Virginia Campaign of '64 and '65*, p. 243.

14. James Nelson Lamkin of the Nelson (Virginia) Light Artillery.

15. EPA crossed out the next eight words.

16. George S. Davidson of Company C, 13th Battalion Virginia Light Artillery, who previously had commanded four batteries in Samuel Jones's Department of Western Virginia.

17. EPA crossed out this sentence.

18. Wade Hampton Gibbes had assumed command of John Floyd King's 13th Battalion Virginia Light Artillery on 10 June 1864; his battery commanders were Capts. David Norvell Walker of Company A (Otey Battery [formerly Capt. George Gaston Otey's]), Crispin Dickenson of Company B (Ringgold Battery), and George S. Davidson of Company C (Davidson's Battery). EPA must have deployed either Walker's or Dickenson's battery in the "smaller salient" to the right of Elliott.

19. Brig. Gen. Gabriel James Rains, a native of North Carolina.

20. EPA wrote "out" in the margin opposite this sentence.

21. Lt. Col. (later Brig. Gen.) Dudley McIver DuBose, a native of Tennessee, commanded H. L. Benning's old brigade in Field's division.

22. John Syng Dorsey Cullen, later the dean of Richmond Medical College.

23. Brig. Gen. John Smith Preston, a native of Virginia with strong associations to South Carolina.

24. Charles Atwood Alexander, third of the Alexander sons, married Ida Calhoun; the wounded man was Private Edwin Calhoun of the 6th South Carolina Cavalry, who had been shot in the face.

25. EPA crossed out the next eight words.

26. Here EPA erased "I only regret that I have lost their name" and left a small space in which he wrote, "Get their name."

27. Born in South America, Pleasants was associated strongly with Pennsylvania.

28. Pleasants's quotation is in William H. Powell, "The Battle of the Petersburg Crater," *B&L*, 4:545–46.

29. EPA first wrote "30 feet."

30. Humphreys, *Virginia Campaign of '64 and '65*, p. 251. EPA marked this passage "Foot note"; it has been placed in sequence within the text.

31. EPA placed a question mark in the margin opposite this sentence. Capt. Samuel T. Wright commanded the Halifax (Virginia) Heavy Artillery, and Capt. Richard Gregory Pegram the Branch Field Artillery (formerly Lee's Life Guard—of Petersburg, Virginia) in Maj. James Campbell Coit's battalion.

32. Humphreys, *Virginia Campaign of '64 and '65*, pp. 251, 254.

33. Ibid., p. 255.

34. EPA crossed out "powerful."

35. EPA placed a question mark in the margin opposite this sentence. Lt. (later Capt.) John Hampden Chamberlayne assumed command of Company C of the 13th Battalion Virginia Light Artillery in August 1864.

36. Brig. Gen. John Caldwell Calhoun Sanders of Alabama.

37. Brig. Gen. William Francis Bartlett of Massachusetts and Col. Elisha Gaylord Marshall of New York, who commanded respectively the 1st and 2nd Brigades of the 1st Division of the IX Corps, were taken prisoner. Why EPA incorrectly identified Marshall as Graham is unknown—he corrected his error in *Military Memoirs*, p. 572.

38. Brig. Gen. James Hewett Ledlie of New York commanded the 1st Division, Ferrero the 4th Division, and Willcox the 3rd Division of the IX Corps; Col. Zenas Randall Bliss of Rhode Island, who led the 1st Brigade of the 2nd Division of the IX Corps, became a major general after the war.

39. The opinion of the court is in *OR*, 40, pt. 1:128–29.

40. Humphreys, *Virginia Campaign of '64 and '65*, p. 264.

41. Harry Reese of the 48th Pennsylvania, the mine boss, who was accompanied by Lt. Jacob Douty.

42. EPA first wrote "150 feet long." Estimates of the size of the Crater vary: see, for examples, Powell, "Battle of the Crater," p. 551 (170 feet long, 60 feet wide, 30 feet deep); Pleasants's report in *OR*, 40, pt. 1:558 (at least 200 feet long, 50 feet wide, 25 feet deep); and the report of Capt. Hugh Thomas Douglas of the Confederate engineers in *OR*, 40, pt. 3:819–20 (125 feet long, 50 feet wide, 20–25 feet deep).

43. An engraving of Virginian John Adams Elder's painting, which EPA pasted in his manuscript, is in *B&L*, 4:566. The original is at the Commonwealth Club in Richmond, Virginia.

44. Powell, "Battle of the Crater," pp. 551–53, 558–59; EPA pasted a clipping with this excerpt in his manuscript.

45. Elisha Gaylord Marshall (see note 37 above).

46. EPA crossed out the next two words.

47. Fitz William McMaster of South Carolina, who commanded the 17th South Carolina.

48. Brig. Gen. Matt Whitaker Ransom of North Carolina led a brigade in Bushrod Johnson's division.

49. Col. (later Brig. Gen.) Henry Goddard Thomas of Maine, whose unit was the 2nd Brigade of the 4th Division of the IX Corps. See his "The Colored Troops at Petersburg," *B&L*, 4:564–65; EPA pasted a clipping with this excerpt in his manuscript.

50. The officers of the regiments of U.S. Colored Troops who were killed or mortally wounded were Capt. Zelotes Fessenden, Lt. William H. Ayers, Capt. Richard K. Woodruff, Capt. Adam C. Liscomb, Capt. John C. Hackhiser, Capt. William H. Flint, Capt. Hector H. Aiken, and Maj. Theodore H. Rockwood.

51. Lt. Col. William Edward Wyatt Ross "and the two officers of his regiment next in rank" are mentioned as casualties in *OR*, 40, pt. 1:598; there is no specific reference to a Captain Wright.

52. Stephen Minot Weld, Jr., of Massachusetts, who commanded the 56th Massachusetts Infantry, left an excellent account of the battle in his superlative *War Diary and Letters of Stephen Minot Weld, 1861–1865* (1912; reprint, Boston, 1979), pp. 352–57.

53. Thomas, "Colored Troops," pp. 565–66; EPA pasted a clipping with this excerpt in his manuscript.

54. EPA crossed out this sentence.

55. Humphreys, *Virginia Campaign of '64 and '65*, p. 260.

56. Brig. Gen. John Wesley Turner, a native of New York, commanded the 2nd Division of the X Corps.

57. EPA partially erased "Otey." In his report of the artillery's part in the battle, William N. Pendleton wrote that Gibbes's "left gun . . . was culpably left for a time unserved, through the misbehavior of Lieut. James C. Otey, who, owing to a combination of circumstances, was the only officer at the time present with the company." *OR*, 40, pt. 1:760. Jennings C. Wise, chronicler of the artillery in the Army of Northern

Virginia, stated in reference to Otey that "this unfortunate young officer" was "the first and the last in the whole career of Lee's Artillery Corps to abandon his guns in cowardice." Wise, *The Long Arm of Lee,* 2 vols. (Lynchburg, Va., 1915), 2:866.

58. EPA placed a question mark in the margin opposite "Captain Davidson." It is possible that he considered omitting criticism of Davidson's conduct during the engagement.

59. EPA placed a question mark in the margin opposite "perhaps 5,000." The effective strength of the black units is not given in *OR.*

Chapter 20

1. Joseph Emerson Brown, a native of South Carolina, was a controversial figure accused by many southerners (EPA among them) of undermining their war effort. For an excellent recent treatment of this subject, see Richard E. Beringer et al., *Why the South Lost the Civil War* (Athens, Ga., 1986), especially chapter 10. Benjamin Harvey Hill of Georgia generally supported Jefferson Davis and became known as one of the president's "pets." For a concise discussion of Davis's reasons for removing Johnston, see Herman Hattaway and Archer Jones, *How the North Won: A Military History of the Civil War* (Urbana, Ill., 1983), pp. 604–7.

2. An almost identical quotation is attributed to Davis regarding Albert Sidney Johnston. In the wake of the loss of Forts Henry and Donelson in 1862 a group of prominent citizens of Tennessee asked Davis to replace Johnston, to which the president replied, "If Sidney Johnston is not a general, we had better give up the war for we have no general." Quoted in Stanley F. Horn, *The Army of Tennessee* (Indianapolis, 1941), p. 105.

3. EPA crossed out this sentence.

4. Joseph E. Johnston, "Opposing Sherman's Advance to Atlanta," *B&L,* 4:274–75; EPA pasted a clipping with this excerpt in the manuscript.

5. Maj. (later Col.) Stephen Wilson Presstman commanded the engineer troops (3rd Regiment) in Johnston's army.

6. EPA crossed out the next nine words.

7. Andrew A. Humphreys, *The Virginia Campaign of '64 and '65: The Army of the Potomac and the Army of the James* (New York, 1883), pp. 267–68.

8. Brig. Gen. John Randolph Chambliss, Jr., of Virginia, whose brigade was in Rooney Lee's division.

9. Brig. Gen. Joseph Hayes, a native of Maine, led the 1st Brigade of the 2nd Division of the V Corps; Brig. Gen. Thomas Lanier Clingman of North Carolina commanded a brigade in Robert F. Hoke's division.

10. Brig. Gen. Johnson Hagood of South Carolina, whose brigade was in Robert F. Hoke's division.

11. EPA crossed out the rest of this paragraph.

12. EPA left a large space here, in which he wrote, "paste in clipping about my telling the fellow to shoot at everything 'a yard high, a foot wide, or a year old.'" He did not include the clipping.

13. EPA crossed out the next two words.

14. Col. John S. Fulton of Tennessee, who commanded Bushrod Johnson's old brigade, was mortally wounded on 30 June 1864 and died five days later. The brigade, then under Col. John M. Hughes (sometimes spelled Hughs), was removed from Johnson's division and shifted north of the James on 7 July.

15. Maj. Gen. Edward Otho Cresap Ord, a native of Maryland, and Maj. Gen. David Bell Birney commanded the two Federal corps; Birney's brother William led the 1st Brigade (Colored Troops) of the 3rd Division of the X Corps.

16. Brig. Gen. Hiram Burnham of Maine, whose unit was the 2nd Brigade of the 1st Division of the XVIII Corps.

17. Lt. Col. John Minor Maury of Virginia, who commanded a battalion of heavy artillery at Fort Harrison. For an exhaustive treatment of the fighting on 29 Sept. and the two succeeding days, see Richard J. Sommers, *Richmond Redeemed: The Siege at Petersburg* (Garden City, 1981).

18. Col. Edgar Burwell Montague, a Virginian, led a brigade in George E. Pickett's division.

19. By the fall of 1864 most of Lee's couriers came from the 39th Battalion Virginia Cavalry, which served as his escort; six months later no one named Evans appeared on the rolls of the battalion or among Lee's headquarters personnel at Appomattox. Still, EPA certainly may have been correct in remembering a courier named Evans.

20. In the 1890s EPA asked Alexander Cheves Haskell for his reminiscences of the action on 7 Oct. 1864, and Haskell responded with a lengthy letter that is reproduced in Louise Haskell Daly, *Alexander Cheves Haskell: The Portrait of a Man* (Norwood, Mass., 1934), pp. 144–53. EPA used that letter to write the following account.

21. Sgt. W. DuBose Snowden of Company B, 7th South Carolina Cavalry.

22. Kautz's report of the engagement in *OR,* 42, pt. 1:823–25, mentions no such a major, though it does note the capture of Capt. M. J. Asch of the 1st New Jersey Cavalry and Lt. Anthony Beers of the 11th Pennsylvania Cavalry.

Chapter 21

1. Col. Francis B. Pond led the 1st Brigade of Ames's division.

2. EPA wrote "get names" in a small space here. EPA's description contains too little detail to permit identification of the battery.

3. Confederate authorities claimed that they placed Federal prisoners in Charleston to prevent continued shelling of civilians in the city by Quincy A. Gillmore's investing Union forces. The Federals responded in August 1864 by selecting 600 Confederate officers held at Fort Delaware (later known in the South as the "Immortal Six Hundred") to be transferred to Morris Island, where they would be subject to Confederate bombardment. See Abram Fulkerson, "The Prison Experience of a Confederate Soldier," *SHSP,* 22:131–33, and *OR,* ser. II, 7:567. The activities at Charleston were not related to the use of captured black soldiers as laborers by Confederates at Petersburg and Richmond. On that topic, see *OR,* ser. II, 7:967–68, 90–93. A concise discussion of the problem of prisoner exchanges is in James M. McPherson, *Ordeal by Fire: The Civil War and Reconstruction* (New York, 1982), pp. 451–56.

4. Maj. Gen. John Grubb Parke of Pennsylvania, who had succeeded Burnside as commander of the IX Corps.

5. Brig. Gen. Samuel Wylie Crawford, a Pennsylvanian, led the 3rd Division of the V Corps.

6. Brig. Gen. Byron Root Pierce of New York commanded the 2nd Brigade of the 3rd Division of the II Corps.

7. Brig. Gen. (later Maj. Gen.) George Washington Custis Lee of Virginia, eldest son of R. E. Lee.

8. Brig. Gen. (later Maj. Gen.) Godfrey Weitzel of Ohio had assumed command of the XVIII Corps in early October 1864.

9. Brig. Gen. Alfred Thomas Archimedes Torbert of Delaware led the 1st Division of the Cavalry Corps.

10. EPA added the losses in another ink and wrote "(Sherman)" beside them; he took his figures from William T. Sherman, "The Grand Strategy of the Last Year of the War," *B&L,* 4:250. Thomas L. Livermore, *Numbers and Losses in the Civil War in America* (1900; reprint, Bloomington, Ind., 1957), p. 127, places Early's effective strength at 17,103 (probably about 3,000 too high) and Sheridan's at 37,771, and their respective losses at 3,921 and 5,018. Robert E. Rodes was killed at Winchester, and S. Dodson Ramseur took over his division.

11. EPA again quotes Sherman, "Grand Strategy," p. 250 for his figures. Livermore, *Numbers and Losses,* pp. 129–30, credits Early with 18,410 effectives (again probably 3,000–4,000 too many) and 2,910 casualties, and Sheridan with 30,829 and 5,665. S. Dodson Ramseur was mortally wounded at Cedar Creek on 19 Oct. and died the next day.

12. Col. (later Brig. Gen.) Thomas Maley Harris was a native of what is now West Virginia. His division became the 4th of E. O. C. Ord's new XXIV Corps, which was organized in early Dec. by combining the white troops from the X and XVIII Corps. The black troops from the Department of Virginia and North Carolina were placed in Godfrey Weitzel's new XXV Corps (the X and XVIII Corps ceased to exist).

13. Hood's attacks resulted in the battles of Peachtree Creek (20 July), Atlanta (22 July), and Ezra Church (28 July).

14. J. B. Hood, "The Invasion of Tennessee," *B&L,* 4:428; EPA pasted a clipping with this excerpt in his manusript.

15. Maj. Gen. John McAllister Schofield, a native of New York, commanded the XXIII Corps and two divisions of the IV Corps.

16. EPA added then crossed out "night of" before "29th."

17. Henry Stone, "Repelling Hood's Invasion of Tennessee," *B&L,* 4:453.

18. Cols. John S. Casement and Israel N. Stiles led respectively the 2nd and 3rd Brigades of the 3rd Division of the XXIII Corps.

19. The fallen Confederates were Brig. Gens. John Adams of Tennessee, Francis Marion Cockrell of Missouri, William Andrew Quarles of Virginia, Hiram Bronson Granbury of Mississippi, Otho French Strahl, a native of Ohio, States Rights Gist of South Carolina, John Calvin Brown of Tennessee, George Washington Gordon of Tennessee, and Maj. Gen. Patrick Ronayne Cleburne. Col. (later Brig. Gen.) Emerson Opdyke of Ohio commanded the 1st Brigade of the 2nd Division of the IV Corps. EPA pasted a clipping with this excerpt in his manuscript.

20. EPA crossed out "veteran."

21. For an excellent brief treatment of the episode at Spring Hill that casts Cheatham in a much more positive light, see Richard M. McMurry, *John Bell Hood and the War for Southern Independence* (Lexington, Ky., 1982), pp. 170–75.

22. This could have been Capt. Willis Wilkinson, an ordnance officer stationed at Richmond.

23. Francis Williamson Smith of Virginia, who was mortally wounded on 5 Apr. 1865 at Amelia Springs and died the next day, commanded a battalion of reserve artillery.

24. EPA placed a question mark in the margin opposite this sentence, added Blair's name in another ink, and left a space below. The overture came from Francis Preston

Blair, Sr., Montgomery Blair's father and a longtime Democrat who had been among Andrew Jackson's closest advisers.

25. EPA placed two question marks in the margin opposite this sentence. John Archibald Campbell of Georgia, a former justice of the U.S. Supreme Court, was Davis's assistant secretary of war; Robert Mercer Taliaferro Hunter of Virginia represented his state in the Confederate Senate.

26. Because neither Lincoln nor Seward left a record of the discussions at Fort Monroe, those interested in what transpired must depend on accounts by the Confederate commissioners. The fullest is in Alexander H. Stephens, *A Constitutional View of the Late War between the States; Its Causes, Character, Conduct and Results,* 2 vols. (Philadelphia, 1868–70), 2:599–619. Stephens claimed that Lincoln suggested slaveowners might be compensated for the loss of their property. See also J. G. Randall and Richard N. Current, *Lincoln the President: Last Full Measure* (New York, 1955), pp. 326–36. On 5 Feb. 1865 Lincoln had recommended to Congress that it pass a joint resolution empowering him to pay $400 million to the Confederate states, apportioned according to their slave populations, on the condition that the states agree to end the rebellion. In a cabinet meeting the following day, Lincoln's advisers voiced strong opposition to the plan. See Roy P. Basler, ed., *The Collected Works of Abraham Lincoln,* 9 vols. (New Brunswick, N.J., 1953), 8:260–61.

27. See chapter 13 of Postmaster General John Henninger Reagan's *Memoirs: With Special Reference to Secession and the Civil War* (1906; reprint, New York, 1973), for an argument that Lincoln made no concrete offer of compensation.

28. Andrew A. Humphreys, *The Virginia Campaign of '64 and '65: The Army of the Potomac and the Army of the James* (New York, 1883), p. 311.

29. This incident inspired a great deal of controversial literature. The best treatment is Marion Brunson Lucas, *Sherman and the Burning of Columbia* (College Station, Tex., 1976), which makes clear that neither side was blameless.

30. Walter H. Taylor, *Four Years with General Lee* (1877; reprint, Bloomington, Ind., 1962), pp. 145–46.

Chapter 22

1. Andrew A. Humphreys, *The Virginia Campaign of '64 and '65: The Army of the Potomac and the Army of the James* (New York, 1883), p. 323; on pp. 433–34, Humphreys gave the figures as 44,500 infantry, 5,000 cavalry, and 6,000 artillery "exclusive of Walker's brigade" and "the heavy artillery, the local troops, and the naval forces." In Walter H. Taylor, *Four Years with General Lee* (1877; reprint, Bloomington, Ind., 1962), p. 186, Taylor placed the army's effective strength on 28 Feb. 1865 at 42,484 infantry, 6,041 cavalry, and 5,399 artillery; by the end of the next month, Taylor argued, desertion and casualties had reduced the total to "but thirty-three thousand muskets" (p. 187). Although Taylor did not say so, his estimate for late March almost certainly referred only to infantry.

2. A small tear in the manuscript removed all but the last three letters of this word.

3. For Humphreys's dicussion of the strength of the Army of the Potomac and Secretary of War Stanton's reports, see *Virginia Campaign of '64 and '65,* pp. 323, 408–11.

4. EPA placed a question mark in the margin opposite the first part of this sentence. Schofield and the XXIII Corps moved from Tennessee to North Carolina in January–

February 1865; once there, Schofield used his own troops and those of Alfred H. Terry to capture Wilmington.

5. EPA crossed out the next four words.

6. EPA added then crossed out "on their journey" after "Canal."

7. Humphreys, *Virginia Campaign of '64 and '65*, p. 349 n. 1. At the time of Sheridan's attack, Pickett and Fitzhugh Lee were enjoying a late afternoon meal of shad at Thomas L. Rosser's camp across Hatcher's Run. Their absence from the front became generally known only in the mid-1880s, when many southerners whispered that they had neglected their duties. For Pickett's report of the battle, which did not mention the meal with Lee and Rosser, see Walter Harrison, *Pickett's Men: A Fragment of War History* (1870; reprint, Gaithersburg, Md., 1984), pp. 142–51.

8. Col. (Brevet Brig. Gen.) Frederick Winthrop of New York, who commanded the 1st Brigade of the 2nd Division of the V Corps.

9. EPA crossed out the rest of this paragraph. On Hill's courtship of Ellen Mary Marcy (the daughter of Maj. Randolph B. Marcy), see James I. Robertson, Jr., *General A. P. Hill: The Story of a Confederate Warrior* (New York, 1987), pp. 27–29.

10. William Johnson Pegram of Virginia led a battalion of artillery in the Third Corps. His brother John had been killed at Hatcher's Run on 6 Feb. 1865. EPA added "at Five Forks" in another ink.

11. EPA deleted "for a whole day even in our broken lines" after "stay."

12. Humphreys, *Virginia Campaign of '64 and '65*, pp. 369–70.

13. Brig. Gen. Robert Sanford Foster, an Indianan whose division was the 1st of the XXIV Corps.

14. Brig. Gen. Thomas Maley Harris, born in what is now West Virginia, commanded the 3rd Brigade of John W. Turner's Independent Division of the XXIV Corps.

15. Edward A. Pollard, *The Lost Cause: A New Southern History of the War of the Confederates* (New York, 1866), pp. 690–92.

16. Marylander Walter Scott Chew's battery was in Lt. Col. David Gregg McIntosh's battalion of the Third Corps.

17. EPA first wrote "before my batteries."

18. Probably Dr. James Bond Read, formerly a captain in Company A, 1st Georgia Infantry, who was a surgeon at a hospital in Richmond.

19. EPA partially erased "I took."

20. EPA crossed out "through."

21. Lt. Col. John Selden Saunders, a Virginian and graduate of West Point a year after EPA, was an artillerist who served for a time on Briscoe G. Baldwin's staff.

22. Probably Col. John J. Clarke, formerly an engineer on James Longstreet's staff, who finished the war as chief engineer with Joseph E. Johnston and his army in North Carolina.

23. Lewis Wardlaw Haskell, who was born in 1847.

24. Perhaps Maj. Louis Webb, who was listed as quartermaster at EPA's headquarters on the roster of Confederates surrendered at Appomattox.

25. EPA left a space here in which he wrote, "perhaps quote some details." For an account of the debacle at Sayler's Creek, see Douglas Southall Freeman, *Lee's Lieutenants: A Study in Command*, 3 vols. (New York, 1942–44), 3:698–711.

26. Brig. Gen. Montgomery Dent Corse of Virginia led a brigade in Pickett's division.

27. Lt. Col. (Brevet Brig. Gen.) Theodore Read, a native of Ohio, was Ord's chief of staff.

28. Francis Washburn of Massachusetts, whose unit was the 4th (not 5th) Massachusetts Cavalry, died on 22 Apr. of wounds received on 6 Apr. at the High Bridge. Col. Reuben Beverley Boston, a Virginian who led the 5th Virginia Cavalry, died on 7 Apr.; Maj. James Walton Thomson of Virginia commanded a battalion of horse artillery and was killed on 6 Apr.; Dearing died on 23 Apr. of wounds received at the High Bridge.

29. Col. John Irvin Gregg of Pennsylvania led the 2nd Brigade of the 2nd Division of the Cavalry Corps.

30. EPA probably used Horace Porter, "The Surrender at Appomattox Court House," *B&L,* 4:729–46, for the text of this note and the remainder of the exchange of correspondence between Lee and Grant on 7–9 April. See also *OR, 46,* pt. 3:619, 641, 664–66.

31. For Longstreet's account of the episode with Pendleton, see James Longstreet, *From Manassas to Appomattox: Memoirs of the Civil War in America* (Philadelphia, 1896), pp. 620–21. Longstreet claimed he told Pendleton that "the Articles of War provided that officers or soldiers who asked commanding officers to surrender should be shot." Pendleton's public version of his visit to army headquarters, which included no hint of displeasure on Lee's part, was recorded in Armistead L. Long, *Memoirs of Robert E. Lee* (New York, 1887), p. 417.

32. EPA pasted a clipping with this note from Grant in his manuscript.

33. On 13 March 1862, Lee was assigned to duty in Richmond "under the direction of the President" and "charged with the conduct of military operations in the armies of the Confederacy" (*OR,* 5:1099). Under these orders Lee functioned as a chief of staff. For a discussion of this appointment and Lee's responsibilities, see Herman Hattaway and Archer Jones, *How the North Won: A Military History of the Civil War* (Urbana, Ill., 1983), pp. 116–19, 189–90.

34. EPA crossed out the rest of this sentence.

35. Between 1865 and 1870, Paraguay fought against an alliance of Brazil, Argentina, and Uruguay. EPA's prediction of a Brazilian victory was accurate; Paraguay lost three-quarters of its population and some 55,000 square miles of territory in a shattering defeat.

36. EPA crossed out "Well, Sir" at the begining of this quotation.

37. EPA crossed out "For" at the beginning of this sentence.

38. EPA crossed out "And" at the beginning of this sentence.

39. EPA crossed out the next six words.

40. EPA crossed out "inestimable."

41. Battery M, 1st U.S. Artillery, lost one gun and a caisson, complete with teams, to the 14th Virginia Cavalry. See *OR, 46,* pt. 1:1246; Fletcher T. Massie, "From Petersburg to Appomattox: Lampkin's Battery of Artillery and How It Fought on Famous Retreat. A Glimpse of General Lee," *SHSP,* 34:246–47; and "The Last Charge of the 14th Virginia Cavalry at Appomattox C. H., Va., April 9, 1865, and Its Battle Flag," *SHSP,* 36:13–16.

42. EPA first wrote "a very superior officer & the company a very fine one."

43. Lt. Col. Charles Albert Whittier, a native of Maine, was assistant adjutant general on the staff of II Corps commander A. A. Humphreys.

44. EPA pasted a clipping containing this exchange of notes in his manuscript.

45. EPA crossed out "Gen." in front of "Lee" and "Fitz Lee."

46. EPA placed a question mark in the margin opposite Field's name, although there is no apparent error in this sentence.

47. Capt. Robert Moorman Sims of South Carolina was Longstreet's assistant adjutant and inspector general.

48. Ord's quotation is in Humphreys, *Virginia Campaign of '64 and '65,* p. 398.

49. Longstreet's version of his confrontation with Custer is in *Manassas to Appomattox,* p. 627; a more dramatic telling is in John Haskell, *The Haskell Memoirs: The Personal Narrative of a Confederate Officer,* ed. Gilbert E. Govan and James W. Livingood (New York, 1960), pp. 94–96. Haskell noted that Custer was wearing Frank Huger's spurs, which he apparently took from Huger while the latter was his prisoner.

50. Through much of the war Samuel Sweeney of this banjo-playing clan provided music for Jeb Stuart's colorful headquarters.

51. Lt. Col. Orville Elias Babcock of Vermont, who was Grant's aide-de-camp.

52. EPA later wrote above this sentence, "No he couldn't & did not. Porter is mistaken."

53. EPA pasted a clipping containing this note in his manuscript.

54. On Grant's insistence that paroles be respected, see Douglas Southall Freeman, *R. E. Lee: A Biography,* 4 vols. (New York, 1934–36), 4:203–5.

55. EPA mistakenly gave 22 Apr. as the date of Johnston's surrender. The three principal Confederate surrenders after Appomattox were: Johnston to Sherman at Durham Station, North Carolina, on 26 Apr.; Richard Taylor (Confederate forces in the Department of Alabama, Mississippi, and East Louisiana) to E. R. S. Canby at Citronelle, Alabama, on 4 May; and E. Kirby Smith (Confederate forces in the Trans-Mississippi) to E. R. S. Canby at New Orleans on 26 May (Smith and Canby were represented respectively by Simon B. Buckner and Peter J. Osterhaus).

56. EPA crossed out "more."

57. EPA left a large space, at the top of which he wrote, "Copies of parole & orders"; however, he included no copies. Lee's farewell order is printed in *B&L,* 4:747.

58. Lt. Col. Edward Raynsford Warner of the 1st New York Light Artillery.

59. A tobacco manufacturer in Petersburg who was active in blockade running, William Cameron made enough money during the war to build a conspicuous house called Mt. Erin (its popular name was Cameron's Castle). John Cheves Haskell recalled that Cameron was "a most hospitable entertainer of Confederate officers," who offered bales of cotton for export to Haskell, Gen. William Mahone, and "several others"— Gibbes presumably among them. Haskell's bale brought him more than $200 in gold. See Haskell, *Memoirs,* pp. 89, 167.

60. P. G. T. Beauregard also wrote a letter of recommendation for EPA, suggesting in a cover note that EPA "should not be surprised to see me join you there [in Brazil] ere long—for I have already offered my services to the Emperor Don Pedro." P. G. T. Beauregard to EPA, n.d. [probably 27 Aug. 1865], and letter of general recommendation dated 27 Aug. 1865, Beauregard Papers, Morristown National Historical Park Library.

61. Elihu Benjamin Washburne, a native of Maine, was a Whig and Republican congressman from Illinois from 1853 to 1869 and minister to France during U. S. Grant's presidency.

62. On this topic, see chapter 21, note 26.

63. Col. (Brevet Brig. Gen.) John Irwin Curtin, commander of the 1st Brigade of the 2nd Division of the IX Corps, was a nephew of Gov. Andrew Gregg Curtin of Pennsylvania.

64. Maj. Gen. Christopher Columbus Augur, born in New York and reared in Michigan, headed the Department of Washington.

65. Joseph Hancock Taylor of Kentucky graduated one class ahead of EPA at West Point.

66. Brig. Gen. William Henry Fitzhugh Payne, a Virginian, was captured near Warrenton, Virginia, the night of Lincoln's assassination and imprisoned until 29 May 1865.

67. A reference to a Chinese character in Bret Harte's "Plain Language from Truthful James": "Which we had a small game, / And Ah Sin took a hand: / It was Euchre. The same / He did not understand; / But he smiled as he sat by the table, / With the smile that was childlike and bland." Ah Sin proceeds to cheat the other players, all the while disarming them with his innocent smile.

68. Brig. Gen. Stewart Van Vliet of Vermont.

69. Brig. Gen. Philippe Regis Denis de Keredern de Trobriand, a native of France, served throughout the war in the Army of the Potomac. There was no General Jeffers (or Jefferson) in the Federal army; however, it is possible that EPA meant Brevet Brig. Gen. Noah Lemuel Jeffries of New York.

70. EPA initially wrote "4th," then crossed it out and replaced it with "5th." He was correct the first time: the 4th was a Thursday, and Davis had been in Washington, Georgia, on the 3rd.

71. EPA wrote "Irwinton" instead of Irwinville, where Davis was captured. For details on Davis's stay in Washington, Georgia, and his surrender, see Burke Davis, *The Long Surrender* (New York, 1985), especially pp. 126–29, 139–48.

72. Neither Maury Klein, *Edward Porter Alexander* (Athens, Ga., 1971) nor Marion Alexander Boggs, ed., *The Alexander Letters, 1787–1900* (1910; reprint, Athens, Ga., 1980) gives the name of the child born on 7 Apr. 1865. Both provide full names and dates of birth for EPA's other five children—Bessie Mason (born 10 Nov. 1861), Edward Porter II and Lucy Roy (twins born 21 Sept. 1863), Adam Leopold (born 24 July 1867), and William Mason (born 23 Nov. 1868). Klein does state that "Bettie had given birth to a girl on April 7" but makes no further mention of the child. She must have died in infancy—perhaps before EPA and Bettie chose a name.

INDEX